Organizational Efficiency through Intelligent Information Technologies

Vijayan Sugumaran
Oakland University, USA & Sogang University, South Korea

Managing Director: Lindsay Johnston
Editorial Director: Joel Gamon
Book Production Manager: Jennifer Romanchak
Publishing Systems Analyst: Adrienne Freeland
Assistant Acquisitions Editor: Kayla Wolfe
Typesetter: Erin O'Dea
Cover Design: Nick Newcomer

Published in the United States of America by
Information Science Reference (an imprint of IGI Global)
701 E. Chocolate Avenue
Hershey PA 17033
Tel: 717-533-8845
Fax: 717-533-8661
E-mail: cust@igi-global.com
Web site: http://www.igi-global.com

Library of Congress Cataloging-in-Publication Data

Organizational efficiency through intelligent information technologies / Vijayan Sugumaran, editor.
p. cm.
Includes bibliographical references and index.
Summary: "This book explores various aspects of design and development of intelligent technologies by bringing together the latest in research in the fields of information systems, intelligent agents, collaborative works and much more"--Provided by publisher.
ISBN 978-1-4666-2047-6 (hardcover) -- ISBN 978-1-4666-2048-3 (ebook) -- ISBN 978-1-4666-2049-0 (print & perpetual access) 1. Information technology--Technological innovations. 2. Organizational effectiveness. 3. Artificial intelligence. 4. Intelligent agents (Computer software) I. Sugumaran, Vijayan, 1960-
HC79.I55O745 2013
658'.0563--dc23

2012013143

British Cataloguing in Publication Data
A Cataloguing in Publication record for this book is available from the British Library.

Associate Editors

List of Reviewers

Table of Contents

Preface xiv

Acknowledgment xxi

Chapter 1
Classifying Consumer Comparison Opinions to Uncover Product Strengths and Weaknesses 1
Kaiquan Xu, City University of Hong Kong, China
Wei Wang, City University of Hong Kong, China
Jimmy S. J. Ren, City University of Hong Kong, China
Jin Xu, Southwest Jiaotong University, China
Long Liu, USTC-CityU Joint Advanced Research Centre, China
Stephen S. Y. Liao, City University of Hong Kong, China

Chapter 2
OntoClippy: A User-Friendly Ontology Design and Creation Methodology 15
Nikolai Dahlem, University of Oldenburg, Germany

Chapter 3
Combining Supervised Learning Techniques to Key-Phrase Extraction for Biomedical
Full-Text 33
Yanliang Qi, New Jersey Institute of Technology, USA
Min Song, New Jersey Institute of Technology, USA
Suk-Chung Yoon, Widener University, USA
Lori Watrous deVersterre, New Jersey Institute of Technology, USA

Chapter 4
Design and Usage of a Process-Centric Collaboration Methodology for Virtual Organizations in
Hybrid Environments 45
Thorsten Dollmann, German Research Center for Artificial Intelligence (DFKI), Germany
Peter Loos, German Research Center for Artificial Intelligence (DFKI), Germany
Michael Fellmann, University of Osnabrueck, Germany
Oliver Thomas, University of Osnabrueck, Germany
Andreas Hoheisel, Fraunhofer Institute for Computer Architecture and Software Technology, Germany
Peter Katranuschkov, TU Dresden, Germany
Raimar J. Scherer, TU Dresden, Germany

Chapter 5
Construction of Domain Ontologies: Sourcing the World Wide Web 65
Jongwoo Kim, University of Massachusetts Boston, USA
Veda C. Storey, Georgia State University, USA

Chapter 6
Self Adaptive Particle Swarm Optimization for Efficient Virtual Machine Provisioning in Cloud 88
R. Jeyarani, Coimbatore Institute of Technology, India
N. Nagaveni, Coimbatore Institute of Technology, India
R. Vasanth Ram, PSG College of Technology, India

Chapter 7
Eliciting User Preferences in Multi-Agent Meeting Scheduling Problem 108
Mohammad Amin Rigi, K. N. Toosi University of Technology, Iran
Farid Khoshalhan, K. N. Toosi University of Technology, Iran

Chapter 8
Wireless Sensor Node Placement Using Hybrid Genetic Programming and Genetic
Algorithms 125
Arpit Tripathi, Indian Institute of Information Technology and Management Gwalior, India
Pulkit Gupta, Indian Institute of Information Technology and Management Gwalior, India
Aditya Trivedi, Indian Institute of Information Technology and Management Gwalior, India
Rahul Kala, Indian Institute of Information Technology and Management Gwalior, India

Chapter 9
Intelligent Agent-Based e-Learning System for Adaptive Learning 145
Hokyin Lai, City University of Hong Kong, Hong Kong
Minhong Wang, The University of Hong Kong, Hong Kong
Huaiqing Wang, City University of Hong Kong, Hong Kong

Chapter 10
Intelligent Information Retrieval Using Fuzzy Association Rule Classifier 159
Sankaradass Veeramalai, Anna University, India
Arputharaj Kannan, Anna University, India

Chapter 11
An Intelligent Operator for Genetic Fuzzy Rule Based System 173
C. Rani, Anna University of Technology Coimbatore, India
S. N. Deepa, Anna University of Technology Coimbatore, India

Chapter 12
Software Effort Estimation: Harmonizing Algorithms and Domain Knowledge in an Integrated Data
Mining Approach 186
Jeremiah D. Deng, University of Otago, New Zealand
Martin K. Purvis, University of Otago, New Zealand
Maryam A. Purvis, University of Otago, New Zealand

Chapter 13
An Ontology Based Model for Document Clustering 199
Sridevi U. K., Sri Krishna College of Engineering and Technology, India
Nagaveni N., Coimbatore Institute of Technology, India

Chapter 14
Towards a Possibilistic Information Retrieval System Using Semantic Query Expansion 216
Bilel Elayeb, ENSI Manouba University, Tunisia
Ibrahim Bounhas, Faculty of Sciences of Tunis, Tunisia
Oussama Ben Khiroun, ENSI Manouba University, Tunisia
Fabrice Evrard, Informatics Research Institute of Toulouse (IRIT), France
Narjès Bellamine-BenSaoud, ENSI Manouba University, Tunisia

Chapter 15
Effective Fuzzy Ontology Based Distributed Document Using Non-Dominated Ranked Genetic Algorithm 243
M. Thangamani, Kongu Engineering College, India
P. Thangaraj, Bannari Amman Institute of Technology, India

Chapter 16
A Dynamically Optimized Fluctuation Smoothing Rule for Scheduling Jobs in a Wafer Fabrication Factory 265
Toly Chen, Feng Chia University, Taiwan

Chapter 17
A Heuristic Method for Learning Path Sequencing for Intelligent Tutoring System (ITS) in E-Learning 285
Sami A. M. Al-Radaei, IT BHU, India
R. B. Mishra, IT BHU, India

Compilation of References 302

About the Contributors 333

Index 341

Detailed Table of Contents

Preface xiv

Acknowledgment xxi

Chapter 1
Classifying Consumer Comparison Opinions to Uncover Product Strengths and Weaknesses 1
Kaiquan Xu, City University of Hong Kong, China
Wei Wang, City University of Hong Kong, China
Jimmy S. J. Ren, City University of Hong Kong, China
Jin Xu, Southwest Jiaotong University, China
Long Liu, USTC-CityU Joint Advanced Research Centre, China
Stephen S. Y. Liao, City University of Hong Kong, China

With the Web 2.0 paradigm, a huge volume of Web content is generated by users at online forums, wikis, blogs, and social networks, among others. These user-contributed contents include numerous user opinions regarding products, services, or political issues. Among these user opinions, certain comparison opinions exist, reflecting customer preferences. Mining comparison opinions is useful as these types of viewpoints can bring more business values than other types of opinion data. Manufacturers can better understand relative product strengths or weaknesses, and accordingly develop better products to meet consumer requirements. Meanwhile, consumers can make purchasing decisions that are more informed by comparing the various features of similar products. In this paper, a novel Support Vector Machine-based method is proposed to automatically identify comparison opinions, extract comparison relations, and display results with the comparison relation maps by mining the volume of consumer opinions posted on the Web. The proposed method is empirically evaluated based on consumer opinions crawled from the Web. The initial experimental results show that the performance of the proposed method is promising and this research opens the door to utilizing these comparison opinions for business intelligence.

Chapter 2
OntoClippy: A User-Friendly Ontology Design and Creation Methodology 15
Nikolai Dahlem, University of Oldenburg, Germany

In this article, the author describes OntoClippy, a tool-supported methodology for the user-friendly design and creation of ontologies. Existing ontology design methodologies and tools are targeted at experts and not suitable for users without a background in formal logic. Therefore, this research develops a methodology and a supporting tool to facilitate the acceptance of ontologies by a wider audience. In this article, the author positions the approach with respect to the current state of the art, formulates the basic principles of the methodology, presents its formal grounding, and describes its phases in detail. To demonstrate the viability of our approach, the author performs a comparative evaluation. The experiment is described, as well as real-world applications of the approach.

Chapter 3
Combining Supervised Learning Techniques to Key-Phrase Extraction for Biomedical Full-Text 33
Yanliang Qi, New Jersey Institute of Technology, USA
Min Song, New Jersey Institute of Technology, USA
Suk-Chung Yoon, Widener University, USA
Lori Watrous deVersterre, New Jersey Institute of Technology, USA

Key-phrase extraction plays a useful a role in research areas of Information Systems (IS) like digital libraries. Short metadata like key phrases are beneficial for searchers to understand the concepts found in the documents. This paper evaluates the effectiveness of different supervised learning techniques on biomedical full-text: Sequential Minimal Optimization (SMO) and K-Nearest Neighbor, both of which could be embedded inside an information system for document search. The authors use these techniques to extract key phrases from PubMed and evaluate the performance of these systems using the holdout validation method. This paper compares different classifier techniques and performance differences between the full-text and it's abstract. Compared with the authors' previous work, which investigated the performance of Naïve Bayes, Linear Regression and SVM(reg1/2), this paper finds that SVMreg-1 performs best in key-phrase extraction for full-text, whereas Naïve Bayes performs best for abstracts. These techniques should be considered for use in information system search functionality. Additional research issues also are identified.

Chapter 4
Design and Usage of a Process-Centric Collaboration Methodology for Virtual Organizations in Hybrid Environments 45
Thorsten Dollmann, German Research Center for Artificial Intelligence (DFKI), Germany
Peter Loos, German Research Center for Artificial Intelligence (DFKI), Germany
Michael Fellmann, University of Osnabrueck, Germany
Oliver Thomas, University of Osnabrueck, Germany
Andreas Hoheisel, Fraunhofer Institute for Computer Architecture and Software Technology, Germany
Peter Katranuschkov, TU Dresden, Germany
Raimar J. Scherer, TU Dresden, Germany

This article describes a collaboration methodology for virtual organizations where the processes can be automatically executed using a hybrid web service, grid or cloud resources. Typically, the process of deriving executable workflows from process models is cumbersome and can be automated only in part or specific to a particular distributed system. The approach introduced in this paper, exemplified by the construction industry field, integrates existing technology within a process-centric framework. The solution on the basis of a hybrid system architecture in conjunction with semantic methods for consistency saving and the framework for modeling VO processes and their automated transformation and execution are discussed in detail.

Chapter 5
Construction of Domain Ontologies: Sourcing the World Wide Web 65
Jongwoo Kim, University of Massachusetts Boston, USA
Veda C. Storey, Georgia State University, USA

As the World Wide Web evolves into the Semantic Web, domain ontologies, which represent the concepts of an application domain and their associated relationships, have become increasingly important as surrogates for capturing and representing the semantics of real world applications. Much ontology development remains manual and is both difficult and time-consuming. This research presents a methodology for semi-automatically generating domain ontologies from extracted information on the World Wide Web. The methodology is implemented in a prototype that integrates existing ontology and web organization tools. The prototype is used to develop ontologies for different application domains, and an empirical analysis carried out to demonstrate the feasibility of the research.

Chapter 6
Self Adaptive Particle Swarm Optimization for Efficient Virtual Machine Provisioning in Cloud 88
R. Jeyarani, Coimbatore Institute of Technology, India
N. Nagaveni, Coimbatore Institute of Technology, India
R. Vasanth Ram, PSG College of Technology, India

Cloud Computing provides dynamic leasing of server capabilities as a scalable, virtualized service to end users. The discussed work focuses on Infrastructure as a Service (IaaS) model where custom Virtual Machines (VM) are launched in appropriate servers available in a data-center. The context of the environment is a large scale, heterogeneous and dynamic resource pool. Nonlinear variation in the availability of processing elements, memory size, storage capacity, and bandwidth causes resource dynamics apart from the sporadic nature of workload. The major challenge is to map a set of VM instances onto a set of servers from a dynamic resource pool so the total incremental power drawn upon the mapping is minimal and does not compromise the performance objectives. This paper proposes a novel Self Adaptive Particle Swarm Optimization (SAPSO) algorithm to solve the intractable nature of the above challenge. The proposed approach promptly detects and efficiently tracks the changing optimum that represents target servers for VM placement. The experimental results of SAPSO was compared with Multi-Strategy Ensemble Particle Swarm Optimization (MEPSO) and the results show that SAPSO outperforms the latter for power aware adaptive VM provisioning in a large scale, heterogeneous and dynamic cloud environment.

Chapter 7
Eliciting User Preferences in Multi-Agent Meeting Scheduling Problem 108
Mohammad Amin Rigi, K. N. Toosi University of Technology, Iran
Farid Khoshalhan, K. N. Toosi University of Technology, Iran

Meeting Scheduling Problem (MSP) arranges meetings between a number of participants. Reaching consensus in arranging a meeting is very diffuclt and time-consuming when the number of participants is large. One efficient approach for overcoming this problem is the use of multi-agent systems. In a multi-agent system, agents are deciding on behalf of their users. They must be able to elicite their users' preferences in an effective way. This paper focuses on the elicitation of users' preferences. Analytical hierarchy process (AHP) - which is known for its ability to determine preferences - is used in this research. Specifically, an adaptive preference modeling technique based on AHP is developed and implemented in a system and the initial validation results are encouraging.

Chapter 8
Wireless Sensor Node Placement Using Hybrid Genetic Programming and Genetic Algorithms 125
Arpit Tripathi, Indian Institute of Information Technology and Management Gwalior, India
Pulkit Gupta, Indian Institute of Information Technology and Management Gwalior, India
Aditya Trivedi, Indian Institute of Information Technology and Management Gwalior, India
Rahul Kala, Indian Institute of Information Technology and Management Gwalior, India

The ease of use and re-configuration in a wireless network has played a key role in their widespread growth. The node deployment problem deals with an optimal placement strategy of the wireless nodes. This paper models a wireless sensor network, consisting of a number of nodes, and a unique sink to which all the information is transmitted using the shortest connecting path. Traditionally the systems have used Genetic Algorithms for optimal placement of the nodes that usually fail to give results in problems employing large numbers of nodes or higher areas to be covered. This paper proposes a hybrid Genetic Programming (GP) and Genetic Algorithm (GA) for solving the problem. While the GP optimizes the deployment structure, the GA is used for actual node placement as per the GP optimized structure. The GA serves as a slave and GP serves as master in this hierarchical implementation. The algorithm optimizes total coverage area, energy utilization, lifetime of the network, and the number of nodes deployed. Experimental results show that the algorithm could place the sensor nodes in a variety of scenarios. The placement was found to be better than random placement strategy as well as the Genetic Algorithm placement strategy.

Chapter 9
Intelligent Agent-Based e-Learning System for Adaptive Learning 145
Hokyin Lai, City University of Hong Kong, Hong Kong
Minhong Wang, The University of Hong Kong, Hong Kong
Huaiqing Wang, City University of Hong Kong, Hong Kong

Adaptive learning approaches support learners to achieve the intended learning outcomes through a personalized way. Previous studies mistakenly treat adaptive e-Learning as personalizing the presentation style of the learning materials, which is not completely correct. The main idea of adaptive learning is to personalize the earning content in a way that can cope with individual differences in aptitude. In this study, an adaptive learning model is designed based on the Aptitude-Treatment Interaction theory and Constructive Alignment Model. The model aims at improving students' learning outcomes through enhancing their intrinsic motivation to learn. This model is operationalized with a multi-agent framework and is validated under a controlled laboratory setting. The result is quite promising. The individual differences of students, especially in the experimental group, have been narrowed significantly. Students who have difficulties in learning show significant improvement after the test. However, the longitudinal effect of this model is not tested in this study and will be studied in the future.

Chapter 10
Intelligent Information Retrieval Using Fuzzy Association Rule Classifier 159
Sankaradass Veeramalai, Anna University, India
Arputharaj Kannan, Anna University, India

As the use of web applications increases, when users use search engines for finding some information by inputting keywords, the number of web pages that match the information increases at a tremendous rate. It is not easy for a user to retrieve the exact web page which contains information he or she requires. In this paper, an approach to web page retrieval system using the hybrid combination of context based and collaborative filtering method employing the concept of fuzzy association rule classification is introduced and the authors propose an innovative clustering of user profiles in order to reduce the filtering space and achieves sub-linear filtering time. This approach can produce recommended web page links for users based on the information that associates strongly with users' queries quickly with better efficiency and therefore improve the recall, precision of a search engine.

Chapter 11
An Intelligent Operator for Genetic Fuzzy Rule Based System 173
C. Rani, Anna University of Technology Coimbatore, India
S. N. Deepa, Anna University of Technology Coimbatore, India

This paper proposes a modified form of operator based on Particle Swarm Optimization (PSO) for designing Genetic Fuzzy Rule Based System (GFRBS). The usual procedure of velocity updating in PSO is modified by calculating the velocity using chromosome's individual best value and global best value based on an updating probability without considering the inertia weight, old velocity and constriction factors. This kind of calculation brings intelligent information sharing mechanism and memory capability to Genetic Algorithm (GA) and can be easily implemented along with other genetic operators. The performance of the proposed operator is evaluated using ten publicly available bench mark data sets. Simulation results show that the proposed operator introduces new material into the population, thereby allows faster and more accurate convergence without struck into a local optima. Statistical analysis of the experimental results shows that the proposed operator produces a classifier model with minimum number of rules and higher classification accuracy.

Chapter 12
Software Effort Estimation: Harmonizing Algorithms and Domain Knowledge in an Integrated Data Mining Approach 186
Jeremiah D. Deng, University of Otago, New Zealand
Martin K. Purvis, University of Otago, New Zealand
Maryam A. Purvis, University of Otago, New Zealand

Software development effort estimation is important for quality management in the software development industry, yet its automation still remains a challenging issue. Applying machine learning algorithms alone often cannot achieve satisfactory results. This paper presents an integrated data mining framework that incorporates domain knowledge into a series of data analysis and modeling processes, including visualization, feature selection, and model validation. An empirical study on the software effort estimation problem using a benchmark dataset shows the necessity and effectiveness of the proposed approach.

Chapter 13
An Ontology Based Model for Document Clustering 199
Sridevi U. K., Sri Krishna College of Engineering and Technology, India
Nagaveni N., Coimbatore Institute of Technology, India

Clustering is an important topic to find relevant content from a document collection and it also reduces the search space. The current clustering research emphasizes the development of a more efficient clustering method without considering the domain knowledge and user's need. In recent years the semantics of documents have been utilized in document clustering. The discussed work focuses on the clustering model where ontology approach is applied. The major challenge is to use the background knowledge in the similarity measure. This paper presents an ontology based annotation of documents and clustering system. The semi-automatic document annotation and concept weighting scheme is used to create an ontology based knowledge base. The Particle Swarm Optimization (PSO) clustering algorithm can be applied to obtain the clustering solution. The accuracy of clustering has been computed before and after combining ontology with Vector Space Model (VSM). The proposed ontology based framework gives improved performance and better clustering compared to the traditional vector space model. The result using ontology was significant and promising.

Chapter 14
Towards a Possibilistic Information Retrieval System Using Semantic Query Expansion 216
Bilel Elayeb, ENSI Manouba University, Tunisia
Ibrahim Bounhas, Faculty of Sciences of Tunis, Tunisia
Oussama Ben Khiroun, ENSI Manouba University, Tunisia
Fabrice Evrard, Informatics Research Institute of Toulouse (IRIT), France
Narjès Bellamine-BenSaoud, ENSI Manouba University, Tunisia

This paper presents a new possibilistic information retrieval system using semantic query expansion. The work is involved in query expansion strategies based on external linguistic resources. In this case, the authors exploited the French dictionary "Le Grand Robert". First, they model the dictionary as a graph and compute similarities between query terms by exploiting the circuits in the graph. Second, the possibility theory is used by taking advantage of a double relevance measure (possibility and necessity) between the articles of the dictionary and query terms. Third, these two approaches are combined by using two different aggregation methods. The authors also benefit from an existing approach for reweighting query terms in the possibilistic matching model to improve the expansion process. In order to assess and compare the approaches, the authors performed experiments on the standard 'LeMonde94' test collection.

Chapter 15
Effective Fuzzy Ontology Based Distributed Document Using Non-Dominated Ranked Genetic Algorithm 243
M. Thangamani, Kongu Engineering College, India
P. Thangaraj, Bannari Amman Institute of Technology, India

The increase in the number of documents has aggravated the difficulty of classifying those documents according to specific needs. Clustering analysis in a distributed environment is a thrust area in artificial intelligence and data mining. Its fundamental task is to utilize characters to compute the degree of related corresponding relationship between objects and to accomplish automatic classification without earlier knowledge. Document clustering utilizes clustering technique to gather the documents of high resemblance collectively by computing the documents resemblance. Recent studies have shown that ontologies are useful in improving the performance of document clustering. Ontology is concerned with the conceptualization of a domain into an individual identifiable format and machine-readable format containing entities, attributes, relationships, and axioms. By analyzing types of techniques for document clustering, a better clustering technique depending on Genetic Algorithm (GA) is determined. Non-Dominated Ranked Genetic Algorithm (NRGA) is used in this paper for clustering, which has the capability of providing a better classification result. The experiment is conducted in 20 newsgroups data set for evaluating the proposed technique. The result shows that the proposed approach is very effective in clustering the documents in the distributed environment.

Chapter 16
A Dynamically Optimized Fluctuation Smoothing Rule for Scheduling Jobs in a Wafer Fabrication Factory 265
Toly Chen, Feng Chia University, Taiwan

This paper presents a dynamically optimized fluctuation smoothing rule to improve the performance of scheduling jobs in a wafer fabrication factory. The rule has been modified from the four-factor bi-criteria nonlinear fluctuation smoothing (4f-biNFS) rule, by dynamically adjusting factors. Some properties of the dynamically optimized fluctuation smoothing rule were also discussed theoretically. In addition, production simulation was also applied to generate some test data for evaluating the effectiveness of the proposed methodology. According to the experimental results, the proposed methodology was better than some existing approaches to reduce the average cycle time and cycle time standard deviation. The results also showed that it was possible to improve the performance of one without sacrificing the other performance metrics.

Chapter 17
A Heuristic Method for Learning Path Sequencing for Intelligent Tutoring System (ITS) in E-Learning 285
Sami A. M. Al-Radaei, IT BHU, India
R. B. Mishra, IT BHU, India

Course sequencing is one of the vital aspects in an Intelligent Tutoring System (ITS) for e-learning to generate the dynamic and individual learning path for each learner. Many researchers used different methods like Genetic Algorithm, Artificial Neural Network, and TF-IDF (Term Frequency- Inverse Document Frequency) in E-leaning systems to find the adaptive course sequencing by obtaining the relation between the courseware. In this paper, heuristic semantic values are assigned to the keywords in the courseware based on the importance of the keyword. These values are used to find the relationship between courseware based on the different semantic values in them. The dynamic learning path sequencing is then generated. A comparison is made in two other important methods of course sequencing using TF-IDF and Vector Space Model (VSM) respectively, the method produces more or less same sequencing path in comparison to the two other methods. This method has been implemented using Eclipse IDE for java programming, MySQL as database, and Tomcat as web server.

Compilation of References 302

About the Contributors 333

Index 341

Preface

INTRODUCTION

Currently, organizations face many business challenges due to the changing business climate, including competition, managerial restructuring due to right-sizing, mergers & acquisitions, and new partnerships. To cope with this fast changing environment, organizations are focusing on services to stay competitive. There is renewed interest in developing efficient services in every business domain to improve the overall performance of the organization. Especially, nowadays, many businesses are focusing on service dominant logic. The core of service dominant logic is that the "value of a product is co-created through activities between service provider and service consumer." Moreover, the main focus of service logic is value, which the customer wants to get from the service that is provided. In order to provide the expected value to customers, services should meet their expectations. The requirements for services should be in line with what customers want from the service. Therefore, it is important to not only gather the right requirements from customers but also include the service provider's requirements in designing appropriate services. The implementation and delivery of services require the integration of a variety of technologies. Thus, IT convergence is also necessary for service implementation and delivery in order to provide a good customer service experience. The IT convergence based service design adds another layer of requirements that also need to be taken into account. Thus, managing the requirements for IT convergence based services is an important issue and is an active area of research.

Eliciting appropriate requirements from both the service providers and consumers is essential for the service identification process. Typically, a Goal and Scenario based methodology is used for eliciting requirements in the context of SOA (Service - Oriented Architecture). To incorporate the notion of value in the service identification methodology, a value based requirements engineering methodology is used. In this approach, one can distinguish and calculate the value associated with each requirement. Thus, through this methodology, one can address the value issue and identify the high value requirements. Since the traditional service identification methodologies just focus on eliciting requirements from existing, known customers without worrying about value concept, a value added requirements elicitation methodology should be used that can be applied for IT convergence based services. Results from requirements engineering field and IT convergence field in the context of services and the design of service systems need to be integrated. In addition, these service systems should provide mechanisms for value co-creation. Hence, novel approaches are required which can combine service identification using goal and scenario in SOA and value based requirement engineering to IT convergence to facilitate value co-creation between provider and customer in a service system.

There are three major factors that impact the success of service design - first, the value co-creation aspect; second, requirements management for service identification; and third, IT convergence. It is important that organizations clearly understand these factors and institute measures to enhance them. Each of these factors is briefly described below. The interaction process between the service provider and customers is referred to as co-creation. Another way of characterizing this phenomenon is through the notion of procurer (consists of producer and consumer). This co-creation activity generates value for all the stakeholders involved, which is then referred to as "value-co-creation." Through this activity, participants can attain their goals which they wanted to achieve before the participation. Value co-creation is an integral part of service systems. Maglio and Spohrer state that "a service system represents any value co-creation configuration of people, technology, value propositions connecting internal and external service systems, and shared information such as language, laws, and measures." In addition, the smaller service systems focus on an individual's interaction with others, while the larger service systems comprise the global economy.

A scenario based approach is used for requirements management and service identification, particularly in the context of IT convergence. This may introduce additional requirements and interactions with system requirements. Goal and scenario methodology has been used for eliciting requirements from a number of stakeholders. In this approach, a goal is something that a stakeholder hopes to achieve in the future. Goals are extracted through the elicitation process from the service provider and customer, and hence represent the objectives of the service provider and customer. Scenarios are the means for achieving the elicited goals. To achieve each scenario, one or more sub-scenarios may be needed. Scenario modeling consists of three levels (Business Level, Service Level and Interaction Level). The first level, called the "Business Level," is the highest among the three levels. This level represents the business requirements given by an organization or a person who plays the role of a business analyst. Thus, this level represents the direction, purpose, and objective of the organization. The second level, called the "Service Level," stands for what the system should provide to an organization to fulfill the business requirements. It means that this level is a sub level of the business level. In addition, this level can consist of more than one component to complete the business objectives. The third level is called the "Interaction Level." Through this level's processes, we can achieve the different components of the service level. Potential changes are elaborated in variable scenarios that describe possible alternative or optional scenarios of a base scenario. The variable scenario model includes variable scenarios as well as all requirements and scenarios of the scenario model. Finally, potential services can be identified from the variable scenario model.

IT Convergence refers to being able to unify and provide a common platform for co-existence. This may involve getting different components to work together in conjunction. With increasing globalization and the growing dynamics of the business environment, technology is definitely an integral part of operations and service delivery. Technological innovations can be used to link and improve services. This is because technology affects the general public, businesses and government in more ways than one. It can be used as a means of providing better services to customers and a cost effective tool for businesses. The concept of integrating technology with different domains has proved to be innovative as well as successful in the recent past. Some of the most noticeable examples include integrating technology into the communications world. For example, the Voice over Internet Protocol service is definitely providing a new method of communication that successfully links the ICT sector with IT convergence. IT convergence comes into play when we are able to provide a better interface for customers. It can be viewed as a mechanism for effectively delivering the required services in accordance with the customer feedback. Thus, there is a great need for integrating value based requirements management and IT convergence to improve service identification, design, and delivery.

ORGANIZATION OF THE BOOK

In Chapter 1, titled "Classifying Consumer Comparison Opinions to Uncover Product Strengths and Weaknesses," Xu et al. discuss opinion mining on the Web. A huge volume of Web content is generated by users in online forums, wikis, blogs, and social networks, among others. These user-contributed contents include numerous user opinions regarding products, services, or political issues. Among these user opinions, certain comparison opinions exist, reflecting customer preferences. Mining comparison opinions is useful as these types of viewpoints can bring more business values than other types of opinion data. Manufacturers can better understand relative product strengths or weaknesses, and accordingly develop better products to meet consumer requirements. Meanwhile, consumers can make purchasing decisions that are more informed by comparing the various features of similar products. In this chapter, a novel Support Vector Machine-based method is proposed to automatically identify comparison opinions, extract comparison relations, and display results with the comparison relation maps by mining the volume of consumer opinions posted on the Web. The proposed method is empirically evaluated based on consumer opinions crawled from the Web.

Nikolai Dahlem, in Chapter 2 titled, "OntoClippy: A User-Friendly Ontology Design and Creation Methodology," describes OntoClippy, a tool-supported methodology for the user-friendly design and creation of ontologies. Existing ontology design methodologies and tools are targeted at experts and not suitable for users without a background in formal logic. Therefore, this research develops a methodology and a supporting tool to facilitate the acceptance of ontologies by a wider audience. In this article, the author positions the approach with respect to the current state of the art, formulates the basic principles of the methodology, presents its formal grounding, and describes its phases in detail. To demonstrate the viability of his approach, the author performs a comparative evaluation. The experiment is described, as well as real-world applications of the approach.

Chapter 3, "Combining Supervised Learning Techniques to Key-Phrase Extraction for Biomedical Full-Text," by Qi et al., discusses extracting key phrases from PubMed. Key-phrase extraction plays a useful a role in research areas of Information Systems (IS) like digital libraries. Short meta-data like key phrases are beneficial for researchers to understand the concepts found in the documents. This chapter evaluates the effectiveness of different supervised learning techniques on biomedical full-text: Sequential Minimal Optimization (SMO) and K-Nearest Neighbor, both of which could be embedded inside an information system for document search. The authors use these techniques to extract key phrases from PubMed and evaluate the performance of these systems using the holdout validation method. This chapter compares different classifier techniques and performance differences between the full-text and it's abstract. It concludes that SVMreg-1 performs best in key-phrase extraction for full-text, whereas Naïve Bayes performs best for abstracts. These techniques should be considered for use in information system search functionality.

In Chapter 4, Dollmann et al. discuss the "Design and Usage of a Process-Centric Collaboration Methodology for Virtual Organizations in Hybrid Environments." This chapter describes a collaboration methodology for virtual organizations where the processes can be automatically executed using a hybrid web service, grid or cloud resources. Typically, the process of deriving executable workflows from process models is cumbersome and can be automated only in part or specific to a particular distributed system. The approach introduced in this chapter, exemplified by the construction industry field, integrates existing technology within a process-centric framework. The solution on the basis of a hybrid system architecture in conjunction with semantic methods for consistency saving and the framework for modeling VO processes and their automated transformation and execution are discussed in detail.

Kim and Storey provide an ontology engineering method in Chapter 5, titled "Construction of Domain Ontologies: Sourcing the World Wide Web." As the World Wide Web evolves into the Semantic Web, domain ontologies, which represent the concepts of an application domain and their associated relationships, have become increasingly important as surrogates for capturing and representing the semantics of real world applications. Much ontology development remains manual and is both difficult and time-consuming. This chapter presents a methodology for semi-automatically generating domain ontologies from extracted information on the World Wide Web. The methodology is implemented in a prototype that integrates existing ontology and web organization tools. The prototype is used to develop anthologies for different application domains, and an empirical analysis carried out to demonstrate the feasibility of the research.

In Chapter 6, titled "Self Adaptive Particle Swarm Optimization for Efficient Virtual Machine Provisioning in Cloud," Jeyarani, Nagaveni, and Ram discuss a novel approach for load balancing in a cloud infrastructure. Cloud Computing provides dynamic leasing of server capabilities as a scalable, virtualized service to end users. Their work focuses on Infrastructure as a Service (IaaS) model where custom Virtual Machines (VM) are launched in appropriate servers available in a data-center. The context of the environment is a large scale, heterogeneous, and dynamic resource pool. Nonlinear variation in the availability of processing elements, memory size, storage capacity, and bandwidth causes resource dynamics apart from the sporadic nature of workload. The major challenge is to map a set of VM instances onto a set of servers from a dynamic resource pool so the total incremental power drawn upon the mapping is minimal and does not compromise the performance objectives. This chapter discusses a novel Self Adaptive Particle Swarm Optimization (SAPSO) algorithm to solve the intractable nature of the above challenge. This approach promptly detects and efficiently tracks the changing optimum that represents target servers for VM placement. The experimental results of SAPSO were compared with Multi-Strategy Ensemble Particle Swarm Optimization (MEPSO) and the results show that SAPSO outperforms the latter.

Rigi and Khoshalhan discuss the meeting scheduling problem in Chapter 7. The chapter, "Eliciting User Preferences in Multi-Agent Meeting Scheduling Problem," applies the analytical hierarchy process to solve this problem. The Meeting Scheduling Problem (MSP) arranges meetings between a number of participants. Reaching consensus in arranging a meeting is very difficult and time-consuming when the number of participants is large. One efficient approach for overcoming this problem is the use of multi-agent systems. In a multi-agent system, agents are deciding on behalf of their users. They must be able to elicit their users' preferences in an effective way. This chapter focuses on the elicitation of users 'preferences. Analytical hierarchy process (AHP) - which is known for its ability to determine preferences - is used in this research. Specifically, an adaptive preference modeling technique based on AHP is developed and implemented in a system and the initial validation results are encouraging.

"Wireless Sensor Node Placement Using Hybrid Genetic Programming and Genetic Algorithms," is Chapter 8 by Tripathi et al. This chapter models a wireless sensor network, consisting of a number of nodes, and a unique sink to which all the information is transmitted using the shortest connecting path. Traditionally the systems have used Genetic Algorithms for optimal placement of the nodes that usually fail to give results in problems employing large numbers of nodes or higher areas to be covered. This chapter provides a hybrid Genetic Programming (GP) and Genetic Algorithm (GA) for solving the problem. While the GP optimizes the deployment structure, the GA is used for actual node placement as per the GP optimized structure. The GA serves as a slave and GP serves as master in this hierarchical implementation. The algorithm optimizes total coverage area, energy utilization, lifetime of the network, and the number of nodes deployed. Experimental results show that the algorithm could place the sensor nodes in a variety of scenarios. The placement was found to be better than random placement strategy as well as the Genetic Algorithm placement strategy.

In Chapter 9, Lai et al. discuss an "Intelligent Agent-Based e-Learning System for Adaptive Learning." Adaptive learning approaches support learners to achieve the intended learning outcomes through a personalized way. Previous studies mistakenly treat adaptive e-Learning as personalizing the presentation style of the learning materials, which is not completely correct. The main idea of adaptive learning is to personalize the earning content in a way that can cope with individual differences in aptitude. In this study, an adaptive learning model is designed based on the Aptitude-Treatment Interaction theory and Constructive Alignment Model. The model aims at improving students 'learning outcomes through enhancing their intrinsic motivation to learn. This model is operationalized with a multi-agent framework and is validated under a controlled laboratory setting. The result is quite promising. The individual differences of students, especially in the experimental group, have been narrowed significantly. Students who have difficulties in learning show significant improvement after the test.

The next chapter, titled "Intelligent Information Retrieval Using Fuzzy Association Rule Classifier," by Veeramalai and Kannan, investigates ways for efficient web page retrieval. As the use of web applications increases, when users use search engines for finding some information by inputting keywords, the number of web pages that match the information increases at a tremendous rate. It is not easy for a user to retrieve the exact web page which contains information he or she requires. In Chapter 10, an approach to web page retrieval system using the hybrid combination of context based and collaborative filtering method employing the concept of fuzzy association rule classification is introduced and the authors propose an innovative clustering of user profiles in order to reduce the filtering space and achieves sub-linear filtering time. This approach can produce recommended web page links for users based on the information that associates strongly with users' queries quickly with better efficiency and therefore improve the recall, precision of a search engine.

Rani and Deepa, in Chapter 11, propose "An Intelligent Operator for Genetic Fuzzy Rule Based System." This chapter proposes a modified form of operator based on Particle Swarm Optimization (PSO) for designing Genetic Fuzzy Rule Based System (GFRBS). The usual procedure of velocity updating in PSO is modified by calculating the velocity using chromosome's individual best value and global best value based on an updating probability without considering the inertia weight, old velocity and constriction factors. This kind of calculation brings intelligent information sharing mechanism and memory capability to Genetic Algorithm (GA) and can be easily implemented along with other genetic operators. The performance of the proposed operator is evaluated using ten publicly available bench mark data sets. Simulation results show that the proposed operator introduces new material into the population, thereby allows faster and more accurate convergence without struck into a local optima. Statistical analysis of the experimental results shows that the proposed operator produces a classifier model with minimum number of rules and higher classification accuracy.

In Chapter 12, titled "Software Effort Estimation: Harmonizing Algorithms and Domain Knowledge in an Integrated Data Mining Approach," Deng et al. discuss effort estimation in software development.

It is important for quality management in the software development industry, yet its automation still remains a challenging issue. Applying machine learning algorithms alone often cannot achieve satisfactory results. This chapter presents an integrated data mining framework that incorporates domain knowledge into a series of data analysis and modeling processes, including visualization, feature selection, and model validation. An empirical study on the software effort estimation problem using a benchmark dataset shows the necessity and effectiveness of the proposed approach.

The next chapter, Chapter 13, is titled "An Ontology Based Model for Document Clustering," by Sridevi and Nagaveni. Existing clustering research emphasizes the development of more efficient clustering method without considering the domain knowledge and user's need. In recent years the semantics of documents have been utilized in document clustering. This chapter focuses on the clustering model where ontology approach is applied. The major challenge is to use the background knowledge in the similarity measure. This chapter presents an ontology based annotation of documents and clustering system. The semi-automatic document annotation and concept weighting scheme is used to create an ontology based knowledge base. The Particle Swarm Optimization (PSO) clustering algorithm can be applied to obtain the clustering solution. The accuracy of clustering has been computed before and after combining ontology with Vector Space Model (VSM). The proposed ontology based framework gives improved performance and better clustering compared to the traditional vector space model.

Chapter 14, by Elayeb et al., presents a possibilistic information retrieval system using semantic query expansion. It utilizes query expansion strategies based on external linguistic resources such as the French dictionary "Le Grand Robert." First, the authors model the dictionary as a graph and compute similarities between query terms by exploiting the circuits in the graph. Second, the possibility theory is used by taking advantage of a double relevance measure (possibility and necessity) between the articles of the dictionary and query terms. Third, these two approaches are combined by using two different aggregation methods. The authors also adapt an existing approach for reweighting query terms in the possibility matching model to improve the expansion process .In order to assess and compare the approaches, the authors have performed experiments on the standard 'LeMonde94'test collection.

"Effective Fuzzy Ontology Based Distributed Document Using Non-Dominated Ranked Genetic Algorithm," is Chapter 15 by Thangamani and Thangaraj. They contend that ontologies are useful in improving the performance of document clustering. An ontology is concerned with the conceptualization of a domain into an individual identifiable format and machine-readable format containing entities, attributes, relationships, and axioms. By analyzing the existing techniques for document clustering, a better clustering technique depending on Genetic Algorithm (GA) is proposed. Non-Dominated Ranked Genetic Algorithm (NRGA) is used in this chapter for clustering, which has the capability of providing a better classification result. An experiment has been conducted using a 20 newsgroups data set for evaluating the proposed technique. The result shows that the proposed approach is very effective in clustering the documents in a distributed environment.

In Chapter 16, Chen and Chia discuss "A Dynamically Optimized Fluctuation Smoothing Rule for Scheduling Jobs in a Wafer Fabrication Factory" in Taiwan. The rule has been modified from the four-factor bi-criteria nonlinear fluctuation smoothing (4f-biNFS) rule, by dynamically adjusting factors. Some properties of the dynamically optimized fluctuation smoothing rule are also discussed theoretically. In addition, production simulation is also applied to generate some test data for evaluating the effectiveness of the proposed methodology. According to the experimental results, the proposed methodology is better than some existing approaches to reduce the average cycle time and cycle time standard deviation. The results also show that it is possible to improve the performance of one without sacrificing the other performance metrics.

The book ends with Chapter 17, titled "A Heuristic Method for Learning Path Sequencing for Intelligent Tutoring System (ITS) in E-Learning," by Al-Radaei and Mishra. In this chapter, heuristic semantic values are assigned to the keywords in the courseware based on the importance of the keyword. These values are used to find the relationship between courseware based on the different semantic values in them. The dynamic learning path sequencing is then generated. A comparison is made with two other important methods of course sequencing using TF-IDF and Vector Space Model (VSM), respectively. The proposed method produces more or less same sequencing path in comparison to the two other methods. This method has been implemented using Eclipse IDE for Java programming, MySQL database, and Tomcat web server.

Vijayan Sugumaran
Oakland University, USA & Sogang University, South Korea

Acknowledgment

Dr. Sugumaran's research has been partly supported by Sogang Business School's World Class University Program (R31-20002) funded by Korea Research Foundation and Sogang University Research Grant of 2011.

Chapter 1
Classifying Consumer Comparison Opinions to Uncover Product Strengths and Weaknesses

Kaiquan Xu
City University of Hong Kong, China

Wei Wang
City University of Hong Kong, China

Jimmy S. J. Ren
City University of Hong Kong, China

Jin Xu
Southwest Jiaotong University, China

Long Liu
USTC-CityU Joint Advanced Research Centre, China

Stephen S. Y. Liao
City University of Hong Kong, China

ABSTRACT

With the Web 2.0 paradigm, a huge volume of Web content is generated by users at online forums, wikis, blogs, and social networks, among others. These user-contributed contents include numerous user opinions regarding products, services, or political issues. Among these user opinions, certain comparison opinions exist, reflecting customer preferences. Mining comparison opinions is useful as these types of viewpoints can bring more business values than other types of opinion data. Manufacturers can better understand relative product strengths or weaknesses, and accordingly develop better products to meet consumer requirements. Meanwhile, consumers can make purchasing decisions that are more informed by comparing the various features of similar products. In this paper, a novel Support Vector Machine-based method is proposed to automatically identify comparison opinions, extract comparison relations, and display results with the comparison relation maps by mining the volume of consumer opinions posted on the Web. The proposed method is empirically evaluated based on consumer opinions crawled from the Web. The initial experimental results show that the performance of the proposed method is promising and this research opens the door to utilizing these comparison opinions for business intelligence.

DOI: 10.4018/978-1-4666-2047-6.ch001

INTRODUCTION

With the emergence of Web 2.0, an increasing number of customers are now afforded opportunities to directly express their opinions and sentiments regarding products/services through various channels, such as online forums, wikis, blogs, social networks, and so on. These opinion data coming directly from customers contain a significant amount of potential business value. Studies on mining customer opinions exist (Ashish & Maluf, 2009; Chau & Xu, 2007; Chen, 2006; Hamdi, 2008; Li, 2008; Liu, 2006; Pang & Lee, 2008; Raghu & Chen, 2007); however, these mainly focus on identifying customer sentiment polarities toward products/services. Less work has been conducted on mining a more important type of opinion data, that is, comparison opinions. Customer reviews are often a rich source of comparison opinions. Users typically prefer to compare several competitive products with similar functions, for example,

Nokia N95 Has a Stronger Signal Than iPhone

- The iPhone has better looks, but a much higher price than the BB Curve.
- Compared with the v3, this V8 has a bigger body, and it has a much worse keyboard than Nokia E71.

For producers, these comparison opinions are precious information sources for identifying the relative strengths and weaknesses of products, analyzing threats from competitors, and designing new products and business strategies. For individual users, these comparison opinions contain rich information for decision-making support through the numerous customer experiences provided.

Mining comparison opinions is a non-trivial task due to the large amount of customer reviews and their informal style. Mature search engine technologies cannot recognize these reviews very well, so for utilizing such a huge volume of user opinion data, a considerable amount of time and labor is spent reading text to recognize and summarize these comparison opinions, which is usually infeasible. But if these comparison opinions can be automatically extracted and expressed succinctly as tuples, such as better (Nokia 95, iPhone, camera) (The Nokia 95 is better than iPhone in the camera attribute.), these tuples are summarized and displayed as comparison relation maps (Figure 1).

These maps visually show which products are better compared with similar products on a given set of features, as expressed by customer reviews. The maps can help product manufacturers quickly recognize their products' strengths or weaknesses, and assist individual users in choosing products according to their preferences.

Building comparison relation maps is extremely complicated and involves several subtasks: identifying product and attribute names, recognizing the comparison relations, and categorizing these relations. A single comparison relation includes more than two entities, and has several possible categories ("better," "worse," and "same"). These new characters make recognizing and extracting comparison relations more difficult than the traditional relation extraction task (Zelenko, Aone, & Richardella, 2003).

In this paper, a novel approach is proposed for building comparison maps, in which the abovementioned task is formally described as a multi-class classification. A multi-step process is put forward. In particular, for identifying and categorizing the comparison relations (a key complicated step), the multi-class Support Vector Machine (SVM) is adopted as it exhibits better performance compared with other methods. In addition, various linguistic features are evaluated on their effectiveness. Empirical results show that the performance of the proposed approach is quite competitive, implying the feasibility of

Figure 1. Product comparison relation map

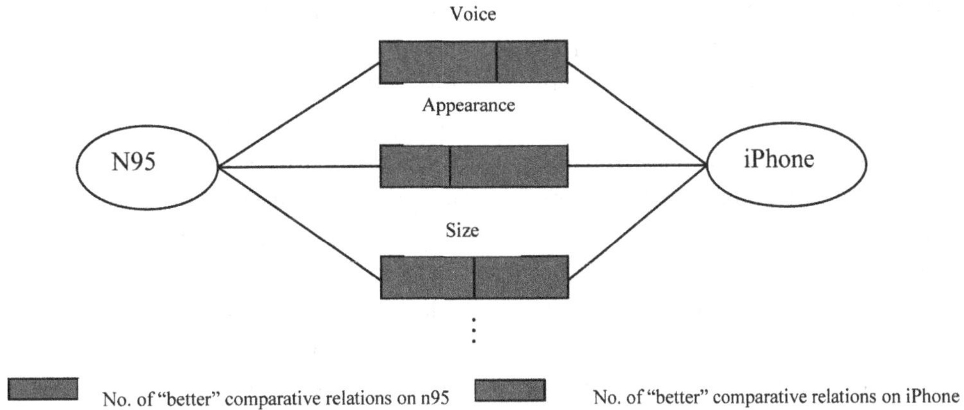

building comparison relation maps for Web 2.0 user opinions.

This paper is organized as follows: the related work is introduced in the next section; then the formal description of the comparison relation mining and the proposed process are described; after that, the process of identifying and categorizing the comparison relations is given; and the empirical evaluation and discussion are presented; and the last section states the conclusion and future work.

RELATED WORK

Sentiment Analysis

Much work has been conducted on analyzing user sentiments from opinion data (Ashish & Maluf, 2009; Chau & Xu, 2007; Chen, 2006; Hamdi, 2008; Li, 2008; Liu, 2006; Pang & Lee, 2008; Raghu & Chen, 2007). These studies mainly recognize the polarities of user reviews. In these studies, three levels of analysis are conducted: document level, sentence level, and attribute level. Sentiment analysis at the document level classifies reviews into different polarities (i.e., positive, negative, or neutral) by summarizing the overall sentiments in the reviews. Usually, classification technologies based on machine learning are adopted (Pang, Lee, & Vaithyanathan, 2002). An innovative methodology for classification of Web forum opinions in multiple languages was proposed by Abbasi and Chen et al. (Abbasi, Chen, & Salem, 2008). Sentiment analysis at the sentence level involves identifying subjective sentences and recognizing their polarities. Certain machine learning methods are adopted for this task (Wiebe, Bruce, & O'Hara, 1999; Yu & Hatzivassiloglou, 2003). However, sentiment analysis at both the document and sentence levels is very general and cannot precisely identify user preferences, while sentiment analysis at the attribute level tries to avoid this disadvantage, focusing on mining opinions on specific product attributes. According to Hu and Liu (2004), the method based on sequence rules is used to extract product attributes, and the context information is then used to recognize the polarities of opinion phrases on the attributes. For sentiment analysis, various linguistic features can be utilized. Among these features, term presence is more effective than term frequency in categorizing the polarities of review documents, and term positions play an important influence on the performance (Pang, Lee, & Vaithyanathan, 2002). The Part of Speech (POS) tags are good indicators in detecting subjectivity and classifying sentiment polarity (Turney, 2001). Some syntax features (such as the dependency tree) exceed the bag-of-words in recognizing sentiment polarity (Kudo & Matsumoto, 2004). The interactions between topic and sentiment play an important role in categorizing sentiment polarity (Hagedorn, Ciaramita, & Atserias, 2007). The techniques for sentiment analysis are mainly categorized into two groups: unsupervised and supervised approaches. Typically, a sentiment lexicon is created in the unsupervised approach, and the polarities are determined by making a number of calculations utilizing the positive and negative phrases (Hatzivassiloglou & Wiebe, 2000; Turney, 2001). The labeled data is used to train classifiers in the supervised approach, which is for predicting unlabeled data (Pang, Lee, & Vaithyanathan, 2002; Wiebe, Bruce, & O'Hara, 1999; Yu & Hatzivassiloglou, 2003). Other studies on sentiment analysis include recognizing the sentiment target/topic and the opinion holder. The objective of identifying the sentiment target/topic is to discover subjectivity and sentiment sentences (Wiebe, Wilson, Bruce, Bell, & Martin, 2004; Yi, Nasukawa, Bunescu, & Niblack, 2003; Yi & Niblack, 2005). Various linguistic clues have been proposed for this task. Semantic parsing techniques have been proposed for identifying the opinion holders associated with particular opinions (Bethard, Yu, Thornton, Hatzivassiloglou, & Jurafsky, 2004; Kim, Jung, & Myaeng, 2007).

As noted, these studies have mainly focused on judging customer sentiment polarities toward products/services. However, few studies have recognized user polarities on comparisons of similar products. Usually, this type of sentiment polarity is more important for producers to learn their products' strengths and weaknesses, and for users to find the products that they like.

Relation Extraction

Another closely related research area is relation extraction, which detects if a specific relation occurs between entities, such as work_in (Tom, IBM: Tom works in IBM). There are a number of methods for relation extraction tasks. One set of these is based on rules/templates, while others adopt various classification techniques. In rule-based methods, the extraction rules are edited manually (Divoli & Attwood, 2005) or automatically generated from annotated training samples (Hakenberg, Plake, Leser, & Kirsch, 2005). The classification-based methods can be divided into two categories: feature-based (Kambhatla, 2004) and kernel-based methods (Bunescu & Mooney, 2005, 2006). In feature-based methods, the feature set (such as words, POS tags, entity types, path in parse tree, and so on) is defined to represent the examples for training classifiers. Although the computing time for these methods is relatively low, choosing appropriate features is intuitive and difficult. The kernel-based methods define kernels to implicitly compute the similarities of examples in a high-dimension space without explicitly representing examples using certain features. For example, the shallow parse tree and dependency tree kernels were proposed separately in (Culotta & Sorensen, 2004) and (Zelenko, Aone, & Richardella, 2003). In (Li, Zhang, Li, & Chen, 2008), a trace kernel was proposed to capture richer contextual information for biomedical relation extraction. Although a defined feature set is not a requirement in these methods, computation complexity is relatively high.

Mining comparison opinion differs from the existing relation extraction in two important aspects. The first aspect is the higher-order of comparison relation, where a single comparison relation usually contains three entities/arguments, while the existing relation extraction methods mainly detect relations with two entities. The second aspect is the multi-directions of comparison relation, where mining comparison relations not only detect if the comparison relations occur or not, but also recognize their directions (i.e., to indicate that product A is better than product B on a particular attribute, or the inverse). In contrast, existing relation extraction methods only detect the occurrences of relations. These two new characteristics bring particular challenges to mining comparison opinions. More linguistic features need to be captured to better extract the comparison relations; multi-class classification technologies should be resorted to for recognizing the directions of the comparison relation, unlike the existing relation extraction problems, which are typically binary-class classification problems.

Competitor Analysis

For competitor analysis, only limited work has been done. Bao et al. (2008) used a number of statistical measures on key words of webpages to find competitors in certain special domains, such as in the SAP vs. Oracle in the ERP domain. However, their work cannot show which producer is better in a particular aspect. Conversely, this paper focuses on mining comparison opinions at the sentence level, which allows the specific identification of what product is better on which attribute.

The lone study thus far on comparison opinion mining is that of Jindal and Liu (2006a). In their work, only comparison sentences are identified, after which relation items are extracted. The comparative relations are categorized into three types: "non-equal gradable", "same", and "superlative" (for the "non-equal gradable" comparison relation, the directions were not differentiated). A very complicated method is adopted. First, a list of key words is used to filter out candidate comparative sentences. A Bayesian classifier is then trained for detecting comparative sentences, using the sequence rules from the training examples and manual compilation. After that, the types of comparison relation are classified with SVM. The single assumption made is that there is only one comparison relation in a sentence.

Jindal and Liu's method has several disadvantages. First, the assumption of only one relation per sentence is untrue in many cases. Users often prefer to compare several products or different attributes of similar products in one sentence. Second, their method requires a manual compilation of rules, making adaptation to new domains difficult. Although the rule-based method usually exhibits good precision, the recall is often low (Riloff, Wiebe, & Phillips, 2005). Another important problem is that their method cannot recognize the directions taken by the "non-equal gradable" comparison relations, and therefore cannot judge which products are better. This leads to inefficient exploration of the business values of these comparison opinions.

In summary, mining user comparison opinions is very important as existing relation extraction methods cannot handle high-order relation extraction problems and cannot recognize comparison relation directions. This study is aimed at overcoming these limitations and developing a new method to better extract comparison relations from customer reviews.

PROBLEM DESCRIPTION AND BASIC PROCESS

Problem Description

The key information in most comparison opinions can be represented in a simple way: the comparison relations, which can capture user sentiment polarities on special attributes of competing products. Usually, the comparison relation is a three-tuple: R (P1, P2, A), where P1 and P2 are the two product names, and A is the attribute name (in later sections, P1, P2, and A are referred to as "entity"). The direction of the comparative relation is represented by R: Better (>), Worse (<), and Same (=). Better (>)/Worse (<) means the product P1 is better/worse than P2 on attribute A; Same (=) means they are similar. Here, No_Comparison (~) is taken as a special direction, which means there is no comparative relation between the two products. Thus, the comparison opinion mining task involves detection if there is a comparative relation R (P1, P2, A); and, if so, recognizes the direction of R.

Thus, for comparison opinion mining and comparison relation extraction, at least two issues should be resolved:

1. Entity Recognition

That is, to recognize product and attribute names distributed in opinion data. For example, in the sentence, "Nokia 95 has a better camera than iPhone" "Nokia 95" and "iPhone" are the product names, and "camera" is the attribute name.

2. Relation Recognition and Categorization

That is, to check if there exists a comparison relation among the recognized entities. If so, what is its direction? For example, in the sentence above, a comparative relation exists among (Nokia 95, iPhone, camera), and the relation direction should be ">." However, in this sentence, "The difference between the Pearl and the Curve is the size and the keyboard" no comparison relation exists.

Basic Process

For recognizing and extracting the comparison relations from user opinions, a pipeline process is proposed (Figure 2).

1. **Opinion Data Collection:** Raw customer reviews are collected from various sources such as online shopping sites, customer review sites, blogs, and social network sites. These opinion data can be directly located and automatically downloaded.
2. **Linguistic Features Annotation:** Various linguistic features such as POS tag, phrase chunking, syntactic tree, and semantic role are annotated on the opinion data for later use. Some preprocessing steps are required, including tokenization, sentence splitting, word stemming, syntactic tree parsing, and dependency parsing. This feature can be implemented via Natural Language Process (NLP) tools.
3. **Entity Recognition:** The two types of entities are recognized: product names and attribute names. In the customer opinions about the mobile phones, which is our focus, some product names always exist in various abbreviations, such as "BlackBerry 8320", "BB 8320", and "8320". Product names usually have some special naming rules, and the attribute names are finite and fixed in one domain; therefore, it is easy to recognize them. Since entity recognition is not the focus of this paper, the simpler, lexicon-based method is adopted here.
4. **Relation Recognition and Categorization:** The existence of comparison relation between entities is checked, and its direction is recognized. As mentioned in the section above, the particular characteristics of comparison relation extraction (i.e., involvement of multiple entities and directions) make this task more complicated than existing relation extractions. Thus, comparison relation extraction is the key and most difficult step. The detailed method for this step is introduced in the succeeding sections.
5. **Comparison Relation Map Generation:** The extracted comparison relations are summarized and represented in comparison relation maps. Some postprocess steps are required, such as merging the different names of the same product and attribute, counting the number of the comparison relations between a pair of competitive products, and displaying these results as comparative relation maps. Finally, the maps can be shown visually to support decision making.

COMPARISON RELATION RECOGNITION AND CATEGORIZATION

As mentioned in the previous sections, comparison relations generally involve three entities, and can belong to one of these four categories: ">," "<," "=," or "~" (No_Comparison). Thus, recognizing and categorizing comparison relations are multi-class classification problems, instead of

Figure 2. Basic process of comparison opinion mining

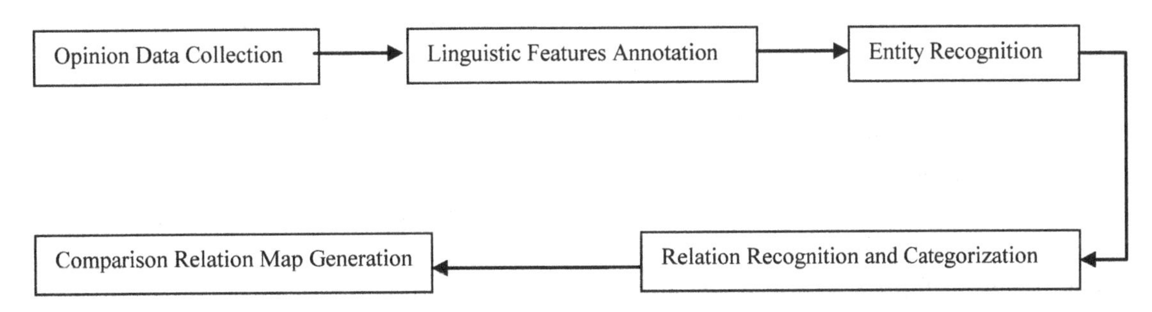

binary-class classification problems. Here, the multi-class SVM (Tsochantaridis, Hofmann, Joachims, & Altun, 2004) is used as it has been proven very effective and efficient.

Multi-Class SVM-Based Method

The SVM was originally designed for binary-class classification problems. Extended multi-class SVM adopts different strategies for multi-class classification problems. Among them, the winner-takes-all strategy adopts the principle: during the training phase, different classifiers are trained for each category, and when predicting, the final prediction is assigned by the classifier with the highest output (Tsochantaridis, Hofmann, Joachims, & Altun, 2004). When mining comparison relations, the winner-takes-all multi-class SVM is extended as follows:

Let R be the feature space of the comparison relations, which indicates the features of different comparison relations. For example, one comparison relation can be represented by entity types, special words, or POS tags.

Let $C = \{>, <, =, \sim\}$ be the category space of the comparison relations.

Let $\Psi(r,c)$ be a feature representation function to represent the combined features of $r \in R$ and $c \in C$. For example, when the sentence containing the relation r includes the words "compared with", and c is ">", a specific element in the feature vector is set to 1.

Our object is to learn a discriminant function $F(r,c,\omega) = \omega \cdot \Psi(r,c)$. For an input comparison relation r, this function assigns a score to each relation/category pair (r, c') $c' \in C$, and the score of the pair (r,c) with c as the right category will be larger than the scores of other pairs (r, c') $c' \in C \,/\, c$. Thus, given a comparison relation r, the prediction category is given by

$$\hat{c} = \arg\max_{c' \in C} F(r, c', \omega).$$

To determine the parameter ω, driven by the idea of the maximum large margin from SVM, the following principle is adopted: for the training examples $\{(r_i, c_i) \mid r_i \in R, c_i \in C\}_{i=1}^{n}$, maximize the minimal margins between $F(r_i, c_i, \omega)$ (the score when the relation r_i has the right category c_i) and $F(r_i, c, \omega)$ $(c \in C \setminus c_i)$ (the score when the relation r_i has other category c). The optimization principle of this method can be formally expressed as

$$\max \min_{i \in \{1...n\}, c \in C \setminus c_i} \{\omega \cdot \Psi(r_i, c_i) - \omega \cdot \Psi(r_i, c)\}.$$

Subject to: $\|\omega\| = 1$

$\omega \cdot \Psi(r_i, c_i) > \omega \cdot \Psi(r_i, c)$, here $i = 1...n$, $c \in C \setminus c_i$.

This learning problem can be transformed into a quadratic programming problem and be efficiently resolved with $O(n^2)$ calculation for a training set with n examples (Platt, 1999).

Linguistic Features

To achieve good performance for comparison relation recognition and categorization, appropriate linguistic features that represent the comparison relations should be captured. By investing the characteristics of comparison opinions, some simple and effective linguistic features are considered. Complex linguistic features (such as semantic roles) are not taken into account because user-generated reviews are always informal expressions (some even including typographical errors), and deep parsing is often inappropriate for this type of data. The adopted features include the following

1. **Entity types:** The patterns in which entity types appear in the comparison relations are usually different, which typically indicate different comparison relation categories. For example,
   a. Nokia N95 has a better camera than iPhone.
   b. The camera of Nokia N95 is better than that of iPhone.

   Although these two sentences express the same comparison relation >(Nokia N95, iPhone, Camera), the entity types appear with different patterns. The pattern of the first sentence is Product- Attribute-Product, but that of the second sentence is Attribute-Product- Product. The entity type feature is used to consider this factor.
2. **Words:** Some important words are good indicators of comparison relations. Here, the two types of words are considered:
   a. **Entity Words:** The words that entities contain, such as, "Nokia N95", "camera".
   b. **Key Words connecting entities:** Some typical words that appear frequently in comparison relations, which are good indicators. Here, the following words and phrases are used:
      i. "In contrast to", "unlike", "compare with", "compare to", "beat", "win", "exceed", "outperform", "prefer", "than", "as", "same", "similar", "superior to", "improvement over", "better", "worse", "best", "worst", "more", "most", "less", "least", and so on.
3. **POS tags:** Comparison relations usually contain the comparative adjective/adverb and superlative adjective/adverb; hence, some POS tags of words and phrase chunking are good indicators of comparative relations. For example, JJR (comparative adjective), JJS (superlative adjective), and Verb.

For these linguistic features, NLP utility tools, such as Gate (GATE, 2009) and Stanford Parser (Stanford NLP Group, 2009), may be used to automatically annotate with high accuracy.

EMPIRICAL EVALUATION

To evaluate the performance of the proposed method and verify the effectiveness of various linguistic features in mining comparison opinions, an empirical evaluation was conducted. In this evaluation, the following two aspects were considered:

1. Compared with other methods, what is the performance of the Multi-class SVM-based method in recognizing and categorizing comparison relations? How does the size of training sample influence the performance?
2. Which kinds of linguistic features are more effective in mining comparison opinions? To what degree do they influence the performance?

Evaluation Design

Data

The web opinion data used in this evaluation were collected from the Amazon online shopping site.

The data include customer reviews on several mobile phones, such as the BlackBerry Curve 8320, the Motorola RAZR2 V8, the BlackBerry Bold 9000, and the Nokia E71. Three domain experts in mobile phones were employed to manually annotate these opinion data. First, the segments containing two different product names were extracted, and these segments typically included all potential comparative relations. Second, for the extracted segments, the product names, attribute names, and sentiment phrases were annotated. Third, comparative relations between different products in one sentence, if any, were detected. If relations existed, the directions of the comparative relations were recognized; otherwise, they were labeled as No_Comparison (~). The final annotating results had to be agreed upon by at least two persons. In summary, the dataset consisted of 750 segments and 2,061 comparative relations. Among these comparative relations, 617 were ">" relations, 456 were "<" relations, 48 are "=" relations, and 940 were "no_comparative" relations.

Data Preprocess

The corpus was preprocessed with NLP tools Gate (GATE, 2009) and Stanford Parser (Stanford NLP Group, 2009) to automatically capture linguistic features. The preprocesses included tokenization, sentence splitting, word stemming, syntactic tree parsing, dependency parsing, and POS tag labeling.

Evaluation Setting and Criteria

The performance of the proposed multi-class SVM-based method was compared with another commonly used multi-class classification technology (Chen & Li, 2010), the maximum entropy model (Berger, Pietra, & Pietra, 1996). The main idea of maximum entropy model is that one should prefer the most uniform models that also satisfy any given constraints. Thus, its learning principle is to maximize distribution entropy on the training data.

In mining comparison opinions, the training examples are always limited, and the numbers of training examples can greatly influence classifier performance. Thus, the performances of these two multi-class classification technologies were compared under the different ratios of the size of training examples to that of testing examples. In the experiment, the ratios were 20:80, 40:60, and 50:50. The features used to represent examples always have a huge impact on classifier performances. Here, different linguistic features were therefore evaluated for their effectiveness in recognizing and categorizing comparison relations. Different conditions (i.e., with all features, with no entity types, with no key words, and with no POS tags) were considered.

The precision, the ratio of the number of properly categorized examples to the number of total examples, was used as the metric in this evaluation. MaxEnt (Zhang, 2009) and SVM-multiclass (Joachims, 2009) software tools were reconfigured and used in this experiment.

Experiment Results and Discussion

Performance with Different Ratios of Training Examples to Testing Examples

Table 1 and Figure 3 show the precision levels of Multi-class SVM and maximum entropy model in recognizing and categorizing comparison relation when the ratios of the size of training examples to that of the testing examples are different. Here, the ratios are respectively 20:80 (20% of all examples as the training examples, 80% as the testing examples), 40:60, and 50:50.

Table 1 shows that the precision of the proposed method is more than 60%, but using only 20% data as the training examples. The performance reaches upwards of 73% if half of the data are used as training examples. These results indicate that the Multi-class SVM-based method achieves quite a competitive performance in recognizing and categorizing the comparison relations, which

Table 1. Precisions of two classifiers with different ratios

Ratio	Maximum Entropy	Multi-class SVM
20:80	60.12%	64.74%
40:60	65.39%	67.69%
50:50	72.22%	73.15%

implies the feasibility of building comparative relation maps from web opinions.

Figure 3 shows that Multi-class SVM-based method is better than the maximum entropy model for this problem. Particularly when the number of training examples is small, the difference is much more evident. Upon increase in training example size, the difference becomes less obvious, probably because of the different learning principles of the two classifiers. The maximum entropy model attempts to learn a classifier that satisfies the constraints of training examples and has the maximum entropy. When the number of training examples is small, the constraints of training examples cannot represent the real distribution of whole examples. Thus, the performance of the maximum entropy model is a little worse compared with the multi-class SVM-based method. However, when the number of training examples increases, the performance of the maximum entropy model improves quickly. In contrast, Multi-class SVM tries to find a hyperplane with a sufficiently large margin that can separate the right examples from the wrong examples. Hence, even with a few training examples, it can still achieve outstanding performance.

Effectiveness of Different Features

Table 2 and Figure 4 show the effectiveness of different features through performance comparison of the two methods under different conditions (i.e., with all feature inclusion, with entity type removal, with key word removal, and with POS tag removal). The rate of performance decrease is checked when removing different kinds of features. This evaluation was conducted with 50:50 as the ratio of the training example size to that of testing examples.

From the table and figure, we can see that for both maximum entropy model and Multi-class SVM, entity type feature extremely affects the performance, showing a decrease of 10.25%. The key words moderately decrease the performance by 7.68%, and POS tag least affects performance. These results indicate that the entity type feature is the most crucial in accurately recognizing and categorizing comparison relations. Key words are also very useful. Thus, in order to achieve good

Figure 3. Comparison of the performance of two classifiers

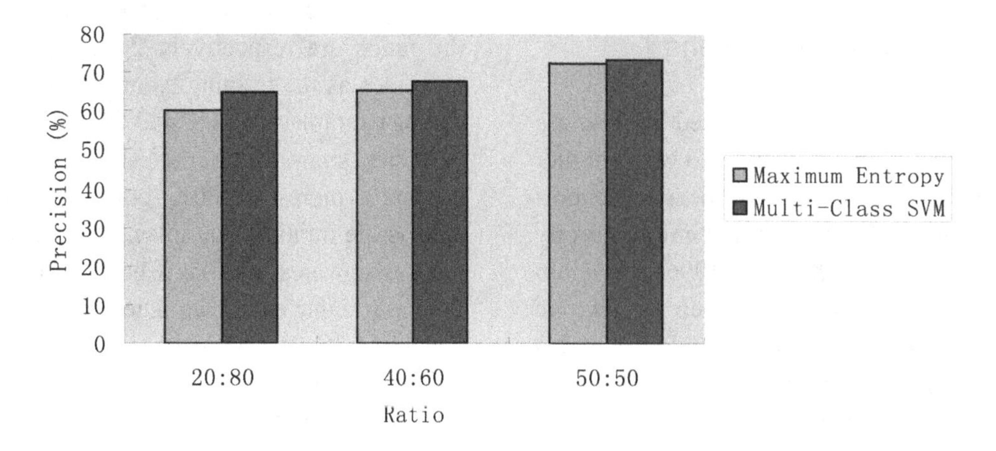

Table 2. Precision when separately removing every type of feature

	All kinds of features	No entity type	No key words	No POS tag
Maximum Entropy Model	72.22	64.82	66.67	68.52
Multi-class SVM	73.15	65.74	67.59	68.52

performance in mining comparison opinions, entity types should be utilized and certain key words explored.

CONCLUSION AND FUTURE WORK

The huge volume of comparison opinions hidden in Web 2.0 user opinion data can bring forth more business values compared with other kinds of opinion data. In this paper, the task of mining these comparison opinions was described to build comparison relation maps of products/services, and a feasible solution process for the task was proposed. The new characteristics of comparison relations make the recognition and categorization of comparison relations much more difficult. The proposed Multi-class SVM-based method achieved good performance with 73.15% precision, a much higher level than the maximum entropy model. Furthermore, the evaluation of effectiveness of different features shows that the entity type is most important in comparison relation recognition and categorization. The experimental evaluation shows the feasibility of mining valuable comparison opinions.

In the future, empirical evaluations of other products aside from mobile phones will be conducted. More linguistic features will be explored to improve the performance of comparison relation recognition and categorization. The joint extraction of product/attribute names and comparison relations will also be studied to reduce the influence of entity recognition on mining comparison relations. In addition, the results of mined comparison opinions will be aligned with the sales figures of products/services to check the influence of these opinions on products sales.

ACKNOWLEDGMENT

An earlier version of the paper appeared in the Proceedings of AMCIS2009.

Figure 4. Precision comparison when separately removing every kind of feature

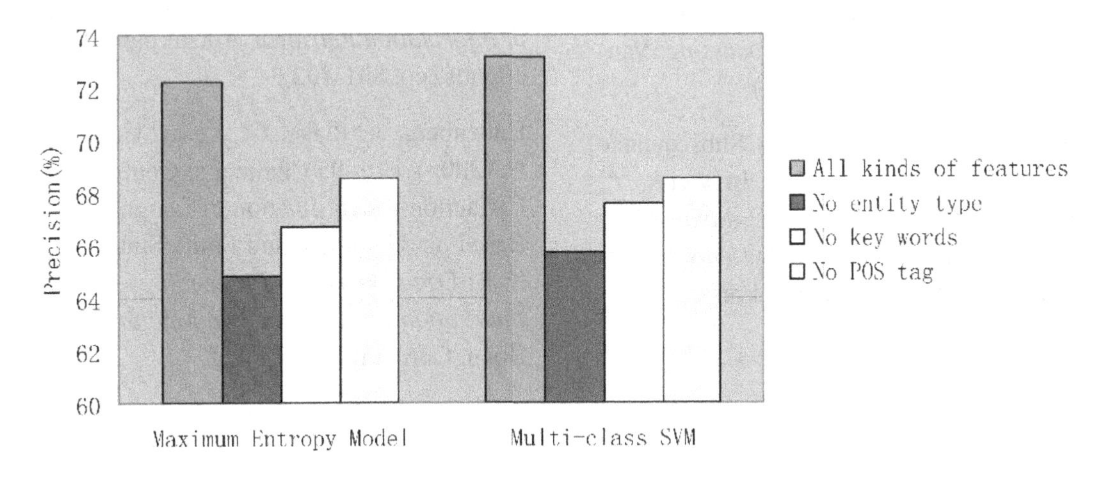

REFERENCES

Abbasi, A., Chen, H., & Salem, A. (2008). Sentiment Analysis in Multiple Languages: Feature Selection for Opinion Classification in Web Forums. *ACM Transactions on Information Systems, 26*(3), 12:1-12:34.

Ashish, N., & Maluf, D. (2009). Intelligent Information Integration: Reclaiming the Intelligence. *International Journal of Intelligent Information Technologies, 5*(3), 28–54.

Bao, S., Li, R., Yu, Y., & Cao, Y. (2008). Competitor Mining with the Web. *IEEE Transactions on Knowledge and Data Engineering, 20*(10), 1297–1310. doi:10.1109/TKDE.2008.98

Berger, A., Pietra, V., & Pietra, S. (1996). A Maximum Entropy approach to Natural Language Processing. *Computational Linguistics, 22*(1), 39–71.

Bethard, S., Yu, H., Thornton, A., Hatzivassiloglou, V., & Jurafsky, D. (2004). Automatic Extraction of Opinion Propositions and their Holders. In Y. Qu, J. Shanahan, & J. Wiebe (Eds.), *Proceedings of the AAAI Spring Symposium on Exploring Attitude and Affect in Text: Theories and Applications,* Stanford, CA (pp. 1-8).

Bunescu, R., & Mooney, J. (2005). A shortest path dependency kernel for relation extraction. In R. Mooney (Ed.), *Proceedings of the Conference on Human Language Technology and Empirical Methods in Natural Language Processing,* Vancouver, BC, Canada (pp. 724-731).

Bunescu, R., & Mooney, R. (2006). Subsequence Kernels for Relation Extraction. In Weiss, Y., Schlkopf, B., & Platt, J. (Eds.), *Advances in Neural Information Processing Systems 18* (pp. 171–178). Cambridge, MA: MIT Press.

Chau, M., & Xu, J. (2007). Mining communities and their relationships in blogs: A study of online hate groups. *International Journal of Human-Computer Studies, 65*(1), 57–70. doi:10.1016/j.ijhcs.2006.08.009

Chen, F., & Li, F. (2010). Comparison of the Hybrid Credit Scoring Models Based on Various Classifiers. *International Journal of Intelligent Information Technologies, 6*(3), 56–74.

Chen, H. (2006). Intelligence and security informatics: information systems perspective. *Decision Support Systems, 41*(3), 555–559. doi:10.1016/j.dss.2004.06.003

Culotta, A., & Sorensen, J. (2004). Dependency tree kernels for relation extraction. In D. Scott (Ed.), *Proceedings of the 42nd Annual Meeting on Association for Computational Linguistics,* Barcelona, Spain (pp. 423:1-423:7).

Divoli, A., & Attwood, T. (2005). BioIE: extracting informative sentences from the biomedical literature. *Bioinformatics (Oxford, England), 21,* 2138–2139. doi:10.1093/bioinformatics/bti296

GATE. (2009). *A General Architecture for Text Engineering*. Retrieved from http://gate.ac.uk/

Hagedorn, B., Ciaramita, M., & Atserias, J. (2007). World knowledge in broad-coverage information filtering. In W. Kraaij & A.P. Vries (Eds.), *Proceedings of the 30th Annual International ACM SIGIR Conference on Research and Development in Information Retrieval,* Amsterdam, The Netherlands (pp. 801-802).

Hakenberg, J., Plake, C., Leser, U., & Kirsch, H. (2005). LLL'05 Challenge: Genic Interaction Extraction - Identification of Language Patterns Based on Alignment and Finite State Automata. In S. Dzeroski (Ed.), *Proceedings of the 22nd International Conference on Machine Learning,* Bonn, Germany (pp. 38-45).

Hamdi, M. (2008). SOMSE: A Neural Network Based Approach to Web Search Optimization. *International Journal of Intelligent Information Technologies*, *4*(4), 31–54.

Hatzivassiloglou, V., & Wiebe, J. (2000). Effects of adjective orientation and gradability on sentence subjectivity. In M. Kay (Ed.), *Proceedings of the 18th Conference on Computational Linguistics*, Saarbrücken, Germany (pp. 299-305).

Hu, M., & Liu, B. (2004). Mining and summarizing customer reviews. In W. Kim & R. Kohavi (Eds.), *Proceedings of the Tenth ACM SIGKDD International Conference on Knowledge Discovery and Data Mining,* Seattle, WA (pp. 168-177).

Jindal, N., & Liu, B. (2006a). Mining Comparative Sentences and Relation. In Y. Gil & R. Mooney (Eds.), *Proceedings of 21st National Conference on Artificial Intelligence,* Boston (pp. 244-251).

Jindal, N., & Liu, B. (2006b). Identifying Comparative Sentences in Text Documents. In E. Efthimiadis (Ed.), *Proceedings of the 29th Annual International ACM SIGIR Conference on Research & Development on Information Retrieval,* Seattle, WA (pp. 244-251).

Joachims, T. (2009). *Multi-Class Support Vector Machine*. Retrieved from http://svmlight.joachims.org/svm_multiclass.html

Kambhatla, N. (2004). Combining lexical, syntactic, and semantic features with maximum entropy models for extracting relations. In J. Chang & Y. Chang (Eds.), *Proceedings of the ACL 2004 on Interactive Poster and Demonstration Sessions,* Barcelona, Spain (p. 2).

Kim, Y., Jung, Y., & Myaeng, S. (2007). Identifying opinion holders in opinion text from online newspapers. In T. Lin, R. Yager, & J. Mendel (Eds.), *Proceedings of the 2007 IEEE International Conference on Granular Computing,* San Jose, CA (p. 699).

Kudo, T., & Matsumoto, Y. (2004). A boosting algorithm for classification of semi-structured text. In D. Lin & D. Wu (Ed.), *Proceedings of the 2004 Conference on Empirical Methods in Natural Language Processing,* Barcelona, Spain (pp. 1-8).

Li, J., Zhang, Z., Li, X., & Chen, H. (2008). Kernel-based learning for biomedical relation extraction. *Journal of the American Society for Information Science and Technology*, *59*(5), 756–769. doi:10.1002/asi.20791

Li, X. (2008). Inference Degradation of Active Information Fusion within Bayesian Network Models. *International Journal of Intelligent Information Technologies*, *4*(4), 1–17.

Liu, B. (2006). *Web Data Mining- Exploring Hyperlinks, Contents and Usage Data.* New York: Springer.

Liu, B. (2008). *Opinion Mining and Summarization.* Paper presented at the 17th International World Wide Web Conference, Beijing, China.

Pang, B., & Lee, L. (2008). Opinion mining and sentiment analysis. In Callan, J., & Sebastiani, F. (Eds.), *Foundations and Trends in Information Retrieval 2*. Boston: Now Publishers.

Pang, B., Lee, L., & Vaithyanathan, S. (2002). Thumbs up? Sentiment Classification using Machine Learning Techniques. In D. Yarowsky & D. Radev (Eds.), *Proceedings of the Conference on Empirical Methods in Natural Language Processing,* Philadelphia (pp. 79-86).

Platt, J. (1999). Fast training of support vector machines using sequential minimal optimization. In Scholkopf, B., Burges, C., & Smola, A. J. (Eds.), *Advances in Kernel Methods: Support Vector Learning* (pp. 185–208). Cambridge, MA: MIT Press.

Raghu, T., & Chen, H. (2007). Cyberinfrastructure for homeland security: Advances in information sharing, data mining, and collaboration systems. *Decision Support Systems*, *43*(4), 1321–1323. doi:10.1016/j.dss.2006.04.002

Riloff, E., Wiebe, J., & Phillips, W. (2005). Exploiting Subjectivity Classification to Improve Information Extraction. In M. Veloso & S. Kambhampati (Eds.), *Proceedings of the 20th National Conference on Artificial Intelligence,* Pittsburgh, PA (pp. 1106-1111).

Stanford, N. L. P. Group. (2009). *The Stanford Parser: A statistical parser.* Retrieved from http://nlp.stanford.edu/software/lex-parser.shtml

Tsochantaridis, I., Hofmann, T., Joachims, T., & Altun, Y. (2004). Support vector machine learning for interdependent and structured output spaces. In C. Brodley (Ed.), *Proceedings of the 21st International Conference on Machine Learning,* Banff, AB, Canada (pp. 104-108).

Turney, P. (2001). Thumbs up or thumbs down? semantic orientation applied to unsupervised classification of reviews. In P. Isabelle (Ed.), *Proceedings of the 40th Annual Meeting on Association for Computational Linguistics,* Philadelphia (pp. 417-424).

Wiebe, J., Bruce, R., & O'Hara, T. (1999). Development and use of a gold-standard data set for subjectivity classifications. In R. Dale & K. Church (Eds.), *Proceedings of the 37th Annual meeting of the Association for Computational Linguistics on Computational Linguistics,* College Park, MD (pp. 246-253).

Wiebe, J., Wilson, T., Bruce, R., Bell, M., & Martin, M. (2004). Learning Subjective Language. *Computational Linguistics*, *30*(3), 277–308. doi:10.1162/0891201041850885

Yi, J., Nasukawa, T., Bunescu, R., & Niblack, W. (2003). Sentiment Analyzer: Extracting Sentiments about a Given Topic using Natural Language Processing Techniques. In J. Shavlik (Ed.), *Proceedings of the Third IEEE International Conference on Data Mining,* Melbourne, FL (pp. 427-434).

Yi, J., & Niblack, W. (2005). Sentiment Mining in WebFountain. In K. Aberer, M. Franklin, & S. Nishio (Eds.), *Proceedings of the 21st International Conference on Data Engineering,* Tokyo (pp. 1073-1083).

Yu, H., & Hatzivassiloglou, V. (2003). Towards answering opinion questions: separating facts from opinions and identifying the polarity of opinion sentences. In M. Collins & M. Steedman (Eds.), *Proceedings of the 2003 Conference on Empirical Methods in Natural Language Processing,* Sapporo, Japan (pp. 129-136).

Zelenko, D., Aone, C., & Richardella, A. (2003). Kernel methods for relation extraction. *Journal of Machine Learning Research*, *3*, 1083–1106. doi:10.1162/153244303322533205

Zhang, L. (2009). *Maximum Entropy Modeling Toolkit for Python and C.* Retrieved from.http://homepages.inf.ed.ac.uk/s0450736/maxent_toolkit.html

This work was previously published in the International Journal of Intelligent Information Technologies, Volume 7, Issue 1, edited by Vijayan Sugumaran, pp. 1-14, copyright 2011 by IGI Publishing (an imprint of IGI Global).

Chapter 2
OntoClippy:
A User-Friendly Ontology Design and Creation Methodology

Nikolai Dahlem
University of Oldenburg, Germany

ABSTRACT

In this article, the author describes OntoClippy, a tool-supported methodology for the user-friendly design and creation of ontologies. Existing ontology design methodologies and tools are targeted at experts and not suitable for users without a background in formal logic. Therefore, this research develops a methodology and a supporting tool to facilitate the acceptance of ontologies by a wider audience. In this article, the author positions the approach with respect to the current state of the art, formulates the basic principles of the methodology, presents its formal grounding, and describes its phases in detail. To demonstrate the viability of our approach, the author performs a comparative evaluation. The experiment is described, as well as real-world applications of the approach.

INTRODUCTION

The acceptance and use of ontologies is hindered by the fact that they are very complex and can only be created by trained ontology engineers. Our goal is making ontologies accessible by designing a methodology and, equally important, a supporting tool, which enable domain-experts and users without a background in logic to design ontologies. We don't want to replace ontology engineers in the ontology building process, but we want to make their work easier by enabling users to build skeleton ontologies, which can be further refined by them.

We envision three use-cases for our approach:

- Average users without a background in computer science, who want to contribute knowledge on their subjects of interest to the semantic web (Berners-Lee, Hendler & Lassila, 2001).
- Domain-experts who create formalized knowledge that is to be used in a software system. Traditionally such ontologies would be created by ontology engineers interviewing domain experts in an iterative process. Enabling domain experts to create initial versions of those ontologies them-

DOI: 10.4018/978-1-4666-2047-6.ch002

selves potentially leads to cost and time benefits when compared to the traditional way.
- Ontology engineers using the methodology for rapid prototyping of ontologies.

We want to reach our goal of increasing the acceptance of ontologies by hiding, as much as possible, the formalism required to build them. Therefore we developed OntoClippy, a user-friendly, tool-supported ontology design and creation methodology with the aim to make ontologies usable by non experts. We want to convey to everybody interested in building ontologies, that ontology design doesn't need to be complex and that by using our tool-supported methodology user will be more productive than with existing methodologies and tools. Eventually we want to test this with an empirical evaluation through experiments and supported by questionnaires.

STATE OF THE ART

In our earlier work we formulated criteria for user-friendly ontology design and creation methodologies and conducted a survey comparing existing methodologies. In the following section we give a short overview over our work and position our work with respect to other approaches for making ontology design and creation more user-friendly.

Criteria for User-Friendly Ontology Design and Creation Methodologies

An ontology creation methodology for domain experts should be efficient to use and easy to learn. The following section gives requirements for such a methodology in the form of criteria the methodology has to meet. These criteria are based on experiences made in the course of the STASIS project (http://www.stasis-project.net). During the project they were discussed and evaluated with users from both academia and industry. Subsequently they have been presented and discussed at the I-ESA conference (Dahlem, Guo, Hahn & Reinelt, 2009).

Besides the methodologies themselves the presented criteria also cover aspects of ontology construction tools and the underlying ontology languages. A methodology should use adequate terminology. It should be well structured, self descriptive, transparent and supported by a tool. The methodology, as well as the supporting tool should help users to avoid errors, they should be robust and consistent and finally they should support conceptualization flexibility (cf. the basic principles of our methodology).

The supporting tools should offer lookahead features, it should hide formality as much as possible and it should present ontology assumptions in a comprehensible manner.

Finally expressiveness is an inherent property of the underlying ontology language, but is also reflected in the methodology itself, as it might restrict the expressiveness to a subset of the underlying language.

Existing Methodologies and Tools

In our earlier work (Dahlem & Hahn, 2009) we conducted a survey comparing ontology creation methodologies found in literature. These methodologies were developed in various communities and with various foci: CommonKADS (Wielinga, Schreiber & Beuker, 1992), Cyc (Lenat, 1995) and KBSI IDEF5 (Benjamin, Menzel, Mayer, Fillion, Futrell, DeWitte & Lingineni, 1994) are geared towards Knowledge Based Systems. The methodologies of Grüninger and Fox (1995) and Uschold and King (1995), as well as METHONTOLOGY (Fernández, Gómez-Pérez & Juristo, 1997), Ontology Development 101 (Noy & McGuinness, 2001) and UPON (De Nicola, Missikoff & Navigli, 1995) are designed for building ontologies from scratch. DILIGENT (Vrandecic, Pinto, Sure & Tempich, 2005) and HCOME (Kotis, Vouros & Alonso, 2005) put the focus on the evolution and collaborative development of ontologies, while SENSUS (Swartout, Patil, Knight & Russ, 1996), KACTUS (Schreiber, Wielinga, Jansweijer, 1995) and ONIONS (Gangemi, Pisanelli & Steve, 1999) build ontologies by deriving domain-ontologies from large scale ontologies, reusing existing ones and reusing other knowledge sources. Finally the On-To-Knowledge methodology (Sure & Studer, 2002) is build for creating and maintaining Knowledge Management applications.

Our survey showed that most methodologies are targeted at experts with backgrounds in formal logic. While some methodologies (Ontology Development 101 and UPON) considered beginners in the field of ontology building and offered a more familiar access (UML) the nonetheless assumed a level of specific knowledge that was too high for non-expert users.

As well as the existing methodologies tools are geared towards experts from different backgrounds (Gruber, Westernthaler & Gahleitner, 2006). To give two prominent examples, the well-known Protégé (http://protege.stanford.edu) is geared towards ontology experts and Altova Semantic Works (http://www.altova.com/products/semanticworks/semantic_web_rdf_owl_editor.html) is geared to users familiar with UML.

We concluded that an approach for improving the usability of ontology creation and design is needed (for further information on the survey cf. Dahlem & Hahn, 2009).

Approaches for Improving Usability of Ontology Design Technologies

There are different existing approaches for improving the usability and user-friendliness of ontology design technology.

One approach is to use controlled vocabularies for creating and interacting with ontologies. Tools using this approach are CLONE (Funk, Tablan, Bontcheva, Cunningham, Davis & Handschuh, 2007), ACE (Kaljurand, 2008) and ROO (Dimitrova, Denaux, Hart, Dolbear, Holt & Cohn, 2008). While natural language is a familiar interface for people controlled vocabularies introduce two new problems. Additionally to learning the ontology model and terms, users also have to memorize the controlled vocabulary. Furthermore it is obviously language dependent and the translation of controlled vocabularies to different languages is more costly than the translation of GUIs.

Another approach is semantic wikis (Schaffert, Gruber & Westenthaler, 2006), which enrich traditional wikis with semantic metadata. While this approach is viable for enriching existing wikis with semantic meta information, it is does not support users in knowledge acquisition and the structuring of knowledge needed for efficiently creating new ontologies.

Yet another approach is the extraction of ontologies from informal representations like concept maps (Simón Cuevas, 2008). While this approach is very user-friendly in using familiar representations it also introduces new problems. The extraction of formal knowledge from informal representations is always error-prone and needs to deal with ambiguity.

Considering the short-comings of the existing approaches and basic principles of ontology modeling (Artz, 2007; March & Allen, 2007) we designed a methodology and a supporting tool that fulfills the following requirements:

- Is geared towards domain-experts and users without a background in formal logic.
- Is grounded in a formal representation, but hides the complexity of the formal models as much as possible.
- Uses a mostly language-independent, easy translatable GUI.
- Supports users in acquiring and structuring knowledge in an intuitive way.

METHODOLOGY

In our methodologies we addressed the aforementioned requirements. We formulated basic principles resulting from the lessons learned while analyzing the shortcomings of existing methodologies. We grounded our methodology in a formal representation and hid the complexity behind an easy to learn graphical representation. Eventually we designed our methodology and the supporting tool based on our basic principles and our formalism and with a GUI based on the graphical representation.

Basic Principles

Our methodology and tool adheres to the following basic principles: hiding of formality, no distinction between A- and T-Box, conceptualization flexibility, flexible hierarchical views and making ontology assumptions explicit. In the following section we will briefly present the single principles.

- **Hiding of formality:** According to Gruber, Westernthaler and Gahleitner (2006) formality tends to increase the user's perception of complexity. Consequently we try to hide all formality by using an intuitive graphical user interface. All steps of our methodology are supported in one view and we provide as much interaction in the form of drag&drop as possible. The only textual interaction is the entering of labels or description, but users won't be confronted with any code. The graphical representation constitutes an intermediate language which is eventually translated in a formalized ontology.
- **No distinction between A- and T-Box:** The distinction whether a concept should be regarded as a class (T-Box) or as an individual (A-Box) is application-specific (cf. Noy & McGuinness, 2001). There is no one way to model a domain of interest. Therefore we introduce so-called entities in our methodology, which in a later stage of our methodology are transformed into either classes or individuals. This makes our approach more flexible and enables user to focus on other aspects of the modeling process. Entities can be arranged in an inheritance hierarchy similar to classes, they can be connected using object properties and have datatype properties (with values) attached to them. Entities can be transformed into individuals if they are leaf nodes of the inheritance hierarchy and if all their datatype and object properties are defined in higher levels of the hierarchy. All other entities are transformed into classes.
- **Conceptualization flexibility:** Is important for novice users as they are prone to committing errors and often learn a new tool by applying a trial&error strategy instead of reading available documentation. We provide flexible means to convert between entities, properties and relationships, thus reducing the amount of work a user has to invest when correcting errors. For example name might be specified as a datatype property, but later in the development process is decided that it should be represented as an entity with datatype properties for salutation, given name and last name. In our approach the user can simply drag the name datatype property out of its parent entity and thus transform it into an entity of its own linked to the original one via an object property. Our approach employs easy drag&drop or wizard-style conversions between all types of entities and properties. This flexibility is also reflected by the entities models, which treads classes and individuals equally and also allows for flexible conversion between them.
- **Flexible hierarchical views:** Confusion between is-a and part-of relations is a com-

mon error by inexperienced users (cf. Noy & McGuinness, 2001). This stems from the fact, that hierarchical structures can be differentiated into logical and partitive (cf. Gaus, 2002) and novice users are used to partitive hierarchical structures (e.g. a university campus contains buildings) not to logical ones (e.g. a full professor is a kind of faculty member). All tools known to the authors use the is-a relations as main structural relationship. Our tool will provide different views on the knowledge model besides the inheritance hierarchy and will allow users to define any given object property as the main relationship for displaying a hierarchy.

- **Making ontology assumptions explicit:** In our evaluation it turned out, that novice users follow the closed-world and unique name assumptions, because it reflects their experiences with the information systems they are used to. The open-world assumption of ontologies and the possible non-uniqueness of names lead to confusion. For example most users in our evaluation automatically assumed that the individuals of a given class constituted a complete set and at first didn't understand the need to explicitly specify this (for more examples see Horrocks, 2008). Our approach will provide users with feedback and ask guidance questions to make ensure that ontology assumptions are made explicit and the encoded meaning is the one the user intended to convey.

Formal Representation

Out methodology is grounded in two formal models, the so-called entity model and ontology model. This is the direct result of our principle to make no distinction between A-Box and T-Box (at first). The entity model is used for the gathering and structuring of knowledge and only in the last step the distinction between A-Box and T-Box is introduced and this model is transformed into ontology-model, which equivalent to a subset of OWL (McGuinness & van Harmelen, 2004).

Entity Model

The entity model is defined as a five tuple $\mathrm{M_E} := (\mathrm{E}, \mathrm{is\_a}, \mathrm{R}, \mathrm{P}, \ell)$:

- E is a set whose elements are called entities.
- $is_a \subseteq E \times E$ defines a partial order on E, where $is\_a(e1, e2)$ indicates that $e1$ is a subentity of $e2$.
- $R \subseteq E \times E \times N$ defines directed, named relationships between entities, where $R(e1, e2, n)$ indicates that $e1$ is the source, $e2$ is the target and n is the name of the relationship.
- $P \subseteq E \times K \times V$ defines properties as a three tuple consisting of e the entity they belong to, k as key and v as value.
- $\ell : E \rightarrow L$ assigns labels to entities.

It is assumed that $L = N = K = V$ and the common case is that they are arbitrary strings.

On this model we formally defined inheritance and the adding, deleting and modifying of elements. To support our basic principle of conceptualization flexibility we also formally defined the conversion between entities, properties and relationships. Thus enabling users to interact with the model in a very flexibly way. As mentioned above eventually the entity is transformed into the ontology model, which we defined formally as well.

Ontology Model

The ontology model is defined as a nine tuple $M_O := (C, is\_a, R_c, P_c, I, type\_of, R_i, P_i, \ell)$:

- C is a set whose elements are called classes.
- $is\_a \subseteq C \times C$ defines a partial order on C, where $is\_a(c_1, c_2)$ indicates that c_1 is a subclass of c_2.
- $R_c \subseteq C \times C \times N$ defines directed, named relationships between classes, where $R_c\ (c_1, c_2, n)$ indicates that c_1 is the source, c_2 is the target and n is the name of the relationship.
- $P_c \subseteq C \times K \times V$ defines properties as a three tuple consisting of c the class they belong to, k as key and v as value.
- I is a set whose elements are called instances.
- $type\_of \subseteq I \times C$ indicates that an instance i is of the type defined by class c.
- $R_i \subseteq I \times I\ with(i_1, i_2) \in R_i \rightarrow (\exists(c_1, c_2, n) \in R_c : (i_1\ type\_of\ c_1 \wedge i_2\ type\_of\ c_2))$ signifies that relationships defined between two classes c_1 and c_2 can be implemented by their associated (via the $type\_of$ relation) instances i_1 and i_2.
- $Pi \subseteq I \times K \times V\ with(i, k, v_i) \in \mathrm{P_i} \rightarrow (\exists(\mathrm{c, k, v_c}) \in \mathrm{P_c} : \mathrm{i\ type\_of\ c})$ defines that instances can implement properties of the class they are belonging to (via the $type\_of$ relation) and assign value v_i to the existing key k.
- $\ell : C \bigcup I \rightarrow L$ assigns labels to classes and instances.

It is assumed that $L = N = K = V$ and the common case is that they are arbitrary strings.

The ontology model is equal to a subset of OWL. As with the entity model we formally defined inheritance, adding, deleting and modifying elements and also the conversion between classes, instances, relationships and properties.

Graphical Representation

Following our basic principle of hiding formality we mapped these two models to a graphical representation, which borrowed concepts from entity relationship and UML diagrams.

Figure 1 shows the graphical notation used in our methodology. Entities are represented as boxes with assigned names. Properties are identified by their names in the upper part of the box and subentities as boxes included in the lower part. Relationships are represented by directed arrows. The relationships between entities and subentities are not shown explicitly, but specified in the diagram description (cf. our basic principle of flexible hierarchical views). The same notation is used for the ontology model, they only difference is, that the box figure is extended by a marked in the upper right corner, which indicates whether the box represents a class or an instance. The semantics of a box being contained in another one is dependent on the types of the boxes, either it is a is_a or a type_of relationship.

Methodology and Supporting Tool

Grounded in the described formal models and using the graphical representation we specified our methodology, which loosely follows the life-cycle described in (Fernández, Gómez-Pérez & Juristo, 1997). It consists of six phases: specification (define scope/purpose), knowledge acquisition, conceptualization (organize knowledge), formalization, evaluation and maintenance, but our primary focus is the beginning of the life cycle (specification, knowledge acquisition, conceptualization and formalization phases). We employ the evolving prototype life-cycle model and there is no fixed order of phases; users can go back and forth between phases as necessary. For this the supporting tool implements all phases in one unified view (see Figure 2). This and the massive use of drag&drop are key differences from Protégé

Figure 1. Graphical notation

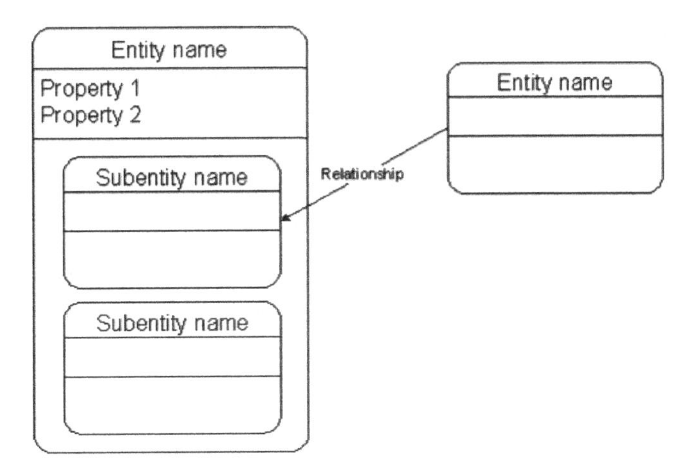

with respect to usability. In the following section we describe the steps of the methodology.

Specification

The specification phase is supported in our tool by a textual interface. The first task in the specification phase is to define the domain of the ontology. The domain can be given as an abstract category, e.g. education. In the next step the goal or purpose of the ontology is described. For this we provide some guiding questions to the user:

- Why is the ontology being build? This question concerns the envisioned outcome of the ontology building process, different motivation for building an ontology are, e.g. solving concrete problems, gathering and formalizing knowledge, optimizing processes.
- What is the intended use of the ontology? This question regards the envisioned use, e.g. using the ontology as basis for software system, using it in a knowledge based system, using it as a common language for data interchange.
- Who uses the ontology? This question regards the envisioned end-users and audience of the ontology, e.g. the ontology is being built for personal use, for use in a company, a basis for an international standard.

In the next step the scope of the ontology is captured by another set of questions:

- Which knowledge should be represented in the ontology?
- What are the boundaries of the ontology; that is which knowledge should explicitly not be included in the ontology?
- What is the intended level of granularity?

Precise answers to the above questions are not always possible and are not strictly required in our methodology.

In another step motivating scenarios for the ontology are formulated in the form of story problems or examples (Grüninger & Fox, 1995). From these motivating scenarios informal competency questions can be extracted by the user. Ideally these questions are defined in a stratified manner, so that the answers to higher level questions require the answers of lower level questions (Uschold & Grüninger, 1996). These competency questions will be used in the evaluation of the ontology.

Furthermore we provide a template to identify and describe possible knowledge sources and we

Figure 2. Ontoclippy: unified view

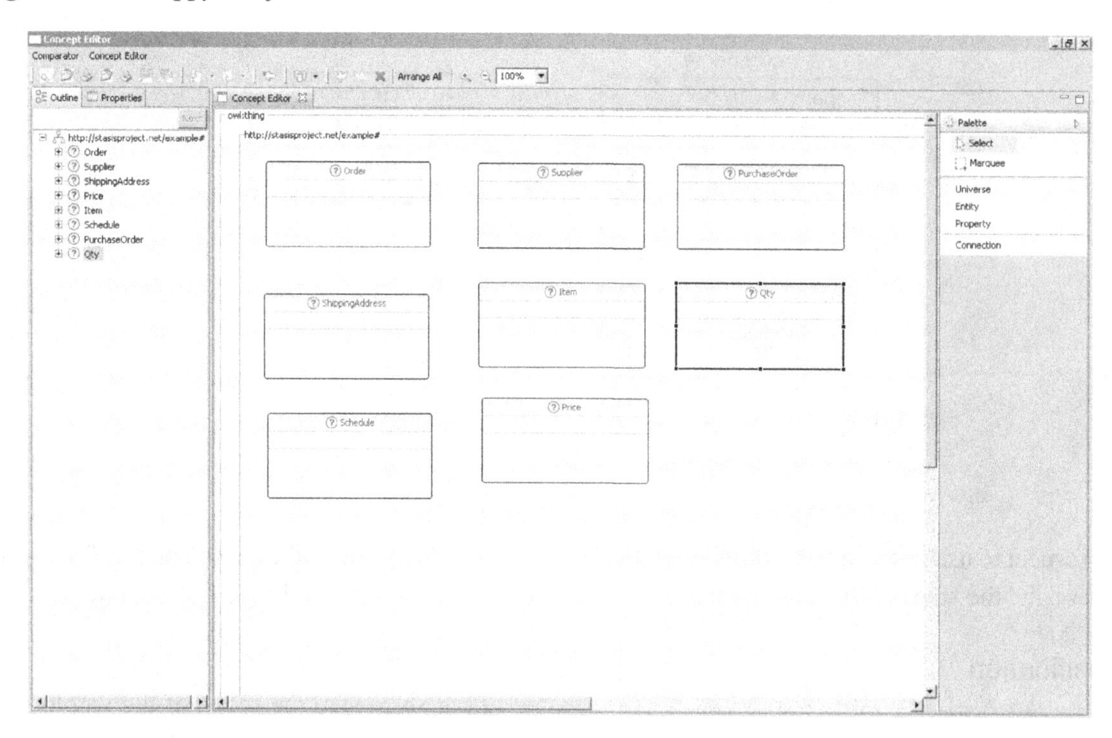

provide design guidelines (e.g. naming conventions) from which the users can choose.

The outcomes of the specification phase are a textual description of the basics of the ontology, list of competency questions, a list of possible knowledge sources and design guidelines.

Knowledge Acquisition

In this phase the knowledge to be represented in the ontology is acquired and further augmented. There a various techniques for acquiring knowledge, e.g. brainstorming, text analysis. In our tool we provide the possibility to manually add knowledge in the form of terms and to automatically extract them from existing sources. In the course of the STASIS project (http://stasis-project.net) we developed import mechanisms for relational databases, XML schema files, EDI messages and Excel files. Our tool features a flexible plugin-interface allows for the usage of other plugins like Natural Language Processing for text mining and the extraction from other sources like MindMap or concept maps.

In a further step the knowledge can be augmented by definitions. These can either be added manually or semi-automatically using search facilities on the lexical ontology Wordnet (Miller, 1995), but our plugin-interface allows for the integration of other glossaries.

Conceptualization

The conceptualization phase is the most important phase of our methodology; it takes the terms and definitions collected in the knowledge acquisitions phase and organizes them into a knowledge model.

All terms are displayed in one view in a desktop-metaphor. Each term is represented by a kind of index card and can be moved around the workplace. In a first step users should arrange related index cards close to each other, so that spatial proximity signifies semantic similarity.

This task can be performed manually by the user or automatically. Our tool uses clustering mechanisms for grouping entities and tries to detect similarity by exploiting the definitions of terms using distance metrics. In literature there exist various clustering methods. We considered exclusive clustering (k-Means Clustering, MacQueen, 1967), overlapping clustering (Fuzzy c-Means (Dunn, 1973)), hierarchical clustering (Single-Linkage Clustering, Johnson, 1967) and probabilistic clustering (EM algorithm, Dempster, Laird & Rubin, 1977). For usage in our prototype we choose the k-means algorithm, but we need to perform further research on the performance of the algorithms with real-world data. The basis for clustering algorithms is the similarity measure between the terms. In our tool we exploit the term names themselves as well as the definitions of the terms. For measuring the similarity of term names we employ edit-distance-like functions, i.e. Levenshtein distance, longest common substring and Jaro-Winkler distance. For exploiting the similarity between the definitions we utilize token-based distance functions, i.e. Jaccard Similarity Coefficient, which counts identical words in definitions and thus utilizes word-to-word similarity measures directly in a bag-of-words way and TFIDF to work on definitions taken from large corpora like Wordnet.

After all the terms are arranged into group the user can start building hierarchies. Our methodology follows a flexible middle-out approach, which we consider to be superior to bottom-up or top-down (cf. Uschold & King, 1995; Raccoon, 1998). The building of hierarchies in our tool is realized using drag&drop, dragging an entity on another one, makes it a sub-entity (cf. Figure 3). The semantics of this depends on the main structural relationship, which is user-definable (cf. the basic principle of flexible hierarchical views). The default relationship is the is-a relation but all other relationships (e.g. part_of) can be used as primary relationship.

Additionally users are prompted with questions in order to ensure that the encoded meaning matches their intended meaning, e.g. asking the user if all sub-entities of an entity should be disjoint. Then properties are added to the entities. These are either created manually, created by converting existing entities, or selected from automatic proposals extracted from the entity definitions. This process is supported by using refactoring mechanisms (as used in object-oriented software development), e.g. if all sub-entities share common properties the user is asked if they should be moved to the parent entity.

Formalization

In a last step the knowledge model is formalized. Therefore entities are transformed to either classes or instances, thus realizing a transformation from the entity model to the ontology model (cf. Formal representations). The integrity of the model is checked on the fly, the pre- and post conditions for the transformation are communicated to the users and methods for dealing with unsatisfied conditions are suggested. This final form of the graphical representation is equivalent to a restricted subset of OWL and is then stored as valid OWL ontology for further usage.

Evaluation

The evaluation of the resulting ontology model can be performed on three levels:

1. A formal evaluation can be carried out automatically checking for logical contradictions and employing predefined metrics. Even if our model doesn't allow the specification of invalid ontologies we use formal checking as a safety net.
2. The second level of evaluation is carried out by a skilled ontology engineers, who can assess the ontology with regard to its

Figure 3. OntoClippy: building a hierarchy

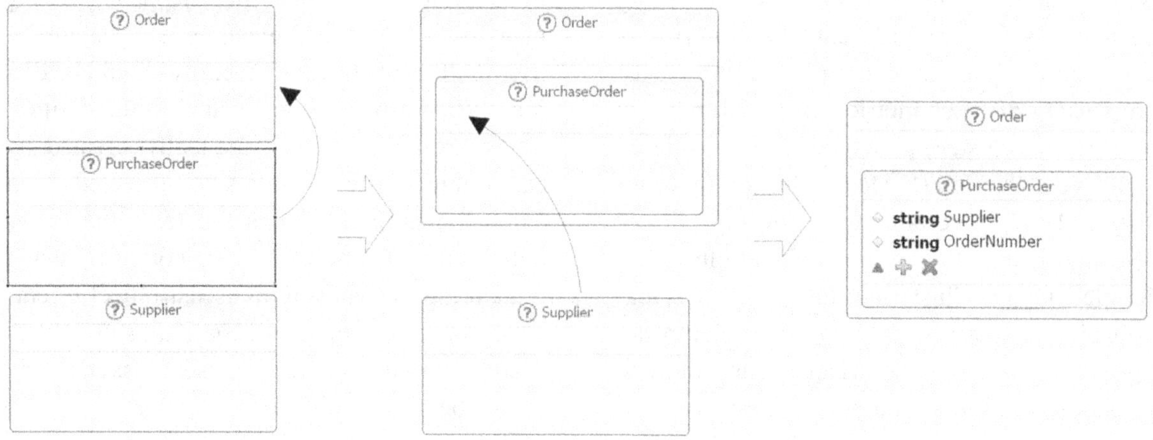

specification and the competency questions formulated in the specification phase. Furthermore he can assess aspects of modeling, which are of a more aesthetic nature and not checkable by automatic means.

3. The third and ultimate level of evaluation is carried out by the users themselves, because the eventual goal of the ontology is the use in a real-world system of some kind and thus its ultimate goal is fitness for its intended application.

In our work we only considered the first level for integration in our tool. Our methodology includes no specific mechanisms for the later two levels of evaluation.

Maintenance

The nature of the graphical representation makes it easy to get an overview over existing large-scale ontologies and the conceptualization flexibility and the integration of all ontology design phases in one unified view enables users to easily modify existing knowledge and add new knowledge. Thus our tool can be used to adapt and maintain existing ontologies, but there is no explicit support for this kind of task, as it was not the focus of our work.

EVALUATION

In order to validate or methodology and tool we conducted an experiment, which was supported by a questionnaire. Our goal was to demonstrate the usability and user-friendliness of our approach over other well-known approaches. We selected 30 teachers from the primary education sector in Germany as participants for our experiment. They had no prior knowledge in the design and creation of ontologies or any related subjects. We choose to compare our approach to Protégé, which is one of the most prominent ontology engineering tools and the Ontology Development 101 methodology, because it is best-suited for non-experts users.

The experiment was carried out in ten groups consisting of three participants each. First the facilitator explained the basic concepts of ontologies and explained the usage of the tools and methodologies by building a simple example ontology. In the next step participants transferred the knowledge to a task stemming from their domain of interest (the education sector). While carrying out the task participants were allowed to ask questions, which were recorded, furthermore other objective data like the time taken, errors committed and features used were recorded. Afterwards every participant filled out a questionnaire.

In the following sections we present the ontologies and questionnaire used in the experiments, the evaluation of the questionnaire and our conclusions drawn from it and our observations made during the experiment.

Ontologies Used in the Experiment

Example

To demonstrate the usage of the methodologies and tools a very simple example ontology was build. The facts constituting the ontology were stated as eight simple declarative sentences:

1. Cars and motorbikes are vehicles.
2. Vehicles are driven by persons.
3. Persons have names.
4. An off-road vehicle is a car.
5. Cars have license plates.
6. There exists an off-road vehicle with the license plate AB-XY 123.
7. There exists a person with the name Hertha Meier.
8. The person with the name Hertha Meier is the driver of the car with the license plate AB-XY 123.

Task

The task given to the participants of the experiment was building an ontology in their domain of interest, which was specified by thirteen declarative sentences.

1. Pupils and teachers are persons.
2. Persons have names.
3. A school has a principal.
4. The principal is teacher.
5. A school has classes.
6. Classes have names.
7. Pupils are assigned to classes.
8. Classes have a form teacher.
9. There exists a class with the name 5a.
10. There exists a teacher with the name Ms. Müller.
11. The teacher with the name Ms. Müller is the form teacher of the class with the name 5a.
12. There exists a pupil with the name Fritz Meyer.
13. The pupil with the name Fritz Meyer is assigned to the class with the name 5a.

Questionnaire and Observations

We recorded observations made during the experiments, namely:

- Which features of our tool where used (search, different hierarchies, drag&drop, transformations, change entities into classes/instances)?
- Did the participants follow the intended ontology design life-cycle as specified by the methodology?
- How much time did it take to complete the task?
- Were the participants able to solve the task? Was the resulting ontology complete?
- Requests made by the participants during the observation were recorded.

The questionnaire used in our experiment is a modified version and extended version of the Computer System Usability Questionnaire (CSUQ) (Lewis, 1995) The answers to the questions of the main parts (parts two and three) were designed as four-point likert scale (Likert, 1932) with no neutral element to force a decision. Responses range from "Disagree" (1) over "Partly disagree" (2) and "Partly agree" (3) to "Agree" (4). An n/a-element meaning "no answer" or "not applicable" was provided for participants to mark if they were unable to answer one of the questions.

The questionnaire consists of five parts, which are explained in the following sections.

Part 1

The first part asks questions regarding the personal experience and background of the participants in order to gain an overview over his or her familiarity with using computer systems and his or her self-assessment regarding mathematical and logical understanding. It was stated that all answers will be treated confidential and that the evaluation will be anonymous. The five questions asked in this part are the following:

1. The participants name (optional)
2. For how many years has the participant been using computers?
3. Which of the following statements apply to the participant? (multiple answers possible)
   a. Able to use office programs
   b. Able to create web pages
   c. Able to install programs
   d. Able to install operating systems
   e. Know how to program
4. Which of the following operating systems has the participant used? (multiple answers possible)
   a. Windows
   b. MacOS
   c. GNU/Linux
   d. Others
5. How does the participant rate his mathematical logical understanding? (on a scale from 1(A) to 5(F))

Parts 2 and 3

The second and third part asked questions regarding the experiences made during the solving of the task with Protégé and OntoClippy. The participants marked their level of agreement or disagreement with the presented statements. There was no neutral element in order to force a decision. If a participant could make a statement regarding a question he was asked to mark n/a (no answer or not applicable). The following 14 statements had to be mark for Protégé and OntoClippy separately.

1. Overall, I am satisfied with how easy it is to use this application.
2. It was simple to use this application.
3. I can effectively complete the task using this system.
4. I was able to efficiently complete the task using this system.
5. I was able to complete the task quickly using this system.
6. It was easy to learn to use this application.
7. I believe I became productive quickly using this application.
8. Whenever I made a mistake using the system, I recovered easily and quickly.
9. The interface of the application is well-structured.
10. The visualization of information is useful.
11. Finding information in the application is easy.
12. The amount of displayed information was adequate.
13. This application has all the functions and capabilities I expect it to have.
14. Overall, the tool is too complex.

The questions were followed by an empty space giving the possibility to make suggestions for enhancing the concerned application.

Part 4

This fourth part asks questions regarding the comparison of the applications Protégé and OntoClippy. First the participants were asked three questions:

1. Which application would the participant rather use?
2. Which application does the participant believe to be more user-friendly?

3. Which application has more features and functions?

After the questions there the participants were asked to write down:

1. What they especially liked about Protégé?
2. What they disliked about Protégé?
3. What they especially liked about OntoClippy?
4. What they dislike about OntoClippy?

Part 5

The fifth part asked the participants two questions about the experiment itself, both on a scale from 1(A) to 5(F):

1. How do they rate clarity and understandability of the task?
2. How do they rate the support by the facilitator?

Evaluation

In this section we give the results of our objective observations, the evaluation of the questionnaires filled out by the participants, analyze them and draw conclusions.

Observations Made During the Experiment

The following observations were made during the experiments:

- In contrast to the sample solution build by an ontology engineer nine out of ten groups included the form teacher as a subclass of teacher, while the ontology engineer modeled it as a relationship between class and teachers. The reason for this was that the form teacher has special duties and privileges which were unknown to the ontology engineer, but very important to the domain experts. This effectively illustrates a benefit of our approach.
- Several participants commented that OntoClippy reminded them of set theory and mindmaps, which actually are two examples we took for building out models and GUI.
- When performing the tasks with Protégé three groups used sketch paper to structure their knowledge before entering it into Protégé. No group did this when using OntoClippy.

Additionally the participants had the following requests (combined from all participants in all groups):

- When performing the task with Protégé participants were confused by the is_a versus part_of relationship, the difference between object and datatype properties. There was confusion between class names and their labels and the distinction between instance and class was not clear.
- When performing the task with OntoClippy participants were confused by the is_a versus part_of relationship.

Part 1

- The participants have been using computers for an average of 15.5 years.
- 28 out of 30 participants know how to use office software.
- 10 out of 30 participants are able to build their own web pages.
- 26 out of 30 participants know how to install new software.
- 16 out of 30 participants know how to install operating systems.
- 3 out of 30 participants know how to program.
- 28 out of 30 participants have used Windows.

- 1 out of 30 participants has used MacOS.
- 5 out of 30 participants have used GNU/Linux.
- 2 out of 30 participants have used different operating systems.
- On a scale from 1(A) to 5(F) the participants rated their mathematical-logical understanding 2.8 (C).

Part 2

Table 1 describes the answers given to part 2 of the questionnaire by means of the median and the mode, the inter-quartile range (IQR) and the range of the results.

The average time it took a group to complete the task was 20 minutes. All solutions were complete, but only 3 groups out of 10 adhered to the intended ontology design life-cycle. The enhancements suggested by the participants were:

- Provide a localized version (in German)
- Use the same icons for the same functionality (different delete buttons: X and minus)

Table 1. Questionnaire results: part 2

Question	Median	Mode	IQR	Range
1	4	4	1	2
2	3	3	1	3
3	3	3	1	3
4	3	3	1	3
5	4	4	1	2
6	3	3	1	3
7	3	3	1	2
8	3	3	1	2
9	3	3	1	3
10	3	4	2	3
11	3	3	1	3
12	4	4	1	2
13	3	4	2	2
14	3	4	1	3

- Make the distinction between data and object properties more clear

Part 3

Table 2 describes the answers given to part 3 of the questionnaire by means of the median and the mode, the inter-quartile range and the range of the results.

The average time it took a group to complete the task was 13.3 minutes. All solutions were complete and all groups adhered to the intended ontology design life-cycle.

- 10 out of 10 groups used OntoClippys drag&drop functionality.
- 8 out of 10 groups used OntoClippys changing entities into classes and instances functionality.
- 9 out of 10 groups used OntoClippys transformation functionality.
- 0 out of 10 groups used OntoClippys search functionality.

The enhancements suggested by the participants were:

- Support copy & paste
- Make more display space available
- Improve the connection routing

Part 4

In this part the participants were asked for a direct comparison between Protégé and OntoClippy.

1. Out of 30 participants 28 prefer OntoClippy over Protégé, which only 2 prefer.
2. Out of 30 participants 27 believe OntoClippy to be more user-friendly than Protégé, which only 2 believe to be more user-friendly. One person opted not to answer the question.
3. Out of 30 participants 9 believe that OntoClippy offers a greater set of features,

while 7 believe Protégé to be more feature-rich. 14 participants could not answer the question. We concluded that the participants were not skilled enough to estimate the feature-sets of the tools.

Additionally they were asked what the liked and disliked about the tools:

- What did you like about Protégé? Intelligible presentation of data, clear and logical design, tree structure.
- What did you dislike about Protégé? No visualization, cumbersome usage, too many tables, ontology scattered around different views, confusing GUI.
- What did you like about OntoClippy? User-friendliness, easy to learn, clear arrangement, visualization, drag&drop, possibility to see the whole ontology in one view.
- What did you dislike about OntoClippy? Connection routing is confusing, there should be more use of colors.

Part 5

This part asked questions regarding the experiment itself:

- On a scale from 1 (A) to 5 (F) the participants rated the comprehensibility of experiment 2.0 (B)
- On a scale from 1 (A) to 5 (F) the participants rated the support by the facilitator 1.23 (A)

Analysis and Conclusion

In general the participants can be characterized as skilled computer users (15.5 years of computer usage in average), who are able to use and install standard software and who mainly use Windows. They are not familiar with programming and rate

Table 2. Questionnaire results: part 3

Question	Median	Mode	IQR	Range
1	4	4	0	2
2	4	4	0	2
3	4	4	0	2
4	4	4	0	2
5	4	4	0	1
6	4	4	0	1
7	4	4	0	2
8	4	4	0	2
9	4	4	0	1
10	4	4	0	2
11	4	4	1	2
12	4	4	0	2
13	4	4	1	2
14	4	4	0	2

their mathematical-logical understanding rather badly.

When comparing the results of part 2 and part 3 one notices that all answers were rather positive (median and mode values 3 and 4). For OntoClippy even all the median and mode values are 4. When comparing the IQR and ranges of the results we note that the participants' attitude towards OntoClippy was more consistent than that towards Protégé. IQR in part 2 is a least 1 and in some cases 2, minimum range is 1 maximum range is 3. In part 3 IQR is almost always 0 and in some cases 1, minimum range is 1, maximum range is 2. We conclude that in general Protégé was rated lower than OntoClippy and that the agreement towards OntoClippy was shared by all participants.

This is backed by the answer is part 4 were almost all participants (28 out of 30) preferred OntoClippy over Protégé and believed it to be more user-friendly (27 out 30).

Additionally we noted that the average time to complete the task was considerably shorted when using OntoClippy (13.5 minutes compared to 20 minutes) and the intended ontology design livecycle was only followed in 3 out of 10 cases when using Protégé. Furthermore the recorded requests show that with Protégé there was generally more confusion on the usage and methodology. From the aforementioned facts and the usage of sketch paper by some groups when using Protégé we conclude that the complexity of Protégé distracts from the ontology design life-cycle.

The suggested enhancements for the tools and show that the simple GUI of OntoClippy is more language independent than that of Protégé (participants were able to work with an English language version and did not request a German one) and that it make ontology principles more clear (less requests when using OntoClippy as compared to Protégé). Most enhancements suggested for OntoClippy will be incorporated in the next prototype (drag&drop support, better connection-routing). The usage of the existing features was very high, only the search functionality wasn't use, which is probably due to the small size of the ontology.

In general OntoClippy performed very well for a prototype and we feel that our approach proved to be viable. Considering the fact that the domain experts modeled the ontology different than the ontology engineer, we feel confident that our approach potentially offers time and cost benefits.

CONCLUSION AND OUTLOOK

In this article we described our efforts for improving the design and creation of ontologies by implementing a user-friendly methodology and tool that better the shortcomings of existing approaches. We have developed a first prototype, which has been used in the course of an EU-funded project (http://www.stasis-project.net) and has proven itself viable in a first evaluation.

Even in the early prototype phase of our approach we found some interesting applications:

- We will use OntoClippy to build a domain ontology for the primary education sector in Germany. This ontology will be build by the members of an online community in order to optimize precision and recall of the search on the 60.000 e-learning materials of this community.
- In a second project websites are described by ontologies, which are used for ontology-based search engine optimization (Enríquez Perdomo, 2006). While this approach yielded promising results the building of the ontologies was too time-consuming. By using OntoClippy the ontology building process can be carried out by the website owners themselves and thus the approach becomes marketable.
- We plan on deploying our methodology in an E-Commerce context (Meng & Chatwin, 2010; Thomas, Redmond & Yoon, 2009) by having customers model their own views on a product domain a thus increasing the search capabilities and user experience of E-Commerce sites.

We are confident that our approach might lead to significant cost and time benefits in the development of ontologies for real-world usage scenarios and enable the build of ontologies for tasks were it wasn't economically feasible before.

In the future we plan to improve our prototype and incorporate the feedback gather from our first evaluation. We also want to research the automatic components of our tool (clustering, etc.) more and evaluate different possibilities with real-world data. Eventually we want to release our methodology and tool to the public.

REFERENCES

Artz, J. M. (2007). Philosophical Foundations of Information Modeling. *International Journal of Intelligent Information Technologies*, *3*(3), 59–74.

Berners-Lee, T., Hendler, J., & Lassila, O. (2001). The Semantic Web. *Scientific American, 284*(5), 28–37. doi:10.1038/scientificamerican0501-34

Dahlem, N., Guo, J., Hahn, A., & Reinelt, M. (2009). *Towards a user-friendly ontology design methodology*. Paper presented at the International Conference on Interoperability for Enterprise Software and Applications (I-ESA 2009).

Dahlem, N., & Hahn, A. (2009). *User-Friendly Ontology Creation Methodologies - A Survey*. Paper presented at the 15th Americas Conference on Information Systems (AMCIS 2009).

De Nicola, A., Missikoff, M., & Navigli, R. (2005). *A proposal for a unified process for ontology building: upon*. Paper presented at Database and Expert Systems Applications.

Dempster, A. P., Laird, N. M., & Rubin, D. B. (1977). Maximum likelihood from incomplete data via the EM algorithm. *Journal of the Royal Statistical Society. Series B. Methodological*, 1–38.

Dimitrova, V., Denaux, R., Hart, G., Dolbear, C., Holt, I., & Cohn, A. G. (2008). Involving Domain Experts in Authoring OWL Ontologies. In *Proceedings of the 7th International Semantic Web Conference, ISWC 2008.*

Dunn, J. C. (1973). A fuzzy relative of the ISODATA process and its use in detecting compact well-separated clusters. *Cybernetics and Systems, 3*(3), 32–57. doi:10.1080/01969727308546046

Enríquez Perdomo, A. (2006). *Enfoque semántico para la gestión de sitios web*. Unpublished master's thesis.

Fernández, M., Gómez-Pérez, A., & Juristo, N. (1997). *Methontology: from ontological art towards ontological engineering*. Paper presented at the AAAI97 Spring Symposium Series on Ontological Engineering, Stanford, CA.

Funk, A., Tablan, V., Bontcheva, K., Cunningham, H., Davis, B., & Handschuh, S. (2007). *CLOnE: Controlled Language for Ontology Editing*. In Proceedings of the 6th International Semantic Web Conference, 2nd Asian Semantic Web Conference, ISWC 2007 + ASWC 2007.

Gangemi, A., Pisanelli, D. M., & Steve, G. (1999). An overview of the ONIONS project: Applying ontologies to the integration of medical terminologies. *Data & Knowledge Engineering, 31*(2), 183–220. doi:10.1016/S0169-023X(99)00023-3

Gaus, W. (2002). *Dokumentations- und ordnungslehre. theorie und praxis des information retrieval* (3rd ed.). Berlin: Springer-Verlag GmbH.

Gruber, A., Westenthaler, R., & Gahleitner, E. (2006). *Supporting domain experts in creating formal knowledge models (ontologies)*. Paper presented at I-KNOW'06, 6th International Conference on Knowledge Management.

Grüninger, M., & Fox, M. S. (1995). *Methodology for the design and evaluation of ontologies*. Paper presented at the Workshop on Basic Ontological Issues in Knowledge Sharing.

Horrocks, I. (2008). *Ontologies and databases*. Paper presented at Semantic Days 2008.

Johnson, S. C. (1967). Hierarchical clustering schemes. *Psychometrika, 32*(3), 241–254. doi:10.1007/BF02289588

Kaljurand, K. (2008). *ACE View — An Ontology and Rule Editor based on Controlled English.* Paper presented at the Poster and Demonstration Session at the 7th International Semantic Web Conference (ISWC2008).

Kotis, K., Vouros, G. A., & Alonso, J. P. (2005). *Hcome: a tool-supported methodology for engineering living ontologies.*

Lenat, D. B. (1995). CYC: a large-scale investment in knowledge infrastructure. *Communications of the ACM, 38*(11), 33–38. doi:10.1145/219717.219745

Lewis, J. R. (1995). IBM Computer Usability Satisfaction Questionnaires: Psychometric Evaluation and Instructions for Use. *International Journal of Human-Computer Interaction, 7*(1), 57–78. doi:10.1080/10447319509526110

Likert, R. (1932). A technique for the measurement of attitudes. *Archives de Psychologie, 22*(140), 1–55.

MacQueen, J. B. (1967). *Some Methods for Classification and Analysis of MultiVariate Observations*. Paper presented at the fifth Berkeley Symposium on Mathematical Statistics and Probability.

March, S. T., & Allen, G. N. (2007). Ontological Foundations for Active Information Systems. *International Journal of Intelligent Information Technologies*, *3*(1), 1–13.

McGuinness, D. L., & van Harmelen, F. (2004). *OWL web ontology language overview.* Retrieved from http://www.w3.org/TR/2004/REC-owl-features-20040210/

Meng, S. K., & Chatwin, C. R. (2010). Ontology-Based Shopping Agent for E-Marketing. *International Journal of Intelligent Information Technologies*, *6*(2), 21–43.

Miller, G. A. (1995). WordNet: a lexical database for English. *Communications of the ACM*, *38*(11), 39–41. doi:10.1145/219717.219748

Noy, N. F., & McGuinness, D. L. (2001). *Ontology development 101: a guide to creating your first ontology* (Tech. Rep. KSL-01-05 and SMI-2001-0880). Stanford, CA: Stanford University.

Raccoon, L. S. B., & Puppydog, P. P. O. (1998). A middle-out concept of hierarchy (or the problem of feeding the animals). *ACM SIGSOFT Software Engineering Notes*, *23*(3), 111–119. doi:10.1145/279437.279489

Schaffert, S., Gruber, A., & Westenthaler, R. (2006). *A semantic wiki for collaborative knowledge formation*. Paper presented at Semantic Content Engineering.

Schreiber, T. G. A., Wielinga, B. J., & Jansweijer, W. (1995). *The KACTUS view on the 'O' word.* Paper presented at the 7th Dutch National Conference on Artificial Intelligence NAIC'95.

Simón Cuevas, A. J. (2008). *Herramientas para el perfeccionamiento de los sistemas de gestión de conocimiento basados en mapas conceptuales*. Unpublished doctoral disseration.

Sure, Y., & Studer, R. (2002). *On-to-knowledge methodology - final version (On-To-Knowledge Deliverable 18)*. Karlsruhe, Germany: Institute AIFB, University of Karlsruhe.

Swartout, W. R., Patil, R., Knight, K., & Russ, T. (1996). *Toward Distributed Use of Large-Scale Ontologies*. Paper presented at the Tenth Workshop on Knowledge Acquisition for Knowledge-Based Systems.

Thomas, M. A., Redmond, R. T., & Yoon, V. Y. (2009). Using Ontological Reasoning for an Adaptive E-Commerce Experience. *International Journal of Intelligent Information Technologies*, *5*(4), 41–52.

Uschold, M. (1996). *Building ontologies: towards a unified methodology.* Paper presented at Expert Systems 96.

Uschold, M., & Grüninger, M. (1996). Ontologies: principles, methods and applications. *The Knowledge Engineering Review*, *11*, 93–136. doi:10.1017/S0269888900007797

Uschold, M., & King, M. (1995). *Towards a methodology for building ontologies*. Paper presented at the Workshop on Basic Ontological Issues in Knowledge Sharing.

Wielinga, B. J., Schreiber, T. G. A., & Breuker, J. A. (1992). KADS: a modelling approach to knowledge engineering. *Knowledge Acquisition*, *4*(1), 5–53. doi:10.1016/1042-8143(92)90013-Q

This work was previously published in the International Journal of Intelligent Information Technologies, Volume 7, Issue 1, edited by Vijayan Sugumaran, pp. 15-32, copyright 2011 by IGI Publishing (an imprint of IGI Global).

Chapter 3
Combining Supervised Learning Techniques to Key-Phrase Extraction for Biomedical Full-Text

Yanliang Qi
New Jersey Institute of Technology, USA

Min Song
New Jersey Institute of Technology, USA

Suk-Chung Yoon
Widener University, USA

Lori Watrous deVersterre
New Jersey Institute of Technology, USA

ABSTRACT

Key-phrase extraction plays a useful a role in research areas of Information Systems (IS) like digital libraries. Short metadata like key phrases are beneficial for searchers to understand the concepts found in the documents. This paper evaluates the effectiveness of different supervised learning techniques on biomedical full-text: Sequential Minimal Optimization (SMO) and K-Nearest Neighbor, both of which could be embedded inside an information system for document search. The authors use these techniques to extract key phrases from PubMed and evaluate the performance of these systems using the holdout validation method. This paper compares different classifier techniques and performance differences between the full-text and it's abstract. Compared with the authors' previous work, which investigated the performance of Naïve Bayes, Linear Regression and SVM(reg1/2), this paper finds that SVMreg-1 performs best in key-phrase extraction for full-text, whereas Naïve Bayes performs best for abstracts. These techniques should be considered for use in information system search functionality. Additional research issues also are identified.

DOI: 10.4018/978-1-4666-2047-6.ch003

INTRODUCTION

In recent years, there has been a tremendous increase in the number of biomedical documents in digital libraries that provide users (researchers, readers) with access to the scientific and technical literature of those biomedical documents (articles or abstract) (Liu, 2007). For example, the PubMed digital library (a free search engine for accessing the MEDLINE database of biomedical research articles) currently contains over 18 million citations from various types of biomedical documents published in the past several decades (www.pubmed.gov). With the rapid expansion of the number of biomedical documents, the ability to effectively determine the relevant documents from a large dataset has become increasingly difficult for users. As it is a challenging task for a reader to examine complete documents to determine whether the document would be useful, short semantic metadata like key-phrases would be an alternative for a reader to understand the concept of the document (Hamdi, 2008). Key phrases are increasingly used as brief descriptors of text document content. However, not all of the biomedical documents in digital libraries have key phrases, so readers have to read through the documents to determine whether they are relevant to their research. Therefore automatically presenting key phrases from a document has become an important task in the biomedical domain.

Automatic key-phrase extraction can be defined as the process of extracting key phrases from a document that an author (or a professional indexer) is likely to assign to that document (El-Beltagy, 2006). Consequently, automatic extraction makes it feasible to generate key phrases for a large number of full-text documents that do not have manually assigned key phrases. It also reduces the cost and time spent manually assigning key phrases to documents (Zhang, Zincir-Heywood, et al., 2005). Key-phrases, short semantic metadata, are useful for various purposes including summarizing as well as search engine optimization. Using key phrases for full-text documents can vary: when they are presented on the first page of the document, the goal is summarization, which enables the users to quickly determine the concept of the document; when they are entered in a search engine query box in a digital library, the goal is to enable the users to make the search more precise (Turney, 2000). Therefore, they play an important role in document descriptions and document search in digital libraries, e.g., PubMed.

Traditionally, key-phrases are assigned manually to documents by authors or professional indexers. The indexers often choose key phrases from a predefined control vocabulary: Medical Subject Heading (MeSH). Authors usually choose key phrases to present their work in a certain way or to maximize its chance of being noticed by particular searchers. However, issues with this manual assignment of key-phrases are (1) it is a time consuming process, (2) it requires knowledge of subject matter, and (3) entails an updated control vocabulary list (Witten, Paynter et al., 1999; Kumar & Srinathan, 2008). Automatic key phrase extraction can be a good practical alternative.

Key-phrases can be automatically generated in two ways: (1) key-phrase assignment (controlled-vocabulary indexing based), which assigns key-phrases from a controlled vocabulary to documents or (2) key-phrase extraction (free-term indexing based), which identifies and selects the most descriptive phrases in that document (Dumais, Platt et al., 1998).

In domain-specific control-indexing, key-phrases are chosen from a controlled vocabulary such as the MeSH terminology list (Medelyan & Witten, 2006). MeSH provides a consistent way to assign phrases to biomedical documents that have the same concept. However the downsides are that the lists are expensive to build and maintain, so they are not always up to date and potentially useful phrases are ignored if they are not in the list (Jones & Paynter, 2003).

In the free-term indexing, the text of a document is analyzed and its most appropriate phrases are identified and associated with the biomedical document (Witten, Paynter, et al., 1999). This means that the selection of key-phrases does not depend on a controlled vocabulary, e.g., MeSH, but rather chooses key phrases in the document.

Both of the approaches use machine learning methods that are the branch of Artificial Intelligence concerned with the design of algorithms. It allows machines to improve their performance over time by learning from data (Abu-Nimeh, Nappa, et al., 2003) and requires, for training purposes, a set of documents with key-phrases which are already attached. Currently, several key phrase extraction techniques have been proposed based on different machine learning techniques, e.g., KEA (Witten, Paynter, et al., 1999), GenEx (Witten, Paynter, et al., 1999; Turney, 2000), and typography (Werner & Bottcher, 2007).

This paper focuses on a key-phrase extraction task from biomedical documents with supervised learning techniques. This is a machine learning technique for learning a function from training data. The tasks we discuss in this paper are to take a biomedical document as input, automatically generate a list (in no particular order) of key-phrases as output, then compare the performance of different algorithms. We also evaluate the effectiveness of automatically extracted key-phrase in terms of how many author-assigned key-phrases are correctly identified (Turney, 1997; Pala & Cicekli, 2008). For this evaluation, we use sequential minimal optimization and k-nearest neighbor classifiers on biomedical full-texts and the abstracts of the documents by comparing the output key-phases with author-assigned key-phrases from PubMed. We evaluate the effectiveness of extracted key-phrases in terms of how many author assigned key-phrases are correctly identified by using a holdout validation method. The primary contribution of the paper is (1) comparison among different classifier techniques and (2) a comparison of performance differences between full-text and abstract. In brief, compared to the updated study (Qi et al., 2009), our results show that Naïve Bayes performs best on abstract, while technique SVMreg-1 performs better than others on full-text.

The rest of this paper is structured as follows; we first discuss the systems and learning algorithms for key phrase extraction. The settings and data collection is explained in the following section. Evaluation experiment and results are presented in the next part. The final section discusses contributions and presents future research direction.

THE SYSTEMS AND LEARNING ALGORITHMS FOR KEY PHRASE EXTRACTION

Key-phrase extraction from a text document is considered a classification task: each phrase is classified as part of a key-phrase or non key-phrase class. To the best of our knowledge, most published literature covers only supervised tasks (Witten, Paynter, et al., 1999; Turney, 2000; Huang, Tian, et al., 2006). In machine learning terminology, the key phrase list in a text document is used as an example, and the learning problem is to find a mapping from the examples to the two classes (key-phrase and non-key-phrase) (Frank, Paynter, et al., 1999). In the context of key phrase extraction, these are simply phrases that have been identified as being either key-phrases or not. Once the learning method has generated the model based on the training data, it can be applied to unlabeled data. The training documents are used to adjust the key-phrase extraction algorithms to attempt to maximize system performance (Turney, 1997). The main difficulties arise from how the system correctly identifies whether a phrase in a document is either a key-phrase or not (Turney, 1999; Turney, 2000).

In general, the key-phrase extraction process can be achieved in the following four steps (El-Beltagy, 2006):

1. Extract candidate phrases and their number of occurrences. A candidate phrase is defined as any sequence of words within the input document that is not separated by

punctuation marks or stop words and then the common suffixes are removed from each candidate phrase by applying a stemmer algorithm, such as the Porter or the Lovins stemmers.

2. Filter candidate phrases. In order to reduce the number of candidate phrases, a number of rules may be applied such as a filtration rule, e.g., a certain number of times a phrase occurs in a text document can be considered a candidate phrase.
3. Calculate the weight of candidate phrases. The weight is calculated to enable ranking by applying linguistic or/and statistical techniques on domain text such as TFIDF and C/NC values. TFIDF weighting is the most common statistical method of measuring the weight of a candidate phrase in a document (Zhang, Zincir-Heywood, et al., 2005). TFIDF value has been used in the candidate phrase extraction step by some of the well-known key phrase extraction systems such as KP-Miner, or KEA. C/NC-value is the other method for calculating the weight of candidate phrases used in the biomedical domain, introduced by Frantzi et al (Frantzi, Ananiadou, et al., 1998). The C/NC-value method combines linguistic (linguistic filter, part-of-speech tagging and stop-list) and statistical analysis (frequency analysis, C/NC-value) to enhance the common statistical techniques (e.g. TFIDF) by making it sensitive to a particular type of multi-word term. C-value enhances the common statistical measure of frequency of occurrence for phrase extraction. NC-value gives a method for the extraction of phrase context words and the incorporation of information from phrase context words to the extraction of terms (Frantzi, Ananiadou, et al., 1998).
4. Refine the results and generate a final key-phrase list. Once the weight calculation step has been performed, a number of key-phrases are listed in rank order of phrases.

In recent years, more effective systems have been developed to improve the performance of a key phrase extraction by integrating data mining techniques (Decision Tree, Naïve Bayes, Support Vector Machine (SVM), etc). For instance, KP-Miner (El-Beltagy, 2006) improves TFIDF by introducing two factors (provide higher weights for terms whose length is greater than one and for terms that appear somewhere in the beginning of the document); LAKE (D'Avanzo, Magnini, et al., 2004) relies on the linguistic features of a document in order to perform key-phrase extraction through the use of a Naïve Bayes classifier as the learning algorithm and TFIDF term weighting with the position of a phrase as a feature; KPSpotter (Song, Song, et al., 2003) uses the information gain measure to rank the candidate phrases based on a TFIDF and distance feature. The following are brief descriptions of the state-of-the art key phrase extraction systems: KEA and GenEx.

Turney was the first to approach the task of key-phrase extraction as a supervised learning problem. Turney proposed a system named Extractor, using frequency-based and part-of-speech information as features, and decision tree and a generic algorithm (called GenEx) as classifiers (Turney, 1997; Turney, 1999; Turney, 2000; Piramuthua & Sikora, 2006; Piramuthua & Sikora, 2009). Extractor uses a set of heuristic and generic algorithms to identify the phrases that are most likely to map to those of the author's. The GenEx system has two components, the Genitor genetic algorithm and the Extractor key-phrase extraction algorithm. Extractor takes a document as input and extracts a list of key-phrases as output. The output of Extractor is controlled by numerical parameters.

KEA is another efficient algorithm for extracting key-phrases from text documents. The KEA system runs in two stages: (a) training and (b) extraction. During the training stage, it creates a model for identifying candidate phrases, using a set of training documents in which the author assigned key-phrases are known. During the extracting stage, it chooses key-phrases from a new document, using the model generated during the training stage. Both stages have two steps: choose a set of candidate phrases from their input documents then calculate the values of certain features (TFIDF and first-occurrence) for each candidate phrase. More explicitly, KEA, by default, generates key-phrases using Naïve Bayes as the classifier. KEA's Naïve Bayes learning model uses a set of training documents with known key-phrases (author assigned) then uses the model to determine which input document's phrases are most likely to be candidate key-phrases. The desired number of key-phrases may be defined in the KEA algorithm. KEA chooses candidate phrases in three steps: input cleaning, phrase identification, and case-folding (Witten, Paynter, et al., 1999). An implementation is available from the New Zealand Digital Library project (www.nzdl.org).

As we highlighted above, key-phrase classification can be affected by various machine learning approaches of classifiers, such as Naïve Bayes, k-nearest neighbor and SVM. A large number of classification algorithms have been used for a majority of automatic key-phrase extraction systems to address key-phrase extraction problems for text documents. Each algorithm has its own strengths and drawbacks. However, Naïve Bayes, k-nearest neighbor and SVM are the most frequently used supervised learning techniques. Indeed, some studies show that the performances of the algorithms are comparable and they achieve very good performance in text classification tasks (Colas & Brazdil, 2006). In the following we describe basic classification algorithms (analyze biological datasets) that we tested in this study: Naive Bayes (Ferrari & Aitken, 2006), regression (Arshadi & Jurisica, 2005), and Support Vector Machine (Brown, 2000).

The Naïve Bayes classifier is popular due to its simplicity, and computational efficiency, and has been widely used for text classification (D'Avanzo, Frixione, et al., 2006). The algorithm uses the joint probabilities of words and categories to estimate the probabilities of categories given in a text document. It computes the posterior probability that the text document belongs to different classes and assigns it to the class with the highest posterior probability. The posterior probability of class is computed using the Bayes rule, and the testing sample is assigned to the class with the highest posterior probability. The advantages of Naïve Bayes are it is quick to train and fast to evaluate; the classifier can also handle missing values by ignoring the examples during model building and classification.

Linear Regression is another important classifier algorithm used to analyze biological datasets. It is from regression analysis which is a mathematical method that describes the relationship between the set of one or more independent variables and a dependent variable (Arshadi & Jurisica, 2005). The goal of linear regression is to find the line that best predicts the dependent variable based on the independent variables. To achieve this goal, linear regression finds the line that minimizes the sum of the squares of the vertical distances of the points from the line.

The other type of learning system is Support Vector Machines (SVMs), which is a relatively new machine learning process, influenced by advances in statistical learning theory. The algorithm is a linear learning system that builds two separate classes (suitable for binary classification tasks), which are generated from training examples. The overall aim is to generalize test-data well. Utilized as binary categorical classifiers, the SVM method performs classification more accurately than most other supervised learning algorithms in biological data analysis applications, especially those applications involving high dimensional datasets (Brown, 2000; Liu, 2007). The SVM method uses a kernel function (the similarity function, which is computed in the original attribute space). The Support Vector Machine can be considered complex, slow and takes a lot of memory (limitation of the kernel), but it is a very effective classifier in a wide range of bioinformatic problems, and in particular performs well in analyzing biological datasets (Brown, 2000). This method is very popular and has been applied in many areas, such as credit scoring model (Chen & Li, 2010) and supply chains (Carbonneau, Vahidov, et al., 2007).

The other two new methods we used and describe in this paper are: Sequential Minimal Optimization and K-Nearest Neighbor classifier.

SMO (Sequential Minimal Optimization) is an algorithm for training support vector machines. SMO breaks the large Quadratic Programming (QP) optimization problem into a series of smallest possible QP problems (Platt, 1999). Avoiding the use of a time-consuming numerical QP optimization as an inner loop, the small QP problems are solved analytically. The main advantage of SMO is that it can handle very large training sets because its required memory is linear in the training set size. It is also the fastest algorithm for linear SVM with a sparse data set.

K-Nearest Neighbor classifier is a supervised learning algorithm. It is a type of instance-based learning method. This algorithm delays the process until a new instance is classified and is sometimes referred to as a "Lazy" learning method. The classification of this algorithm is based on majority vote of the K-nearest neighbor category. K is the parameter in this algorithm. It is a positive integer. If k=1, it means the object is simply assigned to the class of its nearest neighbor. The performance of K-nearest neighbor algorithm can be improved by varying the k value (Islam, Wu, et al., 2007). The key advantage of K-nearest neighbor method is that instead of estimating the target function once for the entire space, this method can estimate locally and differently for each new instance to be classified. Two applications of K-Nearest Neighbor method are text retrieval (Werner & Böttcher, 2007) and web page (Yao & Choi, 2007).

As we highlighted earlier, estimating classifier accuracy is one of the most important criteria for evaluating the systems. Classifier accuracy can be measured by using several evaluation methods: holdout, k-fold cross validation, leave-one-out-cross-validation, bootstrapping, and counting the cost (Kohavi, 1995; Jones & Paynter, 2003). Although a debate continues in machine learning and text mining circles about what is the best method for evaluation, holdout validation has been the widely used schema in practice (Witten, Paynter, et al., 1999; Zhang, Zincir-Heywood, et al., 2005). The holdout method is the simplest kind of cross validation. In this method, the data set is separated into two sets: training and testing. A certain amount of data is held over testing (also called the hold-out set), and the remaining data set is used for training. In this study, we also tested classifiers accuracy using the holdout validation method.

In this paper, we approach the key phrase extraction problem as a classification task using supervised learning. We aim to conduct a benchmark study in order to investigate whether there is a significant difference between the various machine learning approaches to automated key phrase extraction from full text documents and document abstracts. First, we compare the classifier approaches using full text document. Second, we compare the classifier approaches using the abstracts of these full text documents. Finally, we compare the classifier performance based on abstract vs. full text.

EXPERIMENTAL SETTING AND DATA COLLECTION

This section reviews the setting and data collection process of our experimental evaluation. The purpose of this experiment is to assess the differences between classifier techniques (SMO and K-Nearest Neighbor) on biomedical full-text documents and the abstracts of these documents. SMO is an algorithm for training support vector machine, especially useful for large data sets and sparse data sets; for more information see (Platt, 1999). We use the option that the data source is neither normalized nor standardized because under this option SMO gets the best performance. We compare the performance of each classifier using the KEA system. We chose to use KEA for numerous reasons: this system evaluation can be carried out automatically; it allows the modifying of parameters such as CutOff points and the number of key-phrases extracted, e.g., 5, 10, and 15 key-phrases per document; and it is considered the current state of the art (Frank, Paynter, et al., 1999; Witten, Paynter, et al., 1999).

We measure the performance of the classifiers by counting the number of matches between the output of the two systems and the key-phrases that were originally assigned by the author. We used this measure instead of traditional information retrieval metrics (recall and precision) for three reasons (Witten, Paynter, et al., 1999). First, a single overall value is more easily interpreted than two values. Second, the common information retrieval metrics of precision and recall can be misleading, for it is easy to increase precision at the expense of system's recall or increase recall at the expense of systems' precision. Third, this measure fits reasonably well into the expected behavior of end-users who are likely to ask for certain numbers of key-phrases for a text document.

Our experiment is divided into three parts: (1) we perform SMO and K-nearest neighbor classifiers on biomedical full-text documents; (2) we perform the two classifiers using the abstracts rather than full-text, when extracting 5, 10, and 15 key-phrases; (3) we consider whether the performance of the classifiers suffers when it only uses abstracts to extract key-phrases.

We measure the performance of the classifiers by comparing key-phrases with author-assigned key-phrases (Chen, 1999; El-Beltagy, 2006). To evaluate the performance of the two techniques, we use the holdout procedure in which the document collection is split into two sets, where the first one serves for training and the second for testing purposes. The training set is analyzed to adjust the model to the characteristics of the data. The test set serves solely for testing purposes. Our data set consists of 1002 full text documents, and is collected from PubMed www.pubmedcentral.nih.gov. From those 1002 full text documents, we picked the first 50 and the last 50 documents to build up our training data set, which has 100 documents. The others are used as a test set. For each document, there is a set of key-phrases, assigned by the authors of the articles (or professional indexers). We extract key-phrases and the abstract of each document and check them one by one. We include the results in a comparative study of all techniques. A sample system output is given in Table 1 which contains 5 key-phrases extracted by the four techniques.

EXPERIMENT AND RESULTS

Each of the performances of the four algorithms is tested. We also compare our results from the previous study (Qi, Yagci, et al., 2009), which evaluated

Table 1. Five extracted key-phrases by all two new systems

Document Title: A Cdt1–geminin complex licenses chromatin for DNA replication and prevents rereplication during S phase in Xenopus **PubMed ID: PMC7601436**		
Author assigned key-phrases	SMO	K-Nearest Neighbor
Cdt1 DNA replication licensing geminin prereplication complex rereplication	Geminin Cdt1 chromatin licenses complex	Loading binding Geminin G2and activates an ATM/ATR-dependent ATM/ATR-dependent

Table 2. Performance of the classifiers using full text

Algorithm	5 Key phrases	10 Key-phrases	15 Key-phrases
	AVG/STDEV	AVG/STDEV	AVG/STDEV
SMO	0.66 +/- 0.86	0.78 +/- 0.98	0.87 +/- 1.02
K-nearest neighbor	0.76 +/- 0.83	1.13 +/- 1.04	1.36 +/- 1.11
SVMreg-1	1.00 +/- 0.94	1.44 +/- 1.16	1.76 +/- 1.28
The best vs the second	31.6%	27.4%	29.4%
The best vs the worst	51.6%	84.6%	102.3%

the performance of three other supervised classifiers: Naïve Bayes, linear regression, and SVM. In the previous study (Qi, Yagci, et al., 2009), Naïve Bayes performed best for key-phrase extraction from the abstract while SVMreg-1 (standardize data source) performed best for full text document extraction. Table 2, Table 3, and Table 4 show the comparison of the performance of SMO, k-nearest neighbor with the performance of Naïve Bayes, and SVMreg-1 on full text and abstract when using the holdout evaluation method. AVG denotes the mean of the number of subjects, and STDEV denotes the standard deviation.

Table 2 shows the first experiment and represents the average number of correct matches with full-text documents by the three techniques. The comparative study results show that (1) SVMreg-1 classifier still performs better than SMO and K-nearest neighbor when we use the full text documents to extract 5, 10, and 15 key-phrases; (2) K-nearest neighbor, the second best performer technique, tends to better perform than SMO when we use the full text to extract 5, 10, 15 key-phrases; (3) It is acknowledged that the SMO performs worse than the others in most of the cases. SVMreg-1 performs better than K-nearest neighbor in 5, 10, 15 key-phrases by 31.6%, 27.4% and 29.4% respectively. SMO was the worst performer compared to the best performer by 51.6%, 84.6% and 102.3% respectively.

In the second experiment, our data set consists of 1002 abstracts of the same documents, which were extracted from the full text documents used in the first experiment. In Table 3, the comparative study results show that (1) Naïve Bayes outperforms SMO and K-nearest neighbor classifier when we use the abstracts only to extract 5, 10, 15 key-phrases. For example, Naïve Bayes can match on average between one and two of key-phrases of the 5, 10, 15 key-phrases assigned by the author. This difference is statistically significant. (2) The second best performer technique, SMO, tends to perform better than K-nearest neighbor when we use the abstracts to extract 5, 10, 15 key-phrases.

Table 3. Performance of the classifiers using abstracts

Algorithm	5 Key phrases	10 Key-phrases	15 Key-phrases
	AVG/STDEV	AVG/STDEV	AVG/STDEV
SMO	0.56 +/- 0.73	0.78 +/- 0.87	0.87 +/- 0.91
K-nearest neighbor	0.44 +/- 0.65	0.49 +/- 0.7	0.51 +/- 0.72
Naïve Bayes	0.81 +/- 0.84	1.10 +/- 1.02	1.22 +/- 1.07
The best vs the second	44.6%	41.0%	40.2%
The best vs the worst	84.1%	124.5%	139.2%

Table 4. Effect of full-text and abstract

	Number of key-phrases	Naïve Bayes	SMO	SVMreg-1	K-nearest neighbor
Full-text	5	0.95 +/- 0.91	0.66 +/- 0.86	1.00 +/- 0.94	0.76 +/- 0.83
	10	1.31 +/- 1.09	0.78 +/- 0.98	1.44 +/- 1.16	1.13 +/- 1.04
	15	1.57 +/- 1.19	0.87 +/- 1.02	1.76 +/- 1.28	1.36 +/- 1.11
Abstract	5	0.81 +/- 0.84	0.56 +/- 0.73	0.38 +/- 0.61	0.44 +/- 0.65
	10	1.10 +/- 1.02	0.78 +/- 0.87	0.69 +/- 0.81	0.49 +/- 0.7
	15	1.22+/- 1.07	0.87 +/- 0.91	0.81 +/- 0.90	0.51 +/- 0.72

(3) K-nearest neighbor performs worse than others in most of the cases. Naïve Bayes performs better than SMO in 5, 10, 15 key-phrases respectively by 44.6%, 41.0%, and 40.2%. K-nearest neighbor was the worst performer compared to the best performer in 5, 10, 15 key-phrases by 84.1%, 124.5% and 139.2% respectively.

Our final analysis checks whether the classifiers perform better when it only uses the full-text documents. We find significant performance differences between full-text and abstracts of the documents. Table 4 represents the number of correct matches with full-text documents and abstracts of these documents. The results show that all classifier techniques extract more matching key-phrases from full-text compared to the abstracts of the documents. One can argue that when using abstracts, the reason for reduced performance is more likely to retrieve a smaller number of key-phrases found in the abstract than in the biomedical full-text document (Witten, Paynter, et al., 1999).

Our result shows that the classifiers can match on average between one and two of the key-phrases assigned by the author in the documents. However, classifiers' incorrect key-phrase choices are not necessarily poor key-phrases for several reasons. Authors do not necessarily choose key-phrases that best describe the content of their paper. Another reason is that authors might choose key-phrases to slant their work in a certain way, or to maximize its chance of being noticed by particular searchers (Witten, Paynter, et al., 1999).

The limitations of this study come from two parts. One is the size of data set, in the future, we will add more documents (may expand to 10k level) into our data set. Because SMO is more appropriated in training a large and sparse data set, if there is large and sparse dataset in future, SMO may perform much better. A larger dataset will also be more appropriated to evaluate each classifier. The third limitation is from the evaluation method. We will use 10-fold cross validation method instead of holdout method in future studies.

CONCLUSION

Automatic key-phrase extraction is important because it makes it feasible to generate key-phrases for a large number of biomedical documents that do not have manually assigned key-phrases. A benefit of automatic key-phrase extraction is in the reduction in cost and time spent in manually assigning key phrases to documents. Naturally, key-phrase extraction from a text document is considered a classification activity using a supervised learning method. In this paper, (1) we compared the performance among different classifier methods (SMO, k-nearest neighbor, Naïve Bayes, and SVMreg-1) using the KEA system; and (2) we compared performance differences between biomedical full-text documents and abstracts of these documents only. Based on the experimental study and comparison with a previous study, we found that the SVMreg-1 classifier improves the performance of key-phrase extraction from biomedical full-text documents when extracting 5, 10, 15 key-phrases, while Naïve Bayes classifier improves the performance of key-phrase extraction from the abstracts of documents when extracting 5, 10, and 15 key-phrases. As future work, we plan to recruit subjects to evaluate the extracted results by the system and measure the perceived accuracy of results by the system without using original author's (or professional indexers) choices; this could be an interesting contribution to this study.

REFERENCES

Abu-Nimeh, S., & Nappa, D. (2003). An empirical comparison of supervised machine learning techniques in bioinformatics. *Research and Practice in Information Technology Series*, *33*, 219–222.

Arshadi, N., & Jurisica, I. (2005). *Feature Selection for Improving Case Based Classifiers on High Dimentional Data Sets*. AAAI.

Brown, J. (2000). Growing up digital: How the web changes work, education, and the ways people learn. *Change*, 10–20.

Carbonneau, R., & Vahidov, R. (2007). Machine Learning-Based Demand Forecasting in Supply Chains. *International Journal of Intelligent Information Technologies*, *3*(4), 40–57.

Chen, F.-L., & Li, F.-C. (2010). Comparison of the Hybrid Credit Scoring Models Based on Various Classifiers. *International Journal of Intelligent Information Technologies*, *6*(3), 56–74.

Chen, K. (1999). Automatic Identification of Subjects for Textual Documents in Digital Libraries.

Colas, F., & Brazdil, P. (2006). *Comparison of SVM and Some Older Classification Algorithms in Text Classification Tasks*. Santiago, Chile: International Federation for Information Processing.

D'Avanzo, E., Frixione, M., et al. (2006). *LAKE system*. Paper presented at DUC-2006.

D'Avanzo, E., Magnini, B., et al. (2004). *Keyphrase Extraction for Summarization Purposes: The LAKE System*. Paper presented at DUC-2004: Document Understanding Workshop, Boston.

Dumais, S. T., Platt, J., et al. (1998). Inductive Learning Algorithms and Representations for Text Categorization. In *Proceedings of the Information and Knowledge Management 7th International Conference*. New York: ACM Press.

El-Beltagy, S. (2006). KP-Miner: A Simple System for Effective Keyphrase Extraction. In *Proceedings of the Innovation in Information Technology Conference*. Washington, DC: IEEE Computer Society.

Ferrari, L. D., & Aitken, S. (2006). Mining housekeeping genes with a Naive Bayes classifier. *BMC Genomics*.

Frank, E., Paynter, G. W., et al. (1999). *Domain-specific keyphrase extraction*. Paper presented at the 6th International Joint Conference on Artificial Intelligence (IJCAI-99).

Frantzi, K. T., Ananiadou, S., et al. (1998). The C-value/NC-value Method of Automatic Recognition for Multi-Word Terms. In *Proceedings of the Second European Conference on Research and Advanced Technology for Digital Libraries*, London. Berlin: Springer-Verlag.

Hamdi, M. S. (2008). SOMSE: A Neural Network Based Approach to Web Search Optimization. *International Journal of Intelligent Information Technologies*, *4*(4), 31–54.

Huang, C., Tian, Y., et al. (2006). *Keyphrase Extraction using Semantic Networks Structure Analysis.*

Islam, M. J., Wu, Q. M. J., et al. (2007). Investigating the Performance of Naive- Bayes Classifiers and K- Nearest Neighbor Classifiers. In *Proceedings of the 2007 International Conference on Convergence Information Technology.* Washington, DC: IEEE Computer Society.

Jones, S., & Paynter, G. W. (2003). An Evaluation of Document Keyphrase Sets. *Journal of Digital Information*, *4*(1).

Kohavi, R. (1995). A study of cross-validation and bootstrap for accuracy estimation and model selection.

Kumar, N., & Srinathan, K. (2008). Automatic keyphrase extraction from scientific documents using N-gram filtration technique. In *Proceedings of the 8th ACM Symposium on Document Engineering,* Sao Paulo, Brazil. New York: ACM Press.

Liu, B. (2007). *Web Data Mining.* New York: Springer.

Liu, X. (2007). Intelligent Data Analysis. *Intelligent Information Technologies: Concepts, Methodologies, Tools and Applications*, 308.

Medelyan, O., & Witten, I. H. (2006). Thesaurus Based Automatic Keyphrase Indexing. In *Proceedings of JCDL.* New York: ACM Press.

Pala, N., & Cicekli, I. (2008). Turkish keyphrase extraction using KEA. In *Proceedings of the Computer and Information Science Conference.* Washington, DC: IEEE Computer Society.

Piramuthua, S., & Sikora, R. T. (2006). *Genetic Algorithm Based Learning Using Feature Construction.* Paper presented at the INFORMS Annual Meeting, Pittsburgh, PA.

Piramuthua, S., & Sikora, R. T. (2009). Iterative feature construction for improving inductive learning algorithms. *Expert Systems with Applications*, *36*(2), 3401–3406. doi:10.1016/j.eswa.2008.02.010

Platt, J. C. (1999). Fast training of support vector machines using sequential minimal optimization. In *Advances in kernel methods: support vector learning* (pp. 185–208). Cambridge, MA: MIT Press.

Qi, Y., Yagci, A. I., et al. (2009). *Extraction of Key-phrases from Biomedical Full-text with Supervised Learning Techniques.* Paper presented at the 15th American Conference on Information Systems (AMCIS), San Francisco.

Song, M., Song, I.-Y., et al. (2003). KPSpotter: a flexible information gain-based keyphrase extraction system. In *Proceedings of the International Workshop on Web Information and Data Management.* New York: ACM Press.

Turney, P. (1997). *Extraction of key Phrases from Text: Evaluation of Four Algorithms.* Ottawa, ON, Canada: National Research Council.

Turney, P. (2000). Learning algorithms for keyphrase extraction. *Journal of Digital Information.*

Turney, P. D. (1999). *Learning to Extract Keyphrases from Text* (Tech. Rep. ERB-1057 NRC #41622). Ottawa, ON, Canada: National Research Council, Institute for Information Technology.

Turney, P. D. (2000). Learning Algorithms for Keyphrase Extraction. *Information Retrieval, 2*(4), 303–336. doi:10.1023/A:1009976227802

Werner, L., & Böttcher, S. (2007). Supporting Text Retrieval by Typographical Term Weighting. *International Journal of Intelligent Information Technologies, 3*(2), 1–16.

Witten, I. H., Paynter, G. W., et al. (1999). KEA: Practical Automatic Keyphrase Extraction. In *Proceedings of the Fourth on Digital Libraries '99*. New York: ACM Press.

Yao, Z., & Choi, B. (2007). Clustering Web Pages into Hierarchical Categories. *International Journal of Intelligent Information Technologies, 3*(2), 17–35.

Zhang, Y., Zincir-Heywood, N., et al. (2005). Narrative text classification for automatic key phrase extraction in web document corpora. In *Proceedings of the 7th Annual ACM International Workshop on Web Information and Data Management,* Bremen, Germany. New York: ACM Press.

This work was previously published in the International Journal of Intelligent Information Technologies, Volume 7, Issue 1, edited by Vijayan Sugumaran, pp. 33-44, copyright 2011 by IGI Publishing (an imprint of IGI Global).

Chapter 4
Design and Usage of a Process-Centric Collaboration Methodology for Virtual Organizations in Hybrid Environments

Thorsten Dollmann
German Research Center for Artificial Intelligence (DFKI), Germany

Andreas Hoheisel
Fraunhofer Institute for Computer Architecture and Software Technology, Germany

Michael Fellmann
University of Osnabrueck, Germany

Peter Katranuschkov
TU Dresden, Germany

Oliver Thomas
University of Osnabrueck, Germany

Raimar J. Scherer
TU Dresden, Germany

Peter Loos
German Research Center for Artificial Intelligence (DFKI), Germany

ABSTRACT

This article describes a collaboration methodology for virtual organizations where the processes can be automatically executed using a hybrid web service, grid or cloud resources. Typically, the process of deriving executable workflows from process models is cumbersome and can be automated only in part or specific to a particular distributed system. The approach introduced in this paper, exemplified by the construction industry field, integrates existing technology within a process-centric framework. The solution on the basis of a hybrid system architecture in conjunction with semantic methods for consistency saving and the framework for modeling VO processes and their automated transformation and execution are discussed in detail.

DOI: 10.4018/978-1-4666-2047-6.ch004

INTRODUCTION

Effective enterprise collaboration and efficient utilization of appropriate information technology are basic prerequisites for a successful cooperation between companies. Cooperation can follow different objectives which differently affect the creation of processes of the cooperation partners. Regarding the integration of different business processes of the cooperation, one can find different objectives of cooperation affecting the integration process. For example, added value units could be created and newly shown up in the model or elements are reduced by redundancies in the process of building conglomerates or pools, where all cooperation partners are taking part and using it. It is also possible that previous inaccessible software systems of a partner could be used.

The degree of variation of the cooperation is also important for the integration. Therefore, the dynamical cooperation is most challenging and hence a case of reference since the integration of business processes has to be often reactivated to react on the changes of the cooperation. Here, most of the coordination effort between the partners is expected. A wide spread form of cooperation is a virtual organization (VO). A virtual organization (VO) is built as a combination of persons, companies and other real organizational entities. It has a transient nature and can be subject to changes throughout its lifespan. Virtual organizations are defined through dynamic, i. e. alterable "relations" such as roles and access privileges, which in term define the participation of the involved real or virtual actors (Camarinha-Matos, Afsarmanesh, & Ollus, 2005). The use of process modeling techniques – an important component of VO management as such – allows to put emphasis on the execution of tasks related to internal or external work orders as well as to their time and space related coordination.

There are various platform approaches regarding the IT support of Virtual Organizations. However, centralized Client-Server systems based on proprietary interfaces as well as Corba-based systems are increasingly being replaced by more flexible technologies that enable stronger distribution of the information, unify the remote access to services by the use of the SOAP standard and warrant structural data interoperability via XML-based language constructs.

The present article aims at offering an improved collaboration methodology for managing and automatically executing collaborative business processes using hybrid web service, grid or cloud resources. This goal is particularly motivated by increasing process integration scenarios of collaborative business relations and the diffusion of the joint usage of distributed resources. The objective of design-science research is to develop technology based solutions for important and relevant business problems (Hevner et al., 2004). This article tends to information system research with new characteristics. The described shortcomings constitute the prerequisites for the beneficial implementation of a hybrid platform in combination with semantic methods for tasks like consistency checking, information retrieval for the different expert-views of the participating parties as well as functionally oriented process management. The central assumption of this concept is that the VO requirements can be fulfilled and the efficiency of the collaboration processes can be increased. This approach is innovative, because it allows all participants to collaborate with justifiable expenses and efforts through utilization of new universal process-oriented working methods and modern information and communication technology, based on an integrated grid platform allowing even mobile access to the platform. In this paper, we will design and apply such a methodology based on a case study from the construction industry field. We will close with an outlook and future research challenges.

BACKGROUND

IT Processes in Distributed Systems

Implemented systems within the scope of IT supported process automation are increasingly processed at distributed computers worldwide instead of executing them on a central server infrastructure. The communication between those computers is carried out over the internet or local networks. A typical realization form of such distributed systems is the service oriented architecture (SOA), which aligns services in a top-down fashion to the functions of the business processes and makes them available on the spatially distributed servers (Thomas & vom Brocke, 2010). A further method for implementing scalable computer networks for the execution of IT processes is the so called cloud computing. The term cloud within the present article is used in the meaning defined by Forrester Research, which sees a cloud as a pool of an abstractable, highly scalable and managed IT infrastructure, which hosts customer applications and bills expenses according to the usage of the hosted services. The main focus of cloud computing is placed on uncoupled or loosely coupled mass services.

Special services, e.g. parallel simulation computing, requiring closely coupled parallel computing power, or cluster computers with quick internal network connection are better realized within a grid infrastructure. Moreover grid computing ensures better support for virtual organizations, comprising many resource operators and users and dedicated to the solution of a particular task. In contrast to a cloud infrastructure, grid computing aims at achieving transparent conjoint resource usage within networks of organizations, groups or even worldwide networks. Resources involved in a grid network comprise not only computing power and storage capacities, but also applications, software, web services, licenses or sensor for data recording. Grid computing aims at providing VOs with the ability to manage resources such as data, sensors, computers and computer networks and thus ensures their effective deployment for achieving a cooperative solution for a particular problem. A grid is a system that coordinates IT resources that are not subject to centralized control (Foster, 2002). Regardless of their operating characteristics, grid computing enables heterogeneous and dispersed IT resources to be virtually shared and accessed across an industry or workgroup. Significant challenges to be addressed still exist at all levels, for example trust and security issues or the development of grid-adopted applications (French, 2009; Vykoukal, Wolf, & Beck, 2009). Projects within the grid community have focused mainly on high performance computing and resource sharing in research and development VOs (Coppola et al., 2008), paying little attention to industry VO needs, even though requirements have been properly identified (Foster & Kesselmann, 2003; Milke, Schiffers, & Ziegler, 2006). The comprehension of the significant potential of grid technologies for solving current industrial problems leads gradually to a change in the development and implementation perspective of VO projects.

Transformation of Business Models into Executable Grid, Cloud and Service Processes

The transformation of business processes into technical processes, which shall be executed in distributed systems, is currently mostly cumbersome and can be automated only in part. The reason for this lies in particular in the gap between the often informal and abstract modeling of business processes on the one hand, and the formal modeling of IT processes with specific technical details on the other hand. Besides the different levels of abstraction, both types of process description are usually organizationally different across the company and differ in terms of their implementation timing. Thus, in the corresponding software development projects process modeling is executed either at a very early or at a very late stage. The early modeling includes the specification of a system from a technical point of view (e.g. technical specifications). The late modeling defines the systems components and their interaction from a technical point of view and is often closely linked to the chosen development environment. Through the existing gap between semi-formal conceptual and formal technical models, a consistent transfer of technical requirements for supporting IT systems cannot be guaranteed. The lack of consistency between the conceptual and technical level leads to both synchronization problems between the conceptual and the technical process model as well as to the risk of multiple reoccurring implementations of identical functionalities, as a result of deviating conceptual model description of one and the same functionality. An example of this inconsistency occurs with ad hoc changes to the business processes inflicted as a result of changed enterprise environment. Those changes can be reflected in the implementation models but could be missed out in the conceptual level models.

Further differences exist regarding the universe of discourse. While conceptual process description addresses primarily goals and organizational responsibilities, the technical processes concentrate mainly on dataflow or distribution of resources such as computer capacities. To sum up, these differences and problems lead to different and sometimes incompatible approaches for the modeling of business processes and use of technology (executable) processes, which are difficult to overcome.

Our contribution consists in the development of an approach for the conversion of business process models into IT processes which are not specific to particular distributed systems such as service oriented architectures, cloud platforms or computing grids and can be executed on all of them. The presented approach is characterized firstly through its generic method, where an executable process model is created automatically with the help of the predefined parameters within the preconfigured workflow engine based on the existing conceptual process model. For the purpose of conceptual modeling the economically oriented, semi-formal modeling language EPC (Event-driven Process Chain) is used (Keller, Nüttgens, & Scheer, 1992), which is commonly met in scientific and practical circles nowadays. A second differentiating characteristic of our approach is the incorporation of relevant grid and cloud computing aspects such as load balance, compensation and scalability of resources.

In order to cope with the problems and shortcomings, i.e. the missing consistency between the conceptual and technical model levels, a common scientific and practical approach is implementing BPMN (Business Process Modeling Notation) (Object Management Group, 2009) for the modeling of the business processes and the consequent realization in WS-BPEL (Web Services Business Process Execution Language) (OASIS, 2007). This approach also has some considerable disadvantages in certain application cases. Both WS-BPEL and BPMN have relatively complex syntax and semantics, which potentially leads to complex and highly-probable faulty transformation. This facilitates difficult checking and inspection of the created models regarding formal criteria. WS-BPEL for example has three ways of defining a loop, although technically a single loop construct would be sufficient. This further necessitates manual process steps in the transformation of BPMN models into executable ones, thus making a close coupling between modeling and execution impossible and leading to higher cost for the support of dynamic processes.

Furthermore, WS-BPEL is specialized in the orchestration of web services in terms of SOAP services and cannot be applied to other component models without further specific extensions such as BPEL-J. The encapsulation of all components' models as web services is plausible for many application cases but also brings complementary complexity and execution speed reduction. For example, IT processes based primarily on database calling procedures can be realized much more effectively over an ODBC interface. A further example constitutes the computing- and data intensive processes based on the execution of textually interfaced programs in multicore, cluster or grid computing environments which can potentially be executed more quickly over, for instance, POSIX interface or intermediate batch systems (LSF, PBS etc.). Furthermore a parallel executed BPEL process must be explicitly specified as this cannot be processed automatically.

WS-BPEL offers only restricted possibility to define processes independently from the executing infrastructure. Such abstraction alternatives are necessary and important, especially in dynamically distributed environments, because part of the infrastructure can drop out, be newly allocated or fail during process execution. Furthermore, the use of abstract processes allows the achievement of better reusability of the available infrastructure. For example, the same test process can be executed locally on a laptop and upon productive state be available and executed on a bigger computer cluster.

Further approaches addressing the conversion process improvement of conceptual process descriptions into executable processes can be found in the field of semantic web services (an overview is provided in Cardoso & Sheth, 2005; Cabral et al., 2004). Through machine readable semantic description of web services an easier discovery and selection and also a bridging of the semantic gaps within service orchestration is to be achieved. This purpose requires extensive ontology based descriptions. Those were realized in the past with the help of ontology languages and vocabularies such as WSMO (Web Service Modeling Ontology) (Arroyo et al., 2005) and OWL-S (Web Ontology Language for Web Services) (Martin et al., 2004).

DESIGN OF A COLLABORATION METHODOLOGY FOR VIRTUAL ORGANIZATIONS

Process-Centered Infrastructure for VO-Management

The open, scalable and extensible system architecture should be capable to support the required security regulations and procedures regarding distributed information management in virtual organizations. The interfaces for service integration are therefore realized on the basis of ontologies. The adaptivity of the services for use on mobile devices is additionally introduced in the architecture because some domain-specific services of the infrastructure would need to be ported on mobile devices.

The targeted process-oriented IT-platform for the semantic VO-management is realized on the basis of a multi layered system architecture, enabling coherent integration of modern technological issues, and allows for clear and well-defined interrelationships and interfaces between grid middleware components, basic VO services, business process services and engineering services and applications. Furthermore, the platform should be supported by a homogeneous semantic model of the environment, facilitating the system-wide identification of all involved users, resources and services – regardless of their particular location, while implementing strict role-based access profiles. Figure 1 shows the principal layers of the suggested platform architecture extending the original grid architecture (Foster, Kesselmann, Nick, & Tuecke, 2002).

The original grid layers are additionally extended by three new layers. The Semantic Grid Services layer is largely adopted from Dolenc, Klinc, Turk, Katranuschkov and Kurowski (2008). It contains all supporting ontology-based VO management services that are responsible for the provision of semantically rich queries and assertions with regard to users, resources, service access etc. The next two layers, i.e. the Grid Gateway layer and the Semantic Web Services Layer are missing in various other known approaches focusing on pure grid environments. Their purpose is to enable co-existence of web service based subsystems and advanced fully gridified applications. Due to the high security standards imposed by the grid middleware – a major benefit for each industry VO – such co-existence is not given per se.

The Semantic Web Services are in fact normal Web Services defined using WSDL. The term "semantic" is applied here to denote that the services, as all other high-level services, on that layer have to commit to the platform ontologies in their relevant areas of interest. This can be achieved by implementing them either to fully "understand" the relevant parts of the OWL-based ontology specifications or, in a more light-weight approach, by ensuring that the relevant subset of queries/responses to the ontologies are properly interpreted and served (Katranuschkov, Gehre, Shaukat, & Scherer, 2008).

The purpose of the intermediate Grid Gateway layer is solely to provide the necessary mechanisms that would allow acceptance of the Web Services in the grid environment. Engineering applications have two principal possibilities to plug-in to the platform. The first includes comprehensive gridification. However, this is also the more difficult and resource-consuming approach, requiring full or at least partial re-engineering of the application. For its achievement, various methods can be applied depending on the actual goals and the specific application context (Mateos, Zunino, & Campo, 2008). Here, a more pragmatic approach is used. Its essence is firstly to provide a web service wrapper for the application logic which is itself wrapped by a grid service wrapper via a standard conversion procedure utilizing the functionality of the Grid Gateway layer. This is an easier way towards gridification for domain developers, due to the clear separation of gridification techniques from the application logic. A further advantage

Figure 1. Layered structure of the collaboration architecture

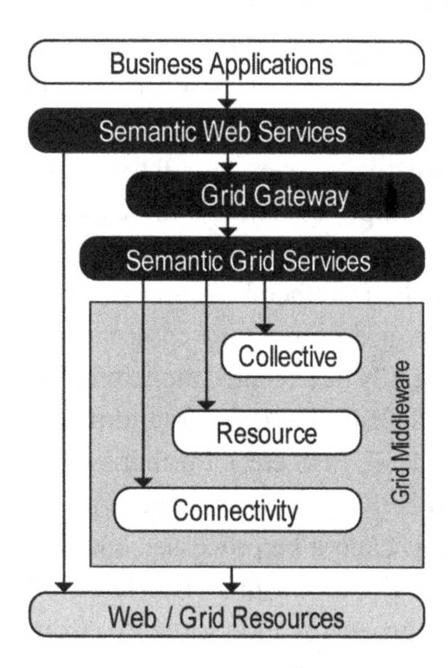

is the co-existence of both grid and web services in the same VO environment and eventually for the same end-user systems, thereby avoiding a mandatory grid solution. The proposed approach sets out to respond the pictured challenges via a flexible and reusable platform. The implementation of the methodology enables:

- Controlled representation of responsibility and authorization structures,
- Fast configuration and management of both global VO processes and local company-specific processes in accordance with the set-up responsibility structure,
- Fast, flexible and secure access to information from different sources (documents, drawings, photographic material etc.), both from headquarters and from the construction site,
- Ad-hoc changes in the process flow, using semiautomatic process simulation, and
- Capturing of processes and process/product data on the site making use of various mobile devices, thereby providing a basis for faster and more efficient decision making with participation of all team members.

Achievement of these goals is grounded on the coherent, integrated use of cutting-edge ICT technologies. First, grid technology provides facilities for secure and efficient use of distributed resources, end-user applications and services in a VO as well as basic services for VO management that can be used as grounding for various domain-specific semantic services. Specifically, grid technology enables an efficient data distribution and computational load balancing in a distributed heterogeneous network. It also enables proper authorization, authentication and access control management with regard to resources and services and enables a secure communication via sophisticated encryption techniques. Additionally, the grid platform provides uniform and secure access to data and documents stored as distributed heterogeneous information sources via standardized grid-based interfaces. Furthermore, it provides standardized and secure access to computational and data storage capacities offered by service providers on the grid.

Thereby, Semantic Web technology enables uniform formal description of the overall system, including all relevant resource, service and information types but also the actors and companies acting on the system and the actual technical processes in the overall value chain. Specifically, Semantic Web technology enables a common semantic commitment of all applications and services of the platform via an explicit formal ontology specification of the concepts describing resources, services, actors as well as project and company organizational structures. The context-dependent definition of work and information profiles for each VO partner and each particular user provides personalized views on the data and services, and company-specific information sources such as different systems are interlinked on the platform in uniform manner.

The integration of meaningful semantics and grid technology possesses great potential, especially with regard to the use of the grid for VO support. However, an important prerequisite for the achievement of semantic interoperability is the use of an expressive formal ontology language. The Ontology Web Language (OWL) (Smith, Welty, & McGuiness, 2004) is currently broadly recognized as such a language, offering great modeling flexibility and warranting syntactic interoperability to other XML-based languages. Already available OWL ontologies can thereby be directly imported and used on the platform. Moreover, via formal semantic description of grid services with the help of OWL-S an efficient VO Service Management can be supported as well. The benefit of ontologies as a basis for the semantic-based management of VOs has already been addressed (Dolenc et al., 2008).

The technique of process modeling allows a semi-formal description of technical processes including the input- and output-documents and data, the performing actors and participating organizational units as well as the required applications and tools. Moreover, it also allows describing the state of the world before and after the execution of a function which is required in order to orchestrate the execution of functions. The technique of process modeling can thus be used to achieve a coherent semi-formal description of the business processes, to describe separate, reusable process fragments and to construct integrated process modules composed of process fragments which are part of the value added chain. The transformation of business-oriented processes into workflow models, i. e. models which are executable on the grid, is a challenging task which still requires human intervention (Thomas, Dollmann & Loos, 2008). In order to improve this transformation, a method for the modeling of VO-processes in grid environments has been developed which constitutes the core methodical concept of the approach.

Framework for Modeling VO Processes in Hybrid Environments

The use of process modeling techniques – an important component of VO management as such – allows to put emphasis on the execution of tasks related to internal or external work orders as well as to their time and space related coordination. A key role is assigned to the creation of abstract representations of reality, adequately simplified for the specifically regarded issues of interest. Current challenges to the process management in a VO can be seen in particular in the distributed modeling imposed via the spatial distance of the VO partners, giving rise to problems related to collaborative process models and heterogeneous, distributed model data stores (Vanderhaeghen, Hofer, & Kupsch, 2006). Hence, it must be possible to integrate VO models on-demand as only directly interacting partners in the VO do need the VO-integrated model data. The semantic enrichment of process models with additional information can provide for easier handling of such heterogeneous models and enable (partial) automation of the integration process (Thomas & Fellmann, 2009).

In order to improve the composition of models in the dynamic context of virtual organizations, a method for modeling VO-processes has been developed, based on the EPC as basic modeling language. This method comprises the three distinct phases modeling, analysis and planning as well as execution and is shown in Figure 2. In the framework different tools for process modeling and automation are being implemented in order to cover and represent the whole construction process chain from the conceptual modeling to the automatic execution of all subjacent IT processes and to reproduce it in the grid infrastructure. This implies that data has to be passed between different tools, and thus, data formats have to be transformed. Due to the tools' different view point over the whole processes and the fact that each of them represents separate process layers, there are different underlying formalities and description languages, which need to be synchronized and integrated with each other. The different tools and methods build up integrated toolbox and method repository for the process modeling. In the process of representing dynamic processes additional information is being created, which enables (semi-) automatic integration and coupling of processes in grid environment.

All reference process models are collected with the help of a standard modeling tool during the modeling phase. During the analysis and planning phase the processes within the specific construction activities are either being newly created or changed based on the process building blocks. The basic idea consists in the fact, that a model must not be created from scratch, but the changes in the process flow can be achieved through new arrangement of process building blocks, thus facilitating easy and less time intensive modeling. The execution of processes during runtime as well as ad hoc process change is thus being realized.

During the execution phase previously created models are being transformed into executable process models. These facilitate the configuration of a workflow management system which supports the cooperative process execution in a network environment of distributed systems. The executable process description of the conceptual models is taken for the purpose of process execution, thus providing the information about the logic flow and the participating information objects as well as the required resources for the process accomplishment.

Unlike the transformation of BPMN to BPEL, our approach offers comparatively simple syntax and semantics, constructed on Event-driven Process Chains (EPC) and Petri Nets. Both later methods are well documented and studied. EPC is taken for the conceptual process description based on its broad practical and scientific acceptance as well as its simplicity and similarity to the Petri Net method. For the description of executable processes the Petri Net based language GWorkflowDL is used which covers the need of grid and cloud processes through its abstraction layer for IT processes in distributed computer architectures. Thus, the proposed approach is not limited to web services as execution technology and allows processes to be defined independently from the execution infrastructure.

Mapping Dynamic Processes to Executable Workflows and Resources

While processes modeled with Event-driven Process Chains only refer to pure business processes that are invoked by human resources, here the automation of business processes as well as their corresponding IT workflows, which are mapped onto IT resources, is considered. In existing systems, these two environments are often represented by two different description formalisms, such as BPEL4People (Kloppmann et al., 2005) for automating processes on human resources and BPEL4WS (OASIS, 2007) for automating processes in a SOA. In order to automate the enactment of the processes the description of the business processes is mapped here to a more formal, executable workflow description language, the so-called "Grid Workflow Description Language" (GWorkflowDL) (Alt, Hoheisel, Pohl, & Gorlatch, 2006). In contrast to other approaches, such as BPEL4WS (OASIS 2007) or SCUFL (Hull et al., 2006), the approach supports several levels of abstractions within one workflow description document, enabling ad-hoc modifications of the workflow during run time. At the same time, the GWorkflowDL is much simpler and more formal than the well-known set of BPEL* description languages. The workflows themselves can be described independently from the underlying infrastructure, thus increasing the reusability of the processes within different execution environments, such as Service-oriented Architectures (SOA), J2EE frameworks, grid, cluster or cloud computing environments.

Preliminary Annotation and Conversion

The GWorkflowDL is based on the formalism of High-Level Petri Nets (HLPN) and is compatible to the international standard ISO/IEC15909-1

Figure 2. Method repository

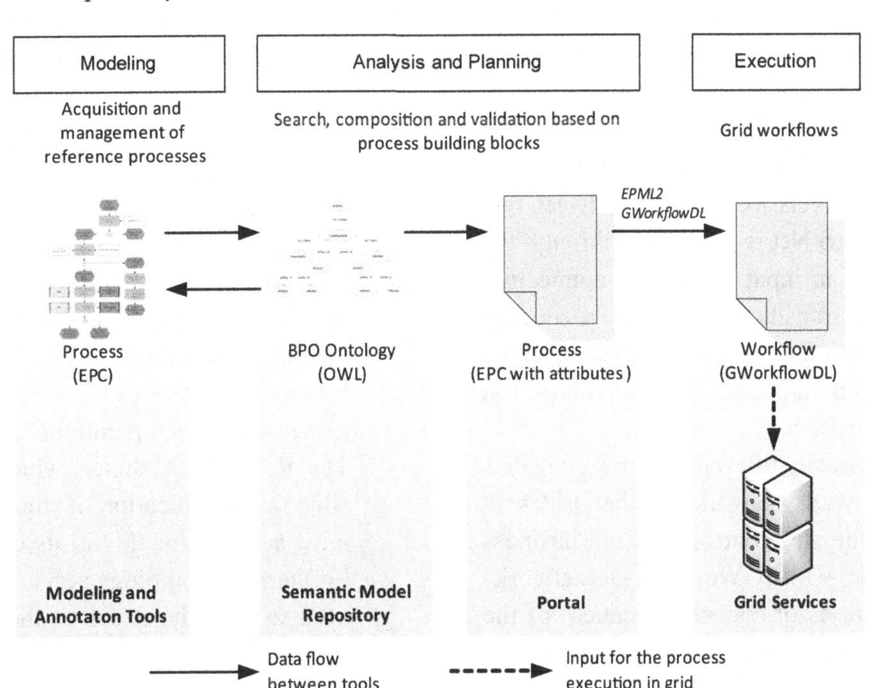

(ISO/IEC, 2004). In contrast to ordinary Petri Nets, the tokens of HLPNs are distinguishable and can be used to model high-level values, such as real input/output data, references to data (e.g. file-names or URLs) and boolean values representing side-effects. The distribution of tokens on places is called marking and represents the state of the distributed system. In order to be able to not only model but also invoke workflows with real data, the concept of HLPN was extended by using the XPath standard to formulate edge expressions and transitions conditions.

To facilitate the translation from abstract (and often informal) business processes into executable workflows, some minor semantic and syntactic extensions to the original Event-driven Process Chains are required, such as annotations for specifying the start events, relations of events or functions to real data as well as the definition of formal operation classes for the functions that need to be mapped onto human or IT resources.

Direct arcs between two functions are not desirable within an EPC depiction of a process model, although they may be encountered in practice. An EPC model can be more compact for the user, if the so-called trivial events are omitted (e. g. "letter is sent by post" as a result for a corresponding function "send letter by post"). Furthermore, most modeling tools also permit such simplified models. To convert these "dirty" EPCs into correct Petri Nets, a connection between two events in the Petri Net is substituted through the combination of an input and output connection separated by a transition. Likewise, a connection between two functions is represented in the Petri Net with an output and an input connection separated by a place.

One significant difference between EPCs and GWorkflowDL networks is that EPCs in general describe the control flow of business process models, while GWorkflowDL networks are representations of concrete instances of the executable (technical) processes including the underlying data which is to be processed. To map an EPC onto an executable process the following additional information, besides the one already given by the modeled functions, events and their connections, is needed:

- **Initial marking (data marks):** Generating the necessary data marks for the places is a complex job. One possibility is the use of transitions, which are associated with a workflow activity that produces data marks from the initial center marking within the specific process ("hole-data-activity"). In this approach, the initial marking consists only of center marks. A second possibility is the explicit modeling of data using EPC information objects. These are typically associated with functions to represent their relation to documents or other data in an EPC. These information objects can be translated into data marks, which will be put on additionally generated input and output places. A third possibility is the use of special event attributes, analogous to the control marks.
- **Executable activities (operation):** The GWorkflowDL aims at the concrete execution of workflows in a distributed system. As a minimum it needs the information of the <oc:operationClass> element, which defines the class of activities that should be executed when a transition is entered. The technically easiest way to provide this information within an EPC is via a naming convention, where the name of a function in the EPC is the same as the name of the <oc:operationClass> element. The Resource Matcher, which is responsible for identification of suitable services, must account for this in its configuration. Furthermore, ontology services can also be used to map the name of the function or

additional identifiers onto appropriate activity classes.

- **Connection addresses:** GWorkflowDL connection addresses establish a relationship between the actual data (marks on places) and certain functional parameters of a workflow activity. However, an EPC describes an abstract process flow, which is generally independent of specific data and therefore does not contain this relationship. In order to generate connections' addresses for the purpose of data flow in a GWorkflowDL network, an external knowledge base is needed, which exemplary can provide the profiles of workflow activities with their input and output parameters. If a compliance with the designated data naming conventions is maintained, then, exemplary, the associated connection addresses can be extracted directly from the WSDL interface description of the corresponding web services.

Process Execution and Monitoring

The Grid Workflow Management System developed by Fraunhofer FIRST enables the automation and interactive monitoring of complex and dynamic processes in service-oriented or grid environments (Hoheisel, 2006; Gubala & Hoheisel, 2007; Hoheisel, 2008; Krefting, Vossberg, Hoheisel, & Tolxdorff, 2010). A unique feature of the solution is the completely virtualized resource allocation based on abstract modeling of the process structure and the powerful resource description formalism. The user is able to invoke workflows without any knowledge of underlying hardware and software specifics, allowing him to concentrate on the real focus of the work.

The Grid Workflow Management System is composed of several services. The "Grid Workflow Execution Service" (GWES) is the core service, which enacts workflows automatically, fault-tolerant and persistent on distributed environments. Besides the GWES, the Grid Workflow Management System is composed of a resource and workflow registry (XML database), a resource matcher for mapping abstract activity requirements onto available hardware and software resources or services, a monitoring system which uses distributed sensors for gathering up-to-date information about short-term (e.g. load) and long-term (e.g. structure) properties of the resources as well as a scheduler which optimizes and plans the selection of resources. Within the enactment of the workflow, the resource matcher first maps abstract activities onto matching resource candidates. For each resource candidate the scheduler calculates a quality measure (e.g. based on the current load and performance of the resource) and assigns resources that are passing a certain quality threshold to matching activities, beginning with activities that possess the highest priority. The priority of an activity can either be specified by the user or by an optimization step within the scheduling process, e.g., giving activities on the critical path a high priority.

The GWES can be used both online as web service – particularly in a distributed grid environment – and offline as Java library on mobile devices. Self-contained local workflows can run on mobile devices and be linked to global workflows using hierarchical process modeling. Figure 3 shows the approach for the successive and mostly automated mapping of business process descriptions onto compatible and available resources. Firstly, business processes are annotated and mapped to abstract technical processes, here by transforming EPC models into GWorkflowDL documents. Then, service candidates providing the appropriate functionality are allocated to the single activities by using the resource matcher service. Finally, a scheduler chooses a candidate and executes the activity using the suitable resources.

USAGE OF THE COLLABORATION METHODOLOGY FOR VIRTUAL ORGANIZATIONS

Introduction to the Case Study

Specific Challenges in the Application Domain

Each industry branch comes along with its own specific features and requirements, which in terms necessitates their separate consideration. Generic solutions without domain specific extensions provide little added value and lead to marginal implementation efficiency in real world problems. The field of construction is ideal for achieving trend-setting research results in regard to the problem mentioned above. The construction industry is characterized by one-of-a-kind products and one-of-a-kind projects, typically leading to complex project structures including intricate contractual relations, frequently changing tasks and high dependability on external factors, effecting in total variegated challenges. There is a continuously growing demand towards improved handling of construction industry projects on the one hand and towards securing and achieving economic efficiency and cost reduction on the other hand. The implementation of different project platforms and computer programs such as document management systems or plan-, time- and construction deficiency management systems is a common necessity. Industry specific characteristics are mostly unique constructions, which build the basis for the respective construction projects and the unique collaboration networks between the participating predominantly small partners.

The resulting project structures are characterized by high complexity. This manifests itself in complex contractual bindings, non-specific, constantly changing duties and responsibilities as well as dependence on external factors (environmental, infrastructural, socio-political aspects), all of which induce ad hoc decision-making.

Figure 3. Mapping business processes onto compatible and available resources

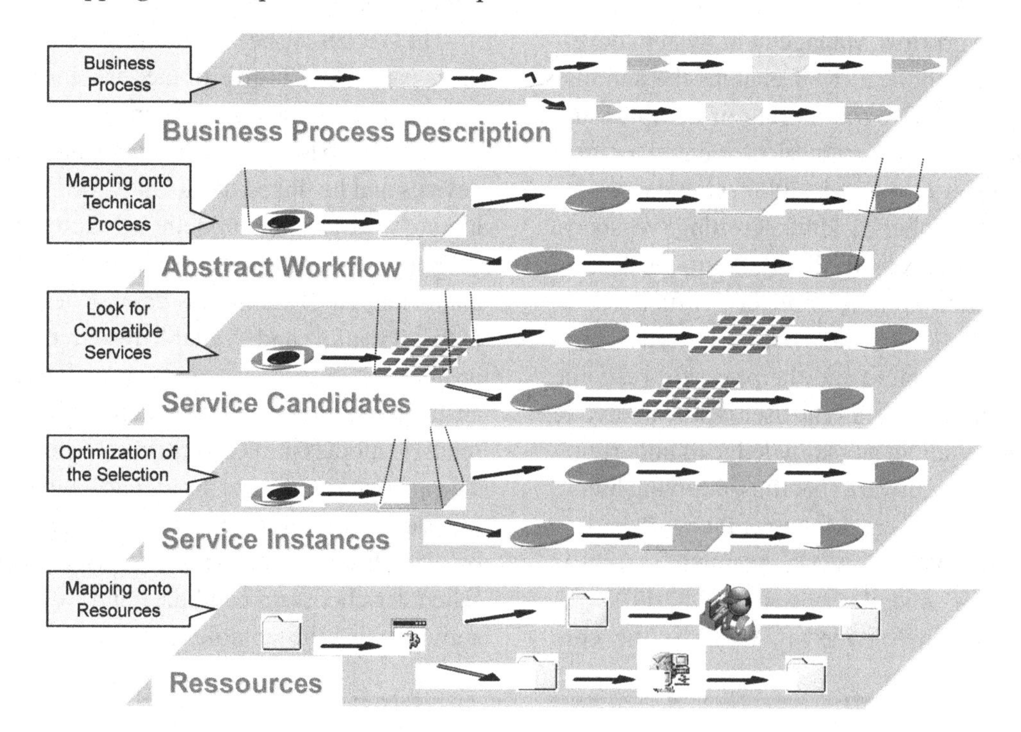

Virtual companies in medium and large constructional projects comprise dozens of sub-contracting partners which in turn are placed on multiple hierarchical levels with highly complex horizontal inter-connectivity. The different processes, accountability, duties and responsibilities build up to intransparent and defective combinations leading to significant time and cost inefficiencies. Resulting project information structures are mostly heterogeneous and highly redundant, as most of the participants are implementing their existing IT-infrastructure. Conventional management instruments do not pose the required abilities to ensure successful management of such a complex infrastructure.

The challenges for virtual organizations in the construction industry result from its complex project structures. Warranting efficient and successful cooperation within a Virtual Organization in construction poses a range of specific requirements on the supporting IT system, e.g.:

- An integrated schema enabling the common understanding about the use of all resources and services, i.e. a system-wide ontology,
- Standardized extensions of the integrated schema to capture discipline-specific aspects,
- Flexible capturing and management of project processes together with the associated resources and services as well as the responsible and cooperating persons and partners,
- Business rules and methods that enable the use of the business objects for VO management and at the same time establish the basis for a harmonized service platform for all VO participants,
- Coherent information logistics providing proper authorization, rigorous access control to resources and services as well as context-dependent views on the overall system for all VO participants.

Defect management processes are vintage processes in the construction industry. Defect management involves three types of actors that need to collaborate for the achievement of fast and cheap problem solutions, even though their views and positions may often be controversial. These are usually the owner, the main contractor and the subcontractors. A typical contractual relationship can be expressed by a 1:1:N relationship, but it does not provide sufficient consideration of complex cases. On a large construction site like the project Campeon visualized by Figure 4 the occurrence of numerous defects during the construction phase may be the case. As considerable cost factor these defects need to be duly managed, largely in parallel. The Campeon consortium involved five main contractors and over hundred subcontractors. 140 locations within the construction site had to be linked, based on a heterogeneous distributed IT-architecture. The execution of the construction project involved several information systems and platforms from different sources (e.g. cross-company communication platforms and data management systems, in-house IT and SAP). Communication among each other was not or only poorly possible. Additional resources and effecting heavy extra costs resulted from the fact that data input and manipulation generated a degree of administrative effort which could not be handled from the customary manpower on the construction site. Figure 4 visualizes the complexity of the parallel procedures by the numerous cranes working in parallel in order to finish the construction project within the technical and financial bounds.

However, whilst circumstances cause and effect can vary, the defect management process itself is generally the same. Activities range from simple message processing to document and media management activities. The latter include taking photos and videos, voice recordings, matching earlier photos to a specific event, classifying media data and so on. Considering the large number of parallel workflows between the in-

Figure 4. Large-scale project Campeon

volved actors, especially with regard to the main contractor, explains the importance of an adequate collaboration platform and collaborative process management.

Application Scenario "Defect Management"

Within the project the transformation of defect management business processes in the construction industry to services of a grid infrastructure was exemplified. Figure 5 shows an exemplary process including the steps from the recording of a constructional defect by the owner to the forwarding of the defect data to the main contractor. During the inspection of the construction site different construction defects are initially recorded by the owner und a defect record entered into the system by using a mobile device (e.g. a pda). Then images from the defects which are taken with another device for documentation purposes are assigned to the respective defects. The assignment happens in form of a decoding of barcodes which have been photographed with the defect. Since only a small area of the images contains the barcode, several image processing steps are required until the codes could be clearly identified. This process step is computationally extensive and is performed using grid computing resources. After assigning pictures and defects, the defect records have to be updated, stored in the central management system and forwarded to the main contractor (MC) who is responsible for eliminating the defects.

The need for the automation of such processes reveals when keeping in mind that hundreds of gigabytes of data and more than 40.000 single defects could occur on larger construction sites and up to 10% of the overall budget has to be used for the remediation of these defects. A new workflow instance has to be instantiated for each defect. Using the proposed methodology, the executable processes could be generated directly from the EPC models and executed on powerful grid resources while users do not have to deal with the technical details of the infrastructure. Dynamic chances within the sequences of action, triggered e. g. from damage at the construction site or the replacement of insolvent subcontractors, could easily be mapped from the business process models onto modified executable IT processes. Also a direct monitoring of the IT processes is possible in the business process layer so that one can immediately react on delays based on IT bottlenecks (e. g. full data storage).

Architecture

The scenario in Figure 6 shows the components of the resulting hybrid system architecture for VO-management in the construction industry, underpinning the hybrid nature as shown on high level in Figure 1. The basis of the environment is the web where the three major end-user Defect Management Systems (DfMS) provided by the owner, the main contractor and the subcontractors are installed. These three systems are "plugged-in" to the platform via the gateway layer as explained above. This provides access to all infrastructure services of the platform, including a Central Defect Management Service and a Workflow Management Service.

Mobile Defect Management Workflows

Mobile information processing technology enables the use of intelligent end-user software on mobile devices. Flexible, context-aware processing of project information as well as fast, ad hoc changes of process execution according to actual specific needs and situations can thus be done on site. In particular, mobile information processing technology provides the availability of any part of the whole information concerning a VO in mobile situations, enabling timely reaction and handling of the mobile work processes.

Corresponding to the presented methodology the instantiation of a process in terms of the creation of a concrete executable procedure

Figure 5. EPC model "record defect"

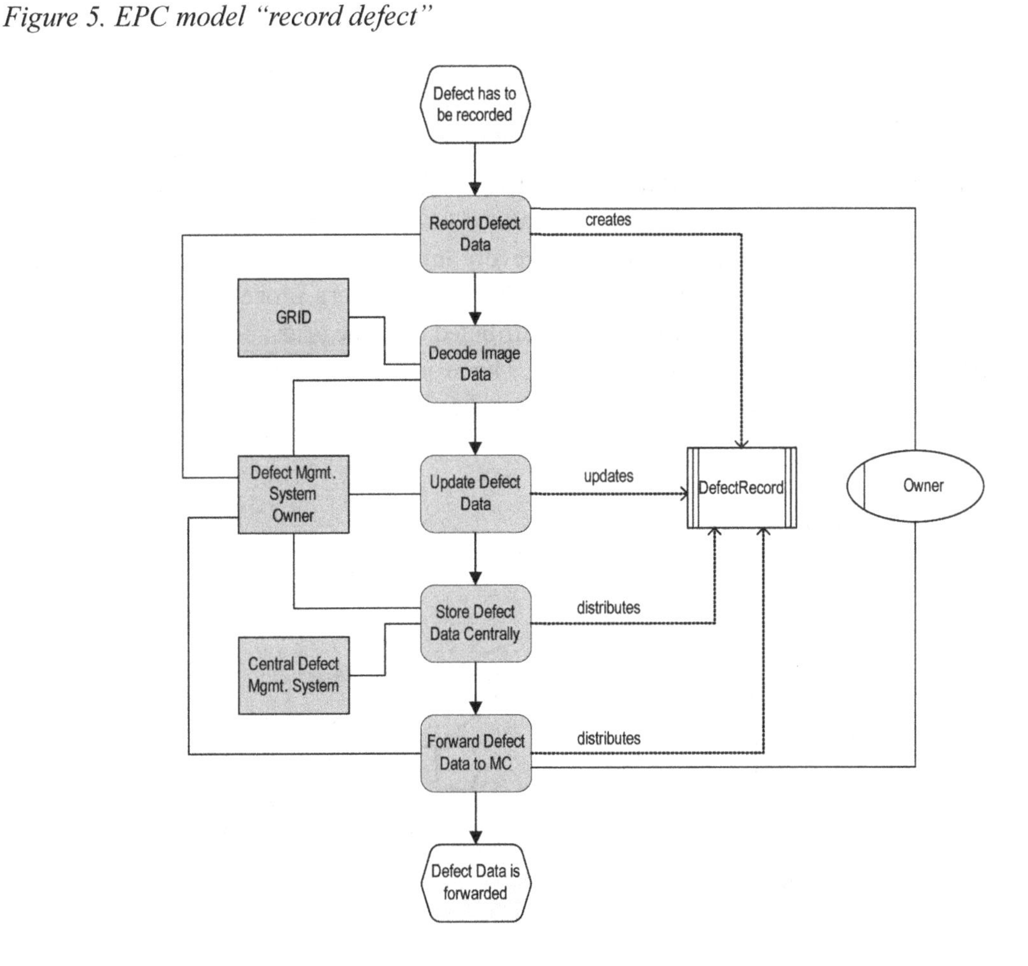

Figure 6. Hybrid BauVOGrid system architecture

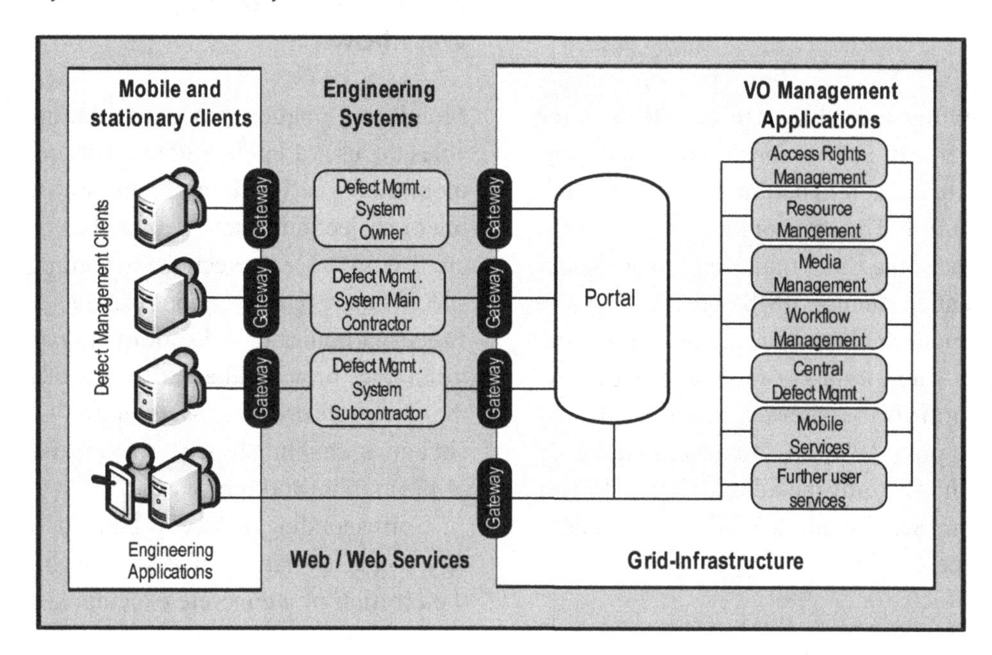

equates to the export of an EPC model from the modeling tool, a conversion to GWorkflowDL and a GWES import. Figure 7 shows the mobile workflow for recording the defect, derived from the process model in Figure 5. In the first step, the user has to record defect data. If the user uses a separate camera for taking a picture of the defect, a 2D-barcode is generated from the defect id and displayed on the pda. The user has to take a picture form the displayed barcode in combination with the defect. When all defects are recorded, the pda is synchronized with the central defect management system using the web service interfaces, along with the upload of all images of the defect to the media management system. For the assignment of the images a service was realized which locates and decodes the barcode in every image. For efficiency reasons subtasks of the procedure are processed in parallel and distributed over the grid.

The workflow is monitored and automated using the Grid Workflow Management System.

Figure 7. Executable grid workflow "record defect"

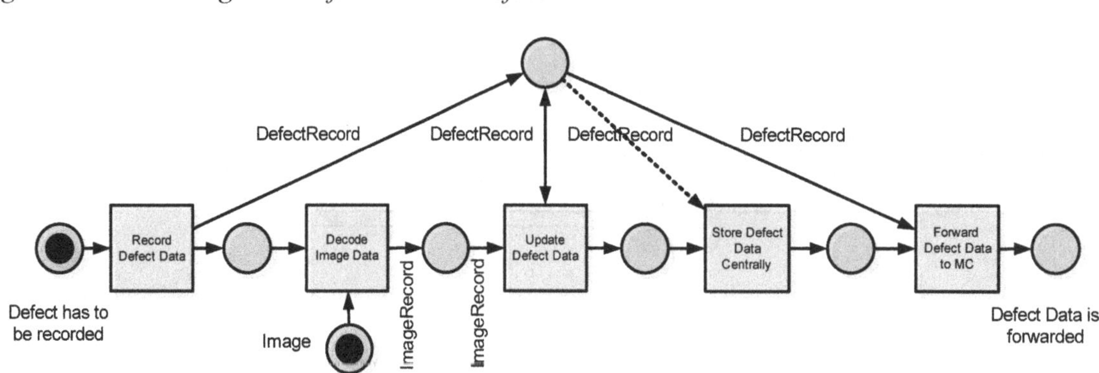

Figure 8 shows the web interface of the GWES online version for the global central defect management system workflow.

CONCLUSION AND OUTLOOK

The effective collaboration and cooperation between enterprises and the efficient utilization of suitable information technologies are basic prerequisites for the successful integration of physical persons, companies and real organizations. There are continuously rising requirements towards the realization of projects and in respect of their profitability and cost reduction. The main idea of the methodology presented in this paper is to substantially enhance the structure, functionality and operability of the multifaceted types of virtual organizations by means of a shared IT-system based on semantic web and grid technology. To do so, a hybrid grid- and web service-based architecture for the next generation of a VO service and gateway solution was developed integrating the process-oriented perspective and prototypically implemented using the construction branch as an example. The research results can be generally applied to collaborative (virtual) organizations and allow the "gridification" of existing applications with justifiable expenses and effort.

In the future, further developments of the approach should support more established tools for the business process description, for example by

Figure 8. GWES web interface and central defect management system workflow

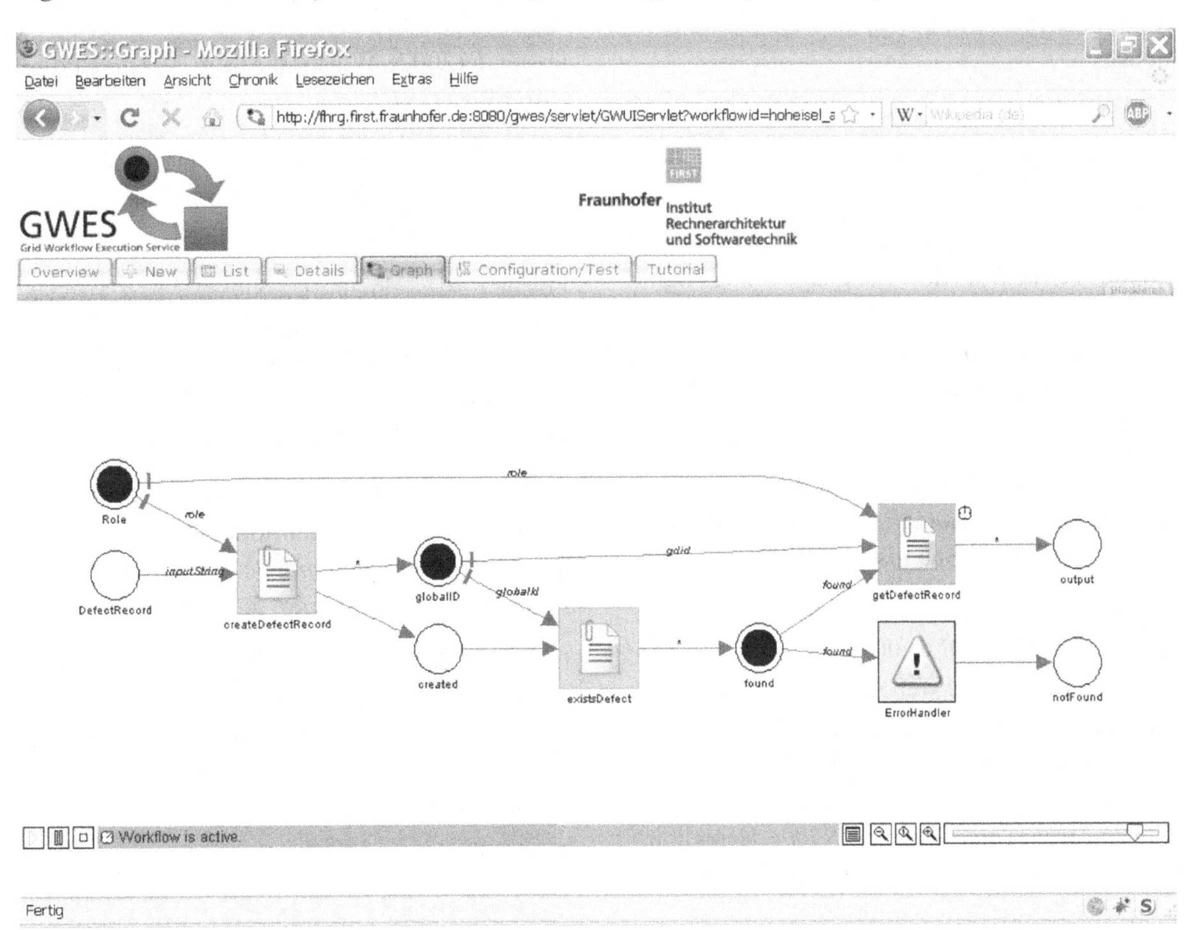

automating the transformation from the BPMN language and thus, deriving generic workflow models dynamically involving grid, service and also cloud resources with as little manual effort as possible.

ACKNOWLEDGMENT

The authors are grateful to the German Federal Ministry of Education and Research for funding the project BauVOGrid which stands for „Grid-Based Platform for the Virtual Organization in the Construction Industry" (promotional reference: 01IG07001A). An earlier version of this paper was presented at the Fifteenth Americas Conference on Information Systems (AMCIS2009), San Francisco, California August 6th-9th 2009 under the title "Process-Oriented Collaboration in Grid-Environments: A Case Study in the Construction Industry"

REFERENCES

Alt, M., Hoheisel, A., Pohl, H.-W., & Gorlatch, S. (2006). A Grid Workflow Language Using High-Level Petri Nets. In Wyrzykowski, R. (Ed.), *Parallel Processing and Applied Mathematics* (pp. 715–722). Berlin: Springer. doi:10.1007/11752578_86

Arroyo, S., Cimpian, E., Domingue, J., Feier, C., Fensel, D., König-Ries, B., et al. (2005). *Web Service Modeling Ontology Primer.* Retrieved from http://www.w3.org/Submission/WSMO-primer/

Cabral, L., Domingue, J., Motta, E., Payne, T. R., & Hakimpour, F. (2004, May 10-12). Approaches to Semantic Web Services: an Overview and Comparisons. In J. Davies, C. Bussler, & R. Studer (Eds.), *The Semantic Web: Research and Applications, Proceedings of the First European Semantic Web Symposium, ESWS 2004,* Heraklion, Crete, Greece (pp. 225-239). Berlin: Springer.

Camarinha-Matos, L. M., Afsarmanesh, H., & Ollus, M. (2005). *Virtual Organizations: Systems and Practices*. Berlin: Springer. doi:10.1007/b102339

Cardoso, J., & Sheth, A. P. (2005). Introduction to Semantic Web Services and Web Process Composition. In J. Cardoso & A. Sheth (Eds.), *First International Workshop on Semantic Web Services and Web Process Composition, SWSWPC 2004* (pp. 1-13). Berlin: Springer.

Coppola, M., Jégou, Y., Matthews, B., Morin, C., Prieto, L. P., & Sánchez, O. D. (2008). Virtual organization support within a grid-wide operating system. *IEEE Internet Computing, 12*(2), 20–28. doi:10.1109/MIC.2008.47

Dolenc, M., Klinc, R., Turk, Z., Katranuschkov, P., & Kurowski, K. (2008). Semantic Grid Platform in Support of Engineering Virtual Organisations. *Informatica, 32*(1), 39–49.

Foster, I. (2002). What is the Grid? A Three Point Checklist. *GRIDtoday, 1*(6), 22–25.

Foster, I., & Kesselmann, C. (2003). *The Grid: Blueprint for a New Computing Infrastructure*. San Francisco: Morgan Kaufmann.

Foster, I., Kesselmann, C., Nick, J. M., & Tuecke, S. (2002). *The Physiology of the Grid: An Open Grid Services Architecture for Distributed Systems Integration*. Retrieved from http://www.globus.org/alliance/publications/papers/ogsa.pdf

French, T. (2009). Virtual Organisational Trust Requirements: Can Semiotics Help Fill The Trust Gap? *International Journal of Intelligent Information Technologies, 5*(2), 1–16.

Gubala, T., & Hoheisel, A. (2007). *Highly Dynamic Workflow Orchestration for Scientific Applications* (Tech. Rep. No. TR-0101). Institute on Grid Information, Resource and Workflow Monitoring Services and Institute on Grid Systems, Tools and Environments, CoreGrid.

Hevner, A. R., March, S. T., Park, J., & Ram, S. (2004). Design science in information systems research. *Management Information Systems Quarterly*, *28*(1), 75–105.

Hoheisel, A. (2006). User tools and languages for graph-based Grid workflows. *Concurrency and Computation*, *18*(10), 1101–1113. doi:10.1002/cpe.1002

Hoheisel, A. (2008). Grid-Workflow-Management. In Weisbecker, A., Pfreundt, F.-J., Linden, J., & Unger, S. (Eds.), *Fraunhofer Enterprise Grids* (pp. 22–25). Stuttgart, Germany: Fraunhofer IRB.

Hull, D., Wolstencroft, K., Stevens, R., Goble, C., Pocock, M., & Li, P. (2006). Taverna: a tool for building and running workflows of services. *Nucleic Acids Research*, *34*, W729–W732. doi:10.1093/nar/gkl320

ISO/IEC. (2004). *High-level Petri Nets – Part 1: Concepts, definitions and graphical notation (ISO/IEC 15909-1)*. Geneva, Switzerland: Author.

Katranuschkov, P., Gehre, A., Shaukat, F., & Scherer, R. J. (2008). Achieving Interoperability in Grid-Enabled Virtual Organisations. In K.-D. Thoben, K. S. Pawar, & R. Goncalves (Eds.), *Proceedings of the 14th International Conference on Concurrent Enterprising, ICE2008* (pp. 835-842). Nottingham, UK: Centre for Concurrent Enterprises.

Keller, G., Nuettgens, M., & Scheer, A.-W. (1992). *Semantische Prozeßmodellierung auf der Grundlage "Ereignisgesteuerter Prozeßketten (EPK)"* (Tech. Rep. No. 89). Saarbruecken, Germany: Universitaet des Saarlandes, Instituts für Wirtschaftsinformatik.

Kloppmann, M., Koenig, D., Leymann, F., Pfau, G., Rickayzen, A., & von Riegen, C. (2005). *WS-BPEL Extension for People - BPEL4People*. IBM and SAP.

Krefting, D., Vossberg, M., Hoheisel, A., & Tolxdorff, T. (2010). Simplified implementation of medical image processing algorithms into a grid using a workflow management system. *Future Generation Computer Systems*, *26*(4), 681–684. doi:10.1016/j.future.2009.07.004

Martin, D., Burstein, M., Lassila, O., Paolucci, M., Payne, T., & McIlraith, S. A. (2004). *Describing Web Services using OWL-S and WSDL*. Arlington, VA: BBN Rosslyn.

Mateos, C., Zunino, A., & Campo, M. (2008). A survey on approaches to gridification. *Software, Practice & Experience*, *38*(5), 523–556. doi:10.1002/spe.847

Milke, J.-M., Schiffers, M., & Ziegler, W. (2006). *Rahmenkonzept für das Management Virtueller Organisationen im D-Grid.*

OASIS. (2007). *Web Services Business Process Execution Language Version 2.0.*

Object Management Group. (2009). *Business Process Modeling Notation (BPMN) – Version 1.2.* Retrieved October 13, 2009, from http://www.omg.org/spec/BPMN/1.2/

Osman, T., Thakker, D., & Al-Dabass, D. (2009). Utilisation of Case-Based Reasoning for Semantic Web Services Composition. *International Journal of Intelligent Information Technologies*, *5*(1), 24–42.

Smith, M.K., Welty, C., & McGuiness, D.L. (2004). *OWL Web Ontology Language Guide.*

Thomas, O., Dollmann, T., & Loos, P. (2008). Rules Integration in Business Process Models – A Fuzzy Oriented Approach. *Enterprise Modelling and Information Systems Architectures*, *3*(1), 18–30.

Thomas, O., & Fellmann, M. (2009). Semantic Process Modeling – Design and Implementation of an Ontology-Based Representation of Business Processes. *Business & Information Systems Engineering*, *1*(6), 438–451. doi:10.1007/s12599-009-0078-8

Thomas, O., & vom Brocke, J. (2010). A Value-Driven Approach to the Design of Service-Oriented Information Systems – Making Use of Conceptual Models. *Information Systems and e-Business Management*, *8*(1), 67-97.

Vanderhaeghen, D., Hofer, A., & Kupsch, F. (2006). Process-Driven Business Integration Management for Collaboration Networks. In Cunha, M. M., & Putnik, G. D. (Eds.), *Knowledge and Technology Management in Virtual Organizations: Issues, Trends, Opportunities and Solutions* (pp. 190–210). Hershey, PA: Idea Group Publishing.

Vykoukal, J., Wolf, M., & Beck, R. (2009). Services Grids in Industry – On-Demand Provisioning and Allocation of Grid-Based Business Services. *Business & Information Systems Engineering*, *1*(2), 206–214. doi:10.1007/s12599-008-0009-0

This work was previously published in the International Journal of Intelligent Information Technologies, Volume 7, Issue 1, edited by Vijayan Sugumaran, pp. 45-64, copyright 2011 by IGI Publishing (an imprint of IGI Global).

Chapter 5
Construction of Domain Ontologies:
Sourcing the World Wide Web

Jongwoo Kim
University of Massachusetts Boston, USA

Veda C. Storey
Georgia State University, USA

ABSTRACT

As the World Wide Web evolves into the Semantic Web, domain ontologies, which represent the concepts of an application domain and their associated relationships, have become increasingly important as surrogates for capturing and representing the semantics of real world applications. Much ontology development remains manual and is both difficult and time-consuming. This research presents a methodology for semi-automatically generating domain ontologies from extracted information on the World Wide Web. The methodology is implemented in a prototype that integrates existing ontology and web organization tools. The prototype is used to develop ontologies for different application domains, and an empirical analysis carried out to demonstrate the feasibility of the research.

INTRODUCTION

The World Wide Web is a massively distributed reservoir of information, but the information does not have well-defined machine-understandable meaning attached to it, prohibiting automated manipulation and reasoning about such information (Ram & Zhao, 2007). The next generation of the World Wide Web, the Semantic Web, is intended to enable more intelligent use of data and information for effective electronic interoperability and collaboration (Horrocks, 2008). A successful Semantic Web, however, depends upon the ability to manage, integrate, and analyze data and is driven by the role of semantics for automated approaches to exploiting Web resources (Berners-Lee, Hendler, & Lassila, 2001). Ontologies, which are at the heart of the Semantic Web, define the concepts and relationships that make global interoperability possible, facilitate sharing and integration (Hor-

DOI: 10.4018/978-1-4666-2047-6.ch005

rocks, 2008; Leukel & Sugumaran, 2009; Tun & Tojo, 2008) and serve as surrogates for semantics. Ontologies are also useful for digital libraries and personalized information management (Katifori, Halatsis, Lepouras, Vassilakis, & Giannopoulou, 2007; Meng & Chatwin, 2010). Although their need is well-documented, ontology development is often performed manually and is challenging and time-consuming (Ding & Foo, 2002; Farquhar, Fikes, & Rice, 1997). One of the major reasons for this difficulty is finding relevant knowledge sources to use to create ontologies.

The World Wide Web is a great resource of information for almost all imaginable domains. If this information could be properly extracted and organized, it should be possible to effectively use it to create domain ontologies, especially if a process to do so could be automated to some extent (Sánchez & Moreno, 2008). The objectives of this research, therefore, are to:

- Develop a methodology for semi-automatically generating domain ontologies by extracting and organizing terms and relationships among those terms using the World Wide Web as a source;
- Establish the feasibility of the ontology creation methodology by creating a prototype; and
- Assess the performance of the methodology through an empirical analysis.

The contribution of the research is to develop a way to semi-automatically create domain ontologies by using the World Wide Web as a source and integrating web tools. Libraries could be used for the Semantic Web and other applications (e.g., heterogeneous databases, conceptual modeling, and web queries (Horrocks, 2008; Ram & Zhao, 2007)).

The section below examines related research on domain ontologies and their role in the Semantic Web. A six-step ontology creation methodology is presented in the section following. Later, this chapter details the implementation of the methodology in a prototype, WebtoOnto. It then evaluates the methodology using an empirical study. A summary and concluding remarks are found in the last section.

RELATED RESEARCH

Ontologies

An ontology is a way of describing one's world and can be used as a surrogate for semantics (Dahlgren, 1995). An ontology represents a set of concepts and the relationships among them for a specific domain. Ontologies have been developed in both Artificial Intelligence and knowledge management research to facilitate knowledge use and reuse with the main idea being to develop an understandable, complete, and sharable system of categories, labels, and relationships that represent the real world in an objective manner (Cristani & Cuel, 2005; Horrocks, 2008; March & Allen, 2007). They are useful because they formalize a shared view of a domain (Grootjen & van der Weide, 2005). An example of an ontology for carpel tunnel syndrome (resulting from repetitive stress) created by our proposed methodology is shown in Figure 1.

There are a number of challenges to developing ontologies. Ontologies are specific to each domain and are time-consuming to create (Herman, 2007; Maedche & Staab, 2000). Large-scale ontologies such as Cyc require a collaborative, community effort from knowledgeable people. Applications can be developed with small, domain specific ontologies (Herman, 2007), the creation of which is the focus of this research.

Organizations may use existing documents for domain ontology creation (Kietz, Maedche, & Volz, 2000; Alexander Maedche & Staab, 2000; Sugiura, Kurematsu, Fukuta, Izumi, & Yamaguchi, 2003). However, when they start a new business or expand an existing one, they may not have

Figure 1. Carpel tunnel syndrome ontology

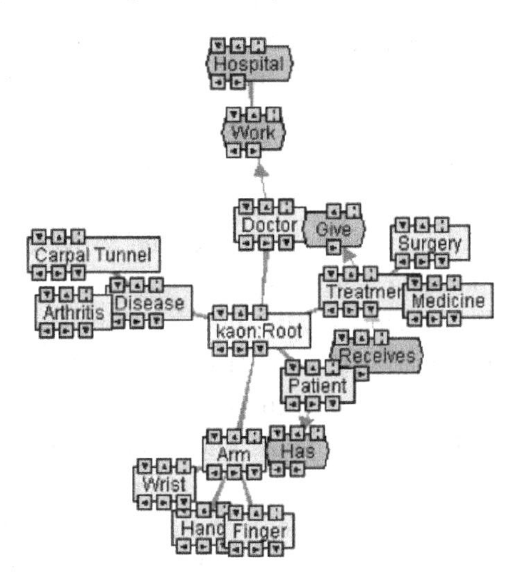

legacy resources upon which to draw. For example, when an organization develops a natural resource protection ontology to improve knowledge management and information sharing, they might have difficulty finding relevant knowledge sources for a specific species (Michener et al., 2007; Xing, Han, & Tao, 2009).

Domain ontologies specify concepts, relationship among concepts, and inference rules for a single application domain (e.g., airline reservations, art galleries, furniture, fishing, gourmet food) or task. They are not applicable across different domains; rather they capture agreed upon concepts, are applied to a specified context (Spyns, Meersman, & Jarrar, 2002), and are often created manually and collaboratively by domain experts (Noy & McGuinness, 2001).

Ontology Creation Methodologies

Ontology creation requires heuristics and expertise, rather than an engineering approach (Pinto & Martins, 2004). Prior research has concentrated on related tasks, such as ontology learning, ontology evaluation, evolution, and merging (Buitelaar & Cimiano, 2008; Corcho, Fernández-López, & Gómez-Pérez, 2003; Omelayenko, 2001). For example, ontology learning seeks to discover ontological knowledge from various forms of data automatically or semi-automatically using methods and tools such as UIMA, GATE, OpenCalais, and WikiOnto (De Silva & Jayaratne, 2009; Lau, Song, Li, Cheung, & Hao; Zhou, 2007). Although prior research assumes that relevant information for ontology creation can easily be found, ontology developers may have difficulty doing so, especially for some specialized domains, which is one reason why this research focuses on the World Wide Web as a source.

Several ontology creation methodologies have been proposed. Zhou (2007) presents a framework for ontology learning, consisting of information extraction, ontology discovery, and ontology organization. Cristani and Cuel (2005) classify ontology creation methodologies, such as DOLCE (Gangemi, Guarino, Masolo, Oltramari, & Schneider, 2002), OTK (Fensel et al., 2000), TOVE (Gruninger & Fox, 1995), METHONTOLOGY (Fernández-López, Gómez-Pérez, & Juristo, 1997), and Enterprise (Uschold, 1996) as top-down and bottom-up. Top-down methods start with an abstract view of a domain and expand it with detailed specifications, for example KACTUS (Schreiber, Wielinga, & Jansweijer, 1995) and DOLCE (Gangemi et al., 2002). Bottom-up methodologies start from the specification of a certain task and obtain generalizations, for example TOVE (Gruninger & Fox, 1995) and OTK (Fensel et al., 2000). A middle-out method starts from the key concepts and moves to generalization and specialization, for example Enterprise (Uschold, 1996) and METHONTOLOGY (Fernández-López et al., 1997).

Ontology development may rely on a stage-based model (e.g. TOVE) and an evolving prototype (e.g. METHONTOLOGY). When the requirements and purposes of the ontology are specific and clear, the stage-based model is more appropriate than an evolving prototype, which is most useful when the environment is difficult to understand.

ONTOLOGY CREATION METHODOLOGY

This section presents a six-step methodology for semi-automated ontology creation using terms from the World Wide Web. The methodology is heuristic in nature and takes advantage of existing tools. The methodology is based on a framework for ontology learning proposed by Zhou (2007) and METHONTOLOGY (Fernández-López et al., 1997), which provides high-level steps for ontology creation as an existing partial solution. Our research expands and augments prior work and integrates tools. Figure 2 provides an overview of our methodology.

Step 1: Identify the scope of domains (Specification and initial conceptualization).

Application domains for which ontologies are needed may be of various sizes. Therefore, the first step in domain ontology creation is to identify the scope of the application domain (e.g., sports versus hockey versus Stanley Cup playoffs or gourmet dining versus gourmet food versus wine versus fine wines. This step is driven by the reason for the ontology development, intended uses, and potential users. The scope requires the identification of the categories of the domains in which the users are interested.

Several attempts have been made to categorize the vast and diverse web pages on the World Wide Web into domains (Boley et al., 1999a, 1999b; Chakrabarti et al., 1999), motivated by the fact that search engines are often unable to provide content-dependent, useful results (Fagni, Perego, Silvestri, & Orlando, 2006). Two major business approaches to web site classification are the interactive tools, DMOZ (www.dmoz.com) and Clusty (www.clusty.com). DMOZ (Directory Mozilla) is an Open Directory Project that attempts to create the most comprehensive human edited directory of the web. DMOZ provides meta-level categorization, expressed in XML. This directory is created and managed by net-citizens' voluntary participation. Each citizen organizes a small portion of the web by removing useless content. When users initiate a search query, DMOZ provides a list of categorized web sites. For example, in Figure 3, when wine is provided as a keyword, DMOZ displays categories related to wine and corresponding web sites.

Clusty hierarchically clusters terms used on web sites by topics and URLs. It uses a clustering engine to organize results from search engines, such as MSN and Lycos, into folders, grouping similar web sites together. Its clustering algorithm puts search results together based on textual and linguistic similarity. Clusty allows users to obtain a quick overview of the domains associated with a given query.

To select the categories of the target domains, users identify and choose relevant categories provided by either DMOZ or Clusty. It also involves specifying key concepts for constructing a target domain. For a small example (for illustration purposes) of a wine ontology, the first two categories (Recreation: Food: Drink: Wine and Shopping: Food: Beverage: Wine) of DMOZ and the 'white wine' section of Clusty can be identified as relevant and selected as illustrated in Figure 3. The key concepts are identified by searching through categories and related topics from DMOZ and Clusty. For example, 'food' and 'drink,' as shown in Figure 3, can be selected as important terms. The keywords selected from DMOZ and Clusty are the initial key concepts.

Step 2: Specify target web sites.

The user specifies target web sites within a domain or category selected from Step 1. Both DMOZ and Clusty identify a set of web sites appropriate for a given domain. DMOZ shows the conceptual hierarchical structure of terms and related web sites. Clusty provides web pages based on two or three-level clustered terms. Using DMOZ and Clusty, the user selects target web

Figure 2. Methodology for domain ontology creation

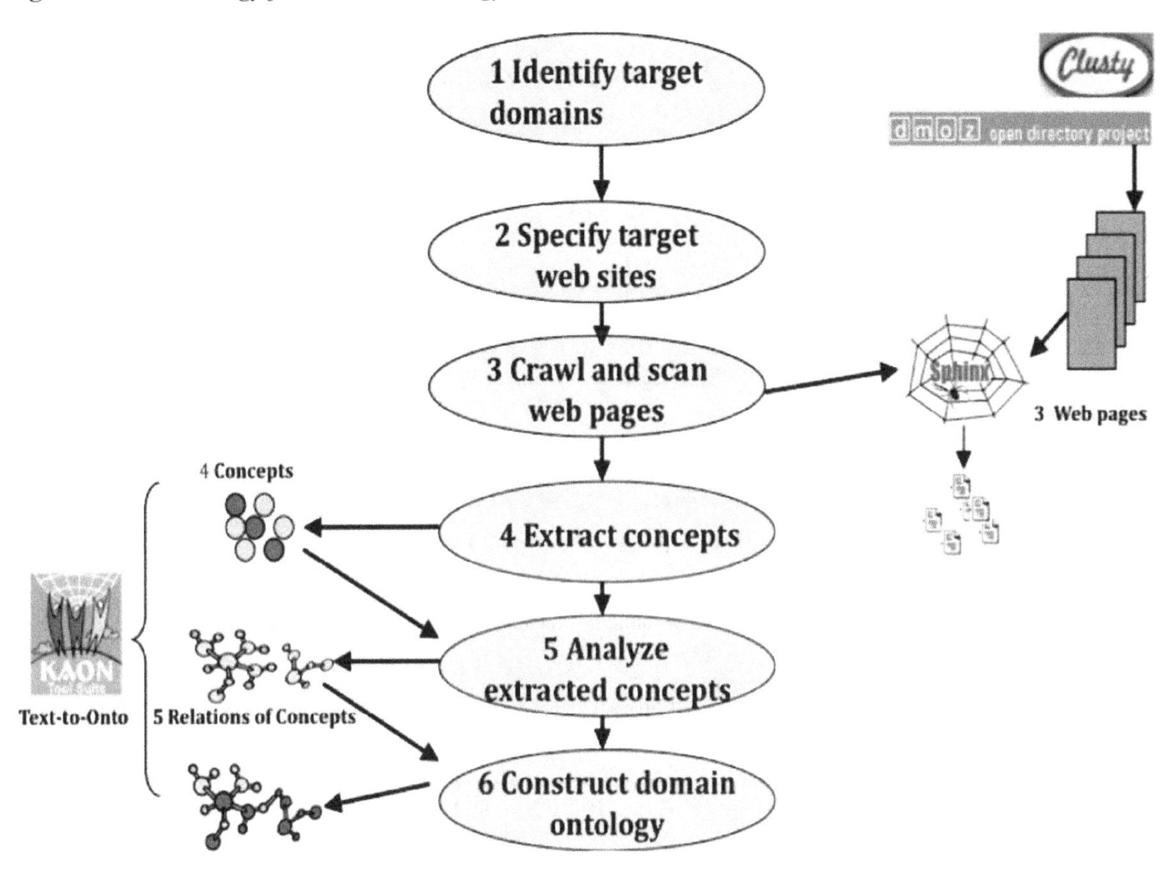

sites related to a given domain. Some categories may have many relevant web sites (e.g., over one hundred). Thus, it is not practical to specify all web sites for each category, so a user needs to browse the web sites before selecting relevant ones to ensure a high level of quality and relevancy of the chosen web sites.

The purpose of this step is to provide the basic resources for the next four steps. When a user selects web sites relevant to a domain, the user will have a better chance of collecting relevant terms and creating domain ontologies with high quality. This is to deal with the well-known context problem (Gu, Wang, Pung, & Zhang, 2004). If there were no interaction with the user for the selection of the web sites, the created ontologies would not be context-dependent, which is a key, required characteristic of domain ontology. However, too much interaction with the users would increase the required time and effort. Since categorized web sites can assist users, users can browse and select relevant ones from DMOZ and Clusty, thus, providing well-organized web sites for a selected domain.

Step 3: Crawl and Scan Web Pages.

Related web pages need to be selected based on the results from Step 2. WebSphinx (http://www.cs.cmu.edu/~rcm/websphinx/) crawls and scans web pages from the selected web sites at DMOZ or Clusty. The user can specify the scope and depth of crawling. The scope refers to the range of data collection. The user can set the scope as a sub directory of the web site, server, or web. The sub directory option restricts WebSphinx

Figure 3. Results from DMOZ and Clusty

dmoz open directory project

Search: wine

Open Directory Categories (1-5 of 23)

1. Recreation: Food: Drink: Wine (1170 matches)
2. Shopping: Food: Beverages: Wine (284)
3. Business: Food and Related Products: Beverages: Wine (190)
4. Recreation: Travel: Specialty Travel: Culinary: Wine (59)
5. Shopping: Home and Garden: Kitchen and Dining: Wine Accessories (86)

[more...]

Open Directory Sites (1-20 of 9693)

1. W3Commerce: Tasting Wine - Covers diverse topics including tasting, food pairing, production regions, and vocabulary.
   -- http://www.tasting-wine.com/ Recreation: Food: Drink: Wine (1170)
2. Wine.com - A retailer offering a large selection of domestic and imported wines. Also a searchable database.
   -- http://www.wine.com/ Shopping: Food: Beverages: Wine (284)
3. Think Global Fine Spanish Wines - Distributor of Spanish wines: Adegas Morgadio, Bodegas Campante, Bodegas Los Lla

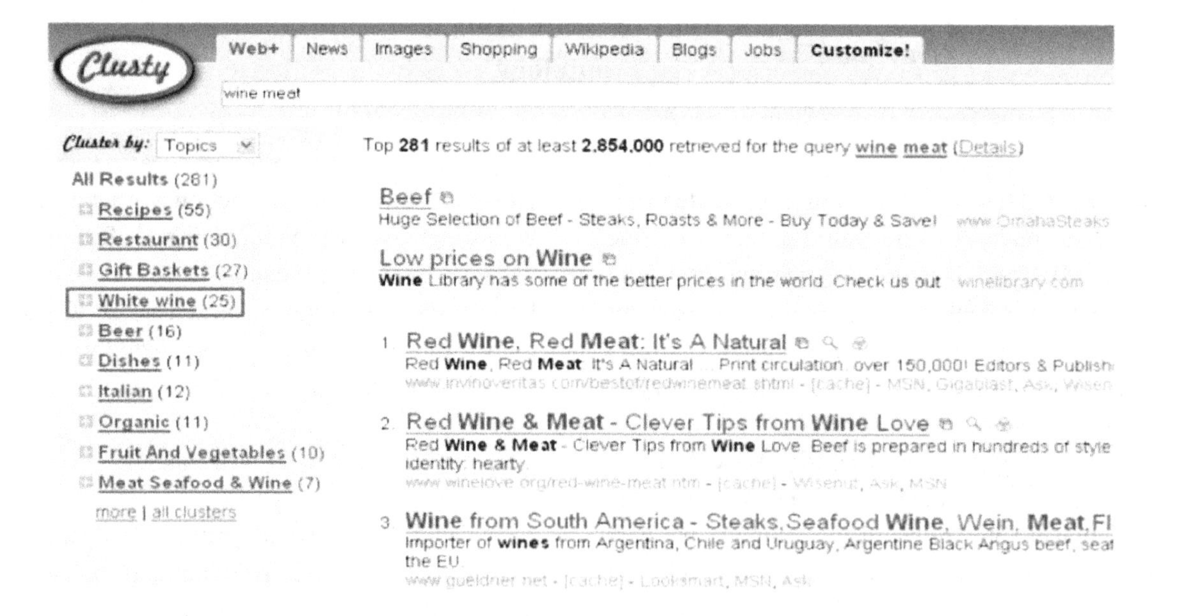

to crawling only the lower levels of the selected web address. Based on the scope of the server, crawling is constrained within the server. When the user selects the web as its scope, WebSphinx crawls documents outside of the server. The depth of crawling refers to the number of hops. For example, when the number of hops is three, WebSphinx will crawl all of the three lower levels. The number of hops, thus, limits the depth, as well as the scope, of crawling.

To obtain web pages related to the selected web sites, the user sets the scope as the server of the target web pages. This setting allows WebSphinx to collect web pages within a specified web site without scrawling beyond that web site as shown in Figure 4. WebSphinx stores web pages as html or txt file format. The scope of the selection is important in controlling the content and the amount of web documents WebSphinx collects.

Step 4: Extract Concepts (Conceptualization).

Candidate terms for ontologies are selected at this step by user. The user browses the results of Step 3 and selects candidate terms related to the domain based upon the importance and the relevance of the term to the domain ontology. Text-to-Onto (Maedche & Volz, 2001) assists the user in the extraction of the concepts by providing relevant information.

The text or html files stored by WebSphinx provide input to Text-to-Onto which provides support for ontology creation from texts. Text-to-Onto is a module of KAON (Karlsruhe Ontology and Semantic web infrastructure), an open-source ontology management infrastructure targeted for business applications (Maedche & Volz, 2001). Text-to-Onto is built on three text mining algorithms: a term extraction algorithm, a concept association extraction algorithm, and an ontology pruning algorithm. It also supports a graphical interface and stores a generated ontology such as XML (RDF schema format). Text-to-Onto constructs an ontology from domain-specific text using machine learning techniques and algorithms. It extracts terms and provides users with information such as frequency, Term Frequency Inverse Document Frequency (TFIDF), Entropy, and C-value.

With this information, relevant ontology terms, as shown in Figure 5, can be selected by the user. TFIDF shows how important a selected term is within a document (Salton & Buckley, 1988). Entropy indicates the rate of disorder of words in a document. The C-value (Collocation-value) improves the extraction of nested multi-word terms and collocations (Frantzi & Ananiadou, 1999) in a domain-independent manner by combining linguistic and statistical information retrieval techniques. The higher the C-value the greater the likelihood of a candidate term being a valid term. For example, 'shark species' has a higher C-value

Figure 4. Crawling and scanning by WebSphinx

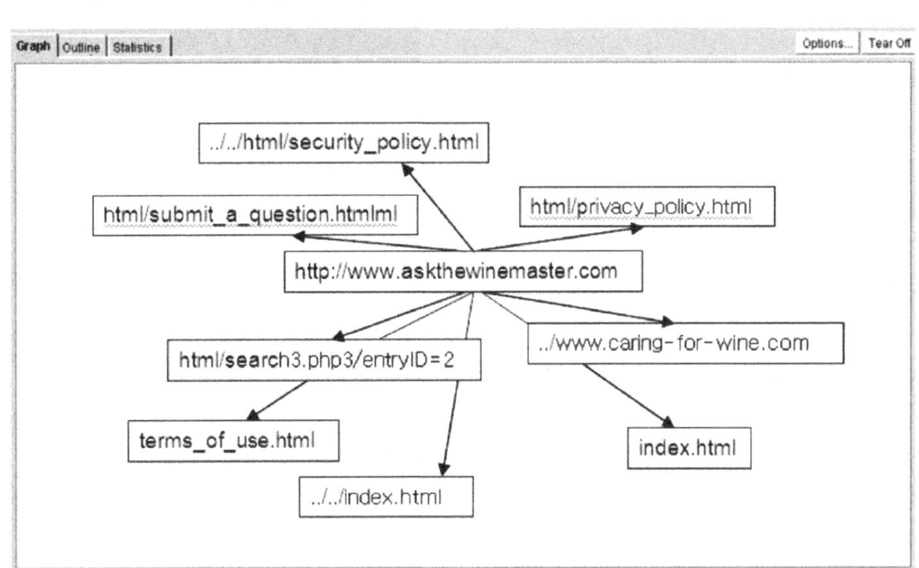

than ‘seafood dealer’ in shark-related documents because ‘shark species’ is more important than ‘seafood dealer’. Relevant terms should be selected by a human user who can understand the domain and the context. Selected concepts are then used in the domain ontology construction.

Step 5: Analyze and Cluster Extracted Features (Conceptualization).

The purpose of this step is to analyze terms and identify relationships among selected terms. Text-to-Onto provides information on the relationships between two terms using its association rules extraction and linguistic patterns. Figure 6 shows that drink and wine have a strong relationship, whereas the relationship between restaurant and wine is weak. Based on these estimations, a user can add terms as hierarchical relationships or properties to begin the ontology construction. Although Text-to-Onto can help users identify and analyze the relationships between terms, users may need to modify the relationships for a specific context. For example, users might want to manually establish a property relationship between restaurant and drink, even though the computed values of support and confidence are low. During this step, the relationships among selected concepts are established to build domain ontologies. This corresponds to the conceptualization process in METHONTOLOGY.

Step 6: Construct Domain Ontology (Formalization and Implementation).

During this step, a domain ontology is actually constructed using terms selected from step 4 and information about the terms provided from step 5. Text-to-Onto supports a graphic interface and a feature to store constructed ontologies in RDF. A portion of a constructed wine ontology is shown in Figure 7. This ontology captures high level concepts related to wine and meat. If the ontology creator is an expert in wine, the creator can expand the branches of red wine and white wine. Price is included as a property of drink, although it would be better for it to be a property of food or drink. Restaurant is also added because it serves both wine and meat. It is linked to ‘Food or Drink’ by the property ‘serve’.

This step corresponds to formalization and implementation suggested by METHONTOLOGY. Users transform the conceptual model into a formal, computable model using the application that supports this step by converting the conceptual model into an XML format.

Figure 5. Term extraction using text-to-onto

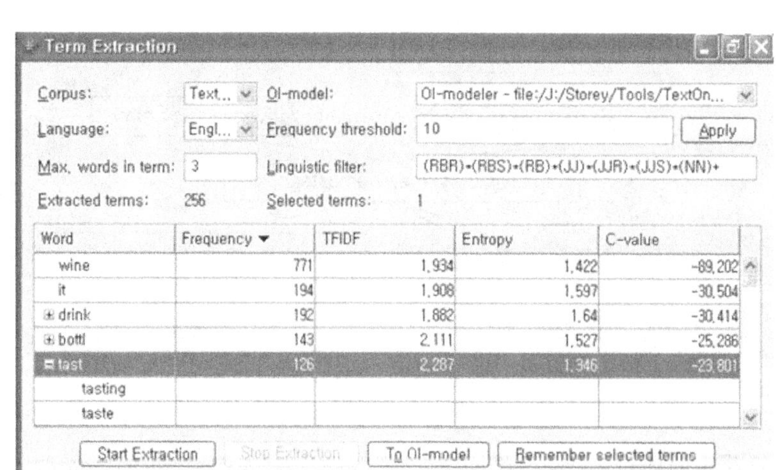

Figure 6. Association extractions by text-to-onto

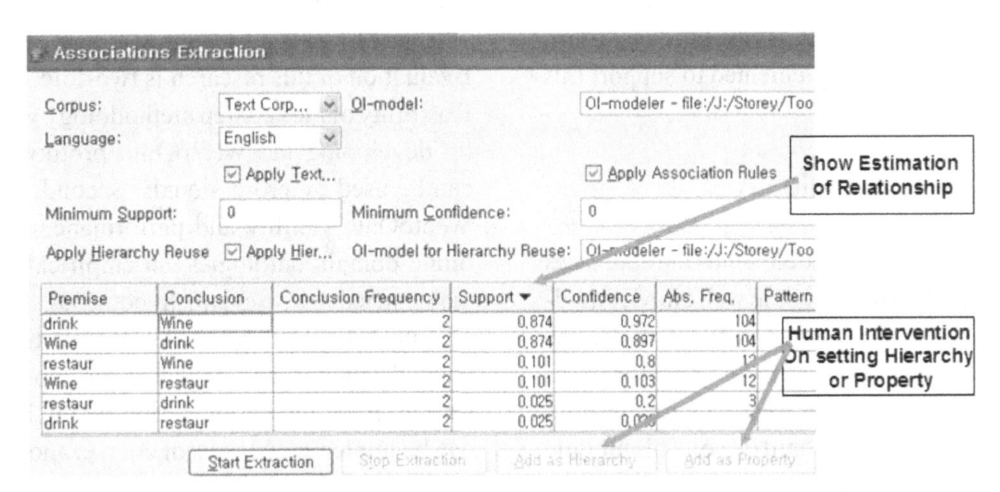

IMPLEMENTATION

The ontology creation methodology has been implemented in a prototype developed as a window program in Java, the architecture of which is shown in Figure 8. The prototype, called WebtoOnto, is comprised of three modules: Category Retrieval Module, Web Crawler Module and Ontology Creation Module. The purpose of the prototype system is to demonstrate that the methodology is feasible and use it as a testbed for empirical assessment and future enhancement.

DMOZ is used in the category retrieval module because it integrates well. The category retrieval module has two sub modules: a category retrieval sub module and a website retrieval sub module, both of which use RDF data files downloaded from the DMOZ web site. One RDF file contains web site category hierarchy information. The other holds web page link information within each category. Figure 9 shows the schema of these two files.

Category Retrieval Sub Module

The category retrieval sub module receives keywords from the user and arranges the strings to be queried onto the RDF file. This module incorporates Step 1 of our proposed methodology. The user interacts with this module to select key terms that set the scope of the domain ontology. This sub module submits the corresponding category list to the user who then selects the categories of interest based upon key terms.

Four flags are implemented to identify the topic from the keywords and to mark the acquisition of the flagged attributes. Four elements (topic, title, description and external) are used to set the flags. Using the Simple API for XML (SAX) parser, this sub module queries the web sites' descriptions provided by DMOZ and receives notification of the XML parsing result. The SAX parser, an event-driven parser, is used because it is faster and has more efficient memory use than the Document Object Model (DOM)-style parsers. The return is comprised of a URL, local name, q-name, and parsing exception. Each entry of a result obtained uses a vector to store the nodes of web pages because a topic can have multiple related web pages.

Website Retrieval Sub Module

This module receives a list of input categories selected by the user as shown in Figure 10. To provide further support, WebtoOnto allows the user to view the selected web pages. This enables the user to make better decisions on relevant web sites by allowing the user to view multiple sites before making a selection, saving time and effort. WindowSwitcher is implemented to support this feature.

Web Crawler Module

The website retrieval module sends the addresses of the selected web sites to the web crawler module. Using the APIs provided by WebSphinx, this module retrieves the corresponding web pages of the selected sites and stores these files in either html or txt format on the local hard drive., This module visualizes a collection of web pages as a graph by using the crawler workbench of WebSphinx. It provides a multithreaded web page retrieval using the WebSphinx class library.

Ontology Creation Module

The ontology creation module, using Text-to-Onto, receives the stored files as input and handles the ontology creation processes from Step 4 to Step 6. Each step is partially automated. For example, the term extraction process is automated with the use of a POS (Part-Of-Speech) tagger (Banko & Moore, 2004) after crawled web pages are provided to the ontology creation module as input by a user. In addition, information such as TFIDF supports the analysis of the selected terms. Finally, the ontology construction is supported by a graphical interface and a RDF conversion feature.

The prototype is an integrated tool for organizations to develop domain ontologies from web documents. It is intended to minimize the effort required for ontology creation with the use of information found in web pages. This tool can help users quickly identify the relevant web pages of a target domain, process them using WebSphinx, and create domain ontologies using Text-to-Onto. It is possible that WebtoOnto could be integrated with existing ontology engineering tools. For example, the category module and website retrieval module of WebtoOnto might serve as a plug-in to Protégé.

EVALUATION

Evaluation of this research is two-fold. First, the feasibility of the six-step methodology was tested by developing the WebtoOnto prototype, so it can be used by professionals. Second, to assess WebtoOnto's utility and performance in developing domain ontologies, an empirical analysis was carried out. Several hypotheses, based on Cognitive Fit Theory (Vessey & Galletta, 1991), were developed and tested in an experimental setting. Even though the proposed methodology can be implemented, it is, of course, another matter to assess whether it is useful. Thus, to assess the usefulness of the methodology, a laboratory experiment was carried out in which ontologies created by two groups were compared.

Performance Test

Hypotheses

This study employs Cognitive Fit Theory (CFT) (Vessey & Galletta, 1991) to assess the perfor-

Figure 7. A part of wine ontology as represented by text-to-onto

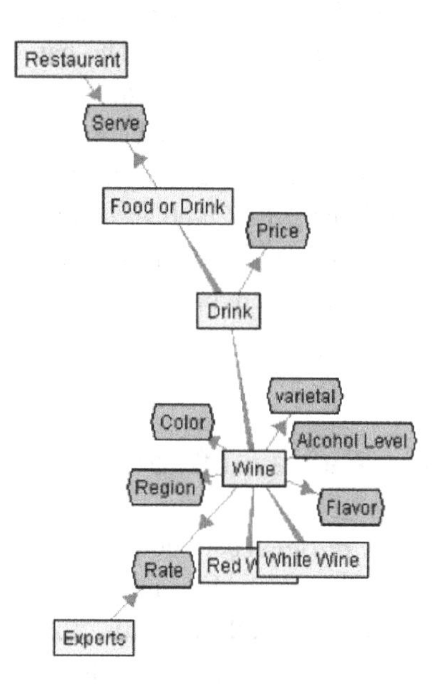

Figure 8. System architecture of web-to-onto

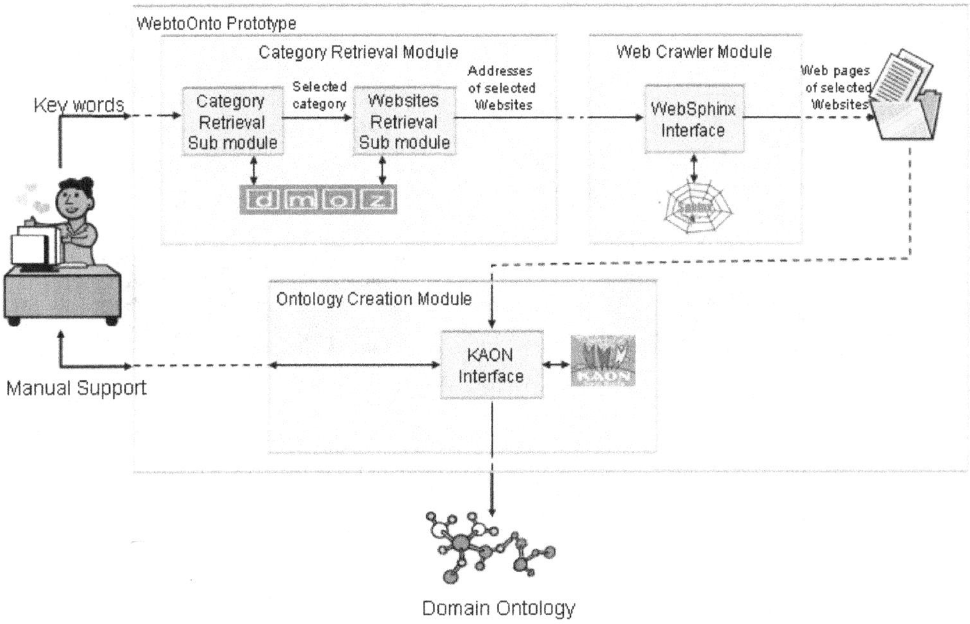

mance of ontology creation with/without information from WebtoOnto. CFT explains how information representation affects the decision processes and decision-making outcomes. CFT has been applied to various areas of information systems, including decision making in geographic information systems (Dennis & Carte, 1998), consumer learning and shopping behavior in e-commerce (Hong, Thong, & Tam, 2004; Suh & Lee, 2005), and software engineering (Shaft & Vessey, 2006).

According to CFT, decision makers develop a mental representation of the task and adopt deci-

Figure 9. Schema of DMOZ category and contents file

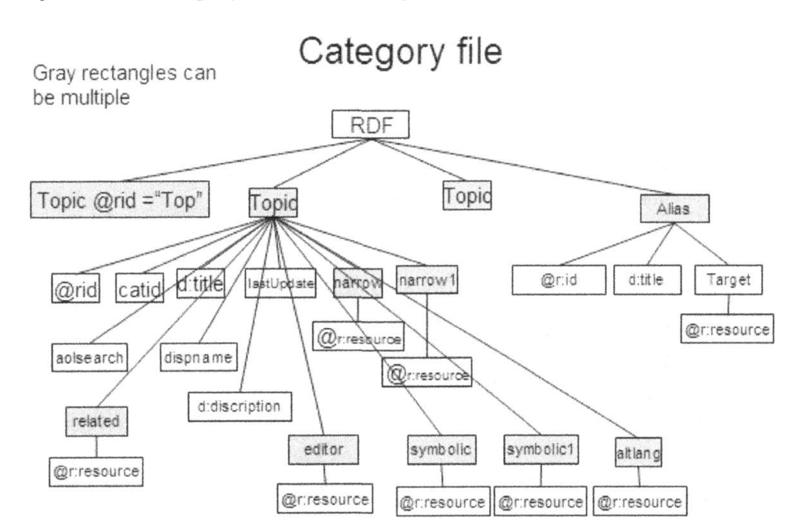

Figure 10. Website retrieval sub module

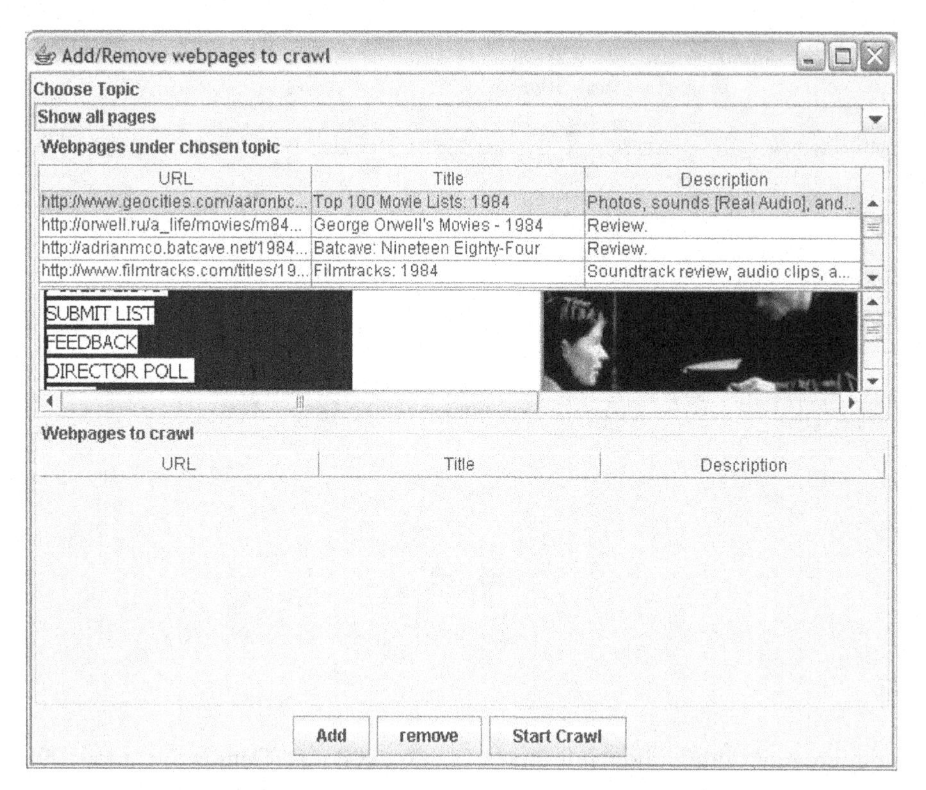

sion processes based upon the task and presentation of task information as shown in Figure 11. Vessey (1991) argues that decision makers can deliver faster and more accurate solutions when the presented information matches the mental representation of the task. This is because the decision makers use the same mental representation and decision processes for both the representation

Figure 11. Cognitive fit for ontology creation task

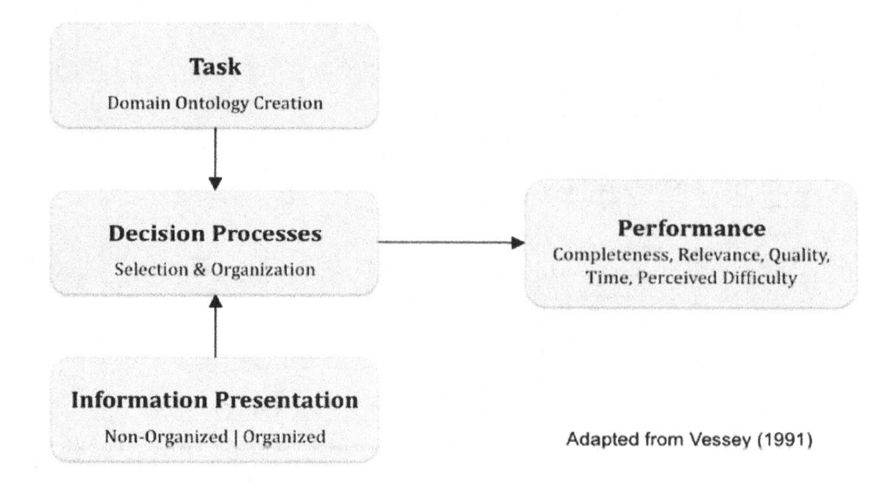

Table 1. Five hypotheses

#	Hypotheses
H1	Cognitive Fit is positively associated with Knowledge Completeness
H2	Cognitive Fit is positively associated with Knowledge Relevance
H3	Cognitive Fit is positively associated with Ontology Quality
H4	Cognitive Fit is negatively associated with Effort.
H5	Cognitive Fit is negatively associated with Mental Effort.

and the task. Thus, the fit between information presentation, task, and decision processes may affect performance.

Cognitive Fit Theory can be applied to a multi-criteria task such as domain ontology creation which evaluates several alternatives based upon a set of criteria. For example, ontology creators must evaluate and select terms, and then organize the selected terms to represent a given domain. Domain ontology creation is neither a spatial, nor a symbolic task; instead, it is more cognitively intensive. Therefore, well-organized information that supports an ontology developer's mental representation, should improve ontology creation. The World Wide Web contains much information that could help an ontology developer, but requires an ontology creator to search through a great deal of irrelevant information. The information provided by WebtoOnto, however, is well-organized, thereby supporting the mental representation needed for the task of ontology creation.

Five hypotheses, shown in Figure 12 and Table 1, were proposed and tested. In Figure 12, constructs are shaped as ovals and elements as rectangles. From step 5, our approach is intended to compare two groups: 1) a control group with ill-represented information, and 2) a treatment group with well-represented information for domain ontology creation. The treatment group received a small number of selected terms with information for ontology developers to refer to when creating a domain ontology. Providing these terms should help ontology developers create ontologies with better quality and less time and effort than searching the World Wide Web.

The five dependent variables representing performance are knowledge completeness (KC), knowledge relevance (KR), ontology quality (OQ), time, and perceived difficulty (Burton-Jones, Storey, Sugumaran, & Ahluwalia, 2005; Dweck, 1986; Lindland, Sindre, & Solvberg, 1994; Paas, 1992; Steinberg, 1989). Knowledge completeness measures the extent of relevant information captured in a domain ontology. Knowledge relevance measures the level of relevance of the knowledge represented, and ontology quality measures the semantic and syntactic quality of a domain ontology. For example, correctness and meaningfulness of inheritance relationships and relevant properties are used for ontology quality measurement. Time and perceived difficulty are measured to represent resources used to develop domain ontologies.

The five hypotheses, shown in Table 1, are based on Cognitive Fit Theory about the relationship between the ontology creation task and information provided by the prototype.

Design

A laboratory experiment was used to test hypotheses H1-H5. This methodology helped to control other factors that might impact a subject's ontology creation.

The experiment used a 1*2 between-group design as shown in Table 2. The control group received instructions that contained information on ontology creation and was asked to search the World Wide Web to find relevant concepts for the ontology. The treatment group received the same instructions on what constitutes a domain ontology and the subjects were asked to create one. Rather than being asked to search the World Wide Web, the subjects in the treatment group received a document containing terms identified by the

Figure 12. Research model

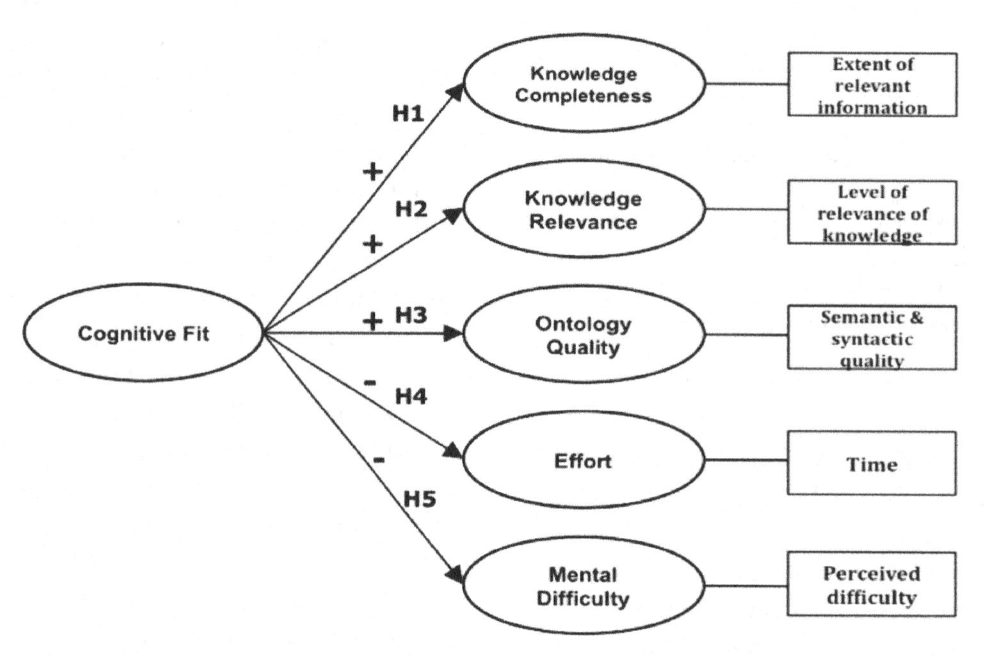

methodology. It might have taken extra time for subjects to run WebtoOnto and learn how to use it. Therefore, subjects received terms generated by WebtoOnto. The participants were randomly assigned to two groups.

A total of 60 students from information systems classes at a large U.S. university participated. All of the subjects were familiar with entity-relationship (ER) diagrams from their coursework. ER diagrams are assumed to be a reasonable precursor to understanding domain ontologies and regarded as a conceptual model shared by stakeholders (Motik, Maedche, & Volz, 2002). Thus, subjects with knowledge of conceptual modeling, such as ER diagrams, should be able to understand and learn how to create an ontology quickly. The control and the treatment groups were equally, and randomly, divided into 30 subjects.

Four of the five dependent variables (all except time) were evaluated using a seven-point scale. The domain ontology diagrams created by the subjects were evaluated by an ontology expert who assessed each domain ontology diagram based upon the dependent variables: KC, KR, and OC (see Appendix). The ontology expert holds a Ph.D. in computer science and has conducted research on ontology creation, ontology integration, and ontology engineering (pruning and refactoring of ontologies). He has applied ontologies to support conceptual modeling activities, e-learning (using upper-level ontologies to enhance the description of learning objects and creating ontologies to define and execute learning processes) and web searches (using very large ontologies to support the disambiguation and expansion of web queries). He teaches conceptual modeling and the semantic web, including evaluating hundreds of students' conceptual models (and ontologies). Thus, the expert was qualified to make a valid assessment.

The expert did not know from which group a domain ontology diagram came. The seven-point scale for these three variables ranged from "very low" (1) to "very high" (7). For time and perceived difficulty, the scores reported by subjects were used. Perceived difficulty was measured using two items that were anchored on a seven-point scale ranging from "very little" (1) to "very much" (7).

Procedure

Five students participated in a pilot study. Minor modifications were made to the materials

*Table 2. 1*2 between-group design*

Information Presentation	
Control Group (Non-Organized)	Treatment Group (Organized)
Internet	A table-format data

and procedures based upon their feedback. The undergraduate students were given the materials after their class had studied entity-relationship diagrams. This was because studying and using entity-relationship diagrams gave the students experience modeling the real world and representing it in a manner that captures concepts and associations between them. The experimental task was given as an assignment to the students who received participation credit. The assignments were completed within one week.

Results

Tables 3 and 4 show the results. One subject neglected to answer questions on perceived difficulty so the values of the subgroup mean were used (Tsikriktsis, 2005). The ANOVA results that tested the hypotheses are shown in Table 4. The first three hypotheses receive support from the data. The differences between the control and treatment groups were significant across three dependent variables: KC, KR, and OC. The treatment group, using the data created by our approach, exceeded the control group in these three areas. For the Time variable, the control group spent more time creating a domain ontology than the treatment group. However, the difference in time was not statistically significant. As for Perceived Difficulty, the treatment group perceived more difficult in creating a domain ontology than the control group, so H5 is not supported.

Discussion

The results of the lab experiment show that the treatment group, working with information from WebtoOnto, created ontologies with better quality than those created by the control group. The first three hypotheses support this finding. For the fourth hypothesis on the time variable, the control group perceived more difficulty than the treatment group. But this difference is not significant. A possible explanation for this result includes the simplicity of the given task, and that more data is needed to establish a statistical difference. However, with the quality being better, even for the same time, the overall approach is worthwhile.

Surprisingly, the fifth hypothesis on the perceived difficulty variable was not supported. A possible reason is that the treatment group was more engaged in organizing terms than the control group. Qualitative verbal data collected from the subjects support this speculation. Only 30% (9/30) of the control group subjects mentioned that term organization was a difficult task whereas 80% (24/30) of the treatment group subjects identified term organization as difficult. Term organization is a more cognitively complex task than web searching or term selection. In that sense, it is understandable that the treatment group perceived more difficulty than the control group. Subjects might have perceived the ontology creation as a relatively simple task to receive extra credit. Therefore, they might have set a certain time limit for the task. Whereas the treatment group spent time on term organization, the control group focused on term identification, which was time-consuming but less cognitively complex. This issue could be addressed by constraining the number of terms in the ontology. Another possibility is that the users found the interface of the prototype difficult to

Table 3. Average values of two groups

	Individuals	KC	KR	OQ	Time	PD
Control Group	30	2.43	4.23	3.53	23.83	4.22
Treatment Group	30	4.93	5.83	4.30	20.53	4.79

Table 4. ANOVA results

Dependent Variables	df	Mean (Standard Dev.) Between Groups	F	Sig.
KC	58,1	4.93 (1.43) (Treatment) > 2.43 (1.10) (Control)	57.09	.00
KR	58,1	5.83 (0.98) (Treatment) > 4.23 (1.65) (Control)	20.71	.00
OQ	58,1	4.30 (1.36) (Treatment) > 3.53 (1.63) (Control)	3.88	.05
Time	58,1	23.83 (14.32) (Control) > 20.53 (11.40)(Treatment)	0.97	.24
PD	58,1	4.79 (1.65) (Treatment) > 4.22 (1.20) (Control)	2.39	.13

manage, which could be addressed with a more complete prototype instead of the proof-of-concept one used in the research (which still improves quality). Finally, the subjects might have been able to formulate associations between categories easier without the constraints of the user interface and, perhaps, similar to their training on entity-relationship diagrams.

Although the overall goal of this research is to develop a methodology for automating domain ontology development, complete automation was not achievable (Zhou, 2007). However, the tool improves KC, KR, and OQ, suggesting that it is most useful to ontology developers to support term selection and organization in the ontology creation process. With regard to term selection, high scores in KC and KR mean that the scope and relevancy of the terms provided by the tool is adequate to develop domain ontologies. As a result, ontology quality in terms of semantic and syntactic quality is high as engineers can better organize relevant terms.

The right rectangle in Figure 13 indicates how much further automation is possible with current tools. Step 1 and Step 2 require human interaction, although DMOZ and Clusty provide support for these steps. Thus, this work successfully integrates existing, separate tools to minimize interruption and improve the related processes.

This research follows the design research guidelines articulated by Hevner et al. (2004). Table 5 summarizes the design research effort.

Figure 13. Analysis of ontology generation methodology steps

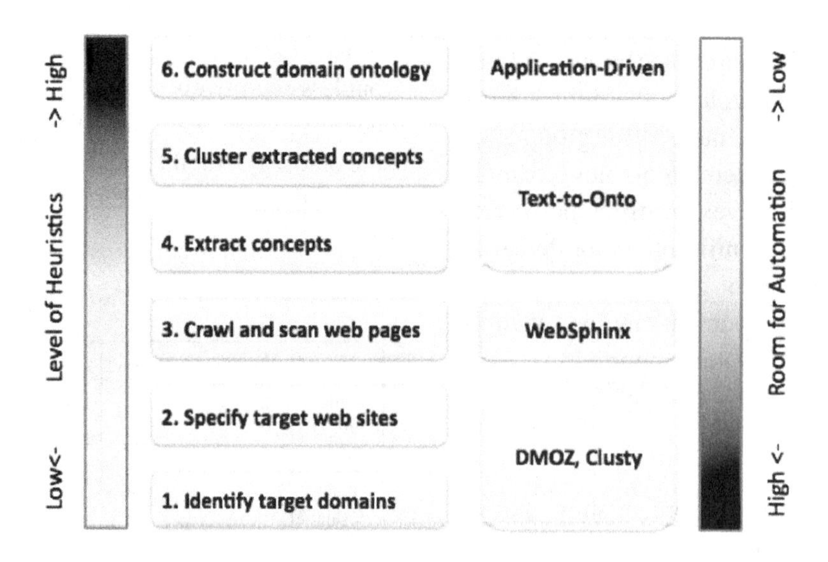

Table 5. Research artifacts

Artifacts	Novelty of Artifacts	Evaluation approach
• Methodology for ontology creation	• World Wide Web as knowledge source	• Iterative design, heuristic development
• Prototype	• Identifies and combine existing partial solutions	• Empirical analysis
• Ontology evaluation metrics: metrics used in statistical evaluation	• Rigorous statistical analysis	• Applications

The main research artifacts are the six-step ontology creation methodology and the prototype system, WebtoOnto. For the prototype, a design science *development pattern* is applied where existing partial solutions are combined to form the entire solution for a research problem (Vaishnavi & Kuechler, 2007, p. 154, p. 159, p. 173). The existing partial solutions that are applied were adapted from DMOZ, WebSphinx, and Text-To-Onto. They were combined, modified and refined for semi-automated ontology creation from information on the World Wide Web. For example, a feature was added so that users can browse web pages while selecting relevant web sites. The research artifacts are summarized in Table 5.

Limitations

The empirical analysis has two main limitations. First, our experiment limits the source to the World Wide Web and a given document to control and treatment groups, respectively, in order to represent a real world context. An attempt was made to be as realistic as possible in creating an initial domain ontology and to control extraneous sources of variance by asking subjects to create an ontology for an unfamiliar domain. Second, the use of student subjects can limit the generalizability of the results. However, student subjects are commonly used in experiments that probe human decision-making (Harrison & Harrell, 1993; Sitkin & Weingart, 1995). Ontology creation requires a series of decision making in terms of selection and organization. Moreover, when professionals need to develop an ontology for an unfamiliar domain, students and professionals are in a similar situation. In this sense, each subject could reasonably represent a professional such as a software engineer or an ontology developer.

The first three propositions are supported by the data. The correlation analysis (Table 6) shows that KC, KR, and OQ are significantly correlated. The correlation between KC and OQ is less significant than the other two correlations: KC vs. KR and KR vs. OQ. When the knowledge completeness of the ontologies is high, this means that the created ontologies cover a wide range of selected domains. When ontologies consist of relevant terms, the semantic and syntactic quality of the ontologies is assessed to be high. Further research is needed to analyze these relationships. In addition, the respondents' prior knowledge on a given domain is difficult to control. To address this issue, an unfamiliar domain was chosen for which respondents were asked to construct ontologies. Of course, even the selected topic might be familiar to certain subjects on some level. Finally, terms with only TFIDF values were given to the treatment group. This was to avoid providing

Table 6. Pearson correlation results

Constructs	KC	KR	OQ	Time	PD
KC	-	.648**	.138	.060	.186
KR		-	.455**	.075	.170
OQ			-	.091	.127
Time				-	.337**
PD					-

**: Correlation is significant at the 0.01 level.

too much information for the treatment group to process during the experiment.

There are several feasible explanations for the insignificant difference in time taken to create a domain ontology. The most likely is a technical explanation. The file size was close to three gigabytes and retrieving relevant information on the domain structure web site from DMOZ's RDF files took more than 10 minutes. With more computing power, this problem could easily be addressed. Another technical issue was that some web pages could not be retrieved when they were developed in programming languages (e.g. ASP and PHP). When users are aware of this issue, they can avoid using these web sites as the source of their domain ontologies. Finally, there might have been early "giving-up" by members of the control group due to cognitive difficulties.

Contribution

There are two main contributions of this research. For practitioners, the six-step methodology and WebtoOnto can help improve ontology creations. The methodology also provides guidance for using the World Wide Web as a source for creating domain ontologies. From a research prospective, this study uses Cognitive Fit Theory to evaluate how the format of information can affect task performance within the context of ontology development. It does so by highlighting how well-organized web sources improve the development of domain ontologies.

CONCLUSION

This research has presented a methodology and prototype implementation for semi-automated ontology generation. The methodology identifies relevant web pages for domain ontology creation, and for extracting terms and relationships from them. This methodology is intended to contribute to the interdisciplinary effort to the World Wide Web as it matures into the Semantic Web through the help of ontologies (Hendler, Shadbolt, Hall, Berners-Lee, & Weitzner, 2008). The prototype integrates a variety of tools to demonstrate how ontology creation can be semi-automated. An empirical assessment revealed support for the effectiveness of the methodology, which may help users create better quality domain ontologies by enabling them to select relevant terms quite easily and focus on organizing them.

Further work is needed to enhance the prototype and to create libraries of ontologies. For example, ontology sources such as DBpedia/Wikipedia and the Linked Data Web could be used. The ontology creation methodology could be integrated with web query tools to provide a more complete solution. Finally, the domain ontologies could be coupled with other repositories of knowledge and applied to various applications.

REFERENCES

Banko, M., & Moore, R. C. (2004). Part of speech tagging in context. In *Proceedings of the 20th International Conference on Computational Linguistics*, Geneva, Switzerland.

Berners-Lee, T., Hendler, J., & Lassila, O. (2001). The Semantic Web. *Scientific American*, *5*, 1–19.

Boley, D., Gini, M., Gross, R., Han, E. H., Hastings, K., & Karypis, G. (1999a). Document categorization and query generation on the World Wide Web using WebACE. *Artificial Intelligence Review*, *13*(5), 365–391. doi:10.1023/A:1006592405320

Boley, D., Gini, M., Gross, R., Han, E. H., Hastings, K., & Karypis, G. (1999b). Partitioning-based clustering for Web document categorization. *Decision Support Systems*, *27*(3), 329–341. doi:10.1016/S0167-9236(99)00055-X

Buitelaar, P., & Cimiano, P. (2008). *Ontology learning and population: Bridging the gap between text and knowledge*. Amsterdam, The Netherlands: IOS Press.

Burton-Jones, A., Storey, V. C., Sugumaran, V., & Ahluwalia, P. (2005). A semiotic metrics suite for assessing the quality of ontologies. *Data & Knowledge Engineering*, *55*(1), 84–102. doi:10.1016/j.datak.2004.11.010

Chakrabarti, S., Dom, B. E., Gibson, D., Kleinberg, J., Kumar, R., & Raghavan, P. (1999). Mining the link structure of the World Wide Web. *IEEE Computer*, *32*(8), 60–67.

Corcho, O., Fernández-López, M., & Gómez-Pérez, A. (2003). Methodologies, tools and languages for building ontologies. Where is their meeting point? *Data & Knowledge Engineering*, *46*(1), 41–64. doi:10.1016/S0169-023X(02)00195-7

Cristani, M., & Cuel, R. (2005). A survey on ontology creation methodologies. *International Journal on Semantic Web and Information Systems*, *1*(2), 49–69. doi:10.4018/jswis.2005040103

Dahlgren, K. (1995). A linguistic ontology. *International Journal of Human-Computer Studies*, *43*(5-6), 809–818. doi:10.1006/ijhc.1995.1075

De Silva, L., & Jayaratne, L. (2009). WikiOnto: A system for semi-automatic extraction and modeling of ontologies using Wikipedia XML corpus. In *Proceedings of the Semantic Web Information Workshop and the 3rd IEEE International Conference on Semantic Computing*, Berkeley, CA.

Dennis, A. R., & Carte, T. A. (1998). Using geographical information systems for decision making: Extending cognitive fit theory to map-based presentations. *Information Systems Research*, *9*(2), 194–203. doi:10.1287/isre.9.2.194

Ding, Y., & Foo, S. (2002). Ontology research and development. Part 1: A review of ontology generation. *Journal of Information Science*, *28*(2), 123.

Dweck, C. S. (1986). Motivational processes affecting learning. *The American Psychologist*, *41*(10), 1040–1048. doi:10.1037/0003-066X.41.10.1040

Fagni, T., Perego, R., Silvestri, F., & Orlando, S. (2006). Boosting the performance of web search engines: Caching and prefetching query results by exploiting historical usage data. *ACM Transactions on Information Systems*, *24*(1), 78.

Farquhar, A., Fikes, R., & Rice, J. (1997). The ontolingua server: A tool for collaborative ontology construction. *International Journal of Human-Computer Studies*, *46*(6), 707–727. doi:10.1006/ijhc.1996.0121

Fensel, D., Van Harmelen, F., Klein, M., Akkermans, H., Broekstra, J., Fluff, C., et al. (2000). On-to-knowledge: Ontology-based tools for knowledge management. In *Proceedings of the eBusiness and eWork Conference*.

Fernández-López, M., Gómez-Pérez, A., & Juristo, N. (1997). *Methontology: From ontological art towards ontological engineering*. Paper presented at the Workshop on Ontological Engineering.

Frantzi, K. T., & Ananiadou, S. (1999). The C-value/NC-value domain independent method for multiword term extraction. *Journal of Natural Language Processing*, *6*(3), 145–180.

Gangemi, A., Guarino, N., Masolo, C., Oltramari, A., & Schneider, L. (2002). Sweetening ontologies with DOLCE. In *Proceedings of the 13th International Conference on Knowledge Engineering and Knowledge Management* (pp. 166-181).

Grootjen, F., & van der Weide, T. (2005). Dualistic ontologies. *International Journal of Intelligent Information Technologies*, *1*(3), 34–55. doi:10.4018/jiit.2005070103

Gruninger, M., & Fox, M. S. (1995). Methodology for the design and evaluation of ontologies. In *Proceedings of the International Joint Conference on Artificial Intelligence and the Workshop on Basic Ontological Issues in Knowledge Sharing.*

Gu, T., Wang, X., Pung, H., & Zhang, D. (2004). An ontology-based context model in intelligent environments. In *Proceedings of the Conference on Communication Networks and Distributed Systems Modelling and Simulation* (pp. 270-275).

Harrison, P. D., & Harrell, A. (1993). Impact of "adverse selection" on managers' project evaluation decisions. *Academy of Management Journal*, *36*, 635–635. doi:10.2307/256596

Hendler, J., Shadbolt, N., Hall, W., Berners-Lee, T., & Weitzner, D. (2008). Web science: An interdisciplinary approach to understanding the web. *Communications of the ACM*, *51*(7), 60–69. doi:10.1145/1364782.1364798

Herman, I. (2007). *Introduction to Semantic Web*. Paper presented at the International Conference on Dublin Core and Metadata Applications.

Hevner, A. R., March, S. T., Park, J., & Ram, S. (2004). Design science in information systems research. *Management Information Systems Quarterly*, *28*(1), 75–105.

Hong, W., Thong, J. Y. L., & Tam, K. (2004). The effects of information format and shopping task on consumers' online shopping behavior: A cognitive fit perspective. *Journal of Management Information Systems*, *21*(3), 149–184.

Horrocks, I. (2008). Ontologies and the Semantic Web. *Communications of the ACM*, *51*(12), 58–67. doi:10.1145/1409360.1409377

Katifori, A., Halatsis, C., Lepouras, G., Vassilakis, C., & Giannopoulou, E. (2007). Ontology visualization methods - a survey. *ACM Computing Surveys*, *39*(4), 11–43. doi:10.1145/1287620.1287621

Kietz, J.-U., Maedche, A., & Volz, R. (2000). A method for semi-automatic ontology acquisition from a corporate intranet. In *Proceedings of the Workshop on Knowledge Engineering and Knowledge Management.*

Lau, R., Song, D., Li, Y., Cheung, T., & Hao, J. (2009). Towards a fuzzy domain ontology extraction method for adaptive e-learning. *IEEE Transactions on Knowledge and Data Engineering*, *21*(6), 800–813. doi:10.1109/TKDE.2008.137

Leukel, J., & Sugumaran, V. (2009). Towards a semiotic metrics suite for product ontology evaluation. *International Journal of Intelligent Information Technologies*, *5*(4), 1–15. doi:10.4018/jiit.2009080701

Lindland, O. I., Sindre, G., & Solvberg, A. (1994). Understanding quality in conceptual modeling. *IEEE Software*, *11*(2), 42–49. doi:10.1109/52.268955

Maedche, A., & Staab, S. (2000). Discovering conceptual relations from text. In *Proceedings of the European Conference on Artificial Intelligence* (pp. 321-325).

Maedche, A., & Staab, S. (2000). Semi-automatic engineering of ontologies from text. In *Proceedings of the 12th International Conference on Software and Knowledge Engineering*, Chicago, IL.

Maedche, A., & Volz, R. (2001). The ontology extraction and maintenance framework text-to-onto. In *Proceedings of the ICDM Workshop on Integrating Data Mining and Knowledge Management.*

March, S., & Allen, G. (2007). Ontological foundations for active information systems. *International Journal of Intelligent Information Technologies*, *3*(1), 1–13. doi:10.4018/jiit.2007010101

Meng, S. K., & Chatwin, C. R. (2010). Ontology-based shopping agent for e-marketing. *International Journal of Intelligent Information Technologies*, *6*(2), 21–43. doi:10.4018/jiit.2010040102

Michener, W., Beach, J., Jones, M., Ludäscher, B., Pennington, D., & Pereira, R. (2007). A knowledge environment for the biodiversity and ecological sciences. *Journal of Intelligent Information Systems*, *29*(1), 111–126. doi:10.1007/s10844-006-0034-8

Motik, B., Maedche, A., & Volz, R. (2002). A conceptual modeling approach for semantics-driven enterprise applications. In. *Proceedings of the Confederated International Coferences of DOA, CoopIS, and ODBASE: On the Move to Meaningful Internet Systems*, *2519*, 1082–1099.

Noy, N. F., & McGuinness, D. L. (2001). *Ontology development 101: A guide to creating your first ontology* (Tech. Rep. No. KSL-01-05, SMI-2001). Stanford, CA: Stanford Knowledge Systems Laboratory and Stanford Medical Informatics

Omelayenko, B. (2001). Learning of ontologies for the Web: The analysis of existent approaches. In *Proceedings of the International Workshop on Web Dynamics*, London, UK.

Paas, F. (1992). Training strategies for attaining transfer of problem-solving skill in statistics: A cognitive-load approach. *Journal of Educational Psychology*, *84*(4), 429–434. doi:10.1037/0022-0663.84.4.429

Pinto, H. S., & Martins, J. P. (2004). Ontologies: How can they be built? *Knowledge and Information Systems*, *6*(4), 441–464. doi:10.1007/s10115-003-0138-1

Ram, S., & Zhao, H. (2007). Opportunities and challenges. *Information Technology Management*, *8*(3), 203–204. doi:10.1007/s10799-007-0018-6

Salton, G., & Buckley, C. (1988). Term-weighting approaches in automatic text retrieval. *Information Processing and Management: An International Journal*, *24*(5), 513–523. doi:10.1016/0306-4573(88)90021-0

Sánchez, D., & Moreno, A. (2008). Learning non-taxonomic relationships from web documents for domain ontology construction. *Data & Knowledge Engineering*, *64*(3), 600–623. doi:10.1016/j.datak.2007.10.001

Schreiber, G., Wielinga, B., & Jansweijer, W. (1995). *The KACTUS view on the 'O' word.* Paper presented at the International Joint Conference on Artificial Intelligence and the Workshop on Basic Ontological Issues in Knowledge Sharing.

Shaft, T. M., & Vessey, I. (2006). The role of cognitive fit in the relationship between software comprehension and modification. *Management Information Systems Quarterly*, *30*(1), 29–55.

Sitkin, S. B., & Weingart, L. R. (1995). Determinants of risky decision-making behavior: A test of the mediating role of risk perceptions and propensity. *Academy of Management Journal*, *38*, 1573–1592. doi:10.2307/256844

Spyns, P., Meersman, R., & Jarrar, M. (2002). Data modelling versus ontology engineering. *SIGMOD Record*, *31*(4), 12–17. doi:10.1145/637411.637413

Steinberg, E. R. (1989). Cognition and learner control: A literature review, 1977-1988. *Journal of Computer Based Instruction*, *16*(4), 117–121.

Sugiura, N., Kurematsu, M., Fukuta, N., Izumi, N., & Yamaguchi, T. (2003). A domain ontology engineeering tool with general ontologies and text corpus. In *Proceedings of the 2nd Workshop on Evaluation of Ontology based Tools* (pp. 71-82).

Suh, K., & Lee, Y. E. (2005). The effects of virtual reality on consumer learning: An empirical investigation. *Management Information Systems Quarterly*, *29*(4), 673–697.

Tsikriktsis, N. (2005). A review of techniques for treating missing data in OM survey research. *Journal of Operations Management*, *24*(1), 53–62. doi:10.1016/j.jom.2005.03.001

Tun, N., & Tojo, S. (2008). enontoModel: A semantically-enriched model for ontologies. *International Journal of Intelligent Information Technologies*, *4*(1), 1–30. doi:10.4018/jiit.2008010101

Uschold, M. (1996). *Building ontologies: Towards a unified methodology*. Edinburgh, UK: University of Edinburgh.

Vaishnavi, V. K., & Kuechler, W. (2007). *Design science research methods and patterns: Innovating information and communication technology*. Boca Raton, FL: Auerbach Publications. doi:10.1201/9781420059335

Vessey, I., & Galletta, D. (1991). Cognitive fit: An empirical study of information acquisition. *Information Systems Research*, *2*(1), 63–84. doi:10.1287/isre.2.1.63

Xing, J., Han, M., & Tao, X. (2009). A wetland protection domain ontology construction for knowledge management and information sharing. *Human and Ecological Risk Assessment: An International Journal*, *15*(2), 298–315.

Zhou, L. (2007). Ontology learning: State of the art and open issues. *Information Technology Management*, *8*(3), 241–252. doi:10.1007/s10799-007-0019-5

APPENDIX

Examples of ontologies and evaluation:

Figure 14. KC: 2, KR: 2, OQ: 1

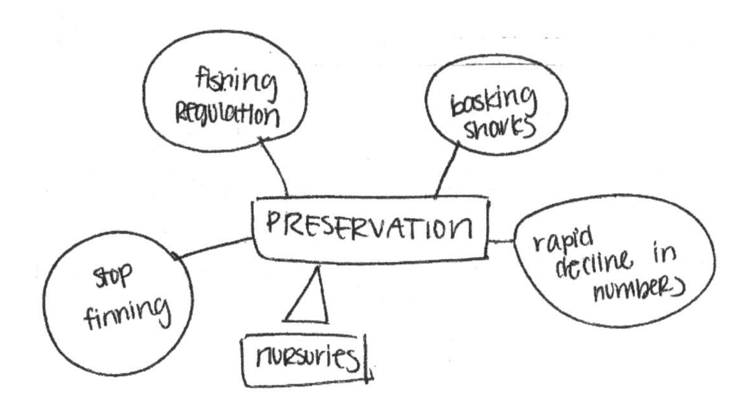

*Figure 15. KC: 6, KR: 7, OQ: 6 * rectangle: class; oval: property; triangle: hierarchical relation*

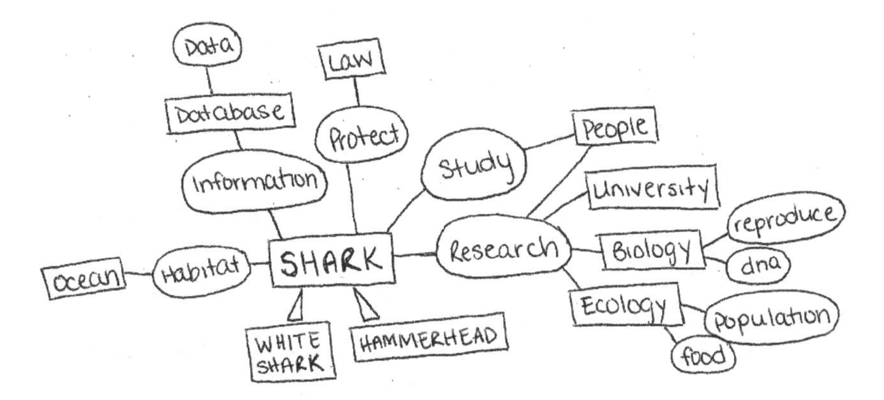

As shown in the figure above, the first figure receives low evaluation points (KC: 2, KR: 2, OQ: 1). KC is low because the number of relevant terms (fishing regulation, stop finning, and preservation) is only three. KR is also low. For example, nursery and basking sharks have little to do with shark and its preservation. Finally as to OQ, the relationships of properties and inheritance are incorrect and irrelevant. As opposed to the previous example, the second figure received high evaluation points (KC: 6, KR: 7, OQ: 6). The total number of selected terms is 20, and the terms cover a large extent of the target ontology. The terms are very relevant to the ontology (e.g., habitat, protect, and DNA). Despite a minor mistake in identifying relevant properties (e.g., properties of biology), inheritance and relevant properties are correctly represented.

This work was previously published in the International Journal of Intelligent Information Technologies, Volume 7, Issue 2, edited by Vijayan Sugumaran, pp. 1-24, copyright 2011 by IGI Publishing (an imprint of IGI Global).

Chapter 6
Self Adaptive Particle Swarm Optimization for Efficient Virtual Machine Provisioning in Cloud

R. Jeyarani
Coimbatore Institute of Technology, India

N. Nagaveni
Coimbatore Institute of Technology, India

R. Vasanth Ram
PSG College of Technology, India

ABSTRACT

Cloud Computing provides dynamic leasing of server capabilities as a scalable, virtualized service to end users. The discussed work focuses on Infrastructure as a Service (IaaS) model where custom Virtual Machines (VM) are launched in appropriate servers available in a data-center. The context of the environment is a large scale, heterogeneous and dynamic resource pool. Nonlinear variation in the availability of processing elements, memory size, storage capacity, and bandwidth causes resource dynamics apart from the sporadic nature of workload. The major challenge is to map a set of VM instances onto a set of servers from a dynamic resource pool so the total incremental power drawn upon the mapping is minimal and does not compromise the performance objectives. This paper proposes a novel Self Adaptive Particle Swarm Optimization (SAPSO) algorithm to solve the intractable nature of the above challenge. The proposed approach promptly detects and efficiently tracks the changing optimum that represents target servers for VM placement. The experimental results of SAPSO was compared with Multi-Strategy Ensemble Particle Swarm Optimization (MEPSO) and the results show that SAPSO outperforms the latter for power aware adaptive VM provisioning in a large scale, heterogeneous and dynamic cloud environment.

DOI: 10.4018/978-1-4666-2047-6.ch006

INTRODUCTION

Cloud Computing is emerging as a promising distributed computing paradigm. It delivers a wide range of services like Infrastructure as a Service (IaaS), Platform as a Service (PaaS) and Software as a Service (SaaS). The cloud resources and services are dynamically provisioned like utilities. The elastic nature of the cloud facilitates users to have as much or little of service depending on their need at any given time. The IaaS model supports on demand provisioning of virtualized resources as a service. In this model, service consumers specify hardware and software configuration of Virtual Machines (VM) to be created and they execute their jobs on each VM (Smith & Nair, 2005). As the nature of the submitted jobs is parallelizable, a VM may require multiple cores for efficient execution. The key challenge is the implementation of efficient VM provisioner which leases suitable hosts for launching VMs that fulfill the customer requirements at the same time minimizing power consumption to facilitate the providers.

Moreover the state of the resource pool gets frequently changed due to the sporadic nature of the resource requirements. Hot migration capabilities of virtualization contribute to resource dynamics where VMs are moved rapidly between physical machines for load balancing and server consolidation (Smith & Nair, 2005). Some servers are shut down periodically for preventive maintenance after migrating the running VMs onto suitable servers, making a few servers unavailable for specific duration (Beltran, 2005; Dikaiakos, Pallis, Katsaros, Mehra, & Vakali, 2009; French, 2009) or the resource dynamics could be due to the failure of hosts. When there is unexpected peak load, few servers are powered on to mitigate the need for resources. Apart from the said dynamics involved due to servers' availability, there are a few more dynamic attributes such as increase or decrease in the number of Processing Elements (PEs) available, size of memory, storage capacity and bandwidth of the servers during VM creation, VM deletion or VM migration. The Dynamic Voltage and Frequency Scaling (DVFS) technique inherent in recent microprocessor technology also introduces variable processing speed based on the load (Hamidi & Vafaei, 2009; Wang, von Laszewskiy, Dayalz, & Wang, 2010; Russell & Yoon, 2009). All of the above mentioned resource dynamics necessitates the need for a Meta-Scheduler which monitors the environment, detects the state change in the resources and finds the optimal or near optimal schedule for placing the VM instances onto available physical servers.

As the main feature of cloud computing is on-demand access to resources, the datacenters are over provisioned to handle the unexpected workload surges. The major issue here is in managing extremely large and dynamic datacenters for power conservation, while fulfilling the incoming VM requests. In the datacenter of a public cloud, generally hundreds and thousands of servers run at any instance of time, hosting many virtual machines and at the same time the cloud system keeps receiving the batches of VM requests. In this scenario, when there is a need to find few target hosts say $'r'$ hosts out of $'n'$ powered on hosts, which can fulfill a batch of incoming VM requests, then there is $'nPr'$ possible permutations of allocating the jobs to hosts making the problem combinatorial (Coffman, 1976).

Although the VM scheduling problem could be formulated as a Linear Programming Problem (LPP) and solved optimally, using such an exact method is computationally inefficient. Complexity class of the scheduling problem belongs to NP-complete involving extremely large search space with correspondingly large number of potential solutions (Garey & Johnson, 1979) and takes much longer time to find the optimal solution. However in cloud, it is sufficient to find near optimal solution, preferably in a short period of time. Meta heuristic methods for scheduling like simulated annealing (SA), genetic algorithms (GA), ant colony optimization (ACO) and particle swarm optimization (PSO) are used to solve the well known NP-complete problems. As the VM provisioning problem is NP-complete, we propose a novel particle swarm optimization based VM provisioner for scheduling Virtual Machines in the cloud system.

The SA is time consuming and the parameter tuning has to be done very carefully (Fidanova, 2006). ACO is better suited for discrete optimization problems. PSO is driven by neighborhood velocity which is a continuous parameter and is very much suitable for continuous optimization problems. It is population based optimization tool and possesses good convergence and diversity maintenance capabilities and could be applied easily to solve various function optimization problems (Sadhasivam, & Rajendran, 2008). Unlike genetic algorithm, PSO gives a feasible solution in a reasonable time as it involves only few parameters and it is easier to find the best combination of parameter values.

As the resource provider agrees to make a set of resources available to the resource consumer, based on service level agreements (SLA), the term VM provisioning is also referred to as 'lease'. Sotomayor, Montero, Llorente, and Foster (2008, 2009) have created open source lease management architecture called 'Haizea' and they have addressed three different types of leases namely advanced reservation leases, best effort leases and immediate leases. To handle different lease types, the Haizea uses back filling strategy. The queue based backfilling strategy is more time consuming and may not be the best choice when the workload scheduling belongs to NP-complete complexity class.

Nurmi et al. (2009) have presented an open source software framework for cloud computing called EUCALYPTUS that implements IaaS cloud. This tool supports immediate VM requests and the host selection for VM placement uses static greedy and round robin method. In this model, the large scale datacenters suffer from poor resource utilization as well as wastage in idle power, which will result in great loss for cloud providers.

Page, Keane, and Naughton (2010) have developed GA based meta scheduler to dynamically schedule heterogeneous tasks on to heterogeneous processors in a distributed system with a single objective of minimizing the execution time. The meta scheduler uses exponential smoothing function to adapt the schedule in a dynamically changing computing resource environment. The paper has not discussed the robustness of adaptive scheduling in dynamically changing environment with experimental results.

Pandey, Wu, Guru, and Buyya (2009) have developed PSO based heuristics for scheduling workflow application to cloud resources taking into consideration the computation cost and data transmission cost and their work has concluded that PSO based approach has achieved three times cost saving compared to Best Resource Selection (BRS) algorithm used in the tool Haizea (Sotomayor, Montero, Llorente, & Foster, 2008, 2009). Most of the existing works on meta scheduling in cloud have focused only on improving the performance of workload facilitating the cloud consumers and less importance have been given to energy efficient datacenter management to facilitate cloud providers. The existing work on power aware VM provisioning follows bin-packing approach such as First Fit Decreasing (FFD) and incremental First Fit Decreasing (iFFD) (Verma, Ahuja, & Neogi, 2008). The FFD unbalances the load as it utilizes more power efficient servers first. The iFFD packs the VMs onto physical servers through VM migration, by considering the fixed target utilization of each server. The FFD and iFFD algorithms will not be efficient for large scale datacenters as they take much longer time for optimal VM provisioning.

Application of PSO based multi objective optimization approach for VM provisioning in a highly dynamic datacenter is the first of its kind. In this paper, we present Adaptive Power Aware Virtual Machine Provisioner (APA-VMP) which implements Self Adaptive Particle Swarm Optimization (SAPSO) algorithm for handling dynamic changes in the resource pool.

The rest of the paper is organized as follows. We first discuss standard PSO and give survey of its variants in handling dynamic environment.

Next we present problem formulation resulting in a mathematical model. We then describe briefly the system architecture of the proposed Meta Scheduler. Next, we describe the novel scheduling heuristic and SAPSO algorithm in detail. The next section deals with the experimental set up and followed by experimental results and inference. Finally we conclude by giving the scope for future research work.

HEURISTIC APPROACH USING PARTICLE SWARM OPTIMIZATION

PSO is a population based optimization tool which could be implemented and applied easily to solve various function optimization problems. It was originally designed by Kennedy and Eberhart in 1995 to imitate the motion of a flock of birds or a school of fish (Engelbrecht, 2007; Kennedy et al., 1995). Each individual called a 'particle' represents a solution point in the search space. The population called a 'swarm' represents the set of potential solutions. PSO is based on the interaction and social communication of the group of particles.

Each particle in PSO can fly only in a limited number of directions which are expected to be good areas. PSO finds a near optimal solution in an acceptable time. The following subsection discusses standard PSO and its variants for handling dynamic environments.

Standard PSO Methodology

The particle is described by a group of vectors denoted as $(\vec{x}_i, \vec{v}_i, \vec{p}_i)$, where $\vec{x}_i = (x_{i1}, x_{i2}, \ldots, x_{iD})$ and $\vec{v}_i = (v_{i1}, v_{i2}, \ldots v_{iD})$ representing position and velocity vectors of the ith particle. D denotes the dimension of the particle. $\vec{p}_i = (p_{i1}, p_{i2}, \ldots p_{iD})$ denotes the personal best representing the best position the particle has achieved so far and $\vec{g}_i = (g_{i1}, g_{i2}, \ldots g_{iD})$ denotes the global best representing the the best position tracked by the entire swarm (Tasgetiren et al., 2004a, 2004b). To begin with, a swarm of particle is randomly generated. Each particle has a position vector in the problem space and velocity vector for moving towards the optimal solution. The dimension of a particle is determined based on the problem to be optimized. The velocity and position of the particles are updated by the Equations (1) and (2) in each iteration.

$$v_{id}(t+1) = wv_{id}(t) + c_1 r_1 [p_{id} - x_{id}(t)] + c_2 r_2 [p_{gd} - x_{id}(t)] \tag{1}$$

$$x_{id}(t+1) = x_{id}(t) + v_{id}(t+1) \tag{2}$$

where i=1,2,..., m denotes the number of particlesand d=1,2,..., D denotes the dimension of particles.

'r_1', 'r_2' are uniformly distributed random numbers in the interval $0, 1$. 'c_1' and 'c_2' are learning factors and usually 'c_1' equals 'c_2' and ranges from $0, 4$ (Shi & Eberhart, 1999). The 'c_1' is the individual cognition component representing the search ability of the particle itself. The 'c_2' is the social communication component representing the influence from the social environment. 'w' is the time dependent inertia weight to avoid unlimited growth of the particle's velocity. The PSO searches for optima by updating generations. The searching is a repeat process and the stopping criteria are that either the maximum number of iterations is reached or minimum error condition is satisfied. The pseudo code for the optimizer is as follows.

- INITIALIZE
    - Randomize position and velocity of all particles in search space.
    - Set each particle's personalBest to particle position.
    - Set globalBest to randomized particle's position.

- REPEAT
    - For each particle:
        - Calculate particle's updated velocity using Equation (1).
        - Calculate particle's position using Equation (2).
        - Calculate the fitness value and evaluate fitness value.
    - If [fitness value corresponding to new position is better than the personalBest in the history]
    - Set personalBest as the new position
    - End For
    - Choose the particle's position with the best fitness value in the population as the gBest.
- UNTIL (Stopping Criteria is met)

The major drawback of the standard PSO is that it gets trapped into local optima, failing to explore the entire population. The local optima occur when each particle is trapped in its own area and so better solutions cannot be found. This is overcome by including Local Improvement Procedure (LIP), which enables each particle to escape from local optima. Eberhart and Shi (2001) reported that a large inertia weight facilitates a global search while a small inertia weight facilitates a local search (Mladenovic & Hansen, 1997; Hu & Eberhart, 2001). They have also pointed out that an inertia weight starting with a value close to one and linearly decreasing to 0.4 through the course of run will give PSO the best performance compared to fixed inertia weight. Shi and Eberhart (1999) illustrated that PSO has the ability to quickly converge and its performance is not sensitive to the population size.

Figure 1. Architecture of Meta Scheduler describing interaction between VM provisioner and other modules

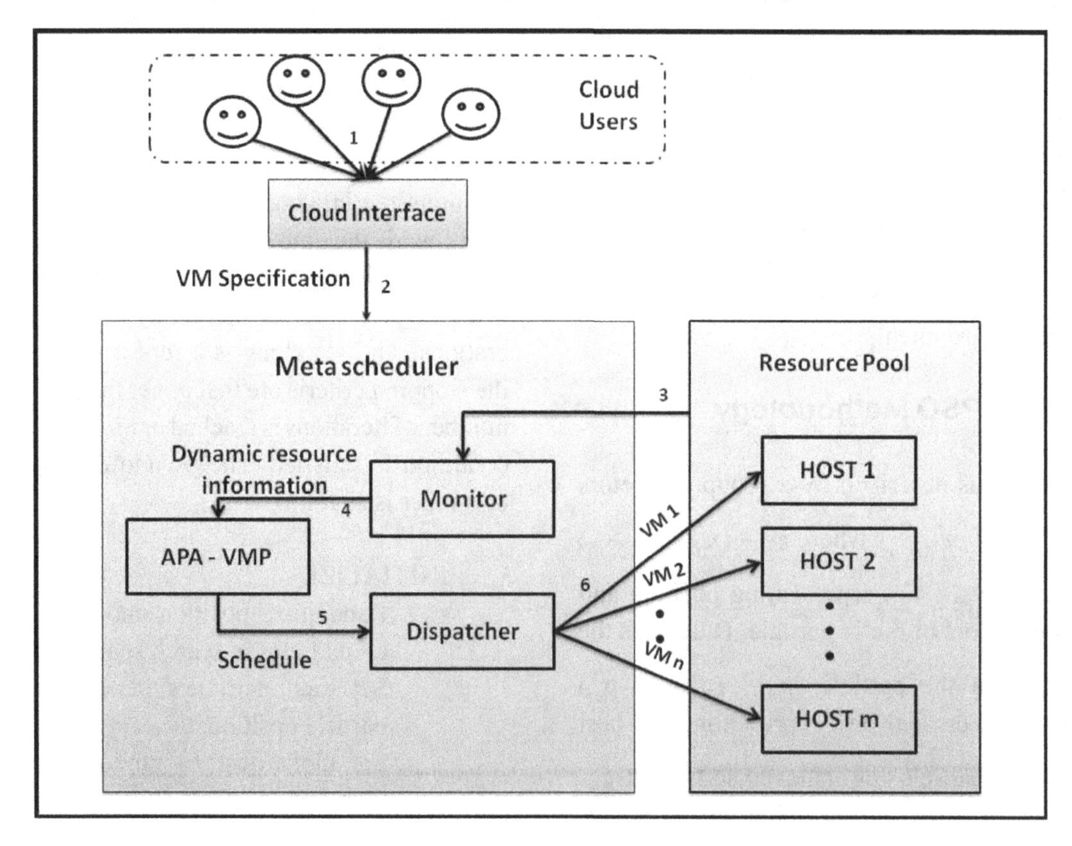

Table 1. Solution representation of a particle

Dimension	x^k_{ij}	s^k_{ij}	r^k_{ij}
0	1.13	3	3
1	3.91	9	1
2	-0.21	1	1
3	-0.39	0	0
4	3.25	7	3
5	3.51	8	0
6	2.74	5	1
7	3.10	6	2
8	0.99	2	2
9	1.62	4	0

PSO Variants for Handling Dynamic Environment

The following section describes four different approaches for handling change in the environment.

1. **Random Inertia Weight:** The first simple approach for handling dynamic environment is using random inertia weight. The authors (Eberhart & Shi, 2001) used the equation [0.5+(Rnd/2.0)] instead of linearly decreasing inertia, to track dynamically moving optima in a chaotic system. Eberhart and Shi (2001) found that when the system change is relatively small, continuing with old swarm configuration may be the better approach and starting with a randomized swarm when the system changes drastically is a more efficient approach.
2. **Re-randomization:** The second approach describes the effect of re-randomization for locating optimum value in dynamic environment. Hu et al. (2001, 2002) introduced two environment detection methods namely "changed-gBest-value" method and "fixed-gBest-value" method. The first one is based on the assumption that when the optimum location of a dynamic system changes, the optimum value of the current location also changes. Resetting particle's memory is used to respond to changes. It is fast but requires extra time to re-evaluate the fitness. The "fixed-gBest-value" method is an effective sensing technique that detects the environment change by re-evaluating the global best and second global best for fixed number of iterations, and if they have not changed, then there is a possible optimum change. The response strategy re-randomizes a portion of the particles for tracking the moving optimum. Re-randomization can be regarded as the death of old particles and the birth of new particles. The authors also suggest that a 10 percent re-randomization is a good choice in most of the cases.
3. **Dynamic PSO using Sentry Particle:** The Third approach is based on sentry particles. Carlisle et al. (2002) illustrated the tracking of changing extrema, in which a fixed number of sentry particles are randomly chosen as stationary particles to identify the change of state in dynamic environments. Each particle replaces its personal best position vector with its current location vector, when an environment is detected and this process is called resetting memory. The authors have also illustrated that instead of blindly replacing all personal best vectors with their corresponding current locations, re-computation of the fitness of the personal best vector is done to accommodate the changed environment and replacement of personal best vector is done with the current location vector only when the fitness value is not better. This strategy preserves information that is still valid. But the overhead involved is additional fitness function evaluation. However, APSO with sentry particle is better for tracking solutions in non stationary environments.

There are a few issues with APSO. The sentry particles can detect only local changes where they are located. It alters the classical PSO's decentralized processing model into centralized control model. All other particles have to depend on one or more number of sentries for detecting and responding to environment changes. Identifying a particle that is capable of working as a sentry to monitor environment makes this variant difficult to use in distributed environment.

Du and Li (2008) designed Multi Ensemble Particle Swarm Optimization (MEPSO) in (Du & Li, 2008) for handling severe environmental changes. In the search space representing dynamic environment, the swarm population is initially divided into two parts and they are termed as Part I and Part II, respectively. They play different roles in the search space by using different strategies. The particles in part I search the global optimum in current environment as quickly as possible. It guarantees good convergence. To improve local search ability of part I, the authors have proposed Gaussian local search.

The movement of particles in part II extend the searching area of the algorithm, and to patrol around the part I to track the changed global optimum that is missed by particles of part I. The strategy of differential mutation enhances the communication between part I and part II. It prevents the algorithm from being premature termination by extending the particle's search area.

4. **Decentralized PSO without Sentry Particles:** Carlisle et al. (2002) proposed a Dynamic Adaptive PSO (DAPSO) for monitoring and automatically reacting to the change in environment. It is used to find moving optimal solution in a dynamically changing and noisy environment. The promising feature of DAPSO is the renewal of a particle's memory without any centralized control (Carlisle et al., 2002). In DAPSO, there is no specially designed particle to monitor the change of the environment and there is no additional fitness evaluation computing to enable the particle to adapt to the changed environment. Here, each particle will compare the fitness value of its current location with that of the personal best location. If the current fitness value does not have any improvement, the particle will use the following equation to update the personal best fitness value Pi.

Figure 2. Scheduling heuristic handler

Algorithm for handler of APA-VMP:
1. Set static power model of resource pool.
2. Get workload list in a scheduler time window and let the number of workloads be n
3. Get present Power Consumption $\boldsymbol{P}$ of the resource pool
4. **Repeat**
5. Get m the number of compute resource available.
6. particle dimension = n
7. Get resource dynamics
8. Optimal-Mapping-Instance = ***SAPSO*** (particle dimension, resource dynamics, $\boldsymbol{P}$)
9. Dispatch the workloads
10. Update resource dynamics of the resource pool
11. Get the workload list
12. **Until** (There are unscheduled workloads in the scheduler time window)
13. Stop

Figure 3. SAPSO algorithm

```
Algorithm SAPSO (dimension, resource dynamics, Pd)
1.  Initialize simulation parameters, see Table 3
2.  Initialize position & velocity vector randomly,
3.  Find sequence vector and operation vector,
4.  Find fitness value using the fitness function eqns (4)
    & (5),
5.  Set personalBest vector of each particle ,
6.  Set globalBest vector of the population ,
7.  Set k=2,
8.  Get resource dynamics and set Evaporation factor
    accordingly
9.  Repeat
10.  For each particle i in the entire population
11.      Update velocity and position vectors
12.      Find fitness value using the fitness function
         eqns (4) & (5)
13.      If ( fitness value of k^th iteration is better than
         that of Evaporated fitness value)
14.          Update personalBest vector and its fitness
             value
15.      Else
16.          Evaporate fitness value
17.  For end

18.  Find the maximum fitness value, Max θ and
     number of particles with Max θ
19.  If (there are more than one particle with Max θ
20.      Find the particle 'q' with minimum Δ using
         eqn (6)
21.  Update globalBest vector and its fitness value
22.  Update inertia w=w*.01
23.  k=k+1,
24.  Until (Termination)
```

$$Pi(t+1) = \begin{cases} Pi(t) * T \\ f(Xi(t+1) \leq Pi(t) * T \\ \\ f(Xi(t+1)) \\ f(Xi(t+1) > Pi(t) * T \end{cases} \quad (3)$$

The evaporation factor T is introduced and it has a value between 0 and 1 (Cui & Potok, 2007). The personal fitness value that is stored in each particle's memory and the global fitness value of the particle swarm will gradually evaporate (decrease) overtime at the rate of the evaporation factor T (Hu, Shi, & Eberhart, 2004). Once the particle continuously fails to improve its current fitness value by using its previous searching experience, the particle's personal best fitness value will gradually decrease. Eventually, the personal and global best fitness value will be lower than the fitness value of the particle's current location and the best fitness value will be replaced by the particle's current fitness value.

The fitness value update equation enables the search particles to self-adapt to the changing environment.

The conventional methods for VM placement mainly driven by performance objectives are not very much suitable for combinatorial problems (Pandey, Wu, Guru, & Buyya, 2009). The application of automatic environment sensing technique such as DAPSO for handling VM placement is more appropriate for a large scale highly dynamic heterogeneous cloud, as it can give near optimal solution within a reasonable of time.

PROBLEM FORMULATION

The two important entities involved in Virtual Machine (VM) provisioning are hosts and VM instances. The hosts in the resource pool representing compute resources subject to space shared allocation policy are assumed to be heterogeneous and dynamic. Each compute resource is associated with the available number of PEs and the size of memory for VM creation and their state changes dynamically. The resource pool is associated with power model which describes the power consumption of compute resources for varying loads. Similarly each VM instance representing workload is associated with the number of required PEs and the required size of memory. The workloads are considered to be independent of each other and are equal in priority. The problem can be stated as follows.

Find a Workload-Compute Resource mapping instance M, such that the total incremental power drawn by the mapped workloads (VM) on to compute resources (CR) is minimized, while maximizing the performance by fulfilling the resource requirements for maximum number of workloads.

We define APA-VMP as a four tuple C = {CR, VM, P, M}. Let CR be a set of 'm' available compute resources denoted by CR(m,t) = {CR_1, CR_2, …CR_m}, available at provisioning start time 't'. Let VM be a set of 'n' workloads denoted by VM(n,t) ={VM_1, VM_2, VM_3, …VM_n} accumulated within a time window 't_o'. Let P(m) = {P_1, P_2 … P_m} be the static power model representing power consumption by the 'm' compute resources in resource pool for varying loads. The problem is multimodal, having more than one mapping which meets the performance constraints of the VM requests. Hence, the goal is to find all of 'a' mapping instances which maximize the performance and then to find which among those minimizes the power consumption.

Here one of the multi- objective optimization approach called hierarchical approach is followed to deal with the multi-criteria condition of the problem. As we need to establish priority among the criteria namely the resource fulfillment and the power consumption and both the criteria are measured in different units namely fulfillment is measured in numbers and power consumption is expressed in watts, we use hierarchical approach for optimization.

To meet performance constraints, a metric called "mean allocation value" denoted by 'θ_r' is defined as follows.

Table 2. Static power consumption model of the resource pool

Host Load	Power Consumption in Watts						
	Intel Xeon Processor				AMD Opteron Processor		
	Xe 2000	Xe 2333	Xe 2666	Xe 3000	Op 1000	Op 1800	Op 2000
0%	283	284	285	286	121	161	167
25%	290	296	305	313	124	171	178
50%	297	309	324	340	127	181	190
75%	305	317	335	354	131	191	200
100%	311	326	347	368	134	202	212

Figure 4. Deployment diagram showing position of APA-VMP in a cloud environment

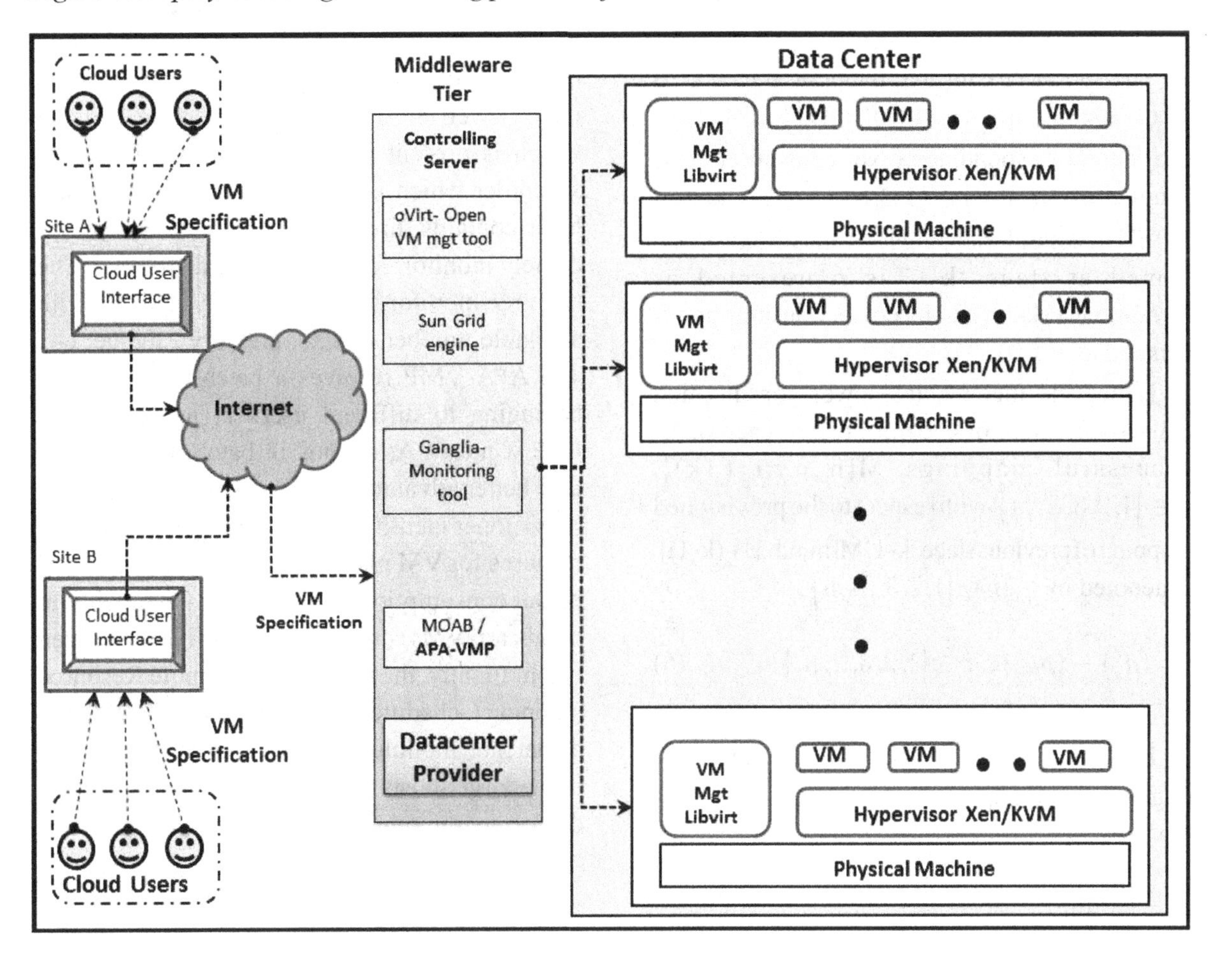

$$\grave{E}_i^j = \begin{cases} 1\_if\, rrVM_i \le arHost_j, \\ i \in \{1,2,3,\ldots,n\} \\ 0\ \_if\, rrVM_i > arHost_j, \\ j \in \{1,2,3,\ldots,m\} \end{cases} \quad (4)$$

Here, $rrVM_i$ denote the minimum resource requirement of ith VM and $arHost_j$ denotes the the available resource of jth host. $\grave{E}_i^j$ denotes the success of allocation of ith job on the jth host.

$$\theta_r = \left[\frac{\sum_{i=1}^{n}\sum_{j=1}^{m}\psi_i^j}{n}\right],$$

$$i \in \{1,2,3,\ldots,n\}, \quad j \in \{1,2,3,\ldots,m\}, \quad r \in \{1,2,3,\ldots,s\} \quad (5)$$

where 's' denotes the total number of mappings. 'θ_r' can vary from 0 to 1. Out of 's' mappings, 'a' mappings with maximum 'θ_r' values give best performance and they are represented as M[m,n,r,t] where 'r' is the ordinality of successful mappings and $r \in \{1,2,3,\ldots,a\}$.

The second metric is based on the power consumption. A 'stage' is defined as the one in which a successful mapping is provisioned. The mappings of successive stages are represented as

M[m,n,r,t+t_0(k)] where 'k' representing a stage, is an integer increasing with successive provisioning.

The 'a' successful mappings at stage 'k' is represented as M[m,n,r,t+t_0(k)], $r \in \{1, 2, 3, \ldots, a\}$ and their corresponding power consumptions is denoted as (ρ_k^r) , $r \in \{1, 2, 3, \ldots, a\}$. The best of 'b' successful mappings that has been provisioned at stage 'k-1' is represented as M[m,n,b,t+t_0(k-1)] and its power consumption is denoted as $(\acute{A}_{k-1})$.

Hence the incremental power consumption collectively in all of CR(m,t), due to each of 'a' successful mappings M[m,n,r,t+t_0(k)], $r \in \{1, 2, 3, \ldots, a\}$ with respect to the provisioned mapping of previous stage 'k-1' M[m,n,b,t+t_0(k-1)], is denoted by $_{r}$, $r \in \{1, 2, 3, \ldots, a\}$.

$$_{r} = (\rho_k^r) - (\rho_{k-1}),\ r \in \{1, 2, 3, \ldots, a\} \quad (6)$$

For better power conservation, $_{r}$ is minimized to get optimal mapping and it is denoted as follows.

$$'_{k} = \min_{a} \ _{r},\ r \in \{1, 2, 3, \ldots, a\} \quad (7)$$

$$\rho_k = \rho_{k-1} + '_{k} \quad (8)$$

Thus the proposed VM provisioner minimizes 'Δ_r' for power efficiency and maximizes 'θ_r' for better performance requirements in order to satisfy both cloud providers and cloud consumers.

SYSTEM ARCHITECTURE

Figure 1 depicts the proposed architecture of Meta Scheduler for cloud environment. It shows the position of provisioner APA-VMP and its interaction with other entities (Akjiratikarl, Yenradee, & Drake, 2007; Jeyarani et al., 2008, 2010; Sadhasivam, Nagaveni, Jayarani, & Ram, 2009). There is a separation of resource provisioning from job execution management. The cloud users submit a list of required VM specification through web interface or cloud interface software which is present in the client layer. The meta scheduler which is a component of middleware layer contains three important software entities namely monitor, APA-VMP, and dispatcher. The resource monitor gets periodically updated with available number of PEs, memory, storage, etc. The APA-VMP receives a batch of workloads belonging to different users in its scheduling time window. As it runs in batch mode, it can take better advantage of resource dynamics. The provisioner identifies the optimal target compute resource for VM placement focusing on minimal power consumption while finding the maximum number of VM requests that are fulfilled in a given batch. Finally, the Workload-Compute Resource mapping (schedule) is given by provisioner to the dispatcher module for launching VM instances in the target hosts. The resource pool represents datacenter containing thousands of hosts.

Table 3. Specific parameter settings of the considered algorithm

Parameter Name	Parameter Value
Swarm size	20
Dimension	10
Generation	40
Runs	10
Self recognition coefficient, c1	2
Social coefficient,c2	2
Inertia weight w	0.9→0.4
r1,r2	U(0,1)
x_i^k	$(0 to 50)$
v_i^k	$(-50 to 50)$

Table 4. Power drawn by Stdpso, Sapso & Mepso

Power Consumption in Watt							
Iter No	Std PSO	ME PSO	SA PSO	IterNo	Std PSO	ME PSO	SA PSO
1	1103	993	1324	21	728	912	499
2	998	728	728	22	728	912	499
3	867	728	728	23	728	912	499
4	728	728	728	24	728	613	499
5	728	971	728	25	728	681	499
6	728	971	728	26	728	681	583
7	728	971	971	27	728	681	583
8	728	971	971	28	728	681	583
9	728	971	971	29	728	583	583
10	728	846	611	30	728	613	499
11	728	846	583	31	728	613	499
12	728	846	583	32	728	613	499
13	728	610	583	33	728	613	499
14	728	610	583	34	728	613	499
15	728	848	728	35	728	613	499
16	728	848	728	36	728	613	499
17	728	730	728	37	728	613	499
18	728	730	728	38	728	613	499
19	728	730	728	39	728	613	499
20	728	1218	499	40	728	613	499

SELF ADAPTIVE PSO METHODOLOGY FOR EFFICIENT VIRTUAL MACHINE (VM) PROVISIONING

This section discusses the design of proposed Self Adaptive PSO algorithm (SAPSO) for VM provisioning in cloud environment.

Solution Representation

The key issue in designing a successful PSO algorithm is the solution representation as it describes a direct relationship between the problem domain and the particles in PSO (Tasgetiren et al., 2004a, 2004b). Here '*n*' workloads are to be allocated to '*m*' different compute resources. So, the particles are represented as '*n*' dimensional vector. Consider the problem of assigning 10 workloads to 3 hosts. Table 1 shows one possible mapping instance given by a particle in the PSO domain. The position vector is denoted by $x_i^k = (x_{i1}^k, x_{i2}^k, \dots x_{ij}^k, \dots x_{in}^k)$, where x_{ij}^k denotes the position of jth dimension of ith particle in kth generation. The velocity vector is denoted by $v_i^k = (v_{i1}^k, v_{i2}^k, \dots v_{ij}^k, \dots v_{in}^k)$, where v_{ij}^k denotes the velocity in jth dimension of ith particle in kth generation. The personal best position vector $p_i^\ell = (p_{i1}^\ell, p_{i2}^\ell, \dots p_{in}^\ell)$ represents the best ever position of each particle and global best position vector $p^g = (p_1^g, p_2^g, \dots p_n^g)$ represents the best position obtained so far in the population. Based on SPV rule (Eberhart & Shi, 2001) the continuous position of the particle is converted to a permutation sequence $s_i^k = (s_{i1}^k, s_{i2}^k, \dots s_{in}^k)$. The last column of Table 1 is the resultant vector $r_i^k = (r_{i1}^k, r_{i2}^k, \dots r_{in}^k)$, representing the target host identifiers of *n* workloads, where $r_{i1}^k = s_{i1}^k \; mod m$. If there are'd' particles, then the swarm size is represented as a two dimensional array of order "*n x d*". Each column is a vector of compute resource ids for *n* workloads. Here in the present problem as we consider assigning '*n*' workloads to '*m*' hosts, where n<<m, the resultant vector will be same as the sequence vector.

Scheduling Heuristic Handler

A scheduling heuristic handler has been designed to invoke SAPSO and it has been shown in Figure 2. The handler gets a list of '*n*' workloads to be processed in a time window 't_0' as well as the number of compute resources available for processing the workloads. Based on their values the dimension of the particle is fixed. It stores the static power model of resource pool. The handler gets the resource dynamics of the resource pool such as PE's count and memory size of all available resources as well as present power consumption and then it invokes SAPSO.

Algorithm SAPSO

The detailed algorithm of SAPSO has been shown in Figure 3. To begin with, the PSO parameters are initialized with empirical values as shown in Table 3 (Shi & Eberhart, 1998). The position vectors and velocity vectors for the entire population are set randomly. The sequence vector and operation vector are found as explained before. The fitness function value of each particle denotes the maximum number of VM requests that can

Figure 5. Performance comparison of Std PSO, MEPSO and SAPSO in detecting and tracking the performance efficient as well as power efficient VM provisioning

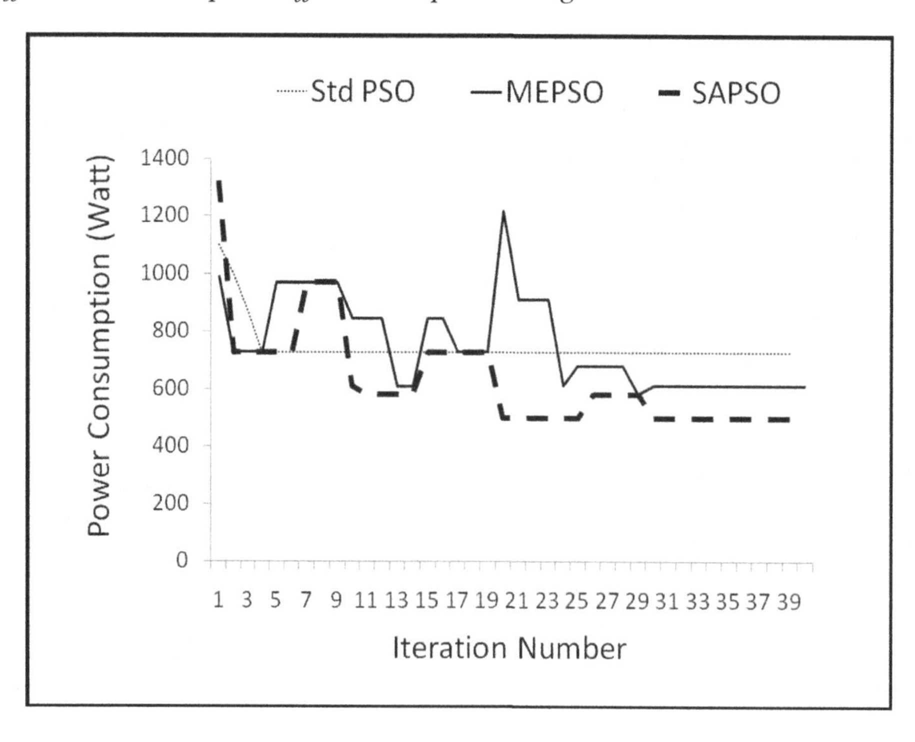

Figure 6. Analysis of Invalid VM provisioning showing increase in the number of failed VM provisioning with increase in the VM requests

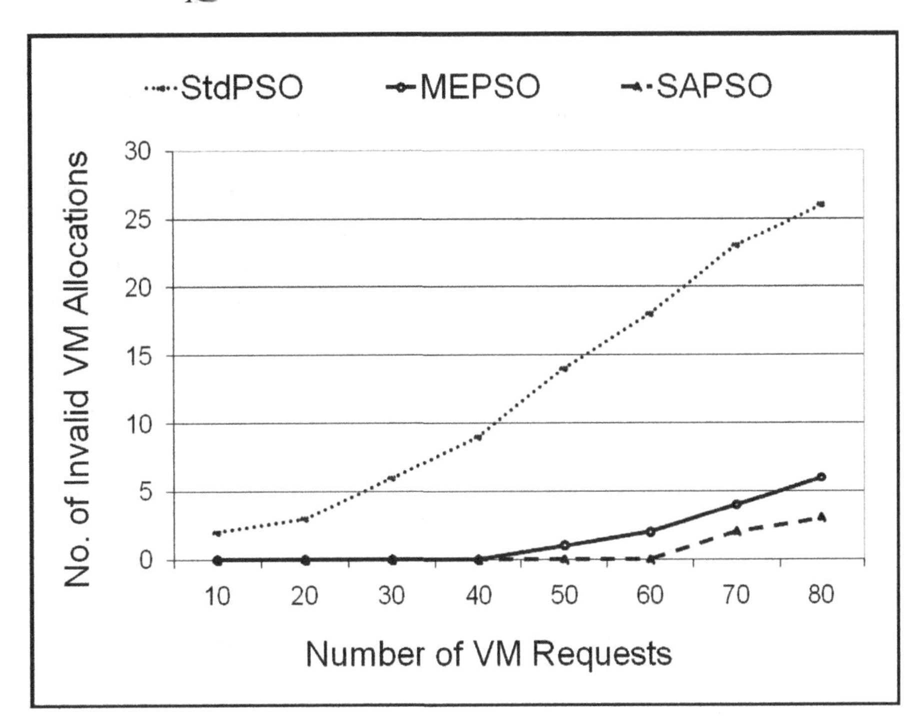

be fulfilled by its mapping using which the mean allocation value is found. For the first iteration, the personal best position vector p_i^ℓ is set with current position vector of each particle. To find p^g, the set of '*a*' particles, which have maximum mean allocation value θ_r ,r $\in \{1, 2, 3, \ldots, a\}$ is found. Next it finds the optimal mapping out of '*a*' particles, which has minimum increment in power consumption by referring to static power model shown in Table 2. The concept used for power aware provisioning takes into consideration that the total incremental power drawn in a lightly loaded host is less compared to heavily loaded host (Verma, Ahuja, & Neogi, 2008).

An evaporation factor 'T' that varies between 0 and 1 is used to sense and track the changes in the resource pool for subsequent iterations. The purpose of 'T' is to remove outdated personal best position representing the obsolete schedule. So, the personal fitness value is made to decrease at the rate of 'T' over time for self adaptive provisioning. Once the particle continuously fails for improving its current fitness value, the particle's personal best value will gradually decrease. Eventually, it will be lower than the current fitness value and so the personal best fitness value will be replaced by the current fitness value corresponding to the changed environment.

Thus the algorithm is able to sense the new powered on hosts as well as recently powered off hosts and considers this updated information for resource provisioning resulting better resource utilization. Moreover, allocating VMs to unavailable hosts leading to failure in provisioning is minimized. In this algorithm, the particles preserve their personal best position in memory, until the best fitness value becomes obsolete. The fitness value update equations help to capture the change in the resource status such as increase or decrease in memory size, number of available cores, etc. and thus new optimum can be very well captured during the process of optimization. Thus the key concept of SAPSO is it adjusts the Evaporation factor depending on the changes in the resource pool. Finally, the position vector corresponding to the global best vector shows the optimal mapping of VMs onto compute resources using self adaptive power-aware provisioning in the meta scheduler. The VMs are scheduled upon finding such a mapping.

EXPERIMENTAL SETUP

Simulation Environment

The simulated dynamic environment was set up using an event driven simulator CloudSIM toolkit (Calheiros, Ranjan, Beloglazov, De Rose, & Buyya, 2010). A resource pool containing 20 servers were created with different size of memory and varying number of processing cores. A batch of 100 Virtual Machine requests belonging to different users, each one with varying resource requirements, was created. A static power model of Xeon and Opteron series running Linux kernel 2.6.17 Table 2 (Ertl, 2008) is used by the Meta scheduler for the finding the best mapping out the successful mappings. The APA-VMP module calls the optimizer which in turn fetches the resource dynamics in an interval of 4 iterations. The optimizer is run for 40 iterations. According to the availability of resources in the resource pool, the optimizer finds the best VM-host mapping and submits to the dispatcher for allocation.

Real Time Cloud Environment

The position of the proposed meta scheduler APA-VMP in a real time cloud environment is depicted in Figure 4. The cloud computing system usually contains three important sections namely client tier, datacenter tier and middleware tier. The client tier represents the cloud user interface. It is generally a web interface, installed in client's computer to access the cloud system. The data center tier

Figure 7. Analysis of rate of failure for fixed and variable evaporation factor

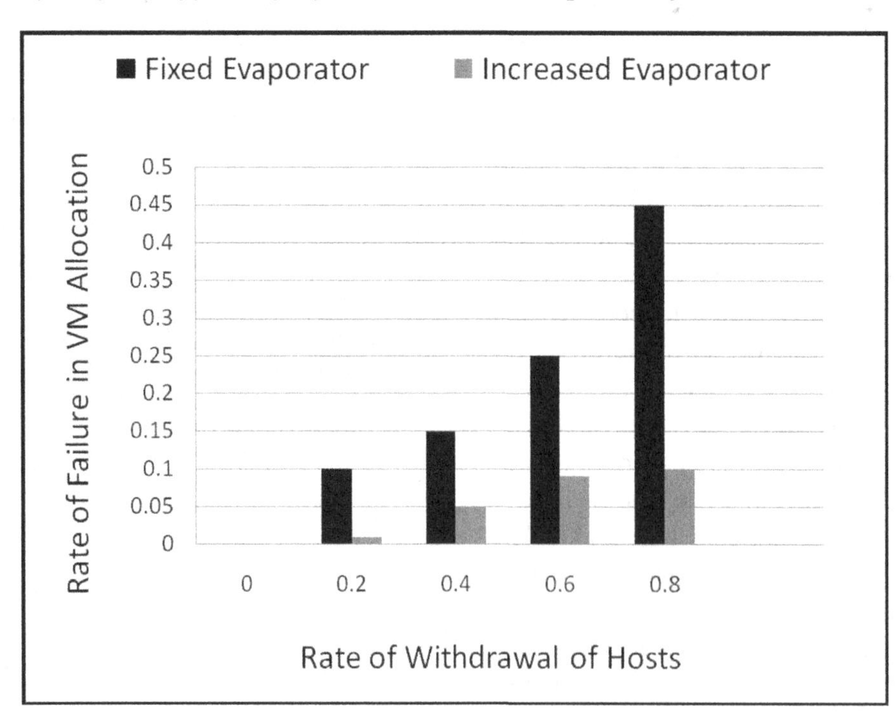

is the physical layer housing thousands of hosts. Each node is installed with a hypervisor either Xen or Kernel Virtual Machine (KVM) for creating virtual machine and it is also installed with local VM management tool called Libvirt which is used to start, stop or migrate a VM. The middleware contains software components for infrastructure management, cluster management, monitoring, and scheduling. Many open source packages are used in the middleware layer. The software oVirt is an open virtual machine management tool which manages large scale infrastructure. It manages many hypervisors and thousands of virtual machines across the hosts. Either Sun Grid Engine (SGE) or XCAT is used as a cluster management tool. Ganglia is monitoring tool used to monitor load on resources. The existing meta scheduler MOAB can be replaced with the proposed APA-VMP for adaptive provisioning in a large scale, dynamic datacenter. The benefit of the proposed tool is power aware VM provisioning in a highly dynamic datacenter.

EXPERIMENTAL RESULTS AND INFERENCE

Experiment 1: Performance comparison of Std PSO, MEPSO and SAPSO in detecting and tracking optimal solution.

A few compute resources were periodically introduced in the resource pool using event driven simulation in every 4th iteration. The VM provisioning was analyzed for standard PSO, MEPSO, and SAPSO. The results were tabulated as given in Table 4 and graphically shown in Figure 5. The Standard PSO does not show any improvement as it has no mechanism to detect the environmental changes; whereas MEPSO and SAPSO are able to detect the arrival of new compute resource and they consider the new one if it is better in fulfilling the VM requirements of the consumer and power conservation requirement of the provider.

Figure 8. Reduction in the number of VM failures by alternate resource mapping

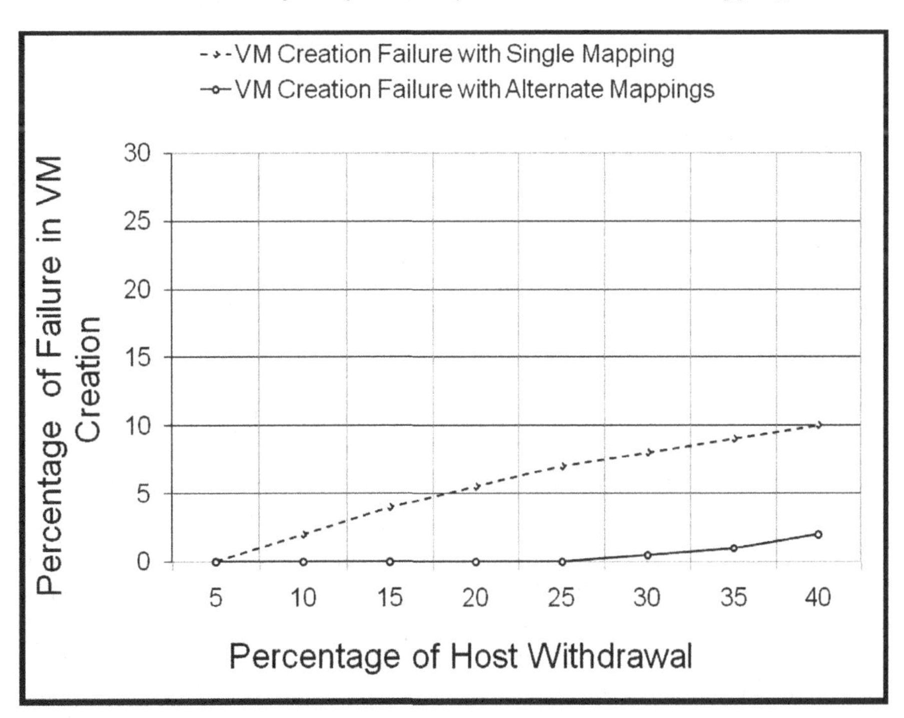

Experiment 2: Analysis of Failure in VM Provisioning.

In the second case, a few computing resources are periodically shutdown. This leads to failure in VM provisioning with stdPSO, because of the unavailability of the mapped host for some VM requests. Figure 6 shows that the increase in the number of invalid provisioning linearly increases with the VM requests. This is because of the outdated memory in Standard PSO, whereas MEPSO and SAPSO are quite efficient in detecting the unavailability of hosts and react in a better manner by reassigning the allocated VMs to the best available hosts.

Experiment 3: Analysis of Rate of Failure for Fixed and Variable Evaporation factor.

This experiment focuses on improving the performance of SAPSO for a highly dynamic resource pool. The rate of failure in VM allocations was recorded for varying withdrawal rate of hosts. The runs were tested with fixed Evaporation factor as well as variable Evaporation factor. The results show that the adjustments in evaporation factor according to the change in resource dynamics reduces the rate of failure in VM allocation and it has been graphically represented in Figure 7. The results of the experiment has also shown that evaporation factor of 0.02 is more suitable to replace the obsolete mapping when the withdrawal rate is less than 30% and evaporation factor of 0.04 performs well when withdrawal rate is in the range of 30-60%.

Experiment 4: Reduction in the number of VM failures by alternate resource mapping.

The SAPSO algorithm has been modified to further minimize VM creation failures, due to the unavailability of provisioned host. This is done by supporting multiple global best representing alternate schedules for VM creation. Instead of single global best vector, the modified SAPSO maintains two global best vectors. The first mapping stores the global best job-host mapping and the second mapping stores the alternate job-host mapping. While first global best vector represents the particle q corresponding to minimum increment in power Δ_q, the second global best vector represents the particle *q'* with second minimum increment in power $\Delta_{q'}$ and is used as an alter mapping.

As the problem considered is multimodal, for a given set of jobs and resources, there are many solutions or job-host mappings which fulfill the resource requirement of jobs, with minimum incremental power. The choice of mapping plays an important role. The second global best is assigned the particle mapping which has a maximum number of mutually exclusive target host ids with the first global best vector. The provisioning process which preserves alternate mapping perform better compared to that with single global mapping, in reducing the number of VM creation failures, especially in scenarios, where resource withdrawal event happens in the interval between end of provisioning and start of dispatching or during dispatching. The result of the experiment 4 is depicted in Figure 8.

CONCLUSION AND FUTURE WORK

As the main purpose of cloud computing is to facilitate consumers to manage unexpected demand in resources, the datacenter becomes inherently dynamic. In the IaaS cloud, there is an instantaneous resource provisioning as well as resource reclamation when the customer no longer requires the resources. As cloud resource pool is enormous, only heuristic method is better in providing reasonable solution within a short duration compared to conventional methods. The dynamic nature of the pool necessitates the application of dynamic PSO to sense the change in the resource state and respond efficiently. The proposed SAPSO is better compared to MEPSO as the former is self adaptive and preserves the fitness value corresponding to the optimal solution until it becomes obsolete. The MEPSO takes more time to find optimal solution compared to SAPSO, as the re-randomization causes the particle to forget the memory and re-computation of fitness value brings computational overhead. The SAPSO can also be used as a resource monitor to find the frequency and degree of change in the resource pool to maintain the supply and demand in equilibrium. Our future work will focus on hybridization of PSO for VM provisioning in large scale dynamic federated datacenters.

REFERENCES

Akjiratikarl, C., Yenradee, P., & Drake, P. R. (2007). PSO-based algorithm for home care worker scheduling in the UK. *Computers & Industrial Engineering, 53*(4), 559–583. doi:10.1016/j.cie.2007.06.002

Beltran, F. (2005). The use of efficient cost-allocation mechanisms for congestion pricing in data networks with priority service models. *International Journal of Business Data Communications and Networking, 1*(1), 33–49. doi:10.4018/jbdcn.2005010103

Calheiros, R. N., Ranjan, R., Beloglazov, A., De Rose, C. A. F., & Buyya, R. (2010). *Cloudsim: A toolkit for modeling and simulation of cloud computing environments and evaluation of resource provisioning algorithms: Software: Practice and experience*. New York, NY: John Wiley & Sons.

Carlisle, A., & Dozler, G. (2002). Tracking changing extrema with adaptive particle swarm optimizer. In *Proceedings of Soft Computing*. Multimedia, Biomedicine, Image Processing and Financial Engineering.

Coffman, E. G. (1976). *Computer and job-shop scheduling theory*. New York, NY: John Wiley & Sons.

Cui, X., & Potok, T. E. (2007). Distributed adaptive particle swarm optimizer in dynamic environment. In *Proceedings of the International Symposium on Parallel and Distributed Processing* (p. 1).

Dikaiakos, M. D., Pallis, G., Katsaros, D., Mehra, P., & Vakali, A. (2009). Cloud computing–distributed internet computing for IT and scientific research. *IEEE Internet Computing, 13*(5), 10–13. doi:10.1109/MIC.2009.103

Du, W., & Li, B. (2008). Multi-strategy ensemble particle swarm optimization for dynamic optimization. *International Journal of Information Sciences, 178*(15), 3096–3109.

Eberhart, R. C., & Shi, Y. (2001). Tracking and optimizing dynamic systems with particle swarms. In. *Proceedings of the Congress on Evolutionary Computation, 1*, 94.

Engelbrecht, A. P. (2007). *Computational intelligence: An introduction* (2nd ed.). New York, NY: John Wiley & Sons.

Ertl, A. (2008). *How much electricity does a computer consume?* Retrieved from http://www.complang.tuwien.ac.at/anton/computer-power-consumption.html

Fidanova, S. (2006). Simulated annealing for grid scheduling problem. In *Proceedings of IEEE International Symposium on Modern Computing* (pp. 41-45).

French, T. (2009). Virtual organizational trust requirements: Can semiotics help fill the trust gap? *International Journal of Intelligent Information Technologies, 5*(2). doi:10.4018/jiit.2009040101

Garey, M. R., & Johnson, D. S. (1979). *Computers and intractability: A guide to the theory of NP-completeness*. San Francisco, CA: Freeman.

Hamidi, H., & Vafaei, A. (2009). Evaluation of fault tolerant mobile agents in distributed systems. *International Journal of Intelligent Information Technologies*, *5*(1). doi:10.4018/jiit.2009010103

Hu, X., & Eberhart, R. C. (2001). Tracking dynamic systems with PSO: Where's the cheese? In *Proceedings of the Workshop on Particle Swarm Optimization*, Indianapolis, IN.

Hu, X., & Eberhart, R. C. (2002). Adaptive particle swarm optimization: Detection and response to dynamic systems. In *Proceedings of the Congress on Evolutionary Computation* (pp. 1666-1670).

Hu, X., Shi, Y., & Eberhart, R. C. (2004). Recent advances in particle swarm. In *Proceedings of the IEEE Congress on Evolutionary Computation* (pp. 90-97).

Jeyarani, R., Vasanth Ram, R., & Nagaveni, N. (2008). Implementation of efficient light weight internal scheduler for high throughput grid environment. In *Proceedings of the National Conference on Advanced Computing in Computer Applications*. Coimbatore, India.

Jeyarani, R., Vasanth Ram, R., & Nagaveni, N. (2010). Design and implementation of an efficient two level scheduler for cloud computing environment. In *Proceedings of the 10th International Conference on Cluster, Cloud and Grid*, Melbourne, Australia (pp. 585-586).

Kennedy, J., & Eberhart, R. C. (1995). Particle swarm optimization. In *Proceedings of the IEEE International Conference on Neural Networks* (Vol. 4).

Mika, M., Waligora, G., & Weglarz, J. (2004). *A meta-heuristic approach to scheduling workflow jobs on a grid, Grid resource management: State of the art and future trend*. Boston, MA: Kluwer Academic.

Mladenovic, N., & Hansen, P. (1997). Variable neighborhood search. *Computers & Operations Research*, *24*(1), 1097–1100. doi:10.1016/S0305-0548(97)00031-2

Nurmi, D., Wolski, R., Grzegorczyk, C., Obertelli, G., Soman, S., Youseff, L., et al. (2009). The eucalyptus open source cloud computing system. In *Proceedings of the 9th IEEE/ACM International Symposium on Cluster Computing and the Grid* (p. 124).

Page, A. J., Keane, T. M., & Naughton, T. J. (2010). Multi-heuristic dynamic task allocation using genetic algorithms in a heterogeneous distributed system. *Journal of Parallel and Distributed Computing*, *70*(7), 758–766. doi:10.1016/j.jpdc.2010.03.011

Page, A. J., & Naughton, T. J. (2005). Dynamic task scheduling using genetic algorithms for heterogeneous distributed computing. In *Proceedings of the IEEE International Symposium on Parallel and Distributed Processing* (p. 189).

Page, J., & Naughton, J. (2005). Framework for task scheduling in heterogeneous distributed computing using genetic algorithms. *Artificial Intelligence*, *24*(3-4), 415–429. doi:10.1007/s10462-005-9002-x

Pandey, S., Wu, L., Guru, S., & Buyya, R. (2009). A particle swarm optimization (PSO)-based heuristic for scheduling workflow applications in cloud computing environment. In *Proceedings of the 24th IEEE International Conference on Advanced Information Networking and Applications*, Perth, Australia (pp. 400-407).

Russel, S., & Yoon, V. Y. (2009). Agents, availability, awareness and decision making. *International Journal of Intelligent Information Technologies*, *5*(4). doi:10.4018/jiit.2009080704

Sadhasivam, S., Nagaveni, N., Jayarani, R., & Ram, R. V. (2009). Design and implementation of an efficient two level scheduler for cloud computing environment. In *Proceedings of the International Conference on Advances in Recent Technologies in Communication and Computing*. Kottayam, India (pp. 884-886).

Sadhasivam, S., & Rajendran, V. (2008). An efficient approach to task scheduling in computational grids. *International Journal of Computer Science and Applications*, *6*(1), 53–69.

Shi, Y. H., & Eberhart, R. C. (1998). Parameter selection in particle swarm optimization. In *Proceedings of* the *Annual Conference on Evolutionary Programming*, San Diego, CA.

Shi, Y. H., & Eberhart, R. C. (1999). Empirical study of particle swarm optimization. In *Proceedings of the Congress on Evolutionary Computation* (Vol. 3).

Smith, J. E., & Nair, R. (2005). *Virtual machines - versatile platforms for systems and processes*. San Francisco, CA: Morgan Kauffman.

Sotomayor, B., Montero, R. S., Llorente, I. M., & Foster, I. (2008). *Capacity leasing in cloud systems using the OpenNebula engine.* Paper presented at the Workshop on Cloud Computing and its Applications, Chicago, IL.

Sotomayor, B., Montero, R. S., Llorente, I. M., & Foster, I. (2009). Virtual infrastructure management in private and hybrid clouds. *IEEE Internet Computing*, *13*(5), 14–22. doi:10.1109/MIC.2009.119

Tasgetiren, M. F., Sevkli, M., Liang, Y.-C., & Gencyilmaz, G. (2004). Particle swarm optimization algorithm for permutation flow shop sequencing problem. In M. Dorigo, M. Birattari, C. Blum, L. M. Gambardella, F. Mondada, & T. Stutzle (Eds.), *Proceedings of the 4th International Workshop on Ant Colony, Optimization, and Swarm Intelligence* (LNCS 3172, pp. 382-390).

Tasgetiren, M. F., Sevkli, M., Liang, Y.-C., & Gencyilmaz, G. (2004). Particle swarm optimization algorithm for single-machine total weighted tardiness problem. In. *Proceedings of the Congress on Evolutionary Computation, 2*, 1412–1419.

Verma, A., Ahuja, P., & Neogi, A. (2008). pMapper: Power and migration cost aware application placement in virtualized systems. In V. Issarny & R. Schantz (Eds.), *Proceedings of Middleware* (LNCS 5346, pp. 243-264).

Wang, L., von Laszewskiy, G., Dayalz, J., & Wang, F. (2010). Towards energy aware scheduling for precedence constrained parallel tasks in a cluster with DVFS. In *Proceedings of the International Conference on Cluster, Cloud and Grid*, Melbourne, Australia (pp. 368-377).

This work was previously published in the International Journal of Intelligent Information Technologies, Volume 7, Issue 2, edited by Vijayan Sugumaran, pp. 25-44, copyright 2011 by IGI Publishing (an imprint of IGI Global).

Chapter 7
Eliciting User Preferences in Multi-Agent Meeting Scheduling Problem

Mohammad Amin Rigi
K. N. Toosi University of Technology, Iran

Farid Khoshalhan
K. N. Toosi University of Technology, Iran

ABSTRACT

Meeting Scheduling Problem (MSP) arranges meetings between a number of participants. Reaching consensus in arranging a meeting is very diffuclt and time-consuming when the number of participants is large. One efficient approach for overcoming this problem is the use of multi-agent systems. In a multi-agent system, agents are deciding on behalf of their users. They must be able to elicite their users' preferences in an effective way. This paper focuses on the elicitation of users' preferences. Analytical hierarchy process (AHP) - which is known for its ability to determine preferences - is used in this research. Specifically, an adaptive preference modeling technique based on AHP is developed and implemented in a system and the initial validation results are encouraging.

INTRODUCTION

Meeting Scheduling Problem (MSP) is a distributed task in which there are several participants, and they are looking for times and places to hold their meetings. Each of the participants has their own preference and calendar (Al-ani, 2007). Meeting scheduling is naturally a time consuming and iterative activity. Tsuruta and Shintani (2000) have defined an MSP as "the process of determining a starting time and an ending time of an event in which several people will participate." Solving a meeting scheduling problem involves satisfying conflicted preferences between individuals. Constraints in the context of scheduling problem are divided into two kinds, hard and soft. Hard constraints are conditions that must be satisfied (like the availability of an individual), whereas soft constraints maybe violated. However, it would be better to satisfy them as much as possible

DOI: 10.4018/978-1-4666-2047-6.ch007

Figure 1. Simplified components of the preference modeling system

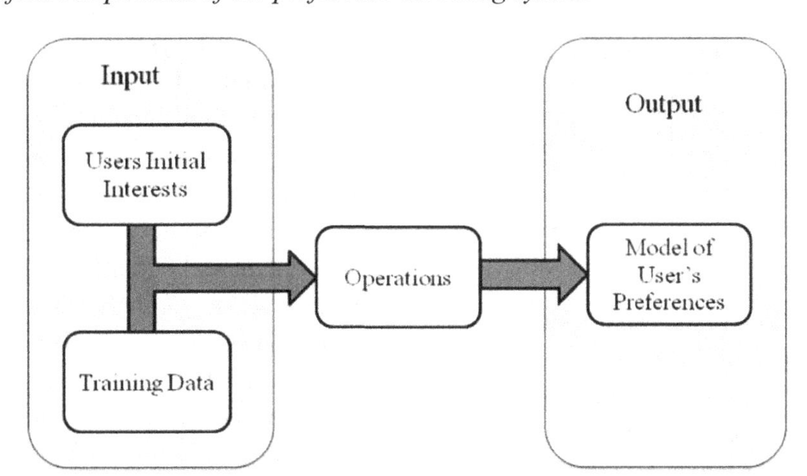

(Abdennadher & Schlenker, 1999). Automated meeting scheduling has two important effects; it will reduce the time that users spend on scheduling, and it will also try to find an efficient schedule. Before we introduce the preference problem, we provide a closer look at the scheduling problem.

There are two main approaches in solving a meeting scheduling problem. The first approach is the centralized approach. In a centralized system each of the participants sends their preferences to the meeting scheduling manager. It is the manager's job to search for a good feasible answer that satisfies all the participants (Ephrati et al., 1994). In this case, a meeting scheduling problem has been seen as a Constraint Satisfaction Problems (CSP) (Chun et al., 2003; BenHassine et al., 2006). However, in recent years many researchers have used distributed and multi-agent systems in order to find good solutions (Mishra & Mishra, 2010; Mazumdar & Mishra, 2010). There have been enormous attempts for solving the CSP in a distributed way such as Distributed CSPs or DCSPs (Maheswaran et al., 2006). Even so, there is another important distributed method in MSP solving, which is the multi-agent negotiation approach. In this method MSP is a treated as a multi-agent agreement problem, and each agent represents a user (Crawford & Veloso, 2004, 2005). Increasingly, software agents perform tasks on behalf of their human counterpart in a variety of application domains (Kuppuswamy & Chithralekha, 2010; Russell & Yoon, 2009).

In this paper, we formulate the MSP as a multi-agent problem and base it on the work

Table 1. Fundamental scale for pairwise comparisons

Intensity of importance	Definition	Explanation
1	Equal importance	Two elements contribute equally to the objective
3	Moderate Importance	Experience and judgment slightly favor one element over another
5	Strong importance	Experience and judgment strongly favor one element over another
7	Very strong importance	One element is favored very strongly over another
9	Extreme importance	The evidence favoring one element over another is of the highest possible order of affirmation
Intensities of 2, 4, 6 and 8 can be used to express intermediate values.		

Table 2. Example of a pairwise comparison matrix

	Choices (Decisions)			
Choices (Decisions)		A	B	C
	A	1	1/3	5
	B		1	7
	C			1

discussed in Crawford (2009) and Ephrati et al. (1996). In Crawford (2009) the author introduces a semi-cooperative learning negotiation agent. This agent could develop a preference model of the user while it is watching the negotiation process. To accomplish this, the agent uses the system log (history). The drawback of this work is that the agent needs a time consuming learning process to understand a user's preference. In addition, there are no facilities for agents that have no information about the history of negotiation (or there exists no information). One solution to circumvent this problem is the use of Analytical Hierarchy Process (AHP) in order to make a prior model of the user's preference. In essence, this research extends the prior work of Crawford (2009) and Ephrati et al. (1996). Our proposed method acquires pairwise preferences of choices from a user in the very first step, and this model can learn as well. This means that when the user negotiates with other participants, the model will update itself. And as times go by, this model will be dependent on learning data (experience), not on the prior knowledge required to be stored in the system. A simplified high level characterization of the MSP system preference modeling is shown in Figure 1.

The rest of the paper is organized as follows. The next section introduces the concept of meeting scheduling problem as an agreement problem and discusses some of the approaches that are used in this model. The following section provides an introduction to analytical hierarchy process (AHP) and shows how AHP can be used to help users to prioritize their choices. After this, we discuss our adaptive preference modeling technique. Later in the chapter, we provide the details of the experimental validation and the results. Finally, the last section includes a conclusion and future work.

MEETING SCHEDULING AS AN AGREEMENT PROBLEM

In this section, we introduce the agreement problem in the multi-agent system based on (Mailler & Lesser, 2003). Specifically, we discuss the Extended Incremental Multi-agent Agreement Problem with Preferences (EIMAPP) (Mailler & Lesser, 2003). An agreement problem (AP) consists of the following elements:

1. A set of decision makers (here agents)
2. A set of variables (each variable has a set of interested decision makers, i.e. agents)
3. A set of options or values

Figure 2. Preference graph with three options

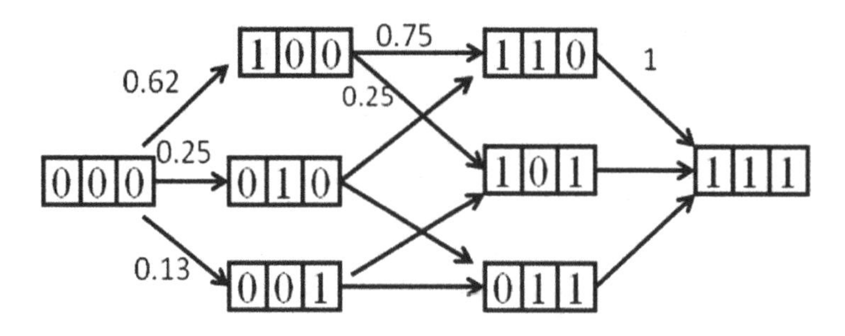

Figure 3. Algorithm for finding weights in a preference graph

```
Make n × n pairwise comparison matrix;
Let user fill the matrix;
Make a preference graph;
Function calculate_weights (bit_vector input)
        Set OPTIONS = options where their corresponding bit in bit vector is zero;
        Build a comparison matrix based on options in OPTIONS;
        Calculate weights of preferences with Eigen Vector.
        For i=0 to OPTIONS.length
        new_bit_vector = Make a new bit_vector by adding a "1" to the input
        bit_vector based on option in the ith place in the set OPTIONS;
        Add corresponding calculated weight on transition "input→
        new_bit_vector" in preference graph;
        Calculate_weights(new_bit_vector);
        End For
End Function
```

For solving an agreement problem, all variables must have an option. In addition, for assigning such an option to a variable, all of the participating decision makers for that variable must agree on the assignment.

In the meeting scheduling domain, consider the following scenario. Decision makers are a set of agents (which are representing their users), e.g. student agent or professor agent. A variable is a meeting, e.g. project report meeting or teacher assistant meeting (for these two meetings, we have two variables). Further, options are available times in the weekly calendar. For example, Wednesday 10 a.m., Wednesday 2 p.m. or Thursday 9 a.m. are three options (values) that could be assigned. A solution is given by assigning options to variables, for example, professor and student agree to meet each other on Wednesday at 2 p.m. Here, decision makers can reach an agreement in more than one round. For example, in the first round, professor agent suggests Wednesday 2 p.m. and the student agent proposes Thursday 9 a.m. In the second round, both professor agent and student agent propose Wednesday 2 p.m. and an agreement is reached.

With this short introduction, we provide the formal definition of an EIMAPP (Extended Incremental Multi-agent Agreement Problem with Preferences) (Mailler & Lesser, 2003).

An EIMAP is a tuple: <A, O, V, T, P> where:

- **A:** Set of agents.
- **O:** Set of options(values).

Table 3. Pairwise comparison matrix for three options

		Options		
		O_1	O_2	O_3
Options	O_1	1	1/3	5
	O_2	3	1	7
	O_3	1/5	1/7	1

Table 4. Priority vector for pairwise comparison matrix in Table 5

Option	Priority
o_1	0.2828
o_2	0.6434
o_3	0.0738

- **V:** Set of variables. Each variable has a set of decision makers ($D_v \in A$). D_v decides which option can be assigned to variable v.
- **T:** Distribution that shows the arrival of new variables. (For example when a new meeting is being held).
- **P:** Set of preference functions. The function shows the preference of assigning an option to a variable by a certain agent.

According to Mailler and Lesser (2003) the solution of EIMAP is a tuple, N = <R, w, M, H>, where:

- R shows restrictions over options. Specifically, R is a function that restricts assignment of options to variables. R(a, O) shows valid options of agent a. (for example with R we make sure that an agent cannot make two meetings at the same time)
- w is a tuple, $<N_p, N_{range}, N_{rule}>$ where
  - The first element (N_p) is the negotiation protocol. The protocol determines how an option can be assigned to a variable. EIMAP uses a round-based negotiation protocol, in which when an option is offered, it will remain on the table. When an intersection is found on the table, we know that an agreement is reached.
  - N_{range} shows how many options an agent can offer in a round by determining the minimum and the maximum of the number of eligible options.
  - N_{rule} is a set of rules about the offers.
- M is a mapping from variables to options. This mapping is the result of negotiation and agreement between agents.
- H stands for history. It is a set that contains all the offers that have been made during the negotiation process.

Having gained familiarity with the negotiation process, it is time to discuss the preference modeling of an agent. As mentioned earlier, AHP (Analytical Hierarchy Process) is used in the preference modeling. Therefore, in the next section, a brief description of AHP and its role in preference modeling is provided.

ANALYTICAL HIERARCHY PROCESS

The AHP is a method for handling complex decision making. AHP assists the decision makers to find and pick an option that best suits their

Figure 4. Preference graph after the first step

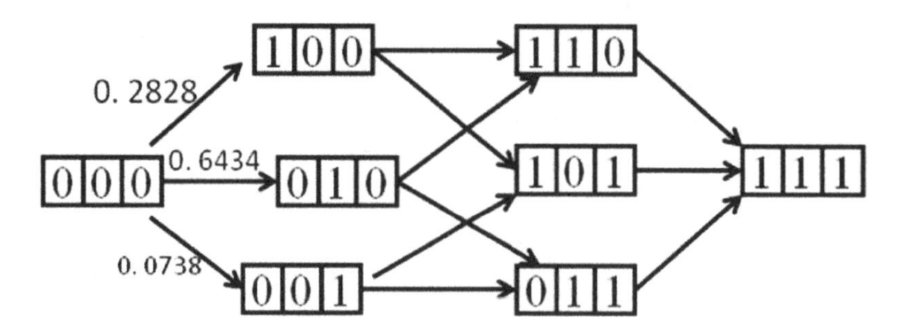

Table 5. Pairwise comparison matrix when transition starts from bit vector "100" (Figure 4)

	Options		
Options		o_2	o_3
	o_2	1	7
	o_3	1/7	1

requirements based on their knowledge of the problem. Rooted in mathematics and psychology, AHP was developed by Thomas L. Saaty in the 1970s. It has been extensively studied and polished since then (Cogger & Yu, 1985; Saaty, 2009). AHP gives a comprehensive and rational framework for structuring a decision problem, representing and quantifying its elements, relating those elements to overall goals, and evaluating alternative solutions.

Users of AHP first decompose their decision problem into a hierarchy of more easily comprehensible sub-problems, each of which can be analyzed separately. The elements of the hierarchy can relate to any aspect of the decision problem — tangible or intangible, carefully measured or roughly estimated, well or poorly-understood —anything that applies to the decision at hand.

Once the hierarchy is created, the decision makers methodically evaluate its various elements by comparing them to one another two at a time. In making the comparisons, the decision makers can use concrete data about the elements, or they can use their judgments about the elements' relative meaning and importance. The essence of AHP is that human judgments, and not just the underlying information, can be used in performing the evaluations. AHP converts these evaluations into numerical values that can be processed and compared over the entire range of the problem. A numerical weight or priority is derived for each element of the hierarchy, allowing diverse and often incommensurable elements to be compared to one another in a rational and consistent way.

Pairwise Comparisons

Decision makers compare the elements two by two, to incorporate their judgments about the various elements in the hierarchy. The Criteria will be compared as to how important they are to the decision makers, with respect to the Goal. The number of comparisons depends on the number of things to be compared. However, how can we compare two decisions? In other words, how can we show the importance of one decision over another? In AHP, there are standards for scaling the importance of available decisions. Table 1 shows the fundamental scales for pairwise comparisons and Table 2 provides an example of a pairwise comparison matrix.

To fill the lower triangular matrix, we use the reciprocal values of the upper diagonal. If a_{ij} is the element of row i column j of the matrix, then the lower diagonal is filled using the following formula:

$$a_{ji}=1/a_{ij} \quad (1)$$

Finding Priority Vectors

In a complex decision making activity with many participants, questions such as the following are common: How to compute priorities? What does it mean to say that the opinions are consistent? How to measure the consistency of subjective judgment? In this section

This section discusses how these questions can be answered, with the use of the example given in Table 2. If a decision maker prefers B to A we

Table 6. Pairwise comparison matrix when transition starts from bit vector "010"

	Options		
Options		o_1	o_3
	o_1	1	5
	o_3	1/5	1

Table 7. Pairwise comparison matrix when transition starts from bit vector "001"

	Options		
Options		o_1	o_2
	o_1	1	1/3
	o_2	3	1

represent it as B>A. If the decision maker prefers A to C, we indicate that as A>C. From a logical perspective we can derive B>C, because B>A and A>C. This logic of preference is called transitive property. Nevertheless, it is notable that human beings make decisions based on logic and feelings. Imagine that in the example above, the decision maker prefers C to B. If the preferences be transitive we call the judgment consistent, otherwise we call it inconsistent. A comparison matrix A is said to be consistent if $a_{ij}*a_{jk} = a_{ik}$ for all i, j and k. However, we shall not force the consistency. Too much consistency is undesirable because we are dealing with human judgments.

Typically, the Eigen vector method is used for computing the priority vector. It consists of the following steps (Cogger & Yu, 1985):

- Let matrix A be the pairwise comparison matrix
- Matrix B = $(A - \lambda I)$
- Calculate λ from (2)

$$\det(A - \lambda I) = 0 \quad (2)$$

- Calculate priority vector from (3)

$$(A - \lambda_{max} I)P = 0 \quad (3)$$

where, P is the priority vector.

In the multi-agent meeting scheduling problem, we use AHP to prioritize the options.

PROPOSED PREFERENCE MODELING APPROACH FOR AGENTS

In this section, we discuss our proposed approach for developing the preference model for agents in the context of Extended Incremental Multi-agent Agreement Problem with Preferences (EIMAPP). We know that agents are negotiating on behalf of their user, and that their users might have complex preferences. However, the problem is how to create such a preference model?

Our approach is a hybrid approach; first we calculate users' preferences through AHP. Then, our model passively observes the user's assignments and updates as they occur. The proposed preference model not only learns about options themselves, it also discovers relationships between options. For example, it gathers that option 2 is rarely offered before option 3. Alternatively, option 4 is likely to be assigned after option 2. As another example, in the multi-agent meeting scheduling problem, many users have time of day preferences, for instance they may prefer afternoon times to morning times. But their users' preferences are also based on relationships between options, such as preferences like back-to-back or spread-out scheduling (Crawford, 2009).

In the rest of this section, we discuss the model in three parts. In the first part, we discuss how we can model user's preference through a graph model. In the second part, we describe how to build this model based on AHP data. In last part we show how this model becomes adaptive and updates itself based on the experience gathered by watching user's actions.

Table 8. Priority vector when transition starts from bit vector "100"

Option	Priority
o_2	0.875
o_3	0.125

Table 9. Priority vector when transition starts from bit vector "010"

Option	Priority
o_1	0.8333
o_3	0.1667

Modeling User Preference

We develop a model of user's preferences by calculating probabilities of the moves between possible states of user's choice assignments. The present state of user's option assignments determines the states that are reachable by the assignment of a new user's preference (by placing probabilities on the transitions).

A user's preference model over options is a weighted directed acyclic graph, P=(S, E), where:

- S is set of possible states of user's assignments. Assignments is a bit vector, one bit for each possible option. For each option, a "1" indicates there is a variable assigned to the option, and a "0" indicates the option is unassigned.
- Let m, n $\in$ S, then (m, n) $\in$ E if and only if we can get to n from m by adding one new assignment. In the bit vector, we will have at least two "1"s indicating the assignment of m and n.
- Each edge (m, n) $\in$ E has a weighting corresponding to the probability of the transition: m => n.

In Figure 2, an example of a preference graph with 3 options is shown. The numbers on the edges show the probability of that transition.

Building the Preference Model Based on Prior Knowledge (AHP)

As indicated earlier, a graph based preference model is used. However, the problem is how to find the weights of the transitions. We use the algorithm shown in Figure 3, which is explained below with an example.

Let a set of options be O = {o_1, o_2, o_3} where o_1 represents a candidate time for meeting on Monday morning at 10 a.m., o_2 is Monday at 2 p.m. and o_3 is Tuesday 9 a.m. We make a 3×3 pairwise comparison matrix and ask the user to fill the matrix. The filled pairwise comparison matrix is shown in Table 3.

Then we use the Eigen vector method to create the priority vector, which is shown in Table 4.

We then assign the calculated weights onto the graph. The output of preference graph up to this point is shown in Figure 4.

The "calculate_weights" function shown in Figure 3 is a recursive function. It calculates the weights of the edges in the graph similar to a DFS (Depth First Search) function. The weights can also be computed similar to a BFS (Breath First Search) function. We demonstrate the rest of example using a BFS. The pairwise comparison matrices for any two of the three options are shown in Tables 5, 6, and 7. These comparisons correspond to the transitions starting from the different bit vectors shown in Figure 4.

Using the Eigen vector method to determine the priorities (weights in preference graph), we get the priority values of the options for each transition. Table 8 shows the priority vector when the transition starts from the bit vector "100". Similarly, Table 9 and Table 10 show the priority vector for transitions from "010" and "001" bit vectors.

Finally, using the priority values from the tables, the complete preference graph is generated, which is shown in Figure 5.

Table 10. Priority vector when transition starts from bit vector "001"

Option	Priority
o_1	0.25
o_2	0.75

Figure 5. Preference graph

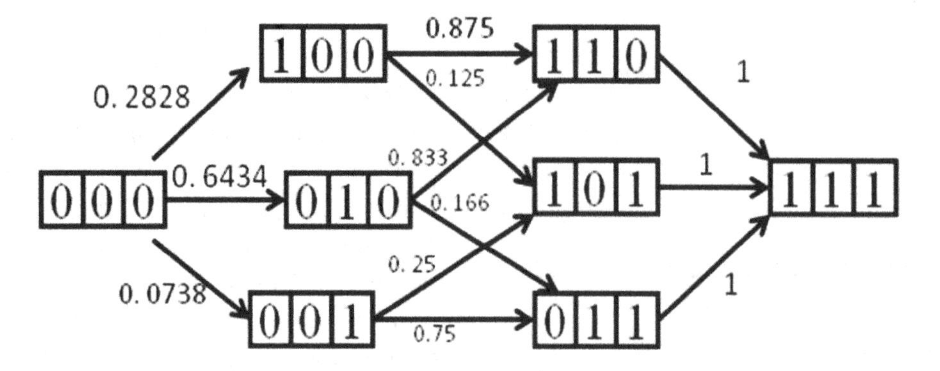

Creating a Learning Model

In this section, we discuss how we can update the preference graph by watching user's negotiation or accessing negotiation history. Training data T is a set of training instance pairs, t_i, where:

T={ t_i | i=1,…,n and t_i= (current_assignment$_i$, new_assignment$_i$) }

where n is the number of options. Once we have the training data, the preference graph is created using the approach discussed in the previous section. Given a preference graph, then we determine the frequency of each transition, and finally we calculate the probability for each of the transitions by dividing the frequency of one assignment by the sum of all frequencies. For example, we can find the weight for transition "a=>b_1" with the following equation.

$$w = \frac{frequency(a, b_1)}{\sum_{i=1}^{m} frequency(a, b_i)} \quad (4)$$

where m is the number of nodes in the preference graph that are adjacent to a.

However, the learning process might be slow, especially when there is no training data. When there is a small training set, and only the learning model is used without AHP, the error rate will be high. In the worst condition, users do not want to participate in the negotiation themselves, because it is a time consuming process. So we are proposing a hybrid approach for finding preferences using both AHP and the learning model.

In other words, we want to find the weights of the graph using both prior knowledge and learning knowledge. Let α be the weight of a transition in the preference graph achieved by AHP and β be

Figure 6. Flowchart of the system

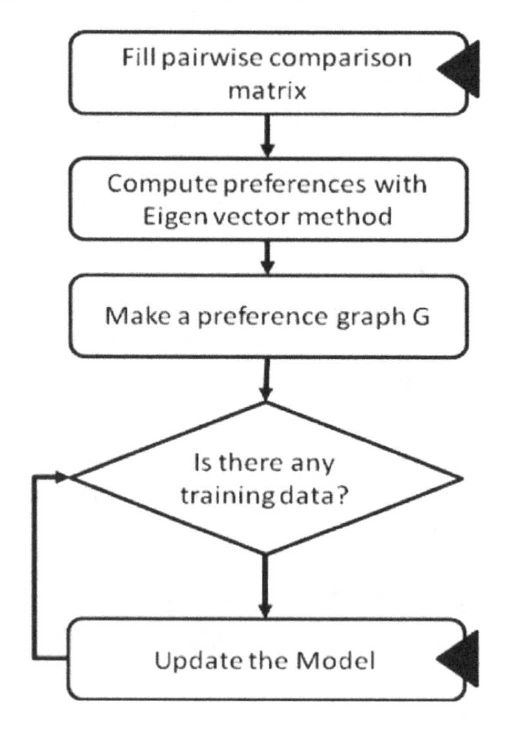

Table 11. Pairwise comparison matrix for meeting scheduling problem

	Mon. 10am	Mon. 11am	Tues. 11am	Tues. 14pm	Wed. 16pm	Thurs. 9am
Mon. 10am	1	3	3	5	7	1
Mon. 11am		1	3	3	7	1
Tues. 11am			1	3	5	1/3
Tues. 14pm				1	3	1/3
Wed. 16pm					1	1/5
Thurs. 9am						1

the weight of that transition calculated using the learning model. The adaptive weight is achieved from the equation below:

$$w = \varphi\alpha + (1 - \varphi)\beta \qquad (5)$$

where φ's value is between zero and one. φ is calculated from following equation:

$$\varphi = \frac{1}{x^{s}} \qquad (6)$$

where x is greater than one and s is the number of training samples.

It is obvious that the calculated weight from (5) is between zero and one and w is the weighted average of α and β. When the training data is small φ is close to one and w is equal to α (the value that AHP calculated). When the agent watches user's negotiation, s grows and φ approaches to zero. Therefore w becomes closer to β (value achieved by learning). Larger x values are used when learning is more important than the injected knowledge. Thus, this model combines two aforementioned methods for finding preferences.

IMPLEMENTATION, EXPERIMENTS, AND EVALUATION

This section presents our experiments and the evaluation of our approach for modeling users' preferences in the multi-agent meeting scheduling problem. This section has two parts; in first part the implementation and technical issues are discussed. The second part discusses the experiments and the results.

For developing a system that is portable across a number of platforms we developed Java-based agents. We used Java Agent Development Environment (JADE) to execute the negotiating agents. As discussed before, our system has two inputs, namely, users' initial interests and the training data (Figure 1). It is notable that the learning model in this system is an adaptive one. It follows the negotiations and updates itself. The training data includes the previously gathered negotiation data (system log) plus the currently running negotiation data. A comprehensive flowchart showing the various operations of the system is depicted in Figure 6. The black triangles show the phases in which the system gets inputs.

Implementation and Technical Issues

The preference graph is a kind of graph (i.e., the preference graph class is a child of graph class). This means that it inherits all the properties of a graph with some additional functionality such as updating the costs of edges by watching the negotiation rounds. When there are *n* options to discuss, the preference graph will has 2^n-1 nodes. There are two choices for implementing preference

Table 12. Assigning symbols to time slots

Time slot	Mon. 10	Mon. 11	Tues. 11	Tues. 14	Wed. 16	Thurs. 9
Symbol	A	B	C	D	E	F

Table 13. Ordered options based on their priorities which is calculated by AHP

Priority	1st	2nd	3rd	4th	5th	6th
Option	Thurs. 9	Mon. 10	Tues. 14	Mon. 11	Tues. 11	Wed. 16

graph, namely, inked lists and matrix (Horowitz et al., 1995). Each one has its own specification.

Using linked list reduces space usage effectively. For example, when we have 10 options to discuss, there will be about 1000 nodes in the preference graph. This means that the graph matrix will have one million elements. On the other hand matrix implementation of the preference graph is much faster. For example, when we calculate real preferences based on Equation (5), the time complexity is O (n^2) when we use the matrix. Using the linked list model results in exponential time complexity because we have to use depth first search (DFS). If the number of options is small, then using it will not be a big problem. So we used linked list for implementing the preference graph. One of the future works of this research is to implement the negotiation system on portable devices such as cell phones. In that case the tradeoff between space and time will be important.

Experiments

In order to test the developed system we asked users to use our system. Negotiation was over choosing a time for a meeting. The available options can be seen in Table 11. At first, the user filled the corresponding pairwise comparison matrix for AHP.

From Table 11 it can be seen that the user prefers morning meetings over afternoon meeting. Also, it seems that the user prefers to arrange the meeting on beginning or ending days of the week. For example, it is obvious that the user is least likely to set a meeting on Wednesday afternoon at 4pm.

To begin with, a user is asked to start negotiation with other agents (users). Meanwhile, the system is modeling the user's preferences. We developed two different type of scenarios for the negotiation. In the first case, the user insisted on what he had chosen before (AHP). In the second case, the user has a non-persistent behavior. For each scenario, there were eleven negotiations. Depending upon when the consensus is reached, each negotiation had different number of rounds.

To simplify tracking the negotiation rounds, some symbols were used instead of time slots. The mapping between time slots and symbols is shown in the Table 12.

Once the user filled the pairwise comparison matrix, we are able to calculate the priorities of options with AHP (Eigen vector method). After the user filled Table 11, the prioritized output of the table is determined (Table 13).

First Scenario: A Persistent User

As mentioned before, there were two different scenarios for the negotiation. In Table 14 we can see the negotiations of a user that he or she followed. A careful look at the negotiations reveals

Table 14. Negotiation scenarios for persistent user with six options

Negotiation	Rounds
1	[A,F]=>F=>B=>C=>D=>E
2	A=>[B,F]=>C=>D=>E
3	F=>C=>B
4	[A,F]=>[B,C]
5	A=>F
6	F=>B=>C
7	[A,F] =>B=>D
8	A
9	[A,F] =>C=>B
10	F=>B
11	[A,F] => [B,D]

Figure 7. Preference of first option (Mon. 10 a.m.) in 11 negotiations when x= 1.1

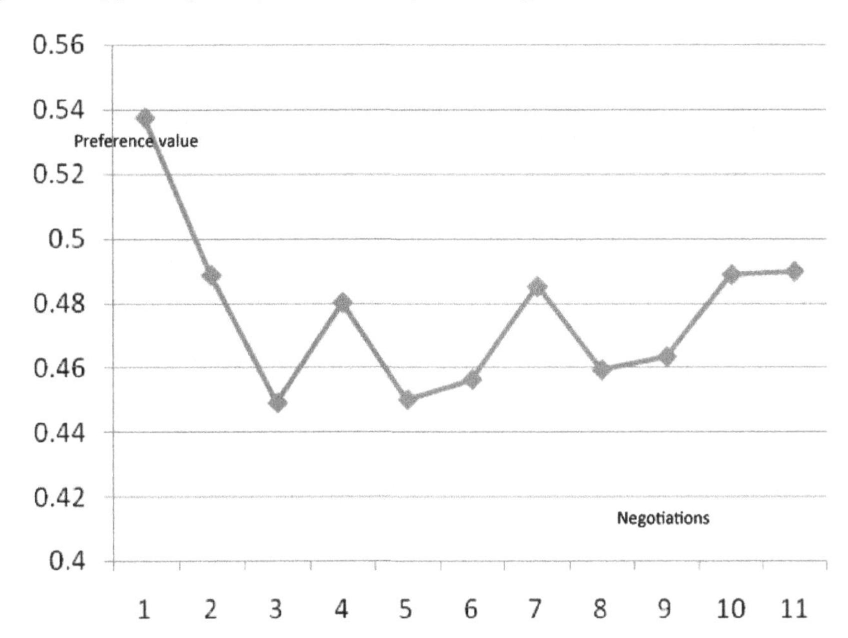

that the user strongly prefers A and F (Monday 10 and Thursday 9).

t is not far from reality if we expect that the results of the above negotiation rounds be similar to the output of the AHP. Results of AHP are shown in Table 13. The Importance of the first option (which is Monday 10 a.m.) with different x values (see Formula (6)) in all negotiation rounds can be seen in Figures 7 through 9.

Figure 8. Preference of first option (Mon. 10 a.m.) in 11 negotiations when x= 2

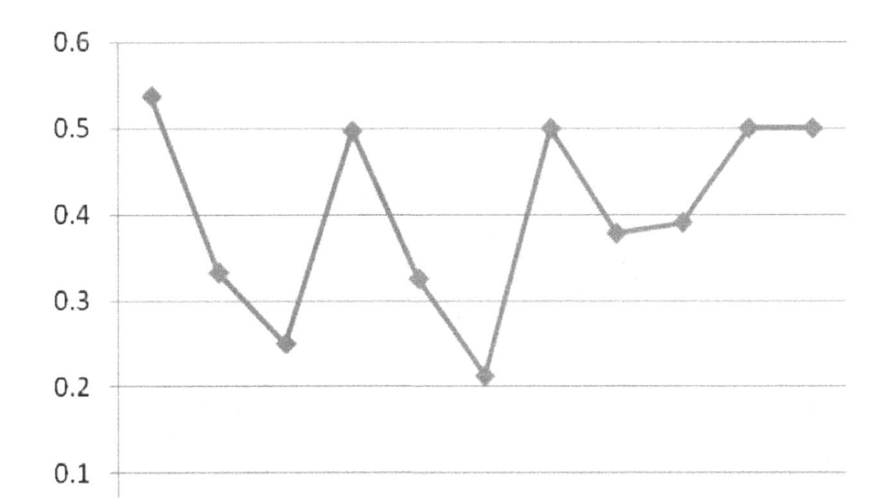

Figure 9. Preference of first option (Mon. 10 a.m.) in 11 negotiations when x= 5

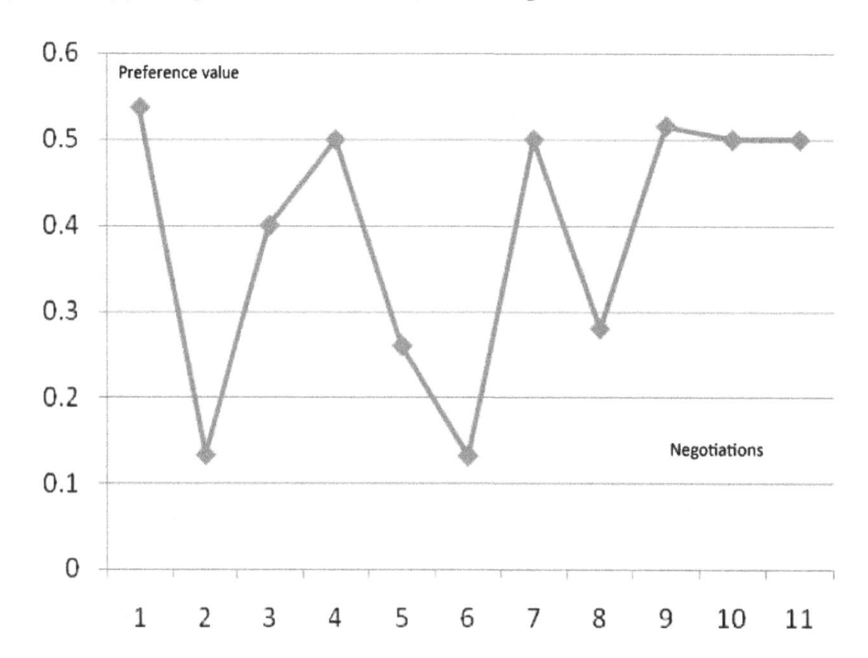

It can be seen that the user's preference is fluctuating smoothly around 0.5. This means that the strong-willed users persist on their previous choices.

As x increases, the preference value of option depends on the learning data than the injected knowledge. Thus, changes in values of preference are more common.

In Figure 9, x is 5. It can be interpreted as paying more attention to the training data than before. Something noteworthy in Figure 9 is the low value of the first option's preference in the sixth round due to the fact that in the sixth round the user offered three other options but not the first one (Table 14). Using larger values of x is very

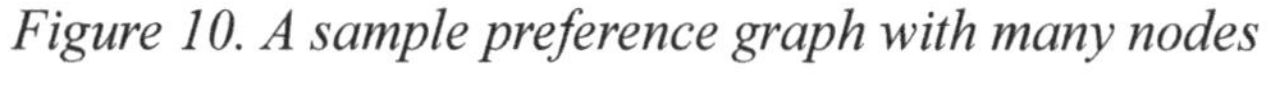
Figure 10. A sample preference graph with many nodes

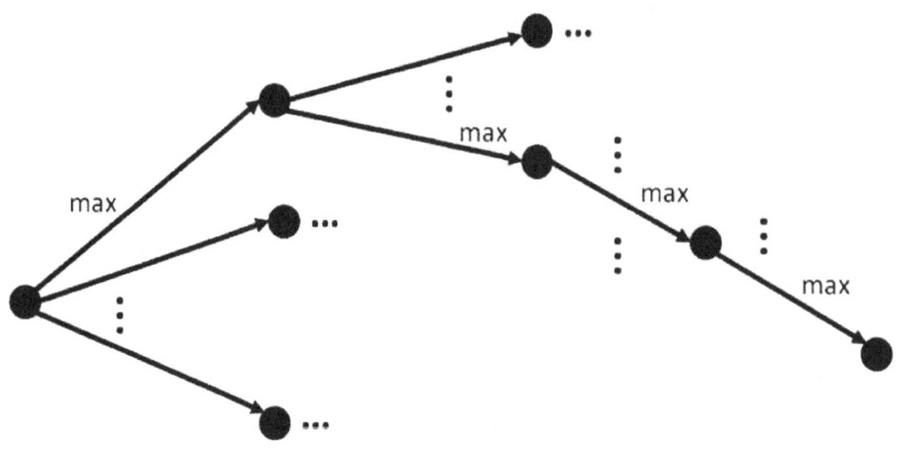

Figure 11. Preference of first option (Mon. 10 a.m.) in 11 negotiations when x= 1.1

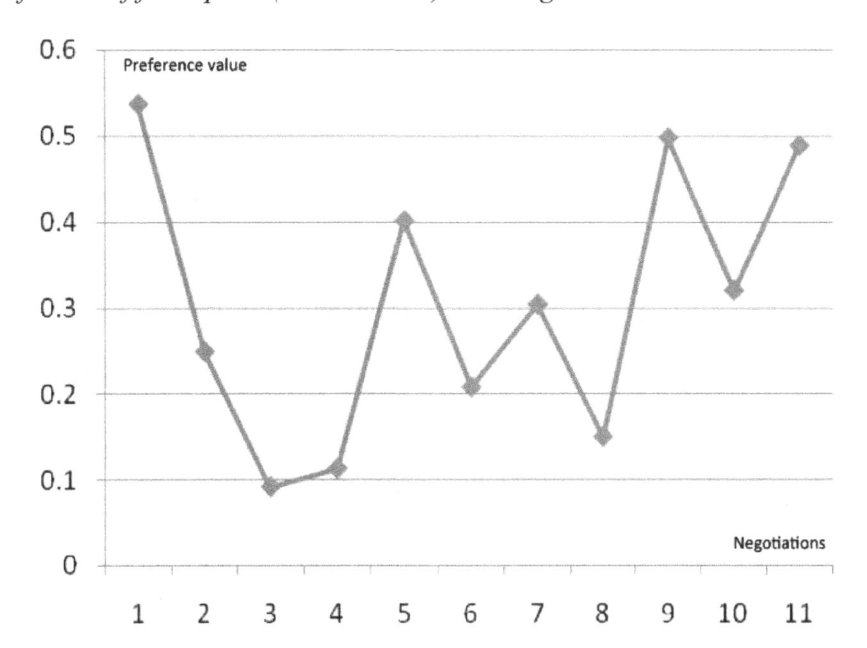

similar to x=5. The only difference is that there is more fluctuation in preference value.

Comparing different values of x, we can conclude that the bigger x is, the greater the fluctuations are. Another result which can be drawn is about having a reasonable number of training data. In all cases, it can be seen that after eight or nine negotiation rounds the preference value converges to a certain value. It is clear that more training data means less error, and a better model of the user. We used only first option because for other options the interpretations are the same.

So far, we have discussed how different values of x can affect a preference value. However, we did not discuss the complete result (preference model) of the negotiations. Consequently, we will examine the outputs now. The main output is the preference graph. As discussed before, a preference graph with n options has about 2^n-1 nodes. In other words, the preference graph of our experiment has 63 nodes which cannot be illustrated here with ease. Therefore, we show only the sequences of important preferences here. In Figure 10, we show the sequence of offers which are important. For example, offer A has the highest preference value so the user offers A. After that, we have to choose an offer from the remaining options. In each step, the highest preference value is chosen from the graph. In short, the output that will be demonstrated here is a branch in the preference

Table 15. Output of negotiations (preference model of user) for persistent user

Negotiation	Priorities					
	1st	2nd	3rd	4th	5th	6th
1	F	A	C	D	B	E
2	F	B	E	A	D	C
3	F	B	C	D	E	A
4	A	B	C	D	E	F
5	F	B	C	D	E	A
6	F	B	C	D	E	A
7	A	B	C	D	E	F
8	F	B	C	D	E	A
9	F	B	C	D	E	A
10	A	B	C	D	E	F
11	A	B	C	D	E	F

Table 16. Negotiation scenarios for non-persistent user with six options

Negotiation	Rounds
1	[A,C] =>B=>D
2	E=>A=>B=>F
3	B=>F=>C=>D=>E
4	C=>B=>E=>F=>A=>C
5	A=>B=>F=>C=>D=>E
6	F=>C=>B=>A=>E=>D
7	B=>A
8	E=>F=>C=>D
9	D=>A=>C=>D
10	E=>F=>C=>A=>B
11	C=>B=>F=>D=>A

graph which begins with the start node (a bit set that consists of 0s only), and it ends with the finish node (a bit set that consists of 1s only).

The output of each negotiation round for persistent user (with x=2) is shown in Table 15.

By analyzing Table 15, we can understand that offers A and B (respectively, Mon. 10 and Thurs. 9) are most likely to be offered at the first rounds of the negotiation. Offers B, C, and D are most likely to be offered in the middle of negotiation rounds (with mentioned orders). Since the user seems likely to continue a particular pattern, changes in preference orders, as negotiation continues, can be seen rarely.

Second Scenario: A Non-Persistent User

A non-persistent user changes his or her preference over time. Mathematically speaking, users have a strong bias toward randomness in their decisions. Negotiation scenarios for the non-persistent user are shown in Table 16.

In accordance with the changing behavior of the user, Figure 11 does not have a particular pattern or even a convergence. Many upwards and downwards trend can be seen in it. Similarly, the diagrams for other values of x are of similar nature and hence we have omitted them.

The output of each negotiation round for the non-persistent user (with x=2) is shown in Table 17.

In contrast to Table 15 in which we could rarely see changes, in Table 17 a considerable number of changes in the preference sequence can be seen. That is because of the ever-changing behavior of the user.

In this section we first discussed the implementation of the system. Then, we developed two scenarios and checked the output for each scenario. The results show that our method works properly in developing the preference model of the user.

CONCLUSION AND FUTURE WORK

Nowadays, many researchers from both academia and industry are interested in designing and implementing automated software agents. The aim of this automation is to allow users to concentrate on more productive tasks and reduce errors caused by human. To effectively act as surrogate for the user, the agent needs to make a good model of

Table 17. Output of negotiations (preference model of user) for persistent user

	Priorities					
Negotia-tion	1st	2nd	3rd	4th	5th	6th
1	F	A	D	C	B	E
2	A	B	D	C	F	E
3	C	A	B	F	E	D
4	C	A	B	F	E	D
5	C	B	D	A	F	E
6	C	B	D	A	F	E
7	C	B	D	A	F	E
8	B	F	C	A	D	E
9	B	F	C	A	D	E
10	B	F	C	A	D	E
11	C	B	D	A	F	E

user's preferences. This model can either be input by the user or learned from interaction with the user (Sen et al., 1997)

Our work has focused on the problem of how to model user's preferences using input from user. This model has the ability to learn. To build such a system we used analytical hierarchy process to obtain the preferences from user. For the learning aspect, we have used a graph based learning model proposed in (Crawford, 2009). Finally, we designed a hybrid model that uses the strengths of the two above mentioned models.

This research is part of a bigger project, which is developing intelligent agents that can optimally negotiate on behalf of their users. Here we only focused on how to understand and model user's preferences. Future works include how to bid optimally in a negotiation process using the proposed preference model.

ACKNOWLEDGMENT

This paper is the extended version of authors' previous paper "Adaptive modeling of user's preferences in multi-agent meeting scheduling problem using analytical hierarchy process" which has been published in IEEE Intl. Conf. on Intelligent Computer Communication and Processing, Cluj-Napoca, Romania, 2010

REFERENCES

Abdennadher, S., & Schlenker, H. (1999). Nurse scheduling using constraint logic programming. In *Proceedings of the 16th National Conference on Artificial Intelligence and the 11th Innovative Applications of Artificial Intelligence Conference* (pp. 838-843).

Al-ani, H. (2007). *A survey: Multi-agent coordination in the meeting-scheduling problem, literature review and survey*. Windsor, ON, Canada: University of Windsor.

BenHassine, A., Ho, T., & Ito, T. (2006). Meeting scheduling solver enhancement with local consistency reinforcement. *International Journal of Applied Intelligence*, *24*(2), 143–154. doi:10.1007/s10489-006-6935-y

Chun, A., Wai, H., & Wong, R. (2003). Optimizing agent-based meeting scheduling through preference estimation. *Engineering Applications of Artificial Intelligence*, *16*(7), 727–743. doi:10.1016/j.engappai.2003.09.009

Cogger, K. O., & Yu, P. L. (1985). Eigen weight vectors and least distance approximation for revealed preference in pairwise weight ratio. *Journal of Optimization Theory and Applications*, *46*, 483–491. doi:10.1007/BF00939153

Crawford, E. (2009). *Learning to improve negotiation in semi-cooperative agreement problem*. Unpublished doctoral dissertation, Carnegie Mellon University, Pittsburgh, PA.

Crawford, E., & Veloso, M. (2004). Mechanism design for multi-agent meeting scheduling, including timepreferences, availability, and value of presence. In *Proceedings of the International Conference on Intelligent Agent Technology* (pp. 253- 259).

Crawford, E., & Veloso, M. (2005). Learning dynamic preferences in multi-agentmeeting scheduling. In *Proceedings of the IEEE/WIC/ACM International Conference on Intelligent Agent Technology.*

Ephrati, E., Zlotkin, G., & Rosenschein, J. (1996). A non-manipulable meeting scheduling system. In *Proceedings of the 13th International Distributed Artificial Intelligence Workshop* (pp. 105-125).

Horowitz, E., Sahni, S., & Mehta, D. (1995). *Fundamentals of data structures in C* (pp. 342–376). New York, NY: W. H. Freeman.

Kuppuswamy, S., & Chithralekha, T. (2010). A new behavior management architecture for language faculty of an agent for task delegation. *International Journal of Intelligent Information Technologies*, *6*(2), 44–64. doi:10.4018/jiit.2010040103

Maheswaran, R., Pearce, J., Bowring, E., Varakantham, P., & Tambe, M. (2006). Privacy loss in distributed constraint reasoning: A quantitative framework for analysis and its applications. *Journal of Autonomous Agents and Multi-Agent Systems*, *34*, 27–60. doi:10.1007/s10458-006-5951-y

Mailler, R., & Lesser, V. (2003). A mediation based protocol for distributed constraint satisfaction. In *Proceedings of the 4th International Workshop on Distributed Constraint Reasoning* (pp. 49-58).

Mazumdar, B. D., & Mishra, R. B. (2010). Multiagent negotiation in B2C e-commerce based on data mining methods. *International Journal of Intelligent Information Technologies*, *6*(4), 46–70. doi:10.4018/jiit.2010100104

Mishra, K., & Mishra, R. B. (2010). Multiagent based selection of tutor-subject-student paradigm in an intelligent tutoring system. *International Journal of Intelligent Information Technologies*, *6*(1), 46–70. doi:10.4018/jiit.2010100904

Russell, S., & Yoon, V. Y. (2009). Agents, availability awareness, and decision making. *International Journal of Intelligent Information Technologies*, *5*(4), 53–70. doi:10.4018/jiit.2009080704

Saaty, T. L. (2009). *Analytic hierarchy process*. New York, NY: McGraw-Hill.

Sen, S., Haynes, T., & Arora, N. (1997). Satisfying user preferences while negotiating meetings. *International Journal of Human-Computer Studies*, *47*, 407–415. doi:10.1006/ijhc.1997.0139

Tsuruta, T., & Shintani, T. (2000). Scheduling meetings using distributed valued constraint satisfaction algorithm. In *Proceedings of the 14th European Conference on Artificial Intelligence* (pp. 383-387).

This work was previously published in the International Journal of Intelligent Information Technologies, Volume 7, Issue 2, edited by Vijayan Sugumaran, pp. 45-62, copyright 2011 by IGI Publishing (an imprint of IGI Global).

Chapter 8
Wireless Sensor Node Placement Using Hybrid Genetic Programming and Genetic Algorithms

Arpit Tripathi
Indian Institute of Information Technology and Management Gwalior, India

Aditya Trivedi
Indian Institute of Information Technology and Management Gwalior, India

Pulkit Gupta
Indian Institute of Information Technology and Management Gwalior, India

Rahul Kala
Indian Institute of Information Technology and Management Gwalior, India

ABSTRACT

The ease of use and re-configuration in a wireless network has played a key role in their widespread growth. The node deployment problem deals with an optimal placement strategy of the wireless nodes. This paper models a wireless sensor network, consisting of a number of nodes, and a unique sink to which all the information is transmitted using the shortest connecting path. Traditionally the systems have used Genetic Algorithms for optimal placement of the nodes that usually fail to give results in problems employing large numbers of nodes or higher areas to be covered. This paper proposes a hybrid Genetic Programming (GP) and Genetic Algorithm (GA) for solving the problem. While the GP optimizes the deployment structure, the GA is used for actual node placement as per the GP optimized structure. The GA serves as a slave and GP serves as master in this hierarchical implementation. The algorithm optimizes total coverage area, energy utilization, lifetime of the network, and the number of nodes deployed. Experimental results show that the algorithm could place the sensor nodes in a variety of scenarios. The placement was found to be better than random placement strategy as well as the Genetic Algorithm placement strategy.

DOI: 10.4018/978-1-4666-2047-6.ch008

INTRODUCTION

From the last few years, Wireless Sensor Networks (WSN) have come out as the most important networking paradigm, both in terms of their viable prospective and also from a scientific point of view. WSNs are important because of their numerous applications; vary from military use to environmental monitoring (measuring temperature, humidity, & solar radiation etc.) and from wildlife to disaster management. Efficient sensor node deployment is essential to sense, gather and process the data. Therefore, in the last few years there is a shift in research activities in this field. Traditionally sensors nodes were distributed randomly or uniformly due to ease and effortlessness. But random or uniform allotment of sensor nodes is sub-optimal and further leads to the Sink Routing-Hole Problem (SRHP).

Sensor nodes transmit the information to the sink via multiple hops as shown in Figure 1. A node near the sink gets data transmitted by farther nodes as well, in addition to its own data, which is finally transmitted to the sink. Thus a node closer to the sink transmits more data than the ones farther from it. The problem with these networks is maximized if some node near the sink fails (Yunhuai, Ngan, & Ni, 2007). The restriction with WSN is their limited source of energy (as they are composed by battery supplied nodes), concern of the coverage constraint, and the trustworthiness and life-time of network. Whenever WSN designers plan WSN they have to consider these considerations along with number of sensor nodes to wrap the region since wireless sensors are still expensive.

The problem of sensor deployment for an optimal sensor network layout can be solved using either of the two strategies: (i) find the minimum number of sensor nodes of given energy to cover the region with appropriate reliability and a good life time, and (ii) for a given number of sensor nodes, find out a set of points and the power levels which give the best trade-off between coverage area, lifetime and energy utilization of the network with appropriate reliability.

While the first strategy limits the maximum area to be covered, keeping the number of sensor nodes variable; the second strategy keeps the number of sensor nodes fixed, making the other parameters variable. In this paper we propose an algorithm for optimizing the number of nodes, as well as the area, lifetime and energy, by using a hybrid of Genetic Programming (GP) and Genetic Algorithms (GA).

Evolutionary Algorithms are an inspiration from the natural species that develop along with generations. The generation of higher generation by the lower generation is done by the application of Evolutionary operators (Melanie, 1999). The Evolutionary Algorithms may be fundamentally categorized into three heads. These are Genetic Algorithms, Genetic Programming and Evolutionary Strategies (Schwefel, 1975; & Rechenberg, 1973). In Genetic Programming (GP) the individual is usually given a tree-based representation and represents a program, solving the fitness of the individuals may be determined (Fogel, 1992). The Genetic Algorithm (GA) makes use of a bit string or a double vector representation where the various properties of the individual are encoded in a contiguous manner to make a vector or string.

Both GP and GA are widely used for a variety of problems. These algorithms however fail to give good results if the fitness landscapes are very complex or highly dimensional in nature. The in-

Figure 1. Passage of information from sensor nodes to sink

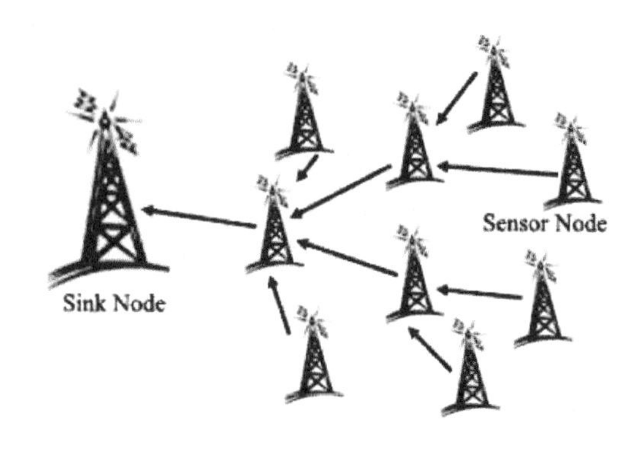

ability of a single evolutionary technique to solve the optimization problem, gives rise to hybridization of two or more evolutionary techniques (Hou, Chen, & Jeng, 2010) for better convergence and optimization (Baffo & Confessore, 2010). In this hybrid algorithm, evolutionary algorithms assist each other to achieve a high degree of optimization in a finite amount of time. Here two evolutionary techniques work in master slave mode (Edwin, Thierens, & Watson, 2004).

The entire problem of node deployment may be fundamentally broken down into parts. The first part of the problem deals with finding the correct connectivity or layout of the WSN. This part of the problem deals with how the various nodes need to be connected to each other and to the sink. It further stresses upon the mechanism by which the various nodes transmit their information to one another, so as to finally reach the sink. The other part of the problem deals with the optimal physical placement of the sensor nodes. This part of the problem computes the exact location in the map where the sensor nodes need to be placed. This part of the problem assumes the connection is already decided. The connection puts a constraint on the range within which a connected node may be placed. The two problems are hence dependent on each other and may not be individually solved.

Increased usage of technology in multiple domains presents a promising future where decision support systems would take over much of tasks being currently done by humans. Automated systems are more efficient in terms of time consuming, work in real time, and give optimal results. Examples include text mining (Qi, Song, Yoon, & Versterre, 2011), power systems (Carrasco, Ternero, Sivianes, Oviedo, & Escudero, 2010). In this paper, we present an intelligent system for wireless sensor node placement which makes wise decision regarding the use of GP to solve the first part of the problem and GA to solve the second part of the problem. GP and GA work in a hierarchical manner with GP as master and GA as the slave. In this paper GA serves as the local search strategy of the GP. The GP fixes some structure of the WSN node deployment. GA is initiated to work over this structure and find the most optimal places in the map for placement of the sensor nodes.

The novelty of the paper is three-fold. Firstly, the region where the sensor nodes may be placed is given in form of a map, which may have any flexible shape or design. It may not strictly be rectangular or circular or any fixed shape as per the problems in literature. Secondly by adjusting the various parameters, we may achieve a clear tradeoff between the optimization of the layout structure (or connectivity) and the region of placement of the nodes. This is done by changing the contributions of the two evolutionary algorithms. Thirdly, to a reasonably high degree, the algorithm is adaptive to the number of nodes and coverage area. The algorithm itself finds out the number of nodes that must be deployed to cover the largest possible area.

This paper is organized as follows. In the next section, we give a review of some related work. The modeling of the problem is given in the section that follows. Afterward, we discuss the GP framework to solve the problem. Later in the chapter, we further discuss the framework of the GA in this hybridized approach of GP and GA. The experimental results are shown in the section following. The conclusion remarks are given in the last section.

RELATED WORK

Yener, Ismail, and Sivrikaya (2007) considered optimization models of WSN subject to distance uncertainty for three classic problems in energy limited WSNs: minimizing the energy consumed, maximizing the data extracted, and maximizing the network lifetime. A characteristic feature of his model was uncertainty which was accounted for using a robust optimization technique. In another work, Shouhong and Ding (2009) considered the issue to approach least square solution for range based positioning. They suggested an algorithm that is based on the equations linearized from range measurement equations and implemented a weighted least square criterion in a computationally efficient way. Lin and Chen (2008) proposed a distributed approach for supporting the randomized scheduling to provide the full coverage. To proficiently achieve this goal, the authors proposed divided their approach into two main stages, field partition and coverage improvement. The managing problems of these two stages had been transferred to two geometry problems, Voronoi polygon construction and circle covering.

Hou, Chen, and Jeng (2010) studied the problem to optimally deploy new sensors in order to improve the coverage of an existing network. In this approach the best- and worst-case coverage problems that are related to the observability of a path were formulated into computational geometry problems. In this work the authors first proved that there exists a duality between the two coverage problems, and then solved the two problems together. Wang, Xu, Takahara, and Hassanein (2007) formulated a generalized node placement optimization problem that aimed at minimizing the network cost with constraints on lifetime and connectivity. As an optimal solution to this problem is difficult to obtain, a two-phase approach was proposed, in which locally optimal design decisions were taken.

Wang, Yang, Ma, He, and Wang (2008) investigated a design approach for minimizing energy consumption and maximizing network lifetime of a multiple-source and single-sink WSN with energy constraints. Both linear and planar network topologies were considered for network lifetime maximization. For planar single-source and single-sink network topologies they successfully used optimality conditions known as Karush-Kuhn-Tucker to obtain analytical expressions of the best possible network lifetime. For planar network topology a decomposition and combination approach was proposed to compute suboptimal solutions. To deal with large scale planar network, an iterative algorithm was proposed.

Gentile proposed convex linear program which ensures that the estimated link distances between neighboring nodes conform to requisite geometrical constraints. He suggested a distributed algorithm to reconstruct the locations of the sensor nodes from the estimated link distances. Shu, Krunz, and Vrudhula (2006) addressed the problem of minimizing energy consumption in a CDMA-based wireless sensor network (WSN). A comprehensive energy consumption model was proposed. Yener, Ismail, and Sivrikaya (2007) considered a multi-hop sensor network and address the problem of minimizing power consumption in each sensor node locally while ensuring two properties: communication connectivity and sensing coverage. Their work presents Markov model and its solution for steady state distributions.

A lot of work is also done by the use of Evolutionary Algorithms to solve the problem optimal node deployment. Genetic Algorithms find a lot of applications in solving the problem because of their real individual representation and optimizing capabilities (Zhao, Yu, & Chen, 2007; Oh, Tan, Kong, Tan, Ng, & Tai, 2007; Seo, Kim, Ryou, & Kang, 2008). The problem has also been solved with the help of Genetic Programming. Johnson, Teredesai, and Saltarelli (2005 and Khanna, Liu, and Chen (2006) proposed a reduced-complexity genetic algorithm for optimization of multi-hop sensor networks. The goal of the system was to generate optimal number of sensor clusters with cluster-heads. Barrett (2007) used Genetic Algorithm for optimizing the sensor node placement in the particular problem of intrusion detection.

The increased amount of research largely results in the growth of the problem complexity that makes it impossible for the simple genetic algorithms to solve. As a result a lot of work is being done for hierarchical implementation of the Genetic Algorithms and other evolutionary techniques, which may many times result in better performance. The model proposed by Kala, Shukla, and Tiwari (2010) is an innovative use of hierarchical GA. Here the authors proposed the use of clustering as a means of dividing the entire fitness landscape into multiple clusters which would be solved by individual slave GAs. The master GA coordinated the location and size of these clusters. The number of clusters reduced from a large size to a very small size which was referred as the finer to coarser approach that suited the highly complex fitness landscapes.

Gautam and Chaudhuri (2007) also proposed an algorithm for optimization in complex landscapes. This approach divided the search space into a number of sub spaces. These sub spaces were redefined after a unit iteration of the algorithm. The individuals could further migrate between the sub-spaces. Another good approach to problem solving by hybrid evolutionary algorithms is Hierarchical Fair Competition based Genetic Algorithms (HFCGA) (Hu, Goodman, Seo, & Pei, 2002, 2005). In this algorithm the entire population pool is divided into classes as per the fitness value. Every individual competes only with the individuals of the same class, or the same range of fitness values. The individuals may migrate between classes, if they reach the required fitness level.

PROBLEM MODELING

Data transmission in WSN takes place through multiple hops. As explained in section 1, inner node transmits more data packets than outer nodes. Assume $T_1, T_2, \ldots, T_N$ are the life times of nodes where N is the number of nodes. The lifetime of the network is given by Equation (1).

$$\text{Life Time of Network} = \text{Min}(T_i) \quad (1)$$

Sensor nodes have distinct output power levels $(OPL_1 < OPL_2 < OPL_3 < \ldots \ldots < OPL_l$ where l is the maximum number of power levels for any node). The transmitting distance $(T_{r1} < T_{r2} < T_{r3} < \ldots \ldots < T_{ri})$ of any node depends upon the output power level at which the particular node is operating. A node can choose any one of the available power levels for operation. The transmitting range depends upon the power levels. Hence the summation of the transmitting range of nodes between source and destination should be greater than distance between source and destination.

If a path from source to destination uses k hops then Equation (2) must hold true.

Sum of the transmitting Ranges of nodes in the Route ≥ Distance between source and destination

$$T_{ri} + T_{ri}^1 + T_{ri}^2 + T_{ri}^3 + \ldots + T_{ri}^k \geq d_{i0} \quad (2)$$

where T_{ri} is the transmitting range of ith node and $T_{ri}^1, T_{ri}^2, T_{ri}^3 \ldots T_{ri}^k$ are the transmitting range of the nodes that lie on the route to sink for the node i. This is shown in Figure 2. d_{io} is the distance between the node i and sink.

If the distance between two nodes is d then d must be less than or equal to transmission range of node to communicate. So distance between any two nodes can take max value T_{rn}.

Sensor nodes either sense the data or forward it to the next node or sink during the lifetime (T_i). Each node when receives or transmits data uses power from the battery. When battery is discharged, the node is considered as dead. It is possible that data packet chooses a route that has a dead node on its way. Thus death of any node in the network is considered as a death of network

If E_{ti} is the energy used by i^{th} node for transmitting data packet, E_S (constant) is the energy used for sensing and processing, and each node transmit an l-bit message over distance d then energy consumed is given by Equation (3) and (4).

$$\text{Transmission Energy } E_t = (1 * E_{elec}) + (1 * E_{amp} * d^2) \text{ if } d < d_0$$

Figure 2. Placement of nodes within the transmitting range

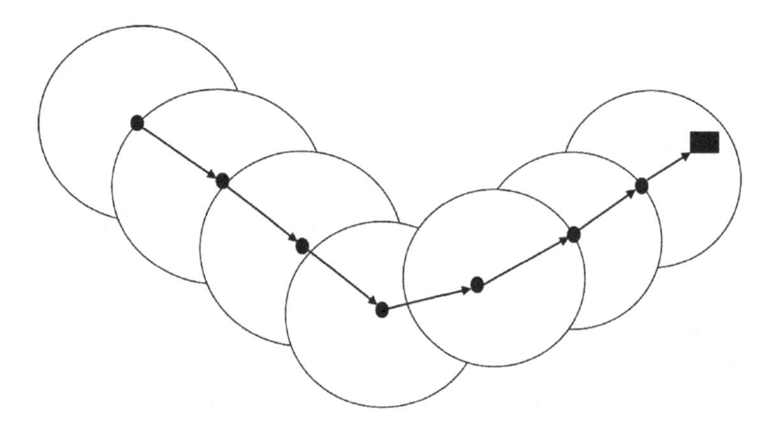

Transmission Energy $E_t =$
$$(1 * E_{elec}) + (1 * E_{amp} * d^4) \text{ if } d > d_0 \quad (3)$$

$$\text{Receiving Energy } E_S = 1 * E_{elec} \quad (4)$$

where E_{amp} is constant of the amount of energy consumed during signal amplification in the amplifier and E_{elec} is constant of the amount of energy consumed when data are converted into radio frequency or from radio frequency and d_0 is constant.

The node is usually sleeps and periodically wakes up for transmission of the data packet. If the node wakes up for the time period of T_a for transferring a data packet and transfers total n data packets during his life time then number of data packets n transmitted is given by Equation (5).

$$n = \frac{T_i}{T_a} \quad (5)$$

Here T_i is the lifetime of the node and T_a is the time to sense and transmit a data packet.

If during the lifetime, a node transmits n number of messages, then whole amount of consumed energy during the lifetime of node i is given by Equation (6)

Total Energy Consumed for node i=
Energy consumed to transmit its own pack.
+Energy consumed to transmit pack.
comes from farther nodes

$$E_i = n(E_{t,i} + E_S) + (j-1) * n(E_{t,i} + E_S)$$

$$E_i = jn(E_{t,i} + E_S) \quad (6)$$

Here j is the index of node from the farther end of the path belonging i^{th} node and the sink.

If initial energy of the node is E_{int} then node dies when total energy consumed by node is equal to the initial energy of node as given in Equation (7).

$$E_{\text{int}} - E_i = 0$$

$$E_{\text{int}} = jn(E_{t,i} + E_S) \quad (7)$$

From Equations (5) and (7) we have

$$E_{\text{int}} = \frac{T_i}{T_a}(E_{t,i} + E_S)$$

$$T_i = E_{\text{int}} \frac{Ta}{j(E_{t,i} + E_S)} \quad (8)$$

If there are N numbers of nodes in the network then the total initial Energy is NE_{int}. Given by (9)

$$\text{Energy Efficiency} = \frac{\sum \text{Energy utilized at the time of sink hole}}{\text{Total Energy}} * 100\%$$

$$E_{utl} = \frac{\sum \frac{T_i}{T_a} j(E_{t,i} + E_S)}{N * E\,\text{int}} * 100\% \quad (9)$$

For a relatively small target area where the farthest node is 5 hops away to the sink, less than 8% of the energy is consumed before the system is down. With the size of application area increased, the problem becomes more serious. For a field with a maximum of 35 hops, when the network fails, only 2% of energy has been spent (Hou, Chen, & Jeng, 2010). Thus random and uniform distribution functions are not suitable for sensor node deployment.

By using path loss models to estimate the received signal level as a function of distance, it become possible to predict the Signal to Noise Ratio (SNR). Log-Normal Shadowing is the most used radio propagation model in WSN application. Measurements have shown that at any value of *d*, the path loss *PL(d)* at particular location is random and distributed log normally(normal in DB) about the mean distance dependent value. This is given by Equations (10) and (11)

$$PL_{(d)}[dB\} = PL(d_0) + 10n \log_{10}(\frac{d}{d_0}) + X_\sigma \quad (10)$$

$$\Pr_{(d)}[dBm] = Pt[dBm] - PL_{(d)}[dB] \quad (11)$$

Here n is the path loss exponent which indicates the rate at which the path loss increases with distance, d_0 is the close-in reference distance which is determined from measurements close to the transmitter, d is the T-R separation distance, $\Pr_{(d)}$ represents the expected signal strength (in dBm) at the receiver placed at distance d (in meters) from the transmitter which delivers Pt as output power (in dBm) and X_σ is zero mean Gaussian distributed random variable (in dB) with standard deviation σ (also in dB). Antenna gains have been considered in channel attenuation $PL_{(d)}$.

For receiving the signal or data packet it is necessary that the SNR is greater than its threshold value $SNR_{\min}$. Probability of successfully receiving the data packets or signals is given by Equation (12).

$$\frac{P_t - PL(d_0) + 10n \log_{10}\left(\frac{d}{d_0}\right) - SNR_{\min} - P_n}{\sigma_x \sqrt{2}} \quad (12)$$

$$P = 1 - \frac{1}{2} e$$

GENETIC PROGRAMMING

The first task in the implementation of the algorithm is the layout optimization that is done by the use of GP. The GP module is given a map that is a representation of the areas where the sensor nodes may be deployed. These may be the areas where the wireless sensor is to be provided. The map consists of a grid of size *p x q*. Any cell located at position *(i,j)* in this map M_{ij} is 1 if it is feasible to place a sensor at that location and 0 otherwise.

Layout in the problem of node deployment in WSN means to specify the general connectionist architecture of the system. Here we specify the total number of nodes that are to be placed as well as the connection between the various nodes. A node i connected to node j means that i can transmit data to j. The connections must be in such a manner that all nodes must be able to transmit data ultimately to the sink.

Individual Representation

The first task in the application of GP is the individual representation. Here we use a tree-like representation of the individual. Every leaf or non-leaf node of the tree represents a sensor node. The root of the tree is always fixed to denote the sink. Suppose that a node i has children $j_1, j_2, j_3, \ldots j_c$. This means that the sensor nodes $j_1, j_2, j_3, \ldots j_c$ are connected to the sensor node i. In other words there is an inward transfer of information from the sensor nodes $j_1, j_2, j_3, \ldots j_c$ to the sensor node i. One such representation is given in Figure 3. Figure 3(a) shows the phenotype representation and Figure 3(b) shows the genotype representation.

Here we may easily see that the inner sensor nodes are found near the root in the GP individual. The transfer of information from the outer sensor nodes to the inner sensor nodes in phenotype representation of Figure 3(a) is analogous to the transfer of information from leaf nodes to the root node in the genotype representation of Figure 3(b). The entire information must reach the sink that is the central node in phenotype representation and the root node in genotype representation.

We place a few constraints in the individual. The maximum height is fixed to some constant value h_{max}. Also the maximum number of children of any node in the GP individual is fixed to some value c_{max}. Also the maximum total number of sensors or nodes is fixed to some value n_{max}.

The GP individuals, along with storage of the connections also store the physical location where the node is placed. These locations are optimized as well as checked for constraints by the GA. Hence each node of the tree is associated with some x_{rel} and y_{rel} value corresponding to the sensor placement position. The *rel* means that the values are stored relating to the parent node. The root has both x_{rel} and y_{rel} as 0. The absolute value x and y may be calculated from the relative values by iterating from the root in a top to bottom manner. The absolute position of x and y for root are assumed to be known before hand. The placement may never happen at an inaccessible location ($m_{xy} = 0$). Further the points must lie within the map ($1 \le x \le p$, $1 \le y \le q$). In case the placement of any node (in the initial individual generation phase or during the operation of any operator) results in the placement violating either of these constraints, it is assumed that further placement of nodes as children of this node would result in placement violating these constraints.

Hence neither this node, nor any of its children are placed. This is because we go radially outward in the phenotype representation, on going down a tree. If a node fails to lie in feasible region, the radially outward nodes would further lie outside the feasible region. This further limits the height of the GP tree. The GP individuals further store the power level at which the node is operating.

We specify another heuristic rule in the placement of the nodes. An outer node is always placed at the maximum possible distance from the inner node. This maximizes the coverage for the same values of the other objectives. The inner node has some coverage area that depends upon the radius of coverage which again depends upon the power level. The center of the outer node is placed on the rim of this coverage area. Further increasing the distance would lead to loss of connectivity between the two nodes which would be illegal.

Genetic Operators

The genetic operators are used for the generation of the higher generation of population from the lower generation. In this algorithm rank based scaling with stochastic uniform selection has been used. Crossover is used by mixing two randomly selected sub-trees from the parents and generating two new trees or individuals by their interchange. The interchange must however ensure that the

Figure 3 (a). Genotype representation of the genetic programming individual; (b). phenotype representation of the genetic programming individual

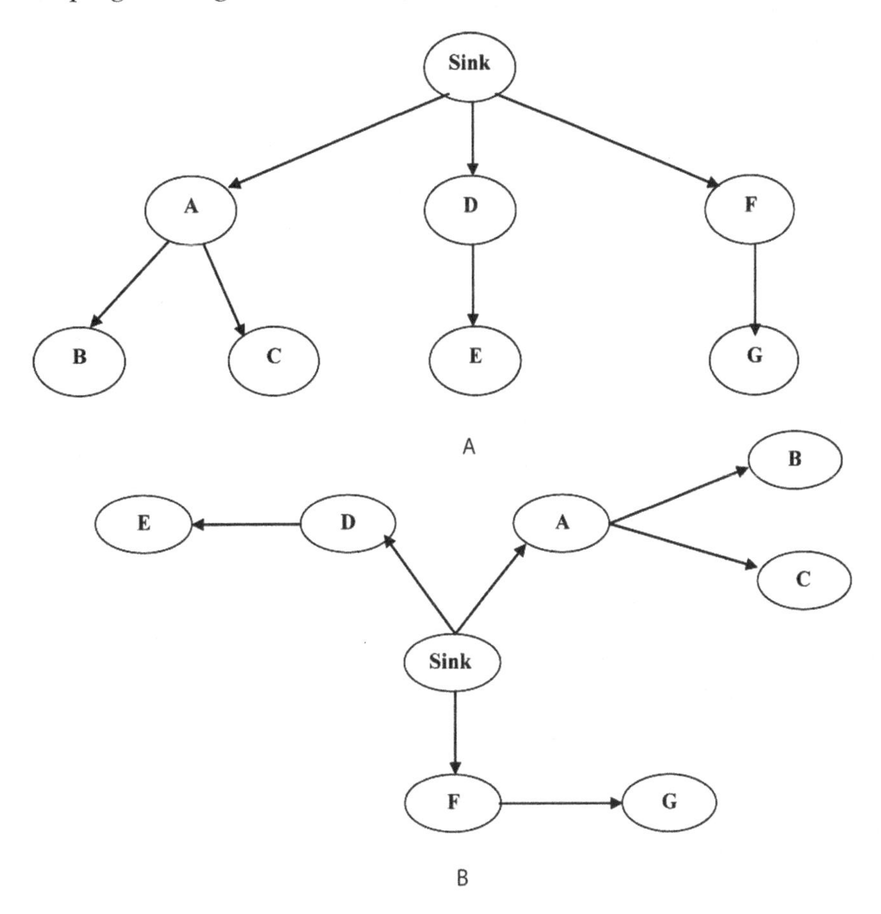

maximum height of any leaf node does not exceed the maximum allowable height. For this we compute the maximum height of both sub-trees and the trees that would be formed upon crossover. In case the crossover may result in crossing of the maximum height threshold, two new sub-trees are selected randomly from the parents.

Mutation in GP is of two types, structural and parametric. The structural mutation tries to change the GP structure. The parametric mutation on the other hand tries to modify the individual property values, stored in each node. In this approach the parametric optimization is carried out by the GA algorithm. The structural mutation tries to select any sub-tree of the selected individual for mutation and replaces it by a completely new and randomly generated sub-tree. The last operator used is elite. This operator transfers the best individual of one generation, directly into the next generation. The parametric mutation has only one role to perform. It randomly selects a node from the entire GP tree. It changes the power level of this tree to some value. In this manner the parametric mutation operator plays a key role in power level optimization. The position of the nodes is not changed in this operation, as this operation is done by the GA.

Fitness Function

The last major task associated with the GP is to formulate the fitness function. The task of fitness function is to assign values to the individual based on their goodness in solving the problem. This problem is a Multi-Objective Optimization problem where 4 objective functions are to be optimized. The objectives to be optimized are lifetime, energy consumption, coverage area and number of sensor nodes. The fitness function is given by Equation (13)

$$Ft = -\alpha_1 * T_{\min} + \alpha_2 * EC - \alpha_3 * A + \alpha_4 * S \quad (13)$$

Here $T_{\min}$ is the lifetime of the node which has minimum lifetime. T_i is the lifetime of the ith node given by Equation (8). T_{min} is given by Equation (14)

$$T_{\min} = T_j : T_j < T_i \text{ for all } i \neq j \quad (14)$$

- EC is the total energy consumed as described by Equation (6).
- A is the total coverage area of all nodes
- S is the total number of sensors.

α_1, α_2 α_3 and α_4 are multi-objective optimization constants

It may be noted that the coefficients α_1 and α_2 have negative signs to convert the whole problem into minimizing problem.

Before using Equation (13) for the fitness evaluation, we need to optimize the physical locations where the nodes may be placed. This is done by the application of GA. The GA optimizes the physical location of the placement of the various nodes and returns the individual with the most optimal fitness. An important characteristic here is that the fitter individual replaced by the GA replaces the original individual whose fitness was being sought in the population pool. Hence next call to the same individual may result in further optimization by the GA.

Relation Between the Two Evolutionary Algorithms

Here we have used two evolutionary techniques, GP and GA for the optimization of the node deployment. GP is used for the optimization of the layout architecture of the problem. GA is used for the optimization of the physical location where the nodes need to be placed. The GP and GA work in a hierarchical mode in this algorithm. The GP gives the GA in individual which primarily considers the information about the nodal layout architecture. The GA carries out the optimization in the placement of the various nodes represented in the layout architecture.

The optimized individual is returned, whose fitness is used as the GP individual fitness. Further this individual is used to replace the original GP individual in the GP population pool. This is shown in Figure 4.

GENETIC ALGORITHM

The other part of the solution is the use of GA that fuses with GP for the optimization task. GA is used for optimizing the physical location where the sensor nodes would be located. While implementation of the GP we assume that the structure or the layout of the system has already been done. Each of the nodes in the GP individual has parameters x_{rel} and y_{rel} that stored the relative position of the node relative to its parent. The GA is used for the optimization of these positions. The constraints that the nodes must lay with the map and at accessible regions are valid for GA as well in its placement strategy. Further the child node must be within the coverage area of the parent node. These constraints must be obeyed by every individual of the population at any generation.

The individual representation in case of the GA consists of a string that stores all the relative values. The maximum and minimum values

Figure 4. The general algorithm framework

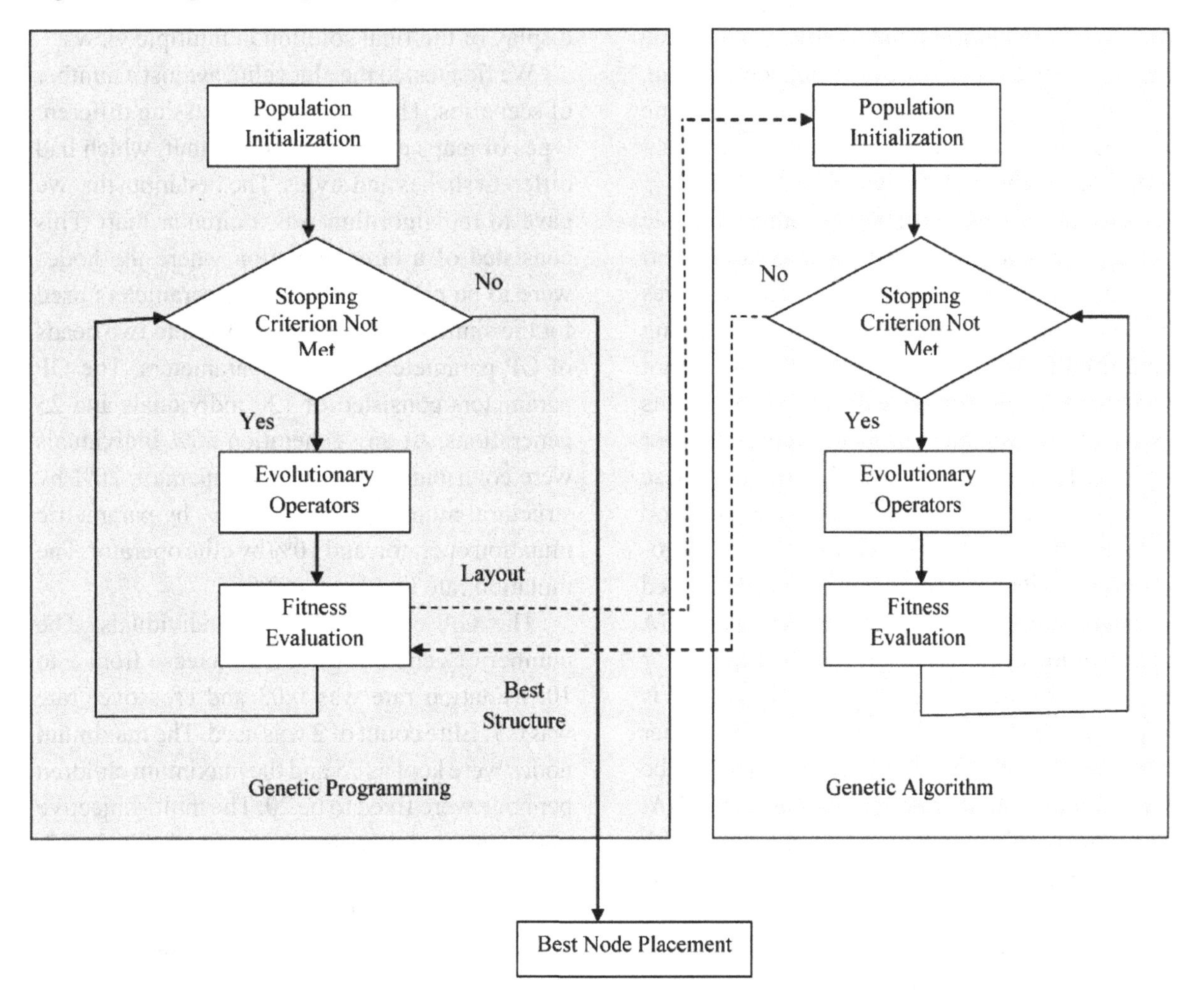

are different for all the locations. This depends upon the power level at which the parent node is operating as fixed by the GP. GA works over a linear architecture, whereas the GP worked over the tree like architecture. We hence need to make a linear representation of the various parameters, based on the supplied GP individual. The final optimized individual again needs to be converted into a tree-like structure, before being returned as the final solution. The conversion from a linear structure to a tree-like structure is also needed before the fitness function calls.

The GA uses the conventional evolutionary operators for the generation of higher generation population from a lower level. These include the stochastic uniform selection, fitness based scaling, weighted crossover, Gaussian mutation and elite. All these in their own mechanism try to influence the evolution of more optimized individuals in the higher generation.

An important operator used here is repair. The various Genetic operators may make the individual disobey some of the constraints. The nodes disobeying the constraints hence need to be repaired by making proper modifications in their values, so that all the constraints are satisfied. This task is performed for all the individuals in the population by the repair operator. If any child lies outside the coverage area of the parent, it is pulled in by random amount. If however the node lies in the inaccessible areas or outside the map, it is simply deleted. All the children of this node are deleted as well. In this manner the resultant individual completely obeys the stated rules.

An important aspect of the algorithm is the role of the two evolutionary algorithms. At the start we may expect completely randomized structures being generated by the GP which go on becoming optimized as the GP iterations precede. It would not be wise to heavily optimize the initial GP layouts as we know they most probably represent poor layouts. Hence we may weakly optimize these layouts, just to get a rough idea to separate good layouts from poor layouts. However as the algorithm proceeds, the layouts start getting optimized in nature. We are now expected to have better GA optimization to clearly determine the fitness. For these reasons the number of generations of GA is kept variable. Let g_{max} be the maximum number of generations that the GA may have and g_{min} be the minimum number of generations of the GA. The number of generations of GA increases with the iterations of the GP. Let any point of time, the GP be at iteration i. Let us further assume that the GP has maximum iterations of G. The number of generations of GA g is given by Equation (15).

$$g = g_{\min} + (g_{\max} - g_{\min})\frac{i}{G} \tag{15}$$

RESULTS

The algorithm was implemented on JAVA platform. Two separate modules were made for the GP and the GA. The algorithm parameters like number of individuals, mutation rate, etc. for both these algorithms was mentioned on a separate parameter file. The algorithm took as input a JPEG image which was used to mark out the accusable and the inaccessible areas. The parsing of the image and formulation of the map as an array was done in a separate file. JAVA Applet was used for the display of the final solution in multiple views.

We first tested the algorithm against a number of scenarios. This was done by passing different types of maps as the algorithm input, which had different shapes and styles. The first input that we gave to the algorithm was a circular map. This consisted of a circular region where the nodes were to be placed. The genetic parameters used for the simulation may be divided into two heads of GP parameters and GA parameters. The GP parameters consisted of 120 individuals and 25 generations. At any generation 50% individuals were contributed by crossover operator, 20% by structural mutation operator, 20% by parametric mutation operator, and 10% by elite operator. The mutation rate was kept as 0.06.

The GA consisted of 40 individuals. The number of generations could increase from 5 to 10. Mutation rate was 0.03 and crossover rate was 0.7. Elite count of 2 was used. The maximum nodes were kept as 75 and the maximum children per node were fixed to be 20. The multi-objective optimization parameters were fixed to 0.3, 0.2, 0.8 and 1.0 for energy, lifetime, area and number of nodes respectively.

The simulation using these parameters took about 5 minutes of execution time when simulated on a 3.0 GHz processor with 1 GB RAM. Figure 5(a) shows the coverage for each node. The transfer of information from the various nodes to the sink is shown in Figure 5(b). From figure it may be seen that the top area is not being covered by any node. This is because of the fact that the coverage of this area would mean an increase in the energy as well as nodal cost. These disadvantages would overcome the benefit of increased area. Another observation that can be made is that the nodes are usually of a larger power level. This is again attributed to the fact that the increase in area coverage by larger power levels overcomes the disadvantage of high energy associated with these levels. The multi-objective parameters play

Figure 5 (a). Area coverage for map 1; (b). layout and placement of the nodes for map 1

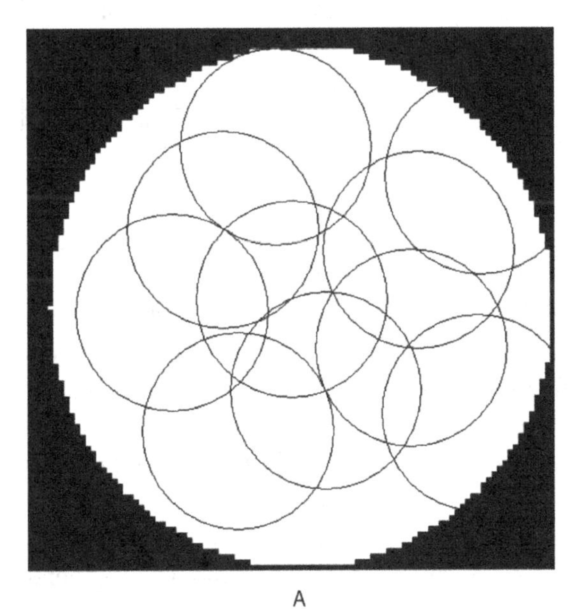

A

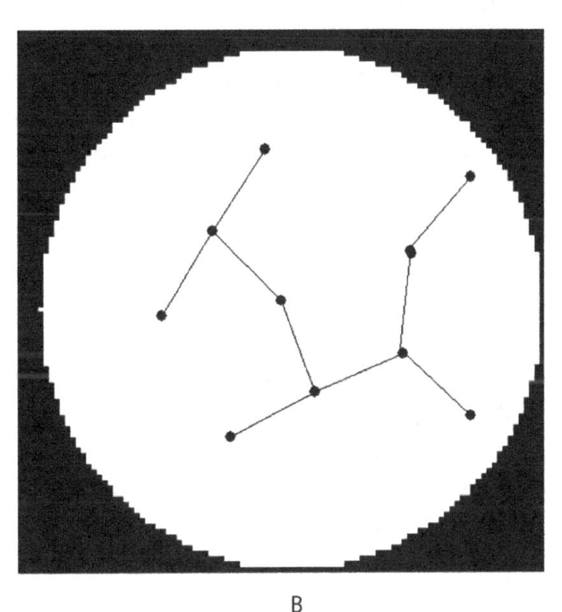

B

a major role in deciding the node placement and their power levels. These are used to lay different stress on different objectives. The value of the different objectives is given in Table 1.

The second experiment was conducted on a square map. The algorithm could place the different sensor nodes anywhere inside the square. The various parameters used were similar to the ones used in the previous experiment, except for the multi-objective weights which had a value of 0.3, 0.2, 0.9 and 0.7 for energy, lifetime, area and number of nodes respectively. The algorithm was allowed to be run for the set number of generations. AT the completion the placement of the nodes was done as per the best fitness individual. Figure 6(a) shows the coverage of the various placed nodes. The transfer of data from all nodes to the sink is given in Figure 6(b).

Here also we observe that the algorithm did not place nodes in the extremes of the square corners. This is because of the penalty of energy and number of nodes. Another observation may be seen that the nodal placement is neither uniform, nor symmetric in nature. This is due to the fact that multiple objectives need to be simultaneously met with and a number of parameters need to be optimized. This would not happen in case the placement is uniform or symmetric. The value of various objectives is given in Table 1

Based on the same lines, the last experiment was performed on a diamond shaped map. Here also same set of values to various parameters was used. The multi-objective weights were changed to 0.3, 0.2, 1.4 and 0.7 for energy, lifetime, area and number of nodes respectively. Here as well the algorithm was efficiently able to place the various nodes in an optimal manner. The coverage area and flow of information is shown in Figure 7(a) and 7(b) respectively. The value of the various objective functions is given in Table 1. Here also the algorithm chose not to cover the entire area, but optimally filled a large part of area, so as to maximize area as well as the energy. The placements were non-uniform and non-symmetric in nature.

In all these experiments we observe that the algorithm did not cover some part of the area. This may also be attributed to the characteristic nature of the map which placed a tradeoff between area maximization and the minimization of the

Table 1. The values of objective functions for the various maps

Map	Energy	Lifetime	Area	Number of Nodes	Total
Map 1	6.138×10^{-3}	5.522×10^{-4}	6478.0	10	0.5520
Map 2	3.797×10^{-3}	4.6757×10^{-4}	4504.0	7	0.2157
Map 3	3.6858×10^{-3}	5.5218×10^{-4}	3826.0	6	-0.1139

energy and number of nodes. In these executions we had assumed that it is not mandatory for these parts of the map to have coverage. However this may not always be the case. Hence we further study the algorithm behavior by adopting an area dominated strategy. This is done by increasing the weight of area and reducing the other weights in the objective function. The coverage in such a case for the circular map is shown in Figure 8 when the weight corresponding to area was increased to 1.8. It may be clearly seen that more nodes are placed that would require more energy. On the contrary a significantly large area is served with very few exceptions.

The evolutionary approach here comprises of the master GP and slave GA. The task of master is to have an overall convergence which decides the final fitness of the individual and hence the most optimal deployment strategy. The fitness of the best individual along with GP generations is shown in Figure 9.

In this algorithm we propped that the number of generations of GA or the slave increase as the algorithm proceeds with the GP iterations. This means a general increase in the time of execution along with GP iterations. We hence study the effect of increasing GA generations on the time.

For this the time needed for the completion of every GP generation is plotted. This is shown in Figure 10. The figure however showcases a characteristic picture where the time of execution first decreases with generations and then constantly increases. Initially the algorithm randomly generates the population that comprise of nodes of multiple power levels.

The lower power levels have smaller energy, but cover smaller areas. The initial few generations have a number of nodes corresponding to smaller power levels. As the generations increase, these nodes migrate to higher power levels because of the large increase in area coverage that outperforms the increasing energy. The initial few generations with large number of nodes require more algorithm processing time. However, as the algorithm proceeds, the increasing power levels result in decrease in the total number of nodes. This causes a general reduction in time. Once the nodes have reached significant power level where a tradeoff is met between energy and area coverage, the reduction in number of nodes is not witnessed. Hence the genera increase in time as a result of increasing GA generations is visible in the curve.

The proposed algorithm was able to solve the problem of node deployment effectively and the

Table 2. Comparative analysis of proposed algorithm with other algorithms

Algorithm	Energy	Lifetime	Area	Number of Nodes	Total
Hybrid GP and GA	**6.138×10^{-3}**	**5.522×10^{-4}**	**6478.0**	**10**	**0.5520**
Random	3.5033×10^{-3}	5.522×10^{-4}	3348.0	6	0.7184
GP	5.2262×10^{-3}	5.522×10^{-4}	5588.0	11	0.5959
Uniform	9.8208×10^{-3}	5.522×10^{-4}	7135.0	16	0.6150

results were convincing as per the set objective weights. We further analyze the algorithm working in comparison to the other commonly used approaches in literature. The comparison is made with Random Placement, Genetic Programming, and Uniform Node Placement. The performance of the various algorithms is shown in Table 2. In random placement strategy, the nodes were randomly placed onto the map, ensuring the specified constraints are met. A large number of placements were done and the performance of each of these was noted. In each of these placement heuristics were used to maximize area and minimize the lifetime, energy and number of nodes. It may be easily seen that as compared to the proposed algorithm, the random placement technique resulted in a smaller energy and placement of a smaller number of nodes. However the total area coverage in this case was reasonably less as compared to the proposed algorithm. This resulted in the random placement having a reasonably poor value of the objective function as compared to the proposed algorithm. This further emphasizes on the point that the possibility of multiple locations of the nodes with different power levels cannot be appreciably done with the use of simple heuristics and requires an intelligent optimization technique.

This algorithm evolved individuals using the same genotype representation as done by the Genetic Programming part of the proposed algorithm. This algorithm was supposed to carry out both structural and parametric optimizations. The algorithm optimized the problem to a fine extent. It resulted in better area coverage as compared to the random algorithm which was however at the cost of placement of a larger number of nodes which resulted in increase of network energy. The value of the net objective function was better as compared to the random node placement. This shows that the algorithm could carry out effective optimizations to increase the coverage area with the least increase in energy and number of nodes. When compared to the proposed algorithm, the genetic programming approach however saw smaller area coverage even with the placement of one more sensor node. The energy was slightly smaller than the proposed algorithm. The proposed algorithm had a worse fitness as compared to the proposed algorithm. This shows the inability of a single evolutionary approach to solve

Figure 6 (a). Area coverage for map 2; (b). layout and placement of the nodes for map 2

A

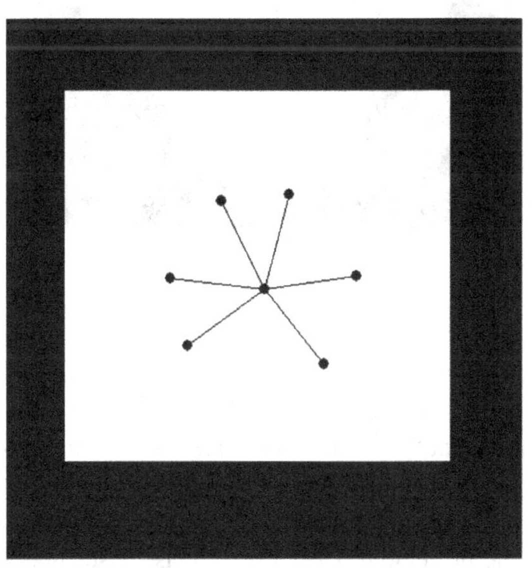

B

Figure 7 (a). Area coverage for map 3; (b). layout and placement of the nodes for map 3

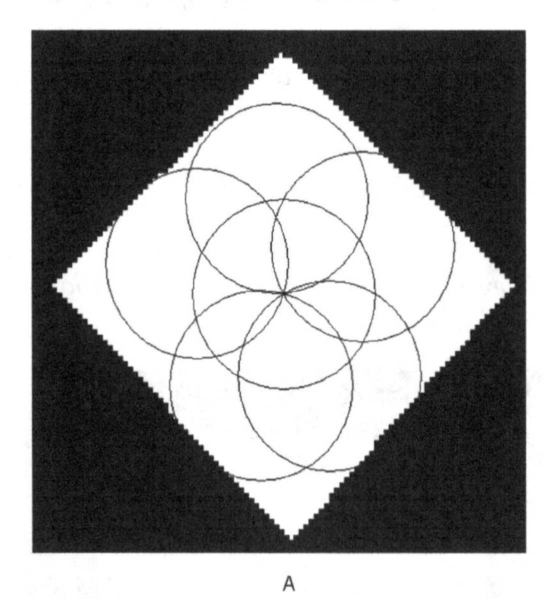

A

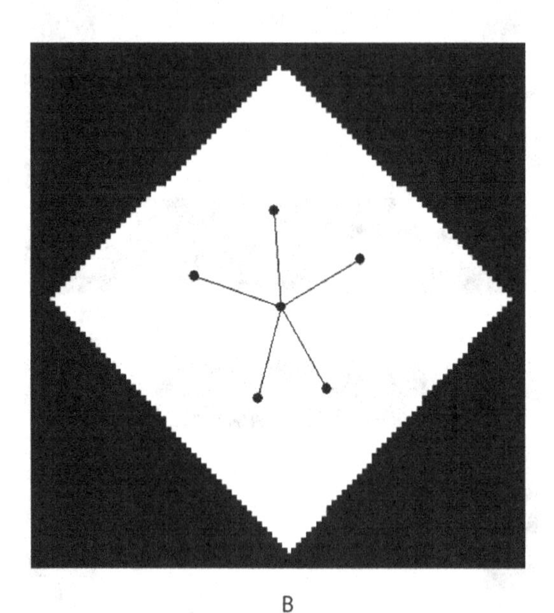

B

the problem that results in hybridization of two evolutionary approaches. Experimental results show that the hybridization results in better performance in optimizing the objective function.

The last algorithm applied was a uniform node placement. Here the various sensor nodes were placed such that the entire area is covered.

Figure 8. Area coverage for map 1 with dominance of area objective function

The uniform placement was done in such a manner that the various sensor nodes are as apart as possible. Each sensor node was operated at the largest power level. This placement technique resulted in a better area coverage that is a natural consequence of the placement strategy. However a very large number of nodes were placed. This resulted in a very large increase in the network energy. The added area coverage did not cope up with the increase in energy. As a result this placement technique had a worse fitness value when compared to the proposed algorithm. This was however better than the random placement and worse than the genetic programming optimized placement.

It may be clearly seen that the proposed approach serves out to be the best in optimizing the objective function. The fusion of the GP and GA carried in this approach is able to remove the weaknesses of the individual algorithms to give a better overall result. Hence the approach may be used for a more effective node deployment in different scenarios.

Figure 9. Convergence in genetic programming

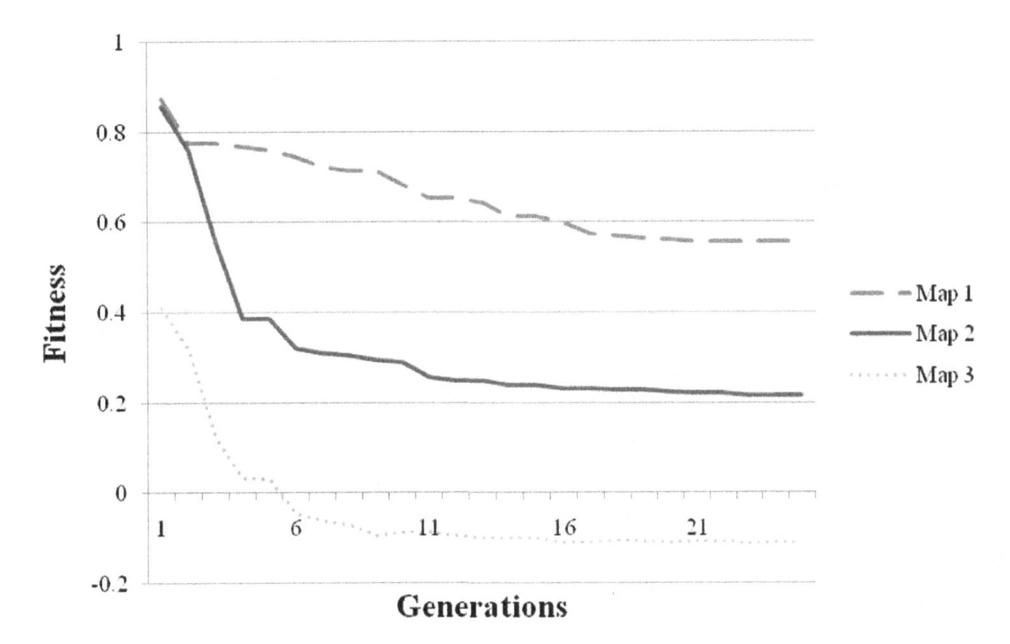

CONCLUSION

The ever growing coverage of wireless networks urges the need of better and more intelligent sensor placement strategies. The multi-objective demand along with the need to optimize multiple parameters makes the complete problem difficult to solve by any trivial technique. In this paper we proposed the use of an algorithm hybrid GP and GA for the same.

The GP was used at the master level and carried forward the layout optimization. It tries

Figure 10. Time of execution for various generations

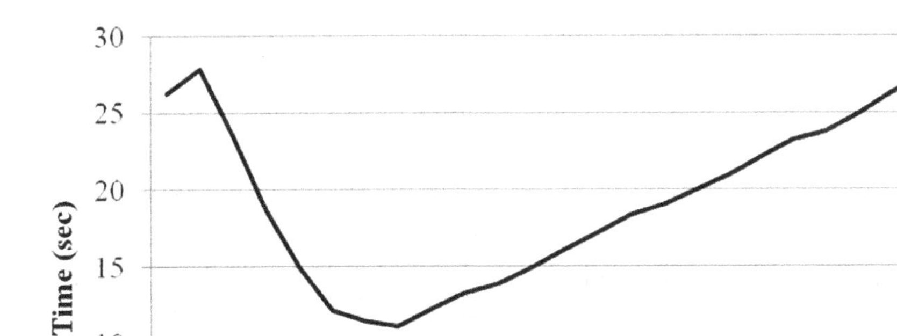

to evolve the most optimal architecture for the sensor placement. The GP individuals were further optimized by means of the GA that tried to fix optimal positions for the various layouts specified by the GP. This led to an optimization of the complete sensor deployment strategy. The algorithm tried to optimize four objectives namely energy, lifetime, area and number of nodes. The contribution of each of these was specified by the multi-objective weights. The area where the node deployment may take place was kept to be variable and could be specified by the user.

The algorithm was tested against a variety of scenarios by changing the maps. The first experiment was on a circular map, which was followed by experiments on square and diamond shaped maps. In all the experiments we observed that the algorithm was able to have an optimal placement of the various nodes with an optimal layout. In our approach, both the evolutionary algorithms in their own way contributed towards the optimization as per these objectives. Experimental results show that the algorithm placed the various nodes in such a manner that all the objectives are satisfied to some extent. In any of the cases a single factor was not allowed to dominate. Rather the mutual effect of all the objectives was taken. For these reasons the area coverage was never complete. It was made to compromise against the increasing energy and node cost. The different multi-objective weights could be adjusted to get different performances to the algorithm.

A major factor behind the algorithm is to strike a balance between the layout and positional optimization. These are controlled by the two evolutionary techniques of GP and GA respectively. This can be easily done by the adjustment of the evolutionary parameters of both the algorithms. In this approach we therefore made an implementation of deterministic adaptation by changing the tradeoff between the two algorithms along with time. The initial few generations are GP dominated, while the domination increases in favor of GA as the algorithm proceeds.

The approach used for solving the problem is an evolutionary approach that is time consuming. More time effective algorithms may be formulated for giving results in shorter time durations. Another problem associated is the scalability. As the dimensionality of the map or the number of placed nodes increase, there is a considerable increase in the search space of the evolutionary algorithm. This lies at both for GP and GA. Very large maps may hence impose a big problem on evolution. The performance may be further improved by framing heuristics for effective guidance of the evolutionary approach. This would result in a considerable reduction of search space at every iteration and an early convergence of the algorithm towards the global minima. All this may be worked over in future.

REFERENCES

Baffo, I., & Confessore, G. (2010). A model to increase the efficiency of a competence-based collaborative network. *International Journal of Intelligent Information Technologies*, *6*(1), 18–30. doi:10.4018/jiit.2010100902

Barrett, S. (2007). Optimizing sensor placement for intruder detection with genetic algorithms In *Proceedings of the IEEE Intelligence and Security Informatics* (pp.185-188).

Carrasco, A., Romero-Ternero, M. C., Sivianes, F., Hernández, M. D., Oviedo, D. I., & Escudero, J. (2010). Facilitating decision making and maintenance for power systems operators through the use of agents and distributed embedded systems. *International Journal of Intelligent Information Technologies*, *6*(4), 1–16. doi:10.4018/jiit.2010100101

Chen, F.-L., & Li, F.-C. (2010). Comparison of the hybrid credit scoring models based on various classifiers. *International Journal of Intelligent Information Technologies*, *6*(3), 56–74. doi:10.4018/jiit.2010070104

Edwin, D. J., Thierens, D., & Watson, R. A. (2004). Hierarchical genetic algorithms. In X. Yao, E. Burke, J. A. Lozano, J. Smith, J. J. Merelo-Guervos, J. A. Bullinaria et al. (Eds.), *Proceedings of the 8th International Conference on Parallel Problem Solving from Nature* (LNCS 3242, pp. 232-241).

Fogel, D. B. (1992). *Evolving artificial intelligence.* Unpublished doctoral dissertation, University of California at San Diego, CA.

Gautam, G., & Chaudhury, B. B. (2007). A distributed hierarchical genetic algorithm for efficient optimization and pattern matching. *Pattern Recognition*, *40*, 212–228. doi:10.1016/j.patcog.2006.04.023

Hou, Y. T., Chen, M. C., & Jeng, B. (2010). An optimal new-node placement to enhance the coverage of wireless sensor networks. *Journal of Wireless Networks*, *16*(4), 1033–1043. doi:10.1007/s11276-009-0186-x

Hu, J., Goodman, E., Seo, K., Fan, Z., & Rosenberg, R. (2005). The hierarchical fair competition (HFC) framework for continuing evolutionary algorithms. *Evolutionary Computation*, *13*(2), 241–277. doi:10.1162/1063656054088530

Hu, J., Goodman, E., Seo, K., & Pei, M. (2002). Adaptive hierarchical fair competition (AHFC) model for parallel evolutionary algorithms. In *Proceedings of Genetic and Evolutionary Computation Conference* (pp. 772-779).

Johnson, D. M., Teredesai, A., & Saltarelli, R. T. (April 2005). Genetic programming in wireless sensor networks. In M. Keijzer, A. Tettamanzi, P. Collet, J. van Hemert, & M. Tomassini (Eds.), *Proceedings of the 8th European Conference on Genetic Programming*, Lausanne, Switzerland (LNCS 3447, pp. 96-107).

Kala, R., Shukla, A., & Tiwari, R. (2010). Clustering based hierarchical genetic algorithm for complex fitness landscapes. *International Journal of Intelligent Systems Technologies and Applications*, *9*(2), 185–205. doi:10.1504/IJISTA.2010.034320

Khanna, R., Liu, H., & Chen, H. (2006). Self organization of sensor networks using genetic algorithms. *International Journal of Sensor Networks*, *1*(3-4), 241–252. doi:10.1504/IJSNET.2006.012040

Lin, J. W., & Chen, Y. T. (2008). Improving the coverage of randomized scheduling in wireless sensor networks. *IEEE Transactions on Wireless Communications*, *7*(12), 4807–4812. doi:10.1109/T-WC.2008.070933

Melanie, M. (1999). *An introduction to genetic algorithms*. Cambridge, MA: MIT Press.

Oh, S. C., Tan, H., Kong, F. W., Tan, Y. S., Ng, K. H., Ng, G. W., & Tai, K. (2007). Multi-objective optimization of sensor network deployment by a genetic algorithm. In *Proceedings of the IEEE Congress of Evolutionary Computation* (pp. 3917-3921).

Qi, Y., Song, M., Yoon, S.-C., & Versterre, L. (2011). Combining supervised learning techniques to key-phrase extraction for biomedical full-text. *International Journal of Intelligent Information Technologies*, *7*(1), 33–44. doi:10.4018/jiit.2011010103

Rechenberg, I. (1973). *Evolutionsstrategie: Optimierung technischer systeme nach prinzipien der biologischen evolution.* Stuttgart, Germany: Frommann-Holzboog-Verlag.

Schwefel, H.-P. (1975). *Evolutionsstrategie and numerische Optimierung.* Unpublished doctoral dissertation, Technische Universitat Berlin, Germany.

Seo, J. H., Kim, Y. H., Ryou, H. B., & Kang, S. J. (2008). Agenetic algorithm for sensor deployment based on two-dimensional operators. In *Proceedings of the ACM Symposium on Applied Computing* (pp. 1812-1813).

Shouhong, Z., & Ding, Z. (2009). A simple approach of range-based positioning with low computational complexity. *IEEE Transactions on Wireless Communications, 8*(12), 5832–5836. doi:10.1109/TWC.2009.12.090905

Shu, T., Krunz, M., & Vrudhula, S. (2006). Joint optimization of transmit power-time and bit energy efficiency in CDMA wireless sensor networks. *IEEE Transactions on Wireless Communications, 5*(11), 3109–3118. doi:10.1109/TWC.2006.04738

Wang, H., Yang, Y., Ma, M., He, J., & Wang, X. (2008). Network lifetime maximization with cross-layer design in wireless sensor networks. *IEEE Transactions on Wireless Communications, 7*(10), 3759–3768. doi:10.1109/T-WC.2008.070079

Wang, Q., Xu, K., Takahara, G., & Hassanein, H. (2007). Device placement for heterogeneous wireless sensor networks: minimum cost with lifetime constraints. *IEEE Transactions on Wireless Communications, 6*(7), 2444–2453. doi:10.1109/TWC.2007.05357

Yener, B., Ismail, M. M., & Sivrikaya, F. (2007). Joint problem of power optimal connectivity and coverage in wireless sensor networks. *Journal of Wireless Networks, 13*(4), 537–550. doi:10.1007/s11276-006-5875-0

Yunhuai, L., Ngan, H., & Ni, L. M. (2007). Power-aware node deployment in wireless sensor network. *International Journal of Distributed Sensor Networks, 3*(2), 225–241. doi:10.1080/15501320701205597

Zhao, C., Yu, Z., & Chen, P. (2007). Optimal deployment of nodes based on genetic algorithm in heterogeneous sensor networks. In *Proceedings of the International Conference on Wireless Communication Networking and Mobile Computing* (pp. 2743-2746).

This work was previously published in the International Journal of Intelligent Information Technologies, Volume 7, Issue 2, edited by Vijayan Sugumaran, pp. 63-83, copyright 2011 by IGI Publishing (an imprint of IGI Global).

Chapter 9
Intelligent Agent-Based e-Learning System for Adaptive Learning

Hokyin Lai
City University of Hong Kong, Hong Kong

Minhong Wang
The University of Hong Kong, Hong Kong

Huaiqing Wang
City University of Hong Kong, Hong Kong

ABSTRACT

Adaptive learning approaches support learners to achieve the intended learning outcomes through a personalized way. Previous studies mistakenly treat adaptive e-Learning as personalizing the presentation style of the learning materials, which is not completely correct. The main idea of adaptive learning is to personalize the earning content in a way that can cope with individual differences in aptitude. In this study, an adaptive learning model is designed based on the Aptitude-Treatment Interaction theory and Constructive Alignment Model. The model aims at improving students' learning outcomes through enhancing their intrinsic motivation to learn. This model is operationalized with a multi-agent framework and is validated under a controlled laboratory setting. The result is quite promising. The individual differences of students, especially in the experimental group, have been narrowed significantly. Students who have difficulties in learning show significant improvement after the test. However, the longitudinal effect of this model is not tested in this study and will be studied in the future.

INTRODUCTION

Individuals learn differently. The concept of adaptive learning is used to cope with individual differences in aptitude. It is assumed that adaptive learning can support individuals to achieve the designated learning outcome by picking the most suitable means. Adaptive learning in fact is not new to the fields of education and information systems. However, most adaptive e-Learning research focuses on applying the available technologies to personalize the presentation style of

DOI: 10.4018/978-1-4666-2047-6.ch009

learning materials. Only few of them have mentioned personalizing learning content to cope with individual differences in aptitude, but without a theoretical foundation.

Aptitude Treatment Interaction (ATI) theory states that if choice of the instruction methods is best matched with the aptitude of individual learner, the probability of having ideal learning outcome will be higher. Aptitude is a quite consistent pattern and may take a long time to change or even cannot be changed while treatment (i.e. instruction method) can be changed.

Snow (1989) suggests that learners who have poor aptitude require a highly structured learning environment or learning content to support their learning. The ATI theory has not been operationalized in previous studies because of the difficulties in evaluating aptitude and matching appropriate instruction method. The ATI theory itself does not provide help in this aspect while Biggs' Constructive Alignment Model may help. Biggs' model is a curriculum design model that addresses the alignments between related items in a curriculum (e.g. teaching and learning activities, learning content and assessment tasks) (Biggs, 2003). Assessment tasks are used to evaluate the level of attainment of learners and can be applied to test whether the learner is capable to advance to the next level of study. If not, highly structured learning content should be provided before advancing to the next level to avoid frustration.

Based on the ATI theory and the constructive alignment model, an adaptive learning model is developed in this study. This model is targeted at enhancing students' learning outcomes by means of strengthening their intrinsic motivation to learn. The logic to operate this model is complicated as the needs vary between individual learners. As such, multi-agent architecture is chosen to operationalize the model. Multi-agent architecture is designed to solve complicated problem which cannot be handled by one single agent while no other technologies can perform better than multi-agent one.

A short curriculum called Introduction to Hang Seng Index has been constructed by two experienced teachers in this discipline, based on Biggs' Constructive Alignment framework. Biggs' framework was referenced because this alignment mechanism concerns the matching between the course objectives and course contents. This framework also suggests that assessment task is a good tool to test the level of development of students. Before advancing to the next level, teachers have to make sure the students have no fundamental problem in the current level with assessment task(s). These characteristic makes this framework a good choice to work as the operation blueprint of the ATI theory. Based on the current aptitude level (or level of development of individual students), the adaptive e-Learning system is able to provide adaptive support without human intervention.

A controlled experiment was conducted, in which 81 undergraduate students who study in the College of Business of one Hong Kong university joined voluntarily. They were randomly assigned to either the experimental group or the control group. Adaptive features were only provided to the experimental group. Each student has spent at most 1.5 hours to go through the curriculum under a controlled laboratory setting, while discussions were prohibited throughout the study. Debriefing was provided after the experiment. Certain individual differences variables, such as gender, age, education level, and preference in presentation mode are well controlled. The pre-test and post-test data were collected both quantitatively and qualitatively. The results showed that students who did badly in the assessment tasks and had received the adaptive support can benefit the most.

LITERATURE REVIEW

People learn differently is absolutely not a new idea (Fizzell, 1984). Keefe (1979) defined individual differences in learning as a consistent pattern of behaviors that an individual approaches educational experiences. It is a relatively stable indicator of how a learner perceives, interacts with, and responds to the learning environment. Conversely, adaptive course design may further enhance learning.

In this section, educational theories related to adaptive learning are described. The emphasis of adaptive e-Learning system is to realize pedagogy with the support of an electronic platform, rather than simply being used as data repository (Hiltz et al., 1999). As such, the reasons why intelligent agent technology is suitable to develop such an adaptive learning model will be discussed.

Adaptive Learning

Adaptive learning means adapting instructional methods to accommodate key individual differences of participants. The concept is that a personalized method of teaching will help learners learn at an efficient and effective way.

Many previous studies were done in adaptive learning, but mainly in classroom setting. One school considers learner preferences, interests, and browsing behavior to determine the personalization mechanisms (Balabanovic & Shoham, 1997; Papanikolaoum & Grigoriadou, 2002). Another school concerns about the distinction in accepting and processing information (Felder & Spurlin, 2005). Gagné (2005) further highlights the relationships between individual differences and learning pace. The processing times of individuals are different and some people are able to process the same piece of information faster than the others. Paramythis and Loidl-Reisinger (2004) identified some key elements of adaptive learning which are: understanding students' needs and preferences, monitoring student activity, interpret learning results, and incorporating such results to implement a way that can facilitate the learning process.

Borgman (1984), Galetta (1984), Gomez et al. (1986) and Olfman et al. (1986) proved that the previous attainment is positively related to learning performance. Von Glasersfeld (1989) supports that sustaining motivation to learn strongly depends on student's confidence in his or her potential to learn. These feelings of competence and belief in potential to solve new challenges are derived from their past experience in solving similar problems rather than any external acknowledgement and motivation (Prawat & Floden, 1994). This links up with Vygotsky (1978) that students are only willing to take a challenge with their current level of development or slightly above. By experiencing the successful completion of challenging tasks, students gain confidence and motivation to embark on more complex challenges. Bernard Weiner's attribution theory further describes how students' beliefs about the causes of academic success or failure. If they believe their failure is due to lack of ability and ability is perceived as uncontrollable, they exert the emotions of shame and frustration and eventually decrease effort and show poorer performance. Teachers intend to avoid these unfavorable conditions to happen by designing a curriculum which starts with their current level of development of students and providing adaptive support at a right time accordingly. As such, students' prior knowledge in the subject is an important consideration. Introduction of milestones in the learning process is crucial. Milestone helps track student's learning progress, as well as provides immediate adaptive support when needed.

Snow (1986) already proved that adaptive learning can achieve an improved learning outcome in the classroom setting. Regarding the proxies that used to measure the learning outcome, most scholars focus on quantitative measurements, such as Mayer (1996) suggested people to weight academic performance by number and types of errors; and Tuckman (2003) proposed to use Grade Point Average (GPA) as a standard measure of learning outcome. However, performance in few subjects like art cannot be measured in such a way. Bostrom et al. (1990) suggested two ways to measure it which are: understanding that can be quantitatively measured by academic performance; and motivation that can be qualitatively measured by attitude change towards learning.

Aptitude-Treatment Interaction (ATI) Theory

The concept of providing adaptive features for individual students in learning is well aligned to the concept in the Aptitude-Treatment Interaction (ATI) theory. ATI theory has been widely discussed for twenty years. ATI theory describes that there is a strong bond between the effectiveness of an instructional strategy (i.e. treatment) and the aptitude level of students (Cronbach & Snow, 1977, 1989). If the aptitude level of student and the instructional strategy are properly matched, student has a higher chance to obtain better educational outcomes (Snow, 1977, 1989). Aptitude has many definitions in wordNet. It can be the inherent ability, talent or ability to do something. Having a high aptitude for something means you are good at doing that something. It is also to be defined as an acquired, learned or developed component of a competency to do a specific task at a certain level. It may be physical or mental. In short, it means the capability to learn in a specific area either because of having talent or having prior knowledge in this area.

Biggs' Constructive Alignment Theory

In order to operationalize the ATI theory, Biggs' constructive alignment theory is referenced. Biggs's theory of constructive alignment inherits the central idea of constructivism that education is a way to train students to be a self-learner (Biggs, 1989). The theory stresses on the fact that developing an effective curriculum rests upon adequately describing the educational goals desired. Biggs views curriculum as a teaching system and the ultimate goals of the system is to guide students towards the desired educational goals. He advocates the alignment of individual components in the system like teaching and learning activities (TLAs) and assessment tasks (ATs). Based on the expertise of teachers in the curriculum design, teachers align learning activities and assessment with the intended learning outcomes appropriately.

Curriculum objectives lie at the central part in the constructive alignment model which means that other constructs in the teaching context are designed based on them. Teachers define the required level of understanding on the subject matter as the curriculum objectives. Referring to the Bloom's Taxonomy, knowledge and skills are categorized in a hierarchical framework (Bloom et al., 1956). Learning at higher levels requires attained pre-requisite knowledge and skills at lower level (Orlich et al., 2004). This implies that the conceptual organization of skills at lower levels contributes to the success in learning the skills at higher levels. The foremost task of teachers is to define the curriculum objectives, which are the expected level of accomplishment, based on their understanding on the learning capabilities.

Teacher then selects TLAs which are able to guide his or her students towards the curriculum objectives that has defined and arranges those activities in a progressive sequence. On the other hand, teacher defined a set of assessment rubrics for measuring the learning performance. Both TLAs and assessments are the reflection of teacher's decision on what their students are to learn, how they are to learn it, and how they will be judged whether they have done or not (Bennett, 2003).

If individual students cannot reach the expected level of accomplishment, teachers might consider provide extra supportive TLAs to strengthening the skills at the current level before escalating the student to next levels. Students with lower cognitive skill require highly structured instructional environments than students with higher cognitive skills (Snow, 1989).

Intelligent Agent for Adaptive E-Learning Systems

Intelligent agent is a computer system that works in an autonomous way which can work in a dynamic environment in order to achieve the goals defined by the system designer (Wooldridge & Jennings, 1995). Intelligent agent system can master complicated problem. It is able to learn new knowledge from experiences and work interactively with each other without human intervention. The characteristics of mobility, ability to interact, ability to cooperate, learn and even reason, based on certain knowledge representations are effective and efficient for personalization or information filtering (Carolan & Collins, 1997; Pankratius et al., 2004; Kuppuswami & Chithralekha, 2010).

IS researchers have begun investigating an emerging, technology-enabled innovation that involves the use of intelligent software agents in e-Learning (Xu & Wang, 2006; Wang, 1997a, 1997b; Kwok et al., 2000; Santos et al., 2004; Conejo et al., 2004; Mishra & Mishra, 2010). Most of the findings have reported that the agent-oriented system infrastructure is good for e-Learning applications, especially for personalization and information filtering.

ADAPTIVE LEARNING MODEL

The ultimate goal of adaptive e-Learning is to deliver right content to right individual at a right time, in the most appropriate way. An adaptive learning model (Figure 1) is built with reference to the ATI theory. Intuitively, the adaptive learning model may not be that useful to those students who already have strong motivation to learn. It is because they are self initiated to search for additional support in order to have a thorough understanding on the subject matter.

Before implementing the adaptive learning model, a well defined curriculum has been constructed with the Biggs' constructive alignment model. The learning objectives are determined by the typical needs in the class and the teaching and learning activities and assessments are clearly aligned with the learning objectives as well (Biggs, 2003). The level of achievement of the learning objectives is referring to the Bloom's taxonomy.

Figure 1. Adaptive learning model

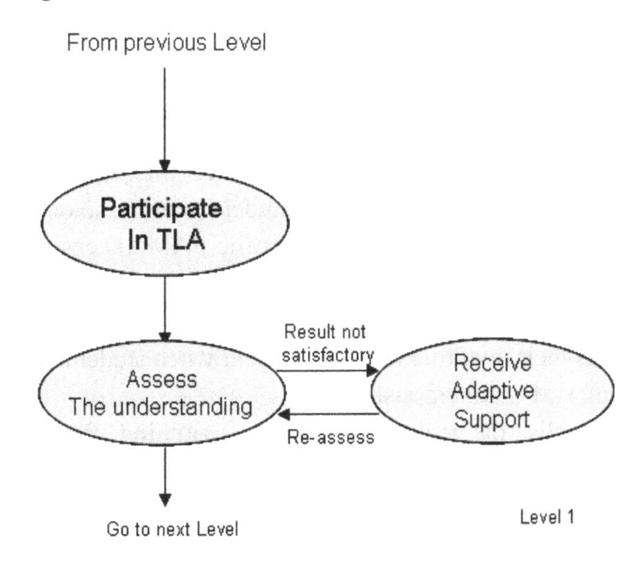

The adaptive learning model is grounded in the recognition that every student is an individual with distinct aptitude (Cronbach & Snow, 1977, 1989). Besides taking student profiles into account at the most beginning of the course, assessment tasks are used to assess the level of development during learning process (Biggs, 2003). Each learning session represents one level of attainment. A session consists of at least one TLA. ATs are put at the end of each learning session. If the assessment result is better than the predefined threshold, then the student is said to be succeed in attaining a certain level in this session without major difficulties and is able to escalate to the next level. Otherwise, adaptive action is triggered and a more detailed explanation on previous task is provided. The revision material, that is a supportive TLA, would explain the session content in a highly structured way. That is with more detailed explanation on the same set of knowledge (Snow, 1989).

THREE-TIER ATI-BASED ADAPTIVE E-LEARNING ARCHITECTURE

Based on the adaptive learning model, a 3-tier ATI-based adaptive e-Learning architecture is designed as shown in Figure 2.

Interface Layer

Students interact with the system through the user interface layer (i.e. the upper layer).

Agent Layer

The middle layer is the agent layer. Four intelligent agents are designed based on the adaptive learning model. Each of them has their own role and responsibilities and they can work autonomously with others in order to accomplish the goals designed by teachers. Their roles and responsibilities are listed as follows:

- **Student Interface Agent (SIA):** A communication hub between students and the agents on the lower tiers of the e-Learning system. Once SIA receives any request from student, it diverts the request to corresponding agent(s) for further processing based on the divert table. Whenever student is about to learn or to retrieve learning material, SIA will divert the request to corresponding agents for further processing.
- **Student Activity Monitoring Agent (SAMA):** The role of SAMA is to monitor the learning progress of each student individually. Other than that, teachers can specify few reporting cases requesting SAMA to report some findings to them. Reporting cases can be defined as a rule in the system, in either individual level or group level. Individual level rule is used to define specific case with respect to individual students. For example, if a particular student cannot reach the assessment thresholds for two consecutive times, SAMA will send a notification to the teacher. Group level rule is used to define case with respect to class rather than individual student. For example, teacher may want to know how many students can get a pass in a particular assessment task. Reporting cases help teachers understand students more such that adjustment in course material and/or adaptive support can be provided in time.

Since this agent is responsible to monitor student activity, so only it can access the student profile. SAMA keeps the student profile, recording students' learning progress and results. It diverts a request to the Learning Process Management Agent when student is about to learn.

- **Learning Process Management Agent (LPMA):** The role of LPMA is to manage the learning process of individual students.

Figure 2. Three-tier ATI-based adaptive e-learning architecture

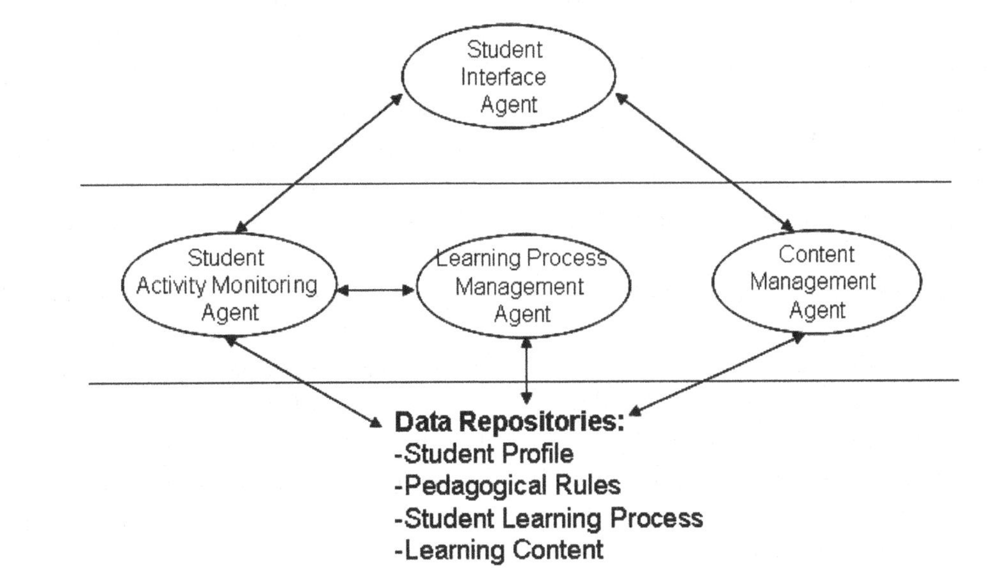

The general curriculum (for the class) is stored in the system as pedagogical rules, while the adaptive action(s) are stored as student learning process. These two databases can only be accessed by LPMA. LPMA is a decision maker such that it picks the appropriate content for individual students to learn when requested and decide whether adaptive support is needed or not. It will divert the result to SAMA for record accordingly.

- **Content Management Agent (CMA):** The role of CMA is to manage the learning contents, such as lecture notes, tutorial notes, exercises, quizzes etc. CMA works closely with LPMA. When receiving request from LPMA, CMA serves it by locating and retrieving the learning content for the student accordingly.

Data Layer

The lower layer is the data layer. It has four data repositories which are implemented in the SQL server database: Student Profile, Pedagogical Rules, Student Learning Process, and Learning Resources.

- **Student Profile:** This component contains both static and dynamic information of individual students. Static information includes GPA before taking the course, prior knowledge in the subject area, and preferred ways of learning etc. Dynamic information includes assessment results. Static information is captured before the course begins and remains unchanged throughout the curriculum, whereas dynamic information is updated when the course is running.
- **Pedagogical Rules:** This component contains the general curriculum design for the course which is applicable to the class. This curriculum is designed based on the averaging ability in class, so the sequence of TLAs is aimed at leading students toward the predefined course objectives. By the end of each teaching session, there is at least one ATs (with preset passing threshold) to test the performance of individual students. If the assessment result cannot

pass the threshold, adaptive feature will be invoked automatically. Adaptive content contains more detailed explanation on the course content.

- **Student Learning Process:** This component stores the individual learning progress. The learning status of each TLA is kept in this storage.
- **Learning Resources (or Learning Material):** This component keeps learning objects (LOs), such as lecture notes, tutorial notes, exercises, quizzes or video chips. The learning objects are compactable with the standard of Sharable Content Object Reference Model (SCORM) (Advanced Distributed Learning, 2001)

EXPERIMENTAL DESIGN

In this section, the experimental design, including the design of the sample curriculum, the selection and grouping of participants and the experimental run-down will be discussed.

Sample Curriculum

A sample curriculum called Introduction to Hang Seng Index is developed by two experienced teachers in this discipline. The general curriculum includes two teaching and learning activities (TLAs): two lectures which are mandatory to all students, and three assessment tasks (ATs): two quizzes and one final examination which are mandatory as well. The sequence of learning in the general curriculum is: lecture 1 (What is Hang Seng Index?) → quiz 1 → lecture 2 (How to calculate the Hang Seng Index figure?) → quiz 2 → final examination whereas the sequence of learning with adaptive TLAs is: lecture 1 → quiz 1 → Revision task 1 (optional) → lecture 2 → quiz 2 → Revision task 2 (optional) → final examination. Figure 3 shows the lecture 1 material of the sample course. The upper part indicates the learning sequence: current task (i.e. lecture 1) is highlighted in red; next available task(s) (i.e. lecture 2 and quiz 1) are highlighted in green and the rest (quiz 2 and final examination) are in grey. This allows learner to have a clear picture of the whole curriculum. The lower part shows the task content. Lecture 1 is a lecture slideshow presentation with audio.

Apart from these, there are two adaptive TLAs which may be triggered in the experiment. (They will only be available in the experimental group.) If individual students cannot get a mark higher than the predefined thresholds of quiz 1 or quiz 2, adaptive TLA will be included in the learning sequence bar (like the circled task in Figure 4) which means that learner needs to go through one more task in the experiment. These TLAs are revision tasks for the current level of study. The revision material would explain the session content in a highly structured way.

Subjects

There were 81 undergraduate students from the College of Business in one Hong Kong university voluntarily joined this study. They are invited to go through the sample curriculum under a controlled laboratory setting and randomly assigned to either the experimental group or the control group. In the experimental group, the adaptive learning model is applied such that adaptive TLA(s) might be initiated if there exists any under threshold assessment result. In the control group, no adaptive TLA is equipped, so no matter how low is the assessment result, no adaptive support will be provided. And the students are allowed to advance to next level. Since the sample curriculum is designed based on the Biggs' constructive alignment model, instruction to learn and the curriculum design details such as the learning objectives are available to all participants before the course begins.

Previous research in adaptive learning considers the course materials' representation methods as an important factor to manipulate adaptive learn-

Figure 3. Sample curriculum

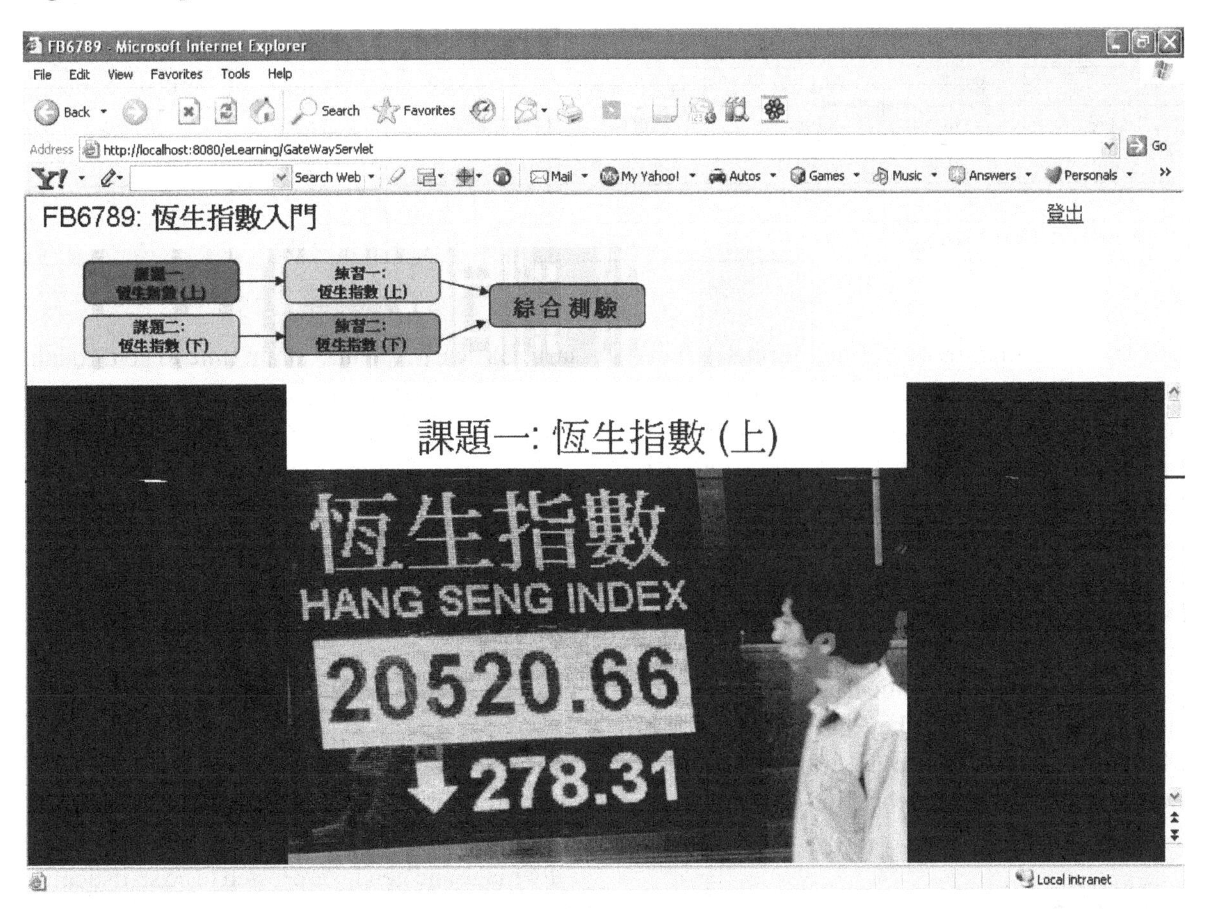

ing, so we have prepared two formats of lecture note and tested the effect too. The lecture note is either in (1) slide show format (i.e. graphical form) or (2) text format. Same set of audio presentation is applied to these two formats. In each group, a sequential assignment of participants into the four sub-groups: {(lecture 1: slide show format, lecture 2: slide show format), (lecture 1: slide show format, lecture 2: text format), (lecture 1: text format, lecture 2: slide show format), (lec-

Figure 4. Sample curriculum with adaptive TLA

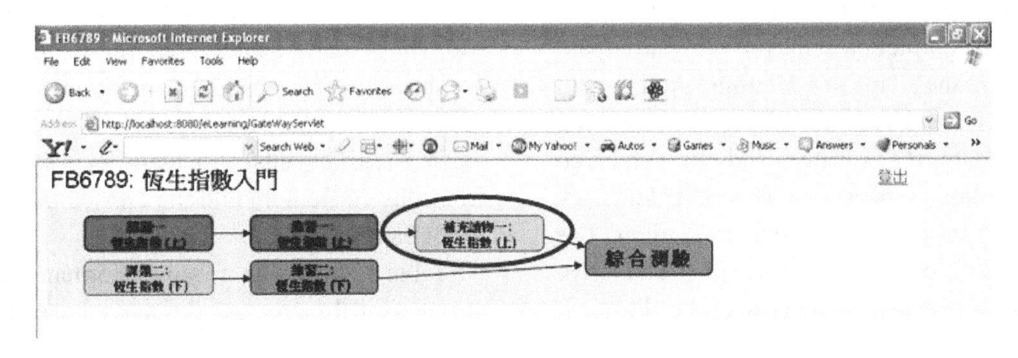

Table 1. Experimental result

Group	Experimental group			Control group		
	Pre-test	Post-test	Change (in %)	Pre-test	Post-test	Change (in %)
Max.	80	100	25.00%	100.00	100.00	0.00%
Min.	0	20	-	0.00	10.00	-
Average	43.33	69.05	59.34%	44.10	68.72	55.81%
SD	23.06	18.10	-21.50%	27.62	23.88	-13.54%

ture 1: text format, lecture 2: text format)}. For instances, the first participant in the experimental group is assigned to the sub-group of (lecture 1: slide show format, lecture 2: slide show format) and the second participant in the same group is assigned to the sub-group of (lecture 1: slide show format, lecture 2: text format) and so on. The format of learning materials is checked to have no impact on the learning outcome in this study.

The grouping arrangement is not opened to the participants before they have finished the whole experiment. We do not want to frustrate any students, so a short debriefing is provided at the end of the experiment.

Experiment

Each participant is given a list of instructions and a set of login ID and password before the experiment has begun. After reading the instruction, they are requested to answer five 4-choice multiple-choice questions about Hang Seng Index. The choices for the same question are very similar to each other to reduce the risk of getting the right answer by luck. The questions act as a pre-test to understand the participant's prior knowledge in this specific area. Upon completion of the pre-test, participant can login to the adaptive e-Learning system with the login ID and password. They are requested to provide the GPA range, and the perceived understanding on the course content before they could start learning the sample curriculum. The participant is required to go through the adaptive TLA(s) (if any) before they can proceed to next task. Basically, the maximum time to go through the sample course is fixed to 1.5 hours. The last TLA for all groups were the same and which was the final examination. The final examination worked as a post-test result. By the end of the experiment, participants are welcome to provide written feedback optionally.

RESULT AND ANALYSIS

In this section, the pre-test and the post-test results are present and discussed. The preference of representation formats of learning materials, GPA range and gender are tested to be statistically insignificant to the learning outcome under this context. Also, the multi-agent framework supports the operation of the experiment very well. The complicated logic has become transparent to the samples as the response time of the system is quite satisfactory.

Pre-Test and Post-Test Analyses

Majority of participants show improvements in the post-test when compared to the pre-test results. 69.05% of participants from the experimental group and 64.10% of participants from the control group show improvement. These figures reflect that most participants can actually learn something from this curriculum and the curriculum design is not bad.

Table 1 shows the group performance in the experiment. In average, the percentages of improvement (in terms of the difference between the post-test and pre-test scores) are 59.34% for the experimental group and 55.81% for the control group. The standard derivations in both groups are decreased (21.50% for the experimental group and 13.54% for the control group). The reduced standard derivations reflect that the learning outcome in terms of academic performance among the group is getting closer and the effect is more prominent in the experimental group. The effect of the individual differences in learning ability affecting the learning outcome is getting lesser.

In the experimental group, 19.05% participants have triggered and used the adaptive TLA(s) in the experiment in which 87.5% of them show significant improvement (that is, maximum improvement: 133.33% and the median of improvement: 44.16%) in the post-test. This figures support the design of the adaptive learning model.

Feedback from Participants

Most feedbacks are related to the perceived difficulties of the curriculum. Comments are optional and only one-third samples have provided, so we cannot have a full picture. By observation, majority of feedbacks given by the experimental group reflect the difficulty of the course. One participant mentioned that the supplementary note (i.e. adaptive support) is very useful and one another expected more explanations on those complicated terms in the material. These reveal that the level of understanding of learners varies. And it is quite contradicting that one participant from the control group made a comment of "content is quite detail with a lot of examples and data, easy to handle". This, again, shows the difference in aptitude between learners. This learner thinks the content provided by the general curriculum is already very detail. Due to the fact that all feedbacks are anonymous, we cannot further inference on the relation between the perceived difficulty of learning content and the actual learning outcome.

CONCLUSION

We conclude that the adaptive learning model derived from the ATI theory and Biggs' constructive alignment model in the e-Learning setting is tested to be useful in improving learning outcome, especially in supporting students who have difficulties in understanding the course content. If the instructional methods consistently align with the aptitude level of individual student throughout the learning process, the learning outcomes are better off. However, one limitation of this study is that this study is not a longitudinal study which cannot show the long-term effect of the adaptive learning model.

E-Learning is in fact less stressful than the traditional learning. This form of learning can eliminate fear of making mistakes in front of people. Students can try the things out without any psychological concerns. We strongly believe that providing adaptive support in e-Learning setting is far more effective than providing adaptive support in normal classroom setting because people are fear of making mistakes in front of people. We may prove this idea in future research.

Also, we will further examine the available education literatures to figure out if there exist any other adaptive actions which can enhance the adaptive learning model.

In addition, multi-agent framework is proved to be a suitable technology to adaptive learning, in terms of the capability to support complicated logics and response time.

REFERENCES

Balabanovic, M., & Shoham, Y. (1997). Fab: Content-based, collaborative recommendation. *Communications of the ACM*, *40*(3), 66–72. doi:10.1145/245108.245124

Beck, H. P., Porrer-Woody, S., & Pierce, L. G. (2001). The relations of learning and grade orientations to academic performance. In Hebl, M. R., Brewer, C. L., & Benjamin, L. T. Jr., (Eds.), *Handbook for teaching introductory psychology: With an emphasis on assessment*. Mahwah, NJ: Lawrence Erlbaum.

Beckstrom, M., Croasdale, H., Riad, S. M., & Kamel, M. M. (2004). *Assessment of Egypt's e-learning readiness*. Retrieved from http://www.ltss.bris.ac.uk/events/egypt/ellen/readiness.doc

Bennett, R. (2003). Determinants of undergraduate student dropout rates in a university business studies department. *Journal of Further and Higher Education, 27*(2), 123–141. doi:10.1080/0309877032000065154

Bhide, A. (1994). Efficient markets, deficient governance: U.S. securities regulations protect investors and enhance market liquidity. But do they alienate managers and shareholders? *Harvard Business Review, 72*(6), 128–140.

Biggs, J. B. (1989). Approaches to the enhancement of tertiary teaching. *Higher Education Research & Development, 8*, 7–25. doi:10.1080/0729436890080102

Biggs, J. B. (2003). *Teaching for quality learning at university*. Buckingham, UK: The Society for Research into Higher Education.

Bloom, B., & Englehart, M. Furst, E., Hill, W., & Krathwohl, D. (1956). *Taxonomy of educational objectives, the classification of educational goals--Handbook I: Cognitive domain*. New York, NY: McKay.

Borgman, C. L. (1984). *The user's mental model of an information retrieval system: Effect on performance*. Unpublished doctoral dissertation, Stanford University, Stanford, CA.

Bostrom, R. P., Olfman, L., & Sein, M. K. (1990). Learning style of end users. *Management Information Systems Quarterly*, 101–119. doi:10.2307/249313

Carolan, T., Collins, B., et al. (1997). *Intelligent agents*. Retrieved from http://ntrg.cs.tcd.ic/cs4/

Conejo, R., Guzman, E., Millian, E., Trella, M., Perez-De-La-Cruz, J. L., & Rioz, A. (2004). SIETTE: A web-based tool for adaptive testing. *International Journal of Artificial Intelligence in Education, 14*, 29–61.

Conrad, K., & TrainningLinks (2000), *Instructional design for web-based training*. Amherst, MA: HRD Press.

Cronbach, L., & Snow, R. (1977). *Aptitudes and instructional methods: A handbook for research on interactions*. New York, NY: Irvington.

Felder, R. M., & Spurlin, J. (2005). Applications, reliability and validity of the index of learning styles. *International Journal of Engineering Education, 32*(1), 103–112.

Fizzell, R. L. (1984). The status of learning styles. *The Educational Forum, 48*(3), 303–312. doi:10.1080/00131728409335909

Gagné, F. (2005). From noncompetence to exceptional talent: Exploring the range of academic achievement within and between grade levels. *Gifted Child Quarterly, 49*(2), 139–153. doi:10.1177/001698620504900204

Galletta, D. (1984). *A learning model of information systems: The effects of orienting materials, ability, expectations and experience on performance, usage and attitudes*. Unpublished doctoral dissertation, University of Minnesota, Minneapolis, MN.

Garrison, R., & Anderson, T. (2003). *E-learning in the 21st century: A framework for research and practice*. London, UK: Routledge. doi:10.4324/9780203166093

Gomez, L. M., Egan, D. E., & Bowers, C. (1986). Learning to use a text editor: Some learner characteristics that predict success. *Human-Computer Interaction, 2*(1), 1-23.

Govindasamy, T. (2002). Successful implementation of e-learning: Pedagogical considerations. *The Internet and Higher Education, 4*, 287–299. doi:10.1016/S1096-7516(01)00071-9

Hiltz, S. R., Fjermestad, J., & Floydlewis, L. (1999). Introduction to the special issue on collaborative learning via Internet. *Group Decision and Negotiation, 8*(5), 367–369. doi:10.1023/A:1008674423058

Keefe, J. W. (1979). Learning style: An overview. In National Association of Secondary School Principals (Eds.), *Student learning styles: Diagnosing and prescribing programs* (pp. 1-17). Reston, VA: National Association of Secondary School Principals.

Kuppuswami, S., & Chithralekha, T. (2010). A new behavior management architecture for language faculty of an agent for task delegation. *International Journal of Intelligent Information Technologies, 6*(2), 44–64. doi:10.4018/jiit.2010040103

Kwork, J., Wang, H., Liao, S., Yuen, J., & Leung, F. (2000). Student profiling system for agent-based educational system. In *Proceedings of the American Conference on Information Systems*.

Mayer, R. E., & Hegarty, M. (1996). The process of understanding mathematical problems. In Sternberg, R. J., & Ben-Zeev, T. (Eds.), *The book of the nature of mathematical thinking*. Mahwah, NJ: Lawrence Erlbaum.

Mcllroy, J., & Jones, B. (1993). *Going to university: The student guide*. Manchester, UK: Manchester University Press.

Mishra, K., & Mishra, R. B. (2010). Multiagent based selection of tutor-subject-student paradigm in an intelligent tutoring system. *International Journal of Intelligent Information Technologies, 6*(1), 46–70. doi:10.4018/jiit.2010100904

Olfman, L., Seiin, M. K., & Bostrom, R. P. (1986). Training for end-user computing: Are basic abilities enough for learning? In *Proceedings of the Twenty-Second Annual Computer Personnel Research Conference*, Calgary, AB, Canada (pp. 1-11).

Orlich, D. C., Harder, R. J., Callahan, R. C., Trevisan, M. S., & Brown, A. B. (2004). *Teaching strategies, a guide to effective instruction* (7th ed.). Boston, MA: Houghton Mifflin.

Pankratius, V., Sandel, O., & Stucky, W. (2004). Retrieving content with agents in web service e-learning systems. In *Proceedings of the First Symposium on Professional Practice in AI and the First IFIP Conference on Artificial Intelligence Applications and Innovations*, Toulouse, France.

Papanikolaoum, K., & Grigoriadou, M. (2002). Towards new forms of knowledge communication: The adaptive dimensions of a web-based learning environment. *Computers & Education, 39*, 333–360. doi:10.1016/S0360-1315(02)00067-2

Paramythis, A., & Loidl-Reisinger, S. (2004). Adaptive learning environments and e-learning standards. *Electronic Journal of eLearning, 2*(1).

Prawat, R. S., & Floden, R. E. (1994). Philosophical-perspectives on constructivist views of learning. *Educational Psychologist, 29*(1), 37–48. doi:10.1207/s15326985ep2901_4

Rosenberg, M. J. (2001). *E-learning strategies for delivering knowledge in the digital age*. New York, NY: McGraw-Hill.

Santos, C. T., & Osorio, F. S. (2004). Integrating intelligent agents, user models, and automatic content categorization in a virtual environment. In J. C. Lester, R. M. Vicari, & F. Paraguacu (Eds.), *Proceedings of the 7th International Conference on Intelligent Tutoring Systems* (LNCS 3220, pp. 128-139).

Sein, M. K., Bostrom, R. P., & Olfman, L. (1987). Conceptual models in training novice users. In *Proceedings of the Third Conference of the British Computer Society Human Computer Interaction*, Stuttgart, West Germany (pp. 861-867).

Snow, R. E. (1986). Individual differences in the design of educational programs. *The American Psychologist, 41*(10), 1029–1039. doi:10.1037/0003-066X.41.10.1029

Snow, R. E. (1989). Aptitude-treatment interaction as a framework for research on individual differences in learning. In Ackerman, P., Strenberg, R. J., & Glaser, R. (Eds.), *Learning and individual differences*. New York, NY: W. H. Freeman.

Tuckman, B. W. (2003). The effect of learning and motivation strategies training on college students' achievement. *Journal of College Student Development, 44*(3), 430. doi:10.1353/csd.2003.0034

Von Glasersfeld, E. (1989). Constructvism in education. In Husen, T., & Postlethwaite, T. N. (Eds.), *The international encyclopedia of education* (pp. 162–163). Oxford, UK: Pergamon Press.

Vygotsky, L. S. (1978). *Mind in society: The development of higher psychological processes*. Cambridge, MA: Harvard University Press.

Wang, H. (1997a). LearnOOP: An active agent-based educational system. *Expert Systems with Applications, 12*(2), 153–162. doi:10.1016/S0957-4174(96)00090-5

Wang, H. (1997b). SQL Tutor+: A co-operative ITS with repository support. *Information and Software Technology, 39*, 343–350. doi:10.1016/S0950-5849(96)01152-4

Wooldridge, M., & Jennings, N. (1995). Intelligent agents: Theory and practice. *The Knowledge Engineering Review, 10*(2), 115–152. doi:10.1017/S0269888900008122

Xu, D., & Wang, H. (2006). Intelligent agent supported personalization for virtual learning environments. *Decision Support Systems, 42*, 825–843. doi:10.1016/j.dss.2005.05.033

This work was previously published in the International Journal of Intelligent Information Technologies, Volume 7, Issue 3, edited by Vijayan Sugumaran, pp. 1-13, copyright 2011 by IGI Publishing (an imprint of IGI Global).

Chapter 10
Intelligent Information Retrieval Using Fuzzy Association Rule Classifier

Sankaradass Veeramalai
Anna University, India

Arputharaj Kannan
Anna University, India

ABSTRACT

As the use of web applications increases, when users use search engines for finding some information by inputting keywords, the number of web pages that match the information increases at a tremendous rate. It is not easy for a user to retrieve the exact web page which contains information he or she requires. In this paper, an approach to web page retrieval system using the hybrid combination of context based and collaborative filtering method employing the concept of fuzzy association rule classification is introduced and the authors propose an innovative clustering of user profiles in order to reduce the filtering space and achieves sub-linear filtering time. This approach can produce recommended web page links for users based on the information that associates strongly with users' queries quickly with better efficiency and therefore improve the recall, precision of a search engine.

INTRODUCTION

As the Internet usage rate has rapidly increased, the volume of electronic documents that matches the user's interest can be seen on the web has also substantially increased. The User gives the keywords as input to a search engine and the search engine returns a set of pages that are related to the key word topics or terms. The result page set consists of too much irrelevant information and may the relevant information of the user's choice cannot be retrieved. In particular, users have to browse and view sites one after another for a long time until they are satisfied to have a good set that is relevant to their interest or more likely, they give up the search.

Earlier recommendation system uses the association concept for classification purpose but Association rule mining does not have a fixed target (Lin, Alvarez, & Ruiz, 2002; Lei, Kang,

DOI: 10.4018/978-1-4666-2047-6.ch010

Lu, & Yan, 2005). That is, any item can appear on any part of a rule. The use of association rules for classification in recommendation system leads to problems where the instances can only belong to a discrete number of classes. The reason is that association rule mining is only possible for attributes that are subjected to the terms of keywords. However, in general the usage of association rules has its own disadvantages. Every item, which is not present in the entire body of the rule, may occur in the head of the rule.

To cope with this problem, we propose a recommendation engine for supporting information retrieval system based on the classification of web pages by fuzzy association rules and also we have introduced user profile clustering concept to reduce retrieval time of the user profile from the group of user profile. The framework of fuzzy classified association rule mining is presented which incorporates fuzzy set modeling based on the time in an existing association rule mining technique (Kumar & Thambidurai, 2004; Lei, Kang, Lu, & Yan, 2005). Interoperability architecture for building customized search engines is developed by Cecil et al. Through this, the existing search engines are decomposed into self-contained components (Chua, Chiang, & Storey, 2009).

In order to implement efficiently these services, information filtering systems rely upon clustering of user profiles (Greening, 1998; Wang, Xie, & Li, 2006; Mostafa, Mukhopadhyay, Lam, & Palakal, 1997). This approach clusters Web site users into different groups and generating common user profiles so that these profiles can be filtered in the recommendation system. This concept improves the ability to capture the precariousness among Web user's navigation behaviour. The usage of clustering methodology increases the filtering efficiency with respect to time.

The goal of Recommender Systems is to generate web pages about new items or to predict the substitute of a specific item for a particular user.

RELATED WORK

The primary goal of information systems is to retrieve or filter objects and classify them based on the rules described in the system. The filtering system may be classified as context based filtering or collaborative filtering (Zhou, Li, Bruza, Wu, Xuusing, & Lau, 2007; Wang, Xie, & Li, 2006). In information-filtering environments, uncertainties associated with changing interests of the user and the dynamic document stream is handled (Mostafa, Mukhopadhyay, Lam, & Palakal, 1997). The classification process is based on association rule mining technique where a rule is defined to make distinct classification. Recommendation using association rules is to predict preference for item k when the user preferred item i and j, by adding confidence of the association rules that have k in the result part and i or j in the condition part. Association rules capture relationships among items based on patterns of co-occurrence across transactions (Kumar & Thambidurai, 2004). The hierarchical structure is also used for classifying a large, heterogeneous collection of web content. The hierarchical structure is initially used to train different second-level classifiers. In the hierarchical case, a model is learned to distinguish a second-level category from other categories within the same top level (Dumais & Chen, 2000).

Recommendation System

The aim of recommendation system is to select information whose content are most relevant to the user's interest from a greater volume of information available and to present them in suitable way for the user (Fernandez, Calderón, Barrenechea, Bustince, & Herrera, 2010). A recommendation system makes suggestions about web pages to a user. Social recommendation methods collect ratings of web pages from many individuals to make recommendations to a user concerned (Basu, Hirsh, & Cohen 1998). Onto-Clippy is a tool-supported methodology for the user-friendly design and creation of ontologies. Existing ontology design methodologies and tools are targeted at experts and not suitable for users without a background in formal logic (Dahlem, 2011). Web information recommendation fall into three categories:

1. Recommendation based on the similarity of web pages.
2. Recommendation based on the preferences and behaviors of user groups.
3. Recommendation based on the preference and behaviour of individual user.

Therefore, when a user inputs "apple" as a keyword of his/her query, the search engine can provide information not only about "pomaceous fruit", but also about "iTune" and "iPhone", according to the same reason.

Fuzzy Association Rule

An association rule is a rule of the form X->Y, where X and Y are set of items. X and Y are respectively called the body and the head of the rule (Lin, Alvarez, & Ruiz 2002). An association rule mining is the major focus in the area of data mining. Its objective is to find certain association relationships among a set of information items in a given database. The relationships among the items are described in asset of rules called association rules. Different from the above three main methods of earlier Recommendation system, association-based approach presents the web pages based on the association relationship of the key words that are extracted from the user and provides web links pointed to web pages associated strongly with the pursuit of the user through concept association.

Web users are most concerned about the important pages may not contain items which cannot be search engine query check, because, it reduces information retrieval efficiency (Shen, 2010). It can help web users to get more useful and interesting information from the WWW, and improve the efficiency and quality of information retrieval of a web search engine, especially its recall (Agarwal, Haque, Liu, & Parsons 2006; Luengo & Herrera, 2010).

The set of association rules is a form of ""IF (pre-conditioned set of Web pages) THEN (post-conditioned Web page)." We keep actual information's user and describe the rules in the user's profile which can be updated at any time to describe the customer's behavior (Puntheeranurak & Tsuji, 2002). There are five kinds of associations of concept described as follows:

Super Class Association

When a specific topic is browsed by a user, it refers to the profiler to discover a broad range of interests, rather than just latching onto one correct topic (Lu, Zhou, Li, Lu, & Zhou, 2002).The word "apple" is associated with "fruit".

Subclass Association

It means associating a key word with its subclass concepts. This kind of association is just opposite to the super class concept association (Lu, Zhou, Li, Lu, & Zhou, 2002). The word "apple" is associated with "iPhone" and "MacOS".

Synonym/Near Synonym Association

It means associating a key word with its synonym or near synonym concepts, including synonyms in other languages (Lu, Zhou, Li, Lu, & Zhou, 2002).The keyword "mobile" has the synonyms which refer to mobility and it is associated with "electronic device".

Historic Association

It means associating a key word with some other concepts related due to some historic causes (Lu, Zhou, Li, Lu, & Zhou, 2002).For instance the word "September 11" is associated with history of "world trade centre attack".

Hotspot Topic Association

It means associating a key word with existing hot news topics which are tying up with it. This is a kind of very useful concept association (Alcal´a, Ducange, Herrera, & Lazzerini, 2009).The keyword "windows" is associated with the upgraded versions of the windows which is released in the recent times.

In general, these systems operate in five stages (Puntheeranurak & Tsuji, 2002):

First, they collect information about the user's preferences based either on observations of user behaviour during Web surf or on explicit user input. Second, they extract related information, such as common words or phrases, and use them as input to an algorithm for creating user profiles. In the third stage, the system discovers similar documents to those that generated the profile. This task requires a Web search mechanism, such as a search engine. Here the filtering mechanism is used to filter the documents based on either context based filtering or collaborative filtering (Zhou, Li, Bruza, Wu, Xuusing, & Lau, 2007).

Next, the system compares the newly discovered documents to the user's profile and presents the most relevant ones to the user. Finally, the system process the user's relevance feedback to modify the profile. In computing systems like grid computing platforms, federated database systems, the database is portioned among a very large number of computers that are dispersed over a wide area, association rule mining is not effective (Wolff & Schuster, 2004). Fuzzy association is used to capture the relationships among different index terms or keywords in the documents, i.e., each pair of words have an associated value to distinguish itself from the others. Therefore, the ambiguity in word usage is avoided (Lei, Kang, Lu, & Yan, 2005).

Filtering Techniques

An information filter that based on user search intents was incorporated in Web search process to quickly filter out irrelevant data (Zhou, Li, Bruza, Wu, Xuusing, & Lau, 2007). Filtering is often meant to imply the removal of data from an incoming stream, rather than finding data in that stream (Belkin & Croft, 1992). Search engines are very effective at filtering pages that match explicit queries in two ways. Simple browsing has given way to filtering as a way to manage web based information based on two ways. Search engines are very effective at filtering pages that match explicit queries (Greening, 1998). Filtering may be classified as:

1. Content based filtering, and
2. Collaborative filtering.

Content Based Filtering

Information retrieval and information filtering systems perform all calculations on the single relation web pages X keywords (Sharma & Sharma, 2010). Content-based recommender systems recommend items with similar content to things the user has liked before (Greening, 1998).

An Autonomous Web Agent for Automatic Retrieval use content-based similarity matching to help search for interesting research papers within a digital library (Greening,1998). Ontology is also used to improve content-based search. Domain ontologies, which represent the concepts of an application domain and their associated relationships, have become increasingly important as surrogates for capturing and representing the semantics of real world applications (Kim & Storey, 2011). When a Web document is fetched to a client, the filtering decision will be done based on the result of the analysis of the contents on the document. This analysis usually takes place in the proxy server in real-time instead of in the browser. At this moment, the content analysis techniques used by most filtering software are some sort of simple keyword matching. Most of the content filtering systems actually share three common approaches (Middleton, Rour,e & Shadbolt, 2001). They are:

1. URL-based on top of content analysis,
2. Text-based content analysis, and
3. Single pass content analysis.

URL Based on Top of Content Analysis

Simply comparing the requested URL address with an URL list in the "access control check" module of the system is always faster than conducting content analysis on the key word (Puntheeranurak & Tsuji, 2002). Content analysis can only determine the subject of the data, but not the habit of the Web surfers. Since the analyzed result of the system access information is usually summarized in the form of Web URL address (Middleton, Roure, & Shadbolt, 2001).

Text-Based Content Analysis

Data objects in a Web request are multimedia in nature. By co-relating the multimedia data with its associated text information in the Web pages text based content analysis is done (Middleton, Roure, & Shadbolt, 2001).

Single-Pass Content Analysis

Content filtering need to satisfy one important constrain. This constraint is related to the block data streaming of the HTTP protocol. Whenever a system receives a block of data, it will pass to its next level or client immediately, where it is difficult for the filtering algorithm to access the previously transmitted information (Middleton, Roure, & Shadbolt, 2001).

Collaborative Filtering

In collaborative systems, all calculations are based on the single relation user × rated web pages. A collaborative recommender system asks people to rate explicitly pages and then recommend new pages that similar users have rated highly (Zhou, Li, Bruza, Wu, Xuusing, & Lau, 2007). Collaborative recommender systems utilize user ratings to recommend items liked by similar people (Prem Melville et al., 2001). After user's rating is received, collaborative filtering is processed by using clustering technique to find the recommended Web page (Vozalis & Margaritis 2003; Greening, 1998).Collaborative filtering is most likely to be used in the small group of users where the individual interest of the user is identified. Web intelligence system focuses on Web 2.0 usage, web mining for personalization service, and brings a different approach to collaborative filtering (Baloglu, Wyne, & Bahcetepe, 2010).

Hybrid Filtering

Hybrid systems, attempting to combine the advantages of content-based and collaborative recommender systems, have proved popular to-date (Middleton, Roure, & Shadbolt, 2001). The hybrid-filtering model can efficiently cope with the faults of traditional filtering models and greatly improve the recommendation (Wang, Xie, & Li, 2006).The feedback required for content-based recommendation is shared, allowing collaborative recommendation as well. If we provide a system with both content-based and collaborative information as separate relations, we get the entity-relationship model (Figure 1).

This approach combines the two filtering methods by first relating each of them to a distinct component and then basing its predictions on the

Figure 1. Hybrid filtering

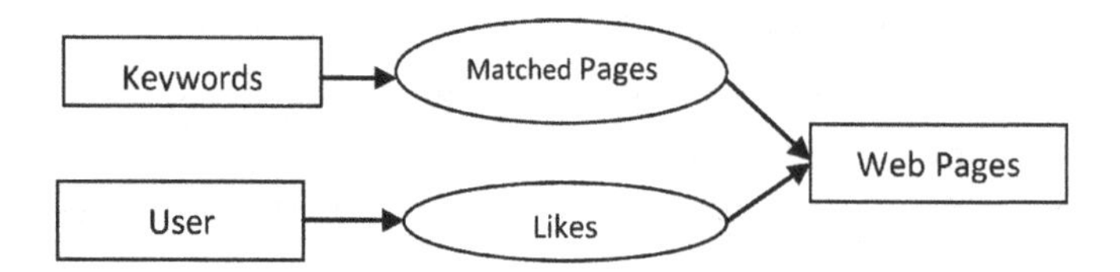

weighted average of the predictions generated by those components. In hybrid filtering the output predictions of both context-based filtering and collaborative filtering is combined improving the overall accuracy of the prediction and thus making a single prediction. It has been shown that a simple linear combination In collaborative filtering technique the number of user ratings is limited and thus, adequate neighborhoods of similar users cannot be created, the content-based component is weighted more heavily (Wang, Xie, & Li, 2006).

In its simplest version, it includes only two components: one component generates predictions based on content-based filtering while the second component is based on the classic collaborative filtering algorithm of scores returned by different Information Retrieval agents can improve the performance of those individual systems on new documents(Vozalis & Margaritis 2003). We can utilize this idea in the filtering components to generate the relevant documents by replacing the Information Retrieval agents with the filtering components of our system and the documents with items for which we want to generate predictions.

ARCHITECTURE

The proposed Recommendation system (Figure 2) utilizes two stages of process as follows:

Figure 2. Proposed recommendation system

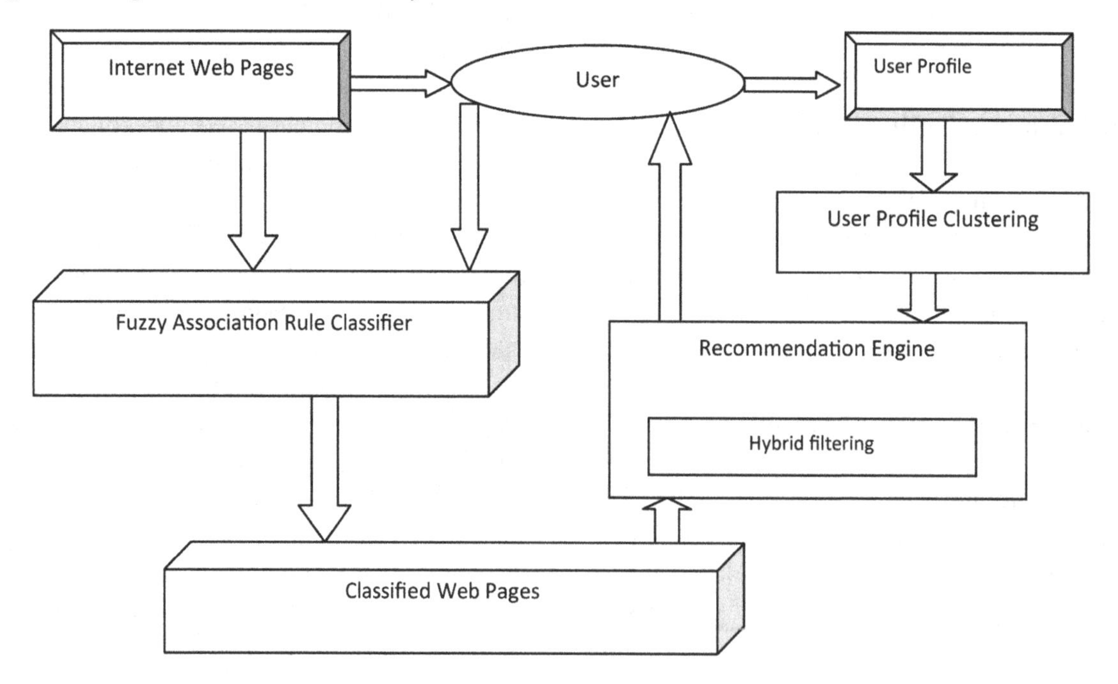

1. User profile processing,
2. Web document Processing.

The User profile processing includes the clustering of the user profiles followed by filtering. The Web document processing includes the classification of web pages followed by filtering process. The filtering process is done by hybrid filtering which combines the efficiency of the context based filtering and collaborative filtering. The user profile clustering methodology reduces the filtering time and space therefore the recall rate of the recommendation system is enhanced.

Proposed Fuzzy Classified Association Rule

Traditional association rule mining algorithms can be applied with limited categorical features. In order to improve the categorical features of the system, it is necessary to transform each quantitative feature into discrete intervals. Fuzzy association rule with appropriate limens can help to design a fuzzy classifier by significantly decreasing the number of rules generated in the previous association rule algorithm. Fuzzy logic which involves the concept of linguistic variables helps the recommendation system to retrieve the web pages in a particular language. Fuzzy logic is considered to be a superior mechanism to enhance the pattern classification by partitioning the web pages in discrete intervals. We propose the fuzzy classification association rule algorithm where the partitioning method takes place on the time attributes where the timing attributes is based on the minimum time of retrieval. The proposed association rule is used to retrieve the web pages based on the user's queries.

Steps in Proposed Fuzzy Classification Association Rules:

Step 1: The user's query and the available items are designated as two vectors. A partitioning method is need to get discrete web pages based on the linguistic and the qualitative attributes in a continuous manner. The applied method is a fuzzy clustering algorithm to determine trapezoidal fuzzy membership functions for each attributes.

Step 2: While the membership functions as fuzzy sets are counted for fuzzy items, the frequent item sets are searched on easy way.

Step 3: The membership values determine the supports of the items according to the linguistic variable with minimum time of retrieval.

Step 4: The web pages generated by the fuzzy sets are classified by the association rule

Figure 3. User profile cluster analysis

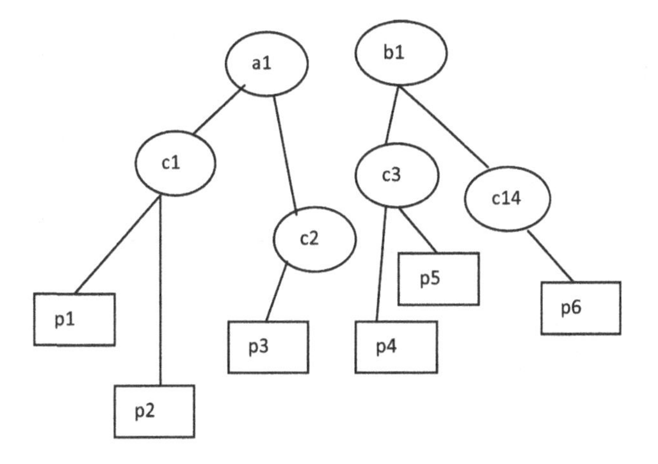

Table 1. Cluster analysis of user profiles

Number of User Profiles filtered	Without clustering (Time in sec)	With Clustering (Time in sec)
100	5	03
200	6	05
300	9	07
400	10	08
500	13	10
600	16	13
700	21	17
800	22	18
900	35	31
1000	43	38

that selects the frequently associated item of the query given by the user.

Step 5: The result of the fuzzy classifier is further classified by the association rule. The classification predictions obtained from the fuzzy sets and association rule removes the complex redundancies in a minimal time.

Proposed Fuzzy Classified Association Rule

We assume every web page d is represented by a weighted concept vector V_d:

$$V_d = \{(v_{1d}),(v_{2d}),.......(v_{nd})\}$$

The key words by the user are represented by weighted concepts vector V_u. These concepts are extracted from user's description V_d, which the user has already rated.

$$V_u = \{(v_{1u}), (v_{2u}),.......(v_{mu})\}$$

Concept's weight represents its interest score for the user.

The keyword correlation matrix M is generated from V_u using the fuzzy RT relation (r_{ij}) using the following equation:

$$r_{ij}=(n_{ij})/(n_i+n_j-n_{ij})$$

The keyword correlation matrix M is an n × m symmetric matrix whose element, m_{ij}, has the value on the interval [0, 1] with 0 indicates no relationship and 1 indicates full relationship between the keywords k_i and k_j. Therefore, m_{ij} is equal to 1 for all i = j, since a keyword has the strongest relationship to itself. The rest of the steps in the fuzzy classified association rule are given below:

- A category set K is created by referring the keywords in M and V_d where k_i does not belong to keyword set k_j.
- Randomly initialize the number of keywords to 'n' where $2 \leq n \leq \sqrt{p}$ and 'p' is the number of web pages present in the database D.
- Find the degree of membership for the keywords K_j where j value ranges from 1< j <= n.
- Find the maximum membership value for the keywords k_j from step (v) and assign appropriate linguistic label to it. Now these keywords are generated as keyword set K= $\{k_1, k_2, ... k_n\}$.
- For i =1 to n do.

Table 2. Efficiency analysis of proposed recommendation system

Number of Documents Retrieved	Efficiency in percentage(%)	
	Existing Recommendation System	Proposed Hybrid Recommendation System
100	93	97
200	90	94
300	87	91
400	85	88
500	84	86
600	81	83
700	79	80

Figure 4. Performance of cluster analysis

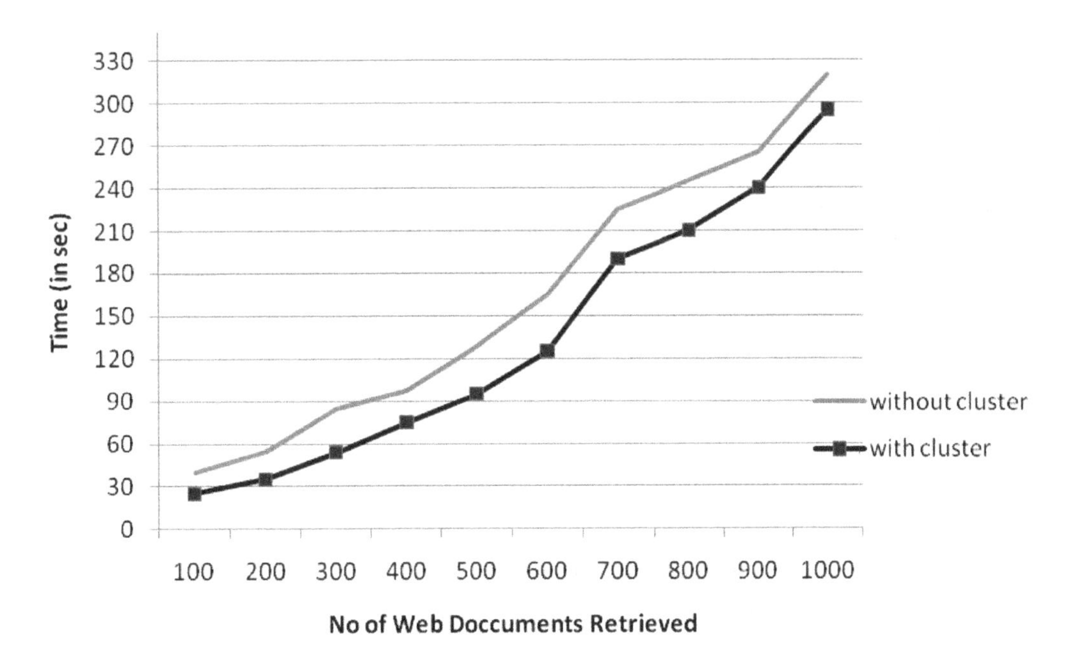

- Use α-, the users limit value; here we propose to calculate the threshold value which has transitivity from the keywords set.
- End for.

The above-generated fuzzy classified keywords are called as keywords, which is a partitioned value. The classified keywords from the above steps are given as input parameters in the web page vector V_d to association rule.

Proposed Algorithm Analysis

Step 1: User's vector V_u is updated when the new web page d is rated. Hence, for each keyword

Figure 5. Performance analysis of hybrid filtering in relevant document retrieval

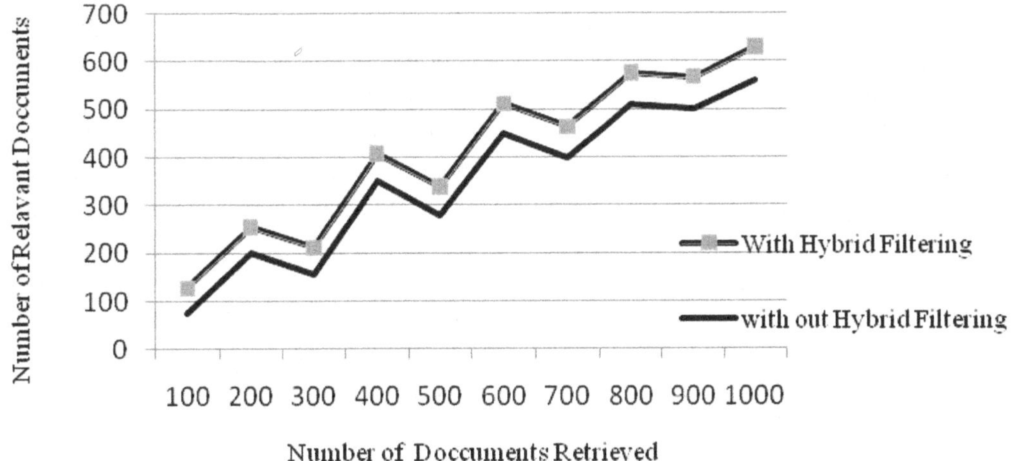

Figure 6. Classification accuracy of proposed fuzzy association algorithm

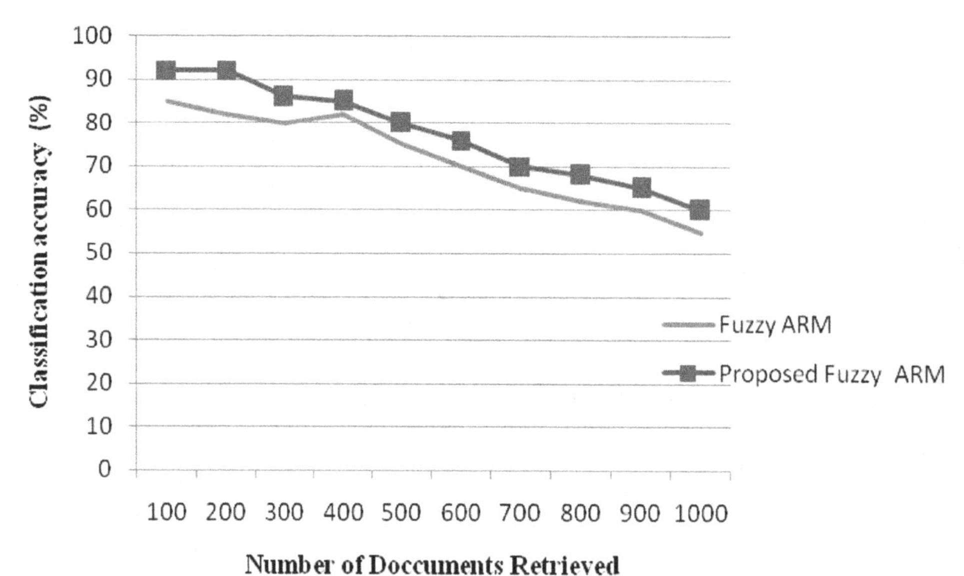

V_u contained in the new keyword set, there are four possible situations:

1. v already exists in K;
2. v is a super class concept of a concept in K;
3. v is a sub class concept of a concept in K;
4. v is a new concept, and is neither a super class nor a subclass concept of a concept in K.

Step 2: For each user keyword belonging to the web page, check the conditions mentioned in step (x):

1. If v already exists in K_u, V_d's weight is updated;
2. v is super class concept of a concept in K_u.

For each v' ∈ v, the result is divided by maximum rating value.

3. If v is a sub class concept of a concept v' in K_u, v is added to V_d
4. Else
5. v is a new concept, v is added to V_u
6. End if.

The classified web pages from the V_d vector is filtered.

User Profile Clustering

The user profile clustering in our proposed recommendation system is used to reduce the filtering space when a large number of users access the web pages. At this time each user profile is considered as a single cluster and the clustering mechanism merges these clusters which are later filtered by the filtering algorithm. Each user profile contains the details of the IP address of the user, the time of requisition from the user, and the size of the data that user has requested. We propose to cluster the user profiles based on the size of the input key words given by the user among the various users in order to reduce the filter space. In every step of the algorithm, two clusters with minimum size are merged to form a single cluster. In the further steps, the cluster profiles with minimum distance from the rest of the users are determined. The user profile with minimum average distance as well as with minimum size of data is formed into a hierarchical tree. Based on the hierarchical model of the tree the user's profile is selected and given as input to the filtering algorithm. In the given figure the following steps are followed:

1. Two profile clusters are merged to form a single cluster.
2. The clusters are merged based on the minimum average distance between the users.
3. Hierarchy clusters are formed.

In Figure 3, a1 and b1 represent the root nodes and the clusters c1 through c4 represents the low level user profiles where as p1 to p6 represent the stored user profile.

Classification

The web pages which are classified by our proposed fuzzy classification association rules are stored as classified web pages in our recommendation system. The classified web pages are filtered in by hybrid filtering mechanism as discussed earlier. The classified web pages improve the efficiency of the filtering mechanism. On the whole the performance of the recommendation system was improved.

Filtering

The User profile which is clustered by the cluster mechanism and the classified web pages which is classified from the proposed fuzzy classification algorithm is filtered in the filtering system of the recommendation engine. The predictions from the context based filtering and the collaborative filtering are combined to form a single prediction to be filtered. The user's rating and the key words from the user profile are matched to filter the web pages from the classified web pages. Thereby the recommendation system returns the relevant information retrieved in our proposed recommendation system.

EXPERIMENTAL RESULTS

Analysis of Clustering

Analysing the cluster mechanism in our proposed system, the time of retrieving the user profiles from the group of users is less since we assume that the user profiles are clustered on the basis of size of the data and the minimum average distance

Figure 7. Precision and recall analysis graph

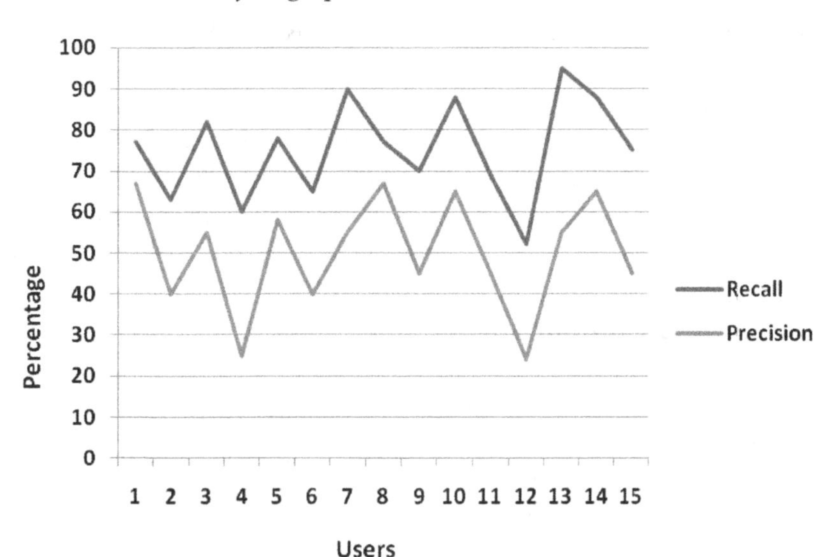

among the users. Table 1 shows the analysis of the clustering.

Since the efficiency of the system has close relation with the cluster performance, the cluster analysis is given in Figure 4, which shows 10 to 15 percent variation in the performance. The user relevant document retrieval time is improved.

Comparison of Hybrid Filtering with Relevancy

Since the hybrid filtering mechanism combine the efficiency of both the context based and collaborative filtering, the usage of hybrid filtering in our system increases the number of relevant document retrieved while comparing with the system that does not incorporate hybrid filtering (Figure 5).

The proposed fuzzy classification association rules are stored as classified web pages in our recommendation system. The accuracy of proposed fuzzy association algorithm was analysed and compared with existing algorithm. Our proposed fuzzy association algorithm accuracy was high since it is giving 10-15 percent high accuracy and the difference is shown in Figure 6. The classified web pages improve the efficiency of the filtering mechanism. On the whole the performance of the recommendation system was improved.

Efficiency of the Proposed System

Using the hybrid filtering combination for filtering the web pages and fuzzy association rule for classifying the web pages, the performance of the recommendation system (Table 2) for the web page retrieval system is increased.

Fuzzy Association Rule Comparison

Compared to non-fuzzy data classification, the exponential combination effect is more severe for datasets with many attributes since multiple fuzzy linguistic values are defined on each attribute's domain.

In Figure 7, the relationship between the precision and recall is shown and we found that there is an improvement in relevancy of the page retrieval. The Precision and Recall relationship is analysized with users.

CONCLUSION

In this paper we have proposed the framework of fuzzy association rule algorithm with minimum time retrieval and the clustering methodologies in case when a large number of users access the system. Furthermore, the recommendation system that is proposed in this paper focused on the minimum retrieval time in an efficient manner. The barrier of retrieving the relevant web pages among many users has been overcome by introducing the clustering of user profiles previous to the hybrid filtering. Our proposed recommendation system could make recommendations in a short time with more relevancies among large number users by predicting the natural language since we had used the fuzzy attributes in the classification algorithm. The filtering space is also highly reduced since the user profiles are clustered based on the size attributes.

REFERENCES

Agarwal, N., Haque, E., Liu, H., & Parsons, L. (2006). A subspace clustering framework for research group collaboration. *International Journal of Information Technology and Web Engineering*, *1*(1), 35–58. doi:10.4018/jitwe.2006010102

Alcal'a, R., Ducange, P., Herrera, F., & Lazzerini, B. (2009). A multi-objective evolutionary approach to concurrently learn rule and data bases of linguistic fuzzy rule-based systems. *IEEE Transactions on Fuzzy Systems*, *17*(5), 1106–1122. doi:10.1109/TFUZZ.2009.2023113

Baloglu, A., Wyne, M. F., & Bahcetepe, Y. (2010). Web 2.0 based intelligent software architecture for photograph sharing. *International Journal of Intelligent Information Technologies*, *6*(4), 17–29. doi:10.4018/jiit.2010100102

Basu, C., Hirsh, H., & Cohen, V. (1998). Recommendation as classification: Using social and content-based information in recommendation. In *Proceedings of the Fifteenth National Conference on Artificial Intelligence*, Madison, WI (pp. 714-720).

Belkin, N., & Croft, B. (1992). Information filtering and information retrieval: Two sides of the same coin? *Communications of the ACM*, *35*(2). doi:10.1145/138859.138861

Chua, C. E. H., Chiang, R. H. L., & Storey, V. C. (2009). Building customized search engines: An interoperability architecture. *International Journal of Intelligent Information Technologies*, *5*(3), 1–27. doi:10.4018/jiit.2009070101

Dahlem, N. (2011). OntoClippy: A user-friendly ontology design and creation methodology. *International Journal of Intelligent Information Technologies*, *7*(1), 15–32. doi:10.4018/jiit.2011010102

Dumais, S. T., & Chen, H. (2000). Hierarchical classification of web content. In *Proceedings of the SIGIR 23rd ACM International Conference on Research and Development in Information Retrieval* (pp. 256-263).

Fernandez, A., Calderón, M., Barrenechea, E., Bustince, H., & Herrera, F. (2010). Solving multi-class problems with linguistic fuzzy rule based classification systems based on pairwise learning and preference relations. *Fuzzy Sets and Systems*, *161*(23), 3064–3080. doi:10.1016/j.fss.2010.05.016

Greening, D. R. (1998). Collaborative filtering for web marketing efforts. In *Proceedings of the AAAI Workshop on Recommender Systems* (pp. 53-55).

Kim, J., & Storey, V. C. (2011). Construction of domain ontologies: Sourcing the World Wide Web. *International Journal of Intelligent Information Technologies*, *7*(2), 1–24.

Kumar, A., & Thambidurai, P. (2004). Collaborative web recommendation systems based on an effective fuzzy association rule mining algorithm. *Indian Journal of Computer Science and Engineering*, *1*(3), 184–191.

Lei, J., Kang, Y., Lu, C., & Yan, Z. (2005). A web document classification approach based on fuzzy association concept. In L. Wang & Y. Jin (Eds.), *Proceedings of the Second International Conference on Fuzzy Systems and Knowledge Discovery* (LNCS 3613, pp. 388-391).

Lin, W. Y., Alvarez, S. A., & Ruiz, C. (2002). Efficient adaptive-support association rule mining for recommender systems. *Data Mining and Knowledge Discovery*, *6*(1), 83–105. doi:10.1023/A:1013284820704

Lu, M., Zhou, Q., Li, F., Lu, Y., & Zhou, L. (2002). Recommendation of web pages based on concept association. In *Proceedings of the 4th IEEE International Workshop on Advanced Issues of E-Commerce and Web-Based Information Systems*, Washington, DC (pp. 221-227).

Luengo, J., & Herrera, F. (2010). Domains of competence of fuzzy rule based classification systems with data complexity measures: A case of study using a fuzzy hybrid genetic based machine learning method. *Fuzzy Sets and Systems*, *161*(1), 3–19. doi:10.1016/j.fss.2009.04.001

Melville, P., Mooney, R. J., & Nagarajan, R. (2002). Content-boosted collaborative filtering for improved recommendations. In *Proceedings of the Eighteenth National Conference on Artificial Intelligence*, Edmonton, AB, Canada (pp. 187-192).

Middleton, S. E., Roure, D. C. D., & Shadbolt, N. R. (2001). Capturing knowledge of user preferences: Ontologies in recommender system. In *Proceedings of the 1st International Conference on Knowledge Capture.*

Mostafa, J., Mukhopadhyay, S., Lam, W., & Palakal, M. (1997). A multilevel approach to intelligent information filtering: Model, system and evaluation. *ACM Transactions on Information Systems*, *15*(4), 368–399. doi:10.1145/263479.263481

Puntheeranurak, P., & Tsuji, H. (2002). Mining web logs for a personalized recommender system based on web usage mining and decision tree induction. *Expert Systems with Applications*, *23*(3), 329–342. doi:10.1016/S0957-4174(02)00052-0

Sharma, D. K., & Sharma, A. K. (2010). Deep web information retrieval process: A technical survey. *International Journal of Information Technology and Web Engineering*, *5*(1), 1–22. doi:10.4018/jitwe.2010010101

Shen, L. Z. (2010). A novel efficient mining association rules algorithm for distributed databases. *Journal of Advanced Materials Research*, *108*(111), 50–56. doi:10.4028/www.scientific.net/AMR.108-111.50

Vozalis, E. G., & Margaritis, K. G. (2003). Recommender systems: An experimental comparison of two filtering algorithms. In *Proceedings of the Ninth Pan-Hellenic Conference in Informatics*, Thessaloniki, Greece (pp.152-166).

Wang, X., Xie, Y., & Li, B. (2006). A hybrid information filtering model. In *Proceedings of the IEEE International Conference on Computational Intelligence and Security*, Guangzhou, China (pp. 1049-1054).

Wolff, R., & Schuster, A. (2004). Association rule mining in peer-to-peer systems. *IEEE Transactions on Cybernetics . Part B: Cybernetics*, *34*(6), 2426–2438. doi:10.1109/TSMCB.2004.836888

Zhou, X., Li, Y., Bruza, P., Wu, S., Xuusing, Y., & Lau, R. Y. K. (2007). Information filtering in web data mining. In *Proceedings of the IEEE/WIC/ACM International Conference on Web Intelligence*, Silicon Valley, CA (pp. 163-169).

This work was previously published in the International Journal of Intelligent Information Technologies, Volume 7, Issue 3, edited by Vijayan Sugumaran, pp. 14-27, copyright 2011 by IGI Publishing (an imprint of IGI Global).

Chapter 11
An Intelligent Operator for Genetic Fuzzy Rule Based System

C. Rani
Anna University of Technology Coimbatore, India

S. N. Deepa
Anna University of Technology Coimbatore, India

ABSTRACT

This paper proposes a modified form of operator based on Particle Swarm Optimization (PSO) for designing Genetic Fuzzy Rule Based System (GFRBS). The usual procedure of velocity updating in PSO is modified by calculating the velocity using chromosome's individual best value and global best value based on an updating probability without considering the inertia weight, old velocity and constriction factors. This kind of calculation brings intelligent information sharing mechanism and memory capability to Genetic Algorithm (GA) and can be easily implemented along with other genetic operators. The performance of the proposed operator is evaluated using ten publicly available bench mark data sets. Simulation results show that the proposed operator introduces new material into the population, thereby allows faster and more accurate convergence without struck into a local optima. Statistical analysis of the experimental results shows that the proposed operator produces a classifier model with minimum number of rules and higher classification accuracy.

INTRODUCTION

Fuzzy Logic has been successfully applied to many control (Gestwa et al., 2003), modeling (Meziane et al., 2007), and classification problems (Pedrycz et al., 2009). The key to the success of the fuzzy logic is its ability to incorporate human expert knowledge. An important issue in the design of fuzzy logic based classifier model is the formation of if-then rules and the membership functions. In general, the rules and membership functions are formed from the experience of the human experts. For the problems with many input variables, the possible number of rules (Ali et al., 2011) increases exponentially, which makes it difficult for experts to define a complete rule set for good system performance.

DOI: 10.4018/978-1-4666-2047-6.ch011

Data-driven approaches (Wang et al., 1992) have been proposed for developing the fuzzy classifier model from numerical data without domain experts. Abe et al. (1995) proposed a rule generation method in which each fuzzy if-then rule was represented by a hyper box in multidimensional pattern space. This approach is very weak in self learning and determining the required number of fuzzy if-then rules. Ishibuchi et al. (1996) proposed a heuristic method for generating fuzzy if-then rules for pattern classification problems using grid-type fuzzy partition. In this method, a prior knowledge on linguistic values is required for specifying the membership function. Also, this method fails to handle high dimensional problems due to curse of dimensionality.

Genetic Fuzzy Rule Based System (GFRBS) (Cordon et al., 2004) is one such approach in which a fuzzy classifier model is augmented by a learning process based on Genetic Algorithm (GA). GA (Goldberg, 1989; Tripathi et al., 2011) is a search algorithm based on the mechanics of natural genetics. The GFRBS proposed in the literature falls into four categories: (1) Learning fuzzy rules with fixed fuzzy membership functions (Ishibuchi et al., 1999) (2) Learning fuzzy membership functions with fixed fuzzy rules (Yuhui et al., 1999), (3) Learning fuzzy rules and membership functions in stages (Setnes et al., 2000) and (4) Learning fuzzy rules and membership functions simultaneously (Russo, 2000). This paper follows the last approach.

Representation of solution variables and genetic operations are the most important issues in designing a fuzzy system using GA. Ishibuchi et al. (1995) coded a set of fuzzy if-then rules using binary string and treated as an individual in genetic algorithm. In Wang et al., (1998) each fuzzy rule set with its associated membership function is first transformed into an intermediary representation and then further encoded as a binary string. Integer string was used in (Yuhui et al., 1999) to represent the rule set and the membership function. Real-coded GA (Roubos et al., 2001) is applied for the simultaneous optimization of the parameters of the antecedent membership functions and the rule consequents. In this paper a mixed form of representation is followed which represents the rule set using integer number and the values of membership function using floating point numbers.

Genetic operators (Herrera, 2003) are used to modify the parameters of chromosomes in order to find better solutions to the problem. Selection, Crossover and Mutation are the commonly used genetic operators. Even though these operators help GA to locate the neighborhood of the optimal or near optimal solutions, but, in general, it takes a large number of generations to converge and even get trapped in local optima. This is because the chromosomes of the genetic population do not have any inherent memory capability and they share information with each other in such a way that the whole population moves like one group towards an optimal area.

To overcome such difficulties, a modified form of operator that uses the concept of velocity updating in Particle Swarm Optimization (PSO) (Jeyarani et al., 2011; Kennedy et al., 2001,) is proposed in addition to genetic operators. The proposed operator initializes a velocity component randomly to every chromosome of the genetic population. At each generation, the velocity is updated using the individual's best chromosome and global best chromosome with a predefined updating probability. Then this updated velocity is used to modify the population along with the common genetic operators. This kind of procedure has no role over inertia weight, old velocity and constriction factors and can be implemented easily along with other genetic operators. The performance of the proposed approach is evaluated using ten bench mark data sets available in the UCI (Newman et al., 1998) machine learning repository.

The structure of the rest of this chapterr is described as follows. The next section briefly introduces the task of classification solved using fuzzy if-then rules. In the following section, components of Genetic Fuzzy Rule Based System are presented. Details of the proposed Particle Swarm Optimization based operation and its implementation issues are discussed afterward. Simulations conducted using ten benchmark data sets are discussed and the results are reported later in the chapter. Concluding remarks are given in the last section.

CLASSIFICATION USING FUZZY IF-THEN RULES

Classification (Chen et al., 2011; Kaiquan et al., 2011,) is a supervised learning technique that takes labeled data samples and generates a classifier model that classifies new data samples into different predefined groups or classes. The classification problem can be solved using fuzzy If-Then rules. The general form of interpretable fuzzy if-then rules representing the input features and the output class of a fuzzy classifier is as below:

R_j: if x_{p1} is A_{ji} and … and x_{pn} is A_{jn} then class C_j

where A_{ji}, …... A_{jn} are antecedent fuzzy sets of the input variable x_{p1} …. x_{pn} and C_j is one of the output class label. Collections of such rules are used as a knowledge base by the classifier upon which qualitative reasoning is performed to derive conclusion. The relation between input and output is expressed using a fuzzy relation constructed on the basis of fuzzy If-Then rules. A fuzzy relation is a fuzzy set defined on universal sets, which are Cartesian products. Mathematically, a fuzzy set A in the universe of discourse X is defined to be a set of ordered pairs,

$$A = \{(x, \mu_A(x)) \mid x \in X\} \quad (1)$$

where $\mu_A(x)$ is called the membership function of x in A. Triangular and trapezoidal membership function are the two most commonly used membership function.

Generally the rules and the membership functions used by the fuzzy logic for solving the classification problem are formed from the experience of the human experts. With an increasing number of variables, the possible number of rules for the system increases exponentially, which makes it difficult for experts to define a complete rule set for good system performance. Also the system performance can be improved by tuning the membership functions. In this paper, genetic algorithm with a modified form of operator is proposed to develop the fuzzy classifier.

GENETIC FUZZY RULE BASED SYSTEM

Genetic Algorithm is a generalized search and optimization technique inspired by the theory of biological evolution. GA maintains a population of individuals that represent candidate solutions to the problem. Each individual in the population is evaluated to give some measure of its fitness to the problem using the objective function. In each generation, a new population is formed by using genetic operators such as selection, crossover and mutation. Evaluation of fitness of the newly created population is repeated carried out until the convergence criterion is satisfied. Thus while designing a fuzzy rule based system using GA; the following issues are to be addressed:

- Representation
- Fitness function formation
- Genetic Operation

Representation

The first important consideration in GFRBS is the representation strategy to be followed. A fuzzy system is specified only when the rule set and the membership function associated with each fuzzy set are specified. The values of membership function are represented using floating point numbers. The range of each input variable is partitioned into three areas (Low, Medium and High) determined by fuzzy sets as shown in Figure 1.

Figure 1. Fuzzy space

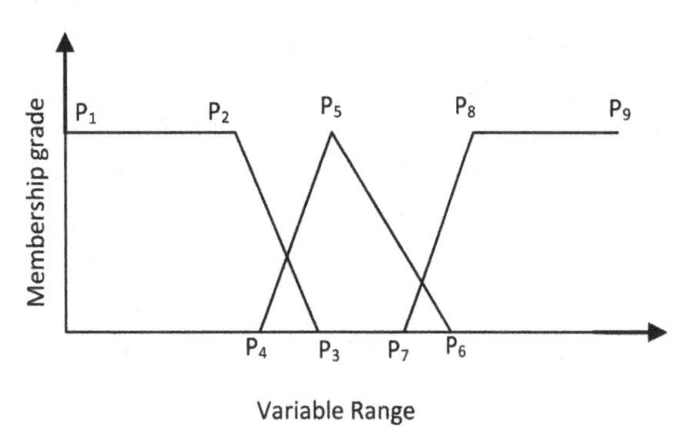

A total of nine membership points (P_1, P_2, P_3, P_4, P_5, P_6, P_7, P_8, P_9) are required for representing each input variable as a fuzzy set. In that nine points, first and last points (P_1 and P_9) are fixed that are the minimum and maximum of the input variable. The remaining seven membership points are evolved between the dynamic range such that P_2 has $[P_1,P_9]$, P_3 has $[P_2,P_9]$, P_4 has $[P_2,P_3]$, P_5 has $[P_4,P_9]$, P_6 has $[P_5,P_9]$, P_7 has $[P_5,P_6]$ and P_8 has $[P_7,P_9]$ as limits.

Integer numbers are used to represent linguistics of each variable in the rule set. In order to design a compact rule set only 'MN_R' rules are represented in the genetic population. Within those 'MN_R' rules, to select the optimal number of rules (ON_R), a rule selection bit is used. The substring corresponding to each rule has three sections: rule selection, representation for the input variables (antecedent) and the representation for the output classes (consequent). Rule selection may take either '1' to select the rule otherwise '0'. Each antecedent part may take an integer value ranges from 1 to 3 such that '1' represents "low", '2' represents "medium", '3' represents "high". The output class is also represented by an integer value whose range depends on the number of class label. With the above representation a typical chromosome will look like the following:

This type of representation increases the efficiency of GA when compared with traditional binary coding for solution variables.

Fitness Function

The next important consideration following the representation is the choice of fitness function. Evaluation of the individuals in the population is accomplished by calculating the objective function value for the problem using the parameter set. The result of the objective function calculation is used to calculate the fitness value of the individual. In the classification problem under consideration, there are two objectives; one is to maximize the correctly classified data and the other one is to minimize the number of rules. These two objectives are conflicting objectives. This is overcome by reformulating the first objective of maximizing the correctly classified data as minimizing the difference between total number of samples and the correctly classified data.

Given the total number of samples ('S') and the maximum number of rules ('MN_R'), the task is to find out the difference between 'S' and the correctly classified data ('Cc') for the selected number of rules('SN_R') of every GA run. During the GA run, the objective is to find out the minimum of the above said value. This is mathematically represented as,

$$Min\ \ f = \left(S - Cc\right) + \left(k \times SN_R\right) \tag{2}$$

where 'k' is a constant introduced to amplify 'SN_R' whose value is usually small. In this paper, the value of 'k' is taken as 5. In general, GA searches for a solution with maximum fitness function value. Hence, the minimization objective function given by (4) is transformed to a fitness function to be maximized as

$$\text{Fitness} = \frac{K}{f} \tag{3}$$

where '*K*' is another constant used to amplify ($1/f$), the value of which is usually small; so that the fitness value of the chromosome will be in a wider range. In this paper, the value of '*K*' is taken as 1000.

Genetic Operation

The selection of individuals and application of crossover and mutation operation to produce new population in every successive generation plays an important role in GA. Tournament selection is used in this work. Arithmetic crossover is applied which randomly selects two chromosomes that represent parent p_i^1 and p_i^2 from a particular variable and produces two offspring as below:

$$C_i^1 = \lambda \cdot p_i^1 + (1-\lambda) p_i^2 \tag{4}$$

$$C_i^2 = \lambda \cdot p_i^2 + (1-\lambda) p_i^1 \tag{5}$$

where $\lambda \in [0,1]$ is a random number with uniform distribution. Uniform Mutation operator is applied which selects a variable from an individual randomly, and then it is set to a uniform random number between the variable's lower and upper limit.

PROPOSED INTELLIGENT OPERATOR BASED ON SWARM INTELLIGENCE

Even though the genetic operators used in GFRBS are central to the success of its search for optimal membership and rule set formation, sometimes these operators make the weak solutions continue to be part of the makeup of future candidate solutions. Further the information sharing mechanism between individual chromosomes of GA is such that the whole population moves like one group towards an optimal area and they do not have any inherent memory capability. To address this issue, a modified operation that uses the concept of velocity updating in PSO is proposed in addition to genetic operators.

PSO is a population based search algorithm and is initialized with a population of random solutions, called particles. Each particle in PSO is associated with a velocity by which they fly through search space. During each iteration, new population is created according to the following two equations:

$$v_i^{g+1} = w_i v_i^g + c_1 rand \times (p_{best} - s_i^g) + c_2 rand \times (g_{best} - s_i^g) \tag{6}$$

$$s_i^{g+1} = s_i^g + v_i^{g+1} \tag{7}$$

where v_i^g = velocity of particle *i* at generation g, v_i^{g+1} = velocity of particle *i* at generation g+*1*, s_i^g = position of particle *i* at generation *g*, s_i^{g+1} = position of particle *i* at generation *g+1*, w = inertia weight, c_1 = self confidence factor, c_2 = swarm confidence factor, p_{best} = particle's individual best, g_{best} = global best at generation g. Since every particle remembers its own previous best value as well as the neighborhood best value, PSO has more memory capability than GA. Also, PSO adopts a one-way information sharing mechanism since only the 'best' particle gives out the information to others. Hence the evolution only looks for the best solution compared with GA.

Considering the merits of velocity updating in PSO and the power of genetic operators in GA, this paper modifies the velocity updating into a new operator that comply with genetic operators. The velocity updating Equation (6) has three components in which first component '$w_i v_i^g$' represents the current motion of the particle, second component '$c_1 rand \times (p_{best} - s_i^g)$' represents the particle's memory influence and finally the third component '$c_2 rand \times (g_{best} - s_i^g)$' rep-

Table 1. Details of dataset used

Area	Dataset Name	# Attributes	Attribute Types	# Classes	Total # Samples	Class wise # Samples
Life Science	Breast Cancer Wisconsin (Original)	10	All are Integer	2	699	458,241
	Pima Indians Diabetes	8	Integer (1,2,3,4,5,8) Real (6,7)	2	768	500,268
	Iris	4	All are Real	3	150	50,50,50
	Ecoli	8	All are Real	8	336	143,77,52, 35,20,5,2,2
	Yeast	8	All are Real	10	1484	463, 429, 244, 163, 51, 44, 37, 30, 20, 5
Physical Science	Magic Gamma Telescope	11	All are Real	2	19020	12332, 6688
	Wine	13	Integer(1,6,13) Real(2,3,4,5,7,8,9, 10,11,12)	3	178	59, 71, 48
	Glass Identification	9	All are Real	6	214	70,17,76, 13,9,29
Financial	Credit Approval	15	Categorical (1,4,5,6,7,9,10,12,13) Integer (3,11,14,15) Real (2,8)	2	690	307,383
Computer	Page Blocks Classification	10	Integer (1,2,3,8,9,10) Real (4,5,6,7)	5	5473	4913, 329, 28, 88, 115

resents the swarm's memory influence. To comply with the genetic operators as well as to equip GA with memory capability and one way information sharing mechanism, the usual procedure of velocity updating is modified as a new form of operator by considering only the self knowledge and group knowledge of the chromosome with an updating probability. Hence the Equation (6 & 7) becomes

$$v_i^g = rand_1 \times (p_{best} - s_i^g) + rand_2 \times (g_{best} - s_i^g) \quad (8)$$

$$s_i^{g+1} = s_i^g + v_i^g \quad (9)$$

This kind of procedure has no role over inertia weight (w), old velocity (v) and constriction factors $(c_1, , c_2)$ and can be implemented easily along with other genetic operators.

Figure 2. Representation of single individual in the population

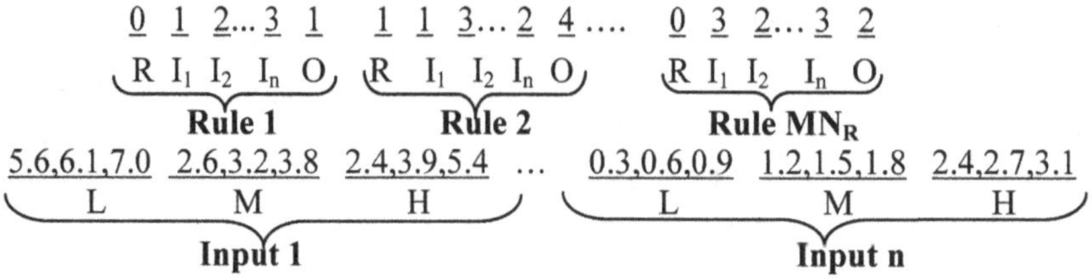

0 1 2...3 1   1 1 3...2 4 .... 0 3 2...3 2
R I1 I2 In O   R I1 I2 In O   R I1 I2 In O
Rule 1   Rule 2   Rule MN_R
5.6,6.1,7.0 2.6,3.2,3.8 2.4,3.9,5.4 ... 0.3,0.6,0.9 1.2,1.5,1.8 2.4,2.7,3.1
L M H   L M H
Input 1   Input n

Figure 3. Optimal membership function

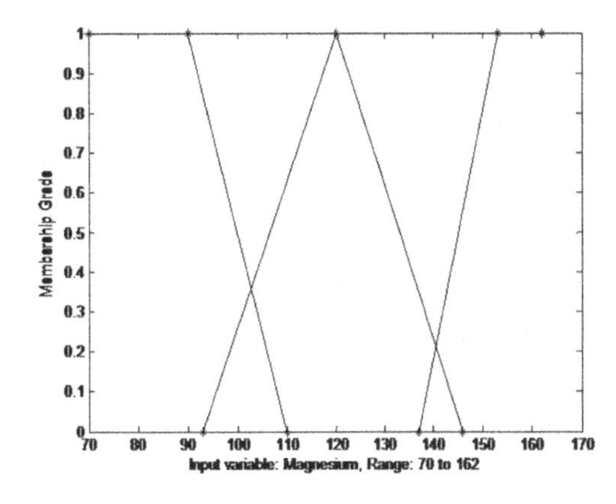

SIMULATION RESULT

This section presents the details of the simulation carried out on ten benchmark datasets available in the UCI machine learning repository. The details of the dataset are given in Table 1.

For comparison, two kinds of simulation are carried out in Matlab R2009 and executed in a PC with Pentium IV processor with 2.40 GHz speed and 256 MB of RAM. First one is RGA with intelligent operator (Proposed RGA) and the other is Simple RGA.

The details of the simulation and the performance of the classifier for the Wine data are presented here. The wine data contains the chemical analysis of 178 wines with 13 input variables and 3 output classes. Among the 13 input variables, 10 variables are real and 3 variables are integer. Each input variable is represented by three fuzzy sets namely, "low", "medium" and "high". Trapezoidal membership function is used to represent the "low" and "high" fuzzy sets. Triangular membership function is used to represent the "medium" fuzzy set.

By following the representation strategy given in Figure 2, the membership function and the rule set are represented by a mixed string. As shown in Figure 1, seven points are required to represent an input variable and hence a total of seventy ($13\times7=91$) membership function points are needed. The range of each membership function point is computed dynamically as discussed in the above Representation section .A maximum of six rules are included in the genetic population. When coded using integer each rule for a wine data set requires fifteen integer numbers (1 for rule selection + 13 for input variables + 1 for output

Figure 4. Convergence of proposed RGA during learning

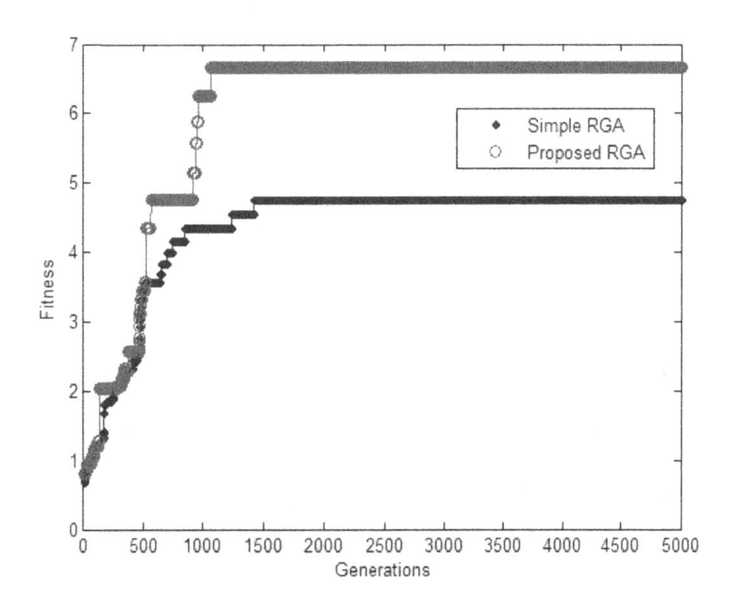

Table 2. Learning ability of proposed RGA for wine data

Performance Parameter	Simple RGA	Proposed RGA
No. of Generations	1485	**1066**
Population Size	30	**30**
Correctly Classified data	171.8	**177.7**
No. of Rules(Average)	3.6	**2.9**
Accuracy in percentage	96.62%	**100%**
CPU Time in Seconds	886.79	**667.48**

class) and hence a total of ninety integer numbers ($6\times15=90$) are needed to represent the complete rule set in the genetic population.

First the learning ability of the proposed RGA and the simple RGA approach are examined by using all the 178 samples as training patterns. Both RGAs are run with 30 independent trials with different values of random seeds and control parameters. The optimal results were obtained with the following setting:

- **Population Size:** 30
- **Crossover Probability:** 0.8
- **Mutation Probability:** 0.1
- **Update Probability:** 0.5 for Intelligent Operator only
- **Tournament Size:** 2

A fuzzy system with three rules and 100% classification accuracy was evolved by the proposed RGA. The three rules evolved by the proposed RGA are given below:

1. If alcohol and color intensity are very low and magnesium is medium and alcalinity of ash and nonflavanoid phenols are very high then it is wine 1.
2. If alcohol and total phenols are low and magnesium and proline are medium and malic acid and color intensity are high then it is wine 2.
3. If magnesium and ash is low and alcohol and color intensity are high and proanthocyanins and hue are very high then it is wine 3.

During the course of run, the ranges of each membership function points are evolved and tuned simultaneously. After 30 generations of the proposed RGA, the points of membership function have begun to distribute uniformly over the range of the variables with halfway overlap between them. The optimal membership function obtained using the proposed RGA for the input

Table 3. Learning ability of proposed RGA for the other data sets

DATA SETS	Simple RGA			Proposed RGA		
	*nCc	*CA	SN_R	nCc	CA	SN_R
Breast Cancer Wisconsin (Original)	672	96.13%	6.4	696	99.57%	3.1
Pima Indians Diabetes	742	96.61%	6.7	761	99.08%	3.3
Iris	150	100%	3.1	150	100%	2.9
Ecoli	318	94.64%	11.9	331	98.51%	8.5
Yeast	1461	98.45%	14.8	1482	99.86%	10.7
Magic Gamma Telescope	18825	98.97%	6.3	19012	99.95%	4.6
Glass Identification	202	94.39%	8.5	211	98.59%	6.2
Credit Approval	678	98.26%	5.2	685	99.27%	3.6
Page Blocks Classification	5248	95.88%	7.6	5466	99.87%	5.8

*nCc=number of Correctly classified data *CA = Classification Accuracy

Table 4. Comparison of LOOCV accuracy

Data Sets	Correct		Incorrect		Unclassified	
	Simple RGA	Proposed RGA	Simple RGA	Proposed RGA	Simple RGA	Proposed RGA
Wine	96.62%	100%	2.13%	0	1.25%	0
Breast Cancer Wisconsin (Original)	96.13%	99.57%	3.24%	0.21%	0.63%	0.22
Pima Indians Diabetes	96.61%	99.08%	3.17%	0.14%	0.22%	0.78%
Iris	100%	100%	0	0	0	0
Ecoli	94.64%	98.51%	4.51%	0.46%	0.85%	1.03%
Yeast	98.45%	99.86%	1.16%	0.05%	0.39%	0.09%
Magic Gamma Telescope	98.97%	99.95%	0.8%	0.01%	0.23%	0.04%
Glass Identification	94.39%	98.59%	3.89%	0.39%	1.72%	1.02%
Credit Approval	98.26%	99.27%	1.2%	0.42%	0.54%	0.31%
Page Blocks Classification	95.88%	99.87%	2.75%	0.04%	1.37%	0.09%

variable 'Magnesium' of wine dataset is shown in Figure 3.

The convergence behavior of the proposed RGA is compared with the simple RGA and is shown in Figure 4.

From the Figure 4, it is found that both the Simple RGA and the Proposed RGA has equivalent increase in the fitness value for the first five hundred generations. After that the Proposed RGA has drastic improvement in its fitness value up to thousand generations and above that it reaches the optimal value. Table 2 compares the learning ability of the two GA models for wine data.

From Table 2, it is inferred that the proposed RGA classifies 178 data correctly in 1066 generations showing very good learning ability when compared with Simple RGA. It is clearly seen from the Table 2, that the proposed RGA is faster than the Simple RGA as the proposed PSO based operation introduces new material into the genetic population and works well in fine tuning the solution variable thereby results in faster convergence. Also from Table 2, it is understood that the proposed mixed form of representation avoids the difficulties of coding the input variables and allows all permissible values for membership function which results in 100% classification accuracy.

Table 3 shows the performance comparison of proposed RGA with Simple RGA during learning for the other data sets. From this table, it is found that the proposed RGA has good learning ability and outperforms the Simple RGA for all the data sets.

Table 5. Statistical comparison of proposed RGA with simple RGA

DATA SETS	Simple RGA	Proposed RGA
Wine	0.581(2)	0.712(1)
Breast Cancer Wisconsin (Original)	0.683(2)	0.875(1)
Pima Indians Diabetes	0.425(2)	0.763(1)
Iris	0.394(1)	0.394(1)
Ecoli	0.656(2)	0.912(1)
Yeast	0.734(2)	0.857(1)
Magic Gamma Telescope	0.526(2)	0.582(1)
Glass Identification	0.849(2)	0.962(1)
Credit Approval	0.469(2)	0.619(1)
Page Blocks Classification	0.325(2)	0.458(1)

Average Rank 1.9 1

Table 6. Performance comparison of proposed GA

Data set	Approaches	Classification accuracy
Wine	Castillo et al., 2001	96.76%
	Setnes et al., 2000	98.31%
	Proposed RGA	**100%**
Breast Cancer Wisconsin (Original)	Pena-Reyes et al., 1999	97.51%
	Ganeshkumar et al., 2008	98.2%
	Proposed RGA	**99.57%**
Iris	Ishibuchi et al., 2004	96.4%
	Devaraj et al., 2010	99.7%
	Proposed RGA	**100%**
Ecoli	Horton et al., 1996	81.1%
	Proposed RGA	**98.51%**
Yeast	Horton et al., 1996	54.9%
	Proposed RGA	**99.86%**
Glass Identification Data	Quinlain, 1987	63.2%
	Ishibuchi et al., 1999	64.4%
	Proposed RGA	**98.59%**
Credit Approval Data	Quinlain, 1987	85.8%
	Ishibuchi et al., 1999	86.7%
	Proposed RGA	**99.27%**

Next, the generalization ability of the proposed system is examined by using standard Leave-One-Out Cross-Validation (LOOCV) (Kohavi et al., 1995) method. The LOOCV procedure works as by dividing all samples into K subsets randomly, where K is the total number of samples. Then K-1 subsets are used to train the model and the remaining K^{th} sample is used for testing. This procedure is repeated for K times such that each sample is given a chance for testing the performance. The LOOCV accuracy is calculated using

$$LOOCV\ Accuracy = \frac{nCc}{K} \quad (14)$$

For wine data set, all the 178 samples were divided into 177 samples for finding the optimal membership function and the rule set and a single sample for testing the performance of the designed fuzzy system. This procedure is iterated 178 times so that each sample is used for evaluating the performance of obtained membership function and rule set. Table 4 shows percent of the samples that are correctly classified, incorrectly classified and unclassified by each method in the LOOCV evaluation for all the data sets.

From this table it is found that proposed RGA has almost zero incorrectly classified samples for all the data sets which clearly depict the superiority of the proposed RGA than the simple RGA in designing a fuzzy rule based system for data classification.

Statistical evaluation of experimental results is considered an essential part of validation of new machine learning methods. For comparing the performance of the proposed algorithm with other algorithms on multiple data sets, Receiver Operating Characteristic (ROC) analysis (Fawcett, 2006) is performed. ROC graphs are useful technique for organizing classifiers and visualizing their performance. Table 5 gives the value of Area under ROC Curve (AUC) for proposed RGA and Simple RGA.

From this statistical analysis, it is found that proposed RGA has the ability to provide a richer measure of classification performance with compact rule set than simple RGA in designing the fuzzy rule based system for all the ten data sets. Table 6 gives the comparison of results obtained by the proposed approach with the already published results for some popular data sets.

From this table, it is clear that the proposed operator for genetic algorithm based fuzzy classifier design outperforms the results of existing classifier in the literature.

CONCLUSION

This paper has proposed a modified form of operator based on velocity updating in Particle Swarm Optimization (PSO) to improve the performance of Genetic Fuzzy Rule Based System (GFRBS). The proposed operator maintains a velocity for each chromosome in the genetic population and is updated only using chromosome's individual best and global best without the role of inertia weight, old velocity and constriction factors. This kind of procedure easily comply with the genetic operator and provide intelligence in terms of memory capability and one way information sharing mechanism similar to PSO. The effectiveness of the proposed operator has been demonstrated using ten publicly available benchmark data sets. For all the data sets, the proposed approach generated a compact fuzzy system with high classification accuracy than the simple real coded genetic algorithm and the other approaches reported in the literature.

REFERENCES

Abe, S., & Lan, M. S. (1995). A method for fuzzy rule extraction directly from numerical data and its application to pattern classification. *IEEE Transactions on Fuzzy Systems*, *3*(1), 18–28. doi:10.1109/91.366565

Ali, M. (2011). Content-based image classification and retrieval: A rule-based system using rough sets framework. *International Journal of Intelligent Information Technologies*, *3*(3), 41–58. doi:10.4018/jiit.2007070103

Castillo, L., Gonzalez, A., & Perez, P. (2001). Including a simplicity criterion in the selection of the best rule in a genetic fuzzy learning algorithm. *Fuzzy Sets and Systems*, *120*(2), 309–321. doi:10.1016/S0165-0114(99)00095-0

Chen, F., & Li, F. (2011). Comparison of the hybrid credit scoring models based on various classifiers. *International Journal of Intelligent Information Technologies*, *6*(3), 56–74. doi:10.4018/jiit.2010070104

Cordon, O., Gomide, F., Herrera, F., Hoffmann, F., & Magdalena, L. (2004). Ten years of genetic fuzzy systems: Current framework and new trends. *Fuzzy Sets and Systems*, *141*(1), 5–31. doi:10.1016/S0165-0114(03)00111-8

Devaraj, D., & Ganeshkumar, P. (2010). Mixed genetic algorithm approach for fuzzy classifier design. *International Journal of Computational Intelligence and Applications*, *9*(1), 49–67. doi:10.1142/S1469026810002768

Fawcett, T. (2006). An introduction to ROC analysis. *Pattern Recognition Letters*, *27*, 861–874. doi:10.1016/j.patrec.2005.10.010

GaneshKumar, P., & Devaraj, D. (2008). Improved genetic fuzzy system for breast cancer diagnosis. *International Journal of Systemics, Cybernetics and Informatics*, 24-28.

Gestwa, M., & Bauschat, J. M. (2003). On the modeling ofhuman pilot using fuzzy logic control . In Mohammadian, M. (Ed.), *Computational intelligence in control* (pp. 148–167). Hershey, PA: IGI Global. doi:10.4018/9781591400370.ch009

Goldberg, D. E. (1989). *Genetic algorithms in search, optimization, and machine learning*. Reading, MA: Addison-Wesley.

Herrera, F., Lozano, M., & Sanchez, A. M. (2003). A taxonomy for the crossover operator for real-coded genetic algorithms: An experimental study. *International Journal of Intelligent Systems*, *18*, 309–338. doi:10.1002/int.10091

Horton, P., & Nakai, K. (1996). A probablistic classification system for predicting the cellular localization sites of proteins. *Intelligent Systems in Molecular Biology*, 109-115.

Ishibuchi, H., Nakashima, T., & Murata, T. (1999). Performance evaluation of fuzzy classifier systems for multidimensional pattern classification problems. *IEEE Transactions on System . Man and Cybernetics-Part B*, *29*(5), 601–617. doi:10.1109/3477.790443

Ishibuchi, H., Nozaki, K., Yamamoto, N., & Tanaka, H. (1995). Selecting fuzzy if-then rules for classification problems using genetic algorithms. *IEEE Transactions on Fuzzy Systems*, *3*, 260–270. doi:10.1109/91.413232

Ishibuchi, H., Nozaki, K., Yamamoto, N., & Tanaka, H. (1996). Adaptive fuzzy rule-based classification systems. *IEEE Transactions on Fuzzy Systems*, *4*(3), 238–250. doi:10.1109/91.531768

Ishibuchi, H., & Yamamoto, T. (2004). Fuzzy rule selection by multi-objective genetic local search algorithms and rule evaluation measures in data mining. *Fuzzy Sets and Systems*, *141*, 59–88. doi:10.1016/S0165-0114(03)00114-3

Jeyarani, R., Nagaveni, N., & Vasanth, R. (2011). Self adaptive particle swarm optimization for efficient virtual machine provisioning in cloud. *International Journal of Intelligent Information Technologies*, *7*(2), 25–44.

Kaiquan, S. J., Wang, W., Ren, J., Jin, S. Y., Liu, L., & Liao, S. (2011). Classifying consumer comparison opinions to uncover product strengths and weaknesses. *International Journal of Intelligent Information Technologies*, *7*(1), 1–14. doi:10.4018/jiit.2011010101

Kennedy, J., Eberhart, R. C., & Shi, Y. (2001). *Swarm intelligence*. San Francisco, CA: Morgan Kaufmann.

Kohavi, R. (1995). A study of cross-validation and bootstrap for accuracy estimation and model selection. In *Proceedings of the Fourteenth International Joint Conference on Artificial Intelligence* (Vol. 2, pp. 1137-1143).

Meziane, F., & Nefti, S. (2007). Evaluating e-commerce trust using fuzzy logic. *International Journal of Intelligent Information Technologies*, *3*(4), 25–39. doi:10.4018/jiit.2007100102

Newman, D. J., Hettich, S., Blake, C. L., & Merz, C. J. (1998). *UCI repository of machine learning databases*. Retrieved from http://www.ics.uci.edu/~mlear/MLRepository.html

Pedrycz, W., & Succi, G. (2009). Fuzzy logic classifiers and models in quantitative software engineering . In Tiako, P. F. (Ed.), *Software applications: Concepts, methodologies, tools and applications* (pp. 3142–3159). Hershey, PA: IGI Global. doi:10.4018/978-1-60566-060-8.ch182

Pena-Reyes, C. A., & Sipper, M. (1999). A fuzzy-genetic approach to breast cancer diagnosis. *Artificial Intelligence in Medicine*, *17*, 131–155. doi:10.1016/S0933-3657(99)00019-6

Quinlain, J. R. (1987). Simplifying decision trees. *International Journal of Man-Machine Studies*, *27*, 221–234. doi:10.1016/S0020-7373(87)80053-6

Roubos, H., & Setnes, M. (2001). Compact and transparent fuzzy models and classifiers through iterative complexity reduction. *IEEE Transactions on Fuzzy Systems*, *9*(4), 516–524. doi:10.1109/91.940965

Russo, M. (2000). Genetic fuzzy learning. *IEEE Transactions on Evolutionary Computation*, *4*(3), 259–273. doi:10.1109/4235.873236

Setnes, M., & Roubos, H. (2000). GA-fuzzy modeling and classification: Complexity and performance. *IEEE Transactions on Fuzzy Systems*, *8*(5), 509–522. doi:10.1109/91.873575

Tripathi, A., Gupta, P., Trivedi, A., & Kala, R. (2011). Wireless sensor node placement using hybrid genetic programming and genetic algorithms. *International Journal of Intelligent Information Technologies*, *7*(2), 63–83.

Wang, C. H., Hong, T., & Tseng, S. (1998). Integrating fuzzy knowledge by genetic algorithms. *IEEE Transactions on Evolutionary Computation*, *2*(4), 138–148. doi:10.1109/4235.738978

Wang, L. X., & Mendel, J. M. (1992). Generating fuzzy rules by learning from examples. *IEEE Transactions on Systems, Man, and Cybernetics*, *22*, 1414–1427. doi:10.1109/21.199466

Yuhui, S., Russell, E., & Yaobin, C. (1999). Implementation of evolutionary fuzzy system. *IEEE Transactions on Fuzzy Systems*, *7*(2), 109–119. doi:10.1109/91.755393

This work was previously published in the International Journal of Intelligent Information Technologies, Volume 7, Issue 3, edited by Vijayan Sugumaran, pp. 28-40, copyright 2011 by IGI Publishing (an imprint of IGI Global).

Chapter 12
Software Effort Estimation:
Harmonizing Algorithms and Domain Knowledge in an Integrated Data Mining Approach

Jeremiah D. Deng
University of Otago, New Zealand

Martin K. Purvis
University of Otago, New Zealand

Maryam A. Purvis
University of Otago, New Zealand

ABSTRACT

Software development effort estimation is important for quality management in the software development industry, yet its automation still remains a challenging issue. Applying machine learning algorithms alone often cannot achieve satisfactory results. This paper presents an integrated data mining framework that incorporates domain knowledge into a series of data analysis and modeling processes, including visualization, feature selection, and model validation. An empirical study on the software effort estimation problem using a benchmark dataset shows the necessity and effectiveness of the proposed approach.

INTRODUCTION

Data mining research has made prominent advances in recent years, with various computational methods contributed from fields such as statistics and machine learning being explored and applied in many application domains. On the other hand, researchers have also realized the lack of incorporating domain knowledge in data mining solutions (Pohle, 2003; Sinha & Zhao, 2008). Without sufficient and proper use of domain knowledge, data mining applications may risk the danger of taking the wrong approach, or choosing inappropriate or suboptimal algorithms or models. Apart from the lacking of domain knowledge incorporation, an automated data mining process is prone to lead to

DOI: 10.4018/978-1-4666-2047-6.ch012

the misinterpretation of data analysis outcomes, and therefore compromise our confidence in using the employed computational methods.

Despite these widely accepted notions, integrating domain knowledge into data mining solutions remains challenging. Some domain knowledge is difficult to put into explicit form, such as rules. Often, there are inconsistencies between what computer algorithms suggest and what human experts understand.

As a promising application area for data mining, making realistic estimates of software development effort has been desired by the software industry for a long time. An accurate effort prediction can benefit project planning and management, and better guarantee the service quality of software development. The importance of software effort modeling is obvious and people have spent considerable effort in collecting project development data in large quantities. While expert judgment is widely used, there is also increasing interest in applying statistics and machine learning techniques to predict software project effort. In recent years, with the release of software development data into the public domain such as those from ISBSG (Chulani et al., 1999), the prospects of building powerful, practical estimation tools seem more favourable, even though formidable challenges still remain.

In this article, we present a case study of software effort estimation that combines the use of data mining algorithms and domain knowledge. While various regression techniques have previously been proposed in software effort estimation, few have paid attention to such important issues as feature selection, model selection and validation. In this paper, we have adopted an integrated data mining approach, where data visualization, feature selection, and modeling have been conducted, and all these processes interact with relevant domain knowledge. Through such interaction, data analysis processes can often be assisted by domain knowledge, and the results get confirmed. When there are discrepancies between algorithmic outcome and domain knowledge, this can help either to draw attention to the corresponding issues (which can be further analyzed in latter data processing), or even correct possible misunderstandings on the human side. In the end, domain knowledge also helps to validate the prediction model as well as assist in the interpretation of its final outcome, making the entire data analysis and modeling process both relevant and effective.

The remainder of the paper is organized as follows. First we briefly review a few relevant works on using data mining techniques for software effort estimation. Then, we present the basic computational methods we have adopted. The case study is presented and finally, we conclude the paper with a discussion on some future directions.

RELEVANT WORK

Machine learning techniques have long found to be useful for software effort development. Two machine learning methods were used in Srinivasan and Fisher (1995) to build estimators from historical data and the model sensitivity of these methods was discussed. A notable work by Shepperd and Schofield (1997) investigated the use of case-based reasoning (CBR). A number of machine learning approaches were investigated by Mair et al. (2000), including CBR, artificial neural networks (ANNs) and rule induction. Olivieira employed support vector regression on the NASA software project data and obtained significantly improved results over linear regression and radial basis functions. Genetic algorithms were used for feature weighting in CBR-based estimation methods (Huang & Chiu, 2006; Li et al., 2009). Elish (2009) studied using multiple additive regression trees to improve the estimation of project effort. Mendes et al. (2002) looked at the comparison of some effort estimation techniques for web hypermedia applications, including case-based reasoning and linear and stepwise regression. Preliminary data analysis for effort estimation data has also been explored by Liu and Mintram (2005). There has been an increased awareness of dealing with outliers using regression and clustering methods (Chan & Wong, 2007; Seo et al., 2008).

On the other hand, feature selection as an indispensable machine learning techniques has found applications in many data mining and pattern recognition areas, such as text mining (Li et al., 2008), music instrument recognition (Deng et al., 2008), bioinformatics (Saeys et al., 2007; Smialowski et al., 2010). For software effort prediction, heuristics such as PCA-based weighting and fuzzy subset selection (Azzeh et al., 2008) have been proposed.

From domain specific aspects, Oligny et al. (2000) explored the relation between effort and duration in software engineering projects. Jeffery et al. (2001) studied using public domain metrics for software development effort. They investigated the ISBSG dataset but warned of its use for prediction purposes, suggesting the use of company-specific data instead. More recently, a systematic review on estimation studies made on cross-company and within company models was conducted (Kitchenham et al., 2007). The result was inconclusive, as it is found both types of models may perform well depending on the data.

Very often the software metric data have been found not to be normally distributed, a number of studies employed transformations on the data, e.g. using natural logarithm, so as to make them suitable for statistical modeling (Liu & Mintram, 2005; Chan & Wong, 2007).

Despite these advances on various fronts, to our knowledge there is little discussion in the literature addressing the use of domain knowledge in a systematic machine-learning based solution, especially for the purpose of software development effort. We argue that we need to bring the outcome obtained from machine learning algorithms into the light of domain knowledge so that the effort prediction system can become most effective.

DATA ANALYSIS AND MODELING

The Framework

The advances of machine learning and data mining techniques have provided powerful means of extracting useful information and knowledge from data, such as text, DNA, images and videos. For software estimation, various techniques can be used for pre-processing, analysis, and modeling. However, we are not aware of any previous work that focused on adopting an integrated approach that combines all these aspects to cope with difficult prediction tasks. Our computational framework that undertakes this integration is shown in Figure 1.

In general a number of machine learning techniques can be employed, including feature selection, visualization, clustering, and regression for modeling. These computational procedures are not isolated from each other; rather, they form some active synergy among them. For instance, visualization can help to identify outliers, and these can be referred back to the preprocessing procedure for removal. Feature selection helps to produce meaningful clustered structure in visualization, and this gives clues for choosing prediction algorithms in the modeling procedure. Feature selection may not only provide better input for the predictor, but also may in turn rely on the use of predictors to evaluate feature selections. Apart from these, we emphasize that domain knowledge plays a central role that oversees and contributes to various computational processes. Domain knowledge can provide direct input into preprocessing and feature selection, for example by

Figure 1. Diagram of the integrated approach

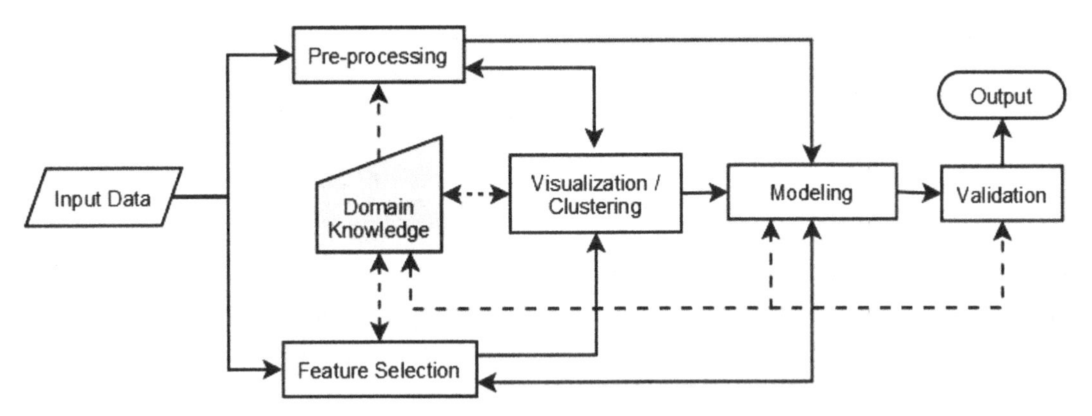

weeding out suspicious data or noise or by suggesting features based on best-practice. It can also provide meaningful measurements to evaluate the performance of the modeling procedure.

On the other hand, findings revealed by clustering analysis and modeling practice can also provide insight that can be added into domain knowledge.

Herewith we go through a few important procedures and briefly introduce some relevant algorithms.

VISUALIZATION

Visualization can play an important part in exploratory data mining processes and provide insight on the modeling of data. Since software metrics data are typically multi-dimensional, to view them on a 2-D display would usually require a multidimensional scaling method, such as principal component analysis (PCA) or Sammon's projection (Sammon, 1969). On the other hand, given the numerous data entries one may have in a dataset, clustering algorithms such as k-means and spectral clustering (Shi & Malik, 2000) become useful in revealing the intrinsic structure of data distribution, and can also help to identify potential outliers in the data.

FEATURE SELECTION

The Pearson correlation test can be used to assess the correlation between two variables. Denoting the two random variables as $\{x_i\}$ and $\{y_i\}$ (i =1, 2, ..., n), their means as m_x and m_y, and standard deviations as σ_x and σ_y, then the Pearson correlation coefficient is defined as

$$p = \frac{1}{n-1} \frac{\sum_{i=1}^{n}(x_i - m_x)(y_i - m_y)}{\tilde{A}_x \tilde{A}_y} \quad (1)$$

Apart from correlation analysis, very few approaches in software effort estimation pay sufficient attention to the problem of feature selection using machine learning techniques. In machine learning, there are a number of attribute evaluators capable of selecting a subset of attributes for classification and regression tasks. For the latter, a common method is the so-called 'wrapper approach', which regression models built on different attribute subsets to find out what an optimal feature selection should be. Another approach is use some pre-defined evaluators, such as ReliefF (Kira & Rendell, 1992), to assess the contribution of attributes to the prediction of the target attribute. The ReliefF evaluator was derived from assessing the quality of attributes for classification. The difference between two values of an attribute A_k in instances i and j can be defined as:

$$diff(A_k, i, j) = \frac{|A_k(i) - A_k(j)|}{\max A_k - \min A_k}. \quad (2)$$

The quality of A_i for classification can thereby be estimated by checking the distance between instances found in the set of nearest neighbours Ω. The estimate is defined as the difference between the distance probabilities measured among neighbours either from the same class, or from different classes:

$$\begin{aligned} W(A_k) = \; & P(\mathrm{diff}(A_k) \mid (i,j) \in \Omega, \\ & \mathrm{class}(i) \neq \mathrm{class}(j)) \\ & -P(\mathrm{diff}(A_k) \mid (i,j) \in \Omega, \\ & \mathrm{class}(i) = \mathrm{class}(j)). \end{aligned} \quad (3)$$

The ReliefF algorithm can be easily extended for attribute evaluation in regression (Robnik-Sikonja & Kononenko, 1997).

MODELING

Various modeling techniques have been applied in previous studies. Many machine learning algorithms can be applied, including statistical regression, multi-layer perceptrons, *k*-nearest neighbour (*k*-NN), radial basis functions, and support vector machines. Here we first take a look on the performance indicators commonly used in the software effort estimation literature.

Performance Evaluation

The predictor needs to go through a validation set for its performance to be evaluated, and in this connection a number of performance indicators can be calculated. For each entry of the validation set, suppose the prediction is f_i', while the actual effort value is f_i. Then the magnitude of relative error (MRE) is defined as

$$\mathrm{MRE}_i = \frac{|f_i' - f_i|}{f_i}. \quad (4)$$

The mean magnitude of relative error (MMRE) is defined as the mean of all MREs produced by the evaluation set:

$$\mathrm{MMRE} = \frac{1}{n}\sum_{i=1}^{n}\frac{|f_i' - f_i|}{f_i}, \quad (5)$$

where n is the number of data entries in the evaluation set.

Another commonly used indicator is the Prediction at level l, denoted as Pred(l), which measures the percentage of estimates that fall within a range of l% difference either side of the actual value. It has been suggested that a good prediction system should satisfy Pred(20)≥75% (Conte et al., 1986), but this is often difficult to achieve in software metrics estimation. Pred(30) is another commonly chosen measurement (Cuadrado-Gallego et al., 2006; Menzies et al., 2005).

It appears that taking the log-transform of numeric attributes is a popular data preprocessing method applied to software metrics data, and software effort values are represented in log-transform as well (Hale et al., 2000; Menzies et al., 2005). When assessing the performance of different methods on effort prediction it is easy to mix the results with or without log-transform and compare them directly. Here we argue that cautions need to be taken when comparing MMRE measures obtained with or without log-transformed effort.

Let us take another look at Equation (4). Suppose, not to lose generality, $f'_i > f_i$, then the MRE value δ can be expressed as

$$\frac{f'_i - f_i}{f_i} = \delta, \tag{6}$$

or

$$f'_i = (1+\delta) f_i. \tag{7}$$

Now, suppose when the effort value is log-transformed, the MRE value is obtained, i.e.,

$$\frac{\ln g_i - \ln f_i}{\ln f_i} = \delta, \tag{8}$$

which then gives the estimated effort when using log-transform:

$$g_i = f_i^{1+\delta}. \tag{9}$$

If $\delta \ln f_i \geq 1$, i.e., $f_i^{\delta} \geq e > 1 + \delta$ since usually $\delta < 1$, it is obvious that $g_i > f'_i$. Otherwise, by applying the Taylor expansion we have

$$g_i = f_i (1 + \delta \ln f_i + \frac{\delta^2}{2!} \ln^2 f_i + ...). \tag{10}$$

As typically $\ln f_i > 1$, which means $g_i > f_i(1+\delta)$, and from Equation (7) we again have $g_i > f'_i$. Obviously, with larger f_i the difference between g_i and f'_i will be larger.

The analysis above clearly shows that given the same MRE value, the prediction when using logarithmic effort data is actually less accurate. This also applies to MMRE assessment. Therefore, effort prediction accuracy with or without log-transform should not be simply compared on MMRE. For predictions using log-transformed effort data, MMRE should be measured by making comparison with the original effort scale, not the log-transformed scale.

Prediction Algorithm

We use a simple *k*-nearest neighbour (*k*-NN) predictor in this study. Given a new input, the predictor will give the average target value of the first *k* nearest neighbours found in the training set, weighted by the reciprocal of their distances to the new input. Suppose the new input is *x*, its *k* nearest neighbours are c_1, c_2, ..., c_k, and their relevant target values (for prediction) are t_1, t_2, ..., t_k respectively, then the *k*-NN estimation is calculated as follows:

$$\text{Est.}(x) = \frac{\sum_{i=1}^{k} \frac{t_i}{d(x, c_i) + \varepsilon}}{\sum_{i=1}^{k} \frac{1}{d(x, c_i) + \varepsilon}}. \tag{11}$$

Here *d*(.,.) gives the distance measure, and ε is a small decimal number used in case of a zero distance causing floating point overflow. The choice of the *k* value very much depends on the actual data and will be discussed later.

A CASE STUDY

The Dataset

The Desharnais dataset is available from the PROMISE Software Engineering Repository (Sayyad Shirabad & Menzies, 2005). It consists of 81 software projects commercially developed by a Canadian software house between 1983 and 1988. The dataset has been widely used in a number of studies (Braga et al., 2008; Li et al., 2009). There are the following eight variables in the dataset:

1. Team experience in years (ExpEqp)
2. Experience of project manager in years (ExpMan)
3. Number of transactions (Trans)

4. Unadjusted function points (RawFPs)
5. Adjusted Function Points (AdjFPs)
6. Adjustment factor (AdjFac)
7. Number of entities (Ent)
8. Duration in months (Dur)
9. Development environment (1,2,3) (DevEnv)
10. Actual effort in hours (Eff)
11. Year finished (Year)

FEATURE SELECTION

Two feature selection indexes were employed to value the worthiness of these attributes in predicting Eff: the Pearson coefficients and the ReliefF index. For ReliefF we used the Weka toolbox (Witten & Frank, 2005), using a neighbourhood size of 20 to match with the *k*-NN predictor setting used in later experiments.

Upon first look of the feature selection results in Table 1, it is tempting to include Dur into the prediction model, since both indexes report the highest on Dur. The Pearson coefficient between Dur and Eff almost indicates a significant correlation. In fact, other software effort data also demonstrate a strong connection between Dur and Eff (Oligny et al., 2000), with linear regression models accurately constructed between the log-transformed data of these two attributes. However, from domain knowledge, we knew both duration and effort are the consequence of software development, not control factors. If we want to estimate software effort by software size and development resources before the project is started, we don't know anything about the project time span yet. Therefore, we chose not to include Dur into our model consideration, since it cannot play a role in real-world software development effort prediction. From domain knowledge we also identified the redundancy between RawFPs and AdjFPs, since the latter is only linearly scaled from the former by AdjFac. The relatively high values for AdjFPs also suggest that it is sufficient to include it alone and ignore the other two attributes.

The Year attribute is interesting. Although experience in software development may intuitively suggest at least a moderate speed-up in project development as time progresses, the feature analysis results denied the connection between Year and Eff. Hence we decided not to include Year. While industry experience would suggest both ExpEqp and ExpMan should be relevant to development effort, it is interesting to note that both feature selection indexes suggest either minor or even negative contribution to a prediction model. In the case of this disagreement, we decided to reconcile it by using domain knowledge. Since these are considered important factors in the software industry, we decided that their inclusion in the prediction model would likely be beneficial.

On the other hand, both our indexes agree that Trans, AdjFPs, and Ent are the most important features. This is well aligned with domain knowledge, since the number of transactions, the number of function points, and the number of entities are all good indicators to the scale and complexity of 4GL software projects. The treatment on DevEnv is however less decisive. Although ReliefF suggests its relevance in effort prediction, the Pearson index would suggest it has poor direct contribution to the prediction result. We decided to keep this

Table 1. Feature selection indexes of the attributes for predicting Eff

Attributes	ReliefF	Pearson coeff.
Dur	0.061	0.65
Trans	0.058	0.58
AdjFPs	0.054	0.70
RawFPs	0.050	0.72
DevEnv	0.041	-0.24
Ent	0.038	0.50
AdjFac	0.012	0.41
ExpEqp	-0.003	0.26
ExpMan	-0.004	0.16
Year	-0.022	-0.03

attribute within the dataset for investigation in later prediction experiments.

Dealing with missing values in a dataset is another topic, but is not our focus in this study. By removing data items with missing values, we have in total 77 data entries. In the reduced dataset, the following 6 attributes are included: ExpEqp, ExpMan, DevEnv, Trans, AdjFPs and Ent, plus a target Eff value. Besides this 6-attribute set, we also considered a further reduced 4-attribute set that does not include ExpEqp and ExpMan. We refer to these as the 'full datasets' since they are not further split into subsets yet.

VISUALIZATION

We used the normal-cut algorithm for spectral clustering (Shi & Malik, 2000) to cluster the data into four possible clusters, and we projected the labeled data onto a 2-D display, as shown in Figure 2. The cluster structure is not easily perceived even after 2-D projection, however. Hence we decided to use nearest neighbour-based algorithm for the modeling of effort data.

Figure 2 also reveals an outlier in the upper right corner of the graph. It is actually the last data entry, which lies quite far away from other data entries. In practice, outliers should be removed from the dataset so that the final prediction model is built free of 'noises'. Here, however, we keep this outlier for benchmarking purpose.

EFFORT PREDICTION

Using the Full Datasets

First we considered the full data set with 77 samples after removing samples with missing values. *k*-NN predictors are built using both the original dataset and a transformed dataset with log-transformed Eff values.

Unless otherwise stated, all results are reported by a 10-fold cross validation over the entire data set with $k = 20$. These performance indexes are reported: average MMRE, minimal MMRE, maximal MMRE, and Pred(30). The results are shown in Table 2.

From the results, it can be seen that using log-transformed effort data can significantly improve the MMRE indexes. The two experience attributes, ExpMan and ExpEqp, included in the $D = 6$ set but not in $D = 4$, do not contribute anything to the

Figure 2. Data clusters visualized by normal-cut with 2-D PCA projection

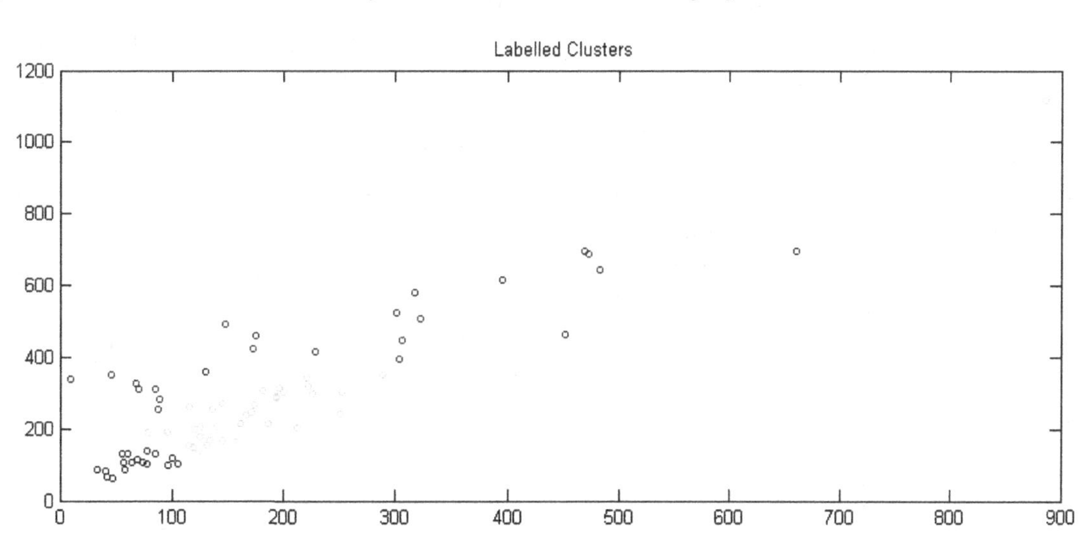

Table 2. Performance on the full datasets

Dataset	avg. MMRE	min MMRE	max MMRE	Pred(30)
D=6	0.61	0.25	1.35	0.40
D=6(Log)	0.54	0.11	1.06	0.40
D=4	0.61	0.24	1.35	0.40
D=4(Log)	0.54	0.11	1.06	0.40

performance. We decided to drop these two attributes in further experiments. On the other hand, the Pred(30) value is rather low for all cases (only 40% predictions fall within 30% difference range), meaning that the prediction is not stable and the model needs to be modified.

Using the Subsets

As indicated by the feature selection indexes, we suspected it is the DevEnv attribute that causes trouble in prediction experiments based on the entire dataset. Again, from domain knowledge, one would favour the use of homogeneous data for modeling. Indeed, data about projects using different program languages often have little relevance to each other. Hence, it makes sense to extract that attribute and split the full set into three homogeneous subsets according to the DevEnv value. The experiments are shown in Table 3. Again, 10-fold cross validation was conducted, and the effort values were also log-transformed. The results obtained from using homogeneous subsets are much improved in two aspects: lower average MMRE (prediction accuracy) and Pred(30) (prediction stability). This also conforms to the earlier findings during feature selection and aligns well with real world practices, where divide-and-conquer is often a preferred approach in dealing with complex data.

Model Selection

We considered a k-NN estimator in this study, however, the optimal setting of k is still an open question. In order to find a good setting of this parameter, we not only considered the average MMRE, but also Pred(30), and the standard deviation of MMRE during cross validation. A good estimation model should give a small average MMRE as well as a small MMRE standard deviation, along with a relatively big Pred(30).

Here we report the results obtained from the homogeneous dataset Subset 1 only, but other results were obtained using similar analysis processes. Figure 3 shows the performance evolution for k to increase from 1 to 40, all with 10-fold cross validation involved. The performance data can be summarized as follows:

1. The average MMRE first smoothly decreases until k=25. Then the trend becomes flat, but it starts to climb up a little bit from k=30.
2. The MMRE standard deviation initially decreases, becomes quite steady for k between 10 and 30, and then starts to rise slowly.
3. The Pred(30) curve climbs up with minor fluctuations, becomes steady when k=23, and then gradually climbs up again when k=33.

This can be explained by the fact that the weighted averaging operation between multiple nearest neighbours can help to reduce prediction errors due to noises, but it can also in the meantime possibly damage the prediction accuracy if k keeps on increasing. A joint assessment of all these tendencies would lead to an optimal choice around $k = 26$, where it seems to be a good trade-off between the estimation bias and variance.

Table 3. Performance on the homogeneous subsets

Subset	MMRE	Pred(30)
DevEnv=1, k=24	0.36	0.60
DevEnv=2, k=11	0.28	0.55
DevEnv=3, k=4	0.70	0.31

Figure 3. Performance evolution of k-NN classifiers against the increasing k value

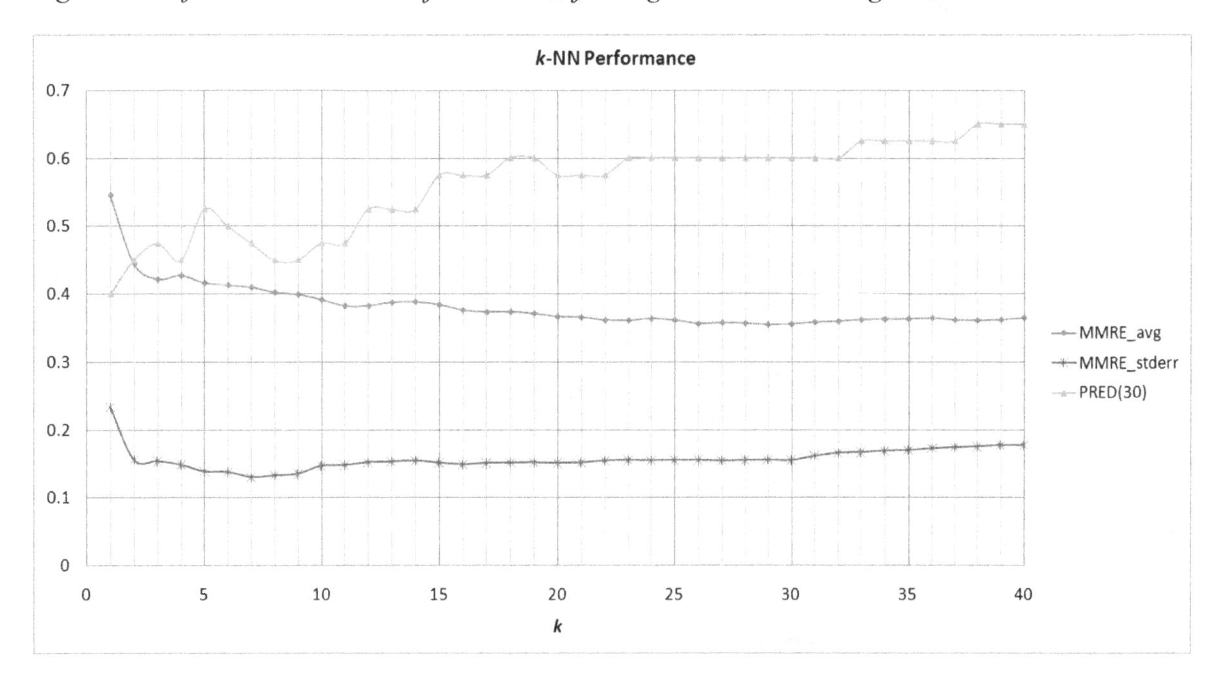

Apart from *k*-NN there are other regression tools that we can use. Here what we want to demonstrate is that it is important not to treat these algorithms as some magic black boxes that produce a one-shot result, but rather to go through a careful model selection process. In this case, we seek the best model using both Pred(30) and MMRE as the selection criteria.

CONCLUSION

Although machine learning and data mining research has made long-stride progress in the past decades, its applications in software metrics domain remain limited. Software effort estimation based on experiences with past projects is difficult, because there are unique factors for each project that can have a significant impact on the overall effort. Those factors that are measurable and that are common across multiple projects need to be treated carefully and combined into an appropriate model for useful predictions to be made. The interpretation of the data and the data analysis outcome still largely relies on inputs of domain knowledge.

In this paper, we have proposed an integrated framework and conducted an empirical study and attempted to investigate the software effort estimation problem using an integrated data mining approach that incorporates data visualization, feature selection, model selection, and evaluation. As we have demonstrated, there are multiple interactions between these computational procedures, and it is found that domain knowledge can be employed to enhance and validate the computational outcomes. At times the findings from direct application of machine learning need to be reconciled with domain knowledge.

On the other hand, by engaging in a substantial data mining study, it is possible for algorithms to make some new findings that would modify or even correct existing domain knowledge. For instance, from the feature selection modeling experiments in our case study, it is found that the two experience factors are not significantly relevant to software effort. Rather, the number of function points, the number entities, and the number of transactions are more relevant. Similar findings may shed light on our software engineering practice in the future.

For sake of simplicity we have included only a nearest-neighbour classifier to demonstrate the effect of feature selection on prediction performance. Other regression analyzers may also be employed, such as support vector machines (Braga et al., 2010) and fuzzy-neural models (Chen & Chia, 2010). Indeed, powerful hybrid predictors can be constructed so as to achieve improved prediction performance, for instance, by using mixture of experts (Wang et al., 2004) or credit scoring models (Chen & Li, 2010).

We have limited our study with 4GL project data, and it is likely that the findings need to be readjusted when other types of software projects are dealt with. There are indeed a variety of newly established software development environments, notably web services (Osman et al., 2009), multi-agent systems (Mazumdar & Mishra, 2010), and knowledge-based system engines (Moisan, 2010). These new trends are mostly oriented towards large-scale system integration in a more complicated and intelligent manner (Ashish & Maluf, 2009). Software effort estimation for such kind of projects will be both interesting and challenging, but the availability of project data is still lacking.

While there still remain many interesting questions to answer on software effort estimation, fundamental techniques such as feature selection for regression are still open research problems. In terms of empirical results this paper presents only a limited case study of software effort estimation, but it aims to highlight the importance of harmonizing data mining algorithms with software development domain knowledge. In the future we intend to experiment with more benchmark datasets, and explore further the possibility of improving software effort estimation practice using the integrated approach that combines more advanced machine learning techniques with the use of domain knowledge.

REFERENCES

Ashish, N., & Maluf, D. A. (2009). Intelligent information integration: Reclaiming the intelligence. *International Journal of Intelligent Information Technologies*, *5*(3), 28–54. doi:10.4018/jiit.2009070102

Azzeh, M., Neagu, D., & Cowling, P. (2008). Improving analogy software effort estimation using fuzzy feature subset selection algorithm. In *Proceedings of the 4th International Workshop on Predictor Models in Software Engineering* (pp. 71-78). New York, NY: ACM Press.

Braga, P. L., Oliveira, A. L. I., & Meira, S. R. L. (2008). A GA-based feature selection and parameters optimization for support vector regression applied to software effort estimation. In *Proceedings of the ACM Symposium on Applied Computing* (pp. 1788-1792). New York, NY: ACM Press.

Chan, V. K. Y., & Wong, W. E. (2007). Outlier elimination in construction of software metric models. In *Proceedings of the ACM Symposium on Applied Computing* (pp. 1484-1488). New York, NY: ACM Press.

Chen, F. L., & Li, F. C. (2010). Comparison of the hybrid credit scoring models based on various classifiers. *International Journal of Intelligent Information Technologies*, *6*(3), 56–74. doi:10.4018/jiit.2010070104

Chen, T., & Chia, F. (2010). A fuzzy-neural approach with collaboration mechanisms for semiconductor yield forecasting. *International Journal of Intelligent Information Technologies*, *6*(3), 17–33. doi:10.4018/jiit.2010070102

Chulani, S., Boehm, B., & Steece, B. (1999). Bayesian analysis of empirical software engineering cost models. *IEEE Transactions on Software Engineering*, *25*(4), 573–583. doi:10.1109/32.799958

Conte, S., Dunsmore, H., & Shen, V. Y. (1986). *Software engineering metrics and models*. Redwood City, CA: Benjamin-Cummings.

Cuadrado-Gallego, J. J., Sicilia, M.-A., Garre, M., & Rodriguez, D. (2006). An empirical study of process-related attributes in segmented software cost-estimation relationships. *Journal of Systems and Software*, *79*(3), 353–361. doi:10.1016/j.jss.2005.04.040

Deng, J. D., Simmermacher, C., & Cranefield, S. (2008). A study on feature analysis for musical instrument classification. *IEEE Transactions on Systems, Man, and Cybernetics. Part B*, *38*(2), 429–438.

Elish, M. O. (2009). Improved estimation of software project effort using multiple additive regression trees. *Expert Systems with Applications*, *36*(7), 10774–10778. doi:10.1016/j.eswa.2009.02.013

Hale, J., Parrish, A., Dixon, B., & Smith, R. (2000). Enhancing the Cocomo estimation models. *IEEE Software*, *17*(6), 45–49. doi:10.1109/52.895167

Huang, S.-J., & Chiu, N.-H. (2006). Optimization of analogy weights by genetic algorithm for software effort estimation. *Information and Software Technology*, *48*(11), 1034–1045. doi:10.1016/j.infsof.2005.12.020

Jeffery, R., Ruhe, M., & Wieczorek, I. (2001). Using public domain metrics to estimate software development effort. In *Proceedings of the 7th IEEE Symposium on Software Metrics* (pp. 16-27). Washington, DC: IEEE Computer Society.

Kira, K., & Rendell, L. A. (1992). A practical approach to feature selection. In *Proceedings of the Ninth International Workshop on Machine Learning* (pp. 249-256). San Francisco, CA: Morgan Kaufmann.

Kitchenham, B. A., Mendes, E., & Travassos, G. H. (2007). Cross versus within-company cost estimation studies: A systematic review. *IEEE Transactions on Software Estimation*, *33*(5), 316–329. doi:10.1109/TSE.2007.1001

Li, Y., Luo, C., & Chung, S. M. (2008). Text clustering with feature selection by using statistical data. *IEEE Transactions on Knowledge and Data Engineering*, *20*(5), 641–652. doi:10.1109/TKDE.2007.190740

Li, Y., Xie, M., & Goh, T. (2009). A study of project selection and feature weighting for analogy based software cost estimation. *Journal of Systems and Software*, *82*(2), 241–252. doi:10.1016/j.jss.2008.06.001

Liu, Q., & Mintram, R. (2005). Preliminary data analysis methods in software estimation. *Software Quality Control*, *13*(1), 91–115.

Mair, C., Kododa, G., Lefley, M., Phalp, K., Schofield, C., Shepperd, M., & Webster, S. (2000). An investigation of machine learning based prediction systems. *System and Software*, *53*(1), 23–29. doi:10.1016/S0164-1212(00)00005-4

Mazumdar, B. D., & Mishra, R. B. (2010). Multiagent negotiation in B2C E-commerce based on data mining methods. *International Journal of Intelligent Information Technologies*, *6*(4), 46–70. doi:10.4018/jiit.2010100104

Mendes, E., & Watson, I. C., T., Mosley, N., & Counsell, S. (2002). A comparison of development effort estimation techniques for web hypermedia applications. In *Proceedings of the 8th IEEE Symposium on Software Metrics* (pp. 131-140). Washington, DC: IEEE Computer Society.

Menzies, T., Port, D., Chen, Z., & Hihn, J. (2005). Simple software cost analysis: Safe or unsafe? In *Proceedings of the Workshop on Predictor Models in Software Engineering* (pp. 1-6). New York, NY: ACM Press.

Moisan, S. (2010). Generating knowledge-based system generators: a software engineering approach. *International Journal of Intelligent Information Technologies, 6*(1), 1–17. doi:10.4018/jiit.2010100901

Oligny, S., Bourque, P., Abran, A., & Fournier, B. (2000). Exploring the relation between effort and duration in software engineering projects. In *Proceedings of the World Computer Congress*, Beijing, China (pp. 175-178).

Osman, T., Thakker, D., & Al-Dabass, D. (2009). Utilisation of case-based reasoning for semantic web services composition. *International Journal of Intelligent Information Technologies, 5*(1), 24–42. doi:10.4018/jiit.2009092102

Pohle, C. (2003). Integrating and updating domain knowledge with data mining. In *Proceedings of the Very Large Data Bases PhD Workshop*, Berlin, Germany.

Robnik-Sikonja, M., & Kononenko, I. (1997). An adaptation of relief for attribute estimation in regression. In *Proceedings of the Fourteenth International Conference on Machine Learning* (pp. 296-304).

Saeys, Y., Inza, I., & Larraaga, P. (2007). A review of feature selection techniques in bioinformatics. *Bioinformatics (Oxford, England), 23*(19), 2507–2517. doi:10.1093/bioinformatics/btm344

Sammon, W. (1969). A nonlinear mapping for data analysis. *IEEE Transactions on Computers, 18*(5), 401–409. doi:10.1109/T-C.1969.222678

Sayyad Shirabad, J., & Menzies, T. (2005). *The PROMISE repository of software engineering databases.* Retrieved from http://promise.site.uottawa.ca/SERepository

Seo, Y.-S., Yoon, K.-A., & Bae, D.-H. (2008). An empirical analysis of software effort estimation with outlier elimination. In *Proceedings of the 4th International Workshop on Predictor Models in Software Engineering* (pp. 25-32). New York, NY: ACM Press.

Shepperd, M., & Schofield, C. (1997). Estimating software project effort using analogies. *IEEE Transactions on Software Engineering, 23*(12), 736–743. doi:10.1109/32.637387

Shi, J., & Malik, J. (2000). Normalized cuts and image segmentation. *IEEE Transactions on Pattern Analysis and Machine Intelligence, 22*(8), 888–905. doi:10.1109/34.868688

Sinha, A. P., & Zhao, H. (2008). Incorporating domain knowledge into data mining classifiers: An application in indirect lending. *Decision Support Systems, 46*(1), 287–299. doi:10.1016/j.dss.2008.06.013

Smialowski, P., Frishman, D., & Kramer, S. (2010). Pitfalls of supervised feature selection. *Bioinformatics (Oxford, England), 26*(3), 440–443. doi:10.1093/bioinformatics/btp621

Srinivasan, K., & Fisher, D. (1995). Machine learning approaches to estimating software development effort. *IEEE Transactions on Software Engineering, 21*(2), 126–137. doi:10.1109/32.345828

Wang, X., & Whigham, P. & Deng, D., & Purvis, M. (2004). "Time-line" hidden markov experts for time series prediction. *Neural Information Processing - Letters and Reviews, 3*(2), 39-48.

Witten, I. H., & Frank, E. (2005). *Data mining: Practical machine learning tools and techniques* (2nd ed.). San Francisco, CA: Morgan Kaufmann.

This work was previously published in the International Journal of Intelligent Information Technologies, Volume 7, Issue 3, edited by Vijayan Sugumaran, pp. 41-53, copyright 2011 by IGI Publishing (an imprint of IGI Global).

Chapter 13
An Ontology Based Model for Document Clustering

Sridevi U. K.
Sri Krishna College of Engineering and Technology, India

Nagaveni N.
Coimbatore Institute of Technology, India

ABSTRACT

Clustering is an important topic to find relevant content from a document collection and it also reduces the search space. The current clustering research emphasizes the development of a more efficient clustering method without considering the domain knowledge and user's need. In recent years the semantics of documents have been utilized in document clustering. The discussed work focuses on the clustering model where ontology approach is applied. The major challenge is to use the background knowledge in the similarity measure. This paper presents an ontology based annotation of documents and clustering system. The semi-automatic document annotation and concept weighting scheme is used to create an ontology based knowledge base. The Particle Swarm Optimization (PSO) clustering algorithm can be applied to obtain the clustering solution. The accuracy of clustering has been computed before and after combining ontology with Vector Space Model (VSM). The proposed ontology based framework gives improved performance and better clustering compared to the traditional vector space model. The result using ontology was significant and promising.

INTRODUCTION

Searching the Web has become more challenging due to the rapid growth in information. The query response time and the scalability issue in the information retrieval can be reduced by cluster retrieval approach. Clustering of retrieved result is used to present more organized result to the user. Clustering simplifies web search engine work by grouping large amount of documents, retrieved according to a given query (Madyloval & Öğüdücü, 2009). Generally, text document clustering methods attempt to group the document based on some topic that is different than those topics represented by the other groups (Frakes & Yates, 1992). For the document clustering, the

DOI: 10.4018/978-1-4666-2047-6.ch013

current keyword-based methodologies tend to be inconsistent and ineffective when the terms are used for cluster analysis. Most of document clustering algorithms use Vector Space Model (VSM) for document representation (Salton, 1989). The vector space model is a widely used data representation for document classification and clustering (Salton & McGill, 1983; Salton, Wong, & Yang, 1975). VSM represents documents as vectors in the space in terms, and measures using inner-products. VSM ignores semantic relations between terms. The research problem of improving relevance in search and ranking of document can be done by considering the semantics of relations. Using ontology as background knowledge can improve document clustering quality with its concept hierarchy knowledge (Zhang et al., 2008).

Ontology based information retrieval matches the relevance of a user generated query against an ontology-based knowledge-base. The ontological information retrieval utilizes the relations between the keywords (Castells, Fernandez, & Vallet, 2007). The vector space model can be combined with the ontology based information retrieval to retrieve the relevant documents (Vallet, Fernande, & Castells, 2005). The efficiency of the information retrieval process can be increased by annotating documents with semantic information.

The motivation of our research is that the terms in the document have multiple meanings. Thus, providing ontology based similarity certainly helps to formulate more effective clustering according to the user's needs. The objective of the research is to define a model for the ontology based annotation and clustering using particle swarm optimization. In this paper we have defined how to apply ontology based annotation method to improve the clustering of the documents. The quality of the solution obtained can be improved by using annotated weights and optimized clustering algorithm.

The idea of the approach is based on concepts and relations extracted from the documents. Our approach consists of three major steps. First, the concepts and their relations are extracted from the document based on ontology based annotation. Second, ontology based indexing is done on the corpus. Third, the PSO-based clustering algorithm finds the optimized clusters.

The main contributions of this paper are:

1. Most of the document clustering approaches do not consider the semantic similarity of terms.
2. We propose a PSO based clustering method on the document represented based on semantic similarity.
3. We conduct experiments to evaluate the ontology based method and the traditional vector space model. The results show that the ontology based model yields better precision and recall.

In the next section, related literature from the field of ontology based methodologies and clustering using particle swarm algorithm is surveyed. The section following describes the proposed methodology that includes the document annotation, similarity measure and clustering framework. The chapter then presents the system architecture that implements the ontology based model for document clustering. A description of the data sets and experimental results follows. The last section of the chapter presents the conclusion and future work.

LITERATURE SURVEY

Ontology in Retrieval

Information retrieval accesses the information as well as its representation, storage and organization. The fundamental issues regarding the effectiveness of information gathering from the web are the mismatch and it is discussed in Li and Zhong (2008). Text clustering methods can cluster the large amounts of web search into a small number of clusters in order to improve the query response time (Yang et al., 2008). The traditional term weighting methods measure the importance of the text in the document (Lan et al., 2009). The keyword-based searches suffer from several inadequacies such as it can miss many highly related pages. Dash, Mishra, Rath, and Acharya (2010) argue that the clustering quality depends on the similarity measure and it has ability to discover the hidden patterns.

The ontologies can be efficiently used in the search for information from the web (Bach, Berger, & Merkl, 2004). Ontology is a general description of all concepts as well as their relationship (Sieg, Mobasher, & Burke, 2007). The basic method for constructing the semantic web is to define the terms in an ontology and to create a metadata to mark the web's content. The semantic annotation system can identify the concept but does not contain relations between them. The main advantage of semantic web is to enhance search mechanisms with the use of ontologies and its efficiency has been discussed in Guha, McCool, and Miller (2003). Boskovic et al. (2010) developed the integration of external services using ontologies and semantic web technologies. The semantic web language uses XML, Resource Descriptive Language (RDF) and Web Ontology Language (OWL). The knowledge base is created using the RDF framework proposed by the W3C to represent their data (Wei, Barjaghi, & Bargiela, 2007).

The semantic web languages are much richer than HTML and they represent the meaning and structure of the content (Maedche et al., 2003). This contributes to make web content understandable. Semantic Web content is annotated according to a particular ontology, which define the meaning of the words or concepts appearing in the content (Li, Yu, & Dai, 2007). The usage of domain ontology is employed for the annotations (Jerome & Pavel, 2007). Song et al. (2005) used an ontology to annotate the documents. Ontology based annotations describe the content of the document and not its general properties (Guarino, Masolo, & Verete, 1999). Annotation ontology describes the kind of property and value types used in representing a resource (Resink, 1999). The KIM platform describes the ontology-based information retrieval based on vector space model using the semantic annotation scheme (Castells, Fernandez, & Vallet, 2007).

Shamsfard, Nematzadeh, and Motiee (2006) have used semantics for improving search results. The relation based search engine "Ontolook" makes use of core ontologies for semantic web (Li, Wang, & Huang, 2007). The term reweighting approaches based on ontology are used in information retrieval applications (Varelas et al., 2005). To improve the recognition of important indexing terms, it is possible to weight the concepts of a document in different ways (Valkeapää, Alm, & Hyvönen, 2007). The manual annotation of document is of high cost and error prone task. Kothari and Russomanno (2008) developed the OWLEnhance prototype using the Web Ontology Language and it includes more semantic relations.

Thomas, Redmond, and Yoon (2009) developed an expert system implementation using the ontology language OWL to express the semantics of the representations and the rule language SWRL to define the rule base for contextual reasoning. The system can be used to guide users in an e-commerce environment. Ontology based approach has been effectively used in information retrieval process in the work of Sridevi and Nagaveni (2009a, 2009b). Iosif and Potamianos (2010) presented web-based metrics for semantic similarity computation between words or terms. The performance of context-based term similarity metrics are evaluated with various feature weighting schemes. Zhang and Wang (2010) showed that the ontology-based clustering algorithm with feature weights do a better job in getting domain knowledge and a more accurate result.

Meng and Chatwin (2010) propose that, the application of ontology can be used in the e-marketing mix of online business and their relationships with different computer applications. Santos and

Madeira (2010) present a semantically enriched middleware for citizen-oriented e-Government services, which facilitates the development and operation of new e-Government applications with higher levels of dynamism. It also introduces the use of composition techniques based on semantic descriptions and ontologies. Baloglu, Wyne, and Bahcetepe (2010) focus on Web 2.0 usage, web mining for personalization service, and brings a different approach to collaborative filtering. The personalization can be combined with ontology to improve the response of the system based on user preference. Shehata, Karray, and Kamel (2010) developed a concept based mining model to capture the semantic structure of each term. Using ontologies produce effective performance in clustering approach. The ontology model can be applied to the fields of information retrieval, web intelligence, recommendation systems and information systems.

Optimization Algorithm in Clustering

Document clustering can be applied to improve the retrieval process. Fast and high quality document clustering algorithms play an important role in effective navigating, summarizing, and organizing information (Cui, Potok, & Palathingal, 2005). The clustering methods may improve the results of text mining application. The goal of document clustering is to partition documents into clusters according to their similarities. Major steps of document clustering include tokenization, stemming, elimination of stop words, index term selection, the term-document matrix setup and clustering. The K-means algorithm is one of the most popular techniques in clustering (Niknam, Amiri, Olamaei, & Arefi, 2009). The drawback of K-means algorithm is it may end in local optima. Therefore, it is necessary to use some other global searching algorithm for generating the clusters.

The Particle Swarm Optimization (PSO) algorithm is a population based stochastic optimization technique that can be used to find an optimal, or near optimal, solution to a numerical and qualitative problem (Eberhart & Kennedy, 1995). The PSO can be used to generate the clusters and it can avoid being trapped in the local optimal solution. PSO can be successfully applied to a wide range of applications and a survey of the method can be found in Kennedy, Eberhart, and Shi (2001). The clustering problem is an optimization problem that locates the optimal centroids of the clusters. In the PSO document clustering algorithm, the multi-dimensional document vector space is modeled as problem space (Cui, Potok, & Palathingal, 2005). In Cuiand Potok (2005), the document clustering is evaluated using the average distance of document to cluster centroid (ADDC).

Hotho, Maedche, and Staab (2002) used the approach of applying background knowledge during preprocessing in order to improve clustering results and allow for selection between results. Zhang et al. (2007) have discussed various semantic similarity measures of terms including path based similarity measure, information content based similarity measure and feature based similarity measure. Alam, Dobbie, and Riddle (2008) describe a new web session clustering algorithm that uses particle swarm optimization. This paper discusses the existing web usage clustering techniques and proposes swarm intelligence based PSO-clustering algorithm for the clustering of web user sessions. Song et al. (2008) discussed how to cluster Deep Web databases semantically. The semantic measure uses ontology and then a hybrid PSO algorithm is provided for deep web databases clustering. Dash et al. (2010) used the hybrid clustering algorithm to find the centroids of a user specified number of clusters, where each cluster groups similar patterns. Killani et al. (2010) present a comparative analysis of K-means and PSO based clustering performances for text datasets. The result in the work shows the PSO based approaches find better solution compared to K-means due to its ability to evaluate many cluster centroids simultaneously in any given time unlike K-means.

In this paper we propose an optimized clustering model that uses ontology based annotation.

The model inherits the advantages of semantics and the relationship between the terms. The method is used to enhance the effectiveness of document clustering algorithms. The clustering performances are evaluated using particle swarm optimization.

PROPOSED METHODOLOGY

Clustering is an important task in information retrieval to improve the precision and recall. The document clustering can be viewed as a utility to assist in document retrieval. Most current document clustering approach work with vector space model and each document is represented by term vector. One major problem with the clustering method does not consider the semantics of the terms. To avoid this problem, we introduce the ontology based semantic similarity model. In contrast to the existing methods, our approach provides effective clustering by using the semantic similarity that is calculated in document annotation process. The proposed approach is composed of two main parts. First, the document annotation is done using ontology and second, the optimized clustering approaches to improve the relevance. The novelty of this approach resides in the ontology based annotation and applying particle swarm optimization to retrieve optimized result. In the traditional retrieval system, keyword-based method cannot meet the need of user's requirements. The main feature of our model compared with the models such as Boolean, statistical and probabilistic are:

1. Combining the conceptual features of documents and to develop an effective ontology based annotation,
2. Semantic similarity score to improve the concept relevance,
3. Optimization algorithm to improve clustering.

Knowledge Representation

The knowledge representation of a document defines the concepts and relations. The ontology model includes the details that are relevant to the content of the document. The similarity measure considers the conceptual structure of model. The words in the documents are mapped to the corresponding domain concepts. RDF and OWL representation can be used to annotate the document. The document is represented using the ontological indexing method given in OntoSearch system (Jiang & Tan, 2006). Annotation of the documents represents the weight and the importance of the concept. The relevance of the document was improved by the ontology based annotation. The importance of a concept in a document is basically computed by the classical term frequency- inverse document frequency (TFIDF) (Salton, 1989). The classical TFIDF cannot represent the semantic relevance between the terms. The TFIDF measure calculates the frequency of occurrence of the concept in each document and is computed as Equation (1)

$$w_x = \frac{freq_{x,d}}{\max_y freq_{y,d}} \cdot \log \frac{|D|}{n_x} \quad (1)$$

The concept weight of x is w_x. The w_x is based on the number of occurrence of concept in the document. The term d represents the document. $freq_{x,d}$ is the number of occurrences of the keyword attached to x concept, $\max_y freq_{y,d}$ is the maximum frequency of the most repeated concept in d, n_x is the number of documents annotated with x and D is set of all document in search space. The number of instance in a document is primarily defined as the number of times the label of the instance appears in the document, if the document is annotated with instance or zero otherwise. See Sridevi and Nagaveni (2010) for more details for ontology based annotation. The term reweighting scheme in Jing, Zhou, Ng, and Huang (2006) has been used and is given in Equation (2)

$$\hat{w} = w_x + \sum_{\substack{t=1 \\ sim(w_x, w_y) \geq \alpha}}^{m} sim(w_x, w_s) \cdot w_s \quad (2)$$

where w_x stands for the weight of the concept terms and $\hat{w}_x$ stands for concept term re-weight. sim(w_x,w_s) stands for the semantic similarity between the two concepts x and s. α is the minimum similarity threshold value. If the terms are semantically identical then the semantic similarity is one. If the terms are unrelated then the semantic similarity is zero. Based on these semantic distances we calculate the concept weight vector of the annotated document.

Semantic Similarity

Semantic similarity represents the concept similarity between the two words. The knowledge base is developed by constructing and populating the ontology for a particular domain. The main goal of ontology based clustering is to enhance searching by making use of semantic annotations. The documents are represented by the concept weight vector and then apply the vector space model for retrieval. The weight calculated reflects how the concept is relevant to the annotated document. The semantic similarity is calculated using Wordnet (Fellbaum, 1998) and the ontology based semantic measure has been applied on the clustering process.

Using ontologies prevents synonyms and misspelling problems during document annotation. Ontology similarity measures can be defined using Wordnet synsets. WordNet (Fellbaum, 1998) is used to represent the senses of the terms in the document. The semantic relationships are defined using synset. In other words, a synset represent the groups of synonyms that represent the concept. Using the ontology similarity method given in Euzenatand Shvaiko (2007), the cosine similarity between term w_1 and w_2 is defined in Equation (3). The cosine similarity between concept terms extracted from the document is calculated using the scheme from Iosif et al. (2006) and Lee, Chauang, and Seamons (1997).

$$Sim\ (w_1, w_2) = \frac{\sum_{i=1}^{N} t_{w1} \cdot t_{w2}}{\sqrt{\sum_{i=1}^{N} (t_{w1})^2} \sqrt{\sum_{i=1}^{N} (t_{w2})^2}} \quad (3)$$

The Sim(w_1,w_2) computes the cosine similarity between the terms w_1 and w_2. The t_{w1} and t_{w2} is the number of occurrence of the concepts related to the words. N is the size of vocabulary. The semantic similarity measure uses the ontology to identify the relations between concepts. The concept frequency is calculated and the weights are assigned to concepts in the document. The concept-document matrix is created using ontology. The optimal document clusters are obtained using PSO.

Optimized Clustering

The clustering problem can be viewed as an optimization problem. The particle swarm optimization algorithm can be applied on the annotated documents to find the optimal centroids of the clusters. In the PSO algorithm, the particle's location represents one solution for the problem. A different problem solution can be generated based on the particle movements to a new location. In each movement of the particle, the velocity and direction will be altered. While most of the clustering procedures perform local searching, the PSO algorithm performs a global searching for solutions. The objective of the PSO clustering algorithm is to discover the proper centroids of clusters for minimizing the intra-cluster distance as well as maximizing the distance between clusters.

The algorithm can be summarized as follows:

1. At the initial stage, each particle randomly selects the document vectors from the document collection as the initial k cluster centroids.
2. For each particle:
   a. The document vector is assigned to the closest centroid vector.

   b. Calculate the fitness value based on the distance between the cluster.
   c. To generate the next solution update the velocity and particle position.
3. Repeat step (2) until one of the following termination conditions is satisfied.
   a. The maximum number of iterations is exceeded, or
   b. The average change in centroid vectors is less than a predefined value.

SYSTEM ARCHITECTURE FOR ONTOLOGY BASED CLUSTERING

The clustering techniques group the documents into unsupervised cluster based on the features of the documents. The ontology based document annotation model is utilized for the clustering of the documents. Figure 1 shows the architecture of the ontology based clustering model.

Ontology-Based Annotation and Indexing

An ontology has good conceptual structure representation and can be combined with the knowledge based representation. Our model makes use of ontology based annotation and indexing. The ontology based model depends on the semantic index terms but the vector space model depends on the keyword index. The semantics of the concepts are used to build a concept term representation. The ontology based similarity measure improves the concept relevance score. The semantically related terms gain more weights and it will improve the term importance in indexing process.

Semantic annotation provides additional information so that a better document relevance can be made. The domain ontology can be used for the annotation and the importance of indexing terms can be improved. The annotation of the corpus is done with concepts from the ontology. The relations between concepts are discovered and the concepts gain more weights based on the semantic relations. The annotation weights are used in the indexing of document. The steps followed in the semantic annotation process are as follows:

1. Read each and every document in the specified folder and identify the terms in each and every document.
2. Remove stop words contained in the terms identified in the document dataset and perform stemming.
3. Document is annotated and ontology based indexing is applied to overall documents.
4. Examine the location of the annotated instance in the document.
5. Semantic similarity measure is used to recalculate the weight measure of each term.
6. Clustering approach is applied on the annotated document.

The concept weight determines the relevance of annotation. Most indexing systems depend on frequency of term within a document. The information retrieval can be improved by combining the ontology similarity and ontology indexing method. In our model, the ranking of the concepts are based on their semantic similarity to other concepts in the document. The concept index of the corpus is built based on the concept vector and the corresponding concept weight vectors generated in the document annotation process.

Clustering Using PSO Algorithm

In PSO system, particles move through the search space. The particle swarm optimization allows the particles to explore more information space and better the chance of finding global optima. One particle's position in the swarm represents one possible solution for clustering the document collection. Therefore, a swarm represents a number of candidate clustering solutions for the document collection (Cui & Potok, 2005). Each particle maintains a matrix $X_i = (C_1, C_2, C_i, .., C_k)$, where C_i represents the ith cluster centroid vector and k is the cluster number. C_i is represented as x_{id}. x_{id} is the

Figure 1. Ontology based model for document clustering

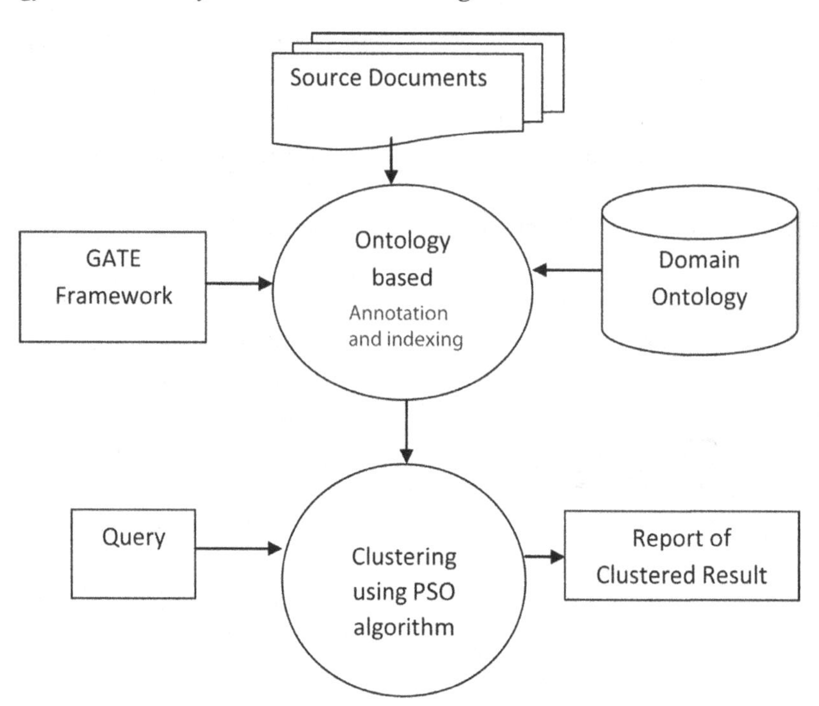

i^{th} element position of the dth particle. The particle in the swarm has its own position and velocity. The movement of the particle is directed by the velocity. The term v_{id} represents the ith element of the velocity vector of the dth particle. For every generation, the particle's new location is computed by adding the particle's current velocity V-vector to its location X-vector. At every generation, the particle's new location is computed by adding the particle's current velocity, v_{id}, to its location, x_{id} using Equation (4) and Equation (5) (Kennedy, Eberhart, & Shi, 2001; Kennedy & Eberhart, 1995) and thus the velocity of the particle is updated.

$$v_{id} = w \times v_{id} + c_1 \times rand_1 \times (Ppbest - x_{id}) + c_2 \times rand_2 \times (Pgbest - x_{id}) \tag{4}$$

$$x_{id} = x_{id} + v_{id} \tag{5}$$

Each particle stores the personal and global best position in the search space. The personal best position of ith particle is the best position visited by the particle so far and is denoted as $Ppbest_i(t)$. Let f be the objective function and the personal best of particle at time step t is updated as Equation (6).

$$Ppbest_i(t+1) = \begin{cases} Ppbest_i(t)\_if \\ f(x_i(t+1) \geq f(Ppbest_i(t)) \\ x_i(t+1)\_if \\ f(x_i(t+1) < f(Ppbest_i(t)) \end{cases} \tag{6}$$

The global best solution is represented as Pgbest. For the Pgbest, the best particle is determined from the entire swarm by selecting the best personal best position. The global best is updated based on best known position of the swarm using Equation (7).

$$Pgbest(t) \in \{Ppbest_0, Ppbest_1, ...Ppbest_k\}$$
$$= \min\{f(Ppbest_0(t), ...Ppbest_k(t)\} \qquad (7)$$

In Equation (4), the random values rand1 and rand2 are used for a wide search. The w factor is the inertia random value. The values of c1 and c2 control the weight in deciding the particle's next movement. The PSO clustering algorithm needs a fitness function to evaluate each particle performance. Each particle maintains a matrix with the cluster centroid vectors.

The PSO algorithm steps are as follows:

Step 1: Randomly initialize the particle velocity and particle position. The K cluster centroids are randomly selected for each particle.
Step 2: For each particle evaluate the fitness of the particle.
Step 3: The document cluster structure should be optimally preserved. The cluster quality can be measured using within cluster, between-cluster and mixture scatter matrices (Howland & Park, 2004) and it is given in Equation (8), Equation (9) and Equation (10). The cluster quality is high if the cluster is tightly grouped, but well separated from the other clusters. The Equation (8) defines the within-cluster and the Equation (9) defines the between cluster measures. The optimization function preserves the cluster structure and maximizes the Equation (9).

$$S_w = \sum_{i=1}^{k} \sum_{j \in N_i} \left(a_j - c^i\right)\left(a_j - c^i\right)^T, \qquad (8)$$

$$S_b = \sum_{i=1}^{k} \sum_{j \in N_i} \left(c^i - c\right)\left(c^i - c\right)^T, \qquad (9)$$

$$S_m = \sum_{j=1}^{n} \left(a_j - c\right)\left(a_j - c\right)^T \qquad (10)$$

where a_j is the document that belongs to the cluster c_i. c_i is the ith cluster centroid. c is the global cluster centroid. The k is the number of clusters and N_i is the number of documents in the cluster i. S_w is the within cluster, S_b is between clustering and S_m is the mixture scatter matrices which is sum of S_w and S_b. The fitness value of the particle is evaluated using S_b.

Step 4: Update the personal best position using Equation (6).
Step 5: Update the global best position among all the individuals using Equation (7).
Step 6: Apply velocity update for each dimension of the particle using Equation (4).
Step 7: Update the position and generate new particle's location using Equation (5).
Step 8: Repeat steps 2–8 until a stopping criteria, such as sufficiently good solution is discovered or a maximum number of generations being completed. The individual which scores the best fitness value in the population is taken as optimal solution.
Step 9: The relevance of documents is evaluated.

EXPERIMENTAL RESULT

Data Set Description

The NewsGroups data set is used for text clustering. Mini News Group is the subset of 20 NewsGroup (http://kdd.ics.uci.edu/databases/20newsgroups/20newsgroups.html) used as a data set and it has a collection about 2000 documents across 20 different newsgroups from Usenet. Each category consists of 1,000 documents assigned

Table 1. Data sets used for evaluation

Dataset	No. of Document	No. of Classes	No. of Unique Terms
20News-group	18,828	20	18,330

Table 2. Dataset description

comp.graphics comp.os.mswindows.misc comp.sys.ibm.pc.hardware comp.sys.mac.hardware comp.windows.x	rec.autos rec.motorcycles rec.sport.baseball rec.sport.hockey	sci.crypt sci.electronics sci.med sci.space
misc.forsale	talk.politics.misc talk.politics.guns talk.politics.mideast	talk.religion.misc alt.atheism soc.religion.christian

to it. Each newsgroup is stored in a subdirectory, with each article stored as a separate file. Some of the newsgroups are closely related with each other while some are highly unrelated. For the purpose of experimentation, clustering is done using up to 10 groups. Based on Jing, Zhou, Ng, and Huang (2006), the four datasets are extracted from the newsgroup datasets. The datasets D1 and D2 contain categories of different topics. The datasets D3, D4 consist of categories of similar topics collected from the collection. Table 1 and Table 2 show the different topics organized into 20 newsgroups (http://people.csail.mit.edu/jrennie/20Newsgroups/). Table 1 describes the dataset used for evaluation and Table 2 shows the topics of the newsgroups.

The documents are annotated using KIM Ontology (KIMO) (Popov et al., 2003) and it is stored using the GATE tool (General Architecture for Text Engineering) (Cunningham, 2002). KIMO is light weight ontology and is encoded in RDF(S). GATE is an open source Java software toolkit and it enables a user to annotate text with respect to one or more ontologies. Gate is used to annotate the corpus and provides an easy to way to indicate which pieces of text denote the concepts. The main purpose of GATE is to develop a model to represent document content and annotations. Using the model, the documents can be retrieved from the corpora not only based on their textual content but also according to their features or annotations. The most popular open source full-text search engine–Lucene API (http://lucene.

Figure 2. Fitness curve comparisons

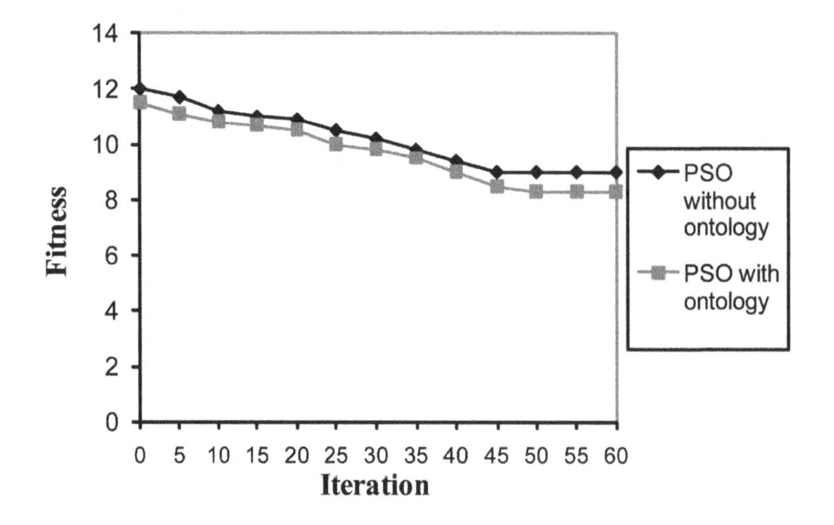

Figure 3. Comparison of clustering quality

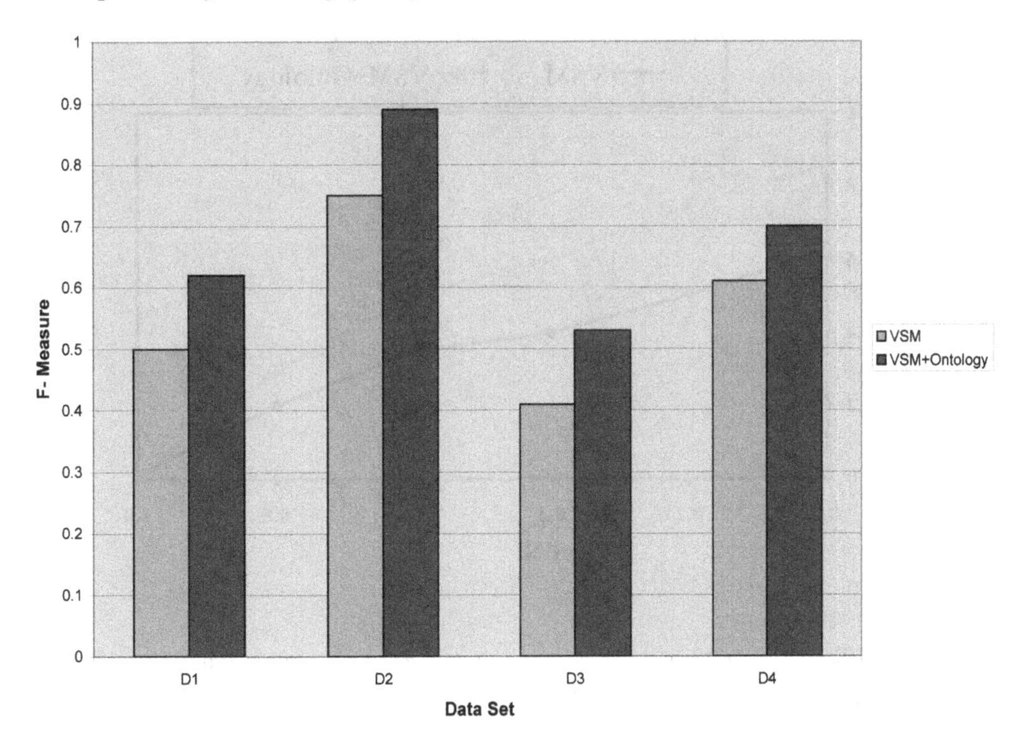

apache.org/) is used for the purpose of indexing and for comparison with ontology based retrieval. Using Jena model, the annotated documents can be retrieved from the corpora based on their textual content and also according to their annotation or features.

Cluster Evaluation

The goal of clustering is to attain high intra-cluster similarity and low inter-cluster similarity. Using Manning, Raghavan, and Schütze (2008), true positive, true negative, false positive and false negative are calculated. Two similar documents in the same cluster are true positive (TP) and two similar documents in different clusters are true negative (TN). The decision of assigning two dissimilar documents to the same cluster is false positive (FP) and two similar documents to different clusters is false negative (FN). Precision (P) and recall(R) are two popular measures for clustering. The higher precision is obtained at the low recall value. The F-measure (F) is used to evaluate the performance measure of the model. The F-measure combines precision and recall, the two most widely used measure. The precision and recall are given in Equation (11). The F-measure is evaluated using the Equation (12). A higher F-measure indicates better performance.

$$P = \frac{TP}{TP + FP} \qquad R = \frac{TP}{TP + FN} \tag{11}$$

$$F = \frac{2 \cdot P \cdot R}{(P + R)} \tag{12}$$

20 random particles are generated. The fitness value is calculated using the distance between the cluster centroid and the documents that are clustered. The fitness values are recorded for ten simulations. In the PSO module, we choose the

Figure 4. Comparison of precision and recall

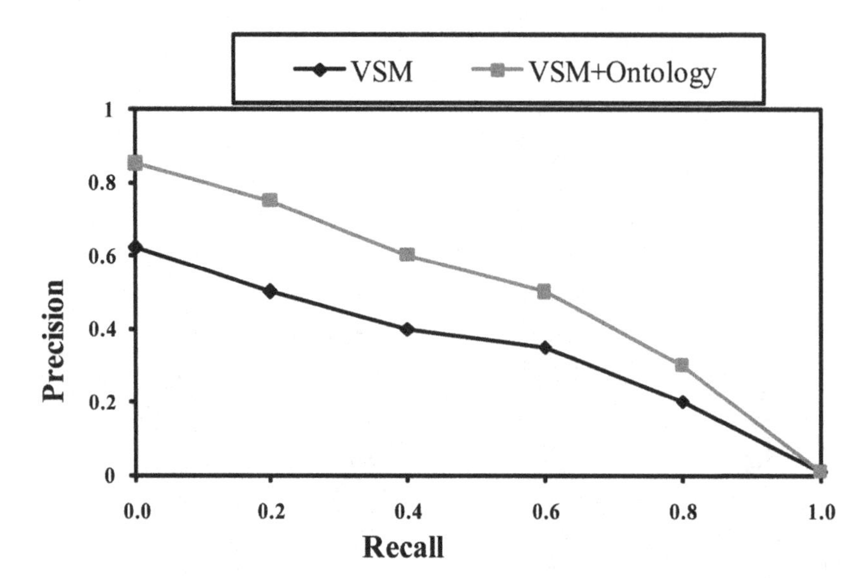

inertia weight w initially set as 0.95 and the acceleration coefficient constants c1 and c2 are set to 1.4. If the fitness value is fixed then it indicates the optimal solution. For each simulation, the initial centroid vectors of each particle are randomly selected. A set of 20 queries was prepared manually for comparative performance measurement. After 100 iterations the same cluster solution is obtained. The F-measure values are the average of 20 runs. Experimental results show that the PSO clustering algorithm using ontology performs better than the PSO clustering algorithms without using ontology. To cluster the large document data sets, PSO requires more iteration to find the optimal solution. The convergence of PSO depends on the particle's best known position and the swarm's best known global position. If global position remain constant throughout the optimization process then the algorithm converge to the optimal.

Figure 2 shows the average fitness comparison using PSO. For a large data set, PSO requires more iteration before optimal clustering. The particle swarm optimization clustering algorithm can generate more compact clustering results. The PSO approach in ontology based VSM have improvements compared to the results of the VSM based PSO. However, when the similarity metric is changed to the ontology based metric, the PSO algorithm has a better performance.

Discussion on the Clustering Quality

The cluster quality for the four data sets from newsgroups is given in Figure 3. For different data sets in 20 Newsgroups the F-measure performance of ontology based VSM increases greatly when compared to the VSM method. It shows consistent performance in F- measure in ontology based VSM and is still the best among these methods.

The aim of the algorithm is to maximize the F-measure. The higher the overall F-measure, the better the clustering accuracy achieved. The semantic similarity measure outperforms the key word based similarity measure model. The relevant documents are returned by a query using ontology index instead of simple keyword index. The average precision is compared using VSM and VSM+Ontology, as shown in Table 3.

Table 4 shows the comparison of F measure. The ontology based VSM approach performance significantly improves. An improvement of 11% is achieved by VSM+Ontology in comparison with VSM keyword search.

Table 3. Comparisons of average precision

Average Precision	VSM	VSM+Ontology	Ratio
Top 10	0.3761	0.4119	1.09519
Top 20	0.1983	0.2074	1.04589

Figure 4 shows the recall and precision comparison. The mean relevance for the top 20 retrieved documents using ontology is 3.1 and using the keyword based search is 2.2. VSM+Ontology obtain the best clustering performance in terms of the results of precision and recall. Evaluation results on the chosen corpus and the annotation ontology have shown the improvements of retrieval performance compared to simple keyword matching approaches. In the traditional VSM the background knowledge is not considered in the term similarity. The performance of ontology based VSM has better improvement than traditional VSM. The clustering results produced by the semantic similarity approach have higher quality than those produced by a keyword based similarity approach. The evaluation results indicate that our semantic annotation, indexing and retrieval approach improves the performances of retrieval not just in terms of recall, but also in terms of precision.

Several observations from the comparison between these methods are worth discussing:

1. Our ontology based VSM results are more accurate than the traditional VSM.
2. The semantic similarity performs consistently and significantly better than the key word based term frequency methods and achieves the best performance in all experiments.
3. The PSO clustering approach combined with semantic similarity performs significantly the best among the traditional clustering method in our experiments.

Ontology based clustering approach has been applied in a wide variety of fields such as pattern recognition, image segmentation, web mining, privacy, remote sensing and marketing business. The semantic knowledge of a domain can be combined with data mining methods to improve the intelligent data analysis method. Semantic based clustering improves the quality of Text summarization. Ontology based clustering concepts can be applied in personalized multimedia content and in filtering process. The proposed method can be used in recommender system which is based on domain ontology. The recommender system clusters the domain concept based on the semantic preference weights of the user's interest.

CONCLUSION AND FUTURE WORK

The proposed model improves the text clustering model by combining the annotation weights. The aim of our current work is to provide qualitative improvement over VSM based search by using an ontology. The document clustering is done through particle swarm optimization. A PSO based ontology model of clustering knowledge documents is presented and compared to the traditional vector space model. The proposed ontology based framework provides improved performance and

Table 4. Comparison of f- measure

Methods	Precision	Recall	F-measure	Time in minutes
VSM	0.737	0.640	0.685	17.37
VSM+Ontology	0.768	0.727	0.747	15.59

better clustering compared to the traditional vector space model. It also overcomes the problems existing in the vector space model commonly used for clustering. The clustering result based on semantic similarity has higher fitness values than those based on the traditional vector space model.

It is worth pointing out that the above observations are made by combining semantic similarity and PSO clustering in terms of F-measure. It will be interesting to see, in our future work, if we can observe similar results using a more general learning algorithm or by using other performance measures. The model can also be enhanced based on personalized concept-based, fuzzy based, and hybrid clustering techniques.

ACKNOWLEDGMENT

The authors express their sincere thanks to the Management and Principal for their encouragement and support.

REFERENCES

Alam, S., Dobbie, G., & Riddle, P. (2008). Particle swarm optimization based clustering of web usage data. In *Proceedings of the IEEE/WIC/ACM International Conference on Web Intelligence and Intelligent Agent Technology* (Vol. 3, pp. 451-454).

Bach, M. D., Berger, H., & Merkl, D. (2004). Improving domain ontologies by mining semantics from text. In *Proceedings of the First Asia Pacific Conference on Conceptual Modeling* (Vol. 31, pp. 91-100).

Baloglu, A., Wyne, M. F., & Bahcetepe, Y. (2010). Web 2.0 based intelligent software architecture for photograph sharing. *International Journal of Intelligent Information Technologies*, *6*(4), 17–29. doi:10.4018/jiit.2010100102

Boskovic, M., Bagheri, E., Gasevic, D., Mohabbati, B., Kaviani, N., & Hatala, M. (2010). Automated staged configuration with semantic web technologies. *International Journal of Software Engineering and Knowledge Engineering*, *20*(4), 459–484. doi:10.1142/S0218194010004827

Castells, P., Fernandez, M., & Vallet, D. (2007). An adaption of the vector space model for ontology based information retrieval. *IEEE Transactions on Knowledge and Data Engineering*, *19*(2), 261–271. doi:10.1109/TKDE.2007.22

Cui, X., & Potok, T. E. (2005). Document clustering analysis based on hybrid PSO+K-means algorithm. *Journal of Computer Sciences*, 27-33.

Cui, X., Potok, T. E., & Palathingal, P. (2005). Document clustering using particle swarm optimization. In *Proceedings of the IEEE Swarm Intelligence Symposium*, Pasadena, CA (pp. 185-191).

Cunningham, H. (2002). GATE, a general architecture for text engineering. *Computers and the Humanities*, *36*, 223–254. doi:10.1023/A:1014348124664

Dash, R., Mishra, D., Rath, A. K., & Acharya, M. (2010). A hybridized K-means clustering approach for high dimensional dataset. *International Journal of Engineering. Science and Technology*, *2*(2), 59–66.

Eberhart, R. C., & Kennedy, J. (1995). A new optimizer using particle swarm theory. In *Proceedings of the Sixth International Symposium on Micromachine and Human Science* (pp. 39-43).

Euzenat, J., & Shvaiko, P. (2007). *Ontology matching*. Berlin, Germany: Springer-Verlag.

Fellbaum, C. (1998). *Wordnet: An electronic lexical databases*. Cambridge, MA: MIT Press.

Frakes, B., & Yates, B. R. (1992). *Information retrieval: Data structures and algorithms*. Upper Saddle River, NJ: Prentice Hall.

Guarino, N., Masolo, C., & Verete, G. (1999). OntoSeek: Content-based access to the web. *IEEE Intelligent Systems*, *14*, 70–80. doi:10.1109/5254.769887

Guha, R., McCool, R., & Miller, E. (2003). Semantic search. In *Proceedings of the 12th International Conference on World Wide Web* (pp. 700-709).

Hotho, A., Maedche, A., & Staab, S. (2002). Ontology based text document clustering. *Kunstliche Intelligenz*, *16*(4), 48–54.

Howland, P., & Park, H. (2004). Cluster preserving dimension reduction methods for efficient classification of text data. In Berry, M. W. (Ed.), *Survey of text mining: Clustering, classification and retrieval* (pp. 3–23). New York, NY: Springer.

Iosif, E., & Potamianos, A. (2010). Unsupervised semantic similarity computation between terms using web documents. *IEEE Transactions on Knowledge and Data Engineering*, *22*(11), 1637–1647. doi:10.1109/TKDE.2009.193

Iosif, E., Tegos, A., Pangos, A., Fosler-Lussie, E., & Potamianos, A. (2006). Combining statistical similarity measures for automatic induction of semantic classes. In *Proceedings of the IEEE/ACL Workshop on Spoken Language Technology* (pp. 86-89).

Jiang, X., & Tan, A. (2006). OntoSearch: A full-text search engine for the semantic web. In *Proceedings of the 21st National Conference on Artificial Intelligence* (pp. 1325-1330).

Jing, J., Zhou, L., Ng, M. K., & Huang, Z. (2006). Ontology-based distance measure for text clustering. In *Proceedings of the SIAM SDM Workshop on Text Mining*, Bethesda, MD.

Kennedy, J., & Eberhart, R. C. (1995). Particle swarm optimization. In. *Proceedings of the IEEE International Joint Conference on Neural Networks*, *4*, 1942–1948.

Kennedy, J., Eberhart, R. C., & Shi, Y. (2001). *Swarm intelligence*. San Francisco, CA: Morgan Kaufmann.

Killani, R., Rao, S. K., Satapathy, S. C., Pradhan, G., & Chandran, K. R. (2010). Effective document clustering with particle swarm optimization. In B. K. Panigrahi, S. Das, P. N. Suganthan, & S. S. Dash (Eds.), *Proceedings of the First International Conference on Swarm, Evolutionary, and Memetic Computing* (LNCS 6466, pp. 623-629).

Kothari, C. R., & Russomanno, D. J. (2008). Enhancing OWL ontologies with relation semantic. *International Journal of Software Engineering and Knowledge Engineering*, *18*(3), 327–356. doi:10.1142/S0218194008003660

Lan, M., Ta, C. L., Su, J., & Lu, Y. (2009). Supervised and traditional term weighting methods for automatic text categorization. *IEEE Transactions on Pattern Analysis and Machine Intelligence*, *31*(4), 721–735. doi:10.1109/TPAMI.2008.110

Lee, D., Chauang, H., & Seamons, K. (1997). Document ranking and the vector space model. *IEEE Software*, *14*(2), 66–75. doi:10.1109/52.582976

Li, G., Yu, S., & Dai, S. (2007). Ontology based query system design and implementation. In *Proceedings of the International Conference on Network and Parallel Computing* (pp. 1010-1015).

Li, Y., Wang, Y., & Huang, X. (2007). A relation- based search engine in semantic web. *IEEE Transactions on Knowledge and Data Engineering*, *19*(2), 273–282. doi:10.1109/TKDE.2007.18

Li, Y., & Zhong, N. (2008). Mining ontology for automatically acquiring web user information needs. *IEEE Transactions on Knowledge and Data Engineering*, *18*(4), 554–568.

Madylova1, A., & Öğüdücü, S. G. (2009). Comparison of similarity measures for clustering Turkish documents. *Intelligent Data Analysis*, *13*(5), 815-832.

Maedche, A., Staab, S., Stojanovic, N., Studer, R., & Sure, Y. (2003). Semantic portal: The SEAL approach. In *Proceedings of the Conference on Spinning the Semantic Web* (pp. 317-359).

Manning, C. D., Raghavan, P., & Schütze, H. (2008). *Introduction to information retrieval*. Cambridge, UK: Cambridge University Press.

Meng, S. K., & Chatwin, C. R. (2010). Ontology-based shopping agent for e-marketing. *International Journal of Intelligent Information Technologies, 6*(2), 21–43. doi:10.4018/jiit.2010040102

Niknam, T., Amiri, B., Olamaei, J., & Arefi, A. (2009). An efficient hybrid evolutionary optimization algorithm based on PSO and SA for clustering. *Journal of Zhejiang University. Science, 10*(4), 512–519. doi:10.1631/jzus.A0820196

Popov, B., Kiryakov, A., Kirilov, A., Manov, D., Ognyanoff, D., & Goranov, M. (2003). KIM - semantic annotation platform. In *Proceedings of the International Semantic Web Conference* (pp. 834-849).

Resink, P. (1999). Semantic similarity in taxonomy: An information-based measure and its application to problems of ambiguity in natural language. *Journal of Artificial Intelligence Research, 11*, 95–130.

Salton, G. (1989). *Automatic text processing*. Reading, MA: Addison-Wesley.

Salton, G., & McGill, M. J. (1983). *Introduction to modern information retrieval*. New York, NY: McGraw-Hill.

Salton, G., Wong, A., & Yang, C. S. (1975). A vector space model for automatic indexing. *Communications of the ACM, 18*(11), 112–117. doi:10.1145/361219.361220

Santos, I. G. D., & Madeira, E. (2010). A semantic-enabled middleware for citizen-centric e-government services. *International Journal of Intelligent Information Technologies, 6*(3), 34–55. doi:10.4018/jiit.2010070103

Shamsfard, M., Nematzadeh, A., & Motiee, S. (2006). ORank: An ontology based system for ranking document. *International Journal of Computer Science, 1*, 225–231.

Shehata, S., Karray, F., & Kamel, M. S. (2010). An efficient concept-based mining model for enhancing text clustering. *IEEE Transactions on Knowledge and Data Engineering, 22*(10), 1360–1371. doi:10.1109/TKDE.2009.174

Sieg, A., Mobasher, B., & Burke, R. (2007). Learning ontology based user profiles: A semantic approach to personalized web search. *IEEE Intelligent Informatics Bulletin, 8*, 7–18.

Song, J. F., Zhang, W. M., Xiao, W., Li, G. H., & Xu, Z. N. (2005). Ontology-based information retrieval model for the semantic web. In *Proceedings of the IEEE Computer Society* (pp. 152-155).

Song, L., Ma, J., Yan, P., Lian, L., & Zhang, D. (2008). Clustering deep web databases semantically. In *Proceedings of the 4th Asia Information Retrieval Conference on Information Retrieval Technology* (pp. 365-376).

Sridev, U. K., & Nagaveni, N. (2010). Ontology based similarity measure in document ranking. *International Journal of Computers and Applications, 1*(26), 125–129.

Sridevi, U. K., & Nagaveni, N. (2009a). Ontology based semantic measures in document similarity ranking. In *Proceedings of the International Conference on Advances in Recent Technologies in Communication and Computing* (pp. 482-486).

Sridevi, U. K., & Nagaveni, N. (2009b). Ontology based correlation analysis in information retrieval. *International Journal of Recent Trends in Engineering, 2*(1), 134–137.

Thomas, M. A., Redmond, T. R., & Yoon, V. Y. (2009). Using ontological reasoning for an adaptive e-commerce experience. *International Journal of Intelligent Information Technologies, 5*(4), 41–52. doi:10.4018/jiit.2009080703

Valkeapää, O., Alm, O., & Hyvönen, E. (2007). An adaptable framework for ontology-based content creation on the semantic web. *Journal of Universal Computer Science, 13*(12), 1825–1853.

Vallet, D., Fernandez, M., & Castells, P. (2005). An ontology based information retrieval model. In *Proceedings of the Second European Semantic Web Conference* (pp. 455-470).

Varelas, G., Voutsakis, E., Raftopoulou, P., Petrakis, E. G., & Milios, E. E. (2005). Semantic similarity methods in wordnet and their application to information retrieval on the web. In *Proceedings of the 7th Annual ACM International Workshop on Web Information and Data Management* (pp. 10-16).

Wei, W., Barjaghi, P. M., & Bargiela, A. (2007). Semantic enhanced information search and retrieval. In *Proceedings of the Sixth International Conference on Advance Language and Web Information Technology* (pp. 218-223).

Yang, X., Guo, D., Cao, X., & Zhou, J. (2008). Research on ontology-based text clustering. In *Proceedings of the Third International Workshop on Semantic Media Adaptation and Personalization* (pp. 141-146).

Zhang, L., & Wang, Z. (2010). Ontology-based clustering algorithm with feature weights. *Journal of Computer Information Systems, 6*(9), 2959–2966.

Zhang, X., Jing, L., Hu, X., Ng, M., Jiangxi, J. X., & Zhou, X. (2008). Medical document using ontology based term similarity measures. *International Journal of Data Warehousing and Mining, 4*(1), 62–73. doi:10.4018/jdwm.2008010104

Zhang, X., Jing, L., Hu, X., Ng, M., & Zhou, X. (2007). A comparative study of ontology based term similarity measures on PubMed document clustering. In *Proceedings of the 12th International Conference on Database Systems for Advanced Applications* (pp. 115-126).

This work was previously published in the International Journal of Intelligent Information Technologies, Volume 7, Issue 3, edited by Vijayan Sugumaran, pp. 54-69, copyright 2011 by IGI Publishing (an imprint of IGI Global).

Chapter 14
Towards a Possibilistic Information Retrieval System Using Semantic Query Expansion

Bilel Elayeb
ENSI Manouba University, Tunisia

Oussama Ben Khiroun
ENSI Manouba University, Tunisia

Ibrahim Bounhas
Faculty of Sciences of Tunis, Tunisia

Fabrice Evrard
Informatics Research Institute of Toulouse (IRIT), France

Narjès Bellamine-BenSaoud
ENSI Manouba University, Tunisia

ABSTRACT

This paper presents a new possibilistic information retrieval system using semantic query expansion. The work is involved in query expansion strategies based on external linguistic resources. In this case, the authors exploited the French dictionary "Le Grand Robert". First, they model the dictionary as a graph and compute similarities between query terms by exploiting the circuits in the graph. Second, the possibility theory is used by taking advantage of a double relevance measure (possibility and necessity) between the articles of the dictionary and query terms. Third, these two approaches are combined by using two different aggregation methods. The authors also benefit from an existing approach for reweighting query terms in the possibilistic matching model to improve the expansion process. In order to assess and compare the approaches, the authors performed experiments on the standard 'LeMonde94' test collection.

INTRODUCTION

The quasi-exponential development of the human knowledge distributed on varied interest fields led to the generation of a big mass of information increasingly difficult to manage and maintain. Within this large scale environment characterised at the same time by the great number of users and the immense mass of data, it becomes essential to conceive and develop tools allowing an effective and organized access. It is crucial to develop

DOI: 10.4018/978-1-4666-2047-6.ch014

automated interfaces which make it possible to formulate and satisfy users' informational needs. Information Retrieval (IR) is a branch of data processing interested to the acquisition, the organization, the storage and the research of information. We need Information Retrieval Systems (IRS) which constitute computer tools aiming to capitalize information and to locate relevant documents. Given an information requirement expressed as a query, the relevance is quantified according to a matching model between the query terms and the documents. Whatever the semantics are given to the representation of the objects (document or query) or the relevance definition; these models have an identical general behaviour (Dos Santos & Madeira, 2010; Baloglu et al., 2010). The majority of them represent the documents and the queries by lists of weighted keywords. Therefore from the concept of query/answer, the relevance of the result given by an IRS depends primarily on the query. However, the user is often unable to give some keywords which describe explicitly and clearly his intentional need what can deteriorate the quality of the awaited results. Query expansion is one of the strategies implemented in IRS to improve their performance and better satisfy users. It consists in enhancing the user's query by adding new terms to better express his need. In fact, there are two main approaches to query expansion in the literature, automatic query expansion (AQE) and interactive query expansion (IQE) (Ruthven, 2003). AQE is simpler for the user, but limits its performance because it has no user involvement. Having user involvement, IQE is more complex for the user, but means it can take more problems such as ambiguous queries. Besides, results of an IRS fail by finding too few relevant documents (low recall) or by retrieving too many irrelevant documents (low precision). Historically, AQE has better recall than IQE (Vélez & Weiss, 1997). Unfortunately, if the terms used to expand a query often changed the query's meaning, AQE frequently decreased precision (Croft & Harper, 1979). The problem is that users typically consider just the first few results (Jansen & McNeese, 2005), which makes precision crucial to search performance. In contrast, IQE has balanced precision and recall leading to an earlier uptake within search. However, like AQE, the precision of IQE approaches needs improvement. Most recently, approaches have started to improve precision by incorporating semantic knowledge (Crabtree, 2009). This can be achieved by various techniques such as corpus analysis and classification (Chevallet & Nie, 1997; Claveau & Sébillot, 2004), user Relevance Feedback (RF) and integration of external linguistic resources (e.g., dictionaries, thesauri and ontologies). We focus in our work on this last interactive query expansion approach using a dictionary as proposed in Elayeb (2009). Several query expansion experiments were conducted for example by using the WordNet lexical database on English IRS (Voorhees, 1994; Smeaton, 1997). The data used for query expansion in these approaches is poor, uncertain and unclear, while possibility theory is naturally appropriate for this kind of application. It allows expressing phenomena of ignorance, imprecision and uncertainty (Brini & Boughanem, 2004). Indeed, it defines two types of relevance. On the one hand, plausible relevance, quantified by the possibility trends to eliminate non-semantically similar terms (irrelevant ones); on the other hand, necessity relevance helps improve our belief in terms not eliminated by possibility measure (i.e., semantically close words useful for expansion). Ben Khiroun et al. (in press) proposed a possibilistic approach for semantic query expansion. Based on this work, we propose a new possibilistic IRS which takes advantage, combine and compare the possibilistic and the circuit-based approaches for semantic query expansion. Moreover in this paper, we propose and investigate the idea of a possibilistic network which models the dependencies between the query terms and the articles of a dictionary. The semantic proximity is quantified through possibility and necessity measures. Expanding a query means adding the most possibly and necessarily articles of the dictionary to its terms. This process is improved by reweighting the old and the new terms to give them relative importance. As a means of assessment, we firstly compare this approach to our circuit-based distance. We combine these two approaches by using two different aggregation methods. We also benefit from an existing approach for reweighting query terms in the possibilistic matching model to improve the expansion process. Experiments are carried out using the standard "LeMonde94" test collection within the French dictionary "Le Grand Robert". Results are evaluated and compared in terms of improving the performance of the proposed IRS. This paper is structured as follows. In the next section, we briefly recall the main concepts of possibility theory. The section following constitutes a literature review in the field. Afterward, we present our approaches for Semantic Query Expansion (SQE) based respectively on Hierarchical Small-Worlds Networks (HSWN) and Possibilistic Networks (PN). The query expansion combining these two approaches with an illustrative example is presented later in the chapter. The existing approach for reweighting query terms in the possibilistic matching model to improve the expansion process is briefly exposed after this. A set of experimentations, results analysis and comparative studies are then made. Near to the chapter's end, a comparison with similar approaches is presented and main directions for future research are proposed. Finally, the last section summarized and concluded the main outcomes of this paper.

POSSIBILITY THEORY

The possibility theory introduced by Zadeh (1978) and developed by several authors, handles uncertainty in the interval [0,1] called the possibility scale, in a qualitative or quantitative way. This section briefly reviews basic elements of possibility theory, for more details see Dubois and Prade (1987, 1998, 2004).

Possibility Distribution

Possibility theory is based on possibility distributions. The latter, denoted by π, are mappings from Ω (the universe of discourse) to the scale [0,1] encoding partial knowledge on the world. The possibility scale is interpreted in two ways. In the ordinal case, possibility values only reflect an ordering between possible states; in the numerical scale, possibility values often account for upper probability bounds (Dubois & Prade, 1998).

Possibility and Necessity Measures

While other approaches provide a unique relevance value, the possibility theory defines two measures. A possibility distribution π on Ω enables events to be qualified in terms of their plausibility and their certainty, in terms of possibility and necessity measures respectively. In the context of IR systems (Indrawan & Loke, 2008; Elayeb & Evrard, 2009), the first measure allows to reject irrelevant documents. The second measure allows reinforcing our belief in the relevant ones.

- The possibility $\Pi(A) = \max_{x \in A} \pi(x)$ of an event A relies on the most normal situation in which A is true.
- The necessity $N(A) = \min_{x \notin A}(1 - \pi(x)) = 1 - \Pi(\neg A)$ of an event A reflects the most normal situation in which A is false.

The width of the gap between *N(A)* and *Π(A)* evaluates the amount of ignorance about *A*. Note that *N(A) > 0* implies *Π(A) = 1*. When *A* is a fuzzy set this property no longer holds but the inequality *N(A) ≤ Π(A)* remains valid (Dubois & Prade, 1987).

Possibilistic Networks

A directed possibilistic network (PN) on a variable set *V* is characterized by a graphical and a numeric component. The first one is a directed acyclic graph. The graph structure encodes independence relation sets just like Bayesian nets (Benferhat & Dubois, 2002; Borgelt & Gebhardt, 1998). The second component quantifies distinct links of the graph and consists of the conditional possibility matrix of each node in the context of its parents. These possibility distributions should respect normalization. For each variable *V*:

- If *V* is a root node and *dom(V)* the domain of *V*, the prior possibility of *V* should satisfy: $\max_{v \in dom(V)} \Pi(v) = 1$;
- If *V* is not a root node, the conditional distribution of *V* in the context of its parents context satisfy: $\max_{v \in dom(V)} \Pi(v \mid Par_V) = 1$; $Par_V \in dom(Par_V)$ where: *dom(V)*: domain of *V*; Par_V: value of parents of *V*; $dom(Par_V)$: domain of parent set of *V*.

In this paper, possibilistic networks are exploited, on the one hand, to help extract candidate terms for semantic query expansion process. In this case, possibilistic network link the dictionary definition of the initial query terms to their index. On the other hand, these resources are validated in the context of a possibilistic IR system. In this case, possibilistic networks link documents to the terms of the reformulated query.

The Possibilistic Matching Model

Possibilistic networks were employed as a matching model in the context of IR systems (Brini & Boughanem, 2003, 2004; Elayeb & Evrard, 2009; Elayeb, 2009). In this case, the goal is to compute a matching score between a query and a document. The query *Q* is composed of a set of weighted terms. We have: Where w_i is the weight of the term t_i.

$$Q = \{(t_1, w_1); (t_2, w_2); \ldots; (t_m, w_m)\}$$

The Degree of Possibilistic Relevance (DPR) of a document (D_j) given the query (*Q*) is computed by the two measures: possibility (Π) and necessity (*N*).

According to Elayeb & Evrard (2009), $\Pi(D_j|Q)$ is proportional to:

$$\Pi'(D_j \mid Q) = \pi(t_1 \mid D_j) * w_1 * \ldots * \pi(t_m \mid D_j) * w_m$$

In the case of an IR system, $\pi(t_i|D_j)$ is estimated by the frequency of the term t_i in the document D_j ($Freq_{ij}$). So we have:

$$\Pi'(D_j \mid Q) = Freq_{1j} * w_1 * \ldots * Freq_{mj} * w_m$$

The necessity of D_j for the query *Q*, denoted $N(D_j|Q)$, is computed as follows:

$$N(D_j \mid Q) = 1 - \Pi(\neg D_j \mid Q)$$

where

$$\Pi(\neg D_j \mid Q) = \frac{\Pi(Q \mid \neg D_j) * \Pi(\neg D_j)}{\Pi(Q)}$$

In the same manner, $\Pi(\neg D_j|Q)$ is proportional to:

$$\Pi'(\neg D_j|Q) = \pi(t_1|\neg D_j) * \ldots * \pi(t_m|\neg D_j)$$

This can be expressed as follows:

$$\Pi'(\neg D_j|Q) = (1 - \frac{\varphi_{1j}}{w_1}) * \ldots * (1 - \frac{\varphi_{mj}}{w_m})$$

where

$$\varphi_{ij} = Log_{10}(\frac{|D|}{nD_i}) * Freq_{ij}$$

In this formula, $|D|$ is the number of documents. nD_i is the number of documents containing the term t_i ($Freq_{ij} > 0$).

The Degree of Possibilistic Relevance of D_j is often computed as the sum of the two measures:

$$DPR(D_j) = \Pi(D_j|Q) + N(D_j|Q)$$

In our system this matching model is employed twice. In the first hand, we match the articles of the dictionary to the query terms to perform expansion. On the second hand, we evaluate documents according to the (reformulated) query.

RELATED WORKS

We present in this section some related query expansion (QE) approaches. According to the source of knowledge exploited for adding new terms, we may distinguish approaches based on 1) relevance feedback, 2) statistical analysis of corpora, and 3) external resources. In the following subsections we review and compare these approaches.

QE Based on Relevance Feedback

Query expansion in existing IRS is mainly based on Relevance Feedback (RF) (Smeaton, 1983; Picariello & Rinaldi, 1998; Lee, 1998; Brini & Boughanem, 2003) used for example in the SMART system (Salton & Buckley, 1990) considering positive and/or negative feedback from the user. Several researches proved that this approach improves the results of search in terms of recall and precision.

According to Harman (1988), the techniques of query expansion are more useful when used to assist the user. However they are less expressive when we try to proceed automatically. Thus one can guide the user by providing him a list of words which correspond to the closest neighbours to the terms of the initial query. The number of terms to be added and the number of iterations are two parameters to be computed automatically. The experiments were carried out by using the Cranfield test collection. The same authors propose in Harman (1992) and Harman and Fox (1992) to add relevant descriptors to the query from the relevant documents and to reduce the weight of the terms which appear in irrelevant ones.

Buckley and Salton (1995) proposed an approach to dynamically change the weights of terms by testing their possible change on the search result. The process is repeated, for each term whose weight was modified, to test if there is an improvement of the result after change. According to Salton, the optimized queries make it possible to obtain a better result (10 -15%) compared to the initial queries.

Within the development of IRS, RF techniques where incorporated into Bayesian model (De Campos & Fernandez-Luna, 2003; Fernandez-Luna & De Campos, 2003) and possibilistic models (Chouaib, 2006). We are particularly interested in this model which we are using in QE and matching. In addition, in the list of restored documents (relevant or irrelevant), a term can exist in several documents, but its possibilistic and necessary weight changes from a document to another. Then, it is necessary to incorporate all the weights of the same term in different documents.

Chouaib (2006) proposed five formulae: two formulae based on the necessity, two others based on the possibility and the fifth is a combination of both. These formulae were defined to calculate the new weights of terms of the new query during the process of RF. Integrating these two degrees of relevance allowed to identify the terms to be added to the new query. Experimental results are carried out using the WT10g document set, which is a part of the TREC-9 test collection. The average precision of the IRS increased of more than 53% for the five formulae. These results show that the introduction of the possibility and the necessity is interesting and reliable for a RF-based QE.

To summarize, the improvements of search results are variable from a test collection to another and depend on the number of added terms, how they are selected and added. However, RF techniques often require heavy intervention rate since the user must evaluate the returned documents. Besides, within this approach, it is possible to introduce into the initial query some terms which do not have a relationship with the user's need thus generating much noise. Finally, the query expansion technique cannot be beneficial in case of short queries as the effect of ambiguous terms will increase. To resolve this problem, we must handle and disambiguate polysemous words. To reduce intervention, avoid noisy words and better understand the meaning of words, we have to use external resources precising explicitly the relationships between words.

QE Based on Corpus Analysis

Latent Semantic Analysis (LSA) and distributional analysis are the main techniques employed in corpus-based QE. Apart from the frequency of terms in a document collection, the distribution of words plays an important role in determining the relevance of documents for a given search query. Galeas and Freisleben (2008) proposed a word distribution analysis as an approach for using descriptive statistics to calculate a compressed representation of word positions in a document. Based on this statistical approximation, two methods for improving the evaluation of document relevance are proposed: (a) a relevance ranking procedure based on how query terms are distributed over initially retrieved documents, and (b) a query expansion technique based on overlapping the distributions of terms in the top-ranked documents. Experimental results obtained for the TREC-8 document collection demonstrate that the proposed approach leads to an improvement of about 6.6% over the Term Frequency-Inverse Document Frequency (TF-IDF) (Salton & Buckley, 1988) weighting scheme without applying query reformulation or relevance feedback techniques.

LSA is a method in vectorial semantics for analyzing relationships between a set of documents and the terms they contain by producing a set of concepts related to the documents and terms. Aiming to resolve the problems existing in traditional method of query expansion, an approach for cross-lingual query expansion based on LSA is proposed by Bi and Su (2009). They used clustering to improve accuracy of expansion word sets and used LSA to implement query expansion without translation. The impact of error in translation is eliminated. Experimental results show that this method achieves better performance of the IRS.

Inspite of its advantages, LSA includes some drawbacks: (1) LSA cannot capture polysemy. Because each word is represented as a single point in space, it is treated as having the same meaning. However, this effect is often lessened because words generally have a predominant sense throughout a corpus (i.e., not all meanings are equally represented), (2) Limitations of bag of words model, where a text is represented as an unordered collection of words, (3) The probabilistic model of LSA does not match observed data: LSA assumes that words and documents form a joint Gaussian model, while a Poisson distribution has been observed. Thus, a newer alternative is probabilistic LSA, based on a multinomial model, which is reported to give better results than standard LSA (Hofmann, 1999).

In all cases, the performance of QE in LSA or distributional analysis based approaches depends on the quality of the corpus which can not cover the whole language. As discussed above, we cannot handle all the senses of a given word. Besides, we are unable to prove that the corpus contains the required relationships between words which are useful for QE. Even if that all relations exist, we cannot guarantee they are handled with LSA or distributional analysis or any other method. That's why, we think that external resources are needed to explicitly represent the meanings and the relations of words.

QE Based on External Resources

Dictionaries and knowledge organisation systems (e.g., thesauri and ontologies) explicitly representing relations between terms are widely used for QE. For example, Adriani and van Rijsbergen (1999) proposed a query expansion technique based on a statistical similarity measure among terms to improve the effectiveness of a dictionary-based cross-lingual information retrieval (CLIR) method. They employed a term similarity-based sense disambiguation technique to enhance the accuracy of the dictionary-based query translation method. The query expansion technique is then applied to query translation to further improve the performance. Authors demonstrated the effectiveness of combining the two techniques using queries in three languages (namely German, Spanish and Indonesian) to retrieve English documents from the standard TREC collection.

Thesauri are also used to expand queries in IRS. They have been frequently integrated thus providing explicit relations of synonymy and semantic similarity. For example, we can refer to Aditi and Hazra (2009) to explain the types and the roles of thesauri in IR and more specifically in QE.

Tuominen and Kauppinen (2009) suggested a QE widget employing the ONKI Ontology Service which contains about 60 ontologies. Authors tested the system with general, domain-specific and spatiotemporal ontologies. However, if a concept appearing in a query is made of many sub-concepts, the expanded query may become inconveniently long as far as the sub-concepts are added. This may influence the performance of the system which may function improperly or become very slow.

Indrawan and Loke (2008) studied the impact of ontology on the performance of information retrieval. A new approach was investigated to test the effectiveness of a generic ontology such as WordNet in improving the performance of information retrieval systems. The test and the analysis of the experiments suggest that WordNet is far from the ideal solution in solving semantic problems in the information retrieval.

Synthesis

The various query expansion approaches include relevance feedback, corpus dependent and independent knowledge models. Based on this review, external resources such as dictionaries, thesauri and ontologies have a higher linguistic coverage compared to corpora. Building ontologies is time consuming and requires sophisticated tools to extract and organise knowledge. Besides, ontologies are not available for all languages and domains. Thesauri are built from the indexes of documents. Consequently they suffer from the problems of ambiguity and coverage since not all the senses of words are represented and clearly distinguished. However dictionaries are exhaustive resources that are built to cover the whole language and they naturally represent the meanings and the relations between words. Also, they exist for all languages. Finally multi-lingual dictionaries may be used in CLIR. We conclude that dictionaries are the most generic resources that may be used to support IRS especially in QE. In this context, we propose, compare and combine the following two semantic query expansion approaches based on a dictionary and used in a possibilistic IRS as follows.

THE CIRCUIT-BASED APPROACH FOR SQE

Elayeb (2009) studied the query expansion problem and its impact on a possibilistic information retrieval system. His method is based on counting circuits in a graph generated from a dictionary considered as Hierarchical Small-World networks. Before we present the circuit-based distance (cf. The Circuit-Based Semantic Proximity section), we briefly recall HSWN in the next section. The following section gives an example of calculus for query expansion.

Hierarchical Small-World Networks (HSWN)

HSWN were defined to exploit statistical characteristics of graphs. They were initially proposed by Watts and Strogatz (1998) in the field of social network analysis. In these networks, it has been remarked that the majority of nodes have few relations with others what allows to constitute small-worlds. Then, the main characteristic of these graphs is their ability to cluster close nodes. This encouraged many authors to use these graphs to model and cluster terms or words (Newman, 2003; Elayeb & Evrard, 2009; Elayeb, 2009).

As a mean of comparison, Gaume and Hathout (2004) show the differences between random graphs (nodes are given, edges are drawn randomly), regular graphs and HSWN. The characteristics of HSWN compared to these graphs (high clustering rate and short paths) allow clustering nodes according to the circuits which link them.

In our case, a dictionary is represented as an HSWN where we consider that it represents a graph characterized by a concentration of relations (arcs) between all French words (nodes) having the same meaning. There is an arc from a term t_i to a term t_j if and only if the entry t_j appears in the definition of entry t_i as a synonym.

The Circuit-Based Semantic Proximity

In the graph of dictionary words maintain relationships that sometimes make circuits. For a given term t_i of an initial query Q^{old}, using the graph of the dictionary we compute the score of semantic proximity of term t_i with any other term t_j according to following formula (Elayeb, 2009):

$$Semantic\_\Pr oximity(t_i,t_j) = \frac{Number\_of\_Circuits(t_i,t_j)}{Maximum\_Number\_of\ Circuits\_in\_the\_Graph}$$

where Number_of_Circuits(t_i, t_j) represents the number of circuits starting from the node t_i and passing through the node t_j in the graph of dictionary (i.e., $t_i \rightarrow \ldots \rightarrow t_j \rightarrow \ldots \rightarrow t_i$).

One of our contributions in comparison with Elayeb's works (Elayeb, 2009) remains especially in the full exploitation of the French dictionary "Le Grand Robert". Unlike Elayeb who was limited to a subset of verbs from this dictionary due to computer resources limitations, we consider all the categories of words such as adverbs, nouns and adjectives.

The maximum length of circuit is one of important parameter in this distance. In fact, more the circuit is long more there is chance to mix various groups of meanings. However, taking into account only too short circuits would cause to cluster terms related to the same hyperonym into different groups. More details about the regrouping

Figure 1. Example of a sub-graph of HSWN of dictionary

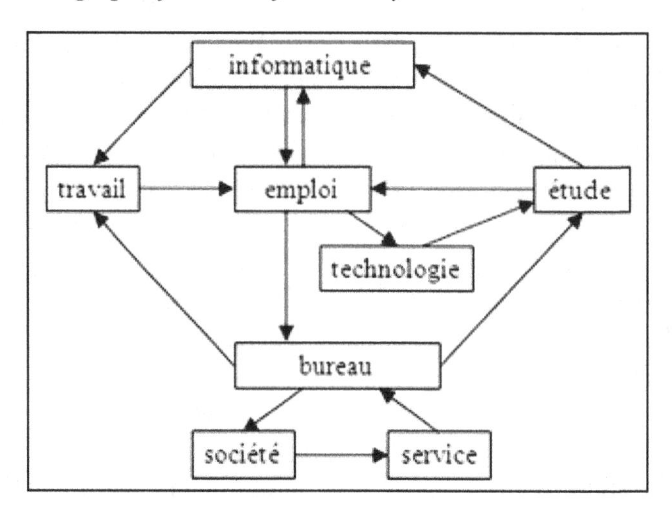

principle can be found in (Elayeb, 2009), where author specify that the maximum length of circuit that we can take into account is about 4 edges.

Illustrative Example

Let us assume a sub-graph of HSWN of dictionary in Figure 1. We detail in the following an example of semantic query expansion using the circuit-based approach. Let also note the initial user's query by Q^{old} = (informatique, bureau). We present different steps to identify some semantic close terms to user's keywords for a maximum length of circuit equal to 3 and 4 (cf. Table 1).

We start by identifying and counting circuits as in Table 1. Then we compute the score of similarity between the query terms and the other words. Finally, the N most similar terms are added to Q^{old} to build Q^{new}:

- If the maximum length of circuit is 3 and if we choose to add only one word to the term "informatique" and 2 words to the term "bureau" for example; the reformulated query will be Q^{new} = (informatique, travail, bureau, emploi, étude).
- Let take the length of circuit equal to 4. If we add only one word to the term "informatique", we should choose "emploi". For the term "bureau", we may decide to add two words. In this case, we must select "étude" and "emploi". Thus Q^{new} contains the following terms: "informatique", "etude", "bureau" and "emploi".

We remark that the number of terms semantically close to the initial keywords increase whenever we augment the length of circuit. Indeed, more the maximum length of circuit is larger more the number of founded circuits is growing; and thus the set of query terms becomes more important. The classification order of these terms is also dependent on the maximum length of circuits.

THE POSSIBILISTIC APPROACH FOR SQE

Our approach is based on possibilistic networks (cf. Model Architecture section). It identifies the most suitable terms to be added to the initial query. An example of this calculus is given in the following section. The added terms are reweighted according to the formulae presented in after this.

Table 1. Results of the example of the circuit-based approach of SQE

Query Terms	Maximum Length of Circuit (MLC)	Semantic Close Terms	Number of Circuit	Score of Semantic Proximity
Informatique	(MLC = 3) informatique → travail → emploi → informatique	travail	1	1
		emploi	1	1
	(MLC = 4) informatique → travail → emploi → informatique informatique → emploi → technologie → étude → informatique informatique → emploi → bureau → étude → informatique	emploi	3	1
		étude	2	0,67
		bureau	1	0,33
		technologie	1	0,33
		travail	1	0,33
Bureau	(MLC = 3) bureau → société → service → bureau bureau → travail → emploi → bureau bureau → étude → emploi → bureau	emploi	2	1
		étude	1	0,5
		service	1	0,5
		société	1	0,5
		travail	1	0,5
	(MLC = 4) bureau → société → service → bureau bureau → travail → emploi → bureau bureau → étude → emploi → bureau bureau → étude → informatique → emploi → bureau	emploi	3	1
		étude	2	0,67
		service	1	0,33
		société	1	0,33
		informatique	1	0,33
		travail	1	0,33

Model Architecture

Our model is inspired from the works of Brini and Boughanem (2003, 2004) who proposed a quantitative possibilistic matching model for information retrieval. This model was subsequently extended by Elayeb and Evrard (2009) and Elayeb (2009) to a qualitative possibilistic framework. We exploit knowledge extracted from the French dictionary "Le Grand Robert" to propose our new possibilistic networks for semantic query expansion. Indeed, the dictionary presents a set of entries which are terms having definitions called articles in the remaining of this paper. Each article is indexed by a set of terms which appear in its definition. The articles and their indexing terms are represented by naive possibilistic networks as shown in Figure 2. A dependency relationship exists between a term and an article.

An arc between a node A_i and a node t_j reflects the possibility and the necessity that t_j is representative (or not) for A_i. The possibility measure is useful to filter the articles and the necessity measure enhances the relevance of the remaining articles. The expansion process renders articles plausibly or necessarily relevant to a user. This dependency between t_j and A_i is computed according to the frequency of t_j in the definition of A_i and to its frequency in the whole collection (dictionary).

Given a query Q_j composed of t_j (or many terms), we presuppose that this mode is able to respond to proposals such as:

- Is it plausible to some degree that an article A_i is a good answer for the query Q_j?
- Is it necessary, certain (in the possibilistic sense), that an article A_i answers the query Q_j?

Figure 2. General architecture of the possibilistic model

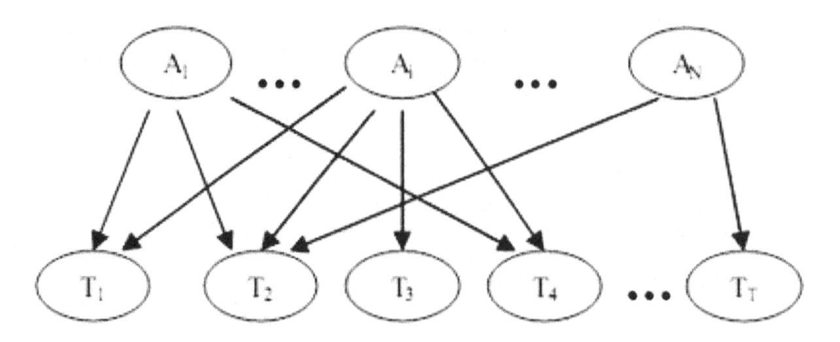

- Is an article A_i preferable than another article A_k to be added to the query Q_j?

The first question is meant to remove articles weakly plausible from the response. The second one focuses on articles that are actually relevant. The third one suggests that since the raw information on term definition (article) is more qualitative than quantitative, ordinal approaches to the problem may be interesting as well. The use of probability theory in the definition of relevance given a query does not account for our limited knowledge of the relevance of an article, since it does not consider imprecision and vagueness intrinsic to relevance (Brini & Boughanem, 2004).

The quantitative relevance of each dictionary article (A_j), given a query $Q = (t_1, t_2, ..., t_T)$, is computed as follows:

According to Elayeb and Evrard (2009), the possibility degree $\Pi(A_j|Q)$ is proportional to:

$$\Pi'(A_j|Q) =$$
$$\Pi(t_1|A_j) * ... * \Pi(t_T|A_j) = nft_{1j} * ... * nft_{Tj}$$

where

$$nft_{ij} = \frac{tf_{ij}}{\max(tf_{kj})}:$$

the normalized frequency of query terms in the dictionary article.

The certainty of retrieving a relevant article A_j for a query, denoted $N(A_j|Q)$, is given by:

$$N(A_j|Q) = 1\text{-}\Pi(\neg A_j|Q)$$

where

$$\Pi(\neg A_j|Q) = \frac{\Pi(Q|\neg A_j) * \Pi(\neg A_j)}{\Pi(Q)}$$

In the same way, $\Pi(\neg A_j|\ Q)$ is then proportional to:

$$\Pi'(\neg A_j|Q) = \Pi(t_1|\neg A_j) * ... * \Pi(t_T|\neg A_j)$$

This numerator can be expressed by:

$$\Pi'(\neg A_j|Q) = (1 - \varphi A_{1j}) * ... * (1 - \varphi A_{Tj})$$

where

$$\varphi A_{ij} = Log_{10}(\frac{nCA}{nA_i}) * nft_{ij}$$

and

Table 2. The degree of possibilistic relevance of the three articles in the example

Number of Index Terms of A_i	Index	DPR(A_1|Q)	DPR(A_2|Q)	DPR(A_3|Q)
1	$Q = (t_1)$	0.75	0.5	0.25
	$Q = (t_2)$	0.588	1.176	0
	$Q = (t_3)$	0.588	0	1.176
	$Q = (t_4)$	1.176	0	0.588
2	$Q = (t_1, t_2)$	0.463	0.676	1
	$Q = (t_1, t_3)$	0.463	1	0.426
	$Q = (t_1, t_4)$	0.926	1	0.213
	$Q = (t_2, t_3)$	0.419	0.176	0.176
	$Q = (t_2, t_4)$	0.676	0.176	0.088
	$Q = (t_3, t_4)$	0.749	0	0.749
3	$Q = (t_1, t_2, t_3)$	0.356	0.176	0.176
	$Q = (t_1, t_2, t_4)$	0.624	0.176	0.088
	$Q = (t_1, t_3, t_4)$	0.624	0	0.374
	$Q = (t_2, t_3, t_4)$	0.565	0.176	0.249
4	$Q = (t_1, t_2, t_3, t_4)$	0.502	0.176	0.249

nCA = total number of articles in dictionary,

nA_i = number of dictionary's articles containing the term t_i.

We define the Degree of Possibilistic Relevance (DPR) for each dictionary article A_i given a query Q by: $DPR(A_i) = \Pi(A_i|Q) + N(A_i|Q)$

The preferred articles are those having the higher DPR(A_i) score. Indeed, these articles are semantically similar to query terms Q and are the best candidates for the expansion of $Q^{old} = (A_1, A_2, ..., A_n)$.

Illustrative Example

Because of the limited space here, we use abstract terms $t_1, t_2, t_3, ..., t_n$ in this example instead of using real terms (having very long dictionary definitions) such as presented in the example of the circuit-based approach for SQE.

Assume a mini-collection of 3 dictionary entries (articles) containing terms t_1, t_2, t_3 and t_4:

$A_1 = \{t_1, t_1, t_1, t_2, t_2, t_3, t_3, t_4, t_4, t_4, t_4\}$, $A_2 = \{t_1, t_1, t_2, t_2, t_2, t_2\}$ and $A_3 = \{t_1, t_3, t_3, t_3, t_3, t_4, t_4\}$

Let us consider the initial user query $Q^{old} = (A_1, A_2, A_3)$. We aim in this case study to reformulate Q^{old} by applying our approach for possibilistic semantic query expansion. We note, in Table 2, the Degree of Possibilistic Relevance of each dictionary article A_i by DPR(A_i).

The evaluation of the three articles A_1, A_2 and A_3 given the query $Q = (t_1, t_2, t_3, t_4)$ gives:

$$\Pi(A_1 \mid Q) = \Pi(t_1 \mid A_1) * \Pi(t_2 \mid A_1) * \Pi(t_3 \mid A_1) * \Pi(t_4 \mid A_1) = (3/4) * (2/4) * (2/4) * (4/4) = 0.1875$$

$$N(A_1 \mid Q) = 1 - [(1 - \phi A_{11}) * (1 - \phi A_{21}) * (1 - \phi A_{31}) * (1 - \phi A_{41})] = 1 - [1 * (1 - 0,088) * (1 - 0,088) * (1 - 0,176)] = 0.3146$$

$$\mathrm{DPR}(A_1) = \Pi(A_1 \mid Q) + N(A_1 \mid Q) = 0.1875 + 0.3146 = 0.502$$

$$\Pi(A_2 \mid Q) = P(t_1 \mid A_2) * \Pi(t_2 \mid A_2) * \Pi(t_3 \mid A_2) * \Pi(t_4 \mid A_2) = (2/4) * (4/4) * (0) * (0) = 0$$

$$N(A_2 \mid Q) = 1 - [(1 - \phi A_{12}) * (1 - \phi A_{22}) * (1 - \phi A_{32}) * (1 - \phi A_{42})] = 1 - [1 * (1 - 0{,}176) * 1 * 1] = 0{,}176$$

$$\mathrm{DPR}(A_2) = \Pi(A_2 \mid Q) + N(A_2 \mid Q) = 0.176$$

$$\Pi(A_3 \mid Q) = \Pi(t_1 \mid A_3) * \Pi(t_2 \mid A_3) * \Pi(t_3 \mid A_3) * \Pi(t_4 \mid A_3) = (1/4) * (0) * (4/4) * (2/4) = 0$$

$$N(A_3 \mid Q) = 1 - [(1 - \phi A_{13}) * (1 - \phi A_{23}) * (1 - \phi A_{33}) * (1 - \phi A_{43})] = 1 - [1 * 1 * (1 - 0.176) * (1 - 0.088)] = 1 - 0.751 = 0.249$$

$$\mathrm{DPR}(A_3) = \Pi(A_3 \mid Q) + N(A_3 \mid Q) = 0.249$$

The query Q, interpreted as a conjunction of terms would be too restrictive, since only article A_1 of the collection contains all four terms of the query $Q = (t_1, t_2, t_3, t_4)$. Thus, to avoid getting an empty list of articles results, we look for articles that contain at least two terms of the query then at least one term (if none of articles in the collection contain two terms). We focus then on articles that deal with sets $\{t_1, t_2\}$ or $\{t_1, t_4\}$, or $\{t_2, t_4\}$.

Applying our new approach, we note that even if the chosen terms tend to select an article, these terms are not the most frequent in the article (for example the term t_1 is not the most frequent in A_2 whereas it has contributed significantly in increasing the score of A_2 in the case of the two queries $Q = (t_1, t_3)$ and $Q = (t_1, t_4)$), what is showing the advantage of the possibilistic approach in the selection of relevant articles. The results summarized in Table 2 allow us to reformulate the query $Q^{old} = (A_1, A_2, A_3)$ as follows:

- If we want to add one term possibly close to each article, we add t_4 to A_1, t_2 to A_2 and t_3 to A_3 because they have the best scores of DPR($A_i|Q$). These additional terms are most frequent in these three articles. As a result the possibilistic expansion proposed is identical to an expansion based on TF-IDF formulae (Salton & Buckley, 1988). The reformulated query will be $Q^{new} = (A_1, t_4, A_2, t_2, A_3, t_3)$.
- If we want to add two terms possibly close to each article, we add $\{t_1$ and $t_4\}$ to A_1, $\{t_1$ and $(t_3$ or $t_4)\}$ to A_2 and $\{t_1$ and $t_2\}$ to A_3. The terms added to A_3 are not the most frequent ones in this article. This shows the contribution of the possibilistic approach compared to TF-IDF. The reformulated query will be $Q^{new} = (A_1, t_1, t_4, A_2, t_3, A_3, t_2)$.
- If we want to add three terms possibly close to each article, we add to A_1 $\{t_1$ and t_4 and $(t_2$ or $t_3)\}$, we add the set $\{t_1$ and t_2 and $(t_3$ or $t_4)\}$ or the set $\{t_2$ and t_4 and $(t_1$ or $t_3)\}$ to A_2 and we add the set $\{t_1$ and t_3 and $t_4)$ to A_3. These additional terms are the most frequent ones in these three articles. The reformulated query will be $Q^{new} = (A_1, t_1, t_4, A_2, t_2, t_3, A_3)$.

We remark here that Q^{new} depends on the number of the added close terms to each article of Q^{old}. We exploit this factor in the following section to define new weights for each term in Q^{new}.

COMBINING THE POSSIBILISTIC AND THE CIRCUIT-BASED APPROACHES FOR SQE

Our goal in this step is to combine the possibilistic approach for SQE with the circuit-based one. Our heuristics here start from the initial tests which prove the effectiveness of the circuit-based approach having the most considerable improvement rate. Thus we propose to improve results provided by the possibilistic approach by integrating knowledge coming from circuits. Indeed, the possibilistic expansion process treats the query terms as a whole. Nevertheless, the circuit-based approach independently applies to each query term. Consequently the only way to aggregate the two approaches consists in reinforcing the possibilistic score of each term by its circuit-based score. We briefly present in the following the formulae for computing the aggregated scores in the next section. An illustrative example is given afterward.

Computing Aggregated Scores

The Degree of Hybrid Relevance (DHR) related to a query $Q = (t_1, t_2, \ldots, t_T)$ is computed as follows. Indeed, we used two formulae of aggregation:

1. **Aggregation using sum:** $DHR(A_i) = DPR(A_i|Q) + ACB(A_i,Q)$
2. **Aggregation using product:** $DHR(A_i) = DPR(A_i|Q) * ACB(A_i,Q)$ where $ACB(A_i,Q)$ is the average of circuit-based scores of the article A_i. It is given by:

$$ACB(A_i,Q) = \sum \mathrm{score}(t_j) / T$$

where T is the number of terms in the query Q and score (t_i) is the circuit-based semantic similarity between t_j and A_i.

Illustrative Example

Let us assume a mini-collection of three dictionary entries (articles) as introduced under The Possibilistic Approach for SQE: Illustrative Example. As we need to apply the circuit-based expansion method in the aggregation method, the graph structure should be studied to extract circuits and to distinguish relevant expansion terms. So, we consider the following sub-dictionary graph example in Figure 3.

Then it exists a set of existing dictionary terms which are not indexing the articles A_1, A_2 and A_3.

Figure 3. Example of dictionary graph representation

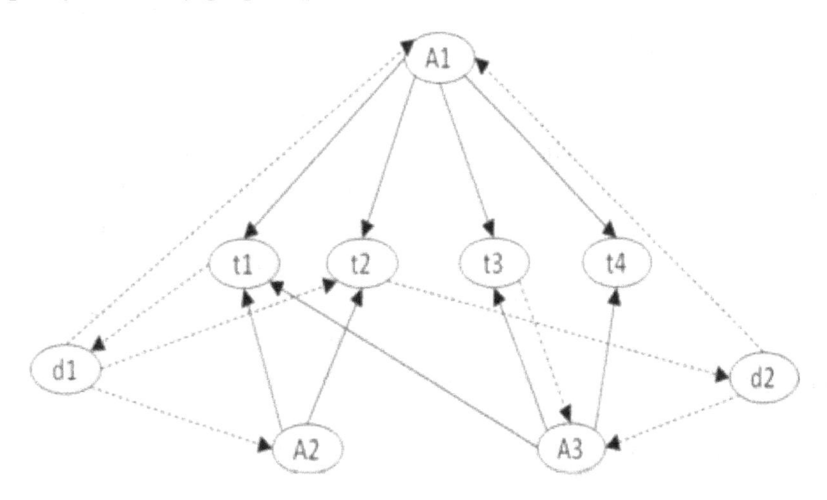

Table 3. Similar terms applying the circuit based expansion method

Query Terms	Maximum Length of Circuit (MLC = 5)	Similar Terms	Number of Circuits	Normalized Circuits Frequency
A_1	$A_1 \rightarrow t_1 \rightarrow d_1 \rightarrow A_1$ $A_1 \rightarrow t_1 \rightarrow d_1 \rightarrow t_2 \rightarrow d_2 \rightarrow A_1$ $A_1 \rightarrow t_2 \rightarrow d_2 \rightarrow A_1$ $A_1 \rightarrow t_3 \rightarrow A_3 \rightarrow t_1 \rightarrow d_1 \rightarrow A_1$	t_1	3	1
		d_1	3	1
		t_2	2	0.67
		d_2	2	0.67
		t_3	1	0.33
		A_3	1	0.33
A_2	$A_2 \rightarrow t_1 \rightarrow d_1 \rightarrow A_2$	t_1	1	1
		d_1	1	1
A_3	$A_3 \rightarrow t_1 \rightarrow d_1 \rightarrow t_2 \rightarrow d_2 \rightarrow A_3$ $A_3 \rightarrow t_1 \rightarrow d_1 \rightarrow A_1 \rightarrow t_3 \rightarrow A_3$ $A_3 \rightarrow t_3 \rightarrow A_3$	t_1	2	1
		d_1	2	1
		t_2	1	0.5
		d_2	1	0.5
		t_3	1	0.5
		A_1	1	0.5

These are presented in the graph by dashed arcs. We search circuits for each article A_i. We notice that the maximum length for circuits is five in this example. Once the circuits are extracted, we search the number of occurrence of each term in the list of circuits related to a query article A_i (only terms appearing at least once are listed in Table 3).

The resulting relevance scores applying Sum and Product aggregation are listed in Table 4.

On the one hand, the product aggregation method reinforces possibilistic relevance if all terms indexing Q are present in the list of similar terms returned by the circuit based distance. On the other hand, the sum aggregation method increases the score if at least one term indexing Q is found in that list.

REWEIGHTING QUERY TERMS

We take advantage here of an existing approach for reweighting query terms to improve an existing possibilistic matching model (Elayeb & Evrard, 2009; Elayeb, 2009). In the first step of query expansion process, the user selects, for each term of its initial query Q^{old}, a number of expansion terms to build its new reformulated query Q^{new}. We define a new weight for each term t_i ($w(t_i)$) given a reformulated query Q^{new} as follows:

$$w(t_i) = [(NTP_{ti}Q^{new}/NTQ^{old}) + 1]*Freq_{ti}Q^{new}$$

where• $NTP_{ti}Q^{new}$: Number of semantically close terms chosen for t_i in Q^{new}.

- **NTQ^{old}:** Number of terms in Q^{old}.
- **$Freq_{ti}Q^{new}$:** Number of occurrences of t_i in Q^{new}.

As an example, we present in Table 5 new weights after applying query expansions corresponding to the example under The Possibilistic Approach for SQE: Illustrative Example.

New weights are considered in the document matching process as defined in Elayeb and Evrard (2009) and Elayeb (2009) and previously detailed under The Possibilistic Matching Model.

Table 4. The degree of hybrid relevance of the three articles in the example

Number of Index Terms of A_i	Index	$DHR(A_1\|Q)$		$DHR(A_2\|Q)$		$DHR(A_3\|Q)$	
		Sum Aggregation	Product Aggregation	Sum Aggregation	Product Aggregation	Sum Aggregation	Product Aggregation
1	$Q = (t_1)$	1.75	0.75	1.5	0.5	1.25	0.25
	$Q = (t_2)$	1.258	0.394	1.176	0	0.5	0
	$Q = (t_3)$	0.918	0.194	0	0	1.676	0.588
	$Q = (t_4)$	1.176	0	0	0	0.588	0
2	$Q = (t_1, t_2)$	1.298	0.387	1.176	0.338	1.75	0.75
	$Q = (t_1, t_3)$	1.128	0.308	1.5	0.5	1.176	0.32
	$Q = (t_1, t_4)$	1.426	0.926	1.5	0.5	0.713	0.107
	$Q = (t_2, t_3)$	0.919	0.463	0.176	0	0.676	0.088
	$Q = (t_2, t_4)$	1.006	0.223	0.176	0	0.338	0.022
	$Q = (t_3, t_4)$	0.914	0.124	0	0	0.999	0.187
3	$Q = (t_1, t_2, t_3)$	1.022	0.237	0.509	0.059	0.843	0.117
	$Q = (t_1, t_2, t_4)$	1.181	0.348	0.509	0.059	0.588	0.044
	$Q = (t_1, t_3, t_4)$	1.067	0.276	0.333	0	0.874	0.187
	$Q = (t_2, t_3, t_4)$	0.898	0.188	0.176	0	0.582	0.083
4	$Q = (t_1, t_2, t_3, t_4)$	1.002	0.251	0.426	0.044	0.749	0.125

IMPLEMENTATION AND EXPERIMENTAL RESULTS

The proposed possibilistic IRS, denoted SPORSER, is implemented in Java and uses the platform Terrier. It provides an information retrieval service and uses the circuit-based and the possibilistic approaches for SQE. We present in Figure 4 the main graphical interface of SPORSER which contains 1) a text zone to write the initial user keywords, 2) a panel where the user can choose the expansion approach, and 3) a zone reserved to present the search results with the score of relevance of each document.

SPORSER offers also a user interface to set the system parameters. First, we can choose the maximum length of circuit if we use the circuit-based approach. Second, we can use the matching model (the possibilistic or the probabilistic Okapi existing in Terrier platform). Third, the user can specify if he wants to reweight the terms while expanding queries. Figure 5 presents the interface allowing selecting these parameters.

Given a query, the system displays a list of possible semantic close words related to its keywords, from which the user can select ones to be added to the initial. He can also visualize the

Table 5. New terms weights in the reformulated query corresponding to the example

Number of Added Terms	A_1	A_2	A_3	t_1	t_2	t_3	t_4
1 term	4/3	4/3	4/3	-	1	1	1
2 terms	5/3	5/3	5/3	3	1	1	2
3 terms	2	2	2	3	2	3	3

HSWN of the dictionary and use some of its words as schematized in Figure 6.

In the next section we introduce the test collection used in our experiments. To improve our assessment, we performed two types of evaluation. We analyse our results at the global and the local scales (cf. Global Results Analysis and Local Results Analysis respectively).

"LeMonde94" Test Collection

We used in our experiments a series of standard tests from the Cross-Language Evaluation Forum (CLEF). It provides necessary tools for the evaluation of information retrieval systems on large corpora including a set of documents, a set of queries and the list of relevant documents for each query. Each query is represented in the XML format by a title containing its terms and a description. In this paper we use the titles as queries to test our approaches. The collection named "LeMonde94" is a sub-collection of CLEF. It includes articles of the French newspaper "LeMonde". This collection consists of 44013 documents and 40 test queries, the whole forming 154 MB.

Global Results Analysis

This section summarises and discusses the overall performance of the various performed tests. Table 6 reports the main runs and evaluation scores for each one. The first column represents the run id which has the following format [P|C|SA|PA][1..4][t|f]. Where: (1) [P|C|SA|PA]: P refers to possibilistic expansion, C to a circuit-based expansion, SA to a sum aggregation expansion and PA to a product aggregation expansion; (2) [1..4]: a number between 1 and 4 related to the number of expansion terms for every word in the

Figure 4. Main user interface of SPORSER

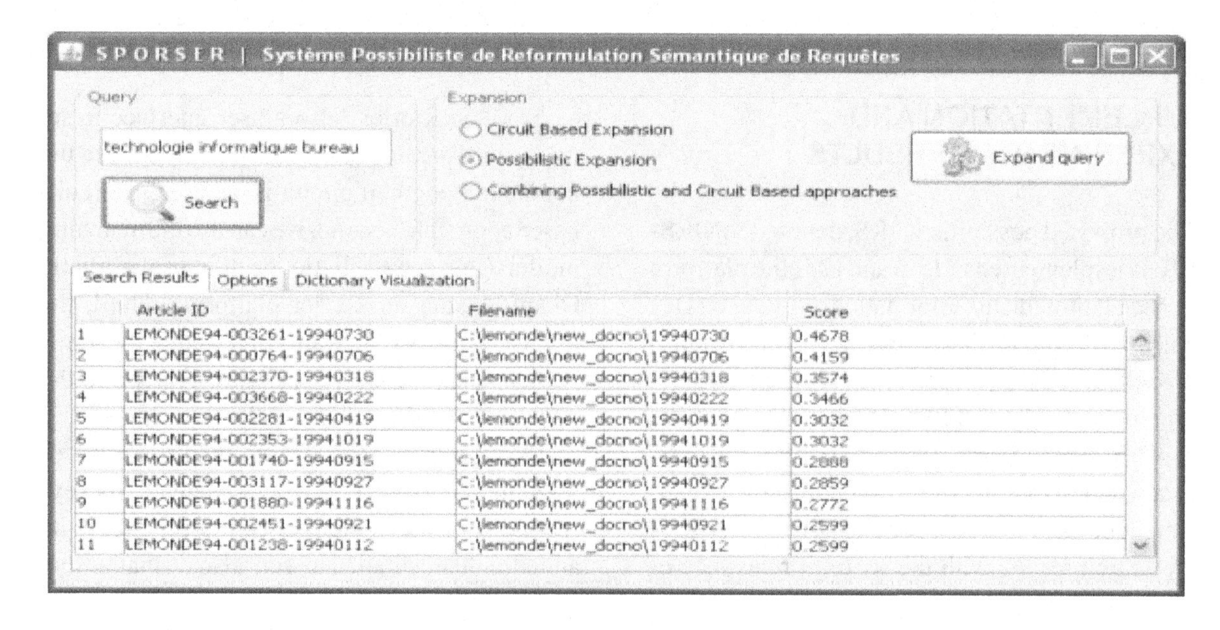

Figure 5. SPORSER interface of parameters' setting of search and query expansion

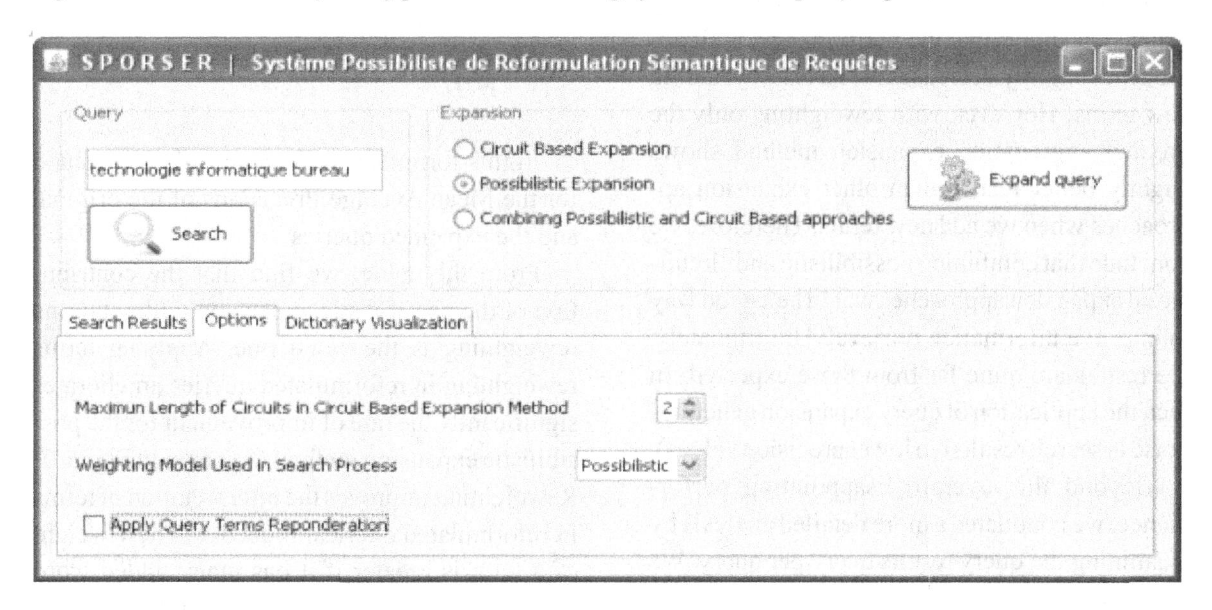

initial query; (3) [t|f]: t (resp. f) for the application (resp. non application) of terms reweighting after expansion.

The last two columns present the Mean Average Precision (MAP), which is the mean of the average precision scores for each query and the exact precision (R-Precision), which is the precision at rank *R*; where *R* is the total number of relevant documents. The first line presents initial tests (without any expansion).

Figure 6. Interface of the HSWN of the dictionary

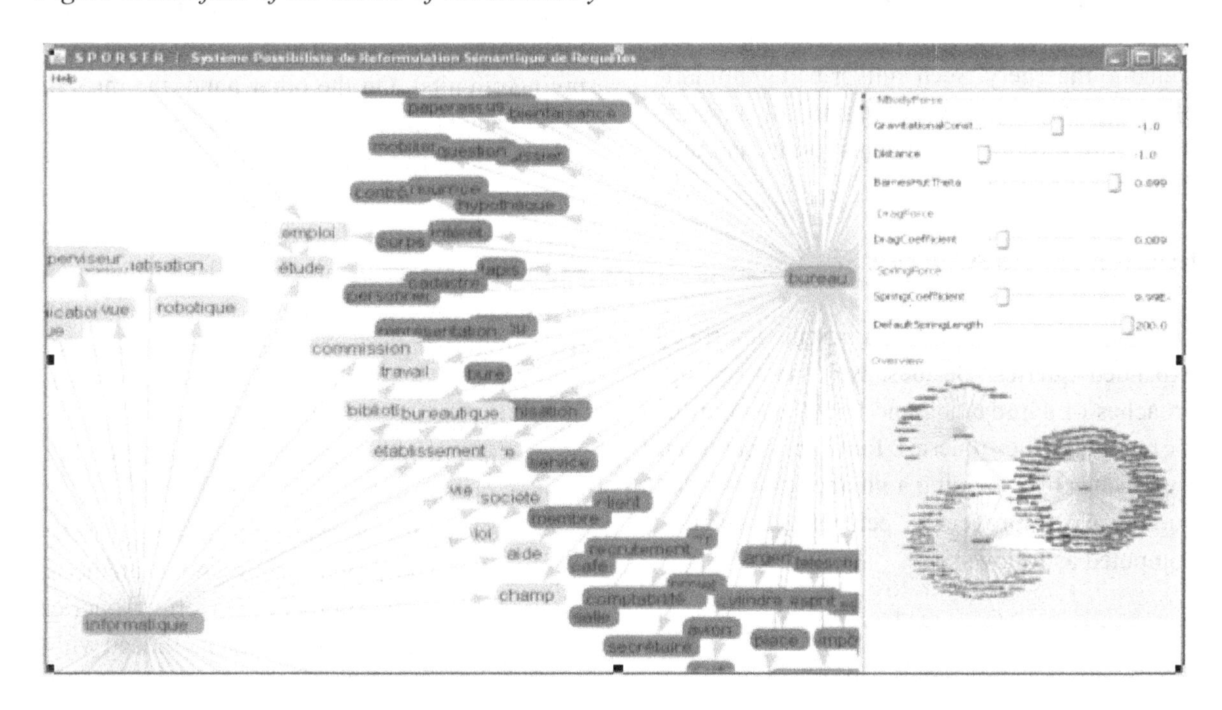

Without reweighting, the application of query expansion shows that the performance of all approaches slightly decreases for all tests by adding new terms. However, with reweighting only the product aggregation expansion method shows slightly better results than other expansion approaches when we add new terms. Therefore, we conclude that combining possibilistic and circuit-based expansion approaches would be a good way to improve information retrieval. Unfortunately, the results are quite far from those expected. In fact, the application of query expansion generates noise in search results (so lower precision values).

Beyond this overall disappointing performance, we conducted a more detailed analysis by examining the query results query per query. We conclude that the overall degradation in the results is generated by some queries that are most of the time misinterpreted due to the linguistic nature of words. For example, in the query "Le syndrome de la guerre du Golfe" ("The Gulf war syndrome") the term "Golfe" ("Gulf") is supposed to reference the Iraq conflict in the Middle East. However, in the expansion process, it has been interpreted as a regular name (not a proper name). Words found from the dictionary like "fleuve" ("river"), "mer" ("sea") and "aplanissement" ("flattening") are added to the query. Such similar bad grammatical interpretations increase substantially noise in the overall retrieved documents results and thus influence the accuracy.

Local Results Analysis

Our goal in this section is to study the improved expanded queries. Besides, we assess our approaches of aggregation and how they improve the number of these queries. Table 7 compares our approaches by providing a number of improved queries and improvement percentage, which is computed as follows:

$$\text{Improvement\_percentage} = \frac{MAP^{NEW} - MAP^{OLD}}{MAP^{OLD}} * 100$$

In this formula, MAP^{OLD} and MAP^{NEW} stand for the Mean Average Precisions of the original and the expanded queries.

From this table, we find that the contribution of the possibilistic expansion without terms reweighting is the worst one. Applying terms reweighting in reformulated queries ameliorates significantly the rate of improvement for the possibilistic expansion method as shown in Figure 7. Reweighting improves the interpretation of terms in reformulated queries. Indeed, the new weight of a term is greater if it has many added word (semantically similar) in the reformulated query; so it is considered more meaningful for user.

We also find that the number of added terms, as shown in Figure 7, is an important factor in all experiments. However, we could not confirm that the optimal number of expansion terms is about 3 as it is shown in Figures 7 and 8. On the one hand, we are limited to 4 terms in all the experiments for computer resources limitation reasons (especially for the circuit-based expansion method that uses excessive resources while computing circuits). On the other hand, the rates of improvement introduced in Table 7 are related to subsets of queries (the cardinality of the subset is presented by the column "Number of improved queries"). Besides, the results of circuit-based expansion are approximately similar whether with or without reweighting due to the used probabilistic proximity distance in the expansion process. This proves the effectiveness of the possibilistic expansion approach which more concretizes the importance of reweighting in the proposed possibilistic IRS.

Table 7 shows also the contribution of applying the sum and product aggregation methods. Figure 8 shows the number of performed queries for each query expansion approach. Indeed with-

Table 6. Overview of performed tests using "LeMonde94" collection

		Run ID	MAP	R-Precision
		topics2000	**0.2358**	**0.2298**
Possibilistic Expansion	Without Reweighting	P1f	0.1681	0.178
		P2f	0.1497	0.1545
		P3f	0.1421	0.1475
		P4f	0.1341	0.143
	With Reweighting	P1t	0.1526	0.1389
		P2t	0.1031	0.1072
		P3t	0.0782	0.0769
		P4t	0.0683	0.0656
Circuit-Based Expansion	Without Reweighting	C1f	0.1792	0.1887
		C2f	0.1644	0.1675
		C3f	0.1522	0.1523
		C4f	0.1426	0.1445
	With Reweighting	C1t	0.1714	0.1861
		C2t	0.1457	0.1432
		C3t	0.1272	0.1142
		C4t	0.1067	0.1036
Sum Aggregation Expansion	Without Reweighting	SA1f	0.1697	0.1623
		SA2f	0.1641	0.1596
		SA3f	0.1583	0.1506
		SA4f	0.1565	0.1481
	With Reweighting	SA1t	0.1862	0.1903
		SA2t	0.1854	0.1856
		SA3t	0.1742	0.1647
		SA4t	0.1739	0.1725
Product Aggregation Expansion	Without Reweighting	PA1f	0.1730	0.1562
		PA2f	0.1690	0.1618
		PA3f	0.1669	0.1604
		PA4f	0.1655	0.1604
	With Reweighting	PA1t	0.1863	0.1817
		PA2t	0.1937	0.1859
		PA3t	0.1964	0.1896
		PA4t	0.1988	0.1873

out aggregation only 2 to 4 queries are improved. When we aggregate the two approaches, we succeed to ameliorate 8 to 11 queries. This shows that each approach is correcting the drawbacks of the other.

However, the average gain rate of these improved queries still lower, comparatively to the gain rate of the possibilistic approach (with terms reweighting) and to the gain rate of the circuit-based approach (with and without terms

Table 7. Improvement rate contribution of different query expansion methods

		Without Reweighting		With Reweighting	
	Number of Terms to Add	**Number of Improved Queries**	**Improvement Percentage**	**Number of Improved Queries**	**Improvement Percentage**
Possibilistic Expansion	1 term	3	5.72	4	49.09
	2 terms	4	1.56	3	93.93
	3 terms	2	1.29	2	97.89
	4 terms	3	0.6	2	96.03
Circuit-Based Expansion	1 term	4	52.5	4	47.63
	2 terms	2	98.85	2	98.64
	3 terms	2	98.5	2	97.79
	4 terms	2	84.52	2	85.2
Sum Aggregation Expansion	1 term	3	31.67	8	23.48
	2 terms	3	13.8	9	17.82
	3 terms	3	14.49	11	31.6
	4 terms	3	6.7	10	27.43
Product Aggregation Expansion	1 term	2	75.15	8	20.94
	2 terms	3	13.95	8	22.71
	3 terms	2	18.45	9	28.5
	4 terms	2	15.59	9	25.19

reweighting). This is due to the reduced number of terms in the test queries. Indeed, a reduced number of terms increases the ambiguity rate and thus reinforces the random selection of the close terms.

DISCUSSION AND FUTURE WORK

In this paper, we proposed and evaluated different dictionary-based approaches for query expansion. Our possibilistic IRS using these approaches encodes dependencies existing between query terms and article definitions of a dictionary in the query expansion process quantifies these relationships by two measures: possibility and necessity. The same model is employed to link the reformulated query terms and documents in the matching process. The possibility degree is convenient to filter documents (resp. articles) out from the response and the necessity degree is useful for document (resp. article) relevance reinforcement. The retrieved documents (resp. articles) are those which are necessarily or possibly relevant given a user's query. The user's query is seen as new information to propagate in a possibilistic network.

Possibility and necessity measures are more effective than the idf factor, since the distribution of terms in the document (resp. article) doesn't only depend on the presence or the absence of the terms in the documents (resp. article) of the collection (like idf), but depends on the distribution of their density in the documents of the collection (resp. article). Thus, compared to idf these measurements are more powerful for negative discrimination.

Moreover, if the basic approach takes account of the quantitative aspect, our system extends it to the qualitative possibilistic framework, by introducing weights (preferences) of query terms. The integration of weights in the possibility and

Figure 7. Average rates of improvement of performed reformulated queries

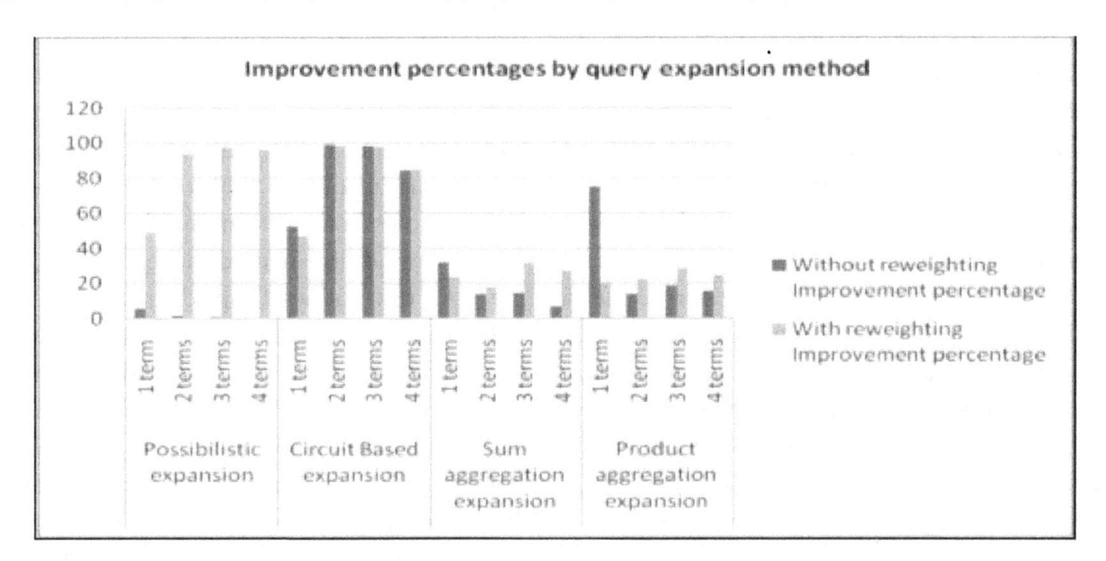

the necessity formulae consists in increasing the scores of possibilistic relevance of the documents containing these terms with an aim of penalizing the scores of relevance of the documents not containing them. The score' penalization or increase is proportional to the capacity of the terms to discriminate between the documents of the collection. In addition, these weights permit to restore documents classified by preference of relevance. It is possible in this case to evaluate at which point a document d_1 (resp. an article a_1) is preferred to a document d_2 (resp. an article a_2) or to measure the preference of a document d_1 (resp. an article a_1) compared to a set of documents $\{d_3, d_4\}$ (resp. a set of articles $\{a_3, a_4\}$).

Figure 8. Number of improved queries by expansion method

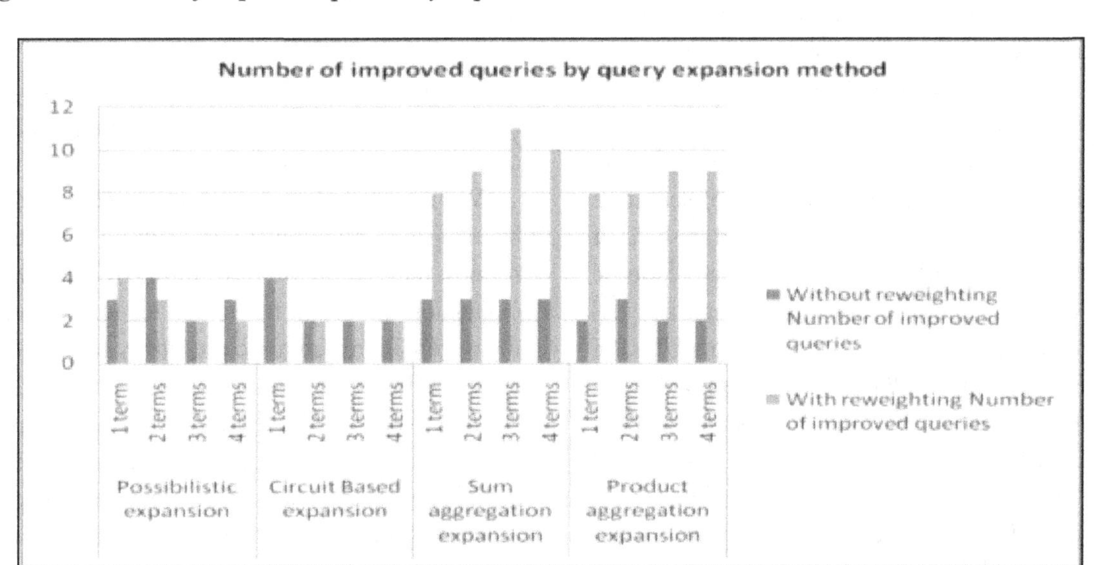

The contribution of PN is enhanced with a circuit-based distance computed in the dictionary graph considered as an HSWN. This distance proved to be useful alone to propose terms to be added to the original query. Furthermore, we proposed to combine the two approaches thus increasing the number of improved queries.

Within the general context of IR and more specifically possibilistic IRS, we summarize our contributions as follows. On the one hand, our work is dedicated to the field of IR where the definition of relevance requires more optimization in the search of information. On the other hand, SPORSER is a contribution in the field of information modelling by structuring the informational space into two possibilistic networks. The first one models dependencies between terms (query items and dictionary entries) and allows query expansion. This type of relations was not taken into account in the basic model of Brini and Boughanem (2004). The second one represents relationships between terms and documents. Indeed, these two networks are mixed to translate the relevance of documents given a reformulated user query.

However, the main focus is centered on the difficulties to improve results of information retrieval independently of the test collection. As a mean of comparison, Lioma and He (2005) employed “LeMonde94” to study the contribution of relevance feedback technique for French IR. They concluded that the poor performance of query expansion may be related to the test collection itself (He & Ounis, 2009). Moreover, Picton and Fabre (2008) presented a study of semantic query expansion methods based on the analysis of the documents collection as a language resource for expanding queries. They implemented a distributional analysis program derived from UPERY system (Bourigault, 2002) and they applied it to a set of articles of “LeMonde” newspaper between 1991 and 2000. They also combined this method with pseudo-relevance feedback giving a new approach for filtered expansion method named distributional feedback. Picton’s works on the distributional expansion led to an overall decrease of system performance due to the existence of some categories of words that should be avoided in the expansion process (the case of adjectives, particular names and named entities). Comparison between our results on “LeMonde94” collection and those of Picton, confirms that the performance of query expansion methods depends directly on the used test queries. Polysemous words may induce noise in the search results after query expansion. To reduce this problem, we plan to integrate a semantic disambiguation mechanism solving the problem of word sense disambiguation in the process of expansion. Furthermore, we plan to investigate the number of added terms to use in automatic query expansion as proposed in Ogilvie and Voorhees (2009).

CONCLUSION

We recapitulate our approaches of semantic query expansion in the SPORSER system based on an external linguistic resource (i.e., the French dictionary “Le Grand Robert”). The first approach models the structure of this dictionary by means of Hierarchical Small-Worlds Networks (HSWN). We enumerate circuits between nodes of the graph HSWN to compute a probabilistic score of semantic proximity between terms. We extend the approach initiated by Elayeb (2009) and limited only to French verbs to all the grammatical categories such as adverbs, nouns and adjectives.

We introduced a second semantic approach based on Possibilistic Networks (PN). This method refines the search of new terms for semantic expansion. Indeed, it takes into account a double measurement of semantic proximity between the articles of the dictionary and query terms. We check for new words of the dictionary which are possibly and necessarily descriptive (relevant) for the initial user query. Then we propose and compare two new query expansion approaches combining the possibilistic and the circuit-based ones. The contribution of these new hybrid approaches is confirmed by the number of improved queries.

Besides, SPORSER constitutes an adaptive information retrieval system which guides the user in the process of query (re)formulation. It proposes an interactive framework which visualizes the structure of the dictionary as a graph and allows the user to select and expand the query terms.

We used the standard "LeMonde94" test collection to assess our approaches. This led to a partial improvement of the results of some test queries using the possibilistic matching model. These improvements, not seen at the global level of analysis, confirm that the performance of any semantic query expansion approach depends on the nature of the test queries in the test collection. As future work, we plan to study other alternatives to enhance the test collection "LeMonde94". Moreover, SPORSER accepts any other gold standard of evaluation which organizes queries and documents in the XML format. Based on the platform Terrier, its architecture is extensible and offers a high level of abstraction. In addition, SPORSER is implemented in Java according to the Model-View-Controller (MVC) design patterns what improves its portability and interoperability at the same time.

REFERENCES

Adriani, M., & van Rijsbergen, C. J. (1999). Term similarity-based query expansion for cross-language information retrieval. In J. L. Borbinha & T. Baker (Ed.), *Proceedings of the European Conference on Research and Advanced Technology for Digital Libraries, Research and Advanced Technology for Digital Libraries* (LNCS 1696, pp. 311-322).

Baloglu, A., Wyne, M. F., & Bahctepe, Y. (2010). Web 2.0 based intelligent software architecture for photograph sharing. *International Journal of Intelligent Information Technologies, 6*(4), 17–29. doi:10.4018/jiit.2010100102

Ben Khiroun, O., Elayeb, B., Bounhas, I., Evrard, F., & Bellamine-BenSaoud, N. (in press). A possibilistic approach for semantic query expansion. In *Proceedings of the 4th International Conference on Internet Technologies and Application*, Wrexham Wales, UK.

Benferhat, S., Dubois, D., Garcia, L., & Prade, H. (2002). On the transformation between possibilistic logic bases and possibilistic causal networks. *International Journal of Approximate Reasoning, 29*(2), 135–173. doi:10.1016/S0888-613X(01)00061-5

Bi, J., & Su, Y. (2009). Expansion method for language-crossed query based on latent semantic analysis. *Computer Engineering, 10*, 49–51.

Borgelt, C., Gebhardt, J., & Kruse, R. (1998). Possibilistic graphical models. In *Proceedings of the International School for the Synthesis of Expert Knowledge*, Udine, Italy (pp. 51-68).

Bourigault, D. (2002). Upery: Un outil d'analyse distributionnelle étendue pour la construction d'ontologies à partir de corpus. In *Proceedings of the Actes de la 9ième Conférence Annuelle sur le Traitement Automatique des Langues*, Paris, France (pp. 75-84).

Brini, A., & Boughanem, M. (2003). Relevance feedback: Introduction of partial assessments for query expansion. In *Proceedings of the 3rd International Conference in Fuzzy Logic and Technology* (pp. 67-72).

Brini, A., Boughanem, M., & Dubois, D. (2004). Towards a possibilistic approach for information retrieval. In *Proceedings of the EUROFUSE Workshop on Data and Knowledge Engineering* (pp. 92-102).

Buckley, C., & Salton, G. (1995). Optimization of relevance feedback weights. In *Proceedings of the 18th Annual International ACM/SIGIR Conference on Research and Development in Information Retrieval* (pp. 351-357).

Chouaib, H. (2006). *Reformulation de requêtes dans un modèle de réseau possibiliste pour la recherche d'information*. Unpublished master's thesis, Liban University, Bayrout, Lebanon.

Claveau, V., Sébillot, P., & De Beaulieu, C. (2004). Extension de requêtes par lien sémantique nom-verbe acquis sur corpus. In *Proceedings of the Actes de la 11ème Conférence de Traitement Automatique des Langues Naturelles*.

Crabtree, D. (2009). Enhancing web search through query expansion. In Wang, J. (Ed.), *Encyclopedia of data warehousing and mining* (2nd ed., pp. 752–757). Hershey, PA: IGI Global.

Croft, B., & Harper, D. J. (1979). Using probabilistic models of document retrieval without relevance information. *The Journal of Documentation, 35*(4), 285–295. doi:10.1108/eb026683

De Campos, L. M., Fernandez-Luna, J. M., & Huete, J. F. (2003). The BNR model: Foundations and performance of Bayesian Network-based retrieval model. *Journal of the American Society for Information Science and Technology, 54*(4), 302–313. doi:10.1002/asi.10210

Dos Santos, I. J. G., & Madeira, E. R. M. (2010). Semantic-enabled middleware for citizen-centric e-government services. *International Journal of Intelligent Information Technologies, 6*(3), 34–55. doi:10.4018/jiit.2010070103

Dubois, D., & Prade, H. (1987). *Théorie des possibilités: Application à la représentation des connaissances en informatique*. Paris, France: Edition Masson.

Dubois, D., & Prade, H. (1998). Possibility theory: Qualitative and quantitative aspects. In Gabbay, D. M., & Smets, P. (Eds.), *Handbook of defeasible reasoning and uncertainty management systems* (*Vol. 1*, pp. 169–226). Dordrecht, The Netherlands: Kluwer Academic.

Dubois, D., & Prade, H. (2004). *Possibility theory: An approach to computerized processing of uncertainty*. New York, NY: Plenum Press.

Elayeb, B. (2009). *SARIPOD: Système multi-agent de recherche intelligente possibiliste de documents web*. Unpublished doctoral dissertation, Institut National Polytechnique de Toulouse, Toulouse, France.

Elayeb, B., Evrard, F., Zaghdoud, M., & Ben Ahmed, M. (2009). Towards an intelligent possibilistic web information retrieval using multiagent system. *International Journal of Interactive Technology and Smart Education, 6*(1), 40–59. doi:10.1108/17415650910965191

Fernandez-Luna, J. M., De Campos, L. M., & Huete, J. F. (2003). Two term-layers: An alternative topology for representing term relationships in the Bayesian Network retrieval mode. In Benítez, J. M., Cordón, O., Hoffmann, F., & Roy, R. (Eds.), *Advances in soft computing-engineering, design and manufacturing* (pp. 213–224). London, UK: Springer.

Galeas, P., & Freisleben, B. (2008). Word distribution analysis for relevance ranking and query expansion. In A. Gelbukh (Ed.), *Proceedings of the 9th International Conference on Computational Linguistics and Intelligent Text Processing* (LNCS 4919, pp. 500-511).

Gaume, B., Hathout, N., & Muller, P. (2004). Désambiguïsation par proximité structurelle. In *Actes de la 11ème*. Conférence de Traitement Automatique des Langues Naturelles.

Harman, D. (1988). Towards interactive query expansion. In *Proceedings of the 11th Annual International ACM SIGIR Conference on Research and Development in Information Retrieval* (pp. 321-331).

Harman, D. (1992). Relevance feedback and other query modification techniques. In Frakes, W. B., & Baeza-Yates, R. (Eds.), *Information retrieval: Data structures and algorithms* (pp. 241–263). Upper Saddle River, NJ: Prentice Hall.

Harman, D., Fox, E., Baeza-Yates, R., & Lee, W. (1992). Inverted files. In Frakes, W. B., & Baeza-Yates, R. (Eds.), *Information retrieval: Data structures and algorithms* (pp. 28–43). Upper Saddle River, NJ: Prentice Hall.

Hazra, I., & Aditi, S. (2009). Thesaurus and query expansion. *International Journal of Computer Science and Information Technology*, *1*(2), 89–97.

He, B., & Ounis, I. (2009). Studying query expansion effectiveness. In M. Boughanem, C. Berrut, J. Mothe, & C. Soulé-Dupuy (Ed.), *Proceedings of the 31st European Conference on Information Retrieval* (LNCS 5478, pp. 611-619).

Hofmann, T. (1999). Probabilistic latent semantic analysis. In K. Laskey & H. Prade (Ed.), *Proceedings of the Fifteenth Conference on Uncertainty in Artificial Intelligence* (pp. 289-296). San Francisco, CA: Morgan Kaufmann.

Indrawan, M., & Loke, S. W. (2008). The impact of ontology on the performance of information retrieval: A case of Wordnet. *International Journal of Information Technology and Web Engineering*, *3*(1), 24–37. doi:10.4018/jitwe.2008010102

Jansen, B. J., & McNeese, M. D. (2005). Evaluating the effectiveness of and patterns of interactions with automated searching assistance: Research articles. *Journal of the American Society for Information Science and Technology*, *56*(14), 1480–1503. doi:10.1002/asi.20242

Lee, J. H. (1998). Combining the evidence of different relevance feedback methods for information retrieval. *Information Processing & Management*, *34*(6), 681–691. doi:10.1016/S0306-4573(98)00034-X

Lioma, C., He, B., Plachouras, V., & Ounis, I. (2005). The University of Glasgow at CLEF 2004: French monolingual information retrieval with Terrier. In C. Peters, P. Clough, J. Gonzalo, G. J. F. Jones, M. Kluck, & B. Magnini (Eds.), *Proceedings of the Cross Language Evaluation Forum* (LNCS 3491, pp. 253-259).

Newman, M. E. J. (2003). The structure and function of complex networks. *SIAM Review*, *45*(2), 167–256. doi:10.1137/S003614450342480

Ogilvie, P., Voorhees, E., & Callan, J. (2009). On the number of terms used in automatic query expansion. *Information Retrieval*, *12*(6), 666–679. doi:10.1007/s10791-009-9104-1

Picariello, A., & Rinaldi, A. M. (2007). User relevance feedback in semantic information retrieval. *International Journal of Intelligent Information Technologies*, *3*(2), 36–50. doi:10.4018/jiit.2007040103

Picton, A., Fabre, C., & Bourigault, D. (2008). Méthodes linguistiques pour l'expansion de requêtes. Une expérience basée sur l'utilisation du voisinage distributionnel. *Revue Française de Linguistique Appliquée*, *13*(1), 83–95.

Ruthven, I. (2003). Re-examining the potential effectiveness of interactive query expansion. In *Proceedings of the 26th Annual International ACM SIGIR Conference on Research and Development in Information Retrieval* (pp. 213-220).

Salton, G., & Buckley, C. (1988). Term-weighting approaches in automatic text retrieval. *Information Processing & Management*, *24*(5), 513–523. doi:10.1016/0306-4573(88)90021-0

Salton, G., & Buckley, C. (1990). Improving retrieval performance by relevance feedback. *Journal of the American Society for Information Science American Society for Information Science*, *41*(4), 288–297. doi:10.1002/(SICI)1097-4571(199006)41:4<288::AID-ASI8>3.0.CO;2-H

Smeaton, A. F. (1983). The retrieval effects of query expansion on a feedback document retrieval system. *The Computer Journal, 26*(3), 239–246. doi:10.1093/comjnl/26.3.239

Smeaton, A. F. (1997). Using NLP or NLP resources for information retrieval tasks. In Strzalkowski, T. (Ed.), *Natural language information retrieval* (pp. 99–111). Dordrecht, The Netherlands: Kluwer Academic.

Tuominen, J., Kauppinen, T., Viljanen, K., & Hyvönen, E. (2009). Ontology-based query expansion widget for information retrieval. In *Proceedings of the 5th Workshop on Scripting and Development for the Semantic Web co-located with the 6th European Semantic Web Conference* (Vol. 449).

Vélez, B., Weiss, R., Sheldon, M., & Gifford, D. (1997). Fast and effective query refinement. In *Proceedings of the 20th Annual International ACM SIGIR Conference on Research and Development in Information Retrieval* (pp. 6-15).

Voorhees, E. M. (1994). Query expansion using lexical-semantic relations. In *Proceedings of the 17th Annual International ACM SIGIR Conference on Research and Development in Information Retrieval* (pp. 61-69).

Watts, D. J., & Strogatz, S. H. (1998). Collective dynamics of 'small-world' networks. *Nature, 393*(6684), 440–442. doi:10.1038/30918

Zadeh, L. A. (1978). Fuzzy sets as a basis for a theory of possibility. *Fuzzy Sets and Systems, 1*(1), 3–28. doi:10.1016/0165-0114(78)90029-5

This work was previously published in the International Journal of Intelligent Information Technologies, Volume 7, Issue 4, edited by Vijayan Sugumaran, pp. 1-25, copyright 2011 by IGI Publishing (an imprint of IGI Global).

Chapter 15
Effective Fuzzy Ontology Based Distributed Document Using Non-Dominated Ranked Genetic Algorithm

M. Thangamani
Kongu Engineering College, India

P. Thangaraj
Bannari Amman Institute of Technology, India

ABSTRACT

The increase in the number of documents has aggravated the difficulty of classifying those documents according to specific needs. Clustering analysis in a distributed environment is a thrust area in artificial intelligence and data mining. Its fundamental task is to utilize characters to compute the degree of related corresponding relationship between objects and to accomplish automatic classification without earlier knowledge. Document clustering utilizes clustering technique to gather the documents of high resemblance collectively by computing the documents resemblance. Recent studies have shown that ontologies are useful in improving the performance of document clustering. Ontology is concerned with the conceptualization of a domain into an individual identifiable format and machine-readable format containing entities, attributes, relationships, and axioms. By analyzing types of techniques for document clustering, a better clustering technique depending on Genetic Algorithm (GA) is determined. Non-Dominated Ranked Genetic Algorithm (NRGA) is used in this paper for clustering, which has the capability of providing a better classification result. The experiment is conducted in 20 newsgroups data set for evaluating the proposed technique. The result shows that the proposed approach is very effective in clustering the documents in the distributed environment.

DOI: 10.4018/978-1-4666-2047-6.ch015

INTRODUCTION

Clustering of document is not only an efficient way of organizing, summarizing, extracting and retrieving of information but also an important method in documentation. Initially, clustering is applied for enhancing the precision or in recalling information retrieval techniques. Clustering analysis is an important field of research intelligence and data mining. The fundamental concept of clustering analysis springs from characteristic to calculate the degree of similar relationship among objects and to attain automatic classification. Recently, clustering data in large data sets (Sharma et al., 2009) has gained a lot of attention in myriad research domains.

Moreover, clustering technique is applicable in certain areas which involve browsing gathered data or in categorizing the outcome, provided by the search engine in terms of replies to the queries provided by the user. Document clustering can also be applied in producing the hierarchical grouping of document. In order to search and retrieve the information efficiently in Document Management Systems (DMSs), the metadata set should be created for the documents with enough details. One metadata per se is not enough for the document management systems. This is because the various document types need various attributes for distinguishing appropriately.

Though there are various document clustering techniques available in the literature but the existing clustering algorithms suffer from problems of practical applicability. The accuracy of the existing clustering approaches is a major concern. The time taken for active clustering of documents is more in large databases. So, a novel technique is needed for effective document clustering with very high accuracy but less complexity.

The discrete use of importance of using the ontology (Grootjen & Weide, 2005) increased in document clustering scheme as this technique seems to the accuracy of clustering. Whereas ontologies provide a position of legitimacy, research in this field leads to superior importance in the arising of different disputes featured in the modern digital situation. With the intention of providing efficacious solutions to the various drawbacks related to present search techniques, ontologies are widely implemented for creating viable document clustering techniques. An example of research concern in the field of ontology (Leukel & Sugumaran, 2009) relates to the Google which serves as search engine for semantic web documents, terms and data found on the internet. For retrieving information from the complex characteristic of the digital information available in digital libraries, ontologies can be successfully used for producing an efficient information retrieval system.

Ontologies (Murthy & Chowdhury, 1996) are introduced as modeling technology for structured metadata definition within the document clustering system. With the obtained metadata the clustering can be performed using the Genetic Algorithms (GAs) (Koller et al., 1997). GA is a search technique that is based on natural genetic and selection merging the idea of survival of the fittest with structured interchanges. Genetic algorithm (Sun et al., 2008) is a famous technique to deal with complex search problems by implementing an evolutionary stochastic search because genetic algorithm can be very effectively applied to various challenging optimization problems. The NP-hard nature of the clustering technique makes genetic algorithm a natural choice for solving it. A common objective function in these implementations is decreasing the square error.

Nowadays, document clustering in distributed environments have become a vibrant area of research. The huge amount of distributed high-dimensional data, such as digital libraries and web accessible text databases necessitate an infrastructure for effective similarity search in Peer-to-Peer (P2P) environments. P2P systems have become promising portals of solutions to deal with data management in case of high degree of distribution. Hence, the main challenge is to offer effective and scalable searching approach, in a highly distributed content, without essentially moving the actual content away from the information providers. Then the drawback of lack of global knowledge, i.e., each peer is conscious of only a small portion of the network topology and content has to be dealt with utmost care.

The principal aim of this research is the development of an improved distributed document clustering technique with very high classification accuracy. Moreover, the research also concentrates on the development of an effective document clustering technique with reduced classification time, less convergence time and less computational complexity. The main contribution of this paper is its usage of fuzzy ontology with the non-dominated ranked genetic algorithm.

This paper uses Ontology Generation using Fuzzy Logic (OGF) with non-dominated ranked genetic algorithm for effective document clustering. This algorithm helps in achieving better classification even for the database that contains huge amount of data. The remaining part of this paper is organized as follows: the next section discusses the related works on ontology generation (Tun & Tojo, 2008) and genetic algorithm based clustering. The section that follows mulls over the motivation of this research. Afterward, the chapter describes the complete methodology of the proposed clustering method. It then exemplifies the experimentation of the proposed clustering technique. The last section concludes the paper with some discussion.

RELATED WORKS

Ontology Based Clustering

Tenenboim et al. (2008) proposed a novel technique on ontology based classification. The author discussed the classification of news items in ePaper, a prototype system of a future personalized newspaper service on a mobile reading device. The ePaper system comprises news items from different news suppliers and distributes to each subscribed user a personalized electronic newspaper, making use of content-based and collaborative filtering techniques. The ePaper can also offer users standard version of chosen newspapers, besides the browsing abilities in the warehouse of news items. This deliberates on the automatic categorization of incoming news with the help of hierarchical news ontology (Dahlem, 2011). Based on this clustering technique on the one hand, and the on the users' profiles on the other, the personalization engine of the system is able to afford a personalized paper to every user onto the mobile reading device.

Hotho et al. (2002) discussed the clustering technique for text data. Text clustering usually involves clustering in a high dimensional space that appears complex with reference to all the virtually practical settings. In this paper, a novel technique is presented for by way of applying background information during preprocessing for improving the clustering outcome. The authors preprocess the input data supplied to ontology-based heuristics for feature selection and feature aggregation. Therefore various choices for text illustrations are constructed. Based on these illustrations, the authors calculate the multiple clustering outcomes using K-Means. The achieved results by the authors compare favorably with a sophisticated baseline preprocessing strategy.

Fuzzy ontology techniques using intuitionistic fuzzy set for knowledge sharing on the semantic web has been proposed by Zhai et al. (2008). Ontology is implemented as a standard benchmark for knowledge representation and sharing of collaborative design on the semantic Web. Fuzzy ontology is an extended version of domain ontology for solving the uncertainty problems. The author proposes a series of fuzzy ontology techniques that consist of fuzzy domain ontology, using intuitionistic fuzzy set, and fuzzy linguistic variable ontologies. They considering semantic relationships between fuzzy concepts, including set relation, order relation and equivalence relation. The fuzzy ontology establishes the fuzzy concepts as values of properties and extends the ordinary relationships to fuzzy relationships and intuitionistic fuzzy relationships.

Fuzzy Based Clustering

The text data of text mining has turned out to be the most favorite research area. Similarly, the study of the text clustering has attracted extensive consideration. Deng et al. (2010) mooted an enhanced fuzzy text clustering, which depends on the fuzzy C-means clustering approach and the edit distance approach. This approach makes use of the feature estimation to decrease the dimensionality of high-dimensional text vector. Since the clustering output of the conventional fuzzy C-means clustering approach requires the stability, the authors are inclined to establish the high-power sample point set, the field radius and weight. Because of the boundary value attribution of the conventional fuzzy C-means clustering approach, the authors suggest the edit distance approach. The experimental outputs confirm that the application of the enhanced approach to the text clustering produces more constant and more precise clustering results than the conventional FCM clustering algorithm.

Pollandt's (1996) work on L-Fuzzy context is an effort to integrate fuzzy logic with Formal Concept Analysis (FCA). The L-Fuzzy context utilizes linguistic variables, which are linguistic terms related with fuzzy sets, to characterize uncertainty in the context. But human interpretation is necessary to define the linguistic variables. Furthermore, the fuzzy concept lattice created from the L-fuzzy context generally generates a combinatorial explosion of concepts as compared to the conventional concept lattice.

Krishnapuram et al. (2001) presented new techniques (Fuzzy C-Medoids FCMdd and Fuzzy C Trimmed Medoids or FCTMaZ) for fuzzy clustering of relational data. The objective functions are based on the choice of c representative objects (medoids) from the data set in such a way that the total dissimilarity within each cluster is minimal. The experimental observations are conducted by comparing FCMdd with the Relational Fuzzy c-Means algorithm (RFCM). The result shows that FCMdd is much faster and more efficient. The worst case complexity of the algorithm is O (n) which occurs while updating the medoids in every iteration. These approaches are very well adopted in web mining applications such as categorization of Web documents, snippets, and user sessions.

Cao et al. (2008) provided fuzzy named entity-based document clustering. Conventional keyword-based document clustering methods have restrictions because of simple treatment of words and rigid partition of clusters. In this paper, the author introduces named entities as objectives into fuzzy document clustering, which are the important elements defining document semantics and in many cases are of user concerns. Initially, the conventional keyword-based vector space representation is adapted with vectors defined over spaces of entity names, types, name-type pairs and identifiers. Next, hierarchical fuzzy document clustering can be applied using a similarity measure of the vectors indicating documents.

Win and Mon (2010) described document clustering with the help of fuzzy c-mean algorithm. Most traditional clustering techniques allocate each bit of data exactly to a single cluster, thereby creating a crisp separation of the provided data. But fuzzy clustering permits for degrees of membership, to which the data fit into various clusters. In this paper, documents are partitioned with the help of fuzzy c-means (FCM) clustering technique. Fuzzy c-means clustering is one of the famous unsupervised clustering methods. But the fuzzy c-means method needs the user to mention the number of clusters and different values of clusters corresponds to different fuzzy partitions earlier. So the validation of clustering result is required. For this purpose, PBM index and F-measure are helpful in validating the cluster.

Genetic Algorithm Based Clustering

Casillas et al. (2003) put forth a novel concept on document clustering using genetic algorithm. The authors present a genetic algorithm that deals with document clustering to compute an approximation of the optimum k value. It also resolves the best clustering of the documents into k clusters. The authors have experimented with the proposed technique with sets of documents that are the output of a query in a search engine. The simulation results show that the proposed genetic algorithm achieves better values of the fitness function and lesser time than the well-known Calinski and Harabasz stopping rule.

Zhang et al. (2008) gives clustering aggregation based on genetic algorithm for documents clustering. In this paper, a technique based on genetic algorithm for clustering aggregation difficulty, named as GeneticCA, is provided to approximate the clustering performance of a clustering division, clustering precision is defined and features of clustering precision are considered. In the evaluation concerning clustering performances of GeneticCA for document clustering, hamming neural network is applied to make clustering partitions with fluctuant and weak clustering performances.

Filho et al. (2005) formulated the Hybrid Genetic Algorithm (HGA, uses the fuzzy c-means clustering technique during the fitness evaluation phase to decrease direct evaluation. The main goal is to enhance the processing speed of the evolutionary process, but it retains a satisfactory level of population diversity and solution quality. That is it increases the chances to acquire as good solutions as traditional GA. Previous experiments in actual practical situations, namely train scheduling and dispatch in freight railroads, have shown the effectiveness of this technique as an approach to solve complex and large scale problems. When population clustering is used, the author mainly concentrates on the quality of solutions obtained and hence investigates a set of classical optimization problems available in the literature.

By considering the difficulty that classical Euclidean distance metric cannot create a suitable separation for data lying in a manifold, a genetic algorithm based clustering method with the help of geodesic distance measure is proposed by Li et al. (2009). In the proposed method, a prototype-based genetic illustration is used, where every chromosome is a sequence of positive integer numbers that indicate the k-medoids. In addition, a geodesic distance based proximity measure is applied to find out the similarity between data points. Simulation results on eight standard synthetic datasets with dissimilar manifold structure illustrate the effectiveness of the algorithm as a clustering technique. Evaluating with generic k-means method for the function of clustering, the proposed technique has the potential to distinguish between complicated non-convex clusters and its clustering performance is obviously better than that of the k-means method for complex manifold structures.

Clustering in Distributed Environment

Text clustering is very important in peer-to-peer networks. The high dimensionality of documents indicates more communication could be saved if each node could get the estimated clustering result by distributed algorithm rather than transferring them into a center and perform clustering. K-means algorithm forms the basis for a lot of existing text clustering algorithms in unstructured peer-to-peer networks. The main issue in the existing approaches is that the clustering quality may decrease with the increase in the network size. A novel text clustering approach based on frequent term sets for peer-to-peer networks are proposed in He et al. (2010). It needs relatively lower communication volume while attaining a clustering result whose quality is not affected by the size of the network. Furthermore, it provides a term set describing each cluster, which makes the user to have a clear comprehension for the clustering result, it and assists the users to find resource in the network or manage the local documents in accordance with the whole network.

Eisenhardt et al. (2003) evolved an approach for document clustering using a distributed peer-to-peer network. The author used the *k*-means clustering approach changed to work in a distributed P2P fashion using a probe and echo system. This is also used by Li and Morris (2002) but the problem is posed from the information retrieval perspective. Cluster signatures are generated from a subset of the document collection by centrally dividing it into clusters. Each cluster is then allotted to a node, and then documents are classified into their relevant clusters by comparing their signature with all cluster signatures.

The P2P k-means approach has its fundamental in a parallel implementation of k-means proposed by Dhillon and Modha (2001). Though k-means monitoring algorithm does not generate a distributed clustering, it assists a centralized *k*-means process and re-computes the clusters by monitoring the distribution of centroids across peers, it triggers a re-clustering if the data distribution changes over time. Alternatively, the P2P *k*-means approach works by updating the centroids at each peer depending on information obtained from their immediate neighbors. The algorithm stops when the information obtained does not result in considerable update to the centroids of all peers.

MOTIVATION

It can be clearly observed that the existing techniques discussed earlier do not produce better accuracy. The time taken for the active clustering algorithms is more when the large databases are considered for clustering. Also in case of determining the initial clusters, the different clusters will result for same dataset. The major limitations in the existing approaches are:

1. Higher Objective function
2. Lesser Silhouette Coefficient
3. Lesser F-Measure
4. Higher separation index
5. Higher number of iterations taken for convergence

The usage of Fuzzy Ontology will provide better classification of large vague database. The early research showed that the usage of Genetic algorithm provided better classification accuracy when compared to the other method. The usage of genetic algorithm will increase of classification. But the convergence time for the usage for genetic algorithm is more and also the number of iterations required for genetic algorithm is more when compared to other techniques. The fuzzy ontology can be initially applied to the database to reduce the convergence time and number of iterations before using genetic algorithm. This motivated the usage of Fuzzy Ontology and Genetic Algorithm for clustering. Fuzzy ontology is combined with the Genetic Algorithm to yield a better, classification accuracy for large databases. In this paper Non-Dominated Ranked Genetic Algorithm (Raghu et al., 2001) is used because of its ability to ensure better accuracy of classification compared to GA.

METHODOLOGY

The proposed approach uses a novel technique for document clustering in a distributed environment. Fuzzy ontology is combined with the Genetic Algorithm to yield good classification accuracy for large databases in the previous approach. It uses Non-Dominated Ranked Genetic Algorithm (Jadaan et al., 2008) because of its capacity to ensure better accuracy of classification compared to GA. The approach uses the distributed architecture, presented in Figure 1.

The proposed clustering approach involves the grouping of electronic documents, extracting vital contents from the document collection and aids effective management of digital library documents. The contents of digital documents are examined and grouped into several categories.

The system is intended to link 'n' number of libraries with 'n' number of digital documents. Thus content analysis, document grouping and content extraction are the main tasks of the proposed approaches.

This section discusses the methodologies implemented in the proposed technique. Initially, Ontology Generation using Fuzzy logic (OGF) is implemented to the database containing a large number of documents. OGF technique will generate the ontology for the given database. With this ontology, the next step is application of Non-Dominated Ranked Genetic Algorithm (NRGA), which is used for clustering the documents in the database with the help of ontology generated by OGF technique. The combination of OGF and NRGA helps to increase the accuracy of clustering.

Ontology Generation Using Fuzzy Logic (OGF)

The OGF framework consists of the following components which are shown in Figure 2:

- Fuzzy Formal Concept Analysis
- Fuzzy Conceptual Clustering
- Fuzzy Ontology Generation.

Fuzzy Formal Concept Analysis: This process considers the database which contains ambiguity data and produces fuzzy formal concepts from it. Additionally, fuzzy formal concepts are created from the fuzzy formal contexts which categorize the generated concepts as a fuzzy concept lattice.

Fuzzy Conceptual Clustering: This process generates conceptual clusters by clustering the fuzzy concept lattice. With the help of fuzzy logic and depending on fuzzy information integrated into the lattice, the clustering process is carried on. The algorithm for Fuzzy Conceptual Clustering is represented in Figure 2.

Hierarchical Relation Generation: This process produces the concept hierarchy by generating the hierarchical relations among conceptual clusters.

Fuzzy Formal Concept Analysis

In OGF, Fuzzy Formal Concept Analysis which integrates fuzzy logic into formal concept analysis is proposed to represent vague data. A fuzzy formal context as a cross-table is shown in Table 1. The context consists of three objects which denote three documents. Those objects are named as D1, D2 and D3. Moreover, it also has three attributes such as "Data Mining" (D), "Clustering" (C) and "Fuzzy Logic" (F) indicating the three research titles. The relationship between an object and an attribute is denoted by a membership value between 0 and 1.

For the purpose of removing the relationships that have low membership values, a threshold called confidence threshold T is introduced. Table 2 represents the cross-table of the fuzzy formal context provided in Table 1 with confidence threshold T as 0.5. Usually, the attributes of a formal concept can be considered as the description of the concept. Thus, the relationships between the object and the concept must be the separation of the relationships between the objects and the attributes of the concept. The relationship between the object and an attribute is denoted as a membership value in fuzzy formal context. Then based on fuzzy theory, the intersection of these membership values must be the minimum of these membership values.

Figure 3 displays the usual concept lattice generated from Table 1. Figure 4 denotes the fuzzy concept lattice generated from the fuzzy formal context provided in Table 2. As illustrated the figures, the fuzzy concept lattice can afford additional information, such as membership values of objects in each fuzzy formal concept and similarities of fuzzy formal concepts that are important for the construction of concept hierarchy.

Fuzzy Conceptual Clustering

The formal concepts are also generated mathematically; likewise the traditional concept lattice

Figure 1. Semantic mechanism with ontology knowledge for modern digital library system

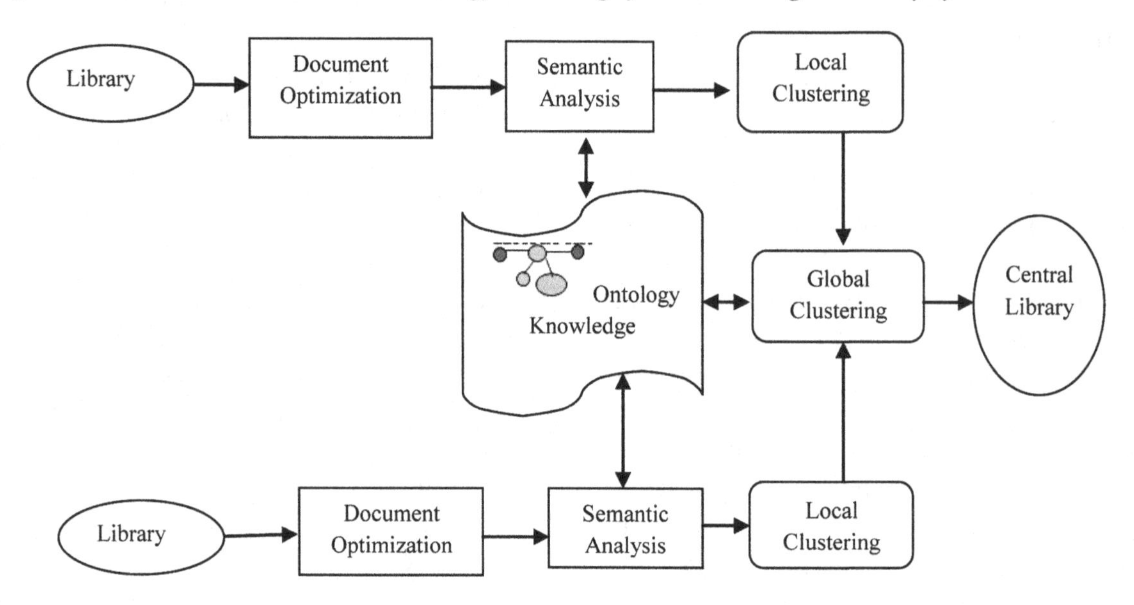

and objects that have small differences in terms of attribute values are categorized into distinct formal concepts. At a higher level, such objects should correspond to the similar concept when they are interpreted by human. According to this observation, a cluster formal concept is proposed into conceptual clusters with the help of fuzzy conceptual clustering. The conceptual clusters created have the following properties:

- The hierarchical relationships are contained in conceptual clusters that can be obtained from fuzzy formal concepts on the fuzzy concept lattice. That is, a concept indicated by a conceptual cluster can be a sub-concept or super-concept of other concepts indicated by other conceptual clusters.
- A formal concept should belong to minimum of one conceptual cluster, but it can also be more than single conceptual cluster. This attribute is obtained from the characteristic of concepts that an object can belong to more than single concept. Consider an illustration that a scientific document can belong to more than single research area.

Conceptual clusters are derived based on the hypothesis that if a formal concept A belongs to a conceptual cluster R, then its sub-concept B also belongs to R if B is similar to A. A similarity confidence threshold Ts can be used to determine the similarity between two concepts.

Fuzzy Ontology Generation

In this step Fuzzy ontology is generated from the fuzzy context with the help of concept hierarchy produced by fuzzy conceptual clustering. As both FCA and ontology support formal definitions of concepts, this approach is carried out.

Fuzzy ontology is created from the fuzzy context with the help of concept hierarchy, produced by fuzzy conceptual clustering. This is performed based on the fact that both FCA and ontology maintain the formal definitions of concepts.

Conversely, a concept defined in FCA constitutes both extensional and intentional data, whereas a concept in ontology just emphasizes its intentional characteristics. For generating the fuzzy ontology, it is necessary to convert both intentional and extensional data of FCA concepts into the equivalent classes and relations of ontology (Figure 5).

Table 1. A cross-table of a fuzzy formal context

	D	C	F
D1	0.8	0.12	0.61
D2	0.9	0.85	0.13
D3	1.0	0.14	0.87

Class Mapping: In this process, the extent and intent of the fuzzy context are mapped into the extent and intent classes of the ontology. Human participation is required to name the label for the extent class. Keyword attributes can be represented by appropriate names and it is used to label the intent class names also.

Taxonomy Relation Generation: With the help concept hierarchy, in place, this phase produces the intent class of the ontology as a hierarchy of classes. The step can be regarded as an isomorphic mapping from the concept hierarchy into taxonomy classes of the ontology. Consider an illustration that the class Research Area can be developed into a hierarchy of classes, in which every class represents a research area, associated with the concept hierarchy.

Non-taxonomy Relation Generation: In this step, the similarity among the extent class and intent classes are generated. Yet this simple task makes it necessary to label the non-taxonomy for a better performance.

Instances Generation: In this process, instances for the extent class are generated. Each instance indicates an object in the initial fuzzy context. Depending on the data existing on the fuzzy concept hierarchy, instances attributes are automatically furnished with suitable values. For example, each instance of the class document that is related to an actual document will be associated with the appropriate research area.

Once the ontology is generated, non-dominated ranked genetic algorithm is used to cluster the documents. The adoption of ontology helps in determining the best classification for clustering by means of a genetic algorithm. The generation process in shown in Figure 6.

Design of Clustering Algorithm Using Non-Dominated Ranked Genetic Algorithm

At first, a random parent population P is formed. The sorting of the population is in accordance with the non-domination. Every solution is allocated a fitness (or rank) equivalent to its non-domination level. Non-domination level of 1 represents the best level and 2 represent the next-best level etc.

Therefore, minimization of fitness is implicit. Initially, the normal Ranked accorded Roulette wheel choosing, recombination, and mutation operators are applied to generate an offspring population Q of size N. As elitism is initiated by contrasting present population with earlier obtained best non-dominated results, the process is varied after the starting generation. Initially the ith generation of the presented algorithm as shown below is explained.

The algorithm represents that Non-Dominated Ranked Genetic is simple and straightforward. Initially, a combined population $P \cup Q$ is created. The mixed population is of size 2N then is obtained and the mixed population sorted based on the non-domination. As every previous and present population members are incorporated in the mixed population elitism is guaranteed. This process will choose N solutions out of 2N.

The new population of size N is utilized for choosing. Next, a two tier ranked dependent Roulette wheel selection is used, one tier to choose the front and the other to choose solution from the front. Here the results obtained for the finest non-dominated set F1 have the higher probabilities to be chosen. Therefore, results from the set F2 are

Table 2. Fuzzy formal context in table 1 with t = 0.5

	D	C	F
D1	0.8	-	0.61
D2	0.9	0.85	-
D3	-	-	0.87

Figure 2. The approach for automatic generation of concept hierarchy

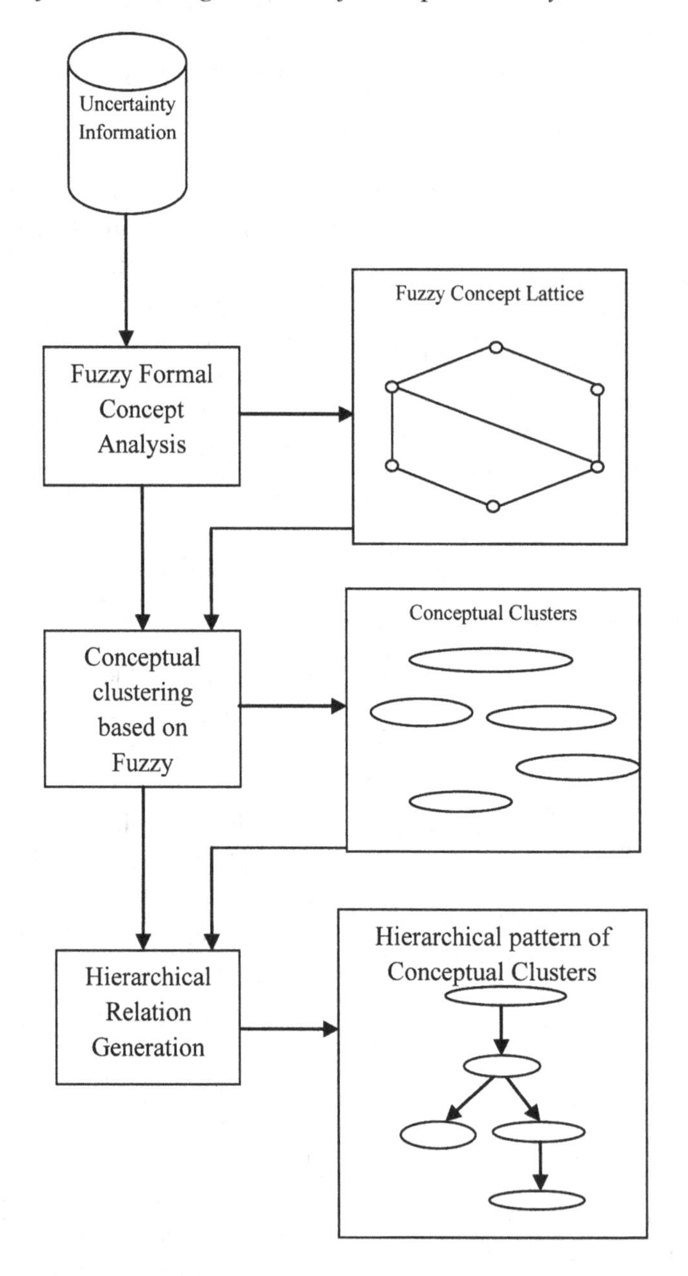

selected with a small probability than the results from the set F1 and so on. After that crossover and mutation are used to generate a new population P of size N. The diversity between non-dominated results is established by the second tier of ranked dependent roulette wheel selection that ranks the results according to their crowding distance. The results with lesser crowding distance will have the higher probabilities.

As solutions contend with their crowding distance, no extra niching attribute is needed. Even though the crowding distance is computed in the objective function space, it can also be obtained in the parameter space, if required. The objective function space niching is utilized in this paper.

Figure 3. A concept lattice generated from traditional FCA

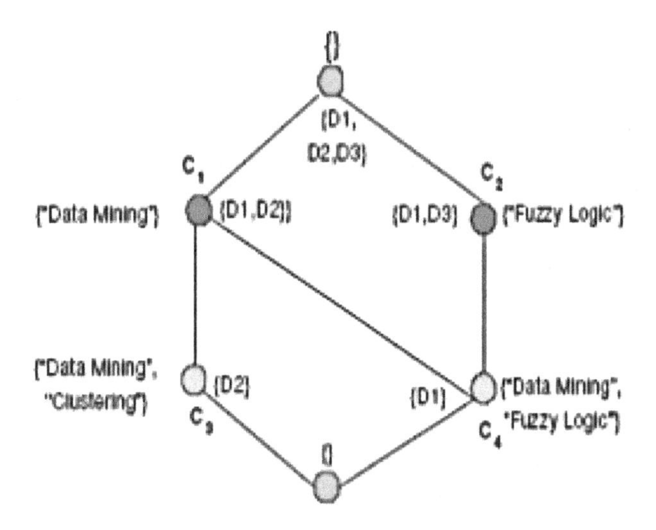

Algorithm: Document Clustering using Ontology Based Document Clustering Using Non-Dominated Ranked Genetic Algorithm

Step 1: Input the documents for clustering.

Step 2: Fuzzy Formal Concept Analysis

- Build cross table for document with the membership value of its attributes.
- The membership value of attribute which does not satisfy confidence threshold T is removed.
- Concept lattice generation

Step 3: Fuzzy Conceptual Clustering

- // S_c – conceptual cluster, C_s – starting concept, T_s – similarity threshold
- $S_C \rightarrow \{\}$
- $F'(K) \leftarrow$ An empty concept lattice

Figure 4. A fuzzy concept lattice generated from FFCA

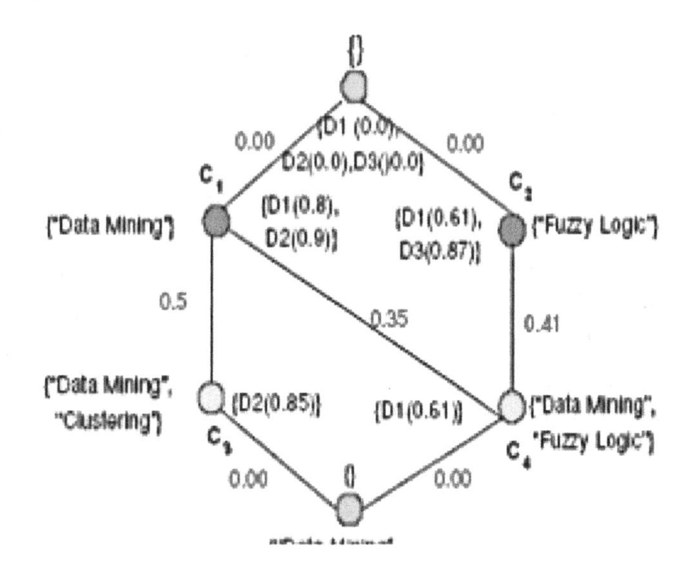

Figure 5. The fuzzy conceptual clustering algorithm

Algorithm: Conceptual Cluster Generation
Input: Starting concept CS of concept lattice F (K) and a similarity threshold T_S
Output: A set of generated conceptual clusters S_C
Process:
1: $S_C \rightarrow \{\}$
2: $F'(K) \leftarrow$ An empty concept lattice
3: Add C_S to $F'(K)$
4: **for** each subconcept C' of C_S in $F(K)$ **do**
5: $F'(C') \leftarrow$ Conceptual_Cluster_Generation(C, $F'(K)$, T_S)
6: **if** $E(C_S, C') = \frac{|C_S \cap C'|}{|C_S \cup C'|} < T_S$ **then**
7: $S_C \leftarrow$ SC {$F'(C')$}
8: **else**
9: Insert $F'(C')$ to $F'(K)$ with sup $(F'(K))$ as a subconcept of C_S
10: **endif**
11: **endfor**
12: $S_C \leftarrow$ SC {$F'(K)$}

- Add C_S to $F'(K)$ for each sub-concept C' of C_S in $F(K)$ do $F'(C') \leftarrow$ Conceptual_Cluster_Generation(C, $F'(K)$, T_S) if $E(C_S,C') = \frac{|C_S \cap C'|}{|C_S \cup C'|} <$ T_S then
- else
- Insert $F'(C')$ to $F'(K)$ with sup $(F'(K))$ as a sub-concept of C_S
- endif
- endfor
- $S_C \leftarrow \mathrm{SC}\{F'(K)\}$

Step 4: Fuzzy Ontology Generation
- Map the extent and intent fuzzy context into extent and intent classes of ontology and name it accordingly
- Isomorphic mapping for Taxonomy relation generation
- Identify relation between extent and intent class for Non- Taxonomy relation generation
- Instances are generated from extent class

Step 5: Initialize Population P using the generated ontology.

Step 6: {Generate random population – size N;
- Evaluate Objective Values;
- Assign Rank (level) Based on Pareto dominance Sort}

Step 7: {Ranked based Roulette Wheel Selection; Recombination and Mutation}

Step 8: For i=1 to g do
- For each member of the combined population ($P \cup Q$) do
- Assign Rank (level) based on Pareto-sort;
- Generate sets of non-dominated fronts;

Figure 6. Fuzzy ontology generation process

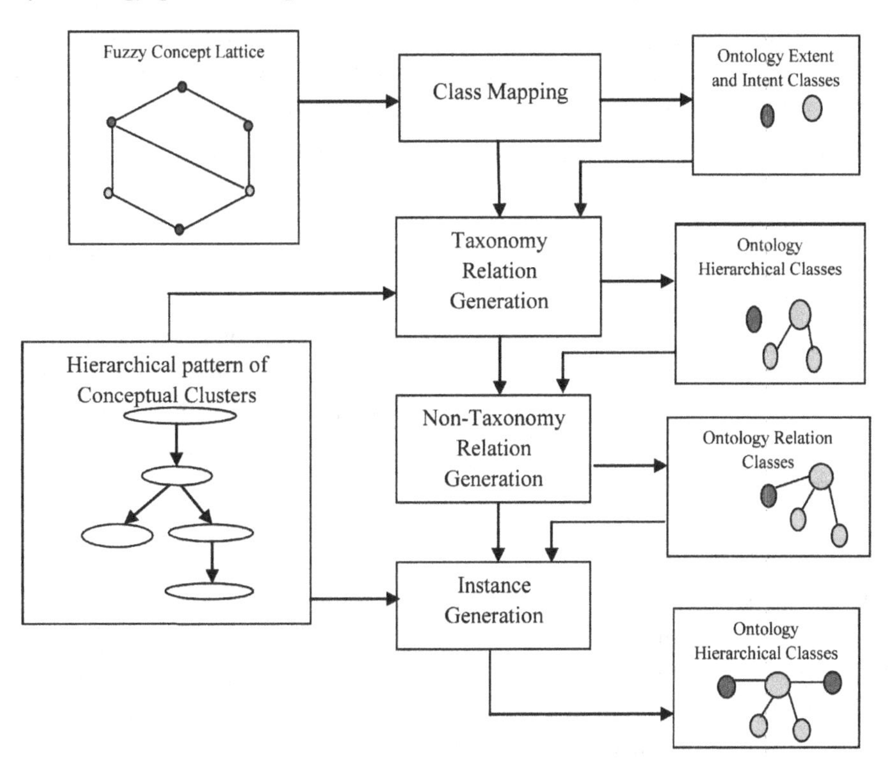

- Calculate the crowding distance between members of each front;
- endfor
- Select the members of the combined population based on least dominated N solution t_i make the population of the next generation. Ties are resolved by taking the less crowding distance;
- Create next generation; {Ranked based Roulette Wheel Selection; Recombination Mutation}
- endfor

This proposed approach uses Non-Dominated Ranked Genetic Algorithm (NRGA) for the document clustering because of the following advantages.

- It provides better convergence
- It yields better accuracy than GA
- It has less computational complexity

EXPERIMENTAL RESULTS

An evaluation study of the proposed document clustering techniques is presented in this chapter. The results of an extensive set of simulation tests are shown, in which the proposed approaches are compared under a wide variety of different scenarios.

A peer-to-peer network environment is constructed with 65 peer nodes and hierarchical level is three. No increase in speed up for nodes > 65 and Hierarchical Level > 3. It is also found that entropy and separation index do not change considerably (Plateau) from 20 to 40 number of nodes. This has been discussed in Hammouda et al. (2009).

The ontology is generated based on the concept hierarchy constructed automatically by OGF. Hence, the quality of the ontology generated depends directly on the concept hierarchy generated.

NRGA is used for clustering. Matlab is used for the evaluation of the proposed approach.

The performance of the proposed approaches is evaluated in the 20 Newsgroup dataset using the following parameters:

- Classification Accuracy
- Objective Function
- Classification Time
- Convergence Behaviors
- Silhouette Coefficient
- F-Measure
- Entropy
- Separation Index

Then the performance of the proposed OGF with NRGA is compared with the clustering techniques like K-means, Hierarchical Peer-to-Peer Clustering (HP2PC), Semantic Enhanced Hierarchical Peer-to-Peer Clustering (HP2PC) and OGF with GA. The 20 Newsgroups data set (http://people.csail.mit.edu/jrennie/20Newsgroups/s) is a collection of approximately 20,000 newsgroup documents, partitioned (nearly) evenly across 20 different newsgroups. The collection of 20 newsgroups has become a popular dataset for experiments in text applications of machine learning techniques, such as text classification and text clustering.

The data are organized into 20 different newsgroups, each corresponding to a different topic. Some of the newsgroups are very closely related to each other (e.g., comp.sys.ibm.pc.hardware/comp.sys.mac.hardware), while others are highly unrelated (e.g., misc.forsale/soc.religion.christian). From the dataset 1000 documents which belong to comp.graphics, misc.forsale, sci.electronics and rec.motorcycles group are randomly chosen for the experiment.

Accuracy of Classification

The classification accuracy A_i of an individual i depend on the number of documents correctly classified (true positives plus true negatives) and it is evaluated by the formula:

$$A_i = \frac{t}{n} \times 100 \quad (1)$$

where t is the number of documents correctly classified and n is the total number of documents.

Table 3 shows a comparison of the accuracy of classification for the proposed OGF with NRGA method with the K-means method, HP2PC, SEHP2PC and OGF with GA. From the Table 3, it can be observed that for comp.graphics category, the accuracy of classification using K-Means and HP2PC algorithm is 89.5% and 91.25% respectively. For the proposed approaches like SEHP2PC, OGF with GA and OGF with NRGA is 94.9, 96.2% and 98.5% respectively. When the misc.forsale category is considered, a better accuracy i.e., 98.2% is achieved by the proposed OGF with NRGA technique the accuracy using K-Means algorithm shows 89.8% and

Table 3. Comparison of clustering techniques based on classification accuracy (%)

Clustering Method	Comp.Graphics	Misc.Forsale	Sci.Electronics	Rec.Motorcycles
K-Means	89.5	89.8	88.7	89.1
HP2PC	91.25	91.4	90.5	91.4
SEHP2PC	94.9	95.9	94.2	96.2
OGF with GA	96.2	96.9	95.1	97.1
OGF with NRGA	98.5	98.2	97.6	99.1

the accuracy using SEHP2PC and OGF with GA indicates 95.9% and 96.9% respectively. When other categories such as sci.electronics and rec. motorcycles are considered, a better accuracy is achieved using the proposed OGF with NRGA technique i.e., 97.6% and 99.1% respectively.

Objective Function

Clustering objective function is defined as.

$$E = \sum_{j=1}^{k} \sum_{x_i \in c_j} (x_i - x_j^*)^2 / n_j \qquad (2)$$

where x_j* indicates the center of cluster c_j, n_j indicates the amount of documents in cluster c_j. The clustering will be better when the value of objective function E is smaller

The resulted objective function is provided in Table 4. It can be seen that the resulted objective function is minimum for using OGF with NRGA, whereas it is higher for the other clustering methods for all the categories like computer graphics, misc.forsale, science electronics and rec.motors. For example, when considering computer graphics, the objective function obtained by OGF with NRGA is 9.55 which is very less when compared with the other clustering techniques.

Classification Time

Table 5 shows the classification time taken by the clustering techniques. It can observed that the time required for classification using the proposed OGF with NRGA technique for comp.graphics, misc.forsale, sci.electronics and rec.motorcycles are 0.58, 0.51, 0.42 and 0.41 seconds respectively, whereas, more time is needed for the other clustering techniques for classification.

Convergence Behaviors

Table 6 conveys the convergence behaviors of proposed approaches and standard K-means technique. The iterations are taken from 0 to 100. Table 5 depicts the statistical analysis of the convergence behaviors of the clustering approaches.

From Figure 7, it can be observed that the proposed OGF with NRGA technique converges in lesser iterations than the other clustering techniques. OGF with NRGA technique takes just 30 iterations for the convergences. It means that the value 13.98 converges to 9.9 in just about 30 iterations. Whereas K-means and HP2PC algorithms take 80 and 70 iterations respectively for the convergence the proposed SEHP2PC and OGF with GA approaches take 60 and 40 iterations respectively for convergence.

Silhouette Coefficient

Silhouette Coefficient is then considered for evaluating the proposed clustering technique. Let $D_M = \{\overline{D}_1, \ldots, \overline{D}_k\}$ describe a clustering result, i.e., it is an exhaustive partitioning of the set of

Table 4. Objective function for different clustering methods

Clustering Methods	Comp.Graphics	Misc.Forsale	Sci.Electronics	Rec.Motorcycles
K-Means	10.23	10.45	10.37	10.55
HP2PC	10.2	10.12	10.14	10.3
SEHP2PC	9.87	9.98	9.845	9.95
OGF with GA	9.84	9.94	9.8	9.85
OGF with NRGA	9.55	9.81	9.68	9.71

Table 5. Classification time for different clustering methods

Clustering Methods	Comp.Graphics	Misc.Forsale	Sci.Electronics	Rec.Motorcycles
K-Means	0.91	0.92	0.89	0.86
HP2PC	0.86	0.89	0.82	0.78
SEHP2PC	0.81	0.84	0.65	0.66
OGF with GA	0.71	0.79	0.59	0.58
OGF with NRGA	0.58	0.51	0.42	0.41

documents $\mathcal{D}$. The distance of a document d ∈ $\mathcal{D}$ to a cluster $D_i \in D_M$ is given as

$$dist\left(d, \bar{D}_i\right) = \frac{\sum_{p \in \bar{D}_i} dist(d, p)}{|\bar{D}_i|} \quad (3)$$

Let there be $a(d, D_M) = dist(d, \bar{D}_l)$ the distance of document d to its cluster $\bar{D}_l$ $(d \in D_l)$, and $b(d, D_M = \min_{\bar{D}_i \int D_M, d \notin \bar{D}_i} dist(d, \bar{\bar{D}}_i)$ the distance of document d to the nearest neighboring cluster.

The silhouette $s(d, D_M)$ of a document d ∈ D is then defined as:

$$s\left(d, D_M\right) = \frac{b\left(d, D_M\right) - a(d, D_M)}{\max\{a\left(d, D_M\right),\ b\left(d, D_M\right)\}} \quad (4)$$

The silhouette coefficient SC (D_M) reads as:

$$SC\left(D_M\right) = \frac{\sum_{p \in \mathcal{D}} s(p, D_M)}{|\mathcal{D}|} \quad (5)$$

Figure 8 provides the silhouette coefficient for the different clustering techniques. It can be observed from Figure 8 that the value of silhouette coefficient for K-Means and HP2PC is 0.52 and 0.56 respectively. The silhouette coefficient of the proposed SEHP2PC and OGF with GA methods is 0.63 and 0.68 respectively. This indicates that

Table 6. Comparison of convergence behaviors of clustering techniques

Iterations	K-Means	HP2PC	SEHP2PC	OGF with GA	OGF with NRGA
0	14.7	14.5	14.3	14.2	13.98
10	14.2	14.4	13.5	13.2	11.6
20	13.6	13.4	12.6	12	10.5
30	13.3	13.15	12.2	11.4	9.9
40	12.9	12.74	11.9	10.7	9.9
50	12.4	12.2	11.8	10.7	9.9
60	12	11.8	11.7	10.7	9.9
70	11.7	11.45	11.7	10.7	9.9
80	11.5	11.45	11.7	10.7	9.9
90	11.5	11.45	11.7	10.7	9.9
100	11.5	11.45	11.7	10.7	9.9

Figure 7. The convergence behaviors of proposed techniques and k-means technique

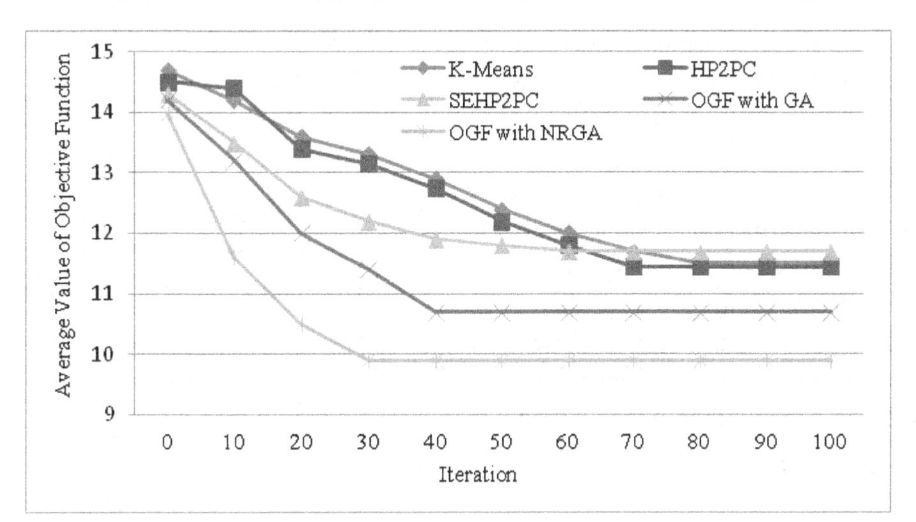

the data points are clearly assigned to cluster centers, whereas the proposed technique yields the silhouette coefficient value of 0.85 which indicates clustering results with excellent separation between clusters.

F-Measure

F-Measure parameter is then considered for evaluating the proposed technique. The F-measure of a class i is defined as:

$$F(i) = \frac{2PR}{P+R} \quad (6)$$

where P is Precision and R is recall.

The overall F-measure for the clustering result C is the weighted average of the F-measure for every class i and it is given by,

$$F_c = \frac{\sum_i (|i| \times F(i))}{\sum_i |i|} \quad (7)$$

Figure 8. Silhouette coefficient of the clustering techniques

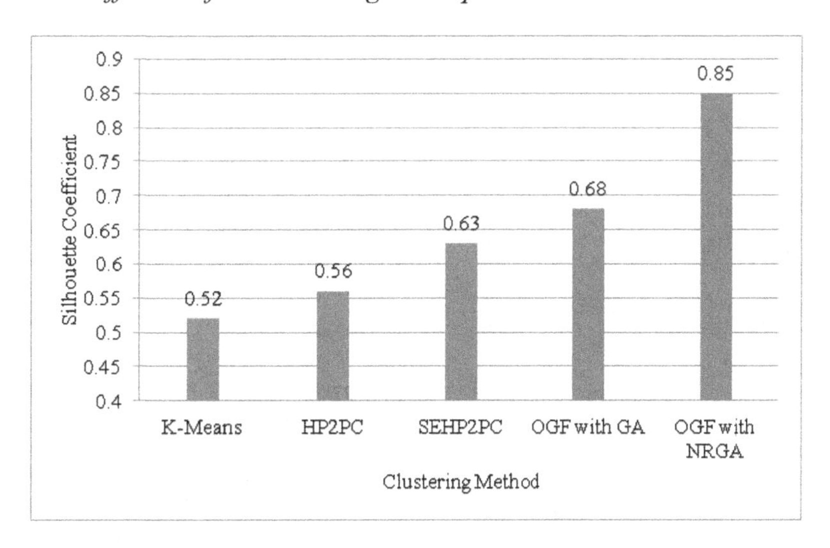

where $|i|$ is the number of objects in class i. When the overall F-measure is higher, the resulting clustering will b better because the higher accuracy of the clusters is due to the mapping of the original classes.

Figure 9 denotes the comparison of the overall F-Measures of the clustering techniques like k-means, HP2PC, SEHP2PC, and OGF with GA and OGF with NRGA. Figure 9 reveals that the value of F-Measure for the standard K-Means and the existing HP2P approaches is 0.5 and 0.53 respectively. F-Measure for the proposed SEHP2PC, OGF with GA and OGF with NRGA clustering approaches is 0.58, 0.62 and 0.68 respectively. This indicates that the proposed OGF with NRGA clustering technique is very significant.

Entropy

Entropy is a measure which helps in determining the goodness of un-nested clusters. It helps in determining the homogeneity of a cluster. When the entropy is higher, it represents the better homogeneity of a cluster. The entropy of a cluster that contains a single object is zero i.e., perfect homogeneity.

For each cluster j in the clustering result C p_{ij} is calculated, the probability that a member of cluster j belong to class i. The entropy of every cluster j is determined using the formula $E_j = \sum_i p_{ij} \log(p_{ij})$, where the sum is taken over all classes. The total entropy for a set of clusters is computed as the sum of entropies for each cluster weighted by the size of each cluster:

$$E_c = \sum_{j=1}^{N_c} (\frac{N_j}{N} \times E_j) \quad (8)$$

where N_j is the size of cluster j and N is the total number of data objects.

Figure 10 expresses the entropy value comparison of the clustering techniques. The entropy value of K-Means and the existing HP2PC is 0.29 and 0.24 respectively. The entropy of the proposed SEHP2PC and OGF with GA clustering is 0.22 and 0.19 respectively. The entropy value resulting for the proposed OGF with NRGA clustering technique is only 0.15 which implies that the homogeneity of clusters is better when compared to the other clustering approaches.

Figure 9. F-measure for proposed techniques and k-means technique

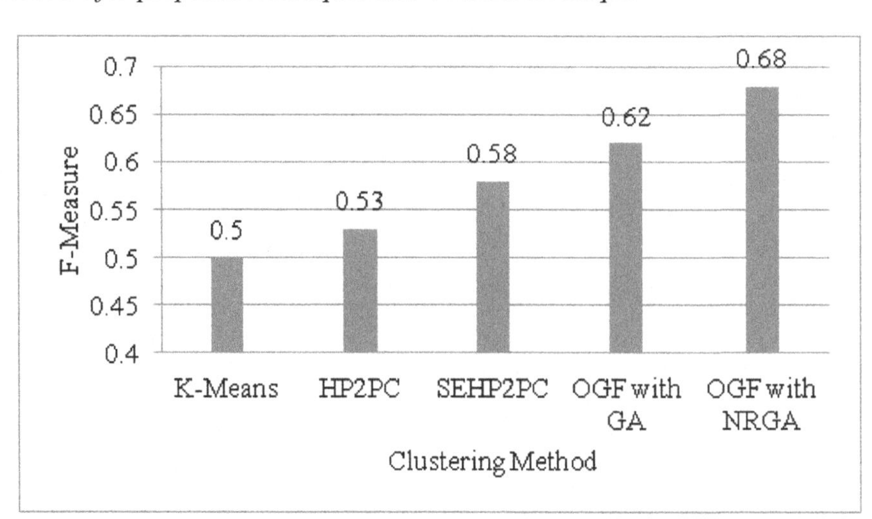

Figure 10. Entropy comparison for proposed techniques and k-means approach

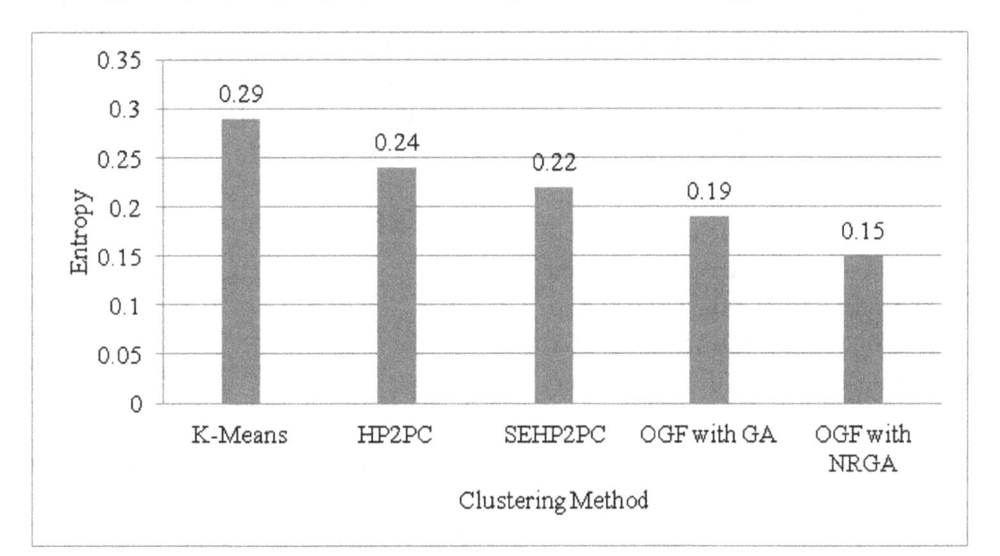

Separation Index

The validity index S is based on the objective function J by determining the average number of data and the square of the minimum distances of the cluster centers. The separation index S is defined as

$$S(c) = \frac{\sum_{i=1}^{c}\sum_{j=1}^{N} u_{ij}^2 d(\underline{x}_j - \underline{v}_i)^2}{N \min_{m,n=1,\ldots c \text{ and } m \neq n} \{d(\underline{v}_m - \underline{v}_n\}^2} = \frac{\sum_{i=1}^{c}\sum_{j=1}^{N} u_{ij}^2 d(\underline{x}_j - \underline{v}_i)^2}{N^*(d_{min})^2} \quad (9)$$

Figure 11. Comparison of the separation index

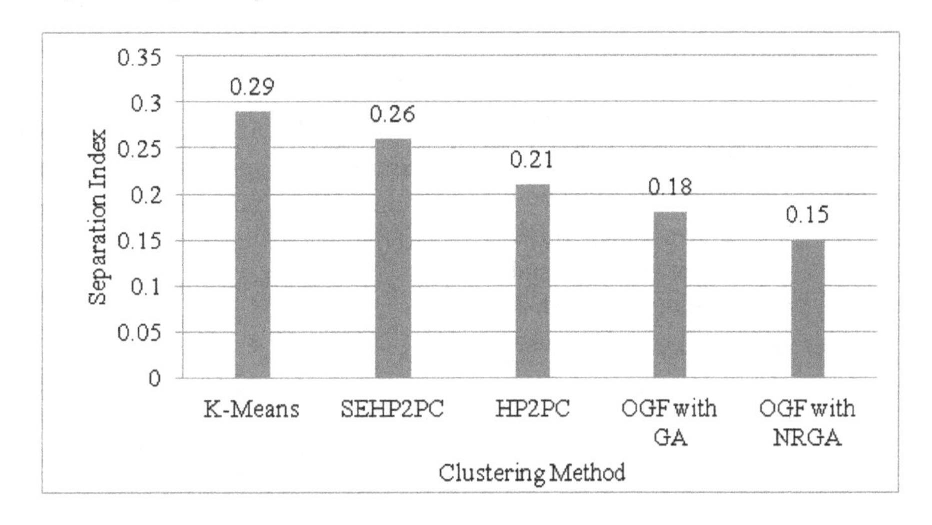

where d_{min} is the minimum Euclidean distance between cluster centers. The more separate the clusters, the larger $(d_{min})^2$, and the smaller S. Thus the smallest S indeed indicates a valid optimal partition.

Figure 11 shows the separation index comparison. The proposed approaches enforce a significant separation index when compared with the K-means approach. Among the proposed approach, proposed OGF with NRGA technique has the least separation index and it achieves very good optimal partition.

CONCLUSION AND FUTURE WORK

In this paper, ontology based document clustering using Non-Dominated Ranked Genetic Algorithm has been proposed. Initially, the fuzzy ontologies are generated for the vague available documents. Then with the help of the generated ontology, the clustering of documents is carried out with the help of Non-Dominated Ranked Genetic Algorithm. This paper utilized a document clustering algorithm based on NRGA to search the best cluster center in the global situation. OGF consists of the following process: Fuzzy Formal Concept Analysis, Fuzzy Conceptual Clustering and Fuzzy Ontology Generation.

The experiments conducted for 20 newsgroup dataset reveal evidently that the proposed technique results in better accuracy when compared to the techniques such as K-Means, HP2PC, SEHP2PC and OGF with Genetic Algorithm. The new approach outperforms the other clustering approaches in terms of accuracy, classification time, objective function, convergence time, F-Measure, silhouette coefficient, entropy and separation index. Thus so this proves approach is very effective in clustering the documents even in large databases.

For future enhancement, better optimization techniques such as Ant Colony Optimization can be used for better efficient performance of the document clustering approach.

REFERENCES

Cao, T. H., Do, H. T., Hong, D. T., & Quan, T. T. (2008). Fuzzy named entity-based document clustering. In *Proceedings of the IEEE International Conference on Fuzzy Systems* (pp. 2028-2034).

Casillas, A., Lena, M. T., & Martínez, R. (2003). Document clustering into an unknown number of clusters using a genetic algorithm. In V. Matoušek & P. Mautner (Eds.), *Proceedings of the 6th International Conference on Text, Speech and Dialogue* (LNCS 2807, pp. 43-49).

Dahlem, N. (2011). OntoClippy: A user-friendly ontology design and creation methodology. *Journal of Intelligent Information Technologies*, *7*(1), 15–32. doi:10.4018/jiit.2011010102

Deng, J., Hu, J. L., Chi, H., & Wu, J. (2010). An improved fuzzy clustering method for text mining. In *Proceedings of the Second International Conference on Networks Security Wireless Communications and Trusted Computing* (pp. 65-69).

Dhillon, I. S., & Modha, D. S. (2001). Concept decompositions for large sparse text data using clustering. *Machine Learning*, *42*, 143–175. doi:10.1023/A:1007612920971

Eisenhardt, M., Muller, W., & Henrich, A. (2003). Classifying documents by distributed p2p clustering. In *Proceedings of the Annual Informatik Meeting on Innovative Information Technology Uses*, Frankfurt, Germany (pp. 286-291).

Filho, F. M., & Gomide, F. (2005). Hybrid genetic algorithms and clustering. In *Proceedings of the Conference of the European Society for Fuzzy Logic and Technology/LFA* (pp. 1009-1014).

Grootjen, F. A., & Weide, T. P. (2005). Dualistic ontologies. *International Journal of Intelligent Information Technologies*, *1*(3), 34–55. doi:10.4018/jiit.2005070103

He, Q., Li, T., Zhuang, F., & Shi, Z. (2010). Frequent term based peer-to-peer text clustering. In *Proceedings of the 3rd International Symposium on Knowledge Acquisition and Modeling* (pp. 352-355).

Hotho, A., Maedche, A., & Staab, S. (2002). Ontology-based text document clustering. *Journal of Kunstliche Intelligenz*, *4*, 48–54.

Jadaan, O. A., Rajamani, L., & Rao, C. R. (2008). Non-dominated ranked genetic algorithm for solving multi-objective optimization problems: NRGA. *Journal of Theoretical and Applied Information Technology*, 60-67.

Kim, J., & Storey, V. C. (2011). Construction of domain ontologies: Sourcing the World Wide Web. *Journal of Intelligent Information Technologies*, *7*(2), 1–24.

Krishnapuram, R., Joshi, A., Nasraoui, O., & Yi, L. (2001). Low-complexity fuzzy relational clustering algorithms for web mining. *IEEE Transactions on Fuzzy Systems*, *9*(4), 595–607. doi:10.1109/91.940971

Leukel, J., & Sugumaran, V. (2009). Towards a semiotic metrics suite for product ontology evaluation. *International Journal of Intelligent Information Technologies*, *5*(4), 1–15. doi:10.4018/jiit.2009080701

Li, G., Zhuang, J., Hou, H., & Yu, D. (2009). A genetic algorithm based clustering using geodesic distance measure. In *Proceedings of the IEEE International Conference on Intelligent Computing and Intelligent Systems* (pp. 274-278).

Li, J., & Morris, R. (2002). Document clustering for distributed full text search. In *Proceedings of the 2nd MIT Student Oxygen Workshop*, Cambridge, MA.

Murthy, C. A., & Chowdhury, N. (1996). In search of optimal clusters using genetic algorithms. *Pattern Recognition Letters*, 825–832. doi:10.1016/0167-8655(96)00043-8

Pollandt, S. (1996). *Fuzzy-tag: Fuzzy formal concept analysis data*. Berlin, Germany: Springer-Verlag.

Quan, T. T., Hui, S. C., & Cao, T. H. (2004). FOGA: A fuzzy ontology generation framework for scholarly semantic web. In *Proceedings of the Knowledge Discovery and Ontologies Workshop*, Pisa, Italy (Vol. 24).

Sharma, A., & Dhir, R. (2009). A wordsets based document clustering algorithm for large datasets. In *Proceedings of the International Conference on Methods and Models in Computer Science* (pp. 1-7).

Sun, H., Liu, Z., & Kong, L. (2008). A document clustering method based on hierarchical algorithm with model clustering. In *Proceedings of the 22nd International Conference on Advanced Information Networking and Applications* (pp. 1229-1233).

Tenenboim, L., Shapira, B., & Shoval, P. (2008). *Ontology-based classification of news in an electronic newspaper* (pp. 89-98). Retrieved from http://sci-gems.math.bas.bg:8080/jspui/handle/10525/1035

Tun, N. N., & Tojo, S. (2008). EnOntoModel: A semantically-enriched model for ontologies. *International Journal of Intelligent Information Technologies*, *4*(1), 1–30. doi:10.4018/jiit.2008010101

Win, T., & Mon, L. (2010). Document clustering by fuzzy c-mean algorithm. In *Proceedings of the 2nd International Conference on Advanced Computer Control* (pp. 239-242).

Zhai, J., Chen, Y., Wang, Q., & Lv, M. (2008). Fuzzy ontology models using intuitionistic fuzzy set for knowledge sharing on the semantic web. In *Proceedings of the 12th International Conference on Computer Supported Cooperative Work in Design*.

Zhang, Z., Cheng, H., Zhang, S., Chen, W., & Fang, Q. (2008). Clustering aggregation based on genetic algorithm for documents clustering. In *Proceedings of the IEEE Congress on Evolutionary Computation* (pp. 3156-3161).

This work was previously published in the International Journal of Intelligent Information Technologies, Volume 7, Issue 4, edited by Vijayan Sugumaran, pp. 26-46, copyright 2011 by IGI Publishing (an imprint of IGI Global).

Chapter 16
A Dynamically Optimized Fluctuation Smoothing Rule for Scheduling Jobs in a Wafer Fabrication Factory

Toly Chen
Feng Chia University, Taiwan

ABSTRACT

This paper presents a dynamically optimized fluctuation smoothing rule to improve the performance of scheduling jobs in a wafer fabrication factory. The rule has been modified from the four-factor bi-criteria nonlinear fluctuation smoothing (4f-biNFS) rule, by dynamically adjusting factors. Some properties of the dynamically optimized fluctuation smoothing rule were also discussed theoretically. In addition, production simulation was also applied to generate some test data for evaluating the effectiveness of the proposed methodology. According to the experimental results, the proposed methodology was better than some existing approaches to reduce the average cycle time and cycle time standard deviation. The results also showed that it was possible to improve the performance of one without sacrificing the other performance metrics.

INTRODUCTION

Semiconductor manufacturing is a capital-intensive industry. A 200mm wafer fabrication factory can cost over a billion dollars. How to effectively use expensive machinery has been a key element for a semiconductor manufacturer to survive and compete in today's marketplace. Job scheduling is one of the most important tasks, to achieve this goal. However, this is not an easy task, because a wafer fabrication factory is a very complex manufacturing system, and has the following characteristics: changes in demand, a variety of product types and priorities, un-balanced capacity, job re-entry into the machines, alternative machines with unequal capacity, and shifting bottleneck (Chen et al., 2010b). Nevertheless, it still attracts the attention of many researchers (Gupta Sivakumar, 2006).

DOI: 10.4018/978-1-4666-2047-6.ch016

In Kim et al. (2001), wafer fabrication factory scheduling problems were divided into three categories: release control, job scheduling in serial processing workstations, and batch scheduling in batch processing workstations. In addition, the scheduling methods can be divided into global approaches and local approaches. Local approaches are usually for specific workstations, while the global approaches can be applied to all workstations in the wafer fabrication factory. On the other hand, the existing methods in this field can be divided into five main categories: dispatching rules, heuristics, data mining-based approaches, agent technologies, and simulation.

This study aims to propose a better dispatching rule. In this regard, some advanced methods have been proposed. For example, Chen (2009a) modified the fluctuation smoothing rule for mean cycle time (FSMCT), and proposed a nonlinear FSMCT (NFSMCT) rule, in which the fluctuation in the estimated remaining cycle time is smoothed, and then its influence is balanced with that of the release time or the mean release rate. Subsequently, the difference among the slack values is enlarged by using the 'division' operator instead. After that, Chen (2009c) presented the one-factor tailored nonlinear FSMCT (1f-TNFSMCT) rule and the one-factor tailored nonlinear fluctuation smoothing rule for cycle time variation (1f-TNFSVCT) rule, including an adjustable parameter to customize the rules. Taking into account the two performance measures (average cycle time and cycle time variation) at the same time, Chen and Wang (2009) proposed a bi-criteria nonlinear fluctuation smoothing rule (1f-biNFS). There is also an adjustable factor. To increase the flexibility of customization, Chen et al. (2010a) extended the rules, and proposed a bi-criteria fluctuation smoothing rule with four adjustable factors (4f-biNFS).

The motivations to introduce the new rule are as follows. In the existing fluctuation smoothing rules, the adjustable factors are static. In other words, they will not change over time. Chen (2009b) therefore designed a mechanism to dynamically adjust the values of the factors in Chen and Wang's bi-criteria nonlinear fluctuation smoothing rule (dynamic 1f-biNFS). However, the adjustment of the factors is based on a predefined rule. This treatment is too subjective, but also not takes into account the status of the wafer fabrication factory. In addition, these rules have not been optimized, and there is considerable room for improvement. To tackle these problems and to further improve the performance of job scheduling in a wafer fabrication factory, a dynamically optimized nonlinear fluctuation smoothing rule is proposed in this study, with the following objectives:

1. It is dynamic. In other words, the content of the new rule can be adjusted dynamically in a convenient way.
2. It is optimized. In other words, its performance meets some requirements of optimality.

Two performance measures, the average cycle time and cycle time standard deviation, are considered. The proposed methodology has the following innovative features:

1. A dynamic adjustment mechanism is designed.
2. A closed-loop continuous feedback mechanism is established to dynamically adjust the new rule to the target wafer fabrication factory. To this end, the cycle time related statistics of the recently completed work are constantly updated and fed back.
3. The adjustment is based on an optimization model to obtain the best results.

In addition, the proposed methodology uses the following intelligent information technologies:

1. **Fuzzy computing:** Fuzzy c-means (FCM) is applied to classify jobs to be scheduled into several categories.
2. **Artificial neural network:** Fuzzy back propagation network (FBPN) is then applied to estimate the remaining cycle time for each job.
3. **Online analysis processing (OLAP):** The cycle time related statistics of the recently completed work are constantly updated and fed back in an online manner.

Through their applications, the accuracy of the remaining cycle time estimation can be greatly improved.

To assess the effectiveness of the proposed methodology, production simulation is also applied in this study. The rest of this paper is organized as follows. Review of the related work is presented first. Next, I describe the dynamically optimized nonlinear fluctuation smoothing rule. Several cases containing the data from a simulated wafer fabrication factory are investigated. Some existing approaches are also applied to such cases. Then, the performance of the proposed methodology is compared with those of the existing approaches. Based on the results, some points are made. Finally, the concluding remarks with a view to the future are given.

RELATED WORK

In the literature review below, the existing methods in the five categories are introduced. The shortcoming and gaps of each category are also discussed.

Dispatching Rule

Some studies (e.g., Wein, 1998) have shown that applying existing dispatching rules (such as first-in first out (FIFO), earliest due date (EDD), least slack (LS), shortest processing time (SPT), shortest remaining processing time (SRPT), critical ratio (CR), FIFO+, SRPT+, and SRPT++) to a wafer fabrication factory does not lead to very good results. Besides, in many wafer fabrication factories scheduling systems have been installed for more than 5 years. Although these systems are considered "satisfactory", it is still believed that more benefits are possible. Specifically, better scheduling/dispatching rules, test environments, and reporting tools are needed (Pfund et al., 2008).

In short, the existing dispatching rules have the following problems. First, most dispatching rules consider only the attributes of the jobs gathered at the same place and lack an effective way of taking into consideration the conditions of the factory as a whole. Second, most dispatching rules are not tailored for a specific wafer fabrication factory. Third, most dispatching rules are static and do not reflect the changes in a wafer fabrication factory. Although there are a few approaches incorporating stochastic variables, such as the fluctuation smoothing rules – FSVCT and FSMCT, they use the average values for these stochastic variables and are in fact not responsive to environmental changes. For tackling this problem, Chen and Lin (2009b) and Chen (2009c) applied the hybrid FCM and FBPN approach to estimate the remaining cycle time of every job to be scheduled. Fourth, most dispatching rules are not optimized. A few studies have applied the response surface methodology (RSM) and the desirability function to deal with multiple-factor and multiple-objective optimization in scheduling (Zhang et al., 2009). However, RSM usually employs second-order multiple-factor regression which might not be accurate enough. The desirability function is a very subjective approach. Finally, most dispatching rules are focused on a single performance measure. In fact, minimizing any performance measure in such a complex job shop is strongly NP-hard. Nevertheless, optimizing multiple performance measures at the same time is still being pursued.

Heuristics

Zhang et al. (2009) proposed the dynamic bottleneck detection (DBD) approach, in which different heuristics are applied to jobs before bottleneck and non-bottleneck workstations. The DBD approach starts from the classification of jobs into several categories. The heuristics for different categories are not the same. The traditional DBD has the following problems:

1. The formation of many ties needs to be broken.
2. To consider the future conditions is favorable to the scheduling performance. However, all the heuristics in DBD are based on historical data only and do not take into account such information.
3. Some advanced dispatching rules have been proposed recently, and can be used to replace the heuristics.

Chen and Lin (2010) proposed a modified DBD approach, by using more advanced heuristics.

Data-Mining Based Approaches

Data-mining based approaches have the potential for scheduling problems. Recently, some studies (e.g., Koonce & Tsai, 2000) proposed methods of data mining to try to follow the best practices in the past. However, the wafer fabrication factory is a highly dynamic environment, so that future circumstances might be very different from those in the past. It is also difficult to find the so-called best practices in such a highly dynamic and complex production system. Another method is to mix some of the existing rules, and every time pick the most appropriate one. For example, Hsieh et al. (2001) used five methods, including FSMCT, FSVCT, largest deviation first (LDF), one step ahead (OSA), and FIFO jointly. However, each time an extensive simulation is required to estimate the performance of each candidate in order to determine the most appropriate one. In addition, the transition from one to the other is radical, which is not conducive to a stable production system.

Agent Technologies

Recently, some studies in this field applied agent technologies. Yoon and Shen (2008) constructed a multiple agent system for scheduling a wafer fabrication factory involving four types of agents (scheduling agents, workcell agents, machine agents, and product agents). The optimal scheduling plan was found by the scheduling agent through enumerating a few possible scenarios. Their proposed methodology was only compared with the two basic scheduling rules FIFO and EDD. In addition, the common batch processing of jobs was not considered, and therefore, the case was not proven to be practical. Recently, data mining has been applied also in scheduling manufacturing systems. For example, in Li and Sigurdur (2004), historic schedules were transformed into appropriate data files that were mined in order to find out which past scheduling decisions corresponded to the best practices. Youssef et al. (2002) proposed a hybrid genetic algorithm (GA) and data mining approach to determine the optimal scheduling plan of a job shop, in which the GA was used to generate a learning population of good solutions. These good solutions were then mined to find some decision rules that could be transformed into a metaheuristic. Koonce and Tsai (2000) proposed a similar methodology. Sourirajan and Uzsoy (2007) proposed a rolling horizon heuristic that decomposes the factory into smaller subproblems that can be solved sequentially over time using a workcenter-based decomposition heuristic.

Simulation

There is scant literature in which the historical data of a real wafer fabrication factory have been collected, since most studies in this field used simulated data. Simulation is a powerful tool supporting the design, layout or re-design of wafer fabrication factories. Recently, some applications proved that it can also support the operations of wafer fabrication factories, especially in the area of scheduling and control (Bremen, 2011). There are two ways of using simulation for improving production planning and scheduling:

1. A simulation model is used to configure, test and fine-tune the results of factory planning.
2. A simulation model is used as part of the planning tool and run in parallel to the real production process, which is known as advanced planning and scheduling (APS).

However, simulation is the most time-consuming approach and the related databases are continuingly updated to maintain enough validity. Nevertheless, it often serves as a benchmark for evaluating the effectiveness of another method.

METHODOLOGY

The proposed methodology has two parts. In the first part, Chen et al.'s (2009) FCM-FBPN approach is applied to estimate the remaining cycle time of each job to be scheduled. The variables are defined as follows:

1. R_i: the release time of job i.
2. LS_i: the size of job i.
3. CS_i: the current stage of job i.
4. NS_i: the number of stages of job i.
5. DD_i: the due date of job i.
6. TPT_i: the total processing time of job i.
7. CR_{ij}: the critical ratio of job i at step j.
8. U_i: the average fab utilization at R_i.
9. Q_i: the queue length on the processing route of job i at R_i.
10. BQ_i: the total queue length before bottlenecks at R_i.
11. FQ_i: the total queue length in the whole fab at R_i.
12. WIP_i: the fab work-in-progress (WIP) at R_i.
13. $D_i^{(k)}$: the delay of the k-th recently completed job, $k = 1 \sim 3$.
14. $B_i^{(l)}$: the l-th bucket of job i, $l = 1 \sim L$.
15. CTE_i: the estimated cycle time of job i.
16. CT_i: the cycle time (actual value) of job i.
17. $SCTE_{ij}$: the estimated step cycle time of job i until step j.
18. SCT_{ij} : the step cycle time (actual value) of job i at step j.
19. SK_{ij} : the slack of job i at step j.
20. $RCTE_{ij}$: the estimated remaining cycle time of job i at step j.

In Chen et al.'s (2009) FCM-FBPN approach, jobs (examples) are pre-classified into K categories with FCM before they are fed into FBPNs. Some past studies (e.g., Chen et al., 2009) showed that the accuracy of the remaining cycle time forecasting can be improved through classification.

FCM performs classification by minimizing the following objective function (Chen, 2010a):

$$\text{Min} \sum_{k=1}^{K}\sum_{i=1}^{n} \mu_{i(k)}^{m} e_{i(k)}^{2} \tag{1}$$

where K is the required number of categories; n is the number of jobs; $\mu_{i(k)}$ represents the membership of job i belonging to category k; $e_{i(k)}$ measures the distance from job i to the centroid of category k; $m \in [1, \infty)$ is a parameter to increase or decrease the fuzziness. The procedure of applying FCM to classify jobs is:

1. Establish an initial classification result.
2. (Iterations) Obtain the centroid of each category as

$$\bar{x}_{(k)} = \{\bar{x}_{(k)j}\} \tag{2}$$

$$\overline{x}_{(k)j} = \sum_{i=1}^{n} \mu_{i(k)}^{m} x_{ij} \Big/ \sum_{i=1}^{n} \mu_{i(k)}^{m} \tag{3}$$

$$\mu_{i(k)} = 1 \Big/ \sum_{l=1}^{K} (e_{i(k)} / e_{i(l)})^{2/(m-1)} \tag{4}$$

$$e_{i(k)} = \sqrt{\sum_{all\ j} (x_{ij} - \overline{x}_{(k)j})^2} \tag{5}$$

where $\overline{x}_{(k)}$ is the centroid of category *k*. $\mu_{i(k)}^{(t)}$ is the membership of job *i* belonging to category *k* after the *t*-th iteration.

3. Re-measure the distance of each job to the centroid of every category, and then recalculate the corresponding membership.
4. Stop if the following condition is satisfied. Otherwise, return to step (2):

$$\max_{k} \max_{i} | \mu_{i(k)}^{(t)} - \mu_{i(k)}^{(t-1)} | < d \tag{6}$$

where *d* is a real number representing the threshold of membership convergence.

Finally, the separate distance test (*S* test) proposed by Xie and Beni (1991) can be applied to determine the optimal number of categories *K*:

Min *S* (7)subject to

$$J_m = \sum_{k=1}^{K} \sum_{i=1}^{n} \mu_{i(k)}^{m} e_{i(k)}^{2} \tag{8}$$

$$e_{\min}^2 = \min_{p \neq q} (\sum_{all\ j} (\overline{x}_{(p)j} - \overline{x}_{(q)j})^2) \tag{9}$$

$$S = \frac{J_m}{n \times e_{\min}^2} \tag{10}$$

$$K \in Z^+ \tag{11}$$

The *K* value minimizing *S* determines the optimal number of categories.

Subsequently, jobs of different categories are then learned with different FBPNs but with the same topology. The configuration of the FBPN is established as follows:

1. **Inputs:** Eight parameters associated with the *i*-th example/job including U_i, Q_i, BQ_i, FQ_i, WIP_i, and $D_i^{(l)}$ (l = 1~3). Reasons for choosing these parameters refer to Chen and Lin (2009a). These parameters must be normalized with the partial normalization approach so that their values fall within [0.1, 0.9], and then multiplied by the value of its importance determined by a team of experts in advance. For details refer to Chen and Lin (2009a). Such a treatment has been proven to be beneficial to FBPN efficiency.
2. **Single hidden layer:** Generally speaking, one or two hidden layers are beneficial for the convergence property of the network.
3. The number of neurons in the hidden layer is the same as in the input layer. This treatment has been adopted by many studies (e.g., Chen & Lin, 2009a).
4. **Output:** Is the estimated (normalized) cycle time (CTE_i) or step cycle time ($SCTE_{ij}$) of the example. In other words, there will be two groups of FBPNs. The first group is for estimating the CTE_i's of all the jobs to be scheduled, while the other group is for estimating their $SCTE_{ij}$'s. Then, the remaining cycle time estimate ($RCTE_{ij}$) can be derived by subtracting $SCTE_{ij}$ from CTE_i.
5. **Network learning rule:** Delta rule.
6. **Transformation function:** Sigmoid function,

$$f(x) = 1/(1 + e^{-x}) \tag{12}$$

7. **Learning rate (η):** 0.01~1.0.
8. Batch learning.

The procedure for determining the parameter values is now described as follows. After pre-classification, a portion of the adopted examples in each category is fed as "training examples" into the FBPN to determine the parameter values for the category. Two phases are involved at the training stage. At first, in the forward phase, inputs are multiplied with weights, summed, and transferred to the hidden layer. Then activated signals are outputted from the hidden layer as:

$$\tilde{h}_j \tag{13}$$

where

$$\tilde{n}_j^h \tag{14}$$

$$\tilde{I}_j^h \tag{15}$$

$\tilde{h}_j$'s are also transferred to the output layer with the same procedure. Finally, the output of the FBPN is generated as:

$$\tilde{o} \tag{16}$$

where

$$\tilde{n}^o = \tilde{I}^o(-)\tilde{\theta}^o \tag{17}$$

$$\tilde{I}^o = \sum_{all\ j} \tilde{w}_j^o(\times)\tilde{h}_j \tag{18}$$

To improve the applicability of the FBPN and to facilitate the comparisons with conventional techniques, the fuzzy-valued output $\tilde{o}$ is defuzzified according to Wrather and Yu's formula (Wrather & Yu, 1982):

$$d(\tilde{o}) = \int_0^1 E(o^\alpha)d\alpha \tag{19}$$

where o^a is the α cut of $\tilde{o}$. Then the output o is compared with the normalized actual cycle time (or step cycle time) a, for which the RMSE is calculated:

$$\text{RMSE} = \sqrt{\sum_{\text{all trained examleps}} (o-a)^2 / \text{number of trained examples}} \tag{20}$$

Subsequently in the backward phase, the deviation between o and a is propagated backward, and the error terms of neurons in the output and hidden layers can be calculated respectively as:

$$\delta^o = o(1-o)(a-o) \tag{21}$$

$$\tilde{\delta}_j^h \tag{22}$$

Based on them, adjustments that should be made for connecting weights and thresholds can be obtained as:

$$\Delta\tilde{w}_j^o = \eta\delta^o\tilde{h}_j \tag{23}$$

$$\Delta\tilde{w}_{ij}^h = \eta\tilde{\delta}_j^h(\times)\tilde{x}_i \tag{24}$$

$$\Delta\theta^o = -\eta\delta^o \tag{25}$$

$$\Delta\tilde{\theta}_j^h = -\eta\tilde{\delta}_j^h \tag{26}$$

To accelerate convergence, a momentum can be added to the learning expressions. For example,

$$\Delta\tilde{w}_j^o = \eta\delta^o\tilde{h}_j + \alpha(\tilde{w}_j^o(t) - \tilde{w}_j^o(t-1)) \tag{27}$$

Theoretically, network-learning stops when the RMSE falls below a pre-specified level, or the improvement in the RMSE becomes negligible with more epochs, or a large number of epochs have already been run. Then test examples are fed into the FBPN to evaluate the accuracy of the network that is also measured with the RMSE. However, the accumulation of fuzziness during the training process continuously increases the lower bound, the upper bound, and the spread of the fuzzy-valued output $\tilde{o}$ (and those of many other fuzzy parameters), and might prevent the RMSE (calculated with the defuzzified output o) from converging to its minimal value. Conversely, the centers of some fuzzy parameters are becoming smaller and smaller because of network learning. It is possible that a fuzzy parameter becomes invalid in the sense that the lower bound is higher than the center. To deal with this problem, the lower and upper bounds of all fuzzy numbers in the FBPN will no longer be modified if Chen's index (Chen & Lin, 2009a) converges to a minimal value.

Finally, the FBPN can be applied to estimate the cycle time or the step cycle time of a new job. When a new job is released into the factory, the eight parameters associated with the new job are recorded. Then the FBPN is applied to estimate the cycle time or step cycle time of the new job.

In traditional fluctuation smoothing rules there are two different formulation methods, depending on the scheduling purpose. One method is aimed at minimizing the mean cycle time with FSMCT:

$$SK_i = i / \lambda - RCTE_{ij} \tag{28}$$

The other method is aimed at minimizing the variance of cycle time with FSVCT:

$$SK_i = R_i - RCTE_{ij} \tag{29}$$

In FSVCT, $RCTE_{ij}$ might be much greater than R_i or i/λ. As a result, the slack of a job becomes determined solely by $RCTE_{ij}$. To deal with this problem, both terms in FSVCT can be normalized:

$$Nor(RCTE_{ij}) = (RCTE_{ij} - \min_{\text{all } i}(RCTE_{ij})) / (\max_{\text{all } i}(RCTE_{ij}) - \min_{\text{all } i}(RCTE_{ij})) \tag{30}$$

$$Nor(R_i) = (R_i - \min_{\text{all } i}(R_i)) / (\max_{\text{all } i}(R_i) - \min_{\text{all } i}(R_i)) \tag{31}$$

After normalization, both terms now range from 0 to 1. Subsequently, to improve the balancing and the responsiveness of FSVCT, the division operator is applied instead of the traditional subtraction operator:

Nonlinear FSVCT rule (NFSVCT):

$$SK_i = Nor(R_i) / Nor(RCTE_{ij}) \tag{32}$$

To tailor the nonlinear FSVCT rule to the wafer fabrication factory that is to be scheduled, the transition from FSVCT to its nonlinear form is analyzed as follows. The nonlinear form can be re-written as

$$SK_i = Nor(R_i) / Nor(RCTE_{ij})$$

$$= \left(\frac{\alpha(RCTE_{ij} - \min(RCTE_{ij}))}{\beta}\right)^{-1} \cdot (R_i - RCTE_{ij} + (RCTE_{ij} - \min(R_i)) \cdot 1) \tag{33}$$

where $\alpha = \max(R_i) - \min(R_i)$ and $\beta = \max(RCTE_{ij}) - \min(RCTE_{ij})$. Conversely, FSVCT can also be re-written as

$$SK_i = R_i - RCTE_{ij} = \left(\frac{\alpha(RCTE_{ij} - \min(RCTE_{ij}))}{\beta}\right)^{-0} \cdot (R_i - RCTE_{ij} + (RCTE_{ij} - \min(R_i)) \cdot 0) \quad (34)$$

These two formulas can be generalized into the following form:

2f-TNFSVCT:

$$SK_i = (R_i - RCTE_{ij} + (RCTE_{ij} - \min(R_i)) \cdot f_1) \cdot \left(\frac{\alpha(RCTE_{ij} - \min(RCTE_{ij}))}{\beta}\right)^{-f_2} \quad (35)$$

where f_1 and f_2 are positive real numbers satisfying the following constraints:

If $f_1 = 0$, then $f_2 = 0$, and vice versa (36)

If $f_1 = 1$, then $f_2 = 1$, and vice versa (37)

Similar analyses can be conducted on FSMCT:

2f-TNFSMCT:

$$SK_i = \left(\frac{i}{\lambda} - RCTE_{ij} + (RCTE_{ij} - \frac{1}{\lambda}) \cdot f_3\right) \cdot \left(\frac{\gamma(RCTE_{ij} - \min(RCTE_{ij}))}{\beta\lambda}\right)^{-f_4} \quad (38)$$

where f_3 and f_4 are positive real numbers satisfying the following constraints:

If $f_3 = 0$, then $f_4 = 0$, and vice versa (39)

If $f_3 = 1$, then $f_4 = 1$, and vice versa (40)

Subsequently, an attempt is made to improve the two performance measures simultaneously by merging the two tailored nonlinear fluctuation smoothing rules into a single scheduling rule:

4f-biNFS:

$$SK_i = (R_i - RCTE_{ij} + (RCTE_{ij} - \min(R_i)) \cdot f_1) \cdot \alpha^{-f_2} \cdot \left(\frac{i}{\lambda} - RCTE_{ij} + (RCTE_{ij} - \frac{1}{\lambda}) \cdot f_3\right) \cdot \left(\frac{\gamma}{\lambda}\right)^{-f_4} \cdot \left(\frac{RCTE_{ij} - \min(RCTE_{ij})}{\beta}\right)^{-(f_2+f_4)} \quad (41)$$

where $f_1 \sim f_4$ are constant-valued parameters. When f_1 and f_2 are equal to 0, 4f-biNFS is equivalent to 2f-TNFSMCT. Conversely, it becomes 2f-TNFSVCT if f_1 and f_2 are equal to 1. The optimal values of the four factors were obtained according to a preliminary analysis considering several possible values, from which the one giving the best result is chosen. However, considering the dynamic fluctuations in factory conditions, in this study the 4f-biNFS dispatching rule is turned into a dynamic one, by specifying dynamic parameters:

$$SK_i = (R_i - RCTE_{ij} + (RCTE_{ij} - \min(R_i)) \cdot f_1(t)) \cdot \alpha^{-f_2(t)} \cdot \left(\frac{i}{\lambda} - RCTE_{ij} + (RCTE_{ij} - \frac{1}{\lambda}) \cdot f_3(t)\right) \cdot \left(\frac{\gamma}{\lambda}\right)^{-f_4(t)} \cdot \left(\frac{RCTE_{ij} - \min(RCTE_{ij})}{\beta}\right)^{-(f_2(t)+f_4(t))} \quad (42)$$

The four adjustable factors satisfy the following constraints:

If $f_1(t) = 1$ and $f_2(t) = 1$, then $f_3(t) = 0, f_4(t) = 0$, and vice versa (43)

If $f_1(t) = 0$ and $f_2(t) = 0$, then $f_3(t) = 1, f_4(t) = 1$, and vice versa (44)

If

$$f_{1a}(t) \geq f_{1b}(t) \text{ and } f_{2a}(t) \geq f_{2b}(t), \text{ then } f_{3a}(t) \leq f_{3b}(t) \text{ and } f_{4a}(t) \leq f_{4b}(t) \quad (45)$$

If

$$f_{1a}(t) \leq f_{1b}(t) \text{ and } f_{2a}(t) \leq f_{2b}(t), \text{ then } f_{3a}(t) \geq f_{3b}(t) \text{ and } f_{4a}(t) \geq f_{4b}(t) \quad (46)$$

where $(f_{1a}(t), f_{2a}(t), f_{3a}(t), f_{4a}(t))$ and $(f_{1b}(t), f_{2b}(t), f_{3b}(t), f_{4b}(t))$ are two different sets of the four dynamic factors. Some models are proposed to form such sets:

Linear model $= f_1(t) = f_2(t), f_3(t) = f_4(t), f_1(t) = 1 - f_3(t)$ (47)

Nonlinear model =

$$f_1(t) = f_2^m(t), f_3(t) = f_4^m(t), f_1(t) = 1 / f_3(t), m \geq 0 \quad (48)$$

Logarithmic model $= f_1(t) = \ln(1 + f_2(t)) / \ln 2$,
$f_3(t) = \ln(1 + f_4(t)) / \ln 2, f_1(t) = 1 / f_3(t)$ (49)

In order to determine the best values of these factors, the traditional way is to try various combinations, from which the one giving the best results is chosen (Chen et al., 2010a). To this end, a series of simulation experiments need to be performed. This is very time-consuming, and can only consider a small number of combinations. In addition, the dynamic changes in the wafer fabrication factory have not been taken into account. Chen (2010b) modeled the relationship between the scheduling performance and these factors with a back propagation network, but the effectiveness was not good enough. In order to solve these problems, a closed-loop continuous feedback mechanism is established in this study, which makes the new rule differ from the existing approaches:

Step 1: (Initialization) Initialize the value of f_1 randomly from [0 2.25], and then derive the values of the other factors based on the nonlinear model:

$$f_2(t) = \sqrt[m]{f_1(t)}; \qquad f_3(t) = 1 / f_1(t);$$
$$f_4(t) = \sqrt[m]{1 / f_1(t)};\ m \geq 0 \quad (50)$$

Step 2: (Job Dispatching) Dispatch jobs using the dynamic rule and the new factor set for q hours.

Step 3: (Performance Evaluation) Calculate the average cycle time and cycle time standard deviation for each product type and priority.

Step 4: (Optimality Checking) Record the dynamic rule as a base rule, if it is not dominated by any of the previous rules. If the number of base rules reaches $u - 1$, go to step 5. Otherwise, go to step 1.

Step 5: (Rule Updating) Add a rule with random factors to the base rule set. Generate u random weights indicated with w_v, $v = 1 \sim u$, and then normalize these weights so that $\sum_{v=1}^{u} w_v = 1$. Subsequently, update the dynamic rule by calculating the weighted geometric mean of the base rules:

$$f_1^{(\tau)}(t) = \prod_{v=1}^{u} f_1^{(v)}(t)^{w_v};$$
$$f_2^{(\tau)}(t) = \prod_{v=1}^{u} f_2^{(v)}(t)^{w_v};$$
$$f_3^{(\tau)}(t) = \prod_{v=1}^{u} f_3^{(v)}(t)^{w_v};$$
$$f_4^{(\tau)}(t) = \prod_{v=1}^{u} f_4^{(v)}(t)^{w_v} \quad (51)$$

where $(f_1^{(\tau)}(t),\ f_2^{(\tau)}(t),\ f_3^{(\tau)}(t),\ f_4^{(\tau)}(t))$ is the factor set of the τ-th base rule. Continue to work with the dynamic rule for q hours. Evaluate the scheduling performance in the same way as in step 3. If any base rule is dominated by the dynamic rule, replace it with the dynamic rule.

Step 6: (Termination) If the simulation horizon is reached, stop. Otherwise, go to step 5.

Subsequently, some properties of the dynamic rule are mentioned below.

Theorem 1: Because all the base rules are based on the nonlinear model, the dynamic rule also meets the nonlinear model.

Proof: Substitute equation (51) into Equation (50),

$$f_2^{(\tau)}(t) = \prod_{v=1}^{u} f_2^{(v)}(t)^{w_v} = \prod_{v=1}^{u} (\sqrt[m]{f_1^{(v)}(t)})^{w_v} = \prod_{v=1}^{u} (\sqrt[m]{f_1^{(v)}(t)^{w_v}}) = \sqrt[m]{\prod_{v=1}^{u} f_1^{(v)}(t)^{w_v}} = \sqrt[m]{f_1^{(\tau)}(t)} \quad (52)$$

$$f_3^{(\tau)}(t) = \prod_{v=1}^{u} f_3^{(v)}(t)^{w_v} = \prod_{v=1}^{u} (1 / f_1^{(v)}(t))^{w_v} = 1 / \prod_{v=1}^{u} f_1^{(v)}(t)^{w_v} = 1 / f_1^{(\tau)}(t) \quad (53)$$

$$f_4^{(\tau)}(t) = \prod_{v=1}^{u} f_4^{(v)}(t)^{w_v} = \prod_{v=1}^{u} (\sqrt[m]{1 / f_1^{(v)}(t)})^{w_v} = \prod_{v=1}^{u} (\sqrt[m]{1 / f_1^{(v)}(t)^{w_v}}) = 1 / \sqrt[m]{\prod_{v=1}^{u} f_1^{(v)}(t)^{w_v}} = 1 / \sqrt[m]{f_1^{(\tau)}(t)} \tag{54}$$

Theorem 1 is proven.

Furthermore, the convergence property of the dynamic rule is discussed. Calculating the weighted geometric mean of the base rules, and then replacing some of which that are outdated, the base rules have become increasingly consistent. Therefore, the dynamic rule, as a moving average, gradually converges to a stable state, which means that changes made to the four factors will be less important. Theorem 2 uses a simple case to illustrate this property.

Theorem 2: The dynamic rule will converge to a stable state and the changes made to the four factors will be less significant.

Proof: We illustrate this property with the simple case with only two base rules r_1 and r_2 that are sorted in ascending order, i.e., $r_1 \leq r_2$. The weighted geometric mean of them is $\sqrt{r_1 r_2}$ if $w_1 = w_2 = 1/2$. Assuming after the first-round evaluation, r_1 is dominated and replaced by $\sqrt{r_1 r_2}$. Then, the dynamic rule is updated to

$$\sqrt{\sqrt{r_1 r_2} r_2} = \sqrt[4]{r_1 r_2^3} \tag{55}$$

Assuming after the second-round evaluation, r_2 is replaced by the dynamic rule. Then, the dynamic rule is updated to

$$\sqrt{\sqrt{r_1 r_2} \sqrt[4]{r_1 r_2^3}} = \sqrt[8]{r_1^3 r_2^5} \tag{56}$$

Since $r_1 \leq r_2$,

$$\sqrt[8]{r_1^3 r_2^5} - \sqrt[4]{r_1 r_2^3} \leq \sqrt[8]{r_1^2 r_2^6} - \sqrt[4]{r_1^2 r_2^2} = \sqrt[4]{r_1 r_2^3} - \sqrt{r_1 r_2} \tag{57}$$

which shows that changes in the dynamic rule diminish gradually. Other possible outcomes associated with this case can be analyzed in a similar way. Theorem 2 is therefore proved.

An example is given in Table 1 to illustrate the calculation of the dynamic rule. The convergence in the dynamic rule can be observed from the series of phase charts in Figure 1.

EXPERIMENTAL RESULTS AND DISCUSSION

To evaluate the effectiveness of the dynamically optimized fluctuation smoothing rule, we used simulated data to avoid disturbing the regular operations of the wafer fabrication factory. To this end, a real wafer fabrication factory located in Taichung Scientific Park of Taiwan with a monthly capacity of about 25,000 wafers was simulated using Visual C++ with the following assumptions:

1. Jobs are uniformly released into the wafer fabrication factory.
2. The distributions of the interarrival times of machine downs are exponential.
3. The distribution of the time required to repair a machine is uniform.
4. Dynamic product mix.
5. The percentages of jobs with different priorities released into the wafer fabrication factory are loosely controlled.
6. The priority of a job cannot be changed during fabrication.
7. Jobs are sequenced on each machine first by their priorities, then by the first-in-first-out (FIFO) policy. Such a sequencing policy is a common practice in many factories.
8. The probabilities of processing a job on alternative machines at a step are all equal.

Table 1. An example

t	$f_1(t)$	$f_2(t)$	$f_3(t)$	$f_4(t)$	Rule #	Replacement
0	0.25	0.50	4.00	2.00	1	
168	1.00	1.00	1.00	1.00	2	
336	2.25	1.50	0.44	0.67	3	
504	0.83	0.91	1.21	1.10	4	replace rule #3 with rule #4
672	0.59	0.77	1.69	1.30	5	replace rule #2 with rule #5
840	0.50	0.70	2.01	1.42	6	replace rule #4 with rule #6
1008	0.42	0.65	2.39	1.55	7	

9. A job cannot proceed to the next step until the fabrication on its every wafer has been finished.
10. No preemption is allowed.

The simulation program has been validated and verified by comparing the actual cycle times with the simulated values and by analyzing the trace report, respectively. The wafer fabrication factory is producing more than 10 types of memory products, and has more than 500 workstations for performing single-wafer or batch operations using 58nm~110nm technologies. Jobs released into the wafer fabrication factory are assigned three types of priorities, i.e., "normal", "hot", and "super hot". Jobs with the highest priorities will be processed first. Such a large scale accompanied with reentrant process flows make job dispatching in the wafer fabrication factory a very tough task. Currently, the longest average cycle time exceeds three months with a variation of more than 300 hours. The wafer fabrication factory is therefore seeking better dispatching rules to replace FIFO, in order to shorten the average cycle times and quicken the delivery to its customers. One hundred replications of the simulation are successively run. The time required for each simulation replication is about 30 minute using a PC with Intel Dual CPU E2200 2.2 GHz and 1.99G RAM. A horizon of twenty-four months is simulated.

To evaluate the effectiveness of the proposed methodology and to make comparison with some existing approaches – FIFO, EDD, SRPT, CR, FSVCT, FSMCT, 1f-TNFSVCT, 1f-TNFSMCT, and 4f-biNFS, all these methods were applied to the simulated wafer fabrication factory so as to collect the data of some jobs that were then separated by their product types and priorities. The data of some cases were so few that they were not discussed. Subsequently, the average cycle time and cycle time standard deviation of various cases were calculated to evaluate the scheduling performance. The results are summarized in Table 2 and Table 3.

In FIFO, jobs were sequenced on each machine first by their priorities, then by their arrival times at the machine. In EDD, jobs were sequenced first by their priorities, then by their due dates. The performance of EDD is dependent on the way of determining the due date of a job. In the experiment, the due date of a job was determined as follows:

$$DD_n = R_n + (\psi - 1.5 * \text{priority}) * TPT_n \quad (58)$$

where ψ indicates the cycle time multiplier. The values of "priority" for normal, hot, and super hot are 1, 2, and 3, respectively. In the experiment, various values of ψ were tried to optimize the performance. In CR, jobs were sequenced first by their priorities, then by their critical ratios. The critical ratio of a job is calculated as follows:

$$CR_{nj} = (t - DD_n) / RPT_{nj} \quad (59)$$

Figure 1. The convergence process of the dynamic rule

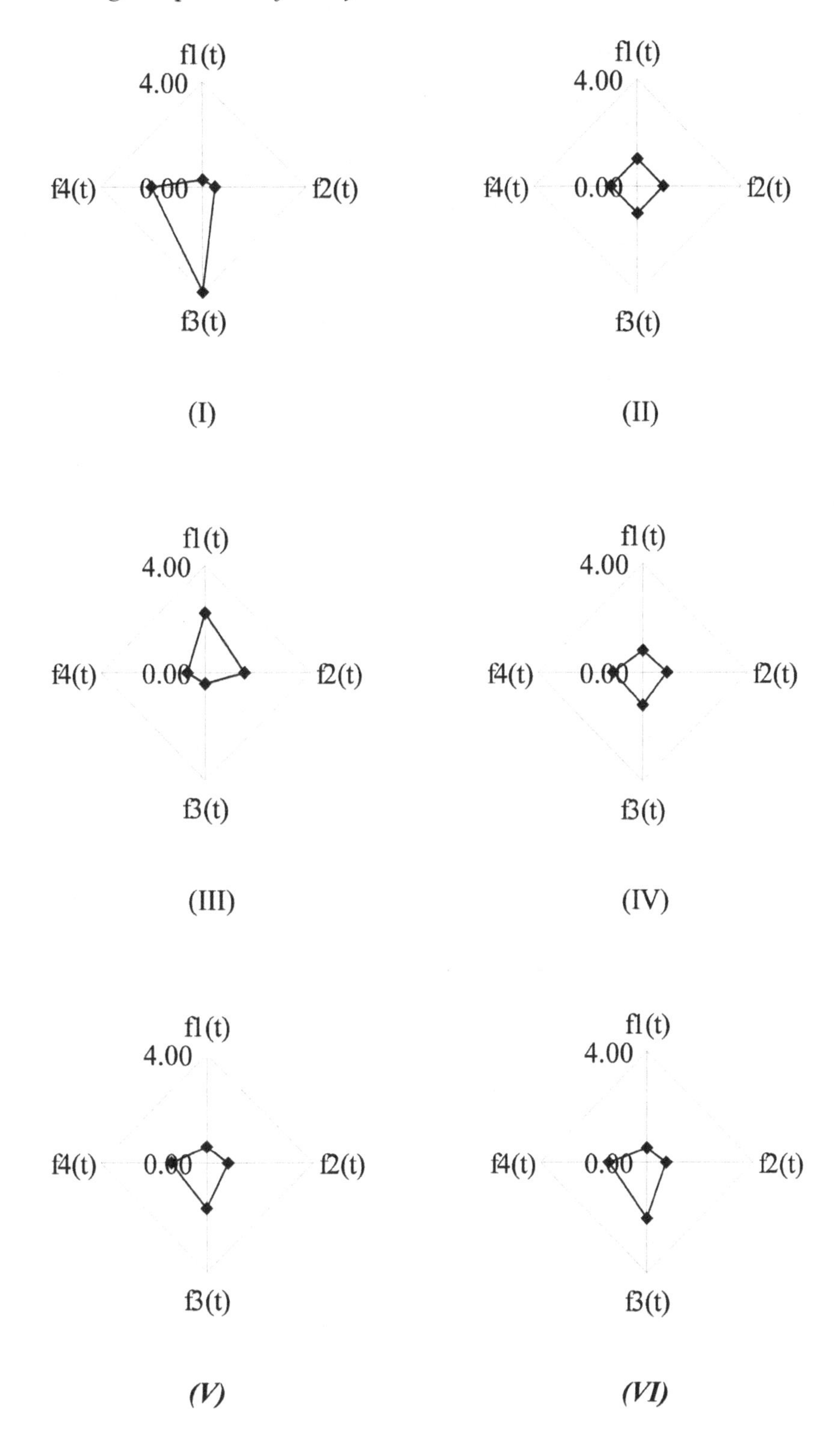

Table 2. The performances of various approaches in the average cycle time

Avg. Cycle Time (hrs)	A (Normal)	A (Hot)	A (Super Hot)	B (Normal)	B (Hot)
FIFO	1256	401	320	1278	457
EDD	1087 (-13%)	346 (-14%)	306 (-4%)	1433 (+12%)	478 (+5%)
SRPT	966 (-23%)	350 (-13%)	309 (-3%)	1737 (+36%)	483 (+6%)
CR	1143 (-9%)	356 (-11%)	301 (-6%)	1497 (+17%)	470 (+3%)
FSMCT	1401 (+12%)	405 (+1%)	320 (+0%)	1408 (+10%)	430 (-6%)
FSVCT	1046 (-17%)	385 (-4%)	317 (-1%)	1745 (+37%)	519 (+14%)
1f-TNFSMCT	1353 (+8%)	379 (-5%)	298 (-7%)	1271 (-1%)	409 (-11%)
1f-TNFSVCT	1368 (+9%)	365 (-9%)	299 (-7%)	1370 (+7%)	413 (-10%)
4f-biNFS	1228 (-2%)	356 (-11%)	289 (-10%)	1223 (-4%)	422 (-8%)
The Proposed Methodology	1224 (-2%)	362 (-9%)	286 (-11%)	1211 (-5%)	387 (-16%)

The performance of CR is dependent on the way of determining the due date of a job. Equation (58) is applied for this purpose. In FSMCT, FSVCT, NFSMCT, and NFSVCT, there were two stages. First, jobs were scheduled with the FIFO policy, for which the remaining cycle times at

Table 3. The performances of various approaches in cycle time standard deviation

Cycle Time Std. Dev. (hrs)	A (Normal)	A (Hot)	A (Super Hot)	B (Normal)	B (Hot)
FSVCT	319	35	28	222	55
FIFO	56 (-82%)	24 (-31%)	23 (-18%)	87 (-61%)	40 (-27%)
EDD	130 (-59%)	25 (-29%)	23 (-18%)	50 (-77%)	39 (-29%)
SRPT	246 (-23%)	32 (-9%)	23 (-18%)	106 (-52%)	30 (-45%)
CR	68 (-79%)	30 (-14%)	19 (-32%)	58 (-74%)	37 (-33%)
FSMCT	42 (-87%)	44 (+26%)	23 (-18%)	35 (-84%)	28 (-49%)
1f-TNFSMCT	81 (+45%)	43 (+79%)	22 (-4%)	49 (-44%)	25 (-38%)
1f-TNFSVCT	44 (-86%)	28 (-20%)	18 (-36%)	31 (-86%)	21 (-62%)
4f-biNFS	65 (-80%)	29 (-16%)	16 (-42%)	51 (-77%)	14 (-75%)
The Proposed Methodology	46 (-85%)	39 (-14%)	11 (-61%)	38 (-83%)	21 (-64%)

each step of all jobs were recorded and averaged. Then, the corresponding policy was applied to schedule jobs based on the average remaining cycle times obtained previously. The remaining cycle times were also updated. In other words, jobs were sequenced on each machine first by their priorities, then by their slack values, which was equal to their release times minus the average remaining cycle times.

With respect to the average cycle time, the FIFO policy was adopted as the basis for comparison. The percentage of improvement in the performance measure by applying another approach is shown in parentheses following the performance measure. On the other hand, the FSVCT policy was adopted as the basis for comparison with respect to cycle time standard deviation. According to the experimental results, the following points can be made:

1. For the average cycle time, the proposed methodology outperformed the baseline approach, the FIFO policy. The most obvious advantage was up to 16%. On the other hand, the proposed methodology also achieved very good performances in reducing cycle time standard deviations. It surpassed the baseline FSVCT policy significantly in all cases with an average advantage of up to 56%, which revealed that the treatments carried out in this study did improve the scheduling performance of the traditional fluctuation smoothing policies. The advantages of the proposed methodology over the existing methods are shown in Figures 2 and 3.
2. Jobs dispatched by the proposed methodology and 4f-biNFS show an average cycle time constantly lower than that of FIFO, while the other compared methods exhibit more variable results.
3. The proposed methodology is a modification of the existing bi-criteria dispatching rule 4f-biNFS by dynamically adjusting the four factors in it. According to the experimental results, the performance of the proposed methodology was also better than that of 4f-biNFS in most cases, which revealed that with dynamic adjustment, the performances of 4f-biNFS was indeed enhanced.
4. As expected, SRPT performed well in reducing the average cycle times, but might give an exceedingly bad performance with respect to cycle time standard deviation.
5. The traditional FSVCT policy performed poorly in the simulation experiment. This might be due to the diversification in product type and priority that made the remaining cycle time of a job highly uncertain and very difficult to estimate. As a result, estimating with the average value might be far from accurate and may impair the scheduling performance of FSVCT.

To make sure whether the differences between the performance of the dynamically optimized fluctuation smoothing rule and those of the nine existing approaches are statistically significant, the following hypotheses were tested:

- **H_{a0}:** The performance in shortening the average cycle time of the dynamically optimized fluctuation smoothing rule is the same as that of the compared existing approach.
- **H_{a1}:** The performance in shortening the average cycle time of the dynamically optimized fluctuation smoothing rule is better than that of the compared existing approach.
- **H_{b0}:** The performance in reducing cycle time standard deviation of the dynamically optimized fluctuation smoothing rule is the same as that of the compared existing approach.

Figure 2. The advantage of the proposed methodology over the existing methods (average cycle time)

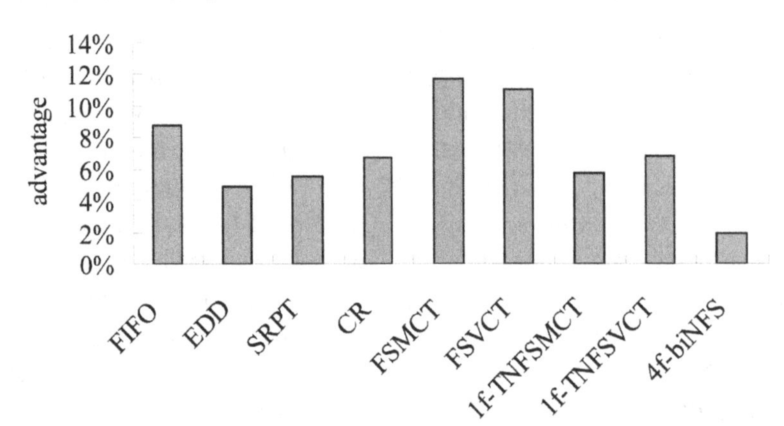

- $\mathbf{H_{b1}}$: The performance in reducing cycle time standard deviation of the dynamically optimized fluctuation smoothing rule is better than that of the compared existing approach.

In the literature, several statistical techniques have been developed for testing these hypotheses at a specified significant level α. Here we applied Wilcoxon's sign-rank test. The results were summarized in Table 4. The null hypothesis H_a was rejected at $\alpha = 0.025$ or 0.05, showing that the dynamically optimized fluctuation smoothing rule was superior to FIFO, FSMCT, 1f-TNFSMCT and 1f-TNFSVCT in reducing the average cycle time. On the other hand, the advantage of the dynamically optimized fluctuation smoothing rule over FIFO, CR and 1f-TNFSMCT in reducing cycle time standard deviation was also significant at $\alpha = 0.025$ or 0.05.

CONCLUSION AND DIRECTIONS FOR FUTURE RESEARCH

A dynamically optimized fluctuation smoothing rule is proposed in this study to improve the scheduling performance in a wafer fabrication

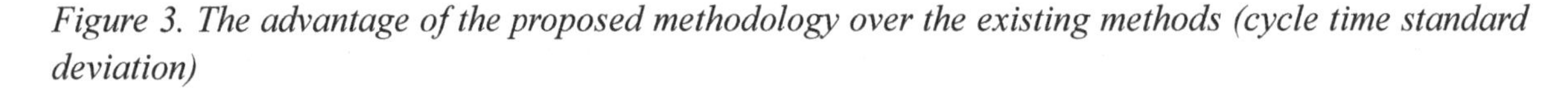

Figure 3. The advantage of the proposed methodology over the existing methods (cycle time standard deviation)

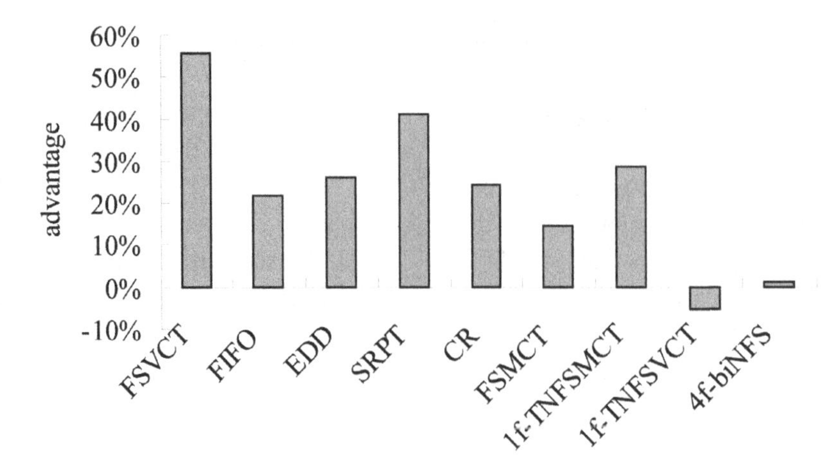

Table 4. The results of wilcoxon sign-rank test

	H_{a0}	H_{b0}
FIFO	Z = 1.89*	Z = 1.75*
EDD	0.67	1.21
SRPT	0.67	1.21
CR	0.94	1.75*
FSMCT	2.02**	1.35
FSVCT	0.94	0.94
1f-TNFSMCT	1.89*	2.02**
1f-TNFSMCT	2.02**	-0.67
4f-biNFS	1.21	0.67

* $p < 0.05$
** $p < 0.025$
*** $p < 0.01$

factory. The dynamically optimized fluctuation smoothing rule was modified from 4f-biNFS. It constantly adjusts the four factors. In addition, such an adjustment is monitored by an optimization mechanism. These characteristics make the dynamically optimized fluctuation smoothing rule differ from the existing methods. Some theoretical properties of the dynamically optimized fluctuation smoothing rule have also been discussed.

To evaluate the effectiveness of the proposed methodology and to compare it with some existing approaches, production simulation was also applied in this study, and then the proposed methodology and some existing approaches were all applied to the simulated wafer fabrication factory. The experimental results were as follows.

1. The proposed methodology adjusts the factors dynamically, which makes it distinct from the existing approaches, and contributes to its advantage over the compared approaches in the practical example.
2. The dynamically optimized fluctuation smoothing rule was shown to be a good compromise between 4f-TNFSMCT and 4f-TNFSVCT. Experimental results also revealed that with dynamic data fusion it was possible to improve one performance measure without raising the expense of another performance measure.

Contribution of this work includes:

1. A dynamic adjustment of the content was proven to be a viable strategy to improve the scheduling performance of a dispatching rule.
2. Some theoretical properties that a dynamic adjustment mechanism should meet have been mentioned.
3. The dynamic adjustment mechanism proposed in this study is easy to implement and therefore more practical.

However, in order to further assess the effectiveness and efficiency of the proposed methodology, it has to be applied to wafer fabrication factories of various sizes and types. As the proposed dynamically optimized fluctuation smoothing rule is a general rule, it can be applied to a variety of systems other than the wafer fabrication plants.

In this study, the new rule is the weighted geometric mean of the base rules. Other methods, such as GA (Tripathi et al., 2011), particle swarm optimization (PSO) (Jeyarani et al., 2011; Rigi & Khoshalhan, 2011), or fuzzy collaborative optimization (Chen, 2011), can be used for the same purpose in future work.

ACKNOWLEDGMENT

This work was supported by National Science Council of Taiwan.

REFERENCES

Bremen, J. K. (2011) *Simulation supports production planning and scheduling.* Retrieved from http://www.sim-serv.com/pdf/news/news_32.pdf

Chen, T. (2009a). A tailored nonlinear fluctuation smoothing rule for semiconductor manufacturing factory scheduling. *Proceedings of the Institution of Mechanical Engineers. Part I, Journal of Systems and Control Engineering, 223*, 149–160. doi:10.1243/09596518JSCE625

Chen, T. (2009b). Dynamic fuzzy-neural fluctuation smoothing rule for jobs scheduling in a wafer fabrication factory. *Proceedings of the Institution of Mechanical Engineers. Part I, Journal of Systems and Control Engineering, 223*, 1081–1094. doi:10.1243/09596518JSCE849

Chen, T. (2009c). Fuzzy-neural-network-based fluctuation smoothing rule for reducing the cycle times of jobs with various priorities in a wafer fabrication factory - a simulation study. *Proceedings of the Institution of Mechanical Engineers. Part B, Journal of Engineering Manufacture, 223*, 1033–1044. doi:10.1243/09544054JEM1459

Chen, T. (2010a). A fuzzy-neural approach with collaboration mechanisms for semiconductor yield forecasting. *International Journal of Intelligent Information Technologies, 6*(3), 17–33. doi:10.4018/jiit.2010070102

Chen, T. (2010b). An optimized tailored nonlinear fluctuation smoothing rule for scheduling a semiconductor manufacturing factory. *Computers & Industrial Engineering, 58*, 317–325. doi:10.1016/j.cie.2009.11.006

Chen, T. (2011). Applying a fuzzy and neural approach for forecasting the foreign exchange rate. *International Journal of Fuzzy System Applications, 1*(1), 36–48.

Chen, T., & Lin, C. H. (2010). A modified DBD system for scheduling jobs in a wafer fabrication factory. *International Review on Computers and Software, 5*(4), 396–405.

Chen, T., & Lin, Y.-C. (2009a). A fuzzy back-propagation-network ensemble with example classification for lot output time prediction in a wafer fab. *Applied Soft Computing, 9*(2), 658–666. doi:10.1016/j.asoc.2008.04.018

Chen, T., & Lin, Y.-C. (2009b). A fuzzy-neural fluctuation smoothing rule for scheduling jobs with various priorities a semiconductor manufacturing factory. *International Journal of Uncertainty Fuzziness and Knowledge-Based Systems, 17*(3), 397–417. doi:10.1142/S0218488509005942

Chen, T., & Wang, Y.-C. (2009). A bi-criteria nonlinear fluctuation smoothing rule incorporating the SOM-FBPN remaining cycle time estimator for scheduling a wafer fab - a simulation study. *International Journal of Advanced Manufacturing Technology, 49*, 709–721. doi:10.1007/s00170-009-2424-x

Chen, T., Wang, Y.-C., & Lin, Y.-C. (2010a). A bi-criteria four-factor fluctuation smoothing rule for scheduling jobs in a wafer fabrication factory. *International Journal of Innovative Computing . Information and Control, 6*(10), 4289–4303.

Chen, T., Wang, Y.-C., & Lin, Y.-C. (2010b). A fuzzy-neural system for scheduling a wafer fabrication factory. *International Journal of Innovative Computing . Information and Control, 6*(2), 687–700.

Chen, T., Wang, Y.-C., & Wu, H.-C. (2009). A fuzzy-neural approach for remaining cycle time estimation in a semiconductor manufacturing factory – A simulation study. *International Journal of Innovative Computing . Information and Control, 5*(8), 2125–2139.

Gupta, A. K., & Sivakumar, A. I. (2006). Job shop scheduling techniques in semiconductor manufacturing. *International Journal of Advanced Manufacturing Technology*, *27*, 1163–1169. doi:10.1007/s00170-004-2296-z

Hsieh, B.-W., Chen, C.-H., & Chang, S.-C. (2001). Scheduling semiconductor wafer fabrication by using ordinal optimization-based simulation. *IEEE Transactions on Robotics and Automation*, *17*(5), 599–608. doi:10.1109/70.964661

Jeyarani, R., Nagaveni, N., & Ram, R. V. (2011). Self adaptive particle swarm optimization for efficient virtual machine provisioning in cloud. *International Journal of Intelligent Information Technologies*, *7*(2), 25–44.

Kim, Y. D., Kim, J. G., & Kim, H. U. (2001). Production scheduling in a semiconductor wafer fabrication facility producing multiple product types with distinct due dates. *IEEE Transactions on Robotics and Automation*, *17*(5), 589–598. doi:10.1109/70.964660

Koonce, D. A., & Tsai, S.-C. (2000). Using data mining to find patterns in genetic algorithm solutions to a job shop schedule. *Computers & Industrial Engineering*, *38*(3), 361–374. doi:10.1016/S0360-8352(00)00050-4

Li, X., & Sigurdur, O. (2004). Data mining for best practices in scheduling data. In *Proceedings of the IIE Annual Conference and Exhibition*.

Pfund, M. E., Balasubramanian, H., Fowler, J. W., Mason, S. J., & Rose, O. (2008). A multi-criteria approach for scheduling semiconductor wafer fabrication facilities. *Journal of Scheduling*, *11*, 29–47. doi:10.1007/s10951-007-0049-1

Rigi, M. A., & Khoshalhan, F. (2011). Eliciting user preferences in multi-agent meeting scheduling problem. *International Journal of Intelligent Information Technologies*, *7*(2), 45–62.

Sourirajan, K., & Uzsoy, R. (2007). Hybrid decomposition heuristics for solving large-scale scheduling problems in semiconductor wafer fabrication. *Journal of Scheduling*, *10*(1), 41–65. doi:10.1007/s10951-006-0325-5

Tripathi, A., Gupta, P., Trivedi, A., & Kala, R. (2011). Wireless sensor node placement using hybrid genetic programming and genetic algorithms. *International Journal of Intelligent Information Technologies*, *7*(2), 63–83.

Wein, L. M. (1998). Scheduling semiconductor wafer fabrication. *IEEE Transactions on Semiconductor Manufacturing*, *1*, 115–130. doi:10.1109/66.4384

Winkler, R., Klawonn, F., & Kruse, R. (2011). Fuzzy c-means in high dimensional spaces. *International Journal of Fuzzy System Applications*, *1*(1), 1–16.

Wrather, C., & Yu, P. L. (1982). Probability dominance in random outcomes. *Journal of Optimization Theory and Applications*, *3*, 315–334. doi:10.1007/BF00934350

Xie, X. L., & Beni, G. (1991). A validity measure for fuzzy clustering. *IEEE Transactions on Pattern Analysis and Machine Intelligence*, *13*, 841–847. doi:10.1109/34.85677

Yoon, H. J., & Shen, W. (2008). A multiagent-based decision-making system for semiconductor wafer fabrication with hard temporal constraints. *IEEE Transactions on Semiconductor Manufacturing*, *21*(1), 83–91. doi:10.1109/TSM.2007.914388

Youssef, H., Brigitte, C. M., & Noureddine, Z. (2002). A genetic algorithm and data mining based meta-heuristic for job shop scheduling problem. In *Proceedings of the IEEE International Conference on Systems, Man and Cybernetics* (Vol. 7, pp. 280-285).

Zhang, H., Jiang, Z., & Guo, C. (2009). Simulation-based optimization of dispatching rules for semiconductor wafer fabrication system scheduling by the response surface methodology. *International Journal of Advanced Manufacturing Technology*, *41*(1-2), 110–121. doi:10.1007/s00170-008-1462-0

This work was previously published in the International Journal of Intelligent Information Technologies, Volume 7, Issue 4, edited by Vijayan Sugumaran, pp. 47-64, copyright 2011 by IGI Publishing (an imprint of IGI Global).

Chapter 17
A Heuristic Method for Learning Path Sequencing for Intelligent Tutoring System (ITS) in E-Learning

Sami A. M. Al-Radaei
IT BHU, India

R. B. Mishra
IT BHU, India

ABSTRACT

Course sequencing is one of the vital aspects in an Intelligent Tutoring System (ITS) for e-learning to generate the dynamic and individual learning path for each learner. Many researchers used different methods like Genetic Algorithm, Artificial Neural Network, and TF-IDF (Term Frequency- Inverse Document Frequency) in E-leaning systems to find the adaptive course sequencing by obtaining the relation between the courseware. In this paper, heuristic semantic values are assigned to the keywords in the courseware based on the importance of the keyword. These values are used to find the relationship between courseware based on the different semantic values in them. The dynamic learning path sequencing is then generated. A comparison is made in two other important methods of course sequencing using TF-IDF and Vector Space Model (VSM) respectively, the method produces more or less same sequencing path in comparison to the two other methods. This method has been implemented using Eclipse IDE for java programming, MySQL as database, and Tomcat as web server.

INTRODUCTION

In a traditional classroom an instructor teaches the course using textbook and syllabus that covers the course in sequence. Students then follow fixed learning path, since they have no alternative learning path. Moreover, these students are with different prior knowledge, performance, preferences and often learning goals. Course sequencing is a well-established technology in the area of intelligent tutoring system (ITS), it is one of the vital aspects in ITS to provide individual course

DOI: 10.4018/978-1-4666-2047-6.ch017

for each learner by dynamically selecting the most suitable and optimal learning path (Mishra & Mishra, 2010). Most of the researchers (Chengling & Liyong, 2006; Nguyen Viet, 2008; Norsham, Norazah, & Puteh, 2009) generate the learning path sequencing based on the relation between the course-wares and they ignore the importance of the semantic of the keywords in the course.

The prime objective of our work is to develop and build dynamic courseware sequencing method based on the relation between the course-wares. This relation is based on the semantic value of the keywords in each courseware. There are two values of the keyword's semantic value, one is courseware semantic value and the other is coursework semantic value. Both values give us the importance of the keyword in the courseware and in the coursework, where coursework consists of almost all the course-wares. We developed a learning system for Java language programming and it is implemented in Java platform, using MySQL for database and Tomcat as web server.

The rest of the contents of the paper are divided into the following sections. The next section provides the background. The following section puts across problem description. Afterward, there is a section that describes our system architecture and its components. Later in the chapter, our courseware design is covered. A discussion of the semantic values computation follows. Implementation Experimentation and Comparison with other models is presented after that, and the Conclusion is given in the last section.

BACKGROUND

In this section we provide an overview of the existing work on course sequencing in an e-learning system. Various approaches have been developed to find the course sequencing. Some of them are based on a set of teaching rules according to the learning style and learner's preferences. These rules are well-defined and commonly accepted, but these rules are domain independent, also in order to design adaptive learning system, huge set of rules are required (Seridi, Sari, Khadir, & Sellami, 2006). Instead of forcing an instructor designer to manually define the set of selection rules, an artificial intelligence (AI) technique has been widely used in E-leaning systems to find the adaptive course sequencing. A Bayesian belief network has been constructed to generate the course sequencing based on learner's profile and courseware difficulty level (Nguyen Viet, 2008). Artificial Neural Network method has been used to discover the connection between the domain concepts contained in the learning object and the learner's learning need by identifying a group of similar learning objects to select the suitable group for a particular student (Norsham et al., 2009). The concept relation matrix between the course-wares has been developed with help of TF-IDF (Term frequency- inverse document frequency), in which matrix values are used for fitness function in genetic Algorithm to construct an optimal learning path for each learner (Huang, Huang, & Chen, 2007). The relationship between the different weighted knowledge nodes in graph structure is described and an algorithm is proposed to find the shortest learning path (Chengling & Liyong, 2006). An individual learning path based on IRT (Item Response Theory) is developed and a collaborative voting approach is proposed to determine the course difficulty level and to estimate the learner ability based on explicit learner feedback and use them in their system (Chen, Lee, & Chen, 2005). A system to understand the semantics of programming languages is proposed by Dadic (2010), this system guides novices in learning syntax and semantic of programming language, problem decomposition, program design and testing. Semantic analysis of student's programs is based on comparison of abstract semantic trees of student's and model-program. Advancement through the course material controlled by computer teacher supports connection of new concepts to the present student's knowledge. An adaptive selection and sequencing of learning objects based on the learning profiles, preferences and abilities of individual learners has been developed (Lung-Hsiang & Chee-Kit, 2010). For e-learning the technical and instructional design of an adaptive learning environment has been created. Instruction design is based on the selection of learning material by individual, subjected to different learning scenarios (Reiners & Sassen, 2008).

Semantic value has been considered in many research works for the different purposes. Semantic values entities assigned to expressions and it has been used in Language grammar and Linguistics (Dever & Keith, 2006). It is used in e-negotiation system by exchange data and semantic values between sellers and buyers agents, both agents convert the meaning of the semantic values to semantic target via ontology server (Lee, 2000; Mazumdar & Mishra, 2010). In another research work three dimensions of value, semantic and the social models are used in personalized blog recommendation system to the emerging blogosphere and improved the user experience for the bologgers in gathering the featured items (Tsai, Shih, & Chou, 2006). The Latent semantic index (LSI) has been widely used to improve the recall of retrieved the documents by analyzing the semantic structure between words and documents (Deerwester, Dumais, Furnas, Landauer, & Harshman, 1990). LSI is based on singular value decomposition of TF-IDF matrix. The result of this decomposition is three matrices which are as follows: the left singular matrix (t X m), right singular matrix (m X d) and S a diagonal matrix with elements being the singular values ranked by their magnitude (m X m) where m is number of dimension (m<= (t, d)).

The latent semantic index can index the documents that contain the words that have similar meaning to the index word. Then it helps users when they submit the query words to get the most relevant information. Some researchers have applied LSI for document categorization tasks (Hull, 1994; Karypis & Han, 2000; Yang, 1995; Zelikovitz & Hirsh, 2001). LSI is used for categorization of multilingual document (Lee, Yang, & Ma, 2006). A new algorithm called Google Latent Semantic distance is proposed and used to extract the most important sequence of keywords to provide the most relevant search result to the user (Chen, Lin, & Chu, 2011). A method for exploited the linguistic information found in source code is proposed using semantic indexing with help of TF-IDF algorithm to present high level concept from the source code (van der Spek, Klusener, & van de Laar, 2008). A method for automatic labelling of high level semantic concept in documentary style videos has been done by acquiring a collection of generic semantic concepts across modalities (audio, video and text) (Iyengar, Nock, Neti, & Franz, 2002). Clustering algorithm is used to identify the similar web pages in content level; the semantic analysis is used to find the similarity between the web pages and then similar pages are grouped using cluster algorithm (De Lucia, Risi, Tortora, & Scanniello, 2007). LSI has been used with the help of ANN algorithms for document classification (Li & Park, 2007).

And particularly in E-learning, semantic analysis has been performed to match the text to the learner's reading ability. If a text is too easy, a learner doesn't learn anything; if a text is too hard, it can be incomprehensible (Foltz, Laham, & Landauer, 1999). Summative and formative assessment of learner's work is generated using latent semantic analysis which infer the meaning of the text during the learning processes (Haley, Thomas, Nuseibeh, Taylor, & Lefrere, 2005). Personalized intelligent web retrieval system can expand field words conceptually through conceptual semantic nets in e-learning. The frequency of users' access to the concept nodes in Semantic net tree reflects their interests in the content of concepts (Lihua, JianPing, & Yunfen, 2009).

PROBLEM DESCRIPTION

The leaning sequencing path is an important issue in E-learning systems. In this paper we address this issue using a computational method based on heuristics. We have used the semantic values of the keywords present in the course-wares to generate the learning path sequencing instead of using the relation between course-wares which is based on the occurrence of the keywords which is only what others researchers like Chen (2008) and Hsieh et al. (2010) have done.

Java programming language has been taken as case study by formulates a computational method for our system. The learning sequencing for eight course-wares is arranged and decided using the relation between the course-wares. This relation is based on the semantic value for the keywords in the courseware and the common keywords between the courseware. Learner can select any courseware randomly, after the selected courseware is completes. Next courseware will be decided based on the lowest difference semantic value between the current courseware and all other course-wares.

We have designed and developed learning system on Java platform with three actors: Administrator, Instructor and learner. The courseware sequencing in the proposed system is based on the semantic values of the course-wares keyword.

SYSTEM ARCHITECTURE

This section describes the system architecture, system components, and details of learning procedures for our proposed method.

System Architecture and Components

The proposed E-learning system is based on Heuristic method for learning path which includes six databases which are: user account database, instructor account database, user profile database, courseware database, Pre-test database and test database. The system consists of three main interfaces for administrator, instructor and learner. The administrator interface aims to provide tools for the administrator to manage, add, remove and update the users' accounts. The instructor interface aims to provide three tools for the instructor 1) add, edit, delete the courseware's materials, keywords, and semantic values for the keywords, 2) add, delete and edit the test and pre-test details (questions, answer, mark, type and difficulty level) and 3) obtain the common keywords among the course-wares and their courseware semantic values and coursework semantic values. The learner interface aims to provide selection for the courseware then online computation for the difference semantic values for the course-wares, learning interface also provides pre-test, courseware materials and evaluation test. System Architecture of the proposed model is shown in Figure 1.

Steps in Procedure

This section explains the procedure of interactions between the system components and the users' (Administrator, instructor, and learners').

Instructor can do the following processes:

1. Through the instructor interface the instructor can add/delete/edit courseware materials.
2. After the courseware materials are added to the database, the instructor can select the important keywords form the keyword-courseware list (calculation is in next section).
3. The instructors' can add/delete/edit the pre-test/test for the particular courseware and assign the answer, mark, domain, and difficulty level.
4. Obtain the common keywords between the course-wares in each level as well as their courseware semantic value and coursework semantic values as we described in next section. The procedure for keyword inserting and semantic value calculation is shown in Figure 2.

The following steps briefly describe the learning strategy and courseware sequencing during interaction between the learner and the proposed system.

Step 1: The new learner has to sign up through the new user page and fills all the information required.

Step 2: learner login to the system (first time) and he select randomly any courseware form course-wares list; this selection will be saved in learner's profile for further calculation and for next login.

Step 3: After completing each courseware a dynamic computation for the next semantic courseware using difference semantic value for all other course-wares is calculated as we will describe in the section on Semantic Value Computation.

COURSEWARE DESIGN AND CONTENTS

In this section we present the details of the courseware design and contents. We make certain assumptions for the courseware contents:

Assumption 1: Each courseware contains some percentage of contents form previous course-wares.

The keywords in each courseware contain some percentage of keywords form all previous course-wares; this relation can be represented in general as:

$$cw'_m = \left(\sum_{i=0}^{m-2} \alpha(1-\alpha)\right) + (1-\alpha)^{m-1} cw_{m-(m-1)} \quad (1)$$

Figure 1. System architecture of the proposed model

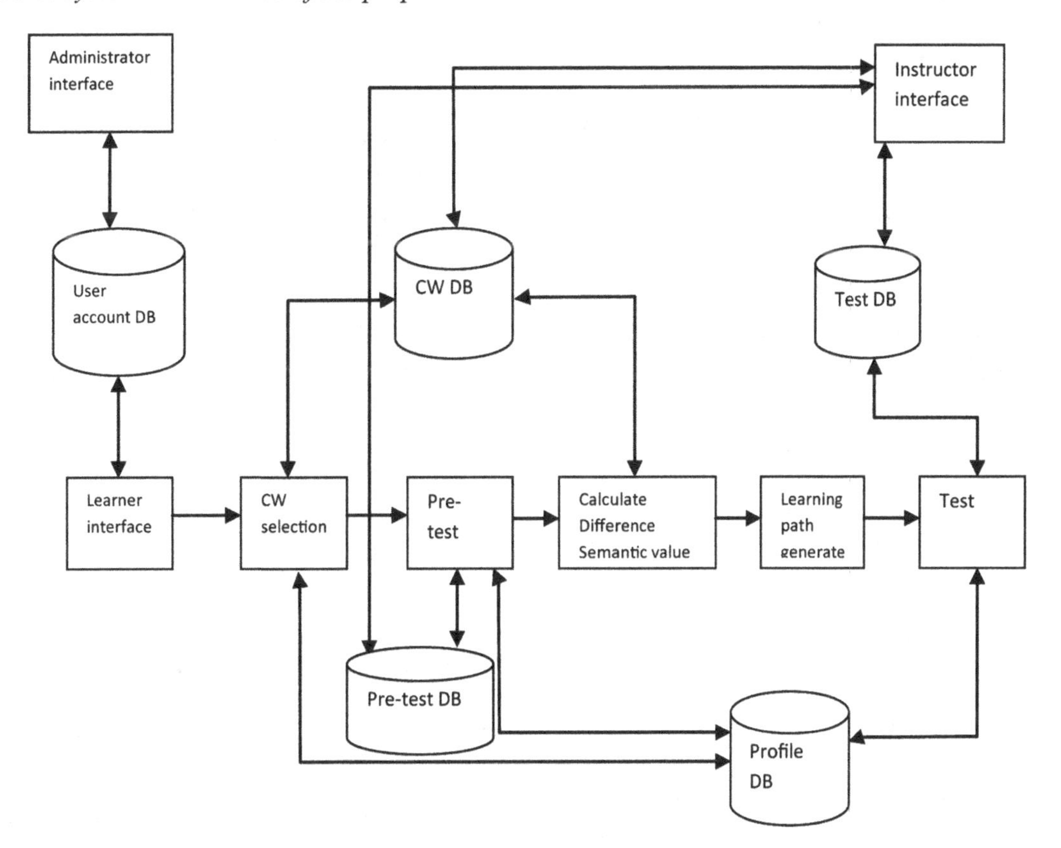

Figure 2. The procedures for keyword extraction and semantic value computation

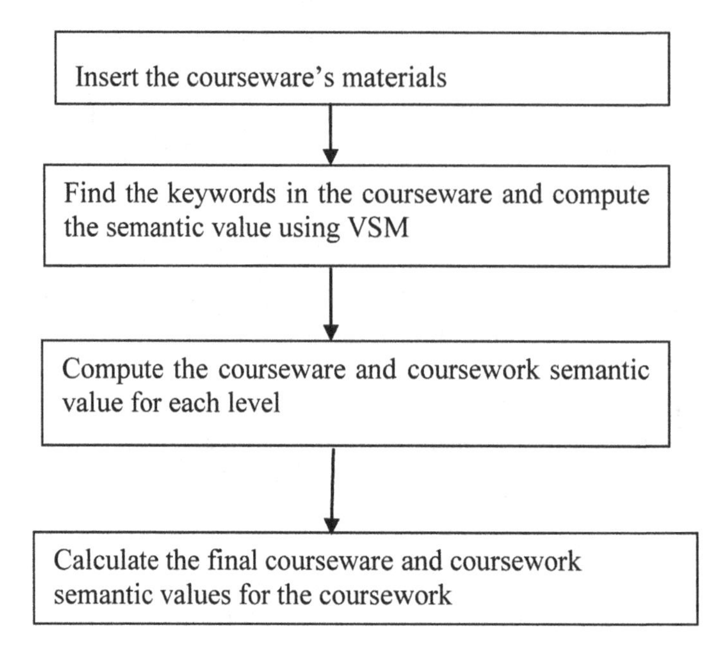

For m=2, 3, 4..., n where n is number of course-wares

For example: the relation between cw'_2 and cw_2 as the following:

$$cw'_2 = \alpha cw_2 + (1-\alpha)cw_1 \quad (2)$$

where cw'_2 is the total number of keyword in courseware 2

cw_2 = The number of specific keywords in course ware2.

cw_1 = The total number of keyword for course-ware1

And for courseware3

$$cw'_3 = \alpha cw_3 + (1-\alpha)cw'_2 \quad (3)$$

Form Equation (2)

$$cw'_3 = \alpha cw_3 + (1-\alpha)cw_2 + (1-\alpha)^2 cw_1 \quad (4)$$

Assumption 2: Each keyword has a semantic value to the particular courseware and it may be different from courseware to another. The keyword "*String*" has the semantic value 0.081121, 0.621897 and 0.030034 in cw_1, cw_2 and cw_8 respectively. The hierarchy of semantic value for the keyword represents the importance of the keyword for the courseware.

The semantic value for the keyword k in level l can be calculated as follows:

$$m = n \times l \quad (5)$$

where m is semantic value for keyword k in level l and n is the semantic value for the keyword.

SEMANTIC VALUE COMPUTATION

Vector Space Model VSM has been widely used in information retrieval, information filtering, information indexing and relevancy ranking (Salton, Wong, & Yang, 1975; Tai, Ren, & Kita,

2002). In this section, we used the VSM to compute Keywords' Semantic value by constructing the Keyword-Courseware Matrix.

In order to compute the semantic values of the keywords in each courseware, every courseware passes through pre-processing steps (stop words filter, common English words filter) to find the keywords-courseware list. The expert lecturer in next step selects the important keywords among all keywords in keywords-courseware list to avoid the occurrence of unrelated keywords in the final keyword-courseware list. The keywords (n) and their occurrence frequency are represented in the matrix A as follows.

$A = K x Q$ keyword-Courseware matrix consist of K rows (keywords) and Q columns (courseware)

This matrix represents one-row matrices and one-column matrices and these represent the vector. The Frobenius Norm of a matrix, also known as the Euclidean Norm, is defined as the square root of the sum of the absolute squares of its elements, which is equal to the length of the vector.

$$f_{cw}^{j} = \sqrt[2]{\sum_{i}^{n} k_i^2} \tag{6}$$

f_{cw}^{j} is the Euclidean norm for the j-th courseware cw

The semantic value of the keywords in the j-th courseware is calculated using the occurrence of the keyword k_i and Euclidean norm as the following:

$$Kw_i = k_i \, / \, f_{cw}^{j} \tag{7}$$

Here only a part of a keyword-courseware matrix is given in Table 1; where it actually consists of 75 keywords and their semantic values for eight course-wares.

Course-wares are represented by keywords and each keyword has semantic value with respect to the courseware as well as with respect to the coursework. The range of the Semantic value is from 0 to 1, which represents the importance of the keywords in the courseware. For example, keyword "*array*" has (0.0) different semantic value in all courseware *cw3, cw5, cw6* and *cw8*, it means that this keyword is not important in those course-wares. The keyword "array" has also the semantic values 0.348822, 0.048251, 0.050437 and 0.035198 in *cw1, cw2, cw4* and *cw7* respectively; keyword "*array*" has most importance in cw1 while it has low importance in *cw2, cw4* and *cw7*.

IMPLEMENTATION

In this study, we developed a web-based learning system to implement the proposed methods above. MySQL server 5.0 is used to promote the fast and secure access from the web application. HTML (HyperText Markup Language) and JavaScript used in the client side, and the Servlet and JSP (Java Server Pages) are designed using Eclipse and they are used in Server side. In this implementation, we have used Apache tomcat as a web server. The typical implementation of the web application using tomcat server is shown in Figure 3.

EXPERIMENTATION AND COMPRESSION

In this section, we are going to compute the learning sequencing path by our method and other two methods in the same set of keywords in the courseware. Then we are going to make a quantitative computational and qualitative (feature's based) comparison for our method evaluation.

Proposed Method

The learning path generating is presented in this section. We compute the semantic values for each courseware at different levels of extraction in the coursework. The coursework for Java language programming contains eight course-wares. The

Table 1. Keyword-courseware semantic values

	Semantic Value							
Keyword	*cw1*	*cw2*	*cw3*	*cw4*	*cw5*	*cw6*	*cw7*	*cw8*
Abstract	0	0	0	0		0	0	0
Access	0	0	0	0.196142	0.224762	0	0	0
Annotate	0	0	0	0.126091	0	0	0	0
Append	0	0.075057	0	0	0.021204	0	0	0
Argument	0	0.166197	0	0.106477	0	0	0.038718	0.01752
Arithmetic	0	0.026806	0	0	0	0	0	0
Array	0.348822	0.048251	0	0.050437	0	0	0.035198	0
Assign	0	0	0	0.04203	0	0	0	0
Attributes	0	0	0	0	0	0	0	0.062571
Boolean	0.081121	0.080418	0	0	0	0	0	0
Buffer	0	0	0	0	0	0	0	0.077588
Byte	0.040561	0.026806	0	0	0	0	0	0.111376
Catching	0	0	0	0	0	0	0.087996	0
Character	0	0.369921	0	0	0	0	0	0.062571
Class	0.210916	0.09114	0.308791	0.448325	0	0.298309	0.123194	0.038794
Constant	0	0	0	0.056041	0.343504	0	0	0

keyword's semantic values of each courseware obtained from previous section are used to compute the different semantic value for the courseware.

The following steps are required for learning path sequencing:

Step 1: Compute the semantic value ($n = Kw_i$) for the courseware's keywords (calculated in previous section). Here we will use the alphabet n because this value will change from one level to another level for the same keyword.

Step 2: The common keywords between the course-wares are obtained as follows:

- Level 1 common keywords are the keywords between $CW_i \cap CW_{i+1}$ and i=1, 2, *n-1*
- Level 2 common keywords are the keywords between $CW_{i \cap i+1} \cap CW_{i+1 \cap i+2}$
- Level 3 common keywords are the keywords between $CW_{i \cap i+1 \cap i+2} \cap CW_{i+1 \cap i+2 \cap i+3}$

Figure 3. Typical web implementation

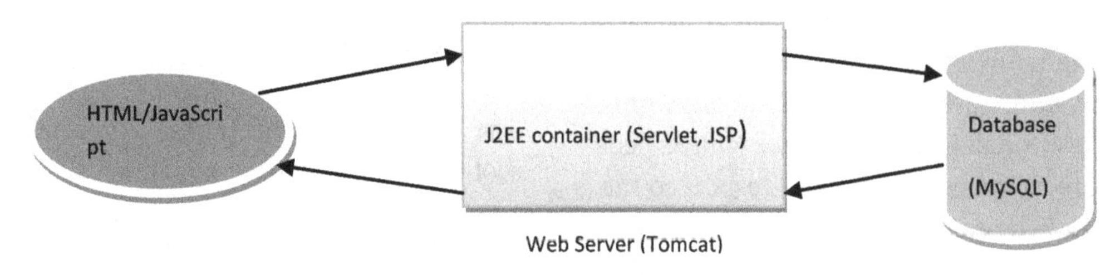

Figure 4. Level of extraction of common and uncommon keyword for course wares

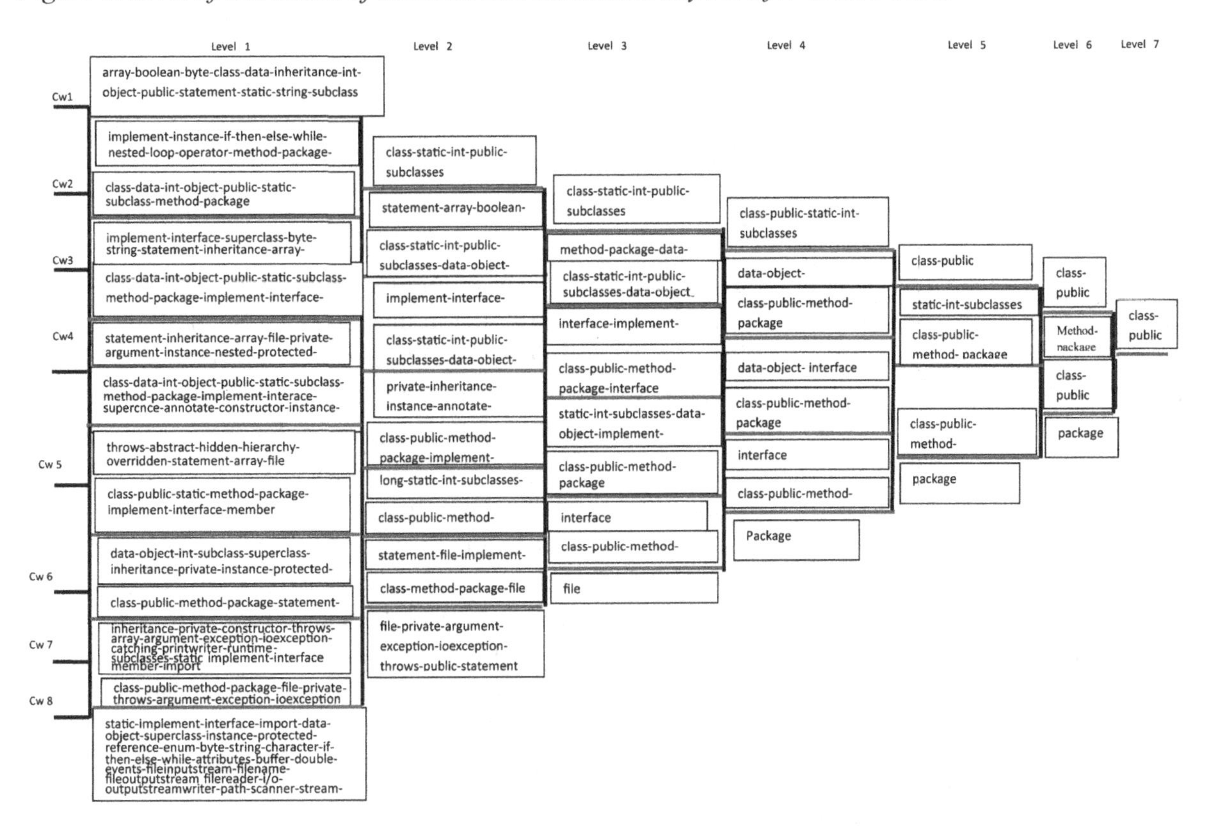

- Level n-1 common keywords are the keywords between $CW_{i \cap i+1 \cap i+2 \dots \cap n-1} \cap cw_{i+1 \cap i+2 \cap i+3 \dots \cap n}$ see Figure 4.

The common keywords between *cw1* and *cw2* in Figure 4 are in the box above the blue line and uncommon keywords are in the box under the blue line (i.e., the box above the blue line is a common keyword and the box under the blue line is uncommon keywords).

Step 3: The keywords in level (l) have less impact on the coursework than the keywords in level $(l+1)$ in the same courseware. We calculate this by multiplying value n of the keyword k in the level (l) as the following: $m = n \times l$.

Step 4: we calculate $\sum p^i K_n^m$ for common keywords in courseware *i* where:

- *n, m* are the courseware and coursework semantic value for common keyword in level (l) respectively,
- *p* is the number of the common keywords in courseware *i*, for each level.

Step 5: Online computation of the difference semantic values for learner's selected courseware as the following:

$$\left|D_{ij}\right| = \sum (n_i - n_j) - (p_i - p_j) - (m_i - m_j)$$

where $i \neq j$ and $j = 1, 2, n$

D_{ij} is used to generate a list of different semantic values for the courseware cw_i to all other course-wares. The courseware with the nearest different semantic value to the

Table 2. Common keyword semantic values for coursework

Courseware	*n*	*p*	*M*
cw1	14.92	61.00	58.79
cw2	24.30	109.00	105.61
cw3	28.10	119.00	171.81
cw4	38.01	159.00	247.72
cw5	33.31	140.00	211.99
cw6	25.32	89.00	113.24
cw7	12.03	75.00	38.81
cw8	20.11	73.00	38.78

courseware cw_i is the next courseware in the sequencing path.

In Table 2 we have calculated the cumulative values of courseware semantic values (*n*), coursework semantic values (*m*) and number of common keywords *(p)* for the course-wares.

The cumulative values of the common semantic values for the selected courseware are used to find the different semantic value between the courseware and the other course-wares, for each courseware cw_i and cw_j where is *i*= 1,2,... to *r* and *j*= 1,2,... to *r*, *r* number of course-wares, and the courseware has the three vector values *n,m* and *p*

$$|D_{ij}| = \sum (n_i - n_j) - (p_i - p_j) - (m_i - m_j)$$

where $i \neq j$

The procedure for learning path sequencing is illustrated in this example: Suppose the learner selects the courseware *cw3* randomly as starting courseware, then the system will compute the different semantic values for this courseware with respect to all other course-wares. After s/he completes the current courseware the next courseware can be found using the computation of the different semantic values for all course-wares except the course-wares which have been selected already, here the courseware with the nearest different semantic value to *cw3* is courseware *cw5* with value (66.40). Similarly we compute the different semantic values for all other course-wares as shown in Table 3.

The learning path with starting courseware cw3 will be *cw3 cw5 cw4 cw2 cw6 cw1 cw8 cw7.*

And with starting courseware cw6 the learning path sequencing will be *cw6 cw2 cw3 cw5 cw4 cw1 cw8 cw7.*

Table 3. Different semantic value for all course-wares

	$\lvert D_{ij}\rvert = \sum (n_i - n_j) - (p_i - p_j) - (m_i - m_j)$							
cw	cw3	cw5	cw4	cw2	cw6	cw1	cw8	cw7
cw1	184.2	250.59	310.02	104.2	92.85	0	------	------
cw2	80	146.39	205.82	0	------	------	------	------
cw3	0	------	------	------	------	------	------	------
cw4	125.82	59.43	0	------	------	------	------	------
cw5	66.39	0	------	------	------	------	------	------
cw6	91.35	157.74	217.17	11.35	0	------	------	------
cw7	193.07	259.46	318.89	113.07	101.72	8.87	6.05	0
cw8	187.02	253.41	312.84	107.02	95.67	2.82	0	------

The computational results based on above example are shown in Figures 5 and 6.

Quantitative Computation and Comparison for Other Method

In learning path perspective, we have compared our result with two different method's (Hsieh & Wang, 2010; Chen, 2008) for the same keywords dataset in the course-wares.

Hsieh and Wang (2010) Method

In Hsieh and Wang (2010) method we have observed:

- Adaptive Term Frequency: Inverse Document Frequency (*ATF-IDF*) algorithm has been used to extract all the significant keywords of every learning object.
- The formal concept analysis approach is used to derive the relationship between concepts using learning objects and attributes (significant keywords) associated with these concepts, these relationships are used to calculate the correlative weighting that represents the coherence between learning objects using Concept Lattice formula.
- The relation between *cwi* and *cwj* is based on the number of co-appearance of *ki, kj* in *cwi*, The relation between *cwj* and *cwi* is based on the number of co-appearance of *kj, ki* in *cwj*.
- The learning path is built based on the learner selection and the correlative matrix with the highest value to the learners' selection.

In Table 4 we have computed the Correlative matrix for the same course-wares using Hsieh and Wang (2010) model.

The learning path obtained using Tung-Cheng's model is *cw3 cw4 cw8 cw5 cw2 cw1 cw6 cw7* which is completely different form the path obtained using our method.

C.-M. Chen, (2008) Method

In Chen (2008) method we have observed:

Figure 5. Selection of the learning course page

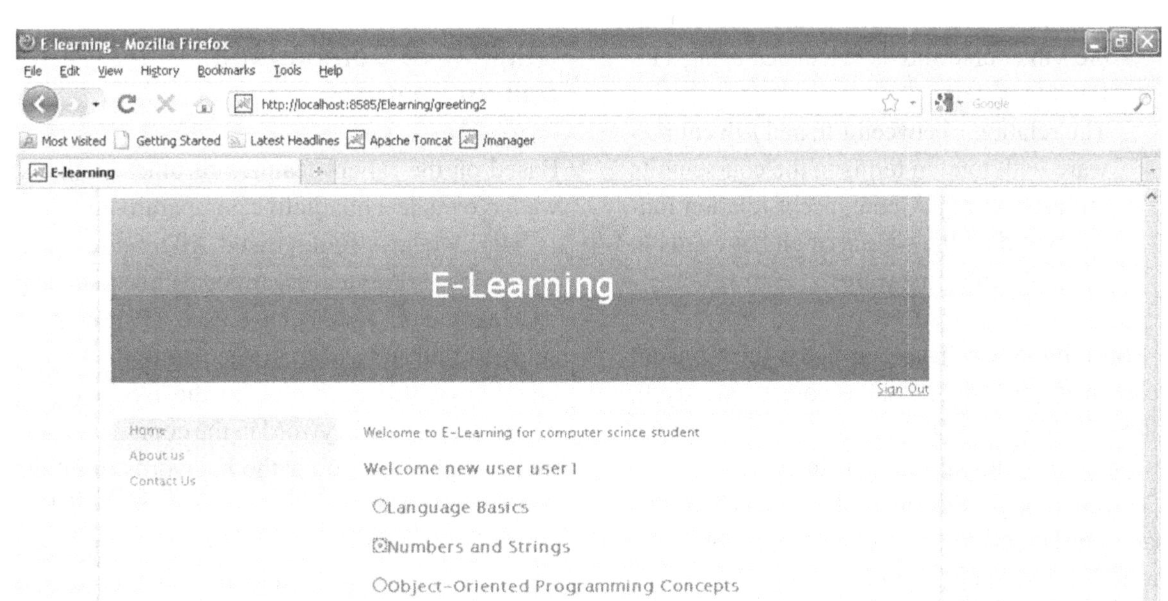

Figure 6. Courseware content for the selected courseware

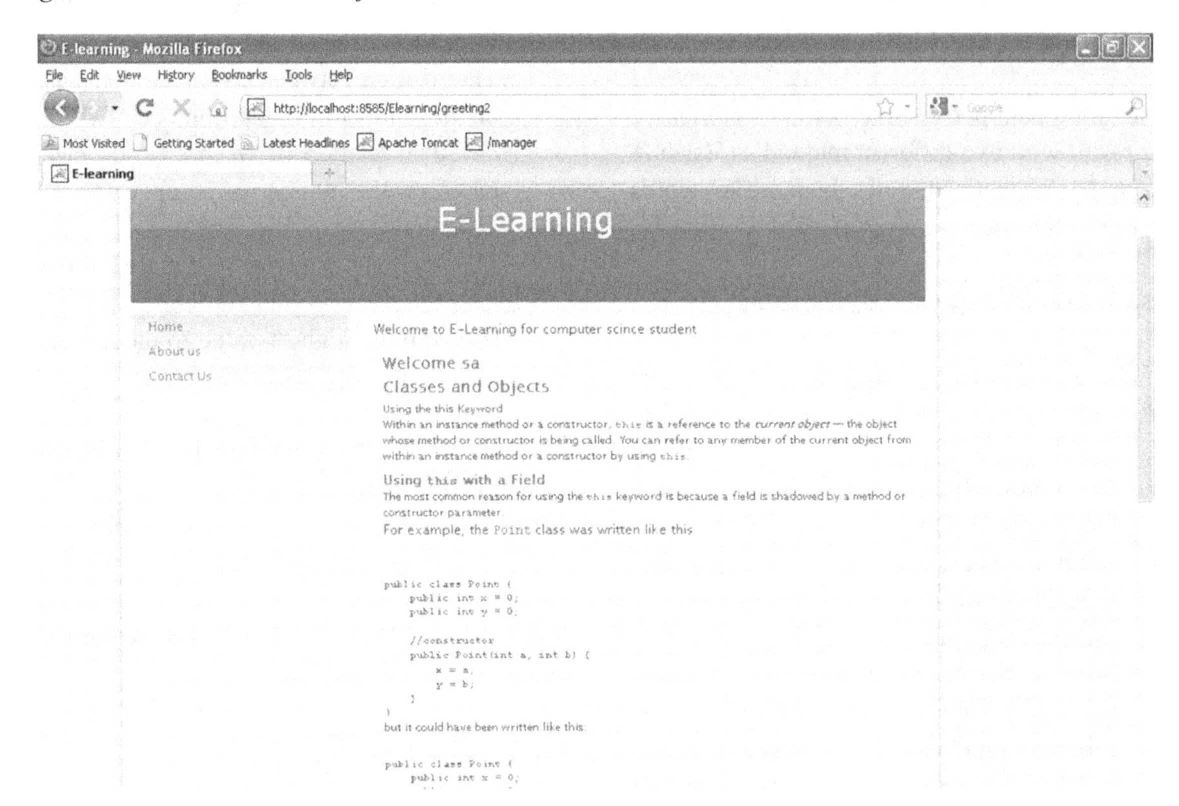

- Vector space model is used to estimate the concept relation degree between two course-wares in multidimensional Euclidean space.
- The importance/weight of the *k*-th term in the *i*-th courseware is calculated using TD-IDF algorithm.
- The relation r between *i*-th and *j*-th courseware with total m terms in the course units are used to build the concept relation matrix based on the weight of all keywords in *i*-th and *j*-th courseware.

In Table 5 we have computed the Concept relation matrix for the same courseware using Chen (2008) model, the comparative view of the two models with our model is in Table 6

Even though the method proposed in this paper is relatively a heuristic one, the path obtained from this method is *cw3 cw5 cw4 cw2 cw6 cw1 cw8 cw7* which is very close to the path *cw3 cw5 cw4 cw2 cw1 cw6 cw8 cw7* obtained using Chen, 2008) model, the difference between paths obtained in our method and Chen, 2008) model is that *cw1* and *cw6* interchanging their positions.

Qualitative Comparison: Salient Features

Based on the salient features of other methods, we have made a qualitative comparative view.

Here we have summarized different research works done in the area of learning path sequencing:

Huang et al. (2007) have used TF-IDF algorithm to find and assign the weight to the importance keywords according to the frequency of occurrence of the keyword in the courseware and their weight is same for the keywords in all the coursework. They calculate the Concept relation matrix or correlative matrix to find the relation between course-wares and use that in fitness

Table 4. Correlative matrix using Hsieh and Wang (2010) method

	cw1	cw2	cw3	cw4	cw5	cw6	cw7	cw8
cw1	1	0.3267	0.1855	0.2735	0.1981	0.0601	0.1021	0.2718
cw2	0.4047	1	0.3723	0.3403	0.2587	0.1389	0.2283	0.3687
cw3	0.1194	0.1617	1	0.2116	0.1813	0.0635	0.0482	0.2228
cw4	0.9999	0.7598	0.9346	1	0.9499	0.4041	0.6993	0.9085
cw5	0.5886	0.4663	0.6543	0.6292	1	0.2816	0.3264	0.5426
cw6	0.1045	0.1987	0.1691	0.2299	0.1655	1	0.1270	0.2306
cw7	0.0925	0.2417	0.0865	0.2471	0.1698	0.0929	1	0.2534
cw8	0.8065	0.8227	0.8049	0.7772	0.6362	0.4174	0.3902	1

function for genetic algorithm to find the optimal learning path.

Nguyen Viet (2008) assigned the weight directly to the courseware (learning object) according to learning object attributes (Prerequisites, Master level, difficulty level, required time, relation, and interaction style). Directed graph is generated to present the learning object, the edge between vertices in the graph represents the relation between course-wares which reveal the difficulty to access a vertex coming from a previous one. Based on knowledge units and the learner's profile (background, skills and style), the shortest path search algorithm and Bayesian Belief Network are used to generate the learning path.

Norsham et al. (2009) have used three weights (1.0, 0.5,0) to the concepts respectively, depending upon the concept if it is very significant and described particularly, slightly described or if the concept is not relevant. The Self organizing map is used to cluster the collection of learning object based on concept similarity. ANN has been used for classification of the combination of learning object and the learner model which consist of personal static data, system usage data and learner's performances to generate the learning path.

Weights of the arrowhead between concepts are given according to the difficulty of the knowledge unit, this knowledge units are represented in a graph. Adjacency matrix is used to find the shortest path in the graph in order to generate the learning path (Chengling & Liyong, 2006).

An analytical hierarchy procedure (AHP) approach has been used to assign a weight to each course using its attitudes, knowledge level, motivation, and learning style. The Neuro-fuzzy

Table 5. Concept relation matrix using Chen (2008)

	cw1	*cw2*	*cw3*	*cw4*	*cw5*	*cw6*	*cw7*	*cw8*
cw1	1	0.2323	0.2503	0.3526	0.2351	0.2804	0.0868	0.0605
cw2	0.2323	1	0.3362	0.5080	0.4140	0.1703	0.1164	0.1970
cw3	0.2503	0.3362	1	0.6167	0.7471	0.2550	0.0829	0.1219
cw4	0.3526	0.5080	0.6167	1	0.7215	0.3812	0.1541	0.1338
cw5	0.2351	0.4140	0.7471	0.7215	1	0.3421	0.1396	0.1251
cw6	0.2804	0.1703	0.2550	0.3812	0.3421	1	0.1453	0.4162
cw7	0.0868	0.1164	0.0829	0.1541	0.1396	0.1453	1	0.1941
cw8	0.0605	0.1970	0.1219	0.1338	0.1251	0.4162	0.1941	1

Table 6. Comparative view of two models with our model

	(Hsieh & Wang, 2010)	(Chen, 2008)	Our Method
Extracting and Assign Weight to the Keyword	ATF-IDF algorithm is used to extract the importance keywords	VSM with TF-IDF are used to extract and assign weight to the important keyword	Keyword-Courseware matrix is calculated using VSM, Euclidean Norm is used to assign the semantic value to the important keyword
The Courseware Relation	The relation depend on the number of co-occurrence of the keywords in two course-wares	The relation depend on the weight of the keywords which is based on TD-IDF algorithm	The relation depends on the difference semantic value between two course-wares which is based on keywords semantic value and number of occurrence the keyword in different levels.
The Obtained Matrix	The matrix is not symmetric because the number of co-appearance of k_i, k_j in cw_i is not equal to and number of co-appearance of k_i, k_j in cw_j	The matrix is symmetric	There is no matrix but the relation between the course-wares are symmetric
Courseware Selection	based on the learners' selection and the courseware with highest value will select as next course	based on the learners' selection and the courseware with highest value will select as next course	based on the learners' selection and the courseware with lowest different semantic value will select as next course
Learning Path	*cw3 cw4 cw8 cw5 cw2 cw1 cw6 cw7*	*cw3 cw5 cw4 cw2 cw1 cw6 cw8 cw7*	*cw3 cw5 cw4 cw2 cw6 cw1 cw8 cw7*

approach has been used to obtain an optimal learning path (Fazlollahtabar & Mahdavi, 2009).

A comparative view of our method with other's method has been shown in Table 7. Most of the researchers in algorithmic methods use ANN, GA and do their implementation in Java,

CONCLUSION

A heuristic method for courseware sequencing for ITS in e-learning system has been developed and implemented using Eclipse IDE for java programming, MySQL as database and Tomcat as a web server. The semantic value of the keyword is obtained based on the importance of the keywords in the courseware at the different levels of extraction. These semantic values are used to find the

Table 7. Comparative view of models

Author	Learning Path Generation Method	Implementation
(Hong, Chen, Chang, & Chen, 2007)	Genetic algorithm	Not specify
(Chen et al., 2005)	Item Response Theory (PEL-IRT)	PHP 4.3 and MySQL server
(Chengling & Liyong, 2006)	Shortest path algorithm	Not specify
(Huang et al., 2007)	Genetic algorithm, Case based reasoning	HTML,JSP
(Norsham et al., 2009)	Artificial neural network	Not specify
(Nguyen Viet, 2008)	Shortest path algorithm, Bayesian Belief Network	Java, MSBNX tool
(Nguyen Viet & Ho Si, 2006)	Bayesian Belief Network	XML
Our Method	Heuristic method	Java, MySql, JSP

relation between the course-wares by computing different semantic values for all course-wares. Another method used the frequency appearance of the keywords, and these methods ignored the importance of the keyword in different courseware which we have kept in our computation of the proposed heuristic method. Other researchers have assigned the weights directly to the course-wares whereas in our work, we have assigned semantic values to the keywords in the courseware. While much of the work of learning path sequencing has been done using ANN and Genetic Algorithm, we have made use of the heuristic method in order to generate the learning path sequencing. Our heuristic method together with other intelligent computing methods like ANN, GA and knowledge based system can be used for this purpose as the scope for further work in this area.

REFERENCES

Chen, C.-M. (2008). Intelligent web-based learning system with personalized learning path guidance. *Computers & Education*, *51*(2), 787–814. doi:10.1016/j.compedu.2007.08.004

Chen, C.-M., Lee, H.-M., & Chen, Y.-H. (2005). Personalized e-learning system using item response theory. *Computers & Education*, *44*(3), 237–255. doi:10.1016/j.compedu.2004.01.006

Chen, P.-I., Lin, S.-J., & Chu, Y.-C. (2011). Using Google latent semantic distance to extract the most relevant information. *Expert Systems with Applications*, *38*(6), 7349–7358. doi:10.1016/j.eswa.2010.12.092

Chengling, Z., & Liyong, W. (2006). A shortest learning path selection algorithm in e-learning. In *Proceedings of the 6th International Conference on Advanced Learning Technologies* (pp. 94-95).

Dadic, T. (2010). Intelligent tutoring system for learning programming. In Stankov, S., Glavinic, V., & Rosic, M. (Eds.), *Intelligent tutoring systems in e-learning environments: Design, implementation and evaluation* (pp. 166–186). Hershey, PA: IGI Global. doi:10.4018/978-1-61692-008-1.ch009

De Lucia, A., Risi, M., Tortora, G., & Scanniello, G. (2007). Clustering algorithms and latent semantic indexing to identify similar pages in web applications. In *Proceedings of the 9th International Workshop on Web Site Evolution* (pp. 65-72).

Deerwester, S., Dumais, S. T., Furnas, G. W., Landauer, T. K., & Harshman, R. (1990). Indexing by latent semantic analysis. *Journal of the American Society for Information Science American Society for Information Science*, *41*(6), 391–407. doi:10.1002/(SICI)1097-4571(199009)41:6<391::AID-ASI1>3.0.CO;2-9

Dever, J., & Keith, B. (2006). *Semantic value encyclopedia of language & linguistics* (pp. 137–142). Oxford, UK: Elsevier.

Fazlollahtabar, H., & Mahdavi, I. (2009). User/tutor optimal learning path in e-learning using comprehensive neuro-fuzzy approach. *Educational Research Review*, *4*(2), 142–155. doi:10.1016/j.edurev.2009.02.001

Foltz, P. W., Laham, D., & Landauer, T. K. (1999). *Automated essay scoring: Applications to educational technology.* Retrieved from http://www-psych.nmsu.edu/ ~pfoltz/reprints/ Edmedia99.html

Haley, D. T., Thomas, P., Nuseibeh, B., Taylor, J., & Lefrere, P. (2005). The learning grid and e-assessment using latent semantic analysis. In *Proceeding of the Conference on Towards the Learning Grid: Advances in Human Learning Services* (pp. 197-202).

Hong, C.-M., Chen, C.-M., Chang, M.-H., & Chen, S.-C. (2007). Intelligent web-based tutoring system with personalized learning path guidance. In *Proceedings of the Seventh IEEE International Conference on Advanced Learning Technologies*, Niigata, Japan (pp. 512-516).

Hsieh, T.-C., & Wang, T.-I. (2010). A mining-based approach on discovering courses pattern for constructing suitable learning path. *Expert Systems with Applications*, *37*(6), 4156–4167. doi:10.1016/j.eswa.2009.11.007

Huang, M.-J., Huang, H.-S., & Chen, M.-Y. (2007). Constructing a personalized e-learning system based on genetic algorithm and case-based reasoning approach. *Expert Systems with Applications*, *33*(3), 551–564. doi:10.1016/j.eswa.2006.05.019

Hull, D. (1994). Improving text retrieval for the routing problem using latent semantic indexing. In *Proceedings of the 17th ACM-SIGIR Conference on Research and Development in Information Retrieval* (pp. 282-291).

Iyengar, G., Nock, H., Neti, C., & Franz, M. (2002). Semantic indexing of multimedia using audio, text and visual cues. In *Proceedings of the Conference on Multimedia Information Systems* (p. 134).

Karypis, G., & Han, E.-H. (2000). Fast supervised dimensionality reduction algorithm with applications to document categorization and retrieval. In *Proceedings of the Ninth International Conference on Information and Knowledge Management* (pp. 12-19).

Lee, C.-H., Yang, H.-C., & Ma, S.-M. (2006). A novel multilingual text categorization system using latent semantic indexing. In *Proceedings of the First International Conference on Innovative Computing, Information and Control* (pp. 503-506).

Lee, M. R. (2000). Context-dependent semantic values for e-negotiation. In *Proceedings of the Second International Workshop on Advanced Issues of E-commerce and Web-based Information Systems* (pp. 41-47).

Li, C. H., & Park, S. C. (2007). Artificial neural network for document classification using latent semantic indexing. In *Proceedings of the International Symposium on Information Technology Convergence* (pp. 17-21).

Lihua, W. JianPing, F., & Yunfen, L. (2009). A personalized intelligent web retrieval system based on the knowledge-base concept and latent semantic indexing model. In *Proceedings of the Seventh ACIS International Conference on Software Engineering Research, Management and Applications* (pp. 45-50).

Lung-Hsiang, W., & Chee-Kit, L. (2010). A survey of optimized learning pathway planning and assessment paper generation with swarm intelligence. In Stankov, S., Glavinic, V., & Rosic, M. (Eds.), *Intelligent tutoring systems in e-learning environments: Design, implementation and evaluation* (*Vol. 14*, pp. 285–302). Hershey, PA: IGI Global.

Mazumdar, B. D., & Mishra, R. B. (2010). Multiagent negotiation in B2C e-commerce based on data mining methods. *International Journal of Intelligent Information Technologies*, *6*(4), 46–70. doi:10.4018/jiit.2010100104

Mishra, K., & Mishra, R. B. (2010). Multiagent based selection of tutor-subject-student paradigm in an intelligent tutoring system. *International Journal of Intelligent Information Technologies*, *6*(1), 46–70. doi:10.4018/jiit.2010100904

Nguyen Viet, A. (2008). Constructing a Bayesian belief network to generate learning path in adaptive hypermedia system. *Journal of Computer Science and Cybermetics*, *1*(24), 12–19.

Nguyen Viet, A., & Ho Si, D. (2006). Applying weighted learning object to build adaptive course in e-learning. In *Proceedings of the Conference on Learning by Effective Utilization of Technologies: Facilitating Intercultural Understanding* (pp. 647-648).

Norsham, I., Norazah, Y., & Puteh, S. (2009). Adaptive course sequencing for personalization of learning path using neural network. *International Journal of Advances in Soft Computing and its Applications*, *4*(1), 49-61.

Reiners, T., & Sassen, I. (2008). A framework for adaptive learning points. In Kidd, T. T., & Song, H. (Eds.), *Handbook of research on instructional systems and technology* (pp. 117–141). Hershey, PA: IGI Global. doi:10.4018/978-1-59904-865-9.ch010

Salton, G., Wong, A., & Yang, C. S. (1975). A vector space model for automatic indexing. *Communications of the ACM, 18*(11), 613–620. doi:10.1145/361219.361220

Seridi, H., Sari, T., Khadir, T., & Sellami, M. (2006). Adaptive instructional planning in intelligent learning systems. In *Proceedings of the Sixth International Conference on Advanced Learning Technologies* (pp. 133-135).

Tai, X., Ren, F., & Kita, K. (2002). An information retrieval model based on vector space method by supervised learning. *Information Processing & Management, 38*(6), 749–764. doi:10.1016/S0306-4573(01)00053-X

Tsai, T., Shih, C.-C., & Chou, S. T. (2006). Personalized blog recommendation using the value, semantic, and social model. In *Proceedings of the Innovations in Information Technology* (pp. 1-5).

van der Spek, P., Klusener, S., & van de Laar, P. (2008). Towards recovering architectural concepts using latent semantic indexing. In *Proceedings of the 12th European Conference on Software Maintenance and Reengineering* (pp. 253-257).

Yang, Y. (1995). Noise reduction in a statistical approach to text categorization. In *Proceedings of the 18th Annual International ACM SIGIR Conference on Research and Development in Information Retrieval*, Seattle, WA (pp. 256-263).

Zelikovitz, S., & Hirsh, H. (2001). Using LSI for text classification in the presence of background text. In *Proceedings of the Tenth International Conference on Information and Knowledge Management*, Atlanta, GA (pp. 113-118).

This work was previously published in the International Journal of Intelligent Information Technologies, Volume 7, Issue 4, edited by Vijayan Sugumaran, pp. 65-80, copyright 2011 by IGI Publishing (an imprint of IGI Global).

Compilation of References

Abbasi, A., Chen, H., & Salem, A. (2008). Sentiment Analysis in Multiple Languages: Feature Selection for Opinion Classification in Web Forums. *ACM Transactions on Information Systems, 26*(3), 12:1-12:34.

Abdennadher, S., & Schlenker, H. (1999). Nurse scheduling using constraint logic programming. In *Proceedings of the 16th National Conference on Artificial Intelligence and the 11th Innovative Applications of Artificial Intelligence Conference* (pp. 838-843).

Abe, S., & Lan, M. S. (1995). A method for fuzzy rule extraction directly from numerical data and its application to pattern classification. *IEEE Transactions on Fuzzy Systems, 3*(1), 18–28. doi:10.1109/91.366565

Abu-Nimeh, S., & Nappa, D. (2003). An empirical comparison of supervised machine learning techniques in bioinformatics. *Research and Practice in Information Technology Series, 33*, 219–222.

Adriani, M., & van Rijsbergen, C. J. (1999). Term similarity-based query expansion for cross-language information retrieval. In J. L. Borbinha & T. Baker (Ed.), *Proceedings of the European Conference on Research and Advanced Technology for Digital Libraries, Research and Advanced Technology for Digital Libraries* (LNCS 1696, pp. 311-322).

Agarwal, N., Haque, E., Liu, H., & Parsons, L. (2006). A subspace clustering framework for research group collaboration. *International Journal of Information Technology and Web Engineering, 1*(1), 35–58. doi:10.4018/jitwe.2006010102

Akjiratikarl, C., Yenradee, P., & Drake, P. R. (2007). PSO-based algorithm for home care worker scheduling in the UK. *Computers & Industrial Engineering, 53*(4), 559–583. doi:10.1016/j.cie.2007.06.002

Alam, S., Dobbie, G., & Riddle, P. (2008). Particle swarm optimization based clustering of web usage data. In *Proceedings of the IEEE/WIC/ACM International Conference on Web Intelligence and Intelligent Agent Technology* (Vol. 3, pp. 451-454).

Al-ani, H. (2007). *A survey: Multi-agent coordination in the meeting-scheduling problem, literature review and survey*. Windsor, ON, Canada: University of Windsor.

Alcal'a, R., Ducange, P., Herrera, F., & Lazzerini, B. (2009). A multi-objective evolutionary approach to concurrently learn rule and data bases of linguistic fuzzy rule-based systems. *IEEE Transactions on Fuzzy Systems, 17*(5), 1106–1122. doi:10.1109/TFUZZ.2009.2023113

Ali, M. (2011). Content-based image classification and retrieval: A rule-based system using rough sets framework. *International Journal of Intelligent Information Technologies, 3*(3), 41–58. doi:10.4018/jiit.2007070103

Alt, M., Hoheisel, A., Pohl, H.-W., & Gorlatch, S. (2006). A Grid Workflow Language Using High-Level Petri Nets. In Wyrzykowski, R. (Ed.), *Parallel Processing and Applied Mathematics* (pp. 715–722). Berlin: Springer. doi:10.1007/11752578_86

Arroyo, S., Cimpian, E., Domingue, J., Feier, C., Fensel, D., König-Ries, B., et al. (2005). *Web Service Modeling Ontology Primer.* Retrieved from http://www.w3.org/Submission/WSMO-primer/

Arshadi, N., & Jurisica, I. (2005). *Feature Selection for Improving Case Based Classifiers on High Dimentional Data Sets*. AAAI.

Artz, J. M. (2007). Philosophical Foundations of Information Modeling. *International Journal of Intelligent Information Technologies, 3*(3), 59–74.

Ashish, N., & Maluf, D. A. (2009). Intelligent information integration: Reclaiming the intelligence. *International Journal of Intelligent Information Technologies, 5*(3), 28–54. doi:10.4018/jiit.2009070102

Azzeh, M., Neagu, D., & Cowling, P. (2008). Improving analogy software effort estimation using fuzzy feature subset selection algorithm. In *Proceedings of the 4th International Workshop on Predictor Models in Software Engineering* (pp. 71-78). New York, NY: ACM Press.

Bach, M. D., Berger, H., & Merkl, D. (2004). Improving domain ontologies by mining semantics from text. In *Proceedings of the First Asia Pacific Conference on Conceptual Modeling* (Vol. 31, pp. 91-100).

Baffo, I., & Confessore, G. (2010). A model to increase the efficiency of a competence-based collaborative network. *International Journal of Intelligent Information Technologies, 6*(1), 18–30. doi:10.4018/jiit.2010100902

Balabanovic, M., & Shoham, Y. (1997). Fab: Content-based, collaborative recommendation. *Communications of the ACM, 40*(3), 66–72. doi:10.1145/245108.245124

Baloglu, A., Wyne, M. F., & Bahctepe, Y. (2010). Web 2.0 based intelligent software architecture for photograph sharing. *International Journal of Intelligent Information Technologies, 6*(4), 17–29. doi:10.4018/jiit.2010100102

Banko, M., & Moore, R. C. (2004). Part of speech tagging in context. In *Proceedings of the 20th International Conference on Computational Linguistics*, Geneva, Switzerland.

Bao, S., Li, R., Yu, Y., & Cao, Y. (2008). Competitor Mining with the Web. *IEEE Transactions on Knowledge and Data Engineering, 20*(10), 1297–1310. doi:10.1109/TKDE.2008.98

Barrett, S. (2007). Optimizing sensor placement for intruder detection with genetic algorithms In *Proceedings of the IEEE Intelligence and Security Informatics* (pp.185-188).

Basu, C., Hirsh, H., & Cohen, V. (1998). Recommendation as classification: Using social and content-based information in recommendation. In *Proceedings of the Fifteenth National Conference on Artificial Intelligence*, Madison, WI (pp. 714-720).

Beck, H. P., Porrer-Woody, S., & Pierce, L. G. (2001). The relations of learning and grade orientations to academic performance. In Hebl, M. R., Brewer, C. L., & Benjamin, L. T. Jr., (Eds.), *Handbook for teaching introductory psychology: With an emphasis on assessment*. Mahwah, NJ: Lawrence Erlbaum.

Beckstrom, M., Croasdale, H., Riad, S. M., & Kamel, M. M. (2004). *Assessment of Egypt's e-learning readiness*. Retrieved from http://www.ltss.bris.ac.uk/events/egypt/ellen/readiness.doc

Belkin, N., & Croft, B. (1992). Information filtering and information retrieval: Two sides of the same coin? *Communications of the ACM, 35*(2). doi:10.1145/138859.138861

Beltran, F. (2005). The use of efficient cost-allocation mechanisms for congestion pricing in data networks with priority service models. *International Journal of Business Data Communications and Networking, 1*(1), 33–49. doi:10.4018/jbdcn.2005010103

Ben Khiroun, O., Elayeb, B., Bounhas, I., Evrard, F., & Bellamine-BenSaoud, N. (in press). A possibilistic approach for semantic query expansion. In *Proceedings of the 4th International Conference on Internet Technologies and Application*, Wrexham Wales, UK.

Benferhat, S., Dubois, D., Garcia, L., & Prade, H. (2002). On the transformation between possibilistic logic bases and possibilistic causal networks. *International Journal of Approximate Reasoning, 29*(2), 135–173. doi:10.1016/S0888-613X(01)00061-5

BenHassine, A., Ho, T., & Ito, T. (2006). Meeting scheduling solver enhancement with local consistency reinforcement. *International Journal of Applied Intelligence, 24*(2), 143–154. doi:10.1007/s10489-006-6935-y

Bennett, R. (2003). Determinants of undergraduate student dropout rates in a university business studies department. *Journal of Further and Higher Education, 27*(2), 123–141. doi:10.1080/030987703200065154

Berger, A., Pietra, V., & Pietra, S. (1996). A Maximum Entropy approach to Natural Language Processing. *Computational Linguistics, 22*(1), 39–71.

Berners-Lee, T., Hendler, J., & Lassila, O. (2001). The Semantic Web. *Scientific American, 284*(5), 28–37. doi:10.1038/scientificamerican0501-34

Bethard, S., Yu, H., Thornton, A., Hatzivassiloglou, V., & Jurafsky, D. (2004). Automatic Extraction of Opinion Propositions and their Holders. In Y. Qu, J. Shanahan, & J. Wiebe (Eds.), *Proceedings of the AAAI Spring Symposium on Exploring Attitude and Affect in Text: Theories and Applications,* Stanford, CA (pp. 1-8).

Bhide, A. (1994). Efficient markets, deficient governance: U.S. securities regulations protect investors and enhance market liquidity. But do they alienate managers and shareholders? *Harvard Business Review, 72*(6), 128–140.

Biggs, J. B. (1989). Approaches to the enhancement of tertiary teaching. *Higher Education Research & Development, 8*, 7–25. doi:10.1080/0729436890080102

Biggs, J. B. (2003). *Teaching for quality learning at university*. Buckingham, UK: The Society for Research into Higher Education.

Bi, J., & Su, Y. (2009). Expansion method for language-crossed query based on latent semantic analysis. *Computer Engineering, 10*, 49–51.

Bloom, B., & Englehart, M. Furst, E., Hill, W., & Krathwohl, D. (1956). *Taxonomy of educational objectives, the classification of educational goals--Handbook I: Cognitive domain.* New York, NY: McKay.

Boley, D., Gini, M., Gross, R., Han, E. H., Hastings, K., & Karypis, G. (1999). Document categorization and query generation on the World Wide Web using WebACE. *Artificial Intelligence Review, 13*(5), 365–391. doi:10.1023/A:1006592405320

Boley, D., Gini, M., Gross, R., Han, E. H., Hastings, K., & Karypis, G. (1999). Partitioning-based clustering for Web document categorization. *Decision Support Systems, 27*(3), 329–341. doi:10.1016/S0167-9236(99)00055-X

Borgelt, C., Gebhardt, J., & Kruse, R. (1998). Possibilistic graphical models. In *Proceedings of the International School for the Synthesis of Expert Knowledge*, Udine, Italy (pp. 51-68).

Borgman, C. L. (1984). *The user's mental model of an information retrieval system: Effect on performance.* Unpublished doctoral dissertation, Stanford University, Stanford, CA.

Boskovic, M., Bagheri, E., Gasevic, D., Mohabbati, B., Kaviani, N., & Hatala, M. (2010). Automated staged configuration with semantic web technologies. *International Journal of Software Engineering and Knowledge Engineering, 20*(4), 459–484. doi:10.1142/S0218194010004827

Bostrom, R. P., Olfman, L., & Sein, M. K. (1990). Learning style of end users. *Management Information Systems Quarterly*, 101–119. doi:10.2307/249313

Bourigault, D. (2002). Upery: Un outil d'analyse distributionnelle étendue pour la construction d'ontologies à partir de corpus. In *Proceedings of the Actes de la 9ième Conférence Annuelle sur le Traitement Automatique des Langues*, Paris, France (pp. 75-84).

Braga, P. L., Oliveira, A. L. I., & Meira, S. R. L. (2008). A GA-based feature selection and parameters optimization for support vector regression applied to software effort estimation. In *Proceedings of the ACM Symposium on Applied Computing* (pp. 1788-1792). New York, NY: ACM Press.

Bremen, J. K. (2011) *Simulation supports production planning and scheduling.* Retrieved from http://www.sim-serv.com/pdf/news/news_32.pdf

Brini, A., & Boughanem, M. (2003). Relevance feedback: Introduction of partial assessments for query expansion. In *Proceedings of the 3rd International Conference in Fuzzy Logic and Technology* (pp. 67-72).

Brini, A., Boughanem, M., & Dubois, D. (2004). Towards a possibilistic approach for information retrieval. In *Proceedings of the EUROFUSE Workshop on Data and Knowledge Engineering* (pp. 92-102).

Brown, J. (2000). Growing up digital: How the web changes work, education, and the ways people learn. *Change*, 10–20.

Buckley, C., & Salton, G. (1995). Optimization of relevance feedback weights. In *Proceedings of the 18th Annual International ACM/SIGIR Conference on Research and Development in Information Retrieval* (pp. 351-357).

Buitelaar, P., & Cimiano, P. (2008). *Ontology learning and population: Bridging the gap between text and knowledge*. Amsterdam, The Netherlands: IOS Press.

Bunescu, R., & Mooney, J. (2005). A shortest path dependency kernel for relation extraction. In R. Mooney (Ed.), *Proceedings of the Conference on Human Language Technology and Empirical Methods in Natural Language Processing,* Vancouver, BC, Canada (pp. 724-731).

Bunescu, R., & Mooney, R. (2006). Subsequence Kernels for Relation Extraction. In Weiss, Y., Schlkopf, B., & Platt, J. (Eds.), *Advances in Neural Information Processing Systems 18* (pp. 171–178). Cambridge, MA: MIT Press.

Burton-Jones, A., Storey, V. C., Sugumaran, V., & Ahluwalia, P. (2005). A semiotic metrics suite for assessing the quality of ontologies. *Data & Knowledge Engineering, 55*(1), 84–102. doi:10.1016/j.datak.2004.11.010

Cabral, L., Domingue, J., Motta, E., Payne, T. R., & Hakimpour, F. (2004, May 10-12). Approaches to Semantic Web Services: an Overview and Comparisons. In J. Davies, C. Bussler, & R. Studer (Eds.), *The Semantic Web: Research and Applications, Proceedings of the First European Semantic Web Symposium, ESWS 2004,* Heraklion, Crete, Greece (pp. 225-239). Berlin: Springer.

Calheiros, R. N., Ranjan, R., Beloglazov, A., De Rose, C. A. F., & Buyya, R. (2010). *Cloudsim: A toolkit for modeling and simulation of cloud computing environments and evaluation of resource provisioning algorithms: Software: Practice and experience*. New York, NY: John Wiley & Sons.

Camarinha-Matos, L. M., Afsarmanesh, H., & Ollus, M. (2005). *Virtual Organizations: Systems and Practices*. Berlin: Springer. doi:10.1007/b102339

Cao, T. H., Do, H. T., Hong, D. T., & Quan, T. T. (2008). Fuzzy named entity-based document clustering. In *Proceedings of the IEEE International Conference on Fuzzy Systems* (pp. 2028-2034).

Carbonneau, R., & Vahidov, R. (2007). Machine Learning-Based Demand Forecasting in Supply Chains. *International Journal of Intelligent Information Technologies, 3*(4), 40–57.

Cardoso, J., & Sheth, A. P. (2005). Introduction to Semantic Web Services and Web Process Composition. In J. Cardoso & A. Sheth (Eds.), *First International Workshop on Semantic Web Services and Web Process Composition, SWSWPC 2004* (pp. 1-13). Berlin: Springer.

Carlisle, A., & Dozler, G. (2002). Tracking changing extrema with adaptive particle swarm optimizer. In *Proceedings of Soft Computing*. Multimedia, Biomedicine, Image Processing and Financial Engineering.

Carolan, T., Collins, B., et al. (1997). *Intelligent agents.* Retrieved from http://ntrg.cs.tcd.ic/cs4/

Carrasco, A., Romero-Ternero, M. C., Sivianes, F., Hernández, M. D., Oviedo, D. I., & Escudero, J. (2010). Facilitating decision making and maintenance for power systems operators through the use of agents and distributed embedded systems. *International Journal of Intelligent Information Technologies, 6*(4), 1–16. doi:10.4018/jiit.2010100101

Casillas, A., Lena, M. T., & Martínez, R. (2003). Document clustering into an unknown number of clusters using a genetic algorithm. In V. Matoušek & P. Mautner (Eds.), *Proceedings of the 6th International Conference on Text, Speech and Dialogue* (LNCS 2807, pp. 43-49).

Castells, P., Fernandez, M., & Vallet, D. (2007). An adaption of the vector space model for ontology based information retrieval. *IEEE Transactions on Knowledge and Data Engineering, 19*(2), 261–271. doi:10.1109/TKDE.2007.22

Castillo, L., Gonzalez, A., & Perez, P. (2001). Including a simplicity criterion in the selection of the best rule in a genetic fuzzy learning algorithm. *Fuzzy Sets and Systems, 120*(2), 309–321. doi:10.1016/S0165-0114(99)00095-0

Chakrabarti, S., Dom, B. E., Gibson, D., Kleinberg, J., Kumar, R., & Raghavan, P. (1999). Mining the link structure of the World Wide Web. *IEEE Computer, 32*(8), 60–67.

Chan, V. K. Y., & Wong, W. E. (2007). Outlier elimination in construction of software metric models. In *Proceedings of the ACM Symposium on Applied Computing* (pp. 1484-1488). New York, NY: ACM Press.

Chau, M., & Xu, J. (2007). Mining communities and their relationships in blogs: A study of online hate groups. *International Journal of Human-Computer Studies*, *65*(1), 57–70. doi:10.1016/j.ijhcs.2006.08.009

Chen , K. (1999). Automatic Identification of Subjects for Textual Documents in Digital Libraries.

Chen, C.-M. (2008). Intelligent web-based learning system with personalized learning path guidance. *Computers & Education*, *51*(2), 787–814. doi:10.1016/j.compedu.2007.08.004

Chen, C.-M., Lee, H.-M., & Chen, Y.-H. (2005). Personalized e-learning system using item response theory. *Computers & Education*, *44*(3), 237–255. doi:10.1016/j.compedu.2004.01.006

Chen, F., & Li, F. (2010). Comparison of the Hybrid Credit Scoring Models Based on Various Classifiers. *International Journal of Intelligent Information Technologies*, *6*(3), 56–74.

Chen, F., & Li, F. (2011). Comparison of the hybrid credit scoring models based on various classifiers. *International Journal of Intelligent Information Technologies*, *6*(3), 56–74. doi:10.4018/jiit.2010070104

Chengling, Z., & Liyong, W. (2006). A shortest learning path selection algorithm in e-learning. In *Proceedings of the 6th International Conference on Advanced Learning Technologies* (pp. 94-95).

Chen, H. (2006). Intelligence and security informatics: information systems perspective. *Decision Support Systems*, *41*(3), 555–559. doi:10.1016/j.dss.2004.06.003

Chen, P.-I., Lin, S.-J., & Chu, Y.-C. (2011). Using Google latent semantic distance to extract the most relevant information. *Expert Systems with Applications*, *38*(6), 7349–7358. doi:10.1016/j.eswa.2010.12.092

Chen, T. (2009). A tailored nonlinear fluctuation smoothing rule for semiconductor manufacturing factory scheduling. *Proceedings of the Institution of Mechanical Engineers. Part I, Journal of Systems and Control Engineering*, *223*, 149–160. doi:10.1243/09596518JSCE625

Chen, T. (2009). Dynamic fuzzy-neural fluctuation smoothing rule for jobs scheduling in a wafer fabrication factory. *Proceedings of the Institution of Mechanical Engineers. Part I, Journal of Systems and Control Engineering*, *223*, 1081–1094. doi:10.1243/09596518JSCE849

Chen, T. (2009). Fuzzy-neural-network-based fluctuation smoothing rule for reducing the cycle times of jobs with various priorities in a wafer fabrication factory - a simulation study. *Proceedings of the Institution of Mechanical Engineers. Part B, Journal of Engineering Manufacture*, *223*, 1033–1044. doi:10.1243/09544054JEM1459

Chen, T. (2010). A fuzzy-neural approach with collaboration mechanisms for semiconductor yield forecasting. *International Journal of Intelligent Information Technologies*, *6*(3), 17–33. doi:10.4018/jiit.2010070102

Chen, T. (2010). An optimized tailored nonlinear fluctuation smoothing rule for scheduling a semiconductor manufacturing factory. *Computers & Industrial Engineering*, *58*, 317–325. doi:10.1016/j.cie.2009.11.006

Chen, T. (2011). Applying a fuzzy and neural approach for forecasting the foreign exchange rate. *International Journal of Fuzzy System Applications*, *1*(1), 36–48.

Chen, T., & Chia, F. (2010). A fuzzy-neural approach with collaboration mechanisms for semiconductor yield forecasting. *International Journal of Intelligent Information Technologies*, *6*(3), 17–33. doi:10.4018/jiit.2010070102

Chen, T., & Lin, C. H. (2010). A modified DBD system for scheduling jobs in a wafer fabrication factory. *International Review on Computers and Software*, *5*(4), 396–405.

Chen, T., & Lin, Y.-C. (2009). A fuzzy back-propagation-network ensemble with example classification for lot output time prediction in a wafer fab. *Applied Soft Computing*, *9*(2), 658–666. doi:10.1016/j.asoc.2008.04.018

Chen, T., & Lin, Y.-C. (2009). A fuzzy-neural fluctuation smoothing rule for scheduling jobs with various priorities a semiconductor manufacturing factory. *International Journal of Uncertainty Fuzziness and Knowledge-Based Systems, 17*(3), 397–417. doi:10.1142/S0218488509005942

Chen, T., & Wang, Y.-C. (2009). A bi-criteria nonlinear fluctuation smoothing rule incorporating the SOM-FBPN remaining cycle time estimator for scheduling a wafer fab - a simulation study. *International Journal of Advanced Manufacturing Technology, 49*, 709–721. doi:10.1007/s00170-009-2424-x

Chen, T., Wang, Y.-C., & Lin, Y.-C. (2010). A bi-criteria four-factor fluctuation smoothing rule for scheduling jobs in a wafer fabrication factory. *International Journal of Innovative Computing. Information and Control, 6*(10), 4289–4303.

Chen, T., Wang, Y.-C., & Lin, Y.-C. (2010). A fuzzy-neural system for scheduling a wafer fabrication factory. *International Journal of Innovative Computing. Information and Control, 6*(2), 687–700.

Chen, T., Wang, Y.-C., & Wu, H.-C. (2009). A fuzzy-neural approach for remaining cycle time estimation in a semiconductor manufacturing factory – A simulation study. *International Journal of Innovative Computing. Information and Control, 5*(8), 2125–2139.

Chouaib, H. (2006). *Reformulation de requêtes dans un modèle de réseau possibiliste pour la recherche d'information*. Unpublished master's thesis, Liban University, Bayrout, Lebanon.

Chua, C. E. H., Chiang, R. H. L., & Storey, V. C. (2009). Building customized search engines: An interoperability architecture. *International Journal of Intelligent Information Technologies, 5*(3), 1–27. doi:10.4018/jiit.2009070101

Chulani, S., Boehm, B., & Steece, B. (1999). Bayesian analysis of empirical software engineering cost models. *IEEE Transactions on Software Engineering, 25*(4), 573–583. doi:10.1109/32.799958

Chun, A., Wai, H., & Wong, R. (2003). Optimizing agent-based meeting scheduling through preference estimation. *Engineering Applications of Artificial Intelligence, 16*(7), 727–743. doi:10.1016/j.engappai.2003.09.009

Claveau, V., Sébillot, P., & De Beaulieu, C. (2004). Extension de requêtes par lien sémantique nom-verbe acquis sur corpus. In *Proceedings of the Actes de la 11ème Conférence de Traitement Automatique des Langues Naturelles*.

Coffman, E. G. (1976). *Computer and job-shop scheduling theory*. New York, NY: John Wiley & Sons.

Cogger, K. O., & Yu, P. L. (1985). Eigen weight vectors and least distance approximation for revealed preference in pairwise weight ratio. *Journal of Optimization Theory and Applications, 46*, 483–491. doi:10.1007/BF00939153

Colas, F., & Brazdil, P. (2006). *Comparison of SVM and Some Older Classification Algorithms in Text Classification Tasks*. Santiago, Chile: International Federation for Information Processing.

Conejo, R., Guzman, E., Millian, E., Trella, M., Perez-De-La-Cruz, J. L., & Rioz, A. (2004). SIETTE: A web-based tool for adaptive testing. *International Journal of Artificial Intelligence in Education, 14*, 29–61.

Conrad, K., & TrainningLinks (2000), *Instructional design for web-based training*. Amherst, MA: HRD Press.

Conte, S., Dunsmore, H., & Shen, V. Y. (1986). *Software engineering metrics and models*. Redwood City, CA: Benjamin-Cummings.

Coppola, M., Jégou, Y., Matthews, B., Morin, C., Prieto, L. P., & Sánchez, O. D. (2008). Virtual organization support within a grid-wide operating system. *IEEE Internet Computing, 12*(2), 20–28. doi:10.1109/MIC.2008.47

Corcho, O., Fernández-López, M., & Gómez-Pérez, A. (2003). Methodologies, tools and languages for building ontologies. Where is their meeting point? *Data & Knowledge Engineering, 46*(1), 41–64. doi:10.1016/S0169-023X(02)00195-7

Cordon, O., Gomide, F., Herrera, F., Hoffmann, F., & Magdalena, L. (2004). Ten years of genetic fuzzy systems: Current framework and new trends. *Fuzzy Sets and Systems, 141*(1), 5–31. doi:10.1016/S0165-0114(03)00111-8

Crabtree, D. (2009). Enhancing web search through query expansion. In Wang, J. (Ed.), *Encyclopedia of data warehousing and mining* (2nd ed., pp. 752–757). Hershey, PA: IGI Global.

Crawford, E. (2009). *Learning to improve negotiation in semi-cooperative agreement problem.* Unpublished doctoral dissertation, Carnegie Mellon University, Pittsburgh, PA.

Crawford, E., & Veloso, M. (2004). Mechanism design for multi-agent meeting scheduling, including timepreferences, availability, and value of presence. In *Proceedings of the International Conference on Intelligent Agent Technology* (pp. 253- 259).

Crawford, E., & Veloso, M. (2005). Learning dynamic preferences in multi-agentmeeting scheduling. In *Proceedings of the IEEE/WIC/ACM International Conference on Intelligent Agent Technology.*

Cristani, M., & Cuel, R. (2005). A survey on ontology creation methodologies. *International Journal on Semantic Web and Information Systems, 1*(2), 49–69. doi:10.4018/jswis.2005040103

Croft, B., & Harper, D. J. (1979). Using probabilistic models of document retrieval without relevance information. *The Journal of Documentation, 35*(4), 285–295. doi:10.1108/eb026683

Cronbach, L., & Snow, R. (1977). *Aptitudes and instructional methods: A handbook for research on interactions.* New York, NY: Irvington.

Cuadrado-Gallego, J. J., Sicilia, M.-A., Garre, M., & Rodriguez, D. (2006). An empirical study of process-related attributes in segmented software cost-estimation relationships. *Journal of Systems and Software, 79*(3), 353–361. doi:10.1016/j.jss.2005.04.040

Cui, X., & Potok, T. E. (2005). Document clustering analysis based on hybrid PSO+K-means algorithm. *Journal of Computer Sciences*, 27-33.

Cui, X., & Potok, T. E. (2007). Distributed adaptive particle swarm optimizer in dynamic environment. In *Proceedings of the International Symposium on Parallel and Distributed Processing* (p. 1).

Cui, X., Potok, T. E., & Palathingal, P. (2005). Document clustering using particle swarm optimization. In *Proceedings of the IEEE Swarm Intelligence Symposium*, Pasadena, CA (pp. 185-191).

Culotta, A., & Sorensen, J. (2004). Dependency tree kernels for relation extraction. In D. Scott (Ed.), *Proceedings of the 42nd Annual Meeting on Association for Computational Linguistics,* Barcelona, Spain (pp. 423:1-423:7).

Cunningham, H. (2002). GATE, a general architecture for text engineering. *Computers and the Humanities, 36*, 223–254. doi:10.1023/A:1014348124664

D'Avanzo, E., Magnini, B., et al. (2004). *Keyphrase Extraction for Summarization Purposes: The LAKE System.* Paper presented at DUC-2004: Document Understanding Workshop, Boston.

Dadic, T. (2010). Intelligent tutoring system for learning programming. In Stankov, S., Glavinic, V., & Rosic, M. (Eds.), *Intelligent tutoring systems in e-learning environments: Design, implementation and evaluation* (pp. 166–186). Hershey, PA: IGI Global. doi:10.4018/978-1-61692-008-1.ch009

Dahlem, N., & Hahn, A. (2009). *User-Friendly Ontology Creation Methodologies - A Survey.* Paper presented at the 15th Americas Conference on Information Systems (AMCIS 2009).

Dahlem, N., Guo, J., Hahn, A., & Reinelt, M. (2009). *Towards a user-friendly ontology design methodology.* Paper presented at the International Conference on Interoperability for Enterprise Software and Applications (I-ESA 2009).

Dahlem, N. (2011). OntoClippy: A user-friendly ontology design and creation methodology. *Journal of Intelligent Information Technologies, 7*(1), 15–32. doi:10.4018/jiit.2011010102

Dahlgren, K. (1995). A linguistic ontology. *International Journal of Human-Computer Studies, 43*(5-6), 809–818. doi:10.1006/ijhc.1995.1075

Dash, R., Mishra, D., Rath, A. K., & Acharya, M. (2010). A hybridized K-means clustering approach for high dimensional dataset. *International Journal of Engineering. Science and Technology, 2*(2), 59–66.

D'Avanzo, E., Frixione, M., et al. (2006). *LAKE system.* Paper presented at DUC-2006.

De Campos, L. M., Fernandez-Luna, J. M., & Huete, J. F. (2003). The BNR model: Foundations and performance of Bayesian Network-based retrieval model. *Journal of the American Society for Information Science and Technology, 54*(4), 302–313. doi:10.1002/asi.10210

De Lucia, A., Risi, M., Tortora, G., & Scanniello, G. (2007). Clustering algorithms and latent semantic indexing to identify similar pages in web applications. In *Proceedings of the 9th International Workshop on Web Site Evolution* (pp. 65-72).

De Nicola, A., Missikoff, M., & Navigli, R. (2005). *A proposal for a unified process for ontology building: upon*. Paper presented at Database and Expert Systems Applications.

De Silva, L., & Jayaratne, L. (2009). WikiOnto: A system for semi-automatic extraction and modeling of ontologies using Wikipedia XML corpus. In *Proceedings of the Semantic Web Information Workshop and the 3rd IEEE International Conference on Semantic Computing*, Berkeley, CA.

Deerwester, S., Dumais, S. T., Furnas, G. W., Landauer, T. K., & Harshman, R. (1990). Indexing by latent semantic analysis. *Journal of the American Society for Information Science American Society for Information Science, 41*(6), 391–407. doi:10.1002/(SICI)1097-4571(199009)41:6<391::AID-ASI1>3.0.CO;2-9

Dempster, A. P., Laird, N. M., & Rubin, D. B. (1977). Maximum likelihood from incomplete data via the EM algorithm. *Journal of the Royal Statistical Society. Series B. Methodological*, 1–38.

Deng, J., Hu, J. L., Chi, H., & Wu, J. (2010). An improved fuzzy clustering method for text mining. In *Proceedings of the Second International Conference on Networks Security Wireless Communications and Trusted Computing* (pp. 65-69).

Deng, J. D., Simmermacher, C., & Cranefield, S. (2008). A study on feature analysis for musical instrument classification. *IEEE Transactions on Systems, Man, and Cybernetics. Part B, 38*(2), 429–438.

Dennis, A. R., & Carte, T. A. (1998). Using geographical information systems for decision making: Extending cognitive fit theory to map-based presentations. *Information Systems Research, 9*(2), 194–203. doi:10.1287/isre.9.2.194

Devaraj, D., & Ganeshkumar, P. (2010). Mixed genetic algorithm approach for fuzzy classifier design. *International Journal of Computational Intelligence and Applications, 9*(1), 49–67. doi:10.1142/S1469026810002768

Dever, J., & Keith, B. (2006). *Semantic value encyclopedia of language & linguistics* (pp. 137–142). Oxford, UK: Elsevier.

Dhillon, I. S., & Modha, D. S. (2001). Concept decompositions for large sparse text data using clustering. *Machine Learning, 42*, 143–175. doi:10.1023/A:1007612920971

Dikaiakos, M. D., Pallis, G., Katsaros, D., Mehra, P., & Vakali, A. (2009). Cloud computing–distributed internet computing for IT and scientific research. *IEEE Internet Computing, 13*(5), 10–13. doi:10.1109/MIC.2009.103

Dimitrova, V., Denaux, R., Hart, G., Dolbear, C., Holt, I., & Cohn, A. G. (2008). Involving Domain Experts in Authoring OWL Ontologies. In *Proceedings of the 7th International Semantic Web Conference, ISWC 2008.*

Ding, Y., & Foo, S. (2002). Ontology research and development. Part 1: A review of ontology generation. *Journal of Information Science, 28*(2), 123.

Divoli, A., & Attwood, T. (2005). BioIE: extracting informative sentences from the biomedical literature. *Bioinformatics (Oxford, England), 21*, 2138–2139. doi:10.1093/bioinformatics/bti296

Dolenc, M., Klinc, R., Turk, Z., Katranuschkov, P., & Kurowski, K. (2008). Semantic Grid Platform in Support of Engineering Virtual Organisations. *Informatica, 32*(1), 39–49.

Dos Santos, I. J. G., & Madeira, E. R. M. (2010). Semantic-enabled middleware for citizen-centric e-government services. *International Journal of Intelligent Information Technologies, 6*(3), 34–55. doi:10.4018/jiit.2010070103

Dubois, D., & Prade, H. (1987). *Théorie des possibilités: Application à la représentation des connaissances en informatique*. Paris, France: Edition Masson.

Dubois, D., & Prade, H. (1998). Possibility theory: Qualitative and quantitative aspects. In Gabbay, D. M., & Smets, P. (Eds.), *Handbook of defeasible reasoning and uncertainty management systems* (*Vol. 1*, pp. 169–226). Dordrecht, The Netherlands: Kluwer Academic.

Dubois, D., & Prade, H. (2004). *Possibility theory: An approach to computerized processing of uncertainty*. New York, NY: Plenum Press.

Dumais, S. T., & Chen, H. (2000). Hierarchical classification of web content. In *Proceedings of the SIGIR 23rd ACM International Conference on Research and Development in Information Retrieval* (pp. 256-263).

Dumais, S. T., Platt, J., et al. (1998). Inductive Learning Algorithms and Representations for Text Categorization. In *Proceedings of the Information and Knowledge Management 7th International Conference.* New York: ACM Press.

Dunn, J. C. (1973). A fuzzy relative of the ISODATA process and its use in detecting compact well-separated clusters. *Cybernetics and Systems*, *3*(3), 32–57. doi:10.1080/01969727308546046

Du, W., & Li, B. (2008). Multi-strategy ensemble particle swarm optimization for dynamic optimization. *International Journal of Information Sciences*, *178*(15), 3096–3109.

Dweck, C. S. (1986). Motivational processes affecting learning. *The American Psychologist*, *41*(10), 1040–1048. doi:10.1037/0003-066X.41.10.1040

Eberhart, R. C., & Kennedy, J. (1995). A new optimizer using particle swarm theory. In *Proceedings of the Sixth International Symposium on Micromachine and Human Science* (pp. 39-43).

Eberhart, R. C., & Shi, Y. (2001). Tracking and optimizing dynamic systems with particle swarms. In. *Proceedings of the Congress on Evolutionary Computation*, *1*, 94.

Edwin, D. J., Thierens, D., & Watson, R. A. (2004). Hierarchical genetic algorithms. In X. Yao, E. Burke, J. A. Lozano, J. Smith, J. J. Merelo-Guervos, J. A. Bullinaria et al. (Eds.), *Proceedings of the 8th International Conference on Parallel Problem Solving from Nature* (LNCS 3242, pp. 232-241).

Eisenhardt, M., Muller, W., & Henrich, A. (2003). Classifying documents by distributed p2p clustering. In *Proceedings of the Annual Informatik Meeting on Innovative Information Technology Uses*, Frankfurt, Germany (pp. 286-291).

Elayeb, B. (2009). *SARIPOD: Système multi-agent de recherche intelligente possibiliste de documents web*. Unpublished doctoral dissertation, Institut National Polytechnique de Toulouse, Toulouse, France.

Elayeb, B., Evrard, F., Zaghdoud, M., & Ben Ahmed, M. (2009). Towards an intelligent possibilistic web information retrieval using multiagent system. *International Journal of Interactive Technology and Smart Education*, *6*(1), 40–59. doi:10.1108/17415650910965191

El-Beltagy, S. (2006). KP-Miner: A Simple System for Effective Keyphrase Extraction. In *Proceedings of the Innovation in Information Technology Conference*. Washington, DC: IEEE Computer Society.

Elish, M. O. (2009). Improved estimation of software project effort using multiple additive regression trees. *Expert Systems with Applications*, *36*(7), 10774–10778. doi:10.1016/j.eswa.2009.02.013

Engelbrecht, A. P. (2007). *Computational intelligence: An introduction* (2nd ed.). New York, NY: John Wiley & Sons.

Enríquez Perdomo, A. (2006). *Enfoque semántico para la gestión de sitios web*. Unpublished master's thesis.

Ephrati, E., Zlotkin, G., & Rosenschein, J. (1996). A non-manipulable meeting scheduling system. In *Proceedings of the 13th International Distributed Artificial Intelligence Workshop* (pp. 105-125).

Ertl, A. (2008). *How much electricity does a computer consume?* Retrieved from http://www.complang.tuwien.ac.at/anton/computer-power-consumption.html

Euzenat, J., & Shvaiko, P. (2007). *Ontology matching*. Berlin, Germany: Springer-Verlag.

Fagni, T., Perego, R., Silvestri, F., & Orlando, S. (2006). Boosting the performance of web search engines: Caching and prefetching query results by exploiting historical usage data. *ACM Transactions on Information Systems*, *24*(1), 78.

Farquhar, A., Fikes, R., & Rice, J. (1997). The ontolingua server: A tool for collaborative ontology construction. *International Journal of Human-Computer Studies*, *46*(6), 707–727. doi:10.1006/ijhc.1996.0121

Fawcett, T. (2006). An introduction to ROC analysis. *Pattern Recognition Letters*, *27*, 861–874. doi:10.1016/j.patrec.2005.10.010

Fazlollahtabar, H., & Mahdavi, I. (2009). User/tutor optimal learning path in e-learning using comprehensive neuro-fuzzy approach. *Educational Research Review*, *4*(2), 142–155. doi:10.1016/j.edurev.2009.02.001

Felder, R. M., & Spurlin, J. (2005). Applications, reliability and validity of the index of learning styles. *International Journal of Engineering Education*, *32*(1), 103–112.

Fellbaum, C. (1998). *Wordnet: An electronic lexical databases*. Cambridge, MA: MIT Press.

Fensel, D., Van Harmelen, F., Klein, M., Akkermans, H., Broekstra, J., Fluff, C., et al. (2000). On-to-knowledge: Ontology-based tools for knowledge management. In *Proceedings of the eBusiness and eWork Conference*.

Fernández, M., Gómez-Pérez, A., & Juristo, N. (1997). *Methontology: from ontological art towards ontological engineering*. Paper presented at the AAAI97 Spring Symposium Series on Ontological Engineering, Stanford, CA.

Fernandez, A., Calderón, M., Barrenechea, E., Bustince, H., & Herrera, F. (2010). Solving multi-class problems with linguistic fuzzy rule based classification systems based on pairwise learning and preference relations. *Fuzzy Sets and Systems*, *161*(23), 3064–3080. doi:10.1016/j.fss.2010.05.016

Fernández-López, M., Gómez-Pérez, A., & Juristo, N. (1997). *Methontology: From ontological art towards ontological engineering*. Paper presented at the Workshop on Ontological Engineering.

Fernandez-Luna, J. M., De Campos, L. M., & Huete, J. F. (2003). Two term-layers: An alternative topology for representing term relationships in the Bayesian Network retrieval mode. In Benítez, J. M., Cordón, O., Hoffmann, F., & Roy, R. (Eds.), *Advances in soft computing-engineering, design and manufacturing* (pp. 213–224). London, UK: Springer.

Ferrari, L. D., & Aitken, S. (2006). Mining housekeeping genes with a Naive Bayes classifier. *BMC Genomics*.

Fidanova, S. (2006). Simulated annealing for grid scheduling problem. In *Proceedings of IEEE International Symposium on Modern Computing* (pp. 41-45).

Filho, F. M., & Gomide, F. (2005). Hybrid genetic algorithms and clustering. In *Proceedings of the Conference of the European Society for Fuzzy Logic and Technology/LFA* (pp. 1009-1014).

Fizzell, R. L. (1984). The status of learning styles. *The Educational Forum*, *48*(3), 303–312. doi:10.1080/00131728409335909

Fogel, D. B. (1992). *Evolving artificial intelligence*. Unpublished doctoral dissertation, University of California at San Diego, CA.

Foltz, P. W., Laham, D., & Landauer, T. K. (1999). *Automated essay scoring: Applications to educational technology.* Retrieved from http:// www-psych.nmsu.edu/ ~pfoltz/reprints/ Edmedia99.html

Foster, I., Kesselmann, C., Nick, J. M., & Tuecke, S. (2002). *The Physiology of the Grid: An Open Grid Services Architecture for Distributed Systems Integration*. Retrieved from http://www.globus.org/alliance/publications/papers/ogsa.pdf

Foster, I. (2002). What is the Grid? A Three Point Checklist. *GRIDtoday*, *1*(6), 22–25.

Foster, I., & Kesselmann, C. (2003). *The Grid: Blueprint for a New Computing Infrastructure*. San Francisco: Morgan Kaufmann.

Frakes, B., & Yates, B. R. (1992). *Information retrieval: Data structures and algorithms*. Upper Saddle River, NJ: Prentice Hall.

Frank, E., Paynter, G. W., et al. (1999). *Domain-specific keyphrase extraction.* Paper presented at the 6th International Joint Conference on Artificial Intelligence (IJCAI-99).

Frantzi, K. T., Ananiadou, S., et al. (1998). The C-value/NC-value Method of Automatic Recognition for Multi-Word Terms. In *Proceedings of the Second European Conference on Research and Advanced Technology for Digital Libraries,* London. Berlin: Springer-Verlag.

Frantzi, K. T., & Ananiadou, S. (1999). The C-value/NC-value domain independent method for multiword term extraction. *Journal of Natural Language Processing*, *6*(3), 145–180.

French, T. (2009). Virtual Organisational Trust Requirements: Can Semiotics Help Fill The Trust Gap? *International Journal of Intelligent Information Technologies*, *5*(2), 1–16.

Funk, A., Tablan, V., Bontcheva, K., Cunningham, H., Davis, B., & Handschuh, S. (2007). *CLOnE: Controlled Language for Ontology Editing*. In Proceedings of the 6th International Semantic Web Conference, 2nd Asian Semantic Web Conference, ISWC 2007 + ASWC 2007.

Gagné, F. (2005). From noncompetence to exceptional talent: Exploring the range of academic achievement within and between grade levels. *Gifted Child Quarterly*, *49*(2), 139–153. doi:10.1177/001698620504900204

Galeas, P., & Freisleben, B. (2008). Word distribution analysis for relevance ranking and query expansion. In A. Gelbukh (Ed.), *Proceedings of the 9th International Conference on Computational Linguistics and Intelligent Text Processing* (LNCS 4919, pp. 500-511).

Galletta, D. (1984). *A learning model of information systems: The effects of orienting materials, ability, expectations and experience on performance, usage and attitudes.* Unpublished doctoral dissertation, University of Minnesota, Minneapolis, MN.

GaneshKumar, P., & Devaraj, D. (2008). Improved genetic fuzzy system for breast cancer diagnosis. *International Journal of Systemics, Cybernetics and Informatics*, 24-28.

Gangemi, A., Guarino, N., Masolo, C., Oltramari, A., & Schneider, L. (2002). Sweetening ontologies with DOLCE. In *Proceedings of the 13th International Conference on Knowledge Engineering and Knowledge Management* (pp. 166-181).

Gangemi, A., Pisanelli, D. M., & Steve, G. (1999). An overview of the ONIONS project: Applying ontologies to the integration of medical terminologies. *Data & Knowledge Engineering*, *31*(2), 183–220. doi:10.1016/S0169-023X(99)00023-3

Garey, M. R., & Johnson, D. S. (1979). *Computers and intractability: A guide to the theory of NP-completeness*. San Francisco, CA: Freeman.

Garrison, R., & Anderson, T. (2003). *E-learning in the 21st century: A framework for research and practice*. London, UK: Routledge. doi:10.4324/9780203166093

GATE. (2009). *A General Architecture for Text Engineering*. Retrieved from http://gate.ac.uk/

Gaume, B., Hathout, N., & Muller, P. (2004). Désambiguïsation par proximité structurelle. In *Actes de la 11ème*. Conférence de Traitement Automatique des Langues Naturelles.

Gaus, W. (2002). *Dokumentations- und ordnungslehre. theorie und praxis des information retrieval* (3rd ed.). Berlin: Springer-Verlag GmbH.

Gautam, G., & Chaudhury, B. B. (2007). A distributed hierarchical genetic algorithm for efficient optimization and pattern matching. *Pattern Recognition*, *40*, 212–228. doi:10.1016/j.patcog.2006.04.023

Gestwa, M., & Bauschat, J. M. (2003). On the modeling of human pilot using fuzzy logic control. In Mohammadian, M. (Ed.), *Computational intelligence in control* (pp. 148–167). Hershey, PA: IGI Global. doi:10.4018/9781591400370.ch009

Goldberg, D. E. (1989). *Genetic algorithms in search, optimization, and machine learning*. Reading, MA: Addison-Wesley.

Gomez, L. M., Egan, D. E., & Bowers, C. (1986). Learning to use a text editor: Some learner characteristics that predict success. *Human-Computer Interaction*, *2*(1), 1-23.

Govindasamy, T. (2002). Successful implementation of e-learning: Pedagogical considerations. *The Internet and Higher Education*, *4*, 287–299. doi:10.1016/S1096-7516(01)00071-9

Greening, D. R. (1998). Collaborative filtering for web marketing efforts. In *Proceedings of the AAAI Workshop on Recommender Systems* (pp. 53-55).

Grootjen, F., & van der Weide, T. (2005). Dualistic ontologies. *International Journal of Intelligent Information Technologies*, *1*(3), 34–55. doi:10.4018/jiit.2005070103

Gruber, A., Westenthaler, R., & Gahleitner, E. (2006). *Supporting domain experts in creating formal knowledge models (ontologies)*. Paper presented at I-KNOW'06, 6th International Conference on Knowledge Management.

Gruninger, M., & Fox, M. S. (1995). Methodology for the design and evaluation of ontologies. In *Proceedings of the International Joint Conference on Artificial Intelligence and the Workshop on Basic Ontological Issues in Knowledge Sharing*.

Gu, T., Wang, X., Pung, H., & Zhang, D. (2004). An ontology-based context model in intelligent environments. In *Proceedings of the Conference on Communication Networks and Distributed Systems Modelling and Simulation* (pp. 270-275).

Guarino, N., Masolo, C., & Verete, G. (1999). OntoSeek: Content-based access to the web. *IEEE Intelligent Systems*, *14*, 70–80. doi:10.1109/5254.769887

Gubala, T., & Hoheisel, A. (2007). *Highly Dynamic Workflow Orchestration for Scientific Applications* (Tech. Rep. No. TR-0101). Institute on Grid Information, Resource and Workflow Monitoring Services and Institute on Grid Systems, Tools and Environments, CoreGrid.

Guha, R., McCool, R., & Miller, E. (2003). Semantic search. In *Proceedings of the 12th International Conference on World Wide Web* (pp. 700-709).

Gupta, A. K., & Sivakumar, A. I. (2006). Job shop scheduling techniques in semiconductor manufacturing. *International Journal of Advanced Manufacturing Technology*, *27*, 1163–1169. doi:10.1007/s00170-004-2296-z

Hagedorn, B., Ciaramita, M., & Atserias, J. (2007). World knowledge in broad-coverage information filtering. In W. Kraaij & A.P. Vries (Eds.), *Proceedings of the 30th Annual International ACM SIGIR Conference on Research and Development in Information Retrieval*, Amsterdam, The Netherlands (pp. 801-802).

Hakenberg, J., Plake, C., Leser, U., & Kirsch, H. (2005). LLL'05 Challenge: Genic Interaction Extraction - Identification of Language Patterns Based on Alignment and Finite State Automata. In S. Dzeroski (Ed.), *Proceedings of the 22nd International Conference on Machine Learning*, Bonn, Germany (pp. 38-45).

Hale, J., Parrish, A., Dixon, B., & Smith, R. (2000). Enhancing the Cocomo estimation models. *IEEE Software*, *17*(6), 45–49. doi:10.1109/52.895167

Haley, D. T., Thomas, P., Nuseibeh, B., Taylor, J., & Lefrere, P. (2005). The learning grid and e-assessment using latent semantic analysis. In *Proceeding of the Conference on Towards the Learning Grid: Advances in Human Learning Services* (pp. 197-202).

Hamdi, M. S. (2008). SOMSE: A Neural Network Based Approach to Web Search Optimization. *International Journal of Intelligent Information Technologies*, *4*(4), 31–54.

Hamidi, H., & Vafaei, A. (2009). Evaluation of fault tolerant mobile agents in distributed systems. *International Journal of Intelligent Information Technologies*, *5*(1). doi:10.4018/jiit.2009010103

Harman, D. (1988). Towards interactive query expansion. In *Proceedings of the 11th Annual International ACM SIGIR Conference on Research and Development in Information Retrieval* (pp. 321-331).

Harman, D. (1992). Relevance feedback and other query modification techniques. In Frakes, W. B., & Baeza-Yates, R. (Eds.), *Information retrieval: Data structures and algorithms* (pp. 241–263). Upper Saddle River, NJ: Prentice Hall.

Harman, D., Fox, E., Baeza-Yates, R., & Lee, W. (1992). Inverted files. In Frakes, W. B., & Baeza-Yates, R. (Eds.), *Information retrieval: Data structures and algorithms* (pp. 28–43). Upper Saddle River, NJ: Prentice Hall.

Harrison, P. D., & Harrell, A. (1993). Impact of "adverse selection" on managers' project evaluation decisions. *Academy of Management Journal*, *36*, 635–635. doi:10.2307/256596

Hatzivassiloglou, V., & Wiebe, J. (2000). Effects of adjective orientation and gradability on sentence subjectivity. In M. Kay (Ed.), *Proceedings of the 18th Conference on Computational Linguistics*, Saarbrücken, Germany (pp. 299-305).

Hazra, I., & Aditi, S. (2009). Thesaurus and query expansion. *International Journal of Computer Science and Information Technology*, *1*(2), 89–97.

He, B., & Ounis, I. (2009). Studying query expansion effectiveness. In M. Boughanem, C. Berrut, J. Mothe, & C. Soulé-Dupuy (Ed.), *Proceedings of the 31st European Conference on Information Retrieval* (LNCS 5478, pp. 611-619).

He, Q., Li, T., Zhuang, F., & Shi, Z. (2010). Frequent term based peer-to-peer text clustering. In *Proceedings of the 3rd International Symposium on Knowledge Acquisition and Modeling* (pp. 352-355).

Hendler, J., Shadbolt, N., Hall, W., Berners-Lee, T., & Weitzner, D. (2008). Web science: An interdisciplinary approach to understanding the web. *Communications of the ACM, 51*(7), 60–69. doi:10.1145/1364782.1364798

Herman, I. (2007). *Introduction to Semantic Web*. Paper presented at the International Conference on Dublin Core and Metadata Applications.

Herrera, F., Lozano, M., & Sanchez, A. M. (2003). A taxonomy for the crossover operator for real-coded genetic algorithms: An experimental study. *International Journal of Intelligent Systems, 18*, 309–338. doi:10.1002/int.10091

Hevner, A. R., March, S. T., Park, J., & Ram, S. (2004). Design science in information systems research. *Management Information Systems Quarterly, 28*(1), 75–105.

Hiltz, S. R., Fjermestad, J., & Floydlewis, L. (1999). Introduction to the special issue on collaborative learning via Internet. *Group Decision and Negotiation, 8*(5), 367–369. doi:10.1023/A:1008674423058

Hofmann, T. (1999). Probabilistic latent semantic analysis. In K. Laskey & H. Prade (Ed.), *Proceedings of the Fifteenth Conference on Uncertainty in Artificial Intelligence* (pp. 289-296). San Francisco, CA: Morgan Kaufmann.

Hoheisel, A. (2006). User tools and languages for graph-based Grid workflows. *Concurrency and Computation, 18*(10), 1101–1113. doi:10.1002/cpe.1002

Hoheisel, A. (2008). Grid-Workflow-Management. In Weisbecker, A., Pfreundt, F.-J., Linden, J., & Unger, S. (Eds.), *Fraunhofer Enterprise Grids* (pp. 22–25). Stuttgart, Germany: Fraunhofer IRB.

Hong, C.-M., Chen, C.-M., Chang, M.-H., & Chen, S.-C. (2007). Intelligent web-based tutoring system with personalized learning path guidance. In *Proceedings of the Seventh IEEE International Conference on Advanced Learning Technologies*, Niigata, Japan (pp. 512-516).

Hong, W., Thong, J. Y. L., & Tam, K. (2004). The effects of information format and shopping task on consumers' online shopping behavior: A cognitive fit perspective. *Journal of Management Information Systems, 21*(3), 149–184.

Horowitz, E., Sahni, S., & Mehta, D. (1995). *Fundamentals of data structures in C* (pp. 342–376). New York, NY: W. H. Freeman.

Horrocks, I. (2008). *Ontologies and databases*. Paper presented at Semantic Days 2008.

Horrocks, I. (2008). Ontologies and the Semantic Web. *Communications of the ACM, 51*(12), 58–67. doi:10.1145/1409360.1409377

Horton, P., & Nakai, K. (1996). A probablistic classification system for predicting the cellular localization sites of proteins. *Intelligent Systems in Molecular Biology*, 109-115.

Hotho, A., Maedche, A., & Staab, S. (2002). Ontology based text document clustering. *Kunstliche Intelligenz, 16*(4), 48–54.

Hou, Y. T., Chen, M. C., & Jeng, B. (2010). An optimal new-node placement to enhance the coverage of wireless sensor networks. *Journal of Wireless Networks, 16*(4), 1033–1043. doi:10.1007/s11276-009-0186-x

Howland, P., & Park, H. (2004). Cluster preserving dimension reduction methods for efficient classification of text data. In Berry, M. W. (Ed.), *Survey of text mining: Clustering, classification and retrieval* (pp. 3–23). New York, NY: Springer.

Hsieh, B.-W., Chen, C.-H., & Chang, S.-C. (2001). Scheduling semiconductor wafer fabrication by using ordinal optimization-based simulation. *IEEE Transactions on Robotics and Automation, 17*(5), 599–608. doi:10.1109/70.964661

Hsieh, T.-C., & Wang, T.-I. (2010). A mining-based approach on discovering courses pattern for constructing suitable learning path. *Expert Systems with Applications*, *37*(6), 4156–4167. doi:10.1016/j.eswa.2009.11.007

Hu, J., Goodman, E., Seo, K., & Pei, M. (2002). Adaptive hierarchical fair competition (AHFC) model for parallel evolutionary algorithms. In *Proceedings of Genetic and Evolutionary Computation Conference* (pp. 772-779).

Hu, M., & Liu, B. (2004). Mining and summarizing customer reviews. In W. Kim & R. Kohavi (Eds.), *Proceedings of the Tenth ACM SIGKDD International Conference on Knowledge Discovery and Data Mining*, Seattle, WA (pp. 168-177).

Hu, X., & Eberhart, R. C. (2001). Tracking dynamic systems with PSO: Where's the cheese? In *Proceedings of the Workshop on Particle Swarm Optimization*, Indianapolis, IN.

Hu, X., & Eberhart, R. C. (2002). Adaptive particle swarm optimization: Detection and response to dynamic systems. In *Proceedings of the Congress on Evolutionary Computation* (pp. 1666-1670).

Hu, X., Shi, Y., & Eberhart, R. C. (2004). Recent advances in particle swarm. In *Proceedings of the IEEE Congress on Evolutionary Computation* (pp. 90-97).

Huang, C., Tian, Y., et al. (2006). *Keyphrase Extraction using Semantic Networks Structure Analysis.*

Huang, M.-J., Huang, H.-S., & Chen, M.-Y. (2007). Constructing a personalized e-learning system based on genetic algorithm and case-based reasoning approach. *Expert Systems with Applications*, *33*(3), 551–564. doi:10.1016/j.eswa.2006.05.019

Huang, S.-J., & Chiu, N.-H. (2006). Optimization of analogy weights by genetic algorithm for software effort estimation. *Information and Software Technology*, *48*(11), 1034–1045. doi:10.1016/j.infsof.2005.12.020

Hu, J., Goodman, E., Seo, K., Fan, Z., & Rosenberg, R. (2005). The hierarchical fair competition (HFC) framework for continuing evolutionary algorithms. *Evolutionary Computation*, *13*(2), 241–277. doi:10.1162/1063656054088530

Hull, D. (1994). Improving text retrieval for the routing problem using latent semantic indexing. In *Proceedings of the 17th ACM-SIGIR Conference on Research and Development in Information Retrieval* (pp. 282-291).

Hull, D., Wolstencroft, K., Stevens, R., Goble, C., Pocock, M., & Li, P. (2006). Taverna: a tool for building and running workflows of services. *Nucleic Acids Research*, *34*, W729–W732. doi:10.1093/nar/gkl320

Indrawan, M., & Loke, S. W. (2008). The impact of ontology on the performance of information retrieval: A case of Wordnet. *International Journal of Information Technology and Web Engineering*, *3*(1), 24–37. doi:10.4018/jitwe.2008010102

Iosif, E., Tegos, A., Pangos, A., Fosler-Lussie, E., & Potamianos, A. (2006). Combining statistical similarity measures for automatic induction of semantic classes. In *Proceedings of the IEEE/ACL Workshop on Spoken Language Technology* (pp. 86-89).

Iosif, E., & Potamianos, A. (2010). Unsupervised semantic similarity computation between terms using web documents. *IEEE Transactions on Knowledge and Data Engineering*, *22*(11), 1637–1647. doi:10.1109/TKDE.2009.193

Ishibuchi, H., Nakashima, T., & Murata, T. (1999). Performance evaluation of fuzzy classifier systems for multidimensional pattern classification problems. *IEEE Transactions on System. Man and Cybernetics-Part B*, *29*(5), 601–617. doi:10.1109/3477.790443

Ishibuchi, H., Nozaki, K., Yamamoto, N., & Tanaka, H. (1995). Selecting fuzzy if-then rules for classification problems using genetic algorithms. *IEEE Transactions on Fuzzy Systems*, *3*, 260–270. doi:10.1109/91.413232

Ishibuchi, H., Nozaki, K., Yamamoto, N., & Tanaka, H. (1996). Adaptive fuzzy rule-based classification systems. *IEEE Transactions on Fuzzy Systems*, *4*(3), 238–250. doi:10.1109/91.531768

Ishibuchi, H., & Yamamoto, T. (2004). Fuzzy rule selection by multi-objective genetic local search algorithms and rule evaluation measures in data mining. *Fuzzy Sets and Systems*, *141*, 59–88. doi:10.1016/S0165-0114(03)00114-3

Islam, M. J., Wu, Q. M. J., et al. (2007). Investigating the Performance of Naive- Bayes Classifiers and K- Nearest Neighbor Classifiers. In *Proceedings of the 2007 International Conference on Convergence Information Technology*. Washington, DC: IEEE Computer Society.

ISO/IEC. (2004). *High-level Petri Nets – Part 1: Concepts, definitions and graphical notation (ISO/IEC 15909-1)*. Geneva, Switzerland: Author.

Iyengar, G., Nock, H., Neti, C., & Franz, M. (2002). Semantic indexing of multimedia using audio, text and visual cues. In *Proceedings of the Conference on Multimedia Information Systems* (p. 134).

Jadaan, O. A., Rajamani, L., & Rao, C. R. (2008). Non-dominated ranked genetic algorithm for solving multi-objective optimization problems: NRGA. *Journal of Theoretical and Applied Information Technology*, 60-67.

Jansen, B. J., & McNeese, M. D. (2005). Evaluating the effectiveness of and patterns of interactions with automated searching assistance: Research articles. *Journal of the American Society for Information Science and Technology*, *56*(14), 1480–1503. doi:10.1002/asi.20242

Jeffery, R., Ruhe, M., & Wieczorek, I. (2001). Using public domain metrics to estimate software development effort. In *Proceedings of the 7th IEEE Symposium on Software Metrics* (pp. 16-27). Washington, DC: IEEE Computer Society.

Jeyarani, R., Vasanth Ram, R., & Nagaveni, N. (2008). Implementation of efficient light weight internal scheduler for high throughput grid environment. In *Proceedings of the National Conference on Advanced Computing in Computer Applications*. Coimbatore, India.

Jeyarani, R., Vasanth Ram, R., & Nagaveni, N. (2010). Design and implementation of an efficient two level scheduler for cloud computing environment. In *Proceedings of the 10th International Conference on Cluster, Cloud and Grid*, Melbourne, Australia (pp. 585-586).

Jeyarani, R., Nagaveni, N., & Vasanth, R. (2011). Self adaptive particle swarm optimization for efficient virtual machine provisioning in cloud. *International Journal of Intelligent Information Technologies*, *7*(2), 25–44.

Jiang, X., & Tan, A. (2006). OntoSearch: A full-text search engine for the semantic web. In *Proceedings of the 21st National Conference on Artificial Intelligence* (pp. 1325-1330).

Jindal, N., & Liu, B. (2006). Mining Comparative Sentences and Relation. In Y. Gil & R. Mooney (Eds.), *Proceedings of 21st National Conference on Artificial Intelligence,* Boston (pp. 244-251).

Jindal, N., & Liu, B. (2006). Identifying Comparative Sentences in Text Documents. In E. Efthimiadis (Ed.), *Proceedings of the 29th Annual International ACM SIGIR Conference on Research & Development on Information Retrieval,* Seattle, WA (pp. 244-251).

Jing, J., Zhou, L., Ng, M. K., & Huang, Z. (2006). Ontology-based distance measure for text clustering. In *Proceedings of the SIAM SDM Workshop on Text Mining*, Bethesda, MD.

Joachims, T. (2009). *Multi-Class Support Vector Machine*. Retrieved from http://svmlight.joachims.org/svm_multiclass.html

Johnson, D. M., Teredesai, A., & Saltarelli, R. T. (April 2005). Genetic programming in wireless sensor networks. In M. Keijzer, A. Tettamanzi, P. Collet, J. van Hemert, & M. Tomassini (Eds.), *Proceedings of the 8th European Conference on Genetic Programming*, Lausanne, Switzerland (LNCS 3447, pp. 96-107).

Johnson, S. C. (1967). Hierarchical clustering schemes. *Psychometrika*, *32*(3), 241–254. doi:10.1007/BF02289588

Jones, S., & Paynter, G. W. (2003). An Evaluation of Document Keyphrase Sets. *Journal of Digital Information*, *4*(1).

Kaiquan, S. J., Wang, W., Ren, J., Jin, S. Y., Liu, L., & Liao, S. (2011). Classifying consumer comparison opinions to uncover product strengths and weaknesses. *International Journal of Intelligent Information Technologies*, *7*(1), 1–14. doi:10.4018/jiit.2011010101

Kala, R., Shukla, A., & Tiwari, R. (2010). Clustering based hierarchical genetic algorithm for complex fitness landscapes. *International Journal of Intelligent Systems Technologies and Applications*, *9*(2), 185–205. doi:10.1504/IJISTA.2010.034320

Kaljurand, K. (2008). *ACE View — An Ontology and Rule Editor based on Controlled English*. Paper presented at the Poster and Demonstration Session at the 7th International Semantic Web Conference (ISWC2008).

Kambhatla, N. (2004). Combining lexical, syntactic, and semantic features with maximum entropy models for extracting relations. In J. Chang & Y. Chang (Eds.), *Proceedings of the ACL 2004 on Interactive Poster and Demonstration Sessions,* Barcelona, Spain (p. 2).

Karypis, G., & Han, E.-H. (2000). Fast supervised dimensionality reduction algorithm with applications to document categorization and retrieval. In *Proceedings of the Ninth International Conference on Information and Knowledge Management* (pp. 12-19).

Katifori, A., Halatsis, C., Lepouras, G., Vassilakis, C., & Giannopoulou, E. (2007). Ontology visualization methods - a survey. *ACM Computing Surveys, 39*(4), 11–43. doi:10.1145/1287620.1287621

Katranuschkov, P., Gehre, A., Shaukat, F., & Scherer, R. J. (2008). Achieving Interoperability in Grid-Enabled Virtual Organisations. In K.-D. Thoben, K. S. Pawar, & R. Goncalves (Eds.), *Proceedings of the 14th International Conference on Concurrent Enterprising, ICE2008* (pp. 835-842). Nottingham, UK: Centre for Concurrent Enterprises.

Keefe, J. W. (1979). Learning style: An overview. In National Association of Secondary School Principals (Eds.), *Student learning styles: Diagnosing and prescribing programs* (pp. 1-17). Reston, VA: National Association of Secondary School Principals.

Keller, G., Nuettgens, M., & Scheer, A.-W. (1992). *Semantische Prozeßmodellierung auf der Grundlage "Ereignisgesteuerter Prozeßketten (EPK)"* (Tech. Rep. No. 89). Saarbruecken, Germany: Universitaet des Saarlandes, Instituts für Wirtschaftsinformatik.

Kennedy, J., & Eberhart, R. C. (1995). Particle swarm optimization. In. *Proceedings of the IEEE International Joint Conference on Neural Networks, 4*, 1942–1948.

Kennedy, J., Eberhart, R. C., & Shi, Y. (2001). *Swarm intelligence*. San Francisco, CA: Morgan Kaufmann.

Khanna, R., Liu, H., & Chen, H. (2006). Self organization of sensor networks using genetic algorithms. *International Journal of Sensor Networks, 1*(3-4), 241–252. doi:10.1504/IJSNET.2006.012040

Kietz, J.-U., Maedche, A., & Volz, R. (2000). A method for semi-automatic ontology acquisition from a corporate intranet. In *Proceedings of the Workshop on Knowledge Engineering and Knowledge Management*.

Killani, R., Rao, S. K., Satapathy, S. C., Pradhan, G., & Chandran, K. R. (2010). Effective document clustering with particle swarm optimization. In B. K. Panigrahi, S. Das, P. N. Suganthan, & S. S. Dash (Eds.), *Proceedings of the First International Conference on Swarm, Evolutionary, and Memetic Computing* (LNCS 6466, pp. 623-629).

Kim, Y., Jung, Y., & Myaeng, S. (2007). Identifying opinion holders in opinion text from online newspapers. In T. Lin, R. Yager, & J. Mendel (Eds.), *Proceedings of the 2007 IEEE International Conference on Granular Computing,* San Jose, CA (p. 699).

Kim, J., & Storey, V. C. (2011). Construction of domain ontologies: Sourcing the World Wide Web. *Journal of Intelligent Information Technologies, 7*(2), 1–24.

Kim, Y. D., Kim, J. G., & Kim, H. U. (2001). Production scheduling in a semiconductor wafer fabrication facility producing multiple product types with distinct due dates. *IEEE Transactions on Robotics and Automation, 17*(5), 589–598. doi:10.1109/70.964660

Kira, K., & Rendell, L. A. (1992). A practical approach to feature selection. In *Proceedings of the Ninth International Workshop on Machine Learning* (pp. 249-256). San Francisco, CA: Morgan Kaufmann.

Kitchenham, B. A., Mendes, E., & Travassos, G. H. (2007). Cross versus within-company cost estimation studies: A systematic review. *IEEE Transactions on Software Estimation, 33*(5), 316–329. doi:10.1109/TSE.2007.1001

Kloppmann, M., Koenig, D., Leymann, F., Pfau, G., Rickayzen, A., & von Riegen, C. (2005). *WS-BPEL Extension for People - BPEL4People*. IBM and SAP.

Kohavi, R. (1995). A study of cross-validation and bootstrap for accuracy estimation and model selection. In *Proceedings of the Fourteenth International Joint Conference on Artificial Intelligence* (Vol. 2, pp. 1137-1143).

Koonce, D. A., & Tsai, S.-C. (2000). Using data mining to find patterns in genetic algorithm solutions to a job shop schedule. *Computers & Industrial Engineering, 38*(3), 361–374. doi:10.1016/S0360-8352(00)00050-4

Kothari, C. R., & Russomanno, D. J. (2008). Enhancing OWL ontologies with relation semantic. *International Journal of Software Engineering and Knowledge Engineering, 18*(3), 327–356. doi:10.1142/S0218194008003660

Kotis, K., Vouros, G. A., & Alonso, J. P. (2005). *Hcome: a tool-supported methodology for engineering living ontologies.*

Krefting, D., Vossberg, M., Hoheisel, A., & Tolxdorff, T. (2010). Simplified implementation of medical image processing algorithms into a grid using a workflow management system. *Future Generation Computer Systems, 26*(4), 681–684. doi:10.1016/j.future.2009.07.004

Krishnapuram, R., Joshi, A., Nasraoui, O., & Yi, L. (2001). Low-complexity fuzzy relational clustering algorithms for web mining. *IEEE Transactions on Fuzzy Systems, 9*(4), 595–607. doi:10.1109/91.940971

Kudo, T., & Matsumoto, Y. (2004). A boosting algorithm for classification of semi-structured text. In D. Lin & D. Wu (Ed.), *Proceedings of the 2004 Conference on Empirical Methods in Natural Language Processing,* Barcelona, Spain (pp. 1-8).

Kumar, N., & Srinathan, K. (2008). Automatic keyphrase extraction from scientific documents using N-gram filtration technique. In *Proceedings of the 8th ACM Symposium on Document Engineering,* Sao Paulo, Brazil. New York: ACM Press.

Kumar, A., & Thambidurai, P. (2004). Collaborative web recommendation systems based on an effective fuzzy association rule mining algorithm. *Indian Journal of Computer Science and Engineering, 1*(3), 184–191.

Kuppuswamy, S., & Chithralekha, T. (2010). A new behavior management architecture for language faculty of an agent for task delegation. *International Journal of Intelligent Information Technologies, 6*(2), 44–64. doi:10.4018/jiit.2010040103

Kwork, J., Wang, H., Liao, S., Yuen, J., & Leung, F. (2000). Student profiling system for agent-based educational system. In *Proceedings of the American Conference on Information Systems.*

Lan, M., Ta, C. L., Su, J., & Lu, Y. (2009). Supervised and traditional term weighting methods for automatic text categorization. *IEEE Transactions on Pattern Analysis and Machine Intelligence, 31*(4), 721–735. doi:10.1109/TPAMI.2008.110

Lau, R., Song, D., Li, Y., Cheung, T., & Hao, J. (2009). Towards a fuzzy domain ontology extraction method for adaptive e-learning. *IEEE Transactions on Knowledge and Data Engineering, 21*(6), 800–813. doi:10.1109/TKDE.2008.137

Lee, C.-H., Yang, H.-C., & Ma, S.-M. (2006). A novel multilingual text categorization system using latent semantic indexing. In *Proceedings of the First International Conference on Innovative Computing, Information and Control* (pp. 503-506).

Lee, M. R. (2000). Context-dependent semantic values for e-negotiation. In *Proceedings of the Second International Workshop on Advanced Issues of E-commerce and Web-based Information Systems* (pp. 41-47).

Lee, D., Chauang, H., & Seamons, K. (1997). Document ranking and the vector space model. *IEEE Software, 14*(2), 66–75. doi:10.1109/52.582976

Lee, J. H. (1998). Combining the evidence of different relevance feedback methods for information retrieval. *Information Processing & Management, 34*(6), 681–691. doi:10.1016/S0306-4573(98)00034-X

Lei, J., Kang, Y., Lu, C., & Yan, Z. (2005). A web document classification approach based on fuzzy association concept. In L. Wang & Y. Jin (Eds.), *Proceedings of the Second International Conference on Fuzzy Systems and Knowledge Discovery* (LNCS 3613, pp. 388-391).

Lenat, D. B. (1995). CYC: a large-scale investment in knowledge infrastructure. *Communications of the ACM*, *38*(11), 33–38. doi:10.1145/219717.219745

Leukel, J., & Sugumaran, V. (2009). Towards a semiotic metrics suite for product ontology evaluation. *International Journal of Intelligent Information Technologies*, *5*(4), 1–15. doi:10.4018/jiit.2009080701

Lewis, J. R. (1995). IBM Computer Usability Satisfaction Questionnaires: Psychometric Evaluation and Instructions for Use. *International Journal of Human-Computer Interaction*, *7*(1), 57–78. doi:10.1080/10447319509526110

Li, C. H., & Park, S. C. (2007). Artificial neural network for document classification using latent semantic indexing. In *Proceedings of the International Symposium on Information Technology Convergence* (pp. 17-21).

Li, G., Yu, S., & Dai, S. (2007). Ontology based query system design and implementation. In *Proceedings of the International Conference on Network and Parallel Computing* (pp. 1010-1015).

Li, G., Zhuang, J., Hou, H., & Yu, D. (2009). A genetic algorithm based clustering using geodesic distance measure. In *Proceedings of the IEEE International Conference on Intelligent Computing and Intelligent Systems* (pp. 274-278).

Li, J., & Morris, R. (2002). Document clustering for distributed full text search. In *Proceedings of the 2nd MIT Student Oxygen Workshop*, Cambridge, MA.

Li, X., & Sigurdur, O. (2004). Data mining for best practices in scheduling data. In *Proceedings of the IIE Annual Conference and Exhibition.*

Lihua, W. JianPing, F., & Yunfen, L. (2009). A personalized intelligent web retrieval system based on the knowledge-base concept and latent semantic indexing model. In *Proceedings of the Seventh ACIS International Conference on Software Engineering Research, Management and Applications* (pp. 45-50).

Li, J., Zhang, Z., Li, X., & Chen, H. (2008). Kernel-based learning for biomedical relation extraction. *Journal of the American Society for Information Science and Technology*, *59*(5), 756–769. doi:10.1002/asi.20791

Likert, R. (1932). A technique for the measurement of attitudes. *Archives de Psychologie*, *22*(140), 1–55.

Lindland, O. I., Sindre, G., & Solvberg, A. (1994). Understanding quality in conceptual modeling. *IEEE Software*, *11*(2), 42–49. doi:10.1109/52.268955

Lin, J. W., & Chen, Y. T. (2008). Improving the coverage of randomized scheduling in wireless sensor networks. *IEEE Transactions on Wireless Communications*, *7*(12), 4807–4812. doi:10.1109/T-WC.2008.070933

Lin, W. Y., Alvarez, S. A., & Ruiz, C. (2002). Efficient adaptive-support association rule mining for recommender systems. *Data Mining and Knowledge Discovery*, *6*(1), 83–105. doi:10.1023/A:1013284820704

Lioma, C., He, B., Plachouras, V., & Ounis, I. (2005). The University of Glasgow at CLEF 2004: French monolingual information retrieval with Terrier. In C. Peters, P. Clough, J. Gonzalo, G. J. F. Jones, M. Kluck, & B. Magnini (Eds.), *Proceedings of the Cross Language Evaluation Forum* (LNCS 3491, pp. 253-259).

Liu, B. (2008). *Opinion Mining and Summarization.* Paper presented at the 17th International World Wide Web Conference, Beijing, China.

Liu, X. (2007). Intelligent Data Analysis. *Intelligent Information Technologies: Concepts, Methodologies, Tools and Applications*, 308.

Liu, B. (2006). *Web Data Mining- Exploring Hyperlinks, Contents and Usage Data*. New York: Springer.

Liu, B. (2007). *Web Data Mining*. New York: Springer.

Liu, Q., & Mintram, R. (2005). Preliminary data analysis methods in software estimation. *Software Quality Control*, *13*(1), 91–115.

Li, X. (2008). Inference Degradation of Active Information Fusion within Bayesian Network Models. *International Journal of Intelligent Information Technologies*, *4*(4), 1–17.

Li, Y., Luo, C., & Chung, S. M. (2008). Text clustering with feature selection by using statistical data. *IEEE Transactions on Knowledge and Data Engineering*, *20*(5), 641–652. doi:10.1109/TKDE.2007.190740

Li, Y., Wang, Y., & Huang, X. (2007). A relation- based search engine in semantic web. *IEEE Transactions on Knowledge and Data Engineering*, *19*(2), 273–282. doi:10.1109/TKDE.2007.18

Li, Y., Xie, M., & Goh, T. (2009). A study of project selection and feature weighting for analogy based software cost estimation. *Journal of Systems and Software*, *82*(2), 241–252. doi:10.1016/j.jss.2008.06.001

Li, Y., & Zhong, N. (2008). Mining ontology for automatically acquiring web user information needs. *IEEE Transactions on Knowledge and Data Engineering*, *18*(4), 554–568.

Lu, M., Zhou, Q., Li, F., Lu, Y., & Zhou, L. (2002). Recommendation of web pages based on concept association. In *Proceedings of the 4th IEEE International Workshop on Advanced Issues of E- Commerce and Web-Based Information Systems*, Washington, DC (pp. 221-227).

Luengo, J., & Herrera, F. (2010). Domains of competence of fuzzy rule based classification systems with data complexity measures: A case of study using a fuzzy hybrid genetic based machine learning method. *Fuzzy Sets and Systems*, *161*(1), 3–19. doi:10.1016/j.fss.2009.04.001

Lung-Hsiang, W., & Chee-Kit, L. (2010). A survey of optimized learning pathway planning and assessment paper generation with swarm intelligence. In Stankov, S., Glavinic, V., & Rosic, M. (Eds.), *Intelligent tutoring systems in e-learning environments: Design, implementation and evaluation* (*Vol. 14*, pp. 285–302). Hershey, PA: IGI Global.

MacQueen, J. B. (1967). *Some Methods for Classification and Analysis of MultiVariate Observations*. Paper presented at the fifth Berkeley Symposium on Mathematical Statistics and Probability.

Madyloval, A., & Öğüdücü, S. G. (2009). Comparison of similarity measures for clustering Turkish documents. *Intelligent Data Analysis, 13*(5), 815-832.

Maedche, A., & Staab, S. (2000). Discovering conceptual relations from text. In *Proceedings of the European Conference on Artificial Intelligence* (pp. 321-325).

Maedche, A., & Staab, S. (2000). Semi-automatic engineering of ontologies from text. In *Proceedings of the 12th International Conference on Software and Knowledge Engineering*, Chicago, IL.

Maedche, A., & Volz, R. (2001). The ontology extraction and maintenance framework text-to-onto. In *Proceedings of the ICDM Workshop on Integrating Data Mining and Knowledge Management*.

Maedche, A., Staab, S., Stojanovic, N., Studer, R., & Sure, Y. (2003). Semantic portal: The SEAL approach. In *Proceedings of the Conference on Spinning the Semantic Web* (pp. 317-359).

Maheswaran, R., Pearce, J., Bowring, E., Varakantham, P., & Tambe, M. (2006). Privacy loss in distributed constraint reasoning: A quantitative framework for analysis and its applications. *Journal of Autonomous Agents and Multi-Agent Systems*, *34*, 27–60. doi:10.1007/s10458-006-5951-y

Mailler, R., & Lesser, V. (2003). A mediation based protocol for distributed constraint satisfaction. In *Proceedings of the 4th International Workshop on Distributed Constraint Reasoning* (pp. 49-58).

Mair, C., Kododa, G., Lefley, M., Phalp, K., Schofield, C., Shepperd, M., & Webster, S. (2000). An investigation of machine learning based prediction systems. *System and Software*, *53*(1), 23–29. doi:10.1016/S0164-1212(00)00005-4

Manning, C. D., Raghavan, P., & Schütze, H. (2008). *Introduction to information retrieval*. Cambridge, UK: Cambridge University Press.

March, S., & Allen, G. (2007). Ontological foundations for active information systems. *International Journal of Intelligent Information Technologies*, *3*(1), 1–13. doi:10.4018/jiit.2007010101

Martin, D., Burstein, M., Lassila, O., Paolucci, M., Payne, T., & McIlraith, S. A. (2004). *Describing Web Services using OWL-S and WSDL*. Arlington, VA: BBN Rosslyn.

Mateos, C., Zunino, A., & Campo, M. (2008). A survey on approaches to gridification. *Software, Practice & Experience*, *38*(5), 523–556. doi:10.1002/spe.847

Mayer, R. E., & Hegarty, M. (1996). The process of understanding mathematical problems. In Sternberg, R. J., & Ben-Zeev, T. (Eds.), *The book of the nature of mathematical thinking*. Mahwah, NJ: Lawrence Erlbaum.

Mazumdar, B. D., & Mishra, R. B. (2010). Multi-agent negotiation in B2C E-commerce based on data mining methods. *International Journal of Intelligent Information Technologies*, *6*(4), 46–70. doi:10.4018/jiit.2010100104

McGuinness, D. L., & van Harmelen, F. (2004). *OWL web ontology language overview*. Retrieved from http://www.w3.org/TR/2004/REC-owl-features-20040210/

McIlroy, J., & Jones, B. (1993). *Going to university: The student guide*. Manchester, UK: Manchester University Press.

Medelyan, O., & Witten, I. H. (2006). Thesaurus Based Automatic Keyphrase Indexing. In *Proceedings of JCDL*. New York: ACM Press.

Melanie, M. (1999). *An introduction to genetic algorithms*. Cambridge, MA: MIT Press.

Melville, P., Mooney, R. J., & Nagarajan, R. (2002). Content-boosted collaborative filtering for improved recommendations. In *Proceedings of the Eighteenth National Conference on Artificial Intelligence*, Edmonton, AB, Canada (pp. 187-192).

Mendes, E., & Watson, I. C., T., Mosley, N., & Counsell, S. (2002). A comparison of development effort estimation techniques for web hypermedia applications. In *Proceedings of the 8th IEEE Symposium on Software Metrics* (pp. 131-140). Washington, DC: IEEE Computer Society.

Meng, S. K., & Chatwin, C. R. (2010). Ontology-based shopping agent for e-marketing. *International Journal of Intelligent Information Technologies*, *6*(2), 21–43. doi:10.4018/jiit.2010040102

Menzies, T., Port, D., Chen, Z., & Hihn, J. (2005). Simple software cost analysis: Safe or unsafe? In *Proceedings of the Workshop on Predictor Models in Software Engineering* (pp. 1-6). New York, NY: ACM Press.

Meziane, F., & Nefti, S. (2007). Evaluating e-commerce trust using fuzzy logic. *International Journal of Intelligent Information Technologies*, *3*(4), 25–39. doi:10.4018/jiit.2007100102

Michener, W., Beach, J., Jones, M., Ludäscher, B., Pennington, D., & Pereira, R. (2007). A knowledge environment for the biodiversity and ecological sciences. *Journal of Intelligent Information Systems*, *29*(1), 111–126. doi:10.1007/s10844-006-0034-8

Middleton, S. E., Roure, D. C. D., & Shadbolt, N. R. (2001). Capturing knowledge of user preferences: Ontologies in recommender system. In *Proceedings of the 1st International Conference on Knowledge Capture*.

Mika, M., Waligora, G., & Weglarz, J. (2004). *A meta-heuristic approach to scheduling workflow jobs on a grid, Grid resource management: State of the art and future trend*. Boston, MA: Kluwer Academic.

Milke, J.-M., Schiffers, M., & Ziegler, W. (2006). *Rahmenkonzept für das Management Virtueller Organisationen im D-Grid*.

Miller, G. A. (1995). WordNet: a lexical database for English. *Communications of the ACM*, *38*(11), 39–41. doi:10.1145/219717.219748

Mishra, K., & Mishra, R. B. (2010). Multiagent based selection of tutor-subject-student paradigm in an intelligent tutoring system. *International Journal of Intelligent Information Technologies*, *6*(1), 46–70. doi:10.4018/jiit.2010100904

Mladenovic, N., & Hansen, P. (1997). Variable neighborhood search. *Computers & Operations Research*, *24*(1), 1097–1100. doi:10.1016/S0305-0548(97)00031-2

Moisan, S. (2010). Generating knowledge-based system generators: a software engineering approach. *International Journal of Intelligent Information Technologies*, *6*(1), 1–17. doi:10.4018/jiit.2010100901

Mostafa, J., Mukhopadhyay, S., Lam, W., & Palakal, M. (1997). A multilevel approach to intelligent information filtering: Model, system and evaluation. *ACM Transactions on Information Systems*, *15*(4), 368–399. doi:10.1145/263479.263481

Motik, B., Maedche, A., & Volz, R. (2002). A conceptual modeling approach for semantics-driven enterprise applications. In. *Proceedings of the Confederated International Coferences of DOA, CoopIS, and ODBASE: On the Move to Meaningful Internet Systems*, *2519*, 1082–1099.

Murthy, C. A., & Chowdhury, N. (1996). In search of optimal clusters using genetic algorithms. *Pattern Recognition Letters*, 825–832. doi:10.1016/0167-8655(96)00043-8

Newman, D. J., Hettich, S., Blake, C. L., & Merz, C. J. (1998). *UCI repository of machine learning databases*. Retrieved from http://www.ics.uci.edu/~mlear/MLRepository.html

Newman, M. E. J. (2003). The structure and function of complex networks. *SIAM Review*, *45*(2), 167–256. doi:10.1137/S003614450342480

Nguyen Viet, A., & Ho Si, D. (2006). Applying weighted learning object to build adaptive course in e-learning. In *Proceedings of the Conference on Learning by Effective Utilization of Technologies: Facilitating Intercultural Understanding* (pp. 647-648).

Nguyen Viet, A. (2008). Constructing a Bayesian belief network to generate learning path in adaptive hypermedia system. *Journal of Computer Science and Cybermetics*, *1*(24), 12–19.

Niknam, T., Amiri, B., Olamaei, J., & Arefi, A. (2009). An efficient hybrid evolutionary optimization algorithm based on PSO and SA for clustering. *Journal of Zhejiang University. Science*, *10*(4), 512–519. doi:10.1631/jzus.A0820196

Norsham, I., Norazah, Y., & Puteh, S. (2009). Adaptive course sequencing for personalization of learning path using neural network. *International Journal of Advances in Soft Computing and its Applications*, *4*(1), 49-61.

Noy, N. F., & McGuinness, D. L. (2001). *Ontology development 101: A guide to creating your first ontology* (Tech. Rep. No. KSL-01-05, SMI-2001). Stanford, CA: Stanford Knowledge Systems Laboratory and Stanford Medical Informatics

Nurmi, D., Wolski, R., Grzegorczyk, C., Obertelli, G., Soman, S., Youseff, L., et al. (2009). The eucalyptus open source cloud computing system. In *Proceedings of the 9th IEEE/ACM International Symposium on Cluster Computing and the Grid* (p. 124).

OASIS. (2007). *Web Services Business Process Execution Language Version 2.0.*

Object Management Group. (2009). *Business Process Modeling Notation (BPMN) – Version 1.2.* Retrieved October 13, 2009, from http://www.omg.org/spec/BPMN/1.2/

Ogilvie, P., Voorhees, E., & Callan, J. (2009). On the number of terms used in automatic query expansion. *Information Retrieval*, *12*(6), 666–679. doi:10.1007/s10791-009-9104-1

Oh, S. C., Tan, H., Kong, F. W., Tan, Y. S., Ng, K. H., Ng, G. W., & Tai, K. (2007). Multi-objective optimization of sensor network deployment by a genetic algorithm. In *Proceedings of the IEEE Congress of Evolutionary Computation* (pp. 3917-3921).

Olfman, L., Seiin, M. K., & Bostrom, R. P. (1986). Training for end-user computing: Are basic abilities enough for learning? In *Proceedings of the Twenty-Second Annual Computer Personnel Research Conference*, Calgary, AB, Canada (pp. 1-11).

Oligny, S., Bourque, P., Abran, A., & Fournier, B. (2000). Exploring the relation between effort and duration in software engineering projects. In *Proceedings of the World Computer Congress*, Beijing, China (pp. 175-178).

Omelayenko, B. (2001). Learning of ontologies for the Web: The analysis of existent approaches. In *Proceedings of the International Workshop on Web Dynamics*, London, UK.

Orlich, D. C., Harder, R. J., Callahan, R. C., Trevisan, M. S., & Brown, A. B. (2004). *Teaching strategies, a guide to effective instruction* (7th ed.). Boston, MA: Houghton Mifflin.

Osman, T., Thakker, D., & Al-Dabass, D. (2009). Utilisation of case-based reasoning for semantic web services composition. *International Journal of Intelligent Information Technologies*, *5*(1), 24–42. doi:10.4018/jiit.2009092102

Paas, F. (1992). Training strategies for attaining transfer of problem-solving skill in statistics: A cognitive-load approach. *Journal of Educational Psychology*, *84*(4), 429–434. doi:10.1037/0022-0663.84.4.429

Page, A. J., & Naughton, T. J. (2005). Dynamic task scheduling using genetic algorithms for heterogeneous distributed computing. In *Proceedings of the IEEE International Symposium on Parallel and Distributed Processing* (p. 189).

Page, A. J., Keane, T. M., & Naughton, T. J. (2010). Multi-heuristic dynamic task allocation using genetic algorithms in a heterogeneous distributed system. *Journal of Parallel and Distributed Computing*, *70*(7), 758–766. doi:10.1016/j.jpdc.2010.03.011

Page, J., & Naughton, J. (2005). Framework for task scheduling in heterogeneous distributed computing using genetic algorithms. *Artificial Intelligence*, *24*(3-4), 415–429. doi:10.1007/s10462-005-9002-x

Pala, N., & Cicekli, I. (2008). Turkish keyphrase extraction using KEA. In *Proceedings of the Computer and Information Science Conference*. Washington, DC: IEEE Computer Society.

Pandey, S., Wu, L., Guru, S., & Buyya, R. (2009). A particle swarm optimization (PSO)-based heuristic for scheduling workflow applications in cloud computing environment. In *Proceedings of the 24th IEEE International Conference on Advanced Information Networking and Applications*, Perth, Australia (pp. 400-407).

Pang, B., Lee, L., & Vaithyanathan, S. (2002). Thumbs up? Sentiment Classification using Machine Learning Techniques. In D. Yarowsky & D. Radev (Eds.), *Proceedings of the Conference on Empirical Methods in Natural Language Processing,* Philadelphia (pp. 79-86).

Pang, B., & Lee, L. (2008). Opinion mining and sentiment analysis. In Callan, J., & Sebastiani, F. (Eds.), *Foundations and Trends in Information Retrieval 2*. Boston: Now Publishers.

Pankratius, V., Sandel, O., & Stucky, W. (2004). Retrieving content with agents in web service e-learning systems. In *Proceedings of the First Symposium on Professional Practice in AI and the First IFIP Conference on Artificial Intelligence Applications and Innovations*, Toulouse, France.

Papanikolaoum, K., & Grigoriadou, M. (2002). Towards new forms of knowledge communication: The adaptive dimensions of a web-based learning environment. *Computers & Education*, *39*, 333–360. doi:10.1016/S0360-1315(02)00067-2

Paramythis, A., & Loidl-Reisinger, S. (2004). Adaptive learning environments and e-learning standards. *Electronic Journal of eLearning*, *2*(1).

Pedrycz, W., & Succi, G. (2009). Fuzzy logic classifiers and models in quantitative software engineering. In Tiako, P. F. (Ed.), *Software applications: Concepts, methodologies, tools and applications* (pp. 3142–3159). Hershey, PA: IGI Global. doi:10.4018/978-1-60566-060-8.ch182

Pena-Reyes, C. A., & Sipper, M. (1999). A fuzzy-genetic approach to breast cancer diagnosis. *Artificial Intelligence in Medicine*, *17*, 131–155. doi:10.1016/S0933-3657(99)00019-6

Pfund, M. E., Balasubramanian, H., Fowler, J. W., Mason, S. J., & Rose, O. (2008). A multi-criteria approach for scheduling semiconductor wafer fabrication facilities. *Journal of Scheduling*, *11*, 29–47. doi:10.1007/s10951-007-0049-1

Picariello, A., & Rinaldi, A. M. (2007). User relevance feedback in semantic information retrieval. *International Journal of Intelligent Information Technologies*, *3*(2), 36–50. doi:10.4018/jiit.2007040103

Picton, A., Fabre, C., & Bourigault, D. (2008). Méthodes linguistiques pour l'expansion de requêtes. Une expérience basée sur l'utilisation du voisinage distributionnel. *Revue Française de Linguistique Appliquée*, *13*(1), 83–95.

Pinto, H. S., & Martins, J. P. (2004). Ontologies: How can they be built? *Knowledge and Information Systems*, *6*(4), 441–464. doi:10.1007/s10115-003-0138-1

Piramuthua, S., & Sikora, R. T. (2006). *Genetic Algorithm Based Learning Using Feature Construction*. Paper presented at the INFORMS Annual Meeting, Pittsburgh, PA.

Piramuthua, S., & Sikora, R. T. (2009). Iterative feature construction for improving inductive learning algorithms. *Expert Systems with Applications*, *36*(2), 3401–3406. doi:10.1016/j.eswa.2008.02.010

Platt, J. C. (1999). Fast training of support vector machines using sequential minimal optimization. In *Advances in kernel methods: support vector learning* (pp. 185–208). Cambridge, MA: MIT Press.

Pohle, C. (2003). Integrating and updating domain knowledge with data mining. In *Proceedings of the Very Large Data Bases PhD Workshop*, Berlin, Germany.

Pollandt, S. (1996). *Fuzzy-tag: Fuzzy formal concept analysis data*. Berlin, Germany: Springer-Verlag.

Popov, B., Kiryakov, A., Kirilov, A., Manov, D., Ognyanoff, D., & Goranov, M. (2003). KIM - semantic annotation platform. In *Proceedings of the International Semantic Web Conference* (pp. 834-849).

Prawat, R. S., & Floden, R. E. (1994). Philosophical-perspectives on constructivist views of learning. *Educational Psychologist, 29*(1), 37–48. doi:10.1207/s15326985ep2901_4

Puntheeranurak, P., & Tsuji, H. (2002). Mining web logs for a personalized recommender system based on web usage mining and decision tree induction. *Expert Systems with Applications, 23*(3), 329–342. doi:10.1016/S0957-4174(02)00052-0

Qi, Y., Yagci, A. I., et al. (2009). *Extraction of Key-phrases from Biomedical Full-text with Supervised Learning Techniques.* Paper presented at the 15th American Conference on Information Systems (AMCIS), San Francisco.

Qi, Y., Song, M., Yoon, S.-C., & Versterre, L. (2011). Combining supervised learning techniques to key-phrase extraction for biomedical full-text. *International Journal of Intelligent Information Technologies, 7*(1), 33–44. doi:10.4018/jiit.2011010103

Quan, T. T., Hui, S. C., & Cao, T. H. (2004). FOGA: A fuzzy ontology generation framework for scholarly semantic web. In *Proceedings of the Knowledge Discovery and Ontologies Workshop*, Pisa, Italy (Vol. 24).

Quinlain, J. R. (1987). Simplifying decision trees. *International Journal of Man-Machine Studies, 27*, 221–234. doi:10.1016/S0020-7373(87)80053-6

Raccoon, L. S. B., & Puppydog, P. P. O. (1998). A middle-out concept of hierarchy (or the problem of feeding the animals). *ACM SIGSOFT Software Engineering Notes, 23*(3), 111–119. doi:10.1145/279437.279489

Raghu, T., & Chen, H. (2007). Cyberinfrastructure for homeland security: Advances in information sharing, data mining, and collaboration systems. *Decision Support Systems, 43*(4), 1321–1323. doi:10.1016/j.dss.2006.04.002

Ram, S., & Zhao, H. (2007). Opportunities and challenges. *Information Technology Management, 8*(3), 203–204. doi:10.1007/s10799-007-0018-6

Rechenberg, I. (1973). *Evolutionsstrategie: Optimierung technischer systeme nach prinzipien der biologischen evolution.* Stuttgart, Germany: Frommann-Holzboog-Verlag.

Reiners, T., & Sassen, I. (2008). A framework for adaptive learning points. In Kidd, T. T., & Song, H. (Eds.), *Handbook of research on instructional systems and technology* (pp. 117–141). Hershey, PA: IGI Global. doi:10.4018/978-1-59904-865-9.ch010

Resink, P. (1999). Semantic similarity in taxonomy: An information-based measure and its application to problems of ambiguity in natural language. *Journal of Artificial Intelligence Research, 11*, 95–130.

Rigi, M. A., & Khoshalhan, F. (2011). Eliciting user preferences in multi-agent meeting scheduling problem. *International Journal of Intelligent Information Technologies, 7*(2), 45–62.

Riloff, E., Wiebe, J., & Phillips, W. (2005). Exploiting Subjectivity Classification to Improve Information Extraction. In M. Veloso & S. Kambhampati (Eds.), *Proceedings of the 20th National Conference on Artificial Intelligence,* Pittsburgh, PA (pp. 1106-1111).

Robnik-Sikonja, M., & Kononenko, I. (1997). An adaptation of relief for attribute estimation in regression. In *Proceedings of the Fourteenth International Conference on Machine Learning* (pp. 296-304).

Rosenberg, M. J. (2001). *E-learning strategies for delivering knowledge in the digital age.* New York, NY: McGraw-Hill.

Roubos, H., & Setnes, M. (2001). Compact and transparent fuzzy models and classifiers through iterative complexity reduction. *IEEE Transactions on Fuzzy Systems, 9*(4), 516–524. doi:10.1109/91.940965

Russel, S., & Yoon, V. Y. (2009). Agents, availability, awareness and decision making. *International Journal of Intelligent Information Technologies, 5*(4). doi:10.4018/jiit.2009080704

Russo, M. (2000). Genetic fuzzy learning. *IEEE Transactions on Evolutionary Computation, 4*(3), 259–273. doi:10.1109/4235.873236

Ruthven, I. (2003). Re-examining the potential effectiveness of interactive query expansion. In *Proceedings of the 26th Annual International ACM SIGIR Conference on Research and Development in Information Retrieval* (pp. 213-220).

Saaty, T. L. (2009). *Analytic hierarchy process*. New York, NY: McGraw-Hill.

Sadhasivam, S., Nagaveni, N., Jayarani, R., & Ram, R. V. (2009). Design and implementation of an efficient two level scheduler for cloud computing environment. In *Proceedings of the International Conference on Advances in Recent Technologies in Communication and Computing*. Kottayam, India (pp. 884-886).

Sadhasivam, S., & Rajendran, V. (2008). An efficient approach to task scheduling in computational grids. *International Journal of Computer Science and Applications*, *6*(1), 53–69.

Saeys, Y., Inza, I., & Larraaga, P. (2007). A review of feature selection techniques in bioinformatics. *Bioinformatics (Oxford, England)*, *23*(19), 2507–2517. doi:10.1093/bioinformatics/btm344

Salton, G. (1989). *Automatic text processing*. Reading, MA: Addison-Wesley.

Salton, G., & Buckley, C. (1988). Term-weighting approaches in automatic text retrieval. *Information Processing and Management: An International Journal*, *24*(5), 513–523. doi:10.1016/0306-4573(88)90021-0

Salton, G., & Buckley, C. (1990). Improving retrieval performance by relevance feedback. *Journal of the American Society for Information Science American Society for Information Science*, *41*(4), 288–297. doi:10.1002/(SICI)1097-4571(199006)41:4<288::AID-ASI8>3.0.CO;2-H

Salton, G., & McGill, M. J. (1983). *Introduction to modern information retrieval*. New York, NY: McGraw-Hill.

Salton, G., Wong, A., & Yang, C. S. (1975). A vector space model for automatic indexing. *Communications of the ACM*, *18*(11), 613–620. doi:10.1145/361219.361220

Sammon, W. (1969). A nonlinear mapping for data analysis. *IEEE Transactions on Computers*, *18*(5), 401–409. doi:10.1109/T-C.1969.222678

Sánchez, D., & Moreno, A. (2008). Learning non-taxonomic relationships from web documents for domain ontology construction. *Data & Knowledge Engineering*, *64*(3), 600–623. doi:10.1016/j.datak.2007.10.001

Santos, C. T., & Osorio, F. S. (2004). Integrating intelligent agents, user models, and automatic content categorization in a virtual environment. In J. C. Lester, R. M. Vicari, & F. Paraguacu (Eds.), *Proceedings of the 7th International Conference on Intelligent Tutoring Systems* (LNCS 3220, pp. 128-139).

Santos, I. G. D., & Madeira, E. (2010). A semantic-enabled middleware for citizen-centric e-government services. *International Journal of Intelligent Information Technologies*, *6*(3), 34–55. doi:10.4018/jiit.2010070103

Sayyad Shirabad, J., & Menzies, T. (2005). *The PROMISE repository of software engineering databases*. Retrieved from http://promise.site.uottawa.ca/SERepository

Schaffert, S., Gruber, A., & Westenthaler, R. (2006). *A semantic wiki for collaborative knowledge formation*. Paper presented at Semantic Content Engineering.

Schreiber, T. G. A., Wielinga, B. J., & Jansweijer, W. (1995). *The KACTUS view on the 'O' word*. Paper presented at the 7th Dutch National Conference on Artificial Intelligence NAIC'95.

Schwefel, H.-P. (1975). *Evolutionsstrategie and numerische Optimierung*. Unpublished doctoral dissertation, Technische Universitat Berlin, Germany.

Sein, M. K., Bostrom, R. P., & Olfman, L. (1987). Conceptual models in training novice users. In *Proceedings of the Third Conference of the British Computer Society Human Computer Interaction*, Stuttgart, West Germany (pp. 861-867).

Sen, S., Haynes, T., & Arora, N. (1997). Satisfying user preferences while negotiating meetings. *International Journal of Human-Computer Studies*, *47*, 407–415. doi:10.1006/ijhc.1997.0139

Seo, J. H., Kim, Y. H., Ryou, H. B., & Kang, S. J. (2008). Agenetic algorithm for sensor deployment based on two-dimensional operators. In *Proceedings of the ACM Symposium on Applied Computing* (pp. 1812-1813).

Seo, Y.-S., Yoon, K.-A., & Bae, D.-H. (2008). An empirical analysis of software effort estimation with outlier elimination. In *Proceedings of the 4th International Workshop on Predictor Models in Software Engineering* (pp. 25-32). New York, NY: ACM Press.

Seridi, H., Sari, T., Khadir, T., & Sellami, M. (2006). Adaptive instructional planning in intelligent learning systems. In *Proceedings of the Sixth International Conference on Advanced Learning Technologies* (pp. 133-135).

Setnes, M., & Roubos, H. (2000). GA-fuzzy modeling and classification: Complexity and performance. *IEEE Transactions on Fuzzy Systems*, *8*(5), 509–522. doi:10.1109/91.873575

Shaft, T. M., & Vessey, I. (2006). The role of cognitive fit in the relationship between software comprehension and modification. *Management Information Systems Quarterly*, *30*(1), 29–55.

Shamsfard, M., Nematzadeh, A., & Motiee, S. (2006). ORank: An ontology based system for ranking document. *International Journal of Computer Science*, *1*, 225–231.

Sharma, A., & Dhir, R. (2009). A wordsets based document clustering algorithm for large datasets. In *Proceedings of the International Conference on Methods and Models in Computer Science* (pp. 1-7).

Sharma, D. K., & Sharma, A. K. (2010). Deep web information retrieval process: A technical survey. *International Journal of Information Technology and Web Engineering*, *5*(1), 1–22. doi:10.4018/jitwe.2010010101

Shehata, S., Karray, F., & Kamel, M. S. (2010). An efficient concept-based mining model for enhancing text clustering. *IEEE Transactions on Knowledge and Data Engineering*, *22*(10), 1360–1371. doi:10.1109/TKDE.2009.174

Shen, L. Z. (2010). A novel efficient mining association rules algorithm for distributed databases. *Journal of Advanced Materials Research*, *108*(111), 50–56. doi:10.4028/www.scientific.net/AMR.108-111.50

Shepperd, M., & Schofield, C. (1997). Estimating software project effort using analogies. *IEEE Transactions on Software Engineering*, *23*(12), 736–743. doi:10.1109/32.637387

Shi, Y. H., & Eberhart, R. C. (1998). Parameter selection in particle swarm optimization. In *Proceedings of the Annual Conference on Evolutionary Programming*, San Diego, CA.

Shi, Y. H., & Eberhart, R. C. (1999). Empirical study of particle swarm optimization. In *Proceedings of the Congress on Evolutionary Computation* (Vol. 3).

Shi, J., & Malik, J. (2000). Normalized cuts and image segmentation. *IEEE Transactions on Pattern Analysis and Machine Intelligence*, *22*(8), 888–905. doi:10.1109/34.868688

Shouhong, Z., & Ding, Z. (2009). A simple approach of range-based positioning with low computational complexity. *IEEE Transactions on Wireless Communications*, *8*(12), 5832–5836. doi:10.1109/TWC.2009.12.090905

Shu, T., Krunz, M., & Vrudhula, S. (2006). Joint optimization of transmit power-time and bit energy efficiency in CDMA wireless sensor networks. *IEEE Transactions on Wireless Communications*, *5*(11), 3109–3118. doi:10.1109/TWC.2006.04738

Sieg, A., Mobasher, B., & Burke, R. (2007). Learning ontology based user profiles: A semantic approach to personalized web search. *IEEE Intelligent Informatics Bulletin*, *8*, 7–18.

Simón Cuevas, A. J. (2008). *Herramientas para el perfeccionamiento de los sistemas de gestión de conocimiento basados en mapas conceptuales*. Unpublished doctoral disseration.

Sinha, A. P., & Zhao, H. (2008). Incorporating domain knowledge into data mining classifiers: An application in indirect lending. *Decision Support Systems*, *46*(1), 287–299. doi:10.1016/j.dss.2008.06.013

Sitkin, S. B., & Weingart, L. R. (1995). Determinants of risky decision-making behavior: A test of the mediating role of risk perceptions and propensity. *Academy of Management Journal*, *38*, 1573–1592. doi:10.2307/256844

Smeaton, A. F. (1983). The retrieval effects of query expansion on a feedback document retrieval system. *The Computer Journal*, *26*(3), 239–246. doi:10.1093/comjnl/26.3.239

Smeaton, A. F. (1997). Using NLP or NLP resources for information retrieval tasks. In Strzalkowski, T. (Ed.), *Natural language information retrieval* (pp. 99–111). Dordrecht, The Netherlands: Kluwer Academic.

Smialowski, P., Frishman, D., & Kramer, S. (2010). Pitfalls of supervised feature selection. *Bioinformatics (Oxford, England)*, *26*(3), 440–443. doi:10.1093/bioinformatics/btp621

Smith, M.K., Welty, C., & McGuiness, D.L. (2004). *OWL Web Ontology Language Guide.*

Smith, J. E., & Nair, R. (2005). *Virtual machines - versatile platforms for systems and processes*. San Francisco, CA: Morgan Kauffman.

Snow, R. E. (1986). Individual differences in the design of educational programs. *The American Psychologist*, *41*(10), 1029–1039. doi:10.1037/0003-066X.41.10.1029

Snow, R. E. (1989). Aptitude-treatment interaction as a framework for research on individual differences in learning. In Ackerman, P., Strenberg, R. J., & Glaser, R. (Eds.), *Learning and individual differences*. New York, NY: W. H. Freeman.

Song, J. F., Zhang, W. M., Xiao, W., Li, G. H., & Xu, Z. N. (2005). Ontology-based information retrieval model for the semantic web. In *Proceedings of the IEEE Computer Society* (pp. 152-155).

Song, L., Ma, J., Yan, P., Lian, L., & Zhang, D. (2008). Clustering deep web databases semantically. In *Proceedings of the 4th Asia Information Retrieval Conference on Information Retrieval Technology* (pp. 365-376).

Song, M., Song, I.-Y., et al. (2003). KPSpotter: a flexible information gain-based keyphrase extraction system. In *Proceedings of the International Workshop on Web Information and Data Management.* New York: ACM Press.

Sotomayor, B., Montero, R. S., Llorente, I. M., & Foster, I. (2008). *Capacity leasing in cloud systems using the OpenNebula engine.* Paper presented at the Workshop on Cloud Computing and its Applications, Chicago, IL.

Sotomayor, B., Montero, R. S., Llorente, I. M., & Foster, I. (2009). Virtual infrastructure management in private and hybrid clouds. *IEEE Internet Computing*, *13*(5), 14–22. doi:10.1109/MIC.2009.119

Sourirajan, K., & Uzsoy, R. (2007). Hybrid decomposition heuristics for solving large-scale scheduling problems in semiconductor wafer fabrication. *Journal of Scheduling*, *10*(1), 41–65. doi:10.1007/s10951-006-0325-5

Spyns, P., Meersman, R., & Jarrar, M. (2002). Data modelling versus ontology engineering. *SIGMOD Record*, *31*(4), 12–17. doi:10.1145/637411.637413

Sridevi, U. K., & Nagaveni, N. (2009). Ontology based semantic measures in document similarity ranking. In *Proceedings of the International Conference on Advances in Recent Technologies in Communication and Computing* (pp. 482-486).

Sridevi, U. K., & Nagaveni, N. (2009). Ontology based correlation analysis in information retrieval. *International Journal of Recent Trends in Engineering*, *2*(1), 134–137.

Sridev, U. K., & Nagaveni, N. (2010). Ontology based similarity measure in document ranking. *International Journal of Computers and Applications*, *1*(26), 125–129.

Srinivasan, K., & Fisher, D. (1995). Machine learning approaches to estimating software development effort. *IEEE Transactions on Software Engineering*, *21*(2), 126–137. doi:10.1109/32.345828

Stanford, N. L. P. Group. (2009). *The Stanford Parser: A statistical parser.* Retrieved from http://nlp.stanford.edu/software/lex-parser.shtml

Steinberg, E. R. (1989). Cognition and learner control: A literature review, 1977-1988. *Journal of Computer Based Instruction*, *16*(4), 117–121.

Sugiura, N., Kurematsu, M., Fukuta, N., Izumi, N., & Yamaguchi, T. (2003). A domain ontology engineeering tool with general ontologies and text corpus. In *Proceedings of the 2nd Workshop on Evaluation of Ontology based Tools* (pp. 71-82).

Suh, K., & Lee, Y. E. (2005). The effects of virtual reality on consumer learning: An empirical investigation. *Management Information Systems Quarterly*, *29*(4), 673–697.

Sun, H., Liu, Z., & Kong, L. (2008). A document clustering method based on hierarchical algorithm with model clustering. In *Proceedings of the 22nd International Conference on Advanced Information Networking and Applications* (pp. 1229-1233).

Sure, Y., & Studer, R. (2002). *On-to-knowledge methodology - final version (On-To-Knowledge Deliverable 18)*. Karlsruhe, Germany: Institute AIFB, University of Karlsruhe.

Swartout, W. R., Patil, R., Knight, K., & Russ, T. (1996). *Toward Distributed Use of Large-Scale Ontologies*. Paper presented at the Tenth Workshop on Knowledge Acquisition for Knowledge-Based Systems.

Tai, X., Ren, F., & Kita, K. (2002). An information retrieval model based on vector space method by supervised learning. *Information Processing & Management, 38*(6), 749–764. doi:10.1016/S0306-4573(01)00053-X

Tasgetiren, M. F., Sevkli, M., Liang, Y.-C., & Gencyilmaz, G. (2004). Particle swarm optimization algorithm for permutation flow shop sequencing problem. In M. Dorigo, M. Birattari, C. Blum, L. M. Gambardella, F. Mondada, & T. Stutzle (Eds.), *Proceedings of the 4th International Workshop on Ant Colony, Optimization, and Swarm Intelligence* (LNCS 3172, pp. 382-390).

Tasgetiren, M. F., Sevkli, M., Liang, Y.-C., & Gencyilmaz, G. (2004). Particle swarm optimization algorithm for single-machine total weighted tardiness problem. In. *Proceedings of the Congress on Evolutionary Computation, 2*, 1412–1419.

Tenenboim, L., Shapira, B., & Shoval, P. (2008). *Ontology-based classification of news in an electronic newspaper* (pp. 89-98). Retrieved from http://sci-gems.math.bas.bg:8080/jspui/handle/10525/1035

Thomas, O., & vom Brocke, J. (2010). A Value-Driven Approach to the Design of Service-Oriented Information Systems – Making Use of Conceptual Models. *Information Systems and e-Business Management, 8*(1), 67-97.

Thomas, M. A., Redmond, T. R., & Yoon, V. Y. (2009). Using ontological reasoning for an adaptive e-commerce experience. *International Journal of Intelligent Information Technologies, 5*(4), 41–52. doi:10.4018/jiit.2009080703

Thomas, O., Dollmann, T., & Loos, P. (2008). Rules Integration in Business Process Models – A Fuzzy Oriented Approach. *Enterprise Modelling and Information Systems Architectures, 3*(1), 18–30.

Thomas, O., & Fellmann, M. (2009). Semantic Process Modeling – Design and Implementation of an Ontology-Based Representation of Business Processes. *Business & Information Systems Engineering, 1*(6), 438–451. doi:10.1007/s12599-009-0078-8

Tripathi, A., Gupta, P., Trivedi, A., & Kala, R. (2011). Wireless sensor node placement using hybrid genetic programming and genetic algorithms. *International Journal of Intelligent Information Technologies, 7*(2), 63–83.

Tsai, T., Shih, C.-C., & Chou, S. T. (2006). Personalized blog recommendation using the value, semantic, and social model. In *Proceedings of the Innovations in Information Technology* (pp. 1-5).

Tsikriktsis, N. (2005). A review of techniques for treating missing data in OM survey research. *Journal of Operations Management, 24*(1), 53–62. doi:10.1016/j.jom.2005.03.001

Tsochantaridis, I., Hofmann, T., Joachims, T., & Altun, Y. (2004). Support vector machine learning for interdependent and structured output spaces. In C. Brodley (Ed.), *Proceedings of the 21st International Conference on Machine Learning,* Banff, AB, Canada (pp. 104-108).

Tsuruta, T., & Shintani, T. (2000). Scheduling meetings using distributed valued constraint satisfaction algorithm. In *Proceedings of the 14th European Conference on Artificial Intelligence* (pp. 383-387).

Tuckman, B. W. (2003). The effect of learning and motivation strategies training on college students' achievement. *Journal of College Student Development, 44*(3), 430. doi:10.1353/csd.2003.0034

Tun, N., & Tojo, S. (2008). enontoModel: A semantically-enriched model for ontologies. *International Journal of Intelligent Information Technologies, 4*(1), 1–30. doi:10.4018/jiit.2008010101

Tuominen, J., Kauppinen, T., Viljanen, K., & Hyvönen, E. (2009). Ontology-based query expansion widget for information retrieval. In *Proceedings of the 5th Workshop on Scripting and Development for the Semantic Web co-located with the 6th European Semantic Web Conference* (Vol. 449).

Turney, P. (2000). Learning algorithms for keyphrase extraction. *Journal of Digital Information.*

Turney, P. (2001). Thumbs up or thumbs down? semantic orientation applied to unsupervised classification of reviews. In P. Isabelle (Ed.), *Proceedings of the 40th Annual Meeting on Association for Computational Linguistics,* Philadelphia (pp. 417-424).

Turney, P. D. (1999). *Learning to Extract Keyphrases from Text* (Tech. Rep. ERB-1057 NRC #41622). Ottawa, ON, Canada: National Research Council, Institute for Information Technology.

Turney, P. (1997). *Extraction of key Phrases from Text: Evaluation of Four Algorithms*. Ottawa, ON, Canada: National Research Council.

Turney, P. D. (2000). Learning Algorithms for Keyphrase Extraction. *Information Retrieval, 2*(4), 303–336. doi:10.1023/A:1009976227802

Uschold, M., & King, M. (1995). *Towards a methodology for building ontologies*. Paper presented at the Workshop on Basic Ontological Issues in Knowledge Sharing.

Uschold, M. (1996). *Building ontologies: Towards a unified methodology*. Edinburgh, UK: University of Edinburgh.

Uschold, M., & Grüninger, M. (1996). Ontologies: principles, methods and applications. *The Knowledge Engineering Review, 11*, 93–136. doi:10.1017/S0269888900007797

Vaishnavi, V. K., & Kuechler, W. (2007). *Design science research methods and patterns: Innovating information and communication technology*. Boca Raton, FL: Auerbach Publications. doi:10.1201/9781420059335

Valkeapää, O., Alm, O., & Hyvönen, E. (2007). An adaptable framework for ontology-based content creation on the semantic web. *Journal of Universal Computer Science, 13*(12), 1825–1853.

Vallet, D., Fernandez, M., & Castells, P. (2005). An ontology based information retrieval model. In *Proceedings of the Second European Semantic Web Conference* (pp. 455-470).

van der Spek, P., Klusener, S., & van de Laar, P. (2008). Towards recovering architectural concepts using latent semantic indexing. In *Proceedings of the 12th European Conference on Software Maintenance and Reengineering* (pp. 253-257).

Vanderhaeghen, D., Hofer, A., & Kupsch, F. (2006). Process-Driven Business Integration Management for Collaboration Networks. In Cunha, M. M., & Putnik, G. D. (Eds.), *Knowledge and Technology Management in Virtual Organizations: Issues, Trends, Opportunities and Solutions* (pp. 190–210). Hershey, PA: Idea Group Publishing.

Varelas, G., Voutsakis, E., Raftopoulou, P., Petrakis, E. G., & Milios, E. E. (2005). Semantic similarity methods in wordnet and their application to information retrieval on the web. In *Proceedings of the 7th Annual ACM International Workshop on Web Information and Data Management* (pp. 10-16).

Vélez, B., Weiss, R., Sheldon, M., & Gifford, D. (1997). Fast and effective query refinement. In *Proceedings of the 20th Annual International ACM SIGIR Conference on Research and Development in Information Retrieval* (pp. 6-15).

Verma, A., Ahuja, P., & Neogi, A. (2008). pMapper: Power and migration cost aware application placement in virtualized systems. In V. Issarny & R. Schantz (Eds.), *Proceedings of Middleware* (LNCS 5346, pp. 243-264).

Vessey, I., & Galletta, D. (1991). Cognitive fit: An empirical study of information acquisition. *Information Systems Research, 2*(1), 63–84. doi:10.1287/isre.2.1.63

Von Glasersfeld, E. (1989). Constructvism in education. In Husen, T., & Postlethwaite, T. N. (Eds.), *The international encyclopedia of education* (pp. 162–163). Oxford, UK: Pergamon Press.

Voorhees, E. M. (1994). Query expansion using lexical-semantic relations. In *Proceedings of the 17th Annual International ACM SIGIR Conference on Research and Development in Information Retrieval* (pp. 61-69).

Vozalis, E. G., & Margaritis, K. G. (2003). Recommender systems: An experimental comparison of two filtering algorithms. In *Proceedings of the Ninth Pan-Hellenic Conference in Informatics*, Thessaloniki, Greece (pp. 152-166).

Vygotsky, L. S. (1978). *Mind in society: The development of higher psychological processes*. Cambridge, MA: Harvard University Press.

Vykoukal, J., Wolf, M., & Beck, R. (2009). Services Grids in Industry – On-Demand Provisioning and Allocation of Grid-Based Business Services. *Business & Information Systems Engineering*, *1*(2), 206–214. doi:10.1007/s12599-008-0009-0

Wang, L., von Laszewskiy, G., Dayalz, J., & Wang, F. (2010). Towards energy aware scheduling for precedence constrained parallel tasks in a cluster with DVFS. In *Proceedings of the International Conference on Cluster, Cloud and Grid*, Melbourne, Australia (pp. 368-377).

Wang, X., & Whigham, P. & Deng, D., & Purvis, M. (2004). "Time-line" hidden markov experts for time series prediction. *Neural Information Processing - Letters and Reviews, 3*(2), 39-48.

Wang, X., Xie, Y., & Li, B. (2006). A hybrid information filtering model. In *Proceedings of the IEEE International Conference on Computational Intelligence and Security*, Guangzhou, China (pp. 1049-1054).

Wang, C. H., Hong, T., & Tseng, S. (1998). Integrating fuzzy knowledge by genetic algorithms. *IEEE Transactions on Evolutionary Computation*, *2*(4), 138–148. doi:10.1109/4235.738978

Wang, H. (1997). LearnOOP: An active agent-based educational system. *Expert Systems with Applications*, *12*(2), 153–162. doi:10.1016/S0957-4174(96)00090-5

Wang, H. (1997). SQL Tutor+: A co-operative ITS with repository support. *Information and Software Technology*, *39*, 343–350. doi:10.1016/S0950-5849(96)01152-4

Wang, H., Yang, Y., Ma, M., He, J., & Wang, X. (2008). Network lifetime maximization with cross-layer design in wireless sensor networks. *IEEE Transactions on Wireless Communications*, *7*(10), 3759–3768. doi:10.1109/T-WC.2008.070079

Wang, L. X., & Mendel, J. M. (1992). Generating fuzzy rules by learning from examples. *IEEE Transactions on Systems, Man, and Cybernetics*, *22*, 1414–1427. doi:10.1109/21.199466

Wang, Q., Xu, K., Takahara, G., & Hassanein, H. (2007). Device placement for heterogeneous wireless sensor networks: minimum cost with lifetime constraints. *IEEE Transactions on Wireless Communications*, *6*(7), 2444–2453. doi:10.1109/TWC.2007.05357

Watts, D. J., & Strogatz, S. H. (1998). Collective dynamics of 'small-world' networks. *Nature*, *393*(6684), 440–442. doi:10.1038/30918

Wei, W., Barjaghi, P. M., & Bargiela, A. (2007). Semantic enhanced information search and retrieval. In *Proceedings of the Sixth International Conference on Advance Language and Web Information Technology* (pp. 218-223).

Wein, L. M. (1998). Scheduling semiconductor wafer fabrication. *IEEE Transactions on Semiconductor Manufacturing*, *1*, 115–130. doi:10.1109/66.4384

Werner, L., & Böttcher, S. (2007). Supporting Text Retrieval by Typographical Term Weighting. *International Journal of Intelligent Information Technologies*, *3*(2), 1–16.

Wiebe, J., Bruce, R., & O'Hara, T. (1999). Development and use of a gold-standard data set for subjectivity classifications. In R. Dale & K. Church (Eds.), *Proceedings of the 37th Annual meeting of the Association for Computational Linguistics on Computational Linguistics,* College Park, MD (pp. 246-253).

Wiebe, J., Wilson, T., Bruce, R., Bell, M., & Martin, M. (2004). Learning Subjective Language. *Computational Linguistics*, *30*(3), 277–308. doi:10.1162/0891201041850885

Wielinga, B. J., Schreiber, T. G. A., & Breuker, J. A. (1992). KADS: a modelling approach to knowledge engineering. *Knowledge Acquisition*, *4*(1), 5–53. doi:10.1016/1042-8143(92)90013-Q

Win, T., & Mon, L. (2010). Document clustering by fuzzy c-mean algorithm. In *Proceedings of the 2nd International Conference on Advanced Computer Control* (pp. 239-242).

Winkler, R., Klawonn, F., & Kruse, R. (2011). Fuzzy c-means in high dimensional spaces. *International Journal of Fuzzy System Applications*, *1*(1), 1–16.

Witten, I. H., Paynter, G. W., et al. (1999). KEA: Practical Automatic Keyphrase Extraction. In *Proceedings of the Fourth on Digital Libraries '99*. New York: ACM Press.

Witten, I. H., & Frank, E. (2005). *Data mining: Practical machine learning tools and techniques* (2nd ed.). San Francisco, CA: Morgan Kaufmann.

Wolff, R., & Schuster, A. (2004). Association rule mining in peer-to-peer systems. *IEEE Transactions on Cybernetics. Part B: Cybernetics*, *34*(6), 2426–2438. doi:10.1109/TSMCB.2004.836888

Wooldridge, M., & Jennings, N. (1995). Intelligent agents: Theory and practice. *The Knowledge Engineering Review*, *10*(2), 115–152. doi:10.1017/S0269888900008122

Wrather, C., & Yu, P. L. (1982). Probability dominance in random outcomes. *Journal of Optimization Theory and Applications*, *3*, 315–334. doi:10.1007/BF00934350

Xie, X. L., & Beni, G. (1991). A validity measure for fuzzy clustering. *IEEE Transactions on Pattern Analysis and Machine Intelligence*, *13*, 841–847. doi:10.1109/34.85677

Xing, J., Han, M., & Tao, X. (2009). A wetland protection domain ontology construction for knowledge management and information sharing. *Human and Ecological Risk Assessment: An International Journal*, *15*(2), 298–315.

Xu, D., & Wang, H. (2006). Intelligent agent supported personalization for virtual learning environments. *Decision Support Systems*, *42*, 825–843. doi:10.1016/j.dss.2005.05.033

Yang, X., Guo, D., Cao, X., & Zhou, J. (2008). Research on ontology-based text clustering. In *Proceedings of the Third International Workshop on Semantic Media Adaptation and Personalization* (pp. 141-146).

Yang, Y. (1995). Noise reduction in a statistical approach to text categorization. In *Proceedings of the 18th Annual International ACM SIGIR Conference on Research and Development in Information Retrieval*, Seattle, WA (pp. 256-263).

Yao, Z., & Choi, B. (2007). Clustering Web Pages into Hierarchical Categories. *International Journal of Intelligent Information Technologies*, *3*(2), 17–35.

Yener, B., Ismail, M. M., & Sivrikaya, F. (2007). Joint problem of power optimal connectivity and coverage in wireless sensor networks. *Journal of Wireless Networks*, *13*(4), 537–550. doi:10.1007/s11276-006-5875-0

Yi, J., & Niblack, W. (2005). Sentiment Mining in WebFountain. In K. Aberer, M. Franklin, & S. Nishio (Eds.), *Proceedings of the 21st International Conference on Data Engineering*, Tokyo (pp. 1073-1083).

Yi, J., Nasukawa, T., Bunescu, R., & Niblack, W. (2003). Sentiment Analyzer: Extracting Sentiments about a Given Topic using Natural Language Processing Techniques. In J. Shavlik (Ed.), *Proceedings of the Third IEEE International Conference on Data Mining*, Melbourne, FL (pp. 427-434).

Yoon, H. J., & Shen, W. (2008). A multiagent-based decision-making system for semiconductor wafer fabrication with hard temporal constraints. *IEEE Transactions on Semiconductor Manufacturing*, *21*(1), 83–91. doi:10.1109/TSM.2007.914388

Youssef, H., Brigitte, C. M., & Noureddine, Z. (2002). A genetic algorithm and data mining based meta-heuristic for job shop scheduling problem. In *Proceedings of the IEEE International Conference on Systems, Man and Cybernetics* (Vol. 7, pp. 280-285).

Yu, H., & Hatzivassiloglou, V. (2003). Towards answering opinion questions: separating facts from opinions and identifying the polarity of opinion sentences. In M. Collins & M. Steedman (Eds.), *Proceedings of the 2003 Conference on Empirical Methods in Natural Language Processing*, Sapporo, Japan (pp. 129-136).

Yuhui, S., Russell, E., & Yaobin, C. (1999). Implementation of evolutionary fuzzy system. *IEEE Transactions on Fuzzy Systems*, *7*(2), 109–119. doi:10.1109/91.755393

Yunhuai, L., Ngan, H., & Ni, L. M. (2007). Power-aware node deployment in wireless sensor network. *International Journal of Distributed Sensor Networks*, *3*(2), 225–241. doi:10.1080/15501320701205597

Zadeh, L. A. (1978). Fuzzy sets as a basis for a theory of possibility. *Fuzzy Sets and Systems*, *1*(1), 3–28. doi:10.1016/0165-0114(78)90029-5

Zelenko, D., Aone, C., & Richardella, A. (2003). Kernel methods for relation extraction. *Journal of Machine Learning Research*, *3*, 1083–1106. doi:10.1162/153244303322533205

Zelikovitz, S., & Hirsh, H. (2001). Using LSI for text classification in the presence of background text. In *Proceedings of the Tenth International Conference on Information and Knowledge Management*, Atlanta, GA (pp. 113-118).

Zhai, J., Chen, Y., Wang, Q., & Lv, M. (2008). Fuzzy ontology models using intuitionistic fuzzy set for knowledge sharing on the semantic web. In *Proceedings of the 12th International Conference on Computer Supported Cooperative Work in Design*.

Zhang, X., Jing, L., Hu, X., Ng, M., & Zhou, X. (2007). A comparative study of ontology based term similarity measures on PubMed document clustering. In *Proceedings of the 12th International Conference on Database Systems for Advanced Applications* (pp. 115-126).

Zhang, Y., Zincir-Heywood, N., et al. (2005). Narrative text classification for automatic key phrase extraction in web document corpora. In *Proceedings of the 7th Annual ACM International Workshop on Web Information and Data Management,* Bremen, Germany. New York: ACM Press.

Zhang, Z., Cheng, H., Zhang, S., Chen, W., & Fang, Q. (2008). Clustering aggregation based on genetic algorithm for documents clustering. In *Proceedings of the IEEE Congress on Evolutionary Computation* (pp. 3156-3161).

Zhang, H., Jiang, Z., & Guo, C. (2009). Simulation-based optimization of dispatching rules for semiconductor wafer fabrication system scheduling by the response surface methodology. *International Journal of Advanced Manufacturing Technology*, *41*(1-2), 110–121. doi:10.1007/s00170-008-1462-0

Zhang, L. (2009). *Maximum Entropy Modeling Toolkit for Python and C*. Retrieved from.http://homepages.inf.ed.ac.uk/s0450736/maxent_toolkit.html

Zhang, L., & Wang, Z. (2010). Ontology-based clustering algorithm with feature weights. *Journal of Computer Information Systems*, *6*(9), 2959–2966.

Zhang, X., Jing, L., Hu, X., Ng, M., Jiangxi, J. X., & Zhou, X. (2008). Medical document using ontology based term similarity measures. *International Journal of Data Warehousing and Mining*, *4*(1), 62–73. doi:10.4018/jdwm.2008010104

Zhao, C., Yu, Z., & Chen, P. (2007). Optimal deployment of nodes based on genetic algorithm in heterogeneous sensor networks. In *Proceedings of the International Conference on Wireless Communication Networking and Mobile Computing* (pp. 2743-2746).

Zhou, X., Li, Y., Bruza, P., Wu, S., Xuusing, Y., & Lau, R. Y. K. (2007). Information filtering in web data mining. In *Proceedings of the IEEE/WIC/ACM International Conference on Web Intelligence*, Silicon Valley, CA (pp. 163-169).

Zhou, L. (2007). Ontology learning: State of the art and open issues. *Information Technology Management*, *8*(3), 241–252. doi:10.1007/s10799-007-0019-5

About the Contributors

Vijayan Sugumaran is Professor of Management Information Systems in the department of Decision and Information Sciences at Oakland University, Rochester, Michigan, USA. He is also WCU Professor of Global Service Management at Sogang University, Seoul, South Korea. He received his PhD in Information Technology from George Mason University, Fairfax, VA. His research interests are in the areas of service science, ontologies and semantic web, intelligent agent and multi-agent systems, component based software development, and knowledge-based systems. He has published more than 150 articles in journals, conferences, and books. His most recent publications have appeared in *Information Systems Research, ACM Transactions on Database Systems, IEEE Transactions on Education, IEEE Transactions on Engineering Management, Communications of the ACM, Healthcare Management Science*, and *Data and Knowledge Engineering*. He has edited twelve books and two journal special issues. He is the Editor-in-Chief of the *International Journal of Intelligent Information Technologies* and also serves on the editorial board of seven other journals. He was the program co-chair for the International Conference on Applications of Natural Language to Information Systems (NLDB 2008 and NLDB 2013). In addition, he has served as the chair of the Intelligent Agent and Multi-Agent Systems mini-track for Americas Conference on Information Systems (AMCIS 1999 - 2013) and Intelligent Information Systems track for the Information Resources Management Association International Conference (IRMA 2001, 2002, 2005 - 2007). He served as Chair of the E-Commerce track for Decision Science Institute's Annual Conference, 2004. He was the Information Technology Coordinator for the Decision Sciences Institute (2007-2009). He also regularly serves as a program committee member for numerous national and international conferences.

* * *

Sami A. M. Al-Radaei is a full time research scholar in the department of computer engineering, IT, BHU, Varanasi-221005 India. He holds a BSc (Engg.) form Technology University, Iraq and MCA degree from Osmania University, India. His research interests include computational method for e-learning, and Semantic Web Services.

Toly Chen received the BS degree, the MS degree, and the PhD degree in industrial engineering from National Tsin Hua University. He is now a professor in the department of industrial engineering and systems management of Feng Chia University. Dr. Chen received IEA/AIE Best Paper Award from International Society of Applied Intelligence in 2009. Dr. Chen is the founding Editor-in-Chief of *International Journal of Fuzzy System Applications* and also on the editorial boards of several international journals.

Nikolai Dahlem holds a masters degree in computer science. He's currently a Ph.D. student with the Business Engineering Group at the Department of Computer Science of the University of Oldenburg, Germany. His research interests are semantic web technologies, ontologies and usability.

S.N.Deepa is currently working as an Assistant Professor in the Department of Electrical and Electronics Engineering, Anna University of Technology Coimbatore, Coimbatore-641047. She has published 32 papers in international journals, 18 papers in national journals and 7 chapters in national/ international books. Her research interest includes Soft Computing Techniques, Linear and Non-Linear System Analysis and Design, Modeling and Simulation.

Jeremiah D. Deng obtained the BEng degree from the University of Electronic Science and Technology of China in 1989, and the MEng and PhD from the South China University of Technology in 1992 and 1995 respectively. He is now a Senior Lecturer at the Department of Information Science, University of Otago. Dr. Deng's research interests include multimedia information retrieval, data mining, neural networks and machine learning. He is a member of IEEE.

Thorsten Dollmann is a researcher at the Institute for Information Systems at the German Research Center for Artificial Intelligence (DFKI). He received diplomas of Business Administration as well as Computer Science from Saarland University. His fields of research are business process management and enterprise architecture. Thorsten Dollmann is currently working on his PhD thesis.

Michael Fellmann is currently working on his PhD thesis at the Institute of Information Management and Corporate Governance, University of Osnabrueck. He has been a research assistant at the Institute for Information Systems at the German Research Center for Artificial Intelligence (DFKI). Michael Fellmann received a Master of Arts in Information Science, Computer Science and Information Systems from the Saarland University. His fields of research are business process management, enterprise modeling and semantic technologies.

Andreas Hoheisel studied geophysics at the University of Cologne/Germany. Since 2000 he works as scientist at the Fraunhofer Institute for Computer Architecture and Software Technology (FIRST) in Berlin/Adlershof. His research topics evolved from coupling mechanisms for simulation models up to generic methods of process management and resource scheduling in distributed systems (SOA, Grid, Cloud). His research results influenced numerous national and international projects, such as the European projects K-Wf Grid and CoreGRID, where he led the research and development activities regarding workflow management. In addition, he was and is active in several joint projects of the German Grid initiative "D-Grid".

R. Jeyarani is working as an Assistant Professor in the department of Computer Technology and Applications, Coimbatore Institute of Technology, India. She has 14 years of teaching experience in computer science. She received her master's degree in Computer Applications from Avinashilingam Deemed University in the year 1994. She received her MPhil degree from PSG College of Technology, Coimbatore in the year 2003. She is currently pursuing her PhD in Anna University, Chennai. Her areas of interest include Grid Computing, Cloud Computing, Service Oriented Architecture, Data Base Management System and Parallel Programming. She has more than six publications in the area of Agent Technology, Grid computing, cloud Computing and Power Aware Scheduling.

Rahul Kala did his Integrated Post Graduate (BTech and MTech in Information Technology) degree at ABV-Indian Institute of Information Technology and Management, Gwalior in 2010. He is currently pursuing PhD in Robotics from School of Cybernetics, University of Reading, UK. His areas of research are hybrid soft computing, robotic planning, autonomous vehicles, biometrics, pattern recognition and soft computing. He is the author of two books and has published about 50 papers in various international and national journals/conferences. He also takes a keen interest toward free/open source software. He is recipient of Commonwealth Scholarship 2010 (UK) and winner of Lord of the Code Scholarship Contest organised by KReSIT, IIT Bombay and Red Hat. He secured All India 8th position in Graduates Aptitude Test in Engineeging-2008 Examinations.

Arputharaj Kannan received MSc degree from Annamalai University-Tamil Nadu in 1986, M.E and PhD degrees from Anna University, Chennai-600 025, Tamil Nadu-India in 1991 and 2000 respectively. He is currently working as a Professor in the Department of Information Science and Technology, Anna University, Chennai-600 025, Tamil Nadu. His areas of interest include Database Systems, Data Mining and Artificial Intelligence.

Peter Katranuschkov received his diploma in civil engineering at the Sofia University and his Ph. D. at the Dresden University of Technology. He has over 30 years of experience in the areas of structural design, CAD, software design and development and building information modeling. Currently he is senior researcher at the Institute of Construction Informatics at the Dresden University of Technology. Dr. Katranuschkov has taken active part in a large number of national and international research projects such as the finished EU projects ToCEE, IStforCE and InteliGrid and the ongoing projects BauVOGrid, Mefisto, REEB and HESMOS. He is member of IAI, co-author of the IFC-ST4 standard extension and co-developer of one of the first BIM server prototypes worldwide. His research interests include product and process modeling and management, ontologies for building construction and concurrent engineering. Dr. Katranuschkov has more than eighty scientific publications.

Farid Khoshalhan is an Associate Professor of Industrial Engineering and Information Technology at the Faculty of Industrial Engineering, K. N. Toosi University of Technology, Tehran-IRAN. His research and client work has focused on evolutionary algorithms, multiple objective decision making, performance and productivity management and ecommerce. Dr. Khoshalhan earned a bachelor's degree in industrial technology from Iran University of Science and Technology, a Master's and PhD in industrial engineering from Tarbiat Modarres University in IRAN.

Hokyin Lai is currently a PhD candidate in the Department of Information Systems at the City University of Hong Kong. She received her master's degrees in business economics and electronic commerce from the Chinese University of Hong Kong and the Hong Kong Polytechnic University, respectively. Her research interests include intelligent systems in finance, e-Learning applications and

Common-sense knowledge management. She has publications in International Journal of Intelligent Information Technologies, Expert Systems with Applications, and International Journal of Business and information. She is a member of the editorial board of the journal of Knowledge Management & E-Learning: an International Journal (KM&EL).

Stephen Liao is Associate Professor of Information Systems at the City University of Hong Kong. His current research interests include use of data mining techniques in mobile commerce applications and intelligent business systems, especially intelligent transportation systems.

Long Liu is currently a PhD student in department of information systems, USTC-CityU Joint Advanced Research Centre. His current research interests include data mining, intelligent transportation systems.

Peter Loos is director of the Institute for Information Systems (IWi) at the German Research Institute for Artificial Intelligence (DFKI) and head of the chair for Business Administration and Information Systems at Saarland University. His research activities include business process management, information modelling, enterprise systems, software development as well as implementation of information systems. In 1997, Prof. Loos received the venia legendi in business administration. During his earlier career Prof. Loos had been chair of information systems & management at University of Mainz (2002-2005), chair of information systems & management at Chemnitz University of Technology (1998-2002), and deputy chair at University of Muenster. Furthermore, he had worked for 6 years as manager of the software development department at the software and consulting company IDS Scheer. Prof. Loos has written several books, contributed to 30 books and published more than 100 papers in journals and proceedings.

R. B. Mishra is the Head and Professor in the department of computer engineering, IT, BHU, Varanasi-221005, India. He holds BSc (Engg.), MTech, and PhD degrees. He has over 31 years in teaching experience and has published around 135 research paper and articles, and one book in Artificial intelligence. He has supervised 8 PhD. and 25 M.Tech dissertations; visited University of Bath, UK on INSA faculty exchange in 1997 from April to June. His research interests are computational methods in E-learning, AI and Multi agent system and their application to medicine, E-commerce, semantic web, Natural language processing, and robotics.

N. Nagaveni received the B.Sc, M.Sc and B.Ed degrees in Mathematics from Bharathiar University, India in 1985, 1987 and 1988 respectively. She received her M.Phil degree from Avinashilingam University, India in 1989, M.Ed degree from Annamalai University, India in 1992 and Ph.D in the area of Topology in Mathematics from Bharathiar University, India in 2000. Since 1992, she has been with the Department of Mathematics, Coimbatore Institute of Technology, Coimbatore Tamil Nadu, India where she is currently working as Assistant Professor. She is engaged as a research supervisor and her research interests includes Topology, Fuzzy sets and Continuous Function, Distributed Computing, Web mining and Privacy Preserving Data Mining. She is a member in the Indian Science congress Association (ICSA). She has presented research papers in the annual conference of ICSA. She has published many papers in International and National journals. She has produced one PhD candidate under her supervision.

Martin Purvis, BS (Yale), MFA (Columbia), MS, PhD, (Massachusetts) is Director of the University of Otago Information Science Department's Software Engineering & Collaborative Modelling Laboratory, a centre for research in distributed information systems, agent-based software engineering, workflow and process modelling, and mobile applications. He is the Director of both the Telecommunications and Software Engineering programmes in Applied Science at the University of Otago, and he has also been the principal investigator on a number of externally-funded research projects. His teaching activities include both mobile telecommunications and software engineering.

Maryam Purvis has worked as a software engineer in the computer industry in the United States. Her experience includes all phases of software development such as requirements analysis, design, implementation, and testing. Her current teaching and research interests are in the areas of dynamic modelling of distributed processes, distributed and dynamic workflow systems, coordination of multi-agent systems as well as the structure of social network interactions.

Yanliang Qi is currently working in the research department of Pfizer Inc. focus on data analysis and business intelligence area. In the past several years, Dr. Qi has been working on text mining, data mining, opinion mining in financial data and biomedical data. Dr. Qi's researches have been published in the International conference, Journal and Book chapters. Dr. Qi got the BS degree from BeiHang University and M.S. degree from New Jersey Institute of Technology.

R. Vasanth Ram has completed his Bachelor's degree in Electronics and Communication Engineering in PSG College of Technology, INDIA. He has published many papers in the area of grid computing and cloud computing. His field of specialization includes robotics, networking, cloud computing and grid computing. He has designed two incredible robots namely Efficient Land Rover and Object Locating Robot. He has presented papers based on his project work titled Improvement in Power Consumption in CMOS Digital Circuits and Design and FPGA implementation of Low Power Content Addressable Memory.

C. Rani is currently a Full Time PhD Research Scholar in the Department of Information Technology, Anna University of Technology Coimbatore, Coimbatore-641047. She has published in 10 national and international conferences. Her research interest includes Soft Computing Techniques and Data Mining.

Jimmy SJ. Ren is currently a PhD student in department of information systems, City University of Hong Kong. He received his bachelor's degree from department of software engineering, East China Normal University.

Mohammad Amin Rigi is a student in IT engineering at Faculty of Industrial Engineering, K. N. Toosi University of Technology, Tehran-IRAN. His research focuses on artificial intelligence, intelligent agents and multi-agent systems. Mr. Rigi earned a bachelor's degree in Computer Software Engineering from Ferdowsi University at Mashhad, IRAN. He is now working on his thesis in order to earn a master's degree in Information Technology Engineering.

Raimar J. Scherer is head of the Institute of Construction Informatics at the Dresden University of Technology. He received his diploma in civil engineering and his Ph. D at the Munich University of Technology. After some years of work in design and software development practice he was appointed professor for CAD and reliability at the University of Karlsruhe in 1987. He moved to the Dresden University of Technology in 1994. Prof. Scherer has been coordinator and outstanding member in a large number of national and international research projects. He is member of several research organizations including ISO 10303 (STEP), ASCE, IABSE, IAI, JCSS and SSA. His research interests include methods and models for cooperative design and concurrent engineering, AI methods in design and construction, product and process modeling and management, and applied stochastic in civil engineering. Prof. Scherer has more than one hundred and fifty scientific publications.

Min Song is an Assistant Professor in the Department of Information Systems and Co-director of the Informatics Research Laboratory at New Jersey Institute of Technology, where the goal of his research is discovery of knowledge from large natural language data such as blogs, doctor's notes, and scientific publications. His research interests are in text mining, bioinfomatics, information retrieval and digital libraries. Min received the outstanding service award from the International Conference on Information and Knowledge Management in 2009. His work received an honorable mention award in the 2006 Greater Philadelphia Bioinformatics Symposium and the Drexel Dissertation Award in 2005. In addition, the paper entitled "Extracting and Mining Protein-protein interaction Network from Biomedical Literature" has received the best paper award from 2004 IEEE Symposium on Computational Intelligence in Bioinformatics and Computational Biology, which was held in San Diego, Calif., on Oct. 7-8, 2004. In addition, Min was nominated for Microsoft Research New Faculty Award in 2008 and Sloan Research Fellow in 2009 by NJIT. He has published one book, five book chapters, 15 journals, and 40 conference papers. Min has received several grants from the National Science Foundation (NSF) and the Institute of Museum and Library Services (IMLS) on developing advanced Digital Libraries systems. He received his PhD in Information Systems from Drexel University, an MS from Indiana University and a BA from Yonsei University in Korea.

U. K. Sridevi received her M.C.A from Bharathiar University, Coimbatore, India in 2001. In 2003 she completed her M.Phil (Computer Science) in Manonmanium Sundaranar University, India. She has an experience of over 10 years in teaching and her areas of interest include Web Mining, Semantic Web, Data Mining, and Artificial Intelligence. She is currently working as Assistant Professor in the Department of Computer Application, Sri Krishna College of Engineering and Technology, Coimbatore, Tamil Nadu, India. She has presented research papers in National and International conferences and published papers in International journals.

Oliver Thomas holds a chair in information management and information systems at the Institute of Information Management and Corporate Governance, University of Osnabrueck, since 2009. He has been the deputy head and a senior researcher of the Institute for Information Systems at the German Research Center for Artificial Intelligence (DFKI). Oliver Thomas is a visiting associate professor at the Aoyama Gakuin University in Tokyo (Japan). His fields of research are business process management, enterprise modeling and product-service systems.

Aditya Trivedi is a Professor in the Information and Communication Technology (ICT) Department at ABV Indian Institute of Information Technology and Management, Gwalior, India. He has about 20 years of teaching experience. He obtained his doctorate (PhD) from IIT Roorkee in the area of Wireless Communication Engineering. He received his bachelor degree in Electronics Engg. from the Jiwaji University. He did his M.Tech. (Communication Systems) from Indian Institute of Technology (IIT), Kanpur. His teaching and research interest include Digital communication, CDMA systems, Signal processing, and Networking. He has published around 30 papers in various national and international journals/conferences. He is a fellow of the Institution of Electronics and Telecommunication Engineers (IETE). Dr. Trivedi is a reviewer of IEEE and Springer journals. In 2007, he was given the IETE's K.S. Krishnan Memorial Award for best system oriented paper.

Sankaradass Veeramalai received the Bachelor's Degree in Electronics and Communication Engineering from Sathyabama Engineering College, Chennai in 1994 and Master Degree in Computer Science and Engineering from SASTRA University in 2002. He is currently a PhD candidate in the Department of Information Science and Technology at Anna University, Chennai, Tamil Nadu. His research interest includes the Database Systems, Data Mining and Web Mining.

Minhong Wang is an Assistant Professor in the Faculty of Education, The University of Hong Kong. She received her Ph.D. in Information Systems from City University of Hong Kong in 2005. Her current research interests include e-learning, Web-based training and professional development, knowledge management, complex process management, and information systems. She has published papers in Information & Management, Computers & Education, IEEE Transactions on Education, Educational Technology & Society, Expert Systems with Applications, Knowledge-based Systems, Journal of Knowledge Management, among others. She is the Editor-in-Chief of Knowledge Management & E-Learning: an International Journal (KM&EL), and serves on the Editorial Board of several international journals.

Wei Wang is currently a PhD student in department of information systems, City University of Hong Kong. He received his bachelor & MPhil degree from Peking University, China. His current research interests include data mining, intelligent transportation systems.

Lori Watrous-deVersterre is a Ph.D. student at NJIT with over 25 years of industry experience in developing software components, leading high-tech commercial software projects, and running multinational groups. She also has 5 years of experience as an adjunct instructor at various universities and has taught sessions for NJIT's Technology for Teachers program. Recently, Lori accepted a faculty position in NJIT's Information Technology Department. As part of her dissertation, Lori is exploring the relationship between digital libraries and social collaboration. She is specifically interested in how an individual's context relates to the way they find information and determine its usefulness.

Jin Xu is a lecturer and PhD Candidate in the Department of Electronic Commerce and Information Management at School of Economics & Management, Southwest Jiaotong University, Chengdu, China. He obtained his M.Phil degree in Management Science & Engineering from the same university. His current research interests include use of data mining techniques in E-commerce applications and intelligent business systems, especially recommender systems and intelligent transportation systems.

Suk-Chung Yoon is currently the chair and William R. Bailey Endowed Professor of the Computer Science Department at Widener University, Chester, Pennsylvania. Dr. Yoon is responsible for two majors, Computer Science and Computer Information Systems. Over the past 20 years, Dr. Yoon has taught Computer Science to all levels of students ranging from non-majors to upper class Computer Science majors and graduate students in our master programs. His research has focused on artificial intelligence, data mining, and large scale computing. His work has been supported by the National Science Foundation as well as corporations such as IBM and J.P. Morgan Chase. Dr. Yoon earned the B.S. from Yonsei University and received my M.S. and Ph.D. degrees from Northwestern University.

Index

A

A-Box 18-19
adaptive learning model 145-147, 149-150, 152, 155
Adaptive Power Aware Virtual Machine Provisioner (APA-VMP) 90
agreement problem (AP) 110
Analytical hierarchy process (AHP) 108, 110
ant colony optimization (ACO) 89
Aptitude Treatment Interaction (ATI) 145-146
Aptitude-Treatment Interaction theory 145
artificial intelligence 13-14, 32, 35, 42, 45, 66, 82, 84-85, 106, 123-124, 143, 156-157, 171-172, 184-185, 213-214, 241, 243, 286
Artificial neural network 267, 285-286, 300
association
    historic 162
    hotspot topic 162
    sub class 161
    super class 161
    synonym/near synonym 161, 223
attributes 3, 5, 54, 73, 89, 160, 165, 170, 189-190, 192-194, 197, 243-244, 249, 251, 253, 267, 295, 297
automatic classification 243-244
automatic query expansion (AQE) 217
axioms 243

B

BauVOGrid 60, 62
Best Value 101, 173, 177
biomedical documents 34-35, 42
bit vector 113-115
blogs 1-2, 6, 12
Business Intelligence 1
Business Process Modeling Notation 48, 63

C

Campeon 57-58
Cartesian products 175
case-based reasoning (CBR) 187
centroid 202, 204-205, 207, 209-210, 269-270
classifier 5, 7, 9-10, 33, 35-42, 159, 165-166, 173-175, 179, 183-184, 196
Class Mapping 251
Cloud Computing 47-48, 53, 88-90, 102, 104-107
clustering
    conceptual 243, 249-250, 253-254, 262
    fuzzy based 246
    genetic algorithm based 245, 247, 263
    ontology based 204-205, 211, 245
    user profile 160, 165, 168
Clusty 68-70, 80
Cognitive Fit Theory (CFT) 74
comparison relations 1-11
competitor analysis 5
compute resources (CR) 96
Computer System Usability Questionnaire (CSUQ) 25
concept weighting scheme 199
construction industry 45-46, 56-59, 62
Constructive Alignment Model 145-146, 148-149, 152, 155
Content Management Agent (CMA) 151
Corpus Analysis 217, 221
Course sequencing 285-286, 301
crawling 69-71
C-value 36, 43, 71, 83

D

data-center 88
data marks 54
Decision Support Systems 1, 12, 14, 82, 127, 158, 198

Dictionary Modelling 216
digital libraries 33-34, 42-44, 66, 239, 244
Directory Mozilla 68
dispatching rules 266-268, 276, 284
Distributed Systems 45, 47-48, 52, 62, 84, 106
Document Management Systems (DMSs) 244
document search 33-34
domain knowledge 186-189, 192, 194-196, 198-199, 201
double relevance measure 216
dynamic bottleneck detection (DBD) 268

E

earliest due date (EDD) 267
Eclipse IDE 285, 298
e-Government 202, 214, 240
Eigen vector 114-115, 118
e-learning 30, 78, 84, 145-147, 149-151, 154-157, 285-288, 298-301
entities 2, 4, 6, 8, 18-20, 23, 25, 28, 46, 96, 98, 192, 195, 238, 243, 246, 287
Entity Model 19-20, 23
entropy 9-14, 71, 255-256, 260-262
extraction
information 1, 14, 67
relation 2, 4-6, 12-14

F

feature selection 12, 42, 186-189, 192, 194-198, 245
filtering
collaborative 159-160, 162-165, 169-172, 202, 245
content based 162
hybrid 159, 163-165, 167, 169-170
first-in first out (FIFO) 267
fitness function 93, 100, 133-135, 175-176, 207, 247, 286, 296
Fluctuation Smoothing 265-267, 272-273, 275, 279-282
fluctuation smoothing rule for mean cycle time (FSMCT) 266
F-Measure 209-210, 212, 246, 248, 256, 259-260, 262
formality 16, 18, 20
formal logic 15, 17, 161
four-factor bi-criteria nonlinear fluctuation smoothing (4f-biNFS) 265
Fuzzy Classified Association Rule 160, 165-166
Fuzzy space 176

G

genetic algorithms (GA) 89, 126
Genetic Fuzzy Rule Based System (GFRBS) 173-174, 183
Genetic Operation 173, 175, 177
genetic operators 132, 135, 173-175, 177-178
GP tree 132-133
graphical notation 20-21, 63
Grid Gateway layer 50
Grid Workflows 45, 63
GWorkflowDL 52-55, 60

H

Heuristic Sequencing Path 285
Hierarchical Genetic Algorithms 125, 143
Hierarchical Small-World Networks (HSWN) 223
High-Level Petri Nets (HLPN) 53
Hong Kong university 146, 152
hybrid Genetic Programming (GP) 125
hybrid system architecture 45, 59
hybrid web service 45-46

I

inertia weight 91-93, 173-174, 177-178, 183, 210
Information Retrieval (IR) 217
Information Systems (IS) 33
Infrastructure as a Service (IaaS) 88-89
Instances Generation 251
Intelligent Agent 123, 145, 147, 149, 158, 212
Intelligent Tutoring System (ITS) 285
interactive query expansion (IQE) 217

J

java programming 285, 288, 298

K

Key-phrase extraction 33-37, 40-42, 143
GenEx 35-36
KEA 35-37, 39, 42-44
keywords 1, 15, 33, 45, 65, 68, 73, 88, 108, 145, 159-160, 162, 166-167, 173, 199-200, 216-217, 224, 231, 243, 265, 285-296, 298-299
K-Nearest Neighbor 33, 35, 37-42
k-nearest neighbour (k-NN) 190-191
knowledge completeness (KC) 77
knowledge model 19, 22-23
knowledge relevance (KR) 77

L

Latent Semantic Analysis (LSA) 221
learning outcomes 145-146, 148, 155
Learning Process Management Agent (LPMA) 150
Le Grand Robert 216, 218, 223, 225, 238
LeMonde94 216, 218, 232, 235, 238-239
Linear Regression 33, 37, 40, 187, 192

M

Machine Learning 1, 3, 12-14, 35, 37-38, 42, 71, 171, 174, 179, 182, 184, 186-190, 195-198, 256, 262
    algorithms 186, 188, 190
mean magnitude of relative error (MMRE) 190
Meeting Scheduling 108-111, 114, 117, 123-124, 283
Meeting Scheduling Problem (MSP) 108
metadata 17, 33-34, 84, 201, 244
model validation 186
multi-agent framework 145, 154-155
multi-agent system 108, 110
multi-layer perceptrons 190
Multi-Strategy Ensemble Particle Swarm Optimization (MEPSO) 88
MySQL 285-286, 291, 298

N

Naïve Bayes 33, 35-37, 40-42
Natural Language Process (NLP) 6
NewsGroup 207-208, 256, 262
node deployment 125-128, 131, 134, 138, 140, 142, 144
Nokia N95 2, 8
Non-Dominated Ranked Genetic Algorithm (NRGA) 243, 249, 255
Non-taxonomy Relation Generation 251

O

old velocity 173-174, 178, 183
Online analysis processing (OLAP) 267
online forums 1-2
OntoClippy 15-16, 22, 24, 26-30, 161, 171, 262
ontology
    creation 16-17, 31, 65-69, 71, 73-83
    design 15-17, 24-25, 28-31, 161, 171, 262
    domain 65-67, 69, 72, 74, 77-78, 80, 82, 162, 171, 212, 263
    model 17, 19-20, 23, 202-203, 211
Ontology Generation Using Fuzzy Logic (OGF) 245, 249
ontology quality (OQ) 77
Ontology Web Language (OWL) 51

P

pairwise comparison matrix 110-115, 117-118
particle swarm optimization (PSO) 89, 173-174, 183, 199, 202, 281
Peer-to-Peer (P2P) 244
planar network 128
Platform as a Service (PaaS) 89
POS (Part-Of-Speech) 74
possibilistic information retrieval 216, 223
Possibilistic Matching Model 216, 218-219, 225, 230, 239
Possibilistic Networks (PN) 218, 238
possibility theory 216-218, 240
POS tags 4, 7-9
power conservation 88-89, 98, 103
Preference Graph 108, 110-112, 115-118, 120-121
Process-Centric Collaboration 45
Process Management 45-46, 52, 58, 150
Proposed RGA 179-183
Protégé 17, 20, 24, 26-30, 74
PubMed 33-35, 39, 215

Q

quality management 186

R

radial basis functions 187, 190
Recommendation System 159-161, 164-166, 168-170, 287
record defect 59-60
relationships 12, 18-20, 23, 65-66, 72, 77, 81-82, 85, 87, 114, 147, 160-162, 197, 201, 204, 221-223, 236, 238, 240, 243, 245-246, 249-250, 295
Relevance Feedback (RF) 217, 220
representation 7, 17-20, 23-24, 50, 64, 75-77, 93, 99, 126, 128, 131-135, 139, 152, 154, 174-176, 178-179, 181, 200, 203, 205, 217, 221, 229, 245-246
re-randomization 93, 105
Resource Descriptive Language (RDF) 201
Resource Dynamics 88-89, 98, 100, 102, 104

S

scheduling 55, 89-91, 94, 98, 100, 103, 105-111, 114, 117, 123-124, 128, 143, 247, 265-269, 272-274, 276, 279-284
search engines 68, 83, 159-160, 162, 171
search space 89, 91, 94, 129, 142, 177, 199, 203, 205-206
Self Adaptive Particle Swarm Optimization (SAP-SO) 88, 90
semantic proximity 218, 223, 238
semantic query expansion 216-219, 223-225, 227, 238-239
Semantic similarity 22, 200-205, 210-215, 222, 229
Semantic Value 286-294, 298-299
Semantic Web 15, 31, 49-51, 61-63, 65-66, 71, 78, 82-84, 198, 201, 212-215, 242, 244-245, 263-264
semi-automatic document annotation 199
Sensor Node Placement 125, 127-128, 185, 283
Sentiment analysis 3-4, 12-13
sentry particles 93-94
Separation Index 248, 255-256, 261-262
Sequential Minimal Optimization (SMO) 33
service oriented architecture (SOA) 47
Silhouette Coefficient 248, 256-259, 262
Simple RGA 179-183
simulated annealing (SA) 89
social networks 1-2
Software as a Service (SaaS) 89
Software development 23, 48, 186-188, 192, 196-198
    automation 186
Software Effort Estimation 186-187, 189-190, 195-198
SPORSER 231-233, 238-239
state of the art 15-16, 39, 86, 106
statistical regression 190
Student Activity Monitoring Agent (SAMA) 150
Student Interface Agent (SIA) 150
Support Vector Machine (SVM) 2, 36
    multi-class 7-11
SVMreg-1 33, 35, 40, 42

T

Taxonomy Relation Generation 251, 254
T-Box 18-19
teaching and learning activities (TLAs) 148, 152
Text-to-Onto 71-74, 81, 84
TF-IDF (Term Frequency- Inverse Document Frequency) 285-286
Tomcat 285-286, 291, 298

U

user-contributed contents 1
User Preferences 3, 108, 124, 172, 283

V

Vector Space Model (VSM) 199-200, 285
Virtual Machines (VM) 88-89
virtual organization (VO) 46
    management 46, 49, 51, 57
visualization 26, 29, 84, 186-189, 193, 195

W

wafer fabrication 265-269, 272, 274-276, 280-284
Web 2.0 1-3, 11, 163, 171, 202, 212, 239
Web Mining 1, 163, 202, 211, 246, 263
Web Ontology Language (OWL) 201
web page retrieval 74, 159, 170
Web Services Business Process Execution Language 48, 63
web site classification 68
WebSphinx 69-71, 74, 81
WebtoOnto 66, 73-75, 77-79, 81-82
wikis 1-2, 17
Wireless Sensor Networks (WSN) 126
WordNet 22-23, 32, 148, 204, 212, 215, 217, 222, 241